Democratic Latin America

This much-expanded and updated second edition of *Democratic Latin America* takes an institutional approach to Latin American politics to discuss contemporary politics and to highlight how past politics have shaped current institutional designs. It draws explicit connections between certain political features—such as fragmentation, efficiency, accountability, instability, consensus, or responsiveness—and the institutional design of a country. Students thus learn not only that a country is unstable or has high rates of participation or low levels of corruption, but they also learn why. And more importantly, they also learn how politics can be shaped by different institutional arrangements.

Features:

- Each chapter focuses on a different institution, such as the executive, political parties, electoral systems, the armed forces, or federalism and compares how they are constructed differently across countries.
- Placing a premium on accessibility, each chapter opens with a story and ends with a detailed country case study, making use of contemporary examples to feed student interest in current events.
- Newly updated comparison-based tables and box features (electoral results, percentage of women legislators, and surveys of partisan identification) are included to stimulate analysis.
- New topics of research have been added to ensure the recognition of the latest changes in the region, including: corruption scandals; the turn of the "pink tide"; protest and social movements; LGBT rights; citizen security and organized crime; new forms of legislative accountability; and the use of social media as a political resource in Latin America.

Democratic Latin America continues to offer an original way of teaching and learning about Latin American politics.

Craig L. Arceneaux is Professor of Political Science at California Polytechnic State University, San Luis Obispo. He served as Chair of the Political Science Department from 2009–2013.

Democratic Latin America

Second Edition

Craig L. Arceneaux

Routledge
Taylor & Francis Group

NEW YORK AND LONDON

Second edition published 2018
by Routledge
711 Third Avenue, New York, NY 10017

and by Routledge
2 Park Square, Milton Park, Abingdon, Oxon, OX14 4RN

Routledge is an imprint of the Taylor & Francis Group, an informa business

First edition published 2012 by Pearson Education, Inc.

Library of Congress Cataloging-in-Publication Data
Names: Arceneaux, Craig L., 1965- author.
Title: Democratic Latin America / Craig L. Arceneaux.
Description: New York, NY : Routledge, 2017. | Includes bibliographical references
and index.
Identifiers: LCCN 2017011195 (print) | LCCN 2017012148 (ebook) | ISBN 9781315544991
(Master) | ISBN 9781134824694 (WebPDF) | ISBN 9781134824762 (ePub) |
ISBN 9781134824830 (Mobipocket/Kindle) | ISBN 9781138682665 (hardback : alk. paper) |
ISBN 9781138682672 (pbk. : alk. paper)
Subjects: LCSH: Democracy—Latin America. | Latin America—Politics and government.
Classification: LCC JL966 (ebook) | LCC JL966 .A74 2017 (print) | DDC 320.98—dc23
LC record available at https://lccn.loc.gov/2017011195

ISBN: 978-1-138-68266-5 (hbk)
ISBN: 978-1-138-68267-2 (pbk)
ISBN: 978-1-315-54499-1 (ebk)

Typeset in TimesNewRomanMTStd
by diacriTech, Chennai

Contents

4 The Executive Branch: Latin American Style 125

**5 The Legislative Branch: The Centerpiece of
Democracy Under Fire** 170

Preface

At my university, I have had the privilege to accompany my students on several study abroad programs. Not too long ago, I traveled with a group of students to Cusco, Peru. As those familiar with Latin America well know, protest activity is common throughout the region, but things were particularly turbulent on our trip. A wide range of groups had latched on to a labor protest by a teacher's union to voice their grievances in a series of marches and work stoppages. Students had difficulty getting to classes, roadblocks threatened our weekend excursions, and the prospects for violence were very real. The reaction from my students was the same I had seen from other student groups and even in companions with whom I have traveled in the past. They commented on the passion they saw in Peruvian politics and compared it to the apathy they more typically observed in the United States. For the students, the protests were an exciting, even commendable thing.

I could hardly disagree with these impressions. When people sense injustice, they have every right to respond. And yes, all too often we do not see this spirited behavior in the United States. But it was not that the reactions of my students were incorrect, it was that they were incomplete. I pressed my students to think more deeply about just why Peruvians had decided to take to the streets. What prompted the sense of injustice in the first place? How did Peruvians come to decide that protest was their only option? And how was it that a narrow protest by teachers transformed into a clamor over inflation, unemployment, indigenous rights in the Amazon, workers' conditions—even a call for a new constitution.

With a little prodding, the students soon linked the protest activity to certain features of government, such as responsiveness, accountability, representation, and efficiency. A healthy democracy exhibits—and fiercely defends—protest activity. Likewise, a healthy democracy recognizes conflict as an inherent property of politics. But when activism becomes almost routine, such that it rather than government appears to be the central forum for popular expression, this tells us that something is wrong, that government institutions are failing to do their job. It is one thing to celebrate the political passion we see as groups take to the streets, but the larger question is how government can uphold its commitment as a representative of the people.

I advised my students that the answer rests within government institutions. Much like a bridge or a building, there are different ways to construct government institutions and to make improvements so that they are geared toward responsiveness, efficiency, and other valued objectives. The struggle for democracy, then, really is all about institutions.

Democratic Latin America seeks to provide that insight. It covers much of the same history, topics, issues, and concepts found in most introductory texts on Latin America, but it does so from the angle of institutions. It therefore not only provides a fresh look at the region, but also does so from a perspective that appropriately represents the prevailing approach in the field of comparative politics.

Other core texts on Latin America tend to leave out or give only brief attention to political institutions. There is a false impression that Latin American political institutions—specifically presidentialism—are little more than a replay of U.S. political institutions and that therefore there is no need to discuss what is already familiar to most people. This is, of course, patently wrong. As I document, political institutions in Latin America are distinct. Presidentialism blends with elements of parliamentarism, both bicameral and unicameral legislatures operate in the region, most countries do not use federalism, the proportional-based electoral systems produce numerous and disparate parties, and the court systems work according to code law rather than common law.

The oversight in most textbooks is curious because it has become fashionable in academic studies to highlight the importance of institutions. But oddly, that same level of appreciation does not find a counterpart in our textbooks on Latin America. This may be due to the long history of colonialism and independent rule in the region—much longer than most other developing areas of the world. It also may be due to the significant influence of the region by the United States. These are no doubt important considerations, and they are not ignored in this text. But in too many texts, they crowd out due attention to institutions and their formative influence on political behavior. Through institutions, students will gain a deeper understanding of the everyday politics they see in Latin America, such as the political protests seen by my students in Peru.

Why institutions? Political institutions provide a road map to the political activity in a country. They offer a straightforward introduction to the politics of a country, one that is readily grasped by students. In addition, they help us to highlight practical politics as we uncover variations in institutional design and the consequences for political outcomes. There is no denying that some political actors will at times use informal institutions, or work outside government institutions. But the fact remains that government institutions provide a primary point of reference as political actors, be they inside or outside of government, pursue and protect their interests.

Features

Drawing on examples from the 18 democratic countries of the region that fell under Spanish or Portuguese colonialism (Argentina, Bolivia, Brazil, Chile, Colombia, Costa Rica, the Dominican Republic, Ecuador, El Salvador, Guatemala, Honduras, Mexico, Nicaragua, Panama, Paraguay, Peru, Uruguay, Venezuela), *Democratic Latin America* works through the major political institutions one by one, granting each a separate chapter, but the use of consistent examples and individual case studies provides the country-based detail desired by students and regional specialists who teach courses on Latin America. While discussing the basic design of different institutions, the text also makes extensive references to current political events in the region. It makes ample use of tables and timely data on electoral results, partisan representation in congress, descriptive statistics on different institutions (e.g., powers of the supreme court and size of the armed forces), and more.

Coverage

Chapter 1 begins the book with an introduction to the institutional approach to politics, and then overviews contemporary democratic Latin America. Both institutions and democratic transitions are approached from a theoretical standpoint. The reader is immediately acquainted with the range of democratic development in the region, and the way in which political rights and civil liberties may vary. Chapter 2 provides the background material required to understand institutional development. After a short section on geography and demography, it traces the history of the region from the pre-Colombian period to independence. Among other concepts, it introduces the important concepts of state and nation to provide a basis upon which to assess development in the region. Chapter 3 launches the survey of contemporary institutions with an examination of their constitutional framework. It picks up on the history of the region since independence, and traces questions of political economy over time. Most of all, it pays particular attention to questions of constitutional change.

Chapters 4, 5, and 6 cover the core constitutions of national government. The chapter on executives emphasizes the distinction of presidentialism in Latin America, and special attention is granted to the design and consequences of presidential power. Chapter 5 looks at legislatures, and highlights how underdevelopment often hinders the ability of a congressional chamber to play its part in a balance-of-power system. It also looks at the growing representation of women and the indigenous in legislative assemblies to recognize the liveliness of Latin American political institutions. Chapter 6 does what few other introductory texts on Latin America do. It discusses the role of the judiciary and lays out the differences between common law and code law practices to once again underscore just how differently institutions in the region work. Here students are asked to think rather deeply about the role of the rule of law in a democratic system, and how judicial institutions can contribute to the rule of law.

Chapter 7 spotlights the focal point of democratic government—elections. It does not simply distinguish between majoritarian and proportional systems, but recognizes that in reality most electoral systems mix these formulas, and it also specifies the other features of electoral systems that affect the distribution of votes. A section on electoral commissions and observation missions raises the point that elections are but one part of a longer electoral cycle that raises democratic concerns throughout. Chapter 8 examines that one institution which stands with one foot in society and one in government—the political party. It identifies the recent rise in social movements and how they have usurped some traditional party functions, but it clarifies the unique contributions that both civil society and parties make in a democracy.

Chapter 9 looks at federalism and unitary government, and the institutions that complete them. Decentralization has been a hallmark of this democratic wave, making the relations between national, regional, and local government pivotal to contemporary issues of democratic consolidation. Finally, Chapter 10 looks at civil-military relations. This is one area that has received attention from other introductory texts on Latin America, but they typically rivet their attention on issues of military intervention given the past history of the region. This chapter is forward-looking and looks expressly at what it takes to construct civil-military relations in a democracy, paying particular attention to the critical role of the ministry of defense and the impact of new military missions.

Pedagogy

As organized, this book strives to answer all the *what* questions that surround political institutions. It is filled with systematic descriptions in a way that encourages comparisons between countries. That is apparent from the organization of the chapters, each of which includes a "Comparing Countries" box that focuses on in-depth cross-national comparison of a specific institutional issue. But it also addresses the *why* and *how* questions that are so important to critical thinking, those questions that probe where political institutions came from, uncover cultural norms and traditions in institutions, and assess the political consequences of institutional choices. By recognizing how institutions both embrace values and attend to problems, it exposes students to normative and practical politics. Each chapter also ends with a "Country in the Spotlight" box that applies the concepts and issues raised in the chapter to a specific case study in detail.

In addition, important terms are highlighted throughout the text, and an effort has been made to ensure that tables and figures do not simply sit aside the narrative, but rather develop and illustrate a significant point. Photos further enliven the text, and remind the reader that the material is not just an academic exercise—it deals with real-life people and events. Readers will find additional helpful readings in annotated bibliographies at the end of each chapter.

New to This Edition

*   Updates to chapter opening vignettes, examples, tables and statistics with references to some of the most recent political developments in Latin America, including the rise of the opposition in Venezuela, the impeachment and removal of Dilma Rousseff in Brazil, electoral reform in Chile, the consolidation of authority by Daniel Ortega in Nicaragua, the end of Kirchnerismo in Argentina, and the turn of the "pink tide."
*   A new section on protest and social movements.
*   A new section and extended discussion of corruption.
*   Expanded references to the struggle for the rights of women, indigenous, and LGBT groups.
*   Extended reference to the impact of technology, such as social media and protest, the use of crowd sourcing to address government accountability, and web source designs used by public officials to enhance transparency.
*   More detailed discussions on the impact of crime and criminal organizations.

Acknowledgments

Few books emerge from the hands of one person alone, and this work is no exception. The motivation to write this book came from the many students at California Polytechnic State University, San Luis Obispo, I have encountered over the years while teaching courses on Latin American Politics. A number of them—too many to name—provided helpful comments on early drafts of the chapters. I would also like to thank my manuscript reviewers from the first edition of the book, including Michelle Bonner, the University of Victoria; Roger Durham, Aquinas College; Ingrid Erickson, University of Florida; Eduardo Magalhães, Simpson College; Scott Morgenstern, the University of Pittsburgh; Gregory Schmidt, University of Texas at El Paso; and Sebastian Urioste, the University of Oregon. Their knowledge of Latin America, students' interests, and pedagogy was evident, and stimulated deep reflections. I have tried to incorporate their suggestions where possible, and I truly hope that the final work lives up to their expectations and that this second edition further addresses their helpful comments. I also would like to acknowledge the contributions of my family, Kathryn and Danielle, who offered—all too often unwillingly—those most precious commodities, time and tolerance. And finally, I would like to extend in advance a note of appreciation to the readers. It is my genuine hope that this book enriches the understanding of Latin American politics by students and enhances the teaching experience of professors, and I welcome any comments from the readers. In closing, I note that any errors of omission or commission remain with the author alone.

1 An Institutional Approach to Democracy and Democratization in Latin America

Photo 1.1 Statue of independence hero General Manuel Belgrano in front of the Presidential Palace in Buenos Aires: Argentine institutions have shaped, embodied, and reacted to the history of the country since independence.

Source: © Shutterstock

Every year international travelers flock to Buenos Aires, Argentina. They are lured by its cosmopolitan charm, famed artistic expressions, and entertaining nightlife. Many come from neighboring Uruguay or Brazil, and many others come from northern horizons on the other side of the world. Their journey is a long one, and most arrive nagged by jet lag and just a bit dazed by the fact that it is no longer summer, but winter—or vice versa. But in many respects Buenos Aires can be approached like other cities, and this provides some comfort to the otherwise flustered traveler. There are taxis, buses, and rental cars for transportation from the airport. Hotels, restaurants, bars, and shops dot its urban core. Crowds flood its streets in synchronicity with the workday. Street peddlers and musicians struggle to make a living. There are signs of fabulous wealth, such as the luxurious flats of Palermo or Recoleta that sit near Audi dealerships and overlook spacious parks. And there are scenes of desperation, found with uncomfortable ease in the working-class streets of La Boca. The inequality is disturbing, but it is also found in most any large city.

Visitors familiar with government institutions in the United States find a superficial sense of familiarity in the large edifices devoted to Congress, the executive branch, and the Supreme Court. There is a separation of powers here too. The congressional palace is laid out in a symmetrical Greco-Roman style, with large fluted columns up front, and a huge dome on top. The U.S. Capitol Building immediately comes to mind. But the subtle differences are unavoidable, and become defining in short order. The dome is copper clad with a green patina finish. It juts upward narrowly to affirm the Italian design in fashion when the architect drafted the blueprints in the 1890s. Statues of majestic birds with their wings spread abut a large monument up front. Eagles come to mind—but these are condors. Up Avenida de Mayo one finds the executive building. It is called the Casa Rosada (Pink House), and that seems to mimic the presidential home in the United States, but still it is pink, not white. Moreover, the president of Argentina only works here. His residence is outside the main city area at an estate known as Quinta de Olivos. Finally, these travelers would not be surprised by the stately building that houses the Supreme Court of Argentina. But few would realize that the magistrates inside mete out justice through a code law tradition influenced by France, and thus work very differently than the judges who practice under common law in Great Britain and the United States.

And as it turns out, Buenos Aires is not just like any other city in the world. It has its own history, culture, and rhythm. The tango, gaucho folklore, passionate nationalism, Boca Juniors (or River Plate) soccer team, appreciation for theater, *mate* drink, grilled meat (*asados*), penchant for mass protests, and an immigrant history all mix to produce a unique city and people. Visitors arrive precisely to experience all that is distinctive about Buenos Aires, and Argentina. And most are not so oblivious—they know that the country offers its own history and politics. But few grasp just how and why the history and politics of Argentina have developed as they have. And those who seek to know more rarely consider the makeup of government institutions, because they appear so comparable to those in the United States. But that is a mistake. After all, when Argentines look at the Casa Rosada, they do not mull over the similarity of the name to the White House. They are more likely to reflect on the rose color. Legend has it that the color came about as a compromise after a civil war that pit those seeking a centralized government—represented by the color white—against those hoping to keep power in the regions—represented by the color red.[1] Relations between the federal and regional governments remain very important to contemporary politics in Argentina.

Put simply, the institutions of Latin America are not simple replays of what we see in the United States. The president of Argentina does share a title with the president of the United States, but he holds different powers. Faced with an uncompromising congress, he can appeal directly to the people with a consultation on desired legislation. Although nonbinding, the consultation can pressure congress. And he holds power not only to veto legislation, but also to veto only selections of a bill and to sign into law other portions. The president of the United States can take neither of these actions. Federalism, parties, congress, and other institutions found in democracies also work in distinct ways in Argentina, such that knowledge of their details and mechanics provides an engaging doorway to the politics of the country. This is a doorway all too often passed by those that glance at institutional labels—such as president, supreme court, ministry of defense, or election—and presume that politics works the same as in other countries with institutions of the same name. And beyond the practice of politics, a survey of institutions also offers a gateway to the history and culture of a country. This is because institutions are reservoirs of national memory that define what is important and cherished by a people.

Raúl Alfonsín knew the power of institutions. He was the president who followed the brutal military regime that ruled Argentina from 1976 to 1983. This was a regime that had dismissed the entire government and proclaimed that it would enact a "process of national reorganization." It even referred to itself as "The 'Proceso' (Process)." Audacious as they were, the military rulers failed miserably. They lacked all legitimacy such that any institution they proposed could survive only if backed by force. But even as they retreated to the barracks, the armed forces held out hope that some of their legislation and institutional reforms would provide a base for the civilian government that followed. Alfonsín rejected that thought. He campaigned on the promise to reinstate the original Constitution of 1853. It was for civilians alone, through democratic procedures, to decide their government. A return to the founding constitution would affirm a popular commitment to the beliefs and values upon which the country stood—and lay bare the folly of military attempts to compose institutions out of thin air.

Institutions cannot, and do not, just appear from nowhere. They echo the historical, cultural, and political consciousness of a nation. But nations do change over time—sometimes dramatically. A wave of immigration at the turn of the nineteenth century literally remade the Argentine nation. Industrialization after World War II gave the working class a powerful voice. Changes like this take place on a stage created by institutions. Over time immigrants and working-class groups found their way into the electoral system as suffrage expanded and new parties reached out to them. Sometimes the changes overwhelm institutions, and powerful actors move in to assert their control. This happened in Argentina when the armed forces, primed by Cold War attitudes and fearful of working-class mobilizations, intervened in 1976. But as noted, that is a difficult task because institutions have roots, and staying power.

And at other times, actors reassess their institutional stage and take it upon themselves to rearrange the set. This happened shortly after the transition to democracy in Argentina. The president who followed Alfonsín, Carlos Menem (1989–1999), pushed constitutional interpretations to their limits as he made ample use of his decree powers to confront an economic crisis, and overhauled the judiciary with sympathetic appointees who would not dare question his actions. But in one respect, the constitution was crystal clear—it prohibited a second term for the president. This was something Menem dearly desired. Alfonsín, now leader of the opposition, saw an opportunity and met with Menem to negotiate constitutional reforms in 1994. One reform allowed Menem to take another run at the presidency (which he won in 1995), but others reduced executive powers and strengthened judicial independence. Political actors in Argentina worked out their differences through institutional changes.

Political actors may gain opportunities to shape institutions, but today it is nearly impossible for them to craft institutions that plainly and durably reflect their interests. The pressures from history and culture, the interests of opposing political leaders and groups, and the complexity of institutions and their interactions ensure that institutions possess autonomy in the long run. Menem did get his second term, but as part of the compromise he relinquished authority over Buenos Aires—the president would no longer appoint its mayor, nor control its massive budget. And as it turns out, the city provided a political and economic base for Menem's opponents to mobilize. Buenos Aires elected a Menem foe, Fernando de la Rúa, as its first mayor in 1996. He would move on to win the presidency in 1999. Carlos Menem could influence a scene in Argentine politics, but he could hardly control the following act.

And what happens when institutions drift from fundamental expectations and beliefs in society, and begin to lose their legitimacy? De la Rúa took the presidency riding a wave of opposition to Menem that grew as corruption scandals came to light and the economy once again went sour. But he did little to address corruption, and did little more than ask Argentines to tighten their belts as the economic crisis deepened. Worst of all, he prohibited access to savings accounts as a stop gag measure to prevent a run on the banks. De la Rúa's supporters took a hit in congressional elections, and the government stagnated. Protestors took to the streets under the banner *"¡Que se vayan todos!"*—"Throw them all out!" Rioting erupted, and more than two dozen died in confrontations with police in late December 2001. Mounting protests forced de la Rúa from office, and triggered a succession of four presidents in three weeks. A commitment to hold early elections on the presidency helped to restore the calm. The Argentine example illustrates how social mobilization and protest often acts as the mirror image of institutional development. Institutions move politics from the street to the halls of government. But when they fail, the opposite occurs.

It would be up to the winner of the 2003 presidential elections, Néstor Kirchner, to restore confidence in democratic institutions. He removed justices tainted by corruption, overturned amnesty laws that shielded soldiers implicated during the military regime, and stood up to international banks that demanded harsh austerity measures for the Argentine public. He left office as the most popular departing president in the history of Argentina in 2007, when he was succeeded by his wife, Cristina Fernández de Kirchner, who would win another term in 2011. But Fernández reignited memories of Menem as she made ample use of executive decrees to address a declining economy and sidestep a fractured congress. And disturbing allegations of corruption emerged. Argentines grew suspicious in 2013 when Fernández pushed judicial reforms that limited investigations into government actions and opened the magistrates council, a body that appoints judges, to elections and partisan affiliation. But the Supreme Court was not about to relinquish the independence it formed during Néstor's term. It declared the reform unconstitutional. Fernández' brashness toward institutions did little for her flagging reputation and opened the door for a member of the opposition, Mauricio Macri, to win the presidency in 2016.

In Argentina and elsewhere, institutions serve as a central forum in the struggle for democracy. Their makeup provides insight to the history and culture of a country. Their rules establish guidelines for political actors to negotiate their differences. Their offices serve as a target for actors seeking political power. Likewise, at any given time a snapshot of institutional offices reveals who has power, and who does not. And their legitimacy reveals the prospects for political instability. Most of all, institutions make for an intriguing subject. It is not only interesting to learn about the manifold ways democratic institutions can be designed. It is practical as well. Latin America is filled with countries on the road toward democratic consolidation—some further than others. Whether or not they succeed will be affected significantly by institutional choices. If we envision democracy as a constellation of institutions, and accept that these institutions can take on different features, we open the possibility of **institutional engineering**. For most countries, success on the road to democracy requires "getting institutions right"—tuning them for the right balance of conflict and consensus required for democratic debate and resolution. This chapter continues with an explanation of just how institutions offer an insightful and pragmatic approach to the study of democracy.

Institutions and the Study of Democratic Politics

There is tremendous interest in the prospects for continued democratization in Latin America. How critical is democracy to stability in Venezuela? What did the 2009 removal of President Manuel Zelaya mean for democracy in Honduras? Can democracy survive the drug war in Mexico? Would a stronger democracy have prevented many of the problems and controversies surrounding the 2016 Olympics in Brazil? Costa Rica is special, because its democracy has lasted so long. But all this interest in democracy usually does not translate into an interest in political institutions. This is odd, because efforts by the United States to "remake" political regimes in Iraq and Afghanistan enlivened debates over how constitutional design affects the prospects for democracy. Should a country choose parliamentarism or presidentialism? How much authority should be delegated to the lower levels of government? How much autonomy should the judiciary receive? Should the president be granted emergency powers? Should some legislative seats be reserved for minority groups? Of course, countries in Latin America have already selected their institutions. But that just leads us to reflect on the wisdom of those choices, why those choices were made, what the impact might be, and if needed, what room there might be for modifications. Latin America provides a compelling backdrop to these questions given the number of democracies resting at different levels of consolidation.

And numbers matter here. When we study institutions in a comparative context—in this case, across 18 different countries—we expose a range of institutional possibilities and the consequences for political behavior that follow. Hence, while we might all agree on democratic rule, it is another matter to recognize that there are multiple ways of "doing" democracy. For example, in several Latin American countries, a constitutional tribunal can be asked to rule on the constitutionality of a bill before it is passed by congress. In the United States, such action must wait not only until after the bill becomes law, but also until after it adversely affects a citizen, who then gains standing to bring the case to court. One might say that there is a question of efficiency here, but there is also a question of political power. Is a court that can rule on the constitutionality of legislation before it is passed more powerful than one that is denied this capacity? Perhaps, but a careful assessment would reveal that it all depends on whether the court can take action on its own—or if it must be prompted to act by some other actor, and it also depends on the conditions under which the request must be made. Are a certain number of legislators required to draft the request, are there time limitations, and, perhaps most importantly, is the ruling binding or advisory? Finally, who appoints these judges? Do short term lengths impair their independence? Different Latin American countries have designed different institutions to answer these questions.

What Is an Institution?

What do we mean by *institution*? At their core, institutions are "humanly devised constraints that shape human interaction" (North, 1990, p. 3). They lay out the rules and procedures we must follow if we are to achieve our goals. We work through institutions on a daily basis in all areas of life as we interact with others. Consider the signals you deliver to another person you might see while walking. Do you make eye contact? Do you hold that contact for a period of time? Do you offer a smile? Do you introduce yourself and extend your hand for a shake? These sorts of social conventions are **informal institutions**—they are not expressly defined and written in some code book—but we all have some sense of the messages they send in a given context. And we tend to follow these rules because they allow us to deliver information rather easily to others—even to strangers. Insofar as most all members of a community instill these informal institutions with shared meanings and find their use convenient (or, more accurately, efficient), they create expectations of behavior and the institutions take on a self-enforcing quality (Knight, 1992, pp. 173–186).

Formal institutions, on the other hand, are explicit and look to a third party for enforcement. One need only reflect on a recent drive for an example of a formal institution. There are published rules for driving, and disobedience elicits an immediate enforcement mechanism through a moving violation ticket or other sort of sanction. You and your fellow drivers represent the parties in this instance, and the local police the third party. Organizations, such as a university or workplace, look to formal institutions to regulate their members and activities. Every student in pursuit of a degree is well aware of the rules that must be followed—in the form of required coursework—to achieve graduation. And every employee typically finds a role within the division of labor established by a business organization, and sits within a well-defined hierarchy. Indeed, nearly every decision and action we take is made within the context of some institution, whether formal and codified or not.

Political institutions represent a subset of all institutions—they are different from social institutions such as a book reading club or economic institutions such as the free market. In particular, political institutions shape the scope of human interaction that expressly revolves around questions of power. And within the family of political institutions, government institutions are those that hold legal authority. The Coordinating Committee for the Defense of Water and Life is a grassroots organization located in Cochabamba, Bolivia. It is a political institution, formed by citizens to support public access to water and utility rates. The Congress of Bolivia also deals with water rights and it is a political institution too, but more specifically it is a government institution. What separates government institutions from other political institutions is that the law grants them the right to act on behalf of all members of a society. And under democratic government institutions, that law emerges from a process of popular consent.

Some of these government institutions take on an informal character, but they can still be formidable. In the United States, there are no vocational requirements for nominees to the Supreme Court, but no president would think of proposing a candidate lacking credentials in the field of law. In Chile, President Michelle Bachelet pushed a gender parity standard for cabinet appointments during her first term (2006–2010). She followed through, and fell victim to criticisms of favoritism even from members of her own party. But the move initiated debate, and a greater awareness of gender disparities. She returned to the presidency in 2014, and this time appointed women to just 40% of cabinet positions. Nonetheless, she did create a new position, the Ministry of Women and Gender Equality. Insofar as Chileans are growing more likely to consider and at some level expect gender parity, this standard may be emerging as an informal institution, if a weak one. And other informal institutions, strong and weak alike, abound in government, as in the expectations of decorum in matters of parliamentary procedure.[2]

Despite the significance and ubiquity of informal institutions in government, this book centers on formal institutions, and it does so for three reasons. First, the approach provides a straightforward introduction to government. We are all generally aware of the formal institutions found in democracies, and this provides the first step to a more thorough inquiry into how they work and contribute to democratic politics. In essence, formal institutions provide a road map to the political activity in a country. Second, countries have more formal government institutions in common than informal government institutions, so that they provide solid basis for comparing the politics of different countries. Insofar as it is interesting to explore how countries approach politics in different ways, the formal institutional framework of a country establishes the groundwork. There is no denying that some political actors will at times use informal institutions, or work outside government institutions, and that these informal institutions might buttress formal democratic institutions (Helmke and Levitsky, 2006). But the fact remains that formal government institutions alone provide a primary point of reference as political actors, be they inside or outside of government, pursue and protect their interests. And finally, there is a normative reason. Namely, even those who emphasize the importance of informal institutions recognize that the rule of law requires the most important matters of politics to be decided through formal institutions (O'Donnell, 1996). As such, political institutions make for a worthy and enticing topic of study (e.g., Cheibub, 2007; Peters 1999; Reynolds, 2002).

What Is an Institutional Approach to Politics?

It does not take much to stir interest in the history and politics of Latin America. The countless tales of conquistadores who laid ruin to rich civilizations and the stories of repressive strongmen who presided over large estates built on the backs of indigent peasants provoke outrage. The seizure of one-half of Mexico's territory in the U.S.-Mexico War, evidence of covert operations from abroad, and continued economic vulnerabilities initiate debates over responsibility for the ills we see in Latin America. The famous and infamous—Pancho Villa, Juan Perón, Che Guevara, Augusto Pinochet,

Alberto Fujimori, Chico Mendes, Hugo Chávez, and Rigoberta Menchú—rouse our curiosity. Long-lasting periods of political instability astonish us—Peru had 69 presidents in its first 100 years, and El Salvador had 62 presidents in just its first 50 years. And then there are the puzzles—Argentina was one of the richest countries in the world at the start of the twentieth century, but that future crumbled in the Great Depression, and was later replaced by brutal military rule. Costa Rica abolished its armed forces in 1948 and saved itself from the scourge of military rule that hit the region later. Venezuela also survived the military rule of the 1960s to 1980s, only to experience an attempted military coup in 1992, and then see the person who led that coup—Hugo Chávez—move into the presidency through democratic elections.

Achievements and challenges have marked more recent times. Argentina has placed many of the officers responsible for human rights violations more than three decades ago behind bars. But impunity reigns in Guatemala, despite a dirty war from 1960 to 1996 that saw almost 200,000 killed. Brazil accelerated its economic growth under the banner of a socialist worker's party, gained worldwide fame with winning bids on the 2014 World Cup and 2016 Olympics, then saw its dreams dashed as an economic downturn, presidential impeachment, and mushrooming corruption scandals brought embarrassment on the world stage. The PRI party in Mexico, which presided over six decades of authoritarian rule during the twentieth century, regained the presidency through competitive elections in 2012. El Salvador elected a former guerrilla insurgent, Salvador Sánchez Céren, to its presidency in 2014. Despite the supposed influence of a *machismo* culture, women have sat in the presidential palaces of five Latin American countries over the past ten years, and female representation in congress is higher than in the United States in over one-half of Latin American countries. Indigenous groups in Ecuador finally realized just how much power they could wield after forming a political party in the 1990s, and in Bolivia, the indigenous saw one of their own—Evo Morales—elected in 2006. Social movements have scored successes as never before and inspired widespread pushes for justice and equality. These include water rights groups in Bolivia, landless movements in Brazil, environmental activists in Ecuador, and trade unions in Costa Rica. Human rights groups use social media to expose abuses that formerly would have remained hidden. Gay and lesbian activists have been able to secure rights to same-sex marriage in Argentina, Brazil, Colombia, and Uruguay, and civil unions in Chile and Ecuador.

It is easy to get caught up in the drama and excitement found in the history and politics of Latin America. Still, at some point it all begs explanation. When looking over the past and present in Latin America, it is one thing to be captivated by events, but it is quite another to understand those events. How should we approach it all? As a first step, we can recognize that if there is one undercurrent to political developments in the region, it is the struggle for democracy. From there, we should note that democracy, at its core, is but a collection of institutions—it requires a set of electoral rules and a party system, an executive, legislature, and judiciary, and there are always the choices of a military and federal arrangements. Hence, to anchor our understanding of political events in Latin America, we can look to political institutions. It is institutions that make the difference between instability and order, and it is the character of those institutions that determines whether that order is forged through autocratic or democratic means. With an institutional approach, we do not simply survey history to document periods of order or disorder. Rather, we ask why and how institutions succeeded or failed and contributed to such conditions.

Because institutions set rules, we can look to them to gain a sense of how political actors are likely to behave, and what sort of outcomes we should expect in a country. **Rational choice institutionalism** is a school of thought that emphasizes how institutions affect the behavior of calculating, self-interested political actors. In this perspective, institutions are collections of incentives and disincentives that tailor individual choice. A political actor has a goal, takes note of how the institutional setting affects the costs and benefits of acting, and then acts upon that goal (or decides against doing so). The behavior chosen to achieve a political goal and the very likelihood of success are largely determined by the institutional setting.

For example, to be elected to office, a candidate may need to collect a certain number of signatures and do so in a minimum number of districts, and may need to secure the nomination of a certified political party. Some of these rules, such as signature requirements and the need to seek support across multiple districts, are expressly designed to create incentives for candidates to take on a broad-based appeal. And rules are rarely neutral. They advantage some and disadvantage others. The eligibility requirements noted above may help create more inclusive, wide-ranging parties, but they might also exclude localized indigenous groups or independent candidates from office. And things grow more intriguing when we place institutions in the context of other institutions. Often, interesting interactions result. For example, electoral systems in Latin America use proportional representation and tend to produce multiple parties. This accommodates diverse perspectives in society, but it also makes it difficult to pass legislation in congress, and thus tends to tilt decision-making power toward presidents in Latin America, who hold more substantial legislative powers than the U.S. president. Holding all else equal, we thus see how the push for greater representation with proportional representation alongside this sort of presidential system can backfire and create a concentration of power (Mainwaring, 1993).

But institutions often do more than just channel our impulses and interact. A second school of thought, **historical institutionalism**, holds that institutions can also create the motivations that initiate our behavior in the first place, and they can even shape our very identities (March and Olsen, 1989; Steinmo, Thelen, and Longstreth, 1992). One scholar of political institutions, Stephen Skowronek, recognizes just how intensely institutions affect political leaders:

> Called upon to account for their actions or to explain their decisions, incumbents have no recourse but to repair to their job descriptions. Thus, institutions do not simply constrain or channel the actions of self-interested individuals, they prescribe actions, construct motives, and assert legitimacy. (1995, p. 94)

Rules first created to check behavior in short order establish patterns of expected behavior, and these in turn shape a sense of appropriate behavior. Political institutions also affect the sensibilities of those outside government, in society, as well.

Consider the impact of federalism, which divides government authority between national and local levels. This political institution not only limits government, but, over time, as people live under federalism, they may grow more endeared toward this form of rule and view it as the only appropriate and legitimate form of rule for them. The point is important because institutions tend to have staying power (Pierson, 2004). Insofar as they channel our behavior, they create routines to which we grow accustomed. And insofar as they benefit some groups that grow more powerful over time, interests emerge to protect them. Further, keep in mind that political institutions are often enshrined in the constitution and require supermajorities to modify. All this means that a small elite might craft a political institution with their own values in mind, or an institution might be designed to accommodate the interests of contending groups, and the institution then has a chance to outlast its creators. As suffrage expands, or new groups rise in importance, and work under such institutions, they may grow accustomed to the values enmeshed within these institutions and embrace them.

For example, in 1993 Brazilians held a referendum to consider whether they wanted to switch from a presidential to a parliamentary form of government. But the presidential tradition in Brazil reaches back to 1889 when Brazil abandoned its monarchy to become a republic. Competition and suffrage were limited at the time, but the seed of presidential government had been planted such that those voting in the 1993 referendum could not help but reflect upon its meaning to the country's political development. Brazil had just transitioned from military rule in 1985. Insofar as military rule was an aberration, and civilians now had the opportunity to restore legitimate rule to the country, Brazilians felt compelled to reaffirm their political traditions. The referendum failed because presidentialism was far too ingrained in Brazilian identity, despite the fact that the architects of Brazilian presidentialism lived long ago.

As both reservoirs of political identities and tools for constitutional engineers, institutions capture both past and present. Countries in Latin America have rich histories that reach back beyond the independence period of the early nineteenth century, farther than the 300 years of colonial rule that preceded independence, and deep into the indigenous civilizations that once governed the region. Political institutions in Latin America draw from political traditions, thought, and culture throughout this history. Indeed, how to synthesize them all remains one of the most pressing topics of contemporary politics. The composure of Latin American political institutions reveals influences from indigenous civilizations, Spanish and Portuguese rule, the ideology of the French Revolution, the tenets of the American Revolution, recurrent periods of instability and *caudillo* rule, and prescriptions of foreign actors such as the World Bank, the International Monetary Fund (IMF), United Nations, and the U.S. State Department and U.S. military.

Institutions thus provide a lens on the past. But their contemporary evolution also exposes the latest political topics of concern in the region. For example, few would deny that gender and indigenous mobilization are prominent issues in contemporary Latin America. They are reflected in institutions as legislatures grapple with gender quotas, parties create female caucuses that bridge partisan lines, courts come to terms with indigenous justice, congressional seats are set aside for indigenous representation, and central governments consider autonomous rule for different ethnic groups. The study of institutional design in Latin America provides a focal point for the broader examination and contemplation of Latin American politics—both its past and its future.

Similarly, institutions also act as a medium between political thought and practical politics. Take, for example, judicial institutions. Common law tradition, as in the United States, tells us to embrace the courts as conservators of our political traditions. Common law thinking offers judges a wide breadth of autonomy, and grants them extensive political powers (most notably, judicial review). But the code law tradition in Latin America questions the democratic credentials of systems that assign powers to nonelected officials. Courts are to be emasculated and treated as advisory bodies. And insofar as they gain political authority, they must be subject to close political oversight from other branches of government. The debate between common law and code law visions is provocative, but ultimately it is a debate that moves from the abstract to the concrete only as it is resolved through institutions—the procedures for judicial appointment, the extent of tenure, the breadth of constitutional review powers, and so on. And when we expose these institutional differences, we have to ask why Latin American countries are so committed to code law. The answer is found in the past—in the influence of the French Revolution on the institutional development of the country. Likewise, the breadth of presidential powers we see in Latin America partly reflects compromises wrought early on as independence leaders worked a middle road between those hoping for monarchic government and others who desired a republic. An institutional approach allows us to merge everyday politics with the history, culture, and traditions of a country and to open discussions on these topics.

COMPARING COUNTRIES

Do Authoritarians Follow Institutional Rules? Military Regimes and Institutional Design

One might assume that institutions resemble little more than felt ropes at a movie theater. They offer guidance and people tend to work within them, but when push comes to shove—when somebody cries "fire" in a movie theater—people are more than willing to violate the rules. If institutions truly are so frail, and readily fall when opposed, they would not be a very valuable subject of study. To counter this skepticism, we can look to the military regimes that preceded the current democratic regimes in Latin America (Arceneaux, 2001). For if institutions have the power to shape military rule, surely they must be influential under democratic rule as well. After all, these militaries came to power by overthrowing the constitutional order and they ruled with brute force.

And as it turns out, institutions are important under military rule as well. No matter the military or its specific goals, all professional militaries have in common the urge to maintain military unity. Order and hierarchy are the prized values of a professional military because they are necessary requisites to its fundamental purpose—the preservation of national security. But governing can upend the disciplined solidarity of the armed forces. Policymaking involves debate. Some officers may make better governors than their superiors. All of this can disrupt the ranks and lead soldiers to call for a withdrawal from government for the sake of military unity, and national security. Hence, the question military regimes face is: do some institutional arrangements preserve military unity better than others?

The armed forces in Brazil experienced one of the longest periods of rule in modern history—from 1964 to 1985. Collegial institutions gave superior officers in each of the services a voice, which also meant that they all held some responsibility for government decisions. A succession of powerful military executives presided over the regime, but a large assembly of superior officers determined who ruled and no president was allowed to succeed himself. Strict promotion, assignment, and retirement regulations ensured a fluid turnover in the ranks, and restricted the rise of personalistic factions. To complement its collegial institutions, the armed forces looked outside the military, to civilians, to staff many government positions. A formal consultation process,

(continued)

known as the *conselho* system, invited civilian policy experts to share their views under the direction of the different government ministries. In addition, civilians filled the legislature, which was granted greater authority over time, and civilians also found posts in the lower levels of Brazil's federal system. The fact that the military did not completely supplant all government positions also helped to prevent the rise of factions. Any officer hoping to amass power could reach only so far into government positions, and thus ultimately had to answer to the military hierarchy first.

Chile also had a long-lasting military regime, but it was in many ways the institutional opposite of the Brazilian military regime. The army commander, Augusto Pinochet, at first took a position alongside the other service commanders in a military *junta* just after the 1973 coup. But in short order he accumulated greater power, first by becoming president of the republic, then by assuming complete control over the armed forces as commander in chief. And in distinction to Brazil, soldiers took on a much more visible presence and civilians did not find their way into notable government positions. The legislature was suspended, military intendants rather than governors administrated the provinces, and civilian ministers sat behind the scenes. Pinochet ruled supremely to 1990. Whereas the Brazilian regime accommodated would-be military factions by allowing their input, but offering little opportunity to control government, Pinochet suppressed prospective rivals. The institutions offered alternative strategies for the forging of a similar goal—military unity.

Military rule in Argentina illustrates how institutional design can have the opposite effect, and spark discord. From 1966 to 1970, General Juan Carlos Onganía presided over a military regime, but his control was uneven. As president, he designed and administered policies with full authority. But he exerted much less control over the armed forces. He was commander in chief, but his service commanders exerted greater control over promotions and assignments. And because this military preferred to stay behind the scenes, he could not curry favor and build a following in military circles by doling out government positions to officers. Over time, the military grew alienated. They were responsible for a government that neither offered participation to it nor exerted authority over it. An internal coup removed Onganía in 1970 and the military struggled to withdraw from power over the following three years. In 1976, after another military coup, the Argentine armed forces would draw all the wrong lessons from the Onganía period. This time, they decided to rule collegially, but unlike Brazil, they did not grant civilians much of a role. They had stayed behind the scenes under Onganía, and so decided that direct involvement would strengthen military rule. The army, navy, and air force essentially split up the government, as each took control of a different policy area. But direct involvement—when combined with collegial rule—spurred divisions, as factions saw that they had the wherewithal to accumulate power and vie for complete control. The divisions tore at military unity and led the regime to collapse in 1983.

Institutional arrangements mattered in these military regimes. Collegial rule and limited military staffing in government positions allowed Brazilian leaders to accommodate factions but at the same time impede moves by military splinters to accumulate power. On the other hand, collegial rule in 1976 Argentina was problematic because too many officers found their way into government positions of power, leading the armed forces to become politicized and divided. Concentrated rule in Chile was successful because it was so complete. Pinochet could rule through the suppression of rivals. Onganía also concentrated government authority, but without a greater fusion of government and military roles, he could not exert authority over the armed forces. The lessons for military rule are clear. If a military is to rule collegially, it should not draw soldiers too deeply into government and instead look to civilians for staffing. If a military is to concentrate authority, it should place officers throughout government to ensure a close tie between the president and the military institution. In a comparative study of military regimes, Karen Remmer (1991) found that regimes that dispersed authority and separated military and government roles (e.g., Brazil) lasted an average of 16.3 years, whereas those that concentrated authority and combined military and government roles (e.g., Chile) lasted an average of 25.1 years. On the other hand, those that dispersed authority but combined military and government roles (e.g., Argentina in 1976) lasted only 6.5 years, whereas those that concentrated authority but separated military and government roles (e.g., Argentina in 1966) lasted just 6.9 years. In the end, we see that institutions are hardly like the felt ropes of a movie theater. Even brutal military regimes behave according to a logic of institutional design.

(continued)

Discussion Questions

1   Beyond institutions, what other factors might help to explain differences in the longevity and impact of military rule in Argentina, Brazil, and Chile?

2   Consider the general influence of institutions in all areas of life. How do institutions tailor your decisions and behavior on a daily basis? How have they shaped where you are today, and what goals you have set for yourself?

Democracy in Latin America

Democracy is not new to Latin America. When the states of the region became independent in the early 1800s, they did so in a time when it was growing more acceptable to look to people rather than kings for the right to rule. This is not to say that some sectors did not embrace monarchy or limited suffrage, but the fact remained that founding fathers of the time had to at least respond to calls for democratic rule. The French and American revolutions were all-too-powerful examples for the nascent states of Latin America. Nonetheless, political elites made significant compromises to democratic rule (see Chapter 3), and those institutions of popular input that did emerge almost uniformly crumbled during the civil strife of the early nineteenth century.

But other efforts to democratize followed. Samuel Huntington (1991) noted that these episodic pushes for democracy occurred in waves across the world in the 1820s and the 1940s. For Latin America, we can identify another wave in the 1890s or so. And like waves, each democratic trend crested and then came crashing down to give way to periods of authoritarian rule. The most recent crash came in the 1960s and 1970s, when a torrent of military interventions tossed popularly elected governments. The 1964 military coup d'état in Brazil signaled the beginning of the end of this **democratic wave**. That history is important, because the most recent democratic wave occurred largely in the 1980s, beginning with the Dominican Republic in 1978. The 1990 transition in Chile capped this wave, although several Central American states followed up on earlier, limited elections with important peace accords in the 1990s. The identification of past waves raises the question of whether or not the current democratic wave has crested, and if it too will come crashing down and allow authoritarianism or something less than democratic rule to return. History shows us that democracy is not necessarily permanent, no matter the desire to maintain it. This is why it is so important to explore how democratic institutions work, and the options available to those that create democratic institutions. A more informed approach to institutional design may spare Latin America from the political waves it suffered in the past.

Figure 1.1 Latin America

Source: © Shutterstock.

Democratic Transition

In his classic study, Robert Dahl noted that the move toward democracy begins when the rulers of an authoritarian regime decide, "the costs of suppression exceed the costs of toleration" (1971, p. 15). While not intending to downplay the human suffering experienced by those living under authoritarianism, we should recognize that repression can take a toll on the regime itself. Widespread protests disrupt economic activity. Human rights abuses draw criticisms from the international arena. And the use of brutal measures tends to causes fissures in the authoritarian government. Resorting to violence empowers some groups, such as the intelligence services or secret police, who grow more unwilling to compromise or accept reform for fear of human rights investigations later on down the road. The interests of these **hard-liners** may conflict with **soft-liners** in the regime that view some level of reform as the only option for the regime to gain some level of legitimacy, and to be able to set aside the costs of blunt repression.

The competing evaluations of hard-liners and soft-liners on the costs of suppression and toleration underscore a fundamental dynamic of transitions from authoritarian rule—namely, that these changes take place in an environment of uncertainty. Hard-liners and soft-liners begin to question each other's motives. Fear, rage, and the thirst for dignity drive social protests in unpredictable directions. Politicians face a constant stream of pivotal moments that require immediate decisions. Should troops be called upon to put down protests? Will the public view a televised speech by the president as a sign of resolve, or as a concession? Will international criticism rally the protestors, or fan nationalism?

Photo 1.2 March for Peace: Several countries in Latin America have yet to consolidate democracy. In Colombia, the FARC guerrilla group used armed struggle rather than institutions to express their interests. In 2016, they negotiated a peace agreement with the government.

Source: © Shutterstock.

Because uncertainty plays such an important role in democratic transitions, scholars have focused more on charting out the processes by which transitions take place, rather than focusing on certain prerequisites that make democracy more or less likely in a country.[3] The recognition that hard-line and soft-line groups emerge does not allow us to predict the prospects for democracy with complete accuracy, but it does provide a sort of map that allows us to chart transition dynamics as they occur. Soft-liners hold an early crucial position as they mediate between hard-liners and the democratic opposition. Moderate and radical elements emerge within the democratic opposition, and their decisions add to the dynamic. Moderates may align with regime softliners to initiate a gradual reform. Or those calling for radical change may be too strong, and pull the moderates into their corner. In this case, regime soft-liners might decide to support the hard-liners and a repressive backlash, or to step aside and allow the regime to collapse. Transition dynamics are like a delicate balance scale that tips as political actors react to each other and move from one weighing pan to the other.

These dynamics—should they lead to democracy—take place within a series of stages that run from **liberalization** to **transition** and then **consolidation**. Liberalization refers to the early reforms made under the authoritarian regime. They may include local elections, the loosening of restrictions on political expression or assembly, or the release of prisoners or general amnesties. Transition occurs the moment authoritarian leaders hand over power after competitive elections, and it signifies the emergence of democracy. Consolidation is a long-term process that sees the new democratic regime gain widespread support within society such that it is accepted as "the only game in town" (Linz, 1990, p. 156).

Why is it important to identify these phases? Liberalization can be a long, drawn-out affair. In the Brazilian military regime of 1964–1985, liberalization occurred as early as 1974 when the regime allowed more competitive congressional elections, and other reforms followed over an 11-year process. Under such long, drawn-out liberalization, members of the democratic opposition often play within the rules of the game established by the authoritarians. This makes it much more difficult for the democratic leaders who emerge after the transition to condemn the regime and take punitive action—too many may have participated in and played by the rules established by the authoritarians. Little wonder that Brazil's democratic leaders have yet to initiate far-reaching trials for the abuses that took place under the military regime. On the other hand, Argentina's military regime never initiated a significant liberalization process. It ultimately collapsed, and human rights trials immediately followed the transition.

The distinction between transition and consolidation is especially important because it reminds us that democracy is a matter of quality, and that institutions cannot stand separate from society. Seminal work by Linz and Stepan (1996, p. 16) gauges consolidation in three areas:

> *Behaviorally*, a democratic regime in a territory is consolidated when no significant national, social, economic, political, or institutional actors spend significant resources attempting to achieve their objectives by creating a nondemocratic regime or by seceding from the state. *Attitudinally*, a democratic regime is consolidated when a strong majority of public opinion, even in the midst of major economic problems and deep dissatisfaction with incumbents, holds the belief that democratic procedures and institutions are the most appropriate way to govern collective life, and when support for antisystem alternatives is quite small, or more or less isolated from prodemocratic forces. *Constitutionally*, a democratic regime is consolidated when governmental and nongovernmental forces alike become subject to, and habituated to, the resolution of conflict within the bounds of the specific laws, procedures, and institutions sanctioned by the new democratic process.

The behavioral, attitudinal, and constitutional features of democratic consolidation remind us that institutions are but one part of democracy. Nonetheless, we can situate institutions as the core element of democracy and the process of democratic consolidation insofar as institutions channel behavior (as rational choice institutionalism reminds us) and engender new attitudes (as noted by historical institutionalists). The institutitional approach to democratization is thus a very practical affair—design the institutions properly, then behavioral and attitudinal changes will follow. Through the following chapters, we will see that some countries in Latin America sit further along in the process of democratic consolidation than others, and we will recognize how institutions have contributed to or hindered such movements.

Defining Democracy

Democracy is now the norm in Latin America. To be authoritarian is to be unusual. There are 33 states in Latin America. This study examines the 18 democratic countries of the region that share a colonial history with Spain or Portugal. That means it includes only the Dominican Republic of the 12 countries in the Caribbean. It excludes Belize in Central America, and it does not examine Guyana or Suriname in South America. The 18 countries that are left share important historical and colonial experiences, which makes it easier to focus on and compare their institutions. Of these 18 countries, only Colombia, Costa Rica, and Venezuela could claim a democratic government before 1978. Now all are democratic, but democracy is a variable, and some are more democratic than others. See Table 1.1 for a summary of democratic transitions in Latin America.

How do we know a democracy when we see one? One of the most simple and widely cited definitions comes from Joseph Schumpeter: "the democratic method is that institutional arrangement for arriving at political decisions in which individuals acquire the power to decide by means of a competitive struggle for the people's vote" (1947, p. 269). Schumpeter focuses on the **political rights** of voting and the competition for votes, but he really does not capture the host of **civil liberties** required to ensure the responsiveness and accountability of government after an election is held, nor does he highlight the importance of maintaining the rule of law on a routine basis. A democracy that lives up to the standards set by Schumpeter can still show glowing democratic deficiencies. In the early 1990s, the Central American countries—less Costa Rica—lived up to the Schumpeterian standard for competitive elections, but analysts still

Table 1.1 **Democratic Transitions in Latin America.** Most Latin American countries became democratic at about the same time in the most recent wave of democratization

	Year of Democratic Transition
Argentina	1983
Bolivia	1983
Brazil	1985
Chile	1990
Colombia	1958
Costa Rica	1949
Dominican Republic*	1978
Ecuador	1979
El Salvador*	1984
Guatemala*	1986
Honduras	1982
Mexico	2000
Nicaragua*	1984
Panama*	1990
Paraguay	1989
Peru*	1980
Uruguay	1985
Venezuela	1958

*El Salvador and Guatemala were embroiled in civil wars until 1992 and 1996, respectively. The countries suffered serious limitations on civil liberties during this time, even while elections took place. Nicaragua shared a similar fate through much of the 1980s. Manuel Noriega severely limited democratic rule in Panama from 1990 to 1994. Alberto Fujimori did the same in Peru from 1992 to 2000. Joaquín Balaguer stole the 1994 presidential elections in the Dominican Republic and ruled until 1997.

viewed their democratic credentials as suspect. At the time, Karl (1995) offered the following description of El Salvador, Guatemala, and Honduras:

> Gains in the electoral arena have not been accompanied by the establishment of civilian control over the military or the rule of law. Elections are often free and fair, yet important sectors remain politically and economically disenfranchised. Militaries support civilian presidents, but they resist efforts by civilians to control internal military affairs, dictate security policy, make officers subject to the judgment of civil courts, or weaken their role as the ultimate arbiters of politics. Impunity is condemned, yet judiciaries remain weak, rights are violated, and contracts are broken.

Such **electoral democracies** may protect political rights, but they are incomplete democracies. They become **liberal democracies** when a full array of civil liberties arise "so that contending interests and values may be expressed and compete through ongoing processes of articulation and representation, beyond periodic elections" (Diamond, 1999, pp. 10–11). In a liberal democracy, the rule of law buttresses these civil liberties so that citizens can ensure the accountability of officeholders through means beyond mere elections (e.g., the availability of the courts to check government abuse and an independent media to act as a watchdog).

Freedom House is a valuable source for the measurement of the political rights associated with participation and competition in elections, and the civil liberties required of a liberal democracy. This U.S.-based organization has been studying and supporting democracy worldwide since 1941. Eleanor Roosevelt was its first chair. Today, Freedom House is known for an annual report, "Freedom in the World." It is used regularly by academics to analyze democratization. The report assigns every country in the world separate scores for its political rights and civil liberties. To create the report, teams of experts discuss and score each country after reviewing a series of questions on political rights and civil liberties.

To assess the quality of political rights in a country, Freedom House has designed specific questions to evaluate different aspects of a political system:

1 **Electoral Process**

    a Is the head of government or other chief national authority elected through free and fair elections?

    b Are the national legislative representatives elected through free and fair elections?

    c Are the electoral laws and framework fair?

2 **Political Pluralism and Participation**

    a Do the people have the right to organize in different political parties or other competitive political groupings of their choice, and is the system open to the rise and fall of these competing parties or groupings?

b Is there a significant opposition vote and a realistic possibility for the opposition to increase its support or gain power through elections?

c Are the people's political choices free from domination by the military, foreign powers, totalitarian parties, religious hierarchies, economic oligarchies, or any other powerful group?

d Do cultural, ethnic, religious, or other minority groups have full political rights and electoral opportunities?

3 **Functioning of Government**

a Do the freely elected head of government and national legislative representatives determine the policies of the government?

b Is the government free from pervasive corruption?

c Is the government accountable to the electorate between elections, and does it operate with openness and transparency?

A separate set of questions addresses features of civil liberties:

4 **Freedom of Expression and Belief**

a Are there free and independent media and other forms of cultural expression? (Note: In cases where the media are state controlled but offer pluralistic points of view, the survey gives the system credit.)

b Are religious institutions and communities free to practice their faith and express themselves in public and private?

c Is there academic freedom, and is the educational system free of extensive political indoctrination?

d Is there open and free private discussion?

5 **Associational and Organizational Rights**

a Is there freedom of assembly, demonstration, and open public discussion?

b Is there freedom for nongovernmental organizations? (Note: Here special attention is given to groups with a focus on human rights and/ or governance issues.)

c Are there free trade unions and peasant organizations or equivalents, and is there effective collective bargaining? Are there free professional and other private organizations?

6 **Rule of Law**

a Is there an independent judiciary?

b Does the rule of law prevail in civil and criminal matters? Are police under direct civilian control?

c Is there protection from political terror, unjustified imprisonment, exile, or torture, whether by groups that support or oppose the system? Is there freedom from war and insurgencies?

d Do laws, policies, and practices guarantee equal treatment of various segments of the population?

7 Personal Autonomy and Individual Rights

    a Do citizens enjoy freedom of travel or choice of residence, employment, or institution of higher education?

    b Do citizens have the right to own property and establish private businesses? Is private business activity unduly influenced by government officials, the security forces, political parties/organizations, or organized crime?

    c Are there personal social freedoms, including gender equality, choice of marriage partners, and size of family?

    d Is there equality of opportunity and the absence of economic exploitation?

The scores for political rights and civil liberties are then tabulated on a 1–7 scale. A lower score indicates more freedom. The two scores are averaged, so that countries scoring 1.0–2.5 are considered "free," 3.0–5.0 are considered "partly free," and 5.5–7.0 are considered "not free." Table 1.2 lists the Freedom House scores for Latin America in the 2011 report. Democracy is indeed the norm in Latin America, but there remains room for improvement. Only 9 of the 18 countries in this study have achieved "free" status as calculated by Freedom House.

It is interesting to note that when deviations between the two scores appear, civil liberties tend to be worse off than political rights. This is the case for Colombia, El Salvador, Panama, and Peru. Both dimensions of the scoring guide incorporate government institutions, but they tend to be more prominently represented in political rights. The discrepancy raises the prospect that political rights may be easier for countries to implement than the deeper aspects of democracy captured by civil liberties (they are what move citizen involvement from periodic elections to "ongoing articulation and representation"). And it may imply that political rights serve as a starting point for democratization and set the groundwork for the expansion civil liberties. Schumpeter's electoral democracy may be incomplete, but it may be the first step to a liberal democracy. Countries can first work on government institutions to ensure basic protections for political rights, and then reach out to matters of civil liberties vested more squarely in society to make a decisive move toward liberal democracy.

Table 1.2 **Freedom House Scores for Latin America, 2015.** Although most countries in Latin America are democratic, they vary in their level of democracy

	Political Rights	*Civil Liberties*	*Aggregate Score*	*Freedom Rating*
Argentina	2	2	79	Free (2)
Bolivia	3	3	68	Partly Free (3)

	Political Rights	Civil Liberties	Aggregate Score	Freedom Rating
Brazil	2	2	81	Free (2)
Chile	1	1	95	Free (1)
Colombia	3	4	63	Partly Free (3.5)
Costa Rica	1	1	90	Free (1)
Dominican Republic	3	3	70	Free (3)
Ecuador	3	3	59	Partly Free (3)
El Salvador	2	3	69	Free (2.5)
Guatemala	4	4	54	Partly Free (4)
Honduras	4	4	45	Partly Free (4)
Mexico	3	3	65	Partly Free (3)
Nicaragua	4	3	54	Partly Free (3.5)
Panama	1	2	83	Free (2)
Paraguay	3	3	64	Partly Free (3)
Peru	2	3	71	Free (2.5)
Uruguay	1	1	98	Free (1)
Venezuela	5	5	35	Partly Free (5)

Source: Data tabulated from Freedom in the World: 2016 Edition (Washington, D.C.: Freedom House). Available at Freedomhouse.org.

COUNTRY IN THE SPOTLIGHT

The Struggle for Democracy in Guatemala

In Guatemala, the struggle for democracy has been long, difficult, and violent. The country is not close to liberal democracy. Freedom House marks it as "partly free," with scores of 4 for both political rights and civil liberties, and a listless aggregate score of 54. Guatemala is an electoral democracy plagued by economic disparity, the exclusion of indigenous communities, political instability, impunity, and rampant crime. In the face of these troubles it brandishes little more than a frail skeleton of democratic institutions. These institutions—their

(continued)

development and all their deficiencies—illuminate the somber prospects for continued democratic growth in Guatemala.

The colonial legacy in Guatemala placed most of the land in the hands of a small economic elite. They harvested dyes from cochineal insects and indigo plants for export to Europe, and moved on to coffee production in the later nineteenth century as synthetic dyes dulled demand for their previous exports. The majority indigenous population found themselves shut out from these economic ventures, and relegated to the smallest plots of land in the most inaccessible areas of the country. And as if the economic disparity did not create enough tension, regional strongmen within the oligarchy looked upon one another with suspicion, and vied for power in the nascent state. The divisions set the stage for a series of civil wars and military intervention in government. Stability came slowly, and only through harsh rule as presidents concentrated power. Toward the end of the nineteenth century, foreign investors emerged as another important actor. Most prominently, the United Fruit Company (UFCO), based in the United States, quickly became the country's largest landowner and employer as bananas joined coffee as a main export.

Guatemala had political parties and elections during this time, but they were limited to the wealthier, urban classes and stained by fraud. The façade of electoral competition was fully exposed under President Jorge Ubico (1931–1944), who ruled dictatorially in the interests of the economic elite. He enforced the Vagrancy Laws, which required all those in the countryside owning fewer than 10 acres to work 90 days on one of the large farming estates, without pay. His rule ended after a revolt led by urban middle-class groups and mid-level military officers. In 1944, the first truly competitive elections in the history of Guatemala brought forth the reformist government of Juan José Arévalo, who broadened civil rights protections, initiated literacy programs, granted greater protections to labor unions, and pushed a voter registration drive. President Jacobo Arbenz followed in 1951 and built upon the reforms with policy changes meant to address the extreme economic inequality in the countryside. In rural areas, about 2 percent of the landowners controlled some 70 percent of the land. Worse yet, much of the land sat fallow, forcing the country to import foodstuffs. But the policy to redistribute land meant confronting UFCO. This gained the attention of policymakers in the United States, who in the midst of the Cold War associated most any move to address economic inequality with communism and ties to the Soviet Union—whether these existed or not. In 1954, Arbenz would be overthrown in a military coup organized by the CIA.

The military governments that followed received support from the United States and quickly reversed the reforms instituted under Arévalo and Arbenz. Guatemala had become a front in the Cold War, despite the fact that most Guatemalans cared only for their own livelihoods and little about global ideological confrontations between capitalism and communism. Over time, several guerrilla groups formed to combat the government, and in 1982 banded together as the Guatemalan National Revolutionary Union (URNG). By this time, effective moves by the military in the eastern side of the country had sent the guerrillas to the western highlands, where the country's indigenous population is concentrated. Ruthless military repression throughout this period included the use of torture, disappearances, massacres, and even scorched-earth campaigns that dropped napalm in the countryside. Some 200,000 perished. The indigenous represented 83 percent of that total, and most were simply caught in the crossfire (Guatemalan Commission for Historical Clarification, 1999).

Growing international isolation, military infighting, and influence from the fledgling democratic wave in Latin America led the military to hand government over to civilians in 1986. Nonetheless, the military continued its repressive military campaign, and the civilian government did little to confront human rights abuses of the past or present. Mediation efforts sponsored by the United Nations, peace initiatives from neighboring Central American countries, and growing warweariness on the part of the military and URNG led to a series of peace accords from 1994 to 1996. The accords addressed a host of issues, including the verification of human rights abuses and the creation of a truth commission, resettlement, judicial reform, social welfare spending, indigenous rights, procedures for a cease-fire and military demobilization, electoral reforms, and civilian control over the military. As a result, the URNG laid down its arms and formed a political party.

Civil war no longer menaces Guatemala, but its democratic institutions remain fragile. These institutions rest upon and reflect the pernicious past of the country, and their standard operations embody the contemporary struggle for democracy. In fact, early on institutional procedures proved critical to the implementation of the peace accords. The reforms addressed in the peace accords required constitutional changes, and under the Guatemalan constitution, this meant

(*continued*)

that Congress had to approve the measures with a two-thirds vote, and then submit the reforms to a national referendum. Consider the dilemma: The reforms were meant to stabilize a teetering democracy, but the process required to implement them presumed that democracy was already in play.

In fact, decades of repression had denied political parties the stability required to form linkages in society and grow. Repression had also produced a culture of fear that dulled ideological bonds within parties, such that most parties looked to unreliable personality appeals to unite their ranks (Sánchez, 2008). In any congress, a two-thirds vote is difficult to achieve, but in Guatemala's brittle party system the effort was far more difficult. Compromises, side deals, and delays led what was a reform package of 12 constitutional amendments to swell to 50 proposed reforms over a two-year period. Furthermore, the breadth of reform—from tax policy to indigenous language rights—overwhelmed an electorate unaccustomed to political expression and still harboring tremendous suspicions of government. Keep in mind that the repressive military campaign continued from 1986 to 1996 even while civilians held government office and elections took place. Finally, voting in Guatemala was a costly process. The electoral law limited the number of polling places, forcing the rural poor to travel long distances. It is not surprising that over 80 percent of registered voters stayed away from the polls for the May 1999 referendum. Nonetheless, turnout was higher in urban areas. These voters were less affected by repression, and had less interest in reforms designed to empower the rural, indigenous population. In the end, none of the reforms passed.

Guatemala's armed forces continue to act with autonomy and impunity (Ruhl, 2005). Congress lacks the resources, let alone the will, to assess security policy or to investigate military proposals. Bribery and threats have sidelined the judiciary, such that it displays little initiative to address human rights abuses during the civil war, despite the official report that laid blame for 93 percent of all killings on the Guatemalan military and security forces (Guatemalan Commission for Historical Clarification, 1999). Guatemala's courts have rebuffed extradition requests and mandates to prosecute from courts in Spain and the Inter-American Court of Human Rights under the banner of sovereignty—though they have shown little initiative to take action on their own (Davis and Warner, 2007). Perpetrators of abuses point to an amnesty signed as part of the peace accords in 1996, but the amnesty did not cover forced disappearances, torture, or genocide. Given the extent of violations during the civil war, this means that prosecutions could still take place. However, it also means that each crime must be carefully and thoroughly investigated. Access to military files and records from the civil war period would be helpful, but the archives are stored in the Ministry of Defense, an institution controlled by the armed forces. The ministry may rest in the executive branch, but the Guatemalan constitution requires the minister to be military officer, and the law holds that only a minister can release classified government documents held within his ministry.

The impunity surrounding human rights abuses is not the only breach in the rule of law. Organized crime, much of it related to drug trafficking, has infiltrated the police, courts, administrative offices, and political positions throughout Guatemala. The independence of the judiciary and its ability to uphold the rule of law are in such grave doubt that the country has allowed an independent, foreign institution to bolster its judicial operations. The government negotiated the creation of the International Commission against Impunity in Guatemala with the United Nations in 2006 to give some credibility to its effort to consolidate the rule of law. The commission has staff from 21 countries and initiates investigations on its own, offers recommendations on judicial reform, and supports the litigation conducted by the public prosecutor's office. Early on, the commission saw some convictions result from its efforts, but it expressed frustration over the lack of commitment on the part of the Guatemalan government to address impunity. For Carlos Castresana, director of the commission, the final straw came when President Alvaro Colom appointed an individual with suspected ties to organized crime, Conrado Reyes, as attorney general. In his resignation statement, Castresana plainly noted, "Nothing that was promised is being done" (*NotiCen*, 2010).

The struggle for democracy in Guatemala is complex and difficult. The civil war has ended, but Guatemala remains one of the most violent countries in the world. The drug war in Mexico has pushed drug trafficking toward Guatemala, such that the country now has a homicide rate twice that of Mexico. With a national police force that has thus far proved incompetent, the crime wave has made it difficult to steer the military from its role in internal security—despite an agreement in the peace accords to limit the armed forces to external missions. The wave has allowed many politicians to emphasize a heavy hand to law and order, even at the expense of human rights concerns, which are

(*continued*)

increasingly associated with being soft on crime. And the indigenous remain largely excluded. Dispersed amongst a rugged, rural geography and divided into at least 24 primary language groups, they find it difficult to mobilize. And though they were the target of repression in the civil war, they were never really represented by the URNG, which was led by disgruntled white, middle-class groups. Absent sociocultural attachments to the rural, indigenous majority, it is little surprise that the URNG has largely floundered as a political party.

Such conditions make a difficult foundation for democratic growth. But an institutional approach provides an ideal entry point to the socioeconomic, historical, cultural, and political aspects of this struggle. We cannot understand the level of military autonomy in Guatemala without a look into the past history of military governance and instability, or the present battle against criminal activity. We can only grasp the deficiencies of judicial institutions with an examination of socioeconomic disparities associated with the rule of law. And the lack of political participation alongside flimsy party organizations must be appreciated in the context of the cultural divisions that mar Guatemala. A survey of institutions thus offers a gateway to a host of questions surrounding development, broadly defined, in Guatemala, and it does so from the perspective of the very crux of democracy—institutional development.

But even more so, a look at Guatemala from the perspective of institutions exposes where reforms can be made to further democracy. Consider that one simple electoral reform in 2007—that of expanding the number of rural polling places (restricted under the previous electoral law)—completely changed electoral dynamics. Alvaro Colom won the 2007 presidential elections largely due to his appeal in rural areas, and he won without carrying Guatemala City—a first in Guatemalan history. The simple reform empowered rural areas, and offers one glimmer of hope for Guatemalan democracy. Institutional reforms could also go a long way toward fostering healthier civil-military relations—the control of the military over the Ministry of Defense is a case in point. We might also consider how appointment and tenure procedures in the court system might advance judicial reform, or how the structure and jurisprudence of the legal system affects the ability of the courts to balance executive and congressional power. And we might survey regulations regarding the creation and financing of parties, their nomination procedures, and the impact of electoral rules to assess how changes might strengthen and stabilize the party system. In the meantime, the institutional crutch provided by the International Commission against Impunity in Guatemala also offers a lesson on how outsiders might stir change. Castresana made his point with a resignation, but his successors made theirs with perseverance. By 2015, the commission amassed evidence implicating over 200 government officials in a scandal that ultimately reached to the office of the presidency, and led to his resignation and detainment. Tens of thousands took part in regular demonstrations in the capital, vowing never again to stay silent in the face of impunity. The commission's mandate will end, but if its legacy is to instill a sense of vigilance in the Guatemalan people, it will have succeeded. Institutions, though created by individuals, can exert a powerful influence on the beliefs and goals of a people. In the chapters that follow, we look at these questions and others in much more detail.

Discussion Questions

1   Do you think there are certain social, economic, or cultural preconditions to democracy? In the case of Guatemala, are the issues it faces in these areas insurmountable?
2   Is it appropriate to set aside human rights concerns and efforts to strengthen civilian control over the military when faced with the level of crime that Guatemala currently confronts? What impact does this decision have on democracy?

Conclusion

This book is about the struggle for democracy, and it envisions this struggle as one of institutional design. The focus is on contemporary politics, but because the construction of democratic institutions is so intimately tied to the lengthy processes of state and nation building, the study begins in Chapter 2 with a look back into the pre-Columbian and colonial periods. Chapter 3 continues with a brief survey of historical eras since independence that affected state and nation building, and set the stage for the construction of constitutions in Latin America. Chapters 4, 5, and 6 cover the principle democratic institutions—the executive, legislature, and judiciary. Chapter 7 then looks at the core of the democratic process, elections, and the rules that determine how voting is done, and what impact it has. Elections have a direct impression on parties and party systems, which are examined in Chapter 8 alongside contributions from civil society. Only four states in the region employ federalism, but they are the largest states—Argentina,

Brazil, Mexico, and Venezuela. Chapter 9 discusses both federal and unitary arrangements, and examines variations in centralization. Finally, because the armed forces have had such a significant impact on democracy in Latin America, they are covered in Chapter 10.

All the chapters share several themes:

- **Institutional Distinction.** When it comes to institutions, details matter. Many institutions throughout Latin America carry the same label as those found in the advanced democracies of Western Europe, North America, or Japan. Nonetheless they work differently and in fact exhibit regional variations of their own.
- **Institutional Context.** Although Chapters 4–10 have their own specific institutional focuses, they all recognize that one institution cannot be examined in isolation from other institutions. Whether an institution effectively addresses any number of goals—representation, efficiency, responsiveness, accountability, capacity building—is often dependent on its relationship with other institutions and their designs.
- **Institutional Development.** Institutions capture history and mingle with culture. The study of institutions is not an abstract process that removes a person from an awareness of the past or the values and beliefs in society. Rather, it sharpens our understanding of how history and culture ultimately affect politics through institutions. Institutions vary from one country to the next largely because of differences in history and culture.
- **Institutional Engineering.** The study of institutions allows us to approach politics as craftspeople. As we grow more aware of available institutional choices, we develop a toolbox that allows us to consider how different institutions should be tailored for the particular problems or goals important to a country. Institutional designs that are suitable for one country may not be appropriate or valued by another.

Comprehensive tables in the following chapters capture many of the institutional variations displayed by the 18 countries of interest to this study. Each chapter has one box feature that compares institutions across countries. In addition, each chapter ends with a more expanded box feature that spotlights how the institution under consideration operates in a given country.

To close, we should note that the instability and violence that wracked Buenos Aires in late 2001 was not new to the country, just as the 1976–1983 period was not Argentina's first experience with military rule. But in one respect, December 2001 was altogether different: The military stayed in the barracks, giving time for democracy to recover through the Kirchner era. Argentina may not exhibit all the signs of a fully consolidated liberal democracy—Freedom House scores the country a "2," and a case study in Chapter 4 on the executive office details lingering concerns over the concentration of power in the presidency—but the country has marked impressive gains in the ability of its civilians to control the military. It now has a ministry of defense staffed by civilians that takes charge of military affairs and ensures that soldiers only execute and do not dictate decisions. That institutional change may have made the difference between a violent protest in December, and something that could have been much worse—a military coup d'état. The road to liberal democracy may be a long one, but it is conquered as one institution after another falls into the democratic fold. Argentina's institutions affirm that the country has never been closer to its destination.

Key Terms

institutional engineering   5
informal institutions   7
formal institutions   7
rational choice institutionalism   10
historical institutionalism   10
democratic wave   16
hard-liners   18
soft-liners   18

liberalization   19
transition   19
consolidation   19
political rights   21
civil liberties   21
electoral democracy   22
liberal democracy   22
Freedom House   22

Discussion Questions

1 Discuss the importance of civil liberties to a democracy. Why are elections alone insufficient to maintain a vibrant democracy?
2 Do culture and values create institutions, or do institutions create culture and values?
3 What institution do you consider to be the most important in a democracy? Why?
4 Identify a recent election in Latin America. Was the election competitive? What were some of the main issues in the election? Did anything in the election strike you as different or unusual?

Suggested Readings

Gretchen Helmke and Steven Levitsky. 2006. *Informal Institutions and Democracy: Lessons from Latin America.* **Baltimore: Johns Hopkins University Press.** This edited volume is one of the few studies of informal institutions. It does not contradict an institutional approach; rather it complements the focus on institutions. About 50 years ago, academics beholden to the "behavioral revolution" rejected the study of institutions after arguing that political activity often veered far from the rules outlined by legal institutions. Rather than "throw the baby out with the bathwater," contributors to this book take a more nuanced approach to institutions in a series of case studies.

Seymour Martin Lipset and Jason M. Lakin. 2004. *The Democratic Century.* **Norman, OK: University of Oklahoma Press.** Seymour Martin Lipset was a sociologist renowned for his pathbreaking studies on, among other things, democratization. He emphasized social modernization and culture; hence his work offers an important counterapproach to the emphasis on institutions. This book provides a general survey of his thoughts on democratization, and although it is not apparent in the title, it focuses on Latin America.

Scott Mainwaring and Aníbal Pérez-Liñán. 2014. *Democracies and Dictatorships in Latin America: Emergence, Survival, and Fall.* **New York: Cambridge University Press.** Like an institutional approach, Mainwaring and Pérez-Liñán emphasize political variables rather than economic changes or class structure to explain democratization in Latin America. Nonetheless, they focus on the more immediate factors (short-term decisions by political leaders) and larger ones (international support for democracy) that couch institutions. This impressive study examines 20 countries from 1900–2010.

Michael Reid. 2016. *Brazil: The Troubled Rise of a Global Power.* **New Haven: Yale University Press.** Michael Reid is a columnist for *The Economist.* In this readable text, he examines the challenges faced by Brazil, a country on the cusp of international ascendence. Although focused on Brazil, the book assesses the pressures exerted by globalization that affect all Latin American countries.

Notes

1   Another legend holds that the color came from the use of bovine blood to paint the structure in the nineteenth century. Rural dwellers hoping to contain the influence and power of Buenos Aires might latch on to this narrative. And others note that the tint probably just represents a fashionable color from when the structure was built in the mid-nineteenth century. The actual story is not important here. What is important is the meaning people place in the institutions that surround them.
2   Under *Robert's Rules of Order*, the guidelines used by most legislative assemblies, the chair of a standing body can declare a member "out of order" for reasons of decorum, but precisely what constitutes decorum can vary from one assembly to the next.
3   Early studies of democratization tended to focus on prerequisites. Some of the presumed requirements for democratization included factors such as the size of the middle class, a certain level of gross domestic product (GDP) per capita, income inequality, urbanization, literacy, the diversity and size of interest groups, and cultural values. For an example, see Lipset (1959).

References

Arceneaux, Craig. 2001. *Bounded Missions: Military Regimes and Democratization in the Southern Cone and Brazil.* University Park, PA: Penn State Press.
Cheibub, José Antonio. 2007. *Presidentialism, Parliamentarism and Democracy.* New York: Cambridge University Press.

Dahl, Robert. 1971. *Polyarchy: Participation and Opposition.* New Haven, CT: Yale University Press.

Davis, Jeffrey, and Edward H. Warner. 2007. "Reaching Beyond the State: Judicial Independence, the Inter-American Court of Human Rights, and Accountability in Guatemala." *Journal of Human Rights* 6:2, pp. 233–55.

Diamond, Larry. 1999. *Developing Democracy: Toward Consolidation.* Baltimore, MD: Johns Hopkins University Press.

Guatemalan Commission for Historical Clarification. 1999. *Guatemala: Memory of Silence.* Available at http://shr.aaas.org/guatemala/ceh/report/english/toc.html.

Helmke, Gretchen, and Steven Levitsky. 2006. *Informal Institutions and Democracy: Lessons from Latin America.* Baltimore, MD: Johns Hopkins University Press.

Huntington, Samuel. 1991. *The Third Wave: Democratization in the Late Twentieth Century.* Norman, OK: University of Oklahoma Press.

Karl, Terry Lynn. 1995. "The Hybrid Regimes of Central America." *Journal of Democracy* 6:3, pp. 72–86.

Knight, Jack. 1992. *Institutions and Social Conflict.* New York: Cambridge University Press.

Linz, Juan J. 1990. "Transitions to Democracy." *Washington Quarterly* 13:3, pp. 143–64.

Linz, Juan J., and Alfred Stepan. 1996. "Toward Consolidated Democracies." *Journal of Democracy* 7:2, pp. 14–33.

Lipset, Seymour Martin. 1959. "Some Social Prerequisites of Democracy, Economic Development and Political Legitimacy." *American Political Science Review* 53, pp. 69–105.

Mainwaring, Scott. 1993. "Presidentialism, Multipartism, and Democracy: A Difficult Combination." *Comparative Political Studies* 26:2, pp. 198–228.

March, James G., and Johan P. Olsen. 1989. *Rediscovering Institutions: The Organizational Basis of Politics.* New York: Free Press.

North, Douglass. 1990. *Institutions, Institutional Change and Economic Performance.* New York: Cambridge University Press.

NotiCen. 2010, July 1. "Guatemala: Head of Anti-Impunity Commission Resigns." University of New Mexico: Latin American Database.

O'Donnell, Guillermo. 1996. "Illusions about Consolidation." *Journal of Democracy* 7:2, pp. 34–51.

Peters, B. Guy. 1999. *Institutional Theory in Political Science: The New Institutionalism.* London: Pinter.

Pierson, Paul. 2004. *Politics in Time: History, Institutions, and Social Analysis.* Princeton, NJ: Princeton University Press.

Remmer, Karen. 1991. *Military Rule in Latin America.* Boulder, CO: Westview Press.

Reynolds, Andrew. 2002. *The Architecture of Democracy: Constitutional Design, Conflict Management, and Democracy.* New York: Oxford University Press.

Ruhl, J. Mark. 2005. "The Guatemalan Military Since the Peace Accords: The Fate of Reform Under Arzú and Portillo." *Latin American Politics and Society* 47:1, pp. 55–85.

Sánchez, Omar. 2008. "Guatemala's Party Universe: A Case Study in Underinstitutionalization." *Latin American Politics and Society* 50:1, pp. 123–51.

Schumpeter, Joseph. 1947. *Capitalism, Socialism, and Democracy.* New York: Harper and Brothers.

Skowronek, Stephen. 1995. "Order and Change." *Polity* 28:1, pp. 91–96.

Steinmo, Sven, Kathleen Thelen, and Frank Longstreth. 1992. *Structuring Politics: Historical Institutionalism in Historical Perspective.* New York: Cambridge University Press.

2　State and Nation in Colonial Latin America

Photo 2.1 The flag of Peru and flag of Cusco wave side by side, but they represent different and often competing national identities.

> The basis of democracy is not maximum consensus. It is the tenuous middle ground between imposed uniformity and implacable hostility.
> —Dankwart Rustow[1]

The city of Cusco, Peru, rests in a lengthy valley, surrounded by grassy hillsides that take on a dry, brown color for much of the year. At an altitude of 10,565 feet, the air is crisp, the sun shines brilliantly, and puffy clouds appear to move with purpose across the deep blue sky. About 348,000 people live in this historically and culturally rich city—the seventh largest in Peru. Long ago, the Incas plotted the contours of Cusco in the shape of a puma, an animal revered in their culture. The Tullumayo River formed the spine of the puma and a hill overlooking the main plaza represented its head. The Incas referred to the city as the navel of the universe, and called the nearby fields irrigated by the Urubamba River the Sacred Valley. The indigenous, in their colorful, traditional clothing and speaking in their native tongue of Quechua, can still be found on almost every corner. The United Nations designated Cusco a World Heritage site in 1983, and this has encouraged its citizens to preserve and thus capture the city in a snapshot that reaches back to the colonial period. The visual impact is stunning. Terra cotta roofs line the valley floor and reach up the hillsides as if they are attempting an escape, or searching for a better view. Many of these building are of adobe construction, with strands of hay poking out from their walls. In the city center, they crowd narrow sidewalks that frame winding, cobbled streets.

One can appreciate Cusco for all its charm, as some one-quarter million tourists do each year. But for the observant, curiosity replaces enchantment over time. Preservation did not begin in 1983, but that late date for more systematic and official preservation efforts tells us how little changed in Cusco since colonial times. In fact, the city was long accessible only by way of winding mountainous roads, many of which were often impassable due to flooding or landslides. More regular contact came only in 1908, with the construction of a railway linking Cusco to Arequipa and Buenos Aires. The "discovery" of Machu Picchu in 1911 spurred outside interest in the region, but real connections did not develop until after the arrival of international flights in the late 1940s. Still, military rule from 1968 to 1980, and a violent insurgency in the 1980s and 1990s, deterred visitors. The snapshot in time provided by Cusco is delightful, but it is also a testimony to the isolation suffered by the entire highland region of Peru. And literally underneath the quaint colonial architecture of Cusco, one notices a dreadful truth. The Spanish demolished the masterful stonework of Incan engineers and used these materials to construct their own churches and government buildings. In some cases, they built directly on top of the ancient foundations, creating a design that moves abruptly from massive rotund stones to whitewashed, mortared bricks. For centuries the architecture served as a reminder that the Spanish were there to remake and dominate.

Cusco offers a stark warning of the difficulties Peru must confront as it strives to consolidate democracy. The city participates in national elections along with large coastal cities such as Lima or Trujillo, but the tabulation of votes to produce a winning candidate masks the deep divides between cosmopolitan Lima and traditional Cusco, or between the advantages Trujillo expects and the distress Cusco fears from free trade. This divide is plainly captured in the main plaza of Cusco, where the red-and-white state flag of Peru waves alongside the rainbow bands that color the flag of Cusco. The Cusco flag is similar to the colorful checkered flags (known as the *whipala*) used by indigenous groups in Ecuador and Bolivia that also look back to Inca heritage. In a ceremony that takes place each Sunday at dusk, members of the Peruvian armed forces line up to lower the state flag, and then they are followed by municipal police officers who lower the Cusco flag. The two flags stand side by side, but they are two flags nonetheless. They reach out to different identities, and remind us all that for democracy to work, it must do so on a foundation of state and nation. This chapter introduces the concepts of state and nation and explains their relevance to democratic politics. It traces the historical development of states and nations in Latin America that preceded the struggles for democracy that would ensue at independence.

Pillars of Democracy: State and Nation

We often hear terms such as *state*, *nation*, *regime*, and even *government* used interchangeably. But these concepts have different meanings, and distinguishing them from one another sheds light on the building blocks and dynamics of political organization. The **state** is a political unit that monopolizes the legitimate use of force over a relatively stationary territory and people. It uses this force to maintain order. Max Weber, perhaps the most prominent analyst of the state, succinctly described it as a "compulsory association with a territorial basis" (1964, p. 156). All states possess sovereignty, which means that they hold sole responsibility and power over their own affairs. In reality, sovereignty is more of a legal right than a reality—states often confront challenges within their confines and submit to influences from abroad. But the concept of the state indicates who has the right to assert sovereignty over a given territory. The **nation** refers to a large group of people who are bound by a common culture. They share a common identity through one or more of the following: language, ethnicity, religion, or history. The term *nation-state* captures the ideal scenario whereby a culturally homogenous people completely populate a territory and enjoy sovereignty. But there are many nations that do not have their own states, such as the Miskito Indians on the eastern coast of Nicaragua. And there are some states that struggle to develop their nations, as in Bolivia where the indigenous people, some two-thirds of the population, found themselves shut out of national politics until the 2006 election of Evo Morales. Very often nations cross state borders, as with many of the indigenous in Bolivia, Ecuador, and Peru, or the indigenous in Mexico and Guatemala, who may see more in common with each other than with the people in their own state capitals.

It is useful to envision the state and the nation as variables. The state is all about political order. But political order is a product of legitimacy and the availability of resources to allow for the administration and enforcement of public policies. And some states have more or less legitimacy and resources than others. The nation, on the other hand, is all about identity and communal bonds, and these too can vary in intensity. Moreover, states and nations can affect each other. A nation may succeed in its battle for self-determination and create a nation-state. But the relationship can be reversed—states can forge nations. Latin America is an area with a shared history, religion, and language—especially among the upper classes and political elites—yet distinct identities have formed such that people do feel Chilean, Colombian, or Mexican. States and nations serve as pillars for democracy because both forge unity, though they do so in different ways, through order or through identity. As the democratic theorist Dankwart Rustow argued more than 40 years ago, "the vast majority of citizens in a democracy-to-be must have no doubt or mental reservations as to which political community they belong to" (1970, p. 350). This then sets the stage for this community to draft rules to settle disputes, and over time, to gain trust in them.

The rules of the game, as it were, brings us to the concept of **regime**, which can be defined as the institutional arrangements of a country that define how politics is organized. If the state is all about order, the regime is all about how that order is achieved. The most obvious distinction here is between authoritarian regimes, which may achieve order through coercion and threats, and democratic regimes, which forge order through consensus and fair play. Linz and Stepan plainly illustrate the mechanics that link the state and nation with democracy: "there can be no complex modern democracy without voting, no voting without citizenship, and no official membership in the community of citizens without a state to certify membership" (1996, p. 28). But the state remains particularly important to a democracy even after free and fair elections. An international organization, such as the Organization of American States or the United Nations, may provide ample support for the voting process in a weak state. But after the international observers have left, what does it matter when the legitimate winners lack the capacity to act on that democratic authority?

The final concept, **government**, refers to a group of people within the state that holds ultimate authority to act on its behalf. In a democracy, these people work according to the rules of the game set by the regime no matter their partisan leaning. To draw these concepts together, we see that the state requires positions of leadership to be filled, the regime defines how those leaders will be selected and behave, and government identifies who those leaders are. And the nation defines that group of people over which the government expresses sovereignty—on behalf of the state.

We can use the concepts of nation, state, regime, and government to draw insightful comparisons among countries. Chile has a unique history that instilled a strong sense of nation in the country—victories in wars with Peru and Bolivia during the nineteenth century certainly helped, and so did the rivalry with Argentina through the twentieth century. Impressive economic development has bolstered the state, and most scholars agreed that the transition from the right-wing government of Sebastián Piñera to the left-wing government of Bachelet in 2014 confirmed the stability and strength of the democratic regime in Chile. The nation in El Salvador was weakened by the violence directed at the peasantry and the indigenous for much of the twentieth century, and by the more recent social dislocation created as family members migrate to the United States to earn income. Long-lasting underdevelopment strains state capacity. Nonetheless, El Salvador features a relatively healthy, competitive democratic regime, one that has brought former protagonists in a civil war to the ballot box to work out their differences. Venezuela has a proud history to bolster its nation, and a state nourished by lucrative oil revenues, but moves by the governments of Hugo Chávez and Nicolás Maduro to consolidate power have strained the democratic credentials of its regime.

This book focuses on the regime, and the democratic regime in particular. But it should be clear by now that context matters. We need to keep our eye on the nation and the state as we assess institutional configurations of the democratic regime, and examine how this background in turn affects the behavior of governments. Before turning to the democratic regime in Latin America, a survey of the historical development of the nation and the state is in order. This chapter covers the history of the region through the colonial period, and charts the weak development of nations and states so that we can better understand the difficulties Latin America faced when it struggled to democratize after independence. And although democracy was never really on the table during the colonial period, it is useful to examine colonial institutions to assess their importance and recognize their influence on the democratic institutions that ultimately emerged.

Land and People

It nearly goes without saying that one cannot have a state without land, or a nation without people. But what may be easily lost in these truisms is how land and people interact to set the stage for the rise of states and nations. Expansive human settlements must address basic needs in regard to climate, soil, and topography if they are to be sustainable. Such dependencies were all the more drastic in the premodern era when the technologies we take for granted—in farming, production, engineering, communications, and transport—were as yet undiscovered. Hence it is worthwhile to consider briefly how the physical geography of Latin America fashioned the indigenous settlement patterns found in the Americas at the start of the Spanish Conquest. It is also important to recognize how geography tailored colonization by Europeans, and their consequent confrontation with indigenous societies (and with each other).

Human Settlements in the Pre-Colombian Period

Recent genetic studies corroborate the widely supported theory that looks to northern Asia as the origin of pre-Columbian peoples in the Americas (Wang et al., 2007).[2] The growth of massive glaciers in the last ice age caused sea levels to drop and exposed a landmass connecting Siberia and Alaska, creating a bridge for groups to migrate from Asia. There is more debate over when the migration occurred, but most scholars agree that the trek took place (in several waves) between 35,000 BCE and 10,000 BCE, and that settlements reached the tip of South America by 9000 BCE. Climate change, the extinction of several species of large mammals due to overhunting, and growing scarcity of nonsettled land stirred intensive farming techniques and set the stage for sizeable, permanent agricultural villages by 3000 to 2000 BCE. The Olmecs farmed on the riverbanks of coastal Mexico (near present-day Veracruz), and emerged as the first notable civilization in about 1200 BCE. They would be the first of many civilizations in the area to design impressive pyramids for religious purposes. Today, tourists in San Lorenzo, Mexico, marvel at the colossal heads sculpted by Olmec craftspeople for use on these ceremonial sites. They were chiseled from basalt found more than 60 miles away, and some stand over 9 feet tall. Olmec archeological sites have uncovered stoneworks crafted from jade mined in Guatemala, and Olmec artworks or their influence have been found as far away as El Salvador. All this points to the existence of a significant ancient trade network.

The Mayans represent the second great ancient Mesoamerican civilization. Their rise was intimately tied to the Olmecs, which essentially vanished after 300 BCE. Centered in the lowlands of the Yucatán Peninsula of Mexico, but reaching through Guatemala, Belize, and El Salvador, the Mayans acted as middlemen in trade networks developed by the Olmecs. By their high point in 300–800 CE, the Mayans had developed a series of city-states, with aristocratic lineages of nobles and chieftains and a complex social organization of merchants, farmers, priests, and other classes. Their scientific and cultural achievements were unsurpassed by their regional contemporaries. The Mayans are the only known ancient civilization of the hemisphere to record a detailed, written historical record from their rise in 2600 BCE to the time of the Spanish arrival. Unfortunately, Spanish missionaries hoping to erase indigenous histories that they viewed as unimportant and heathen set out to destroy all Mayan documents. Today only four books from this civilization survive. The Spanish thus lost out on the opportunity to learn about the highly accurate Mayan calendar, or to appreciate advances in Mayans mathematics. The Spanish never realized that the supposedly backward Mayans made use of the number zero well in advance of European mathematicians, who had waited until the eleventh century.

Archeologists and anthropologists still debate why the Olmecs and Mayans declined. War certainly played a role. Olmec ruins show signs of invasion around 400 BCE, and the constant warfare among Mayan city-states certainly contributed to the decline of larger population settlements after 800 CE. But physical geography also played a role. Both of these civilizations were centered in the lowlands where poor soils sit below hot, humid weather. In these tropical areas, slash-and-burn methods of cultivation and farming alongside flooded riverbanks could yield impressive harvests at times, but they would be difficult to sustain in the face of rapid population growth, or as populations concentrate in larger city-states. The highland areas, on the other hand, offered rich soils often enriched by volcanic activity. And while rainfall was less plentiful here, the streams that ran from the mountains could be used to irrigate fields. Not to be overlooked, the drier climate allowed food to be stored without rotting for longer periods of time than in the humid lowlands so that that a bad harvest might not lead to famine. Consider how this setting encouraged political organization. Somebody had to coordinate the irrigation channels that worked their way through various fields and settlements. Somebody had to collect the agricultural surpluses and distribute them to craftspeople, engineers, traders, and soldiers who did not farm. And somebody had to mandate that a portion of the harvest was to be held in reserve. The need to irrigate land, distribute food, and store supplies thus set the conditions for centralized political authority, and state building.

And so it is little wonder that the largest concentrations of population and civilizations in the Americas would develop in the highlands of Latin America, ranging from about 8,000 to 14,000 feet. It is easy to overlook the appeal of the highlands from the perspective of today, especially in view of the productive agricultural activity that currently takes place in the pampas of Argentina, the savannas of Brazil, and further north in the plains of the United States. These regions are breadbaskets of the modern world. Why were they not the basis for huge population centers in the pre-Columbian era? The puzzle is solved when we realize that the Americas of this time lacked large draft animals such as oxen, cattle, or horses. The largest mammal that could be domesticated was the llama, which makes a fine pack animal, but proves less useful for tilling land (and it was found only in the Andes). And the fact is, those breadbaskets that are so bountiful today have hard soils with nutrients buried deep below. The digging sticks used by the indigenous were far more useful in the fertile soils of the highlands. Finally, we should also realize that modern fertilizers have made many of these contemporary farmlands possible (especially in Brazil).

Population growth in the highlands of central Mexico followed quickly on the heels of the Olmec civilization. Early on, the city of Teotihuacán stood dominant. With a population of perhaps 200,000 at its height in 450–650 CE, it was probably larger than any city in Europe. When the Aztecs began to consolidate power in the fourteenth century, they looked upon the ancient pyramids of Teotihuacán as a model for their own settlements, the twin cities of Tenochtitlán and Tlatelolco. These cities sat upon islands in a vast lake, which has since been drained and covered by the modern metropolis of Mexico City. The Aztecs carved canals to serve as streets, and manipulated the water flow and elevation to irrigate farmland and support fishing hatcheries. The Spanish compared the city to Venice, and marveled at the ability of the site to sustain a population of some 200,000–300,000. The Aztecs oversaw an extensive tribute-based empire through the valley of central Mexico and engaged in constant warfare to subdue rivals.

When the Spanish moved to conquer the Aztecs, these rivals gladly supported the attack.

Like in Mesoamerica, the larger, early settlements in northern South America developed alongside rivers on the coast, although they appear to have made more use of ocean resources and fish. But the population centers moved inland to higher elevations in order to access more productive farmland, most prominently under the Chavin civilization (900 BCE–200 CE) in modern-day Peru. At about this same time, significant settlements appeared on the shores of Lake Titicaca, in the highlands between Peru and Bolivia. Communities developed throughout the central Andes, but it would take the Incas to unite them. The Incas formed the second great highland civilization in existence when the Spanish arrived. Their architectural achievements, including the stacking of massive boulders for construction without mortar, are legendary. They consolidated power in relatively short order through the 1400s, when Incan cities peppered the Andes Mountains from northern Chile, through Bolivia and Peru, and just past Ecuador. With their administrative center in Cusco, Peru, the Incas incorporated communities not through tribute payment, but by intense assimilation. They brought regional leaders to Cusco for education, resettled or dispersed defiant populations, and blended their religious beliefs with those found locally. Relay runners carried messages on an intricate road system across high mountain divides. It was a system that worked for the dispersed settlements of the Andes. The Incan Empire held about 10 million—it may have been the largest empire of its time. But unlike the Aztecs, it was not a very urban empire. Cusco stood at an impressive 300,000 in population. But it was a religious and administrative capital and off-limits to settlement. Most individuals in the Inca Empire lived in smaller cities of under 1,000 individuals (Fiedel, 1992).

The physical geography of the Americas directed human settlement toward the highlands. Nonetheless, it is imperative to recognize that indigenous populations radiated throughout the Americas, including the supposedly inhospitable area of greater Amazonia, which may have housed some 6 million inhabitants. Much of what we presume to be virgin rainforest had in fact been slashed and burned for millennia, with much of the growth so affected or manipulated by indigenous groups that it is almost fitting to regard it as "man-made." Diseases introduced by European settlements decimated many of these populations in advance of actual contact, and this promoted the myth that much of the "New World" was untouched, pristine land there for the taking. An authoritative estimate of the population at the time of the Spanish arrival places almost 54 million in the hemisphere—3.8 million in North America, 17 million in Mexico, 5.5 million in Central America, 3 million in the Caribbean, 15.6 million in the Andes, and 8.5 million in lowland South America. At about this same time, Europe had a population of roughly 70 million (Spain had about 10 million) (Denevan, 1992).

Despite the considerable population size, geography fragmented the peoples of the Americas. Latin America is an immense region, stretching over 7,000 miles through a diverse range of ecological zones—from arid deserts to lofty mountain ranges, tropical rainforests, steppe plains, and even polar regions. Historically, the terrain has impeded the movement of people, as well as the exchange ideas and goods. The Silk Road connected peoples in China, the Indus Valley, Persia, the Arab region, and Europe for nearly 3,000 years and over 4,000 miles. If the ancient civilizations of Mesoamerica attempted to reach the burgeoning population in South America, just over 1,000 miles away, they would confront sweltering tropical lowlands in Central America culminating in the thick rainforest of the narrow Panamanian isthmus. Even today, the Pan-American Highway ends at the unforgiving marshlands of the Darien Gap in Panama. Equally difficult terrain sat to the north, separating the Mesoamericans from contact with the peoples of southwest and southeast North America just 700 miles away. Any attempts to travel in this direction faced inhospitable desert barriers. And if the topography itself was not enough of a barrier, also consider how the Americas largely rest on a north-south axis. This setting hinders the diffusion of crop seeds and animal species, which are so sensitive to changes in the seasons and daylight patterns. It took ancient peoples hundreds and often thousands of years to domesticate animals or transform wild plants into crop foods. But once these animals or seeds moved to another latitude, the process would essentially have to begin anew. Llamas, guinea pigs, and potatoes were staples of the South American highlands and suitable for use in the highlands of Mexico. But topography and latitudinal change conspired to prevent the dispersal of these and other resources (Diamond, 1999, pp. 176–191).

The Colonial Impact on Settlement and Demography

As fate would have it, just as the indigenous were drawn to highland areas, so too were the Spanish. But the allure was completely different for the Spanish. The rich veins of silver and gold that layered the Andes of Peru and Bolivia as well as the mountains of central Mexico enticed the Spanish. In the eyes of the colonizers, happening upon large indigenous populations in these areas was a stroke of good fortune. Mining is a labor-intensive activity, and the Spanish would immediately make use of indigenous labor. Mining is also a very dangerous undertaking. The mother lode was found in a mountain near present-day Potosí, Bolivia. The locals assert that millions died in the local mines. Even if they have trebled their claims, it is difficult to overstate the extent of the human tragedy. The indigenous fell victim to collapsing caves, explosions, exposure, and even poisoning after being forced to mix silver ore and mercury with their bare feet. As the drudgery took its toll, the Spanish imported African slaves to make up the work. Africans had already been brought in larger numbers to cultivate agricultural fields where the indigenous most quickly succumbed to disease. This occurred in the Caribbean, portions of Central America, and the coasts of Venezuela and Colombia. Islands offered little refuge from contagion, the humidity of the lowlands accelerated the spread of viruses, and the constant passage of Europeans in the coastal areas ensured a steady array of infectious diseases—if not smallpox or measles on a recently docked ship, then chicken pox or diphtheria from another in passage, or influenza or typhus from yet another just setting sail from the port of Seville in Spain.

The trade routes established to support Spanish interests in the mines of Bolivia and central Mexico shaped colonial settlements. The discovery of mercury in Huancavelica, Peru, and the desire to secure a stable supply of indigenous labor pushed the trade route from Potosí not directly to the Atlantic, but north through the Andes and toward the Pacific. Ships then set sail from Lima, and offloaded cargo in Panama for a land journey. From Portobelo on the Atlantic coast of Panama, another ship would make its way to Havana Harbor to meet up with galleons that had departed Veracruz loaded with bullion from the mines of central Mexico. The ships would then travel as one large fleet for protection against pirates and privateers. When the extraction of metals was at its height in the sixteenth century, the transatlantic journey took place once per year.

The colonial period lasted just over 300 years, and by the end of it, some things had changed, but others had remained the same. Disease and abuse had ravaged the indigenous populations. By 1800, Spanish America was left with a population of 13.5 million, and the indigenous composed less than 50 percent of this total. And it was not simply the addition of Europeans and Africans (and some Asians) that remade the social landscape. Miscegenation brought new racial categories. Those of mixed indigenous blood came to be known as *mestizos*, and those of mixed African blood as *mulattos*. Together they formed about one-third of the population at independence, but over time *mestizos* alone would emerge as the largest group in most Latin American countries. Aside from these stark demographic changes, the

Photo 2.2 Mining operations first initiated under colonialism remain important to the economy in Bolivia. The work is difficult, and dangerous.

Source: © Shutterstock

layering of Spanish economic interests and settlements over prior indigenous settlements meant that the distribution of population had actually changed little. Of the 13.5 million in 1800, about 41 percent lived in central and south Mexico, and about 26 percent lived in the Andean regions of Bolivia, Peru, Ecuador, Colombia, and just into Venezuela (Sánchez-Albornoz, 1984). Nonetheless, despite the general similarity of *regional* population distribution, the growth of the modern economy and its reliance on global trade magnified the importance and wealth of coastal areas, leaving the indigenous populations behind in the deep valleys and inaccessible highlands. In a cruel twist of fate, the prized lands of ancient civilizations became the backwaters of modern society.

Geography also tailored confrontations between European powers in Latin America. The English and the French established their colonies in North America, and the Dutch were also occupied elsewhere and never really had the population for large landholdings. Nonetheless, all saw an opportunity to engage in illicit trade with Spanish and Portuguese colonials or to prey on unsuspecting ships. And the layout of the Antilles—the chain of islands that rings the Caribbean Sea—provided the ideal staging ground. Prying ships could take refuge in sheltered bays, captains with knowledge of local reefs, shallows, and channels gained a chance to evade larger warships, and best of all, an island territory legitimated a country's presence in the region. Britain prized Jamaica not only for its sugar, but also because the island essentially acted as a warehouse. Upon hearing word of the desire for some good or another in the Spanish colonies, British merchants could fill their order in Port Royal, Jamaica. The very geography of the Caribbean made the Spanish colonies much more porous and vulnerable than they otherwise would have been.

And just as geography drew settlement to some regions, other areas came to be viewed as backwaters. El Salvador lacked a Caribbean coast, and was largely neglected. Chile was important just as a transshipment area, and only lightly populated. The port at Buenos Aires struggled to gain the attention of the interior cities of Argentina, which looked to the activity out of Potosí for trade. The impact was enduring and quickly felt after independence. El Salvador expressed tremendous reticence when Central America attempted to unify. Chile, lacking the large indigenous populations found in Peru or Bolivia and not significantly affected by continued European immigration, developed a solid *mestizo* identity. And Argentina fragmented in the face of the distrust that had developed between Buenos Aires and the cities of the interior.

The Colonial Period

The colonial period lasted some 300 years and forever changed the region. Upon conquest, Spain and Portugal quickly gained the upper hand against the indigenous. Nonetheless, their impact was uneven. Multitudes of ancient civilizations disappeared, never to be heard from again. But others, especially the larger settlements in the highlands, survived. And although the Spanish and Portuguese ran roughshod over old political orders, they failed to eradicate them completely. Indigenous beliefs, customs, and institutions persisted. Some of them blended with the project to instill colonial authority throughout the region, and found their way into colonial institutions. Similarly, many indigenous spiritual beliefs survived as they mixed with Catholic traditions. And in some places the residuals of indigenous civilizations were simply shut out, and allowed to linger in isolated indigenous communities. The constant battle to secure monarchic authority played itself out in colonial institutions up to the moment of independence.

The Arrival and Conquest

Christopher Columbus consolidated the early settlement of the Spanish on a large island that would take the name Hispaniola (present-day Haiti and the Dominican Republic). Tales of instant wealth attracted others, creating tension with the Spanish crown, which hoped to ensure a steady stream of precious metals for itself. The small shavings of gold that littered the rivers of Hispaniola disappointed both. Nonetheless, the tension only intensified as Columbus and others mapped out the contours of the Caribbean Sea, exposing yet more unexplored territories. To control the acquisition of land the monarchy threatened severe punishments—including the loss of arms or legs—for those thinking of sailing off to prospect on their own. Further lands were to be settled only under royal order. Puerto Rico came first in 1508, Jamaica followed in 1509, and then Cuba in 1511. Still, the finds of precious metals remained far from encouraging. Early encounters with native populations offering gifts of gold jewelry usually stirred hopes, and the pillage of small villages often made for quick fortunes. But time and again, it was panning and not mining that awaited the Spanish. Denied an easy road to riches, the colonizers exploited the one resource they found plentiful—indigenous labor. The Spanish directed the Indians to work the rivers for gold, and over time, to harvest the sugar cane fields created as an alternative export to gold or silver. The level of brutality may have been at its height in these early years, and even those indigenous that survived soon succumbed to disease.

The Expansion of Spanish Colonialism

The impact of the Spanish in the Caribbean was immediate and lasting. Many countries in the area today still look to sugar as a primary export, and the importation of African slaves to address the population decline forever remade the demographics of the region. But the "Island Era" of Spanish colonialism quickly passed as the search for precious metals continued unabated. In 1513, Juan Ponce de León landed in Florida, and Vasco Núñez de Balboa crossed Panama to view the Pacific Ocean. Francisco Hernández de Córdoba made his way from Cuba to the Yucatán in 1517. He brought back news of an impressive civilization after sighting Mayan ruins, and this prompted the governor of Cuba to declare the area open to colonization. Hernán Cortés, who had acquired a substantial plot of land in Cuba after his participation in the conquest of the island, received word of the proclamation and famously declared, "I did not come to America to till the soil like a peasant." The craving for gold and glory was alive and well in Cortés and the conquistadors who followed. So motivated, Cortés made his way to the shores near Veracruz, Mexico, in 1519. With 508 soldiers, 16 horses, and fewer than one dozen cannons, he would subdue the mighty Aztec empire in just under two years. A similar story unfolded for Francisco Pizarro, who had traveled with Balboa and taken a position in the local government of Panama. There he heard of a rich civilization in the Andean highlands to the south. In 1532, he captured the Inca leader Atahualpa at Cajamarca, Peru, after defeating an army of 80,000 with just 168 men.

How did the Spanish do it? They did keep detailed records, but accounts from the victorious rarely offer an unblemished glimpse of history. As a case in point, a common explanation for the conquest is that the indigenous stood in awe of the Spanish and welcomed them as gods. Their beards, armor, and clothing, not to mention the horses they rode in on and their use of gunpowder, were no doubt wholly unfamiliar to the indigenous. But consider how this explanation plays into the conception of the indigenous as naive barbarians, a conception that would be used to legitimate their subjugation by the "civilized" Spanish. And in fact, recent historical analysis notes that this explanation only began to appear well after the actual conquest, in the 1560s. Cortés himself logged a copious amount of notes, but never declared to be taken as a god. Nor did the Franciscan priests who accompanied him and accumulated equally detailed records (Townsend, 2003).

A better explanation for the conquest looks to the combination of Spanish strategy and technology, and the long-term effects of disease. Both the Aztec and Incan empires had their share of enemies, which Cortés and Pizarro skillfully manipulated to their advantage. And horses, armor, and gunpowder do make a difference, one that is difficult to appreciate today as an element of surprise and for the relative advantages they afforded. The Aztecs fought with the *macuahitl*, a wooden club lined with obsidian shards. Swung properly, it could create a fatal gash with a single strike. But obsidian was no match for Spanish armor. It just shattered. And for defense, Aztecs protected themselves with the *chimalli*, a wooden shield that could deflect the blow of a *macuahitl*, but not the swing of a heavy Spanish sword. Beyond the discrepancies in military technology, disease probably offers the most compelling explanation for the Spanish conquest. Little did Cortés know that the most powerful weapon in his arsenal was an African slave of his who carried the smallpox virus. As Cortés planned his attack on the outskirts of Tenochtitlan, microbes made the first advance and unleashed an epidemic.

COMPARING COUNTRIES

Conquest in Brazil Contrasted with Spanish America

How did a different experience with conquest in Brazil initiate a different path of state and nation building compared to that seen in the Spanish colonies? News that Columbus had discovered new lands and peoples (despite his insistence that he had set anchor in the Indies) rattled the maritime rivalry between Spain and Portugal. To secure its claims, Spain found a willing ally in the Catholic Church— Pope Alexander VI was of Spanish (Catalan) descent. With the aim to prevent Portuguese colonization in the western hemisphere, the pope demarcated the **Line of Tordesillas** in the Atlantic Ocean, and proclaimed all territories beyond this north-south running line to be under the dominion of Spain. Portugal was compelled to respect the authority of the Church, but respectfully noted that as demarcated, the line restricted access to its colonies in Africa. Strong currents and winds often sent its ships farther west than expected as they sailed around the protruding landmass of western Africa. To accommodate this possibility, the line was pushed west, so that it rested about half-way between the Cape Verde Islands (Portuguese territory sitting just off of Africa) and Hispaniola (Spanish territory). With little beyond the Caribbean mapped, Spain and Pope Alexander VI did not realize that the compromise granted Portugal a nub of South America that jutted out to the Atlantic.

Pedro Alvarés Cabral, a Portuguese explorer on his way to India, discovered what would become Brazil in 1500. Assured that Spain would let the land alone because of the papal demarcation, and finding few desirable resources, Portugal did not aggressively pursue colonization. Besides, it already controlled a lucrative spice trade from Asia. But European powers not party to the Treaty of Tordesillas did see opportunities in Brazil. France moved first, attracted by the abundant brazilwood forests, leading Portugal to redouble efforts to settle the area in the mid-sixteenth century. While fending off the French, the Portuguese quickly discovered another opportunity. Europe could not get enough of the sugar milled in the Americas, but Spain had neglected many of its prospective lands due to its fixation on mining. Brazil's vast tropical lowlands in the northeast offered ideal growing conditions. Other European states knew this and sought out Brazil's sugar fields. The newfound Portuguese resolve turned back the intruders, who instead settled on territories (often taken from Spain) in

(continued)

the Caribbean. France took Haiti, England took Jamaica, and the Dutch cultivated their cane in the Lesser Antilles. Many grew wealthy from the sugar exports, but by the 1680s, supply far outstripped demand. The market crashed, and took Brazil down with it. Luckily for the Portuguese, at about this time gold and diamonds would be found in the interior of Brazil to reenergize the colonial economy.

The Portuguese crown closely coordinated the settlement of Brazil, and it did not have to face the avaricious attitudes held by many of the Spanish conquistadors. In fact, the monarchy had to offer substantial land grants (*capitanias*) to prompt colonization. This fostered a more intimate relationship between the colonials and the crown in Brazil compared to Spanish America, and allowed the transition to independence to evolve with greater stability. Another colonial legacy would be the merciless use of African slaves, which over time made the demography in Brazil more like the Caribbean than mainland Spanish America. The Portuguese made use of indigenous slaves when they could, but they did not find populations like in the highlands of the Americas. Those they did find soon succumbed to disease. From about 1550 to 1850, about 4 million Africans landed in the ports of Brazil, whereas 3 million arrived in the Caribbean and 1.5 million reached mainland Spanish America. Dependence on slavery created a stark social hierarchy in Brazil—one that largely lacked a middle class. This made elites all the more reluctant to break with the Portuguese monarchy, even as they saw Spanish colonials gain their independence. Brazilian elites needed only to reflect on the revenge unleashed during the slave revolts of the Haitian Revolution in 1791.

Discussion Questions

1   Describe how differences from hundreds of years ago set Brazil on a different path of development compared to Spanish America.
2   Brazil did not experience the instability seen in Spanish America during the nineteenth century. Would you attribute this to differences in state building, nation building, some other factor, or just plain luck?

Colonial Institutions

God, glory, and gold. These are the motivations typically associated with Spanish and Portuguese colonialism. They were there to baptize the indigenous, to feed the appetites of rapacious conquistadors, and to guarantee the flow of precious metals to the coffers of the monarchy. While each of these ambitions was no doubt in play, together they might be better referenced as "God, glory, *or* gold." The actors behind these motives were typically devoted more to one than another, and they often saw the other goals as obstacles to their interests. Colonial authorities designed institutions to mediate these differences. Even so, sometimes these institutions gave rise to new interests, and new quarrels. And although elites remained the protagonists of institutional design, the colonial project also had to come to terms with long-standing indigenous customs that could not so easily be set aside.

As noted, the Spanish crown attempted to keep the ambitions of conquistadors at bay by carefully controlling the opening of new territories. But as more land opened, the more pressing question became how to consolidate authority on that land. The last thing the monarchy wanted to see was the rise of a nobility in the Americas due to the concerns it had at home. The expulsion of the Moors from the Iberian peninsula—the 700-year war known as the *reconquista* (711–1492)—had left much uncertainty in its wake. The peninsula was little more than an assemblage of kingdoms at the time, only gradually dominated by the principalities of Aragón and Castile (the marriage of Ferdinand and Isabella united the regions in 1469). Expansion came at the cost of conceding government offices and privileges to the nobles and knights that led the charge in the *reconquista*. As the Moorish threat subsided, the first priority of the state was to ensure that Aragón and Castile rather than these local strongmen consolidated power. The opening of new territories in the Americas only broadened this concern.

To prevent the rise of a noble class, the first step was to deny prestige to the conquerors. Other than the exceptional cases of Cortés and Pizarro, the crown stood firm in its policy to deny conquistadors titles of nobility. But a noble class could still emerge in practice if the conquistadors were able to subject individuals to servitude. And this is precisely what the crown feared after hearing of the large indigenous populations in the Americas. The Island Era led the conquistadors to conclude that the indigenous were the most valuable commodity in the Americas. The plunder of a village might produce a windfall gain, but the results were unpredictable and often meager, and land was of little value without labor. How then, was the monarchy to reward the conquistadors, but prevent their transformation into a class of lords with serfs beneath them? The monarchy would quickly emerge as a protector of indigenous independence, not because of any devotion to altruistic principles, but to curb the power of the conquistadors and later settlers. The Catholic Church, with its commitment to evangelize native souls, had interests that dovetailed with those of the monarchy.

The institution designed to accommodate these interests was the **encomienda**—a royal grant of labor (and in some cases, the right to extract tribute). The *encomienda* was based upon the idea that the indigenous were first and foremost subjects of the king, and as such fell under the royal duty to spread the Christian faith. In principle, the *encomienda* was a practical arrangement. A conquistador granted one would be expected to offer religious instruction to a group of indigenous in the stead of the king. In return, the conquistador received full benefits to their labor. In practice, the *encomienda* masked slavery even after the Law of Burgos (1512) charged *encomenderos* with a broader set of responsibilities regarding the treatment and general welfare of the indigenous. The *encomienda* did create a feudal relation based on the mutual, uneven exchange of services, but so long as individual *encomiendas* existed only at the pleasure of the crown it could not form the basis for a new nobility in the Americas. To underscore its opposition to the rise of a new noble class, the crown even passed regulations to prohibit *encomenderos* from living in the same village as the indigenous so as to preclude any resemblance to the personal bonds that laid beneath lord and vassal relations in Europe.

The Church was a partner in the *encomienda*. In fact, many priests were granted their own *encomiendas*. But the difficulty of reconciling spiritual enlightenment and the brutality of forced labor was too much for some. Fray Bartolomé de Las Casas harshly criticized the treatment of the indigenous in several publications, including one tellingly entitled *The Devastation of the Indies*. Although he and others had influence in Spain, it was just as much the successful consolidation of authority under Charles V (1516–1556) that inspired the monarchy to follow up on the Law of Burgos with the New Laws in 1542. The decree placed new restrictions on the use of indigenous labor and payment of tribute, forbade new *encomiendas*, withdrew all grants to church officials and government administrators, and declared all remaining *encomiendas* to be nonhereditary. *Encomenderos* rebelled against the New Laws, and often resorted to violence to protect their interests. But even as the New Laws slowly took effect, the brutality of the *encomenderos* and the continued spread of disease also undid the system—over time, many *encomenderos* saw their grant of labor die off.

The discovery of rich silver mines in Mexico and Upper Peru (Bolivia) assured the mercantilist interests of the Spanish monarchy that had prompted colonization in the first place. **Mercantilism** is an economic theory that envisions the accumulation of wealth, primarily in the form of precious metals, as a zero-sum game between states. Economic development thus occurs not through trade and competition (as in capitalism), but through the strident accumulation of mineral wealth. Interest in mining also meant that the monarchy had its own designs for indigenous labor. To ensure a steady workforce the monarchy created a new government position, the **corregidor**. This official had direct authority over a territorially defined indigenous population, and could require a certain percentage of that population to work in the mines or on agricultural fields for a period of time. This allotment of labor was known as a **repartimiento**. The *encomienda* was more personal insofar as it made demands on individuals, but the *repartimiento* entailed a collective responsibility, and it was based loosely on traditional indigenous customs that required subjugated populations to offer up a portion of their population for work on an annual basis (the *mita* in the Andes, and the *coatequitl* in

Mexico). In fact, the *repartimiento* reinforced traditional customs by relying on a local chief to coordinate matters for the *corregidor*. Initially *corregidores* were only to administrate labor and collect royal tribute, but plans changed after a series of bankruptcy declarations by the crown beginning in 1557—due in no small part to rising military costs in the Americas. To raise funds, *corregidor* offices were put up for sale, and to make them more lucrative, *corregidores* were allowed to own land, use labor for their own purposes, exact their own tribute, and even to force villages to purchase their goods as part of the *repartimiento*. The position could only be purchased for some two or three years, so *corregidores* had a strong incentive to exploit their *repartimento* swiftly, making conditions all the more harsh for the indigenous. To facilitate the access to labor, the Spanish uprooted indigenous villages and consolidated them into larger settlements called *reducciones*. Little thought was given to how this policy also uprooted localized traditions and customs, and further decimated the diversity of indigenous culture. One sample of colonial settlements in Bolivia ("Upper Peru") documented the reduction of 900 villages to just 44 settlements. Before the *reducciones*, the average village held 142 individuals. Afterward, the villages had an average population of 2,900 (Klein, 2003, p. 36). "Community" as it was previously understood was forever changed.

The importance of the indigenous to the monarchy cannot be underestimated. If they were not directed toward the mines, or their labor contracted for agricultural work, they were targeted for tribute payments. In the province of Guatemala, which had no significant mining activity, indigenous tribute represented 70 percent of fiscal resources in the seventeenth century (Pérez-Brignoli, 1989, p. 48). This tribute was often collected in-kind—as corn, wool, cotton, indigo, or cocoa. But increasingly, demands on the indigenous also came from private interests. The *corregidor* system clashed with another institution that sat outside the public realm, the *hacienda*. These were the large landed, private estates that farmed or ranched primarily for the colonial domestic market. Many had their start with a royal grant of land designed to encourage Spanish settlement, and expanded rapidly through land purchases or by annexing indigenous lands (by force, or sometimes as these lands opened due to depopulation from disease).

The burgeoning colonial municipalities represented a lucrative opportunity for the haciendas, but one that would be lost so long as the *corregidores* monopolized the labor required to produce marketable goods. Greedy *corregidores* had unwittingly contributed to the early growth of the haciendas. Their cruelty convinced many indigenous to abandon the *reducciones*. This created a floating peasant population that eventually settled in many of the budding haciendas. But more labor was needed. Over time, hacienda owners convinced the crown to apply a tax structure directly to the indigenous, and thereby draw all of them into the Spanish economy. Now obligated to pay taxes, many indigenous had no choice but to work on a hacienda to gain an income. Once they arrived, hacienda owners used a number of schemes to retain them. Salary advances put laborers into debt the day they began work. Loans would be extended for land, tools, and seed. Conversion to Christianity also had its costs, and initiated more loaning activity. Every holy day had festivals and rituals attached to it, requiring the faithful to purchase various items—candles, religious icons, beads, and various forms of tribute. Of course, the advances and loans came with exacting interest rates. As the obligations passed from one generation to the next, debt peonage guaranteed much of the hacienda labor.

Spain created a network of offices to administrate the colonies. Responsibility for rule making, execution, and adjudication often overlapped, as did many of the territories of the offices. While the overlay in responsibilities allowed the monarchy to capitalize on divide-and-rule tactics, the administrative structure resulted just as much from practical considerations and local pressures. Initially, to settle the lands the monarchy conferred the title of governor on many of the conquistadors who took charge of large swaths of territory. Again, to thwart those seeking titles as a basis for nobility, the crown took specific measures. The governor positions could be held for only three to eight years, and were expressly nonhereditary. The Spanish monarchy enacted a long legal battle against the grandson of Christopher Columbus, Luis Colón, to have him renounce his family claim to a governorship in 1536. Spain created up to 35 governorships in Latin America. Many would become the basis for the future states of Latin America.

The governors set the early groundwork for settling the Americas, but as the monarchy consolidated its power at home, it formed new institutions to ensure its authority abroad. It already had a system of councils for advice in the different territories of the Spanish kingdom, and so developed a **Council of the Indies** for the new colonies. The council came into being in 1524, though it had existed previous to this time at a more informal level—usually as an *ad hoc* subcommittee of the Council of Castile. Still, the Council of the Indies met in Spain. It could devise all the royal decrees it desired, but an ocean separated the discharge and application of those decrees. As such, real power rested in the administration and adjudication of decrees. The monarchy knew full well that the chancellery seal of a royal order would not be enough—a more personal touch would be required to remind the colonials of the authority behind the parchment. In the territories of the Spanish kingdom beyond Castile, the **viceroy** played this role, and this same institution would be applied in the colonies. Viceroy literally means "vice-king," and the position was duly cloaked in pomp and ceremony. The viceroy lived in a palace, had royal bodyguards, and received a generous salary. In fact, the office took on such a stately appearance that it was easy to confuse it with royalty itself. It is of little surprise that the Spanish monarchy eliminated the office in all its European dominions save Navarre by the end of the eighteenth century. But distance meant that the crown would still have to rely on the viceroy in the Americas.

The monarchy enacted several measures to ensure that the viceroy would not emerge as a source of power. The term of office was set officially at three years. But it was understood that the viceroy served at the pleasure of the king, and could be removed early, or asked to stay on. Few lasted more than five years. The monarchy also curtailed the powers of the viceroy in the Americas. In Europe, the viceroy wielded administrative and judicial powers. In Spanish America, the viceroy held only administrative powers, whereas an independent institution, the *audiencia*, exercised judicial powers and acted as a final court of appeal in their regions. This still left the viceroy with primary control over military and police matters, which could clearly be used to consolidate power. To prevent this from happening, the monarchy carved out certain territories to create captaincies general. This was done in more hostile territories such as Chile, Central America (Guatemala), and Venezuela, and also on the strategic islands of Cuba and Santo Domingo.

Aside from limiting the powers of the viceroys, the monarchy also ensured control with oversight mechanisms. At any given time, a *visitador-general* might arrive to pour through the accounts of the viceroy. During the visit, the powers of the viceroy could be suspended and handed over to the *visitador-general*. The *audiencia* offered a more routine method of supervision. About nine judges (*oidores*) sat on the *audiencia*, and their terms were not set. Most saw several viceroys come and go while in office. To more firmly guarantee that the viceroy did not abuse his power while in office, the *audiencia* would conduct an official inquiry (*juicio de residencia*) into the performance of the viceroy at the end of his term. A charge of corruption or other misdemeanor could bring a hefty fine, thereby allowing an *audiencia* to wield an effective threat over a viceroy during his term. The *audiencia* was created expressly to check the authority of the viceroy. In fact, it was the only institution in Spanish America other than the viceroy that could directly contact the monarchy. All other government communications had to make their way through the viceroy. The collective nature of the *audiencia* dampened its potential as a threat to monarchic authority. Still, the crown held a check on its authority as a contingency. Specifically, the *audiencia* was never allowed to interfere with the work of a *visitador-general*. Hence, in the worst-case scenario, the crown could always send a *visitador-general* to enact policy and remake government (Smith, 1913).

The first viceroy managed the area of New Spain beginning in 1535. Peru gained its own viceroy in 1543 because of its economic importance. Later on, viceroys would be added in New Granada (1717), and Río del la Plata (1776). A total of 13 *audiencas* would eventually preside over Spanish America: Santo Domingo (1511), Mexico (1527), Panama (1538), Guatemala (1543), Lima (1543), Guadalajara (1548), Santa Fe de Bogotá (1548), Charcas (1559), Chile (1563), Quito (1563), Buenos Aires (1661), Caracas (1786), and Cusco (1787). Oversight by the *audiencia* put the viceroy in a rather ambiguous position. As a representative to the king, the viceroy had wide discretion in how he applied the law. The Laws of the Indies, a sort of constitution for the colonial government, asked viceroys, "in all matters and business that comes before them to do what seems to them right." And yet the *juicio de residencia* opened the viceroy to detailed and often subjective scrutiny by the members of the *audiencia*. To accommodate these conflicting pressures, over time viceroys began to draw a distinction between the obedience and the execution of the law. Hence, when charged with a failure to comply (sometimes unfairly, or by a vengeful *oidor*), the viceroy would answer, "I obey but I do not execute" (**obedezco pero no cumplo**). Over time, the defense would provide a cover for government officials at all levels to proclaim devotion to the law, even as they pursued their own interests. The thinking lasted well beyond the colonial era, and set the stage for the corrupt practices that still plague contemporary government in Latin America.

The web of authority at the higher reaches of colonial administration may have served its purpose—after all, the colonial period lasted more than 300 years. But if the monarchy succeeded in preventing the rise of a rival, it did so at the cost of devolving considerable power to the local level. While viceroys, *visitadores-general*, *audiencias*, captains-general, and governors checked one another's actions, lands had to be settled, fields cultivated, mountains mined, rebellions put down, shipments processed, taxes collected, and so on. Much of the authority fell to the level just below the governors, to the *corregidores*. Those *corregidores* that did not supervise indigenous lands administered large territories that contained several municipalities. In some regions, such as New Spain, these *corregidores* took the name *alcaldías-mayores*. Underneath them and in each municipality a local council called a *cabildo* governed routine affairs, such as land grants or extensions, land use, residency rules, the appointment of local officials, and the organization of religious feasts. Formally, members were elected, but the largest landowners almost always dominated the offices, and used the *cabildo* to perpetuate their interests. The sheer number of municipalities, the location of many in isolated areas, and the overlap of powers and interests among higher administrative offices created a government structure that allowed the *cabildos* to act with a great deal of autonomy on those issues that ultimately had the most direct bearing on the daily lives of individuals in the colonies.

Religious Institutions in Colonial Latin America

The Catholic Church is an influential actor in contemporary Latin American politics. Its role can be traced back to colonial times, when the Church held a very visible place in Spanish America. Upon the initiation of any attack, a conquistador would read to the indigenous the **Requerimiento**. This document outlined the history of the Church, and demanded submission to the monarchy and the pope. If the indigenous failed to submit or resisted conversion, the reading duly informed them that they would be enslaved, and that any death or losses of property would be entirely their fault. The document was expressly designed to absolve the conquistadors of any sins (murder, rape, robbery, etc.) they might commit, and in fact placed the blame for these actions on the shoulders of the noncompliant indigenous—even when the Spanish failed to read the document in their language. Despite the use of religion to justify the actions of the conquistadors, the monarchy in Spain and Portugal had a mixed relationship with the Church, one that stemmed directly from the institutional organization of the Church.

Papal authority worked its way through two clergies in the Americas. One was organized around bishoprics and parishes at the local level. Spanish and Portuguese monarchies exercised considerable control over this structure through the **patronato real**, which gave the crown control over higher-level ecclesiastical appointments, and the collection and distribution of church funds. The *patronato real* even required all church communications from the colonies to Rome to be channeled through Spain or Portugal. Because this clergy tended primarily to the spiritual needs of Europeans and *mestizos* in the urban colonial settlements, it came to be known as the **secular clergy**. On the other hand, the **religious orders** also answered to the pope, but they did so through their commitments to religious vows, and not through the monarchy. Some of the more important religious orders were the Franciscans, Dominicans, Augustinians, Mercedarians, and Jesuits.

The religious orders did cooperate and work with colonial authorities, but on an irregular basis. Early on, they took the primary responsibility for missionary work in the hinterlands of the colonies—in part because the secular clergy monopolized spiritual affairs in the urban areas. The establishment of a mission required permission from the viceroy, *audiencia*, and bishop. Missions would congregate indigenous settlements, much like the *reducciones*, though they did not have the same harsh reputation. Once established, their isolation would often allow for considerable autonomy, and this is where tensions often developed. In the eyes of the colonial authorities, the religious orders were taking the first steps toward the creation of new municipalities. After the indigenous received sufficient training in Spanish language and culture, and developed a rudimentary agricultural or even manufacturing base, the *pueblo* could open to settlement and the mission would be converted into a parish under the secular clergy. But many in the religious orders, having spent so much time in remote areas with the indigenous, grew protective of indigenous interests, critical of colonial encroachment, and reluctant to hand over management of the territories. Still, the religious orders were not entirely innocent. Many grew quite wealthy and acted as semiautonomous governments in the frontier regions of the colonies. In 1759, the Portuguese monarchy concluded that the Jesuits had grown too independent, and expelled them from Brazil. In 1767, the Spanish followed suit in their colonies.

The Long Road to Independence

Mercantilism seemed to offer such a simple route to power and prosperity. After all, what country would refuse a steady flow of precious metals? But in the long run, mercantilism did not make economic sense, and did more to frustrate than to foster economic growth. At the time, gold and silver were synonymous with money, so the increase in bullion from the colonies meant that the Spanish economy quickly had much more money chasing the same amount of goods. The ensuing inflation compelled Spanish craftspeople and manufacturers to charge higher prices to stay afloat. Their goods could no longer compete in the emerging markets of Europe, nor, over time, could they even sell at home, as Spanish consumers used their newfound wealth to purchase cheaper goods from London, Paris, or Venice. Many historians wryly note the manufacturing decline made Spain, in essence, the "Indies of Europe." Precious metals made their way to Spain, and then almost immediately left to finance the purchase of manufactured goods from elsewhere in Europe. As early as the sixteenth century, Spain fell into an economic situation that, ironically enough, presaged that of contemporary developing countries—it exported raw materials such as gold, silver, spices, sugar, or dyes and imported manufactured goods (Stein and Stein, 1970).

The predicament would have a defining influence on relations between Spain and its holdings in the Americas. If Spanish industry could not compete in Europe, at least it could monopolize the sale of manufactured goods in its colonies. But this meant regulating the development of manufacturing in the Americas, and restricting the rights of the colonials to purchase goods from other European states. Importantly, the policies did not affect the colonists uniformly. A privileged set of merchants and landowners would receive exclusive rights to sell steel, iron, or livestock for mining activity, or to purchase and mint silver coinage and control shipments to Spain. Most of these elites lived in the most important administrative centers of the empire, Mexico City or Lima, and also in Potosí during the heyday of silver extraction in the seventeenth century. These elites also used their control over important political offices to engage in contraband trade with impunity. On the other hand, those merchants and estate owners on the colonial periphery—Argentina, Chile, Paraguay, Ecuador, the interior of Colombia and Venezuela, and many parts of Central America—were left to enterprise on their own. They did not have monopoly access to markets, and their involvement in the contraband trade, while pervasive by necessity, represented a serious risk. Neglect by the crown meant that they had to confront hostile indigenous groups on their own, regularly suffered from shortages of goods, and lacked extravagant cathedrals and religious establishments (Mahoney 2010, pp. 50–119). More than economic interests would come into play as the colonists mulled independence, but mercantilism ensured that any change in relations with Spain would inevitably pit some colonists against others, and make the move toward independence all the more complex.

Mercantilism remained relevant throughout the colonial period because the system perpetuated a sort of vicious circle. The more silver that flowed into Spain, the worse off its manufacturers, and the greater the need to regulate the rights of the colonists and increase silver imports so that manufactured items could be purchased from elsewhere in Europe. Add to this the political problems of Spain. The Netherlands rebelled and finally broke away from the empire in 1648, and Spain soon found itself in near-constant warfare with its primary rivals, France and England. In fact, between 1650 and 1770, the country experienced just 18 years of peace. The battles extended to the western hemisphere as the French, English, and now even the Dutch picked away at Spain's colonies. With the colonies under siege, more and more of the precious metals had to remain in the Americas to fund defenses there. As late as the mid-seventeenth century, one large fleet per year left Havana Harbor stocked with bullion. By the end of the seventeenth century, the defensive needs of the colonies or the threat of attack meant that fleets would sail, or make it, only every four to five years.

Mercantilism and imperial overstretch took their toll on Spain, but the policies designed to address economic problems and military entanglements opened opportunities for *criollos* in the Americas. *Criollos* were Spaniards who had been born in the colonies. Though part of the elite, the crown always viewed them with slightly more suspicion than the *peninsulares*—Spaniards born in Spain. But debt forced the monarchy to put more and more government offices up for sale, and necessity compelled the monarchy to accept bids from *criollos* as well as *peninsulares*. Over time, only the viceroy was off limits, but with its powers so curtailed by design, this hardly slowed the rise of *criollo* authority. Newfound commercial relations and wealth bolstered this growing political influence, as many *criollos* took advantage of the increasingly preoccupied Spanish navy, and ignored the restrictions on intercolonial or contraband trade. But the budding prominence of the *criollos* would mean little if not for one more factor—*criollos* increasingly viewed themselves as a distinct class. Many families had lived in the Americas for generations. Their past and their future rested in Guatemala, Quito, Cartagena, Santiago, or elsewhere in the Americas—not in Spain. In spite of shared physical attributes, *peninsulares* were looking like foreigners, and some *criollos* were even starting to see more in common with *mestizos*.

Charles II (1661–1700) personified the increasingly decrepit state of Spain. He was last in the line of the Habsburg Dynasty, which had grown so protective of its family fortunes that it had practiced interbreeding in earnest for generations. The final result was the physically and mentally impaired Charles II. In a move to reestablish prestige in the crown, Charles II accepted an offer to marry Marie Louise of Orléans in 1679. The proposal came from her uncle, Louis XIV of France—the Sun King himself—who hoped that the union would secure access to the Spanish throne for his Bourbon Dynasty. She would die within 10 years, perhaps due to trauma created by the impossible and frightening task of producing an heir with an impotent lunatic. But time with Marie created the only bond known by Charles II. Upon his death he willed the crown to a Bourbon, Philip of Anjou, grandson of Louis XIV. Distant Habsburg relatives in Austria cried foul, and found support from Britain, Portugal, and certain principalities of the Holy Roman Empire. They were disturbed by how Bourbon access to the Spanish throne would upset the balance of power in Europe. The War of the Spanish Succession would last from 1700 to 1714, but the Bourbons prevailed.

After the war, the Bourbons realized that they had inherited an inefficient and corrupt empire, and responded with reforms to centralize authority—reforms clearly influenced by the regal absolutism developed under Louis XIV. This was a considerable departure from the administrative style of the Habsburgs, who had dedicated advisory councils to almost every issue and territory. The councils were a legacy of empire building, wrought as different kingdoms and principalities fell under the authority of Castile, and then Spain proper. In essence, they were designed to accommodate input from regional aristocrats.

The reformist push targeted Spain and its European holdings first, but the **Bourbon Reforms** would be implemented aggressively in the Americas beginning with the reign of Charles III (1759–1788). A new office inspired by French administrative thought, the intendant, replaced the provincial governors and received a direct line of communication with the monarchy, thereby sidestepping the viceroys and *audiencias*. These officers instituted new tax structures and responsibilities that directly undermined the authority of the *corregidores*. Most significantly, centralization occurred at the expense of *criollos*. The Bourbons reversed their hard-won gains in government as they looked to the more trustworthy *peninsulares* to take on new powers and responsibilities. The Bourbons also undermined the role of the Church with its novel approach to monarchic rule. Absolutism claimed that the crown carried an inherit divine right from God, a right not subject to scrutiny or mediation by the papacy. Reason rather than doctrine would guide the monarchy, and if this meant the confiscation of unproductive church lands, new tax obligations on the indigenous that interfered with evangelism, or the removal of church officials from administrative offices, so be it.

The Bourbon Reforms could not be implemented by decree alone. They threatened the advances made by the *criollos*, withdrew the advantages of the Church, and increased the tax burden for all. Spain would have to rely on force, and this required the military to assume greater control over local policing and judicial proceedings. In some cases, military officers took positions in government to more effectively address concerns of law and order. But the armed forces underwent further change as events continued to develop in Europe. Colonial entanglements drew France and England into conflict and initiated the Seven Years' War (1756–1763). Other states joined the fight to expand or protect their interests. Spain followed its Bourbon ally

France in 1761, and immediately felt the wrath of the powerful British navy, which took control of Havana and Manila. After the occupations, Spain rethought its military policy in the colonies, which allowed no more than 20 percent of the conscripts in the most significant garrisons to come from the colonies. Spain needed more manpower to defend its extensive empire, even if this meant increasing recruitment of the less trustworthy colonials. From 1760 to 1800 the share of officer corps held by *criollos* swelled from 33 percent to 60 percent. More dramatic changes took place in the hinterlands of the colonial empire. By the end of the eighteenth century, colonials represented 90 percent of the troops in Buenos Aires. The armed forces, then, were not only becoming a more important actor, but they also were becoming a more "American" actor. Government, on the other hand, staffed by *peninsulares*, was growing more foreign and illegitimate. Brazil experienced some administrative restructuring similar to the Bourbon Reforms at this time, but the dissent was contained because the changes did not drastically discriminate against Brazilian-born elites (Loveman, 1999, pp. 13–22).

The impact of the Bourbon Reforms on *mestizos*, *mulattos*, Africans, and the indigenous cannot be underplayed. In fact, they felt the brunt of the changes in tax structures and collections procedures. The Church recognized this immediately, and some of its sectors, especially the more autonomous religious orders, prodded the masses to rebel and instigated riots. Local church officials supported indigenous tax rebellions in New Granada in 1780 known as the *comunero* rebellions. But sparking the kindling of grievances held by the masses was a dangerous affair. The Túpac Amaru Revolt (1780–1783) clarified this for even the most aggrieved *criollos* and church elites. The upheaval began near Cusco, Peru, when José Gabriel Condorcanqui, a *mestizo*, protested the mounting exactions of Spanish officials. He sought support from the *criollos*, but his objections resonated more strongly with the vast indigenous population of the area, especially after he claimed descent from the Inca Túpac Amaru, and took on the name Túpac Amaru II. The revolt spread like wildfire. Indigenous militia groups moved through the valleys of the Andes, burning haciendas, churches, and other colonial institutions, and indiscriminately slaughtering every Spaniard they confronted. *Peninsulares* and *criollos* alike saw the inevitable consequences of their colonial policies—a race war—and responded with overwhelming force. An estimated 100,000 persons, about 10 percent of the viceroyalty, died in the fighting. After his capture, colonial officials brought Túpac Amaru II to the main plaza in Cusco, where he was forced to watch the hanging of his wife, brother-in-law, and son. Then came Túpac Amaru's turn. An executioner cut off his tongue, tied his limbs to four horses to dislocate his bones, and chopped off his head. Colonial officials engaged in other forms of torture and public executions over the course of several months as a warning to those thinking of reviving the rebellion.

By the late eighteenth century, the authority of the Spanish monarchy rested on the shoulders of the *criollos*. As part of the upper classes, they had the resources to tip the balance toward the *peninsulares* and Spain, or toward the lower classes. The *criollos* craved political change and denounced the privileged status of the *peninsulares*, but they cringed at the thought of how any changes to the social or economic structure would take them down along with the *peninsulares*. Fear usually has a definitive impact on behavior—it creates a risk-averse stance that can be upset only by extraordinary changes. For the *criollos*, these extraordinary changes would come from abroad, with the advance of the French Revolution in 1789. Because this revolution challenged monarchic authority, and ultimately led to war in Europe, it had consequences far beyond France. The Spanish monarchy joined a coalition of forces hoping to reverse the tide in France, but France prevailed, and compelled Spain to ally with it in 1796. Great Britain mobilized a second effort to confront Napoleon's France—and its new collaborator, Spain. British supremacy on the seas immediately affected Spain's colonial relations. The number of ships leaving the port of Cádiz for the colonies fell from 105 in 1796 to just 12 in 1797 (Adelman, 2006, p. 104).

The final blow would come at the Battle of Trafalgar in 1805, when Admiral Nelson led his British fleet to a decisive victory over the French and Spanish navies. For Spain, the loss effectively severed economic relations with its colonies. As the war effort continued, in 1807 France moved its troops into Portugal to enforce an embargo between Lisbon and the British. The Portuguese monarchy escaped to Brazil with the support of Great Britain, but Spain would not be so lucky. In 1808, Napoleon turned on his Spanish ally and placed his brother Joseph Bonaparte on the throne. The French faced intense resistance from the Spanish people, who formed juntas at the regional level to govern in the absence of King Ferdinand VII. *Criollos* in the Americas now faced a decision—none supported Joseph Bonaparte, but did this mean submitting to the authority of the Supreme Junta in Seville, and proclaiming provisional authority alongside the Supreme Junta until the reestablishment of Ferdinand VII to the throne? Or did it mean declaring that the absence of a legitimate monarch meant that they now held full sovereignty and independence was theirs?

The issue grew more complicated when the Supreme Junta retreated to Cádiz, and took on a more liberal tone from 1810 to 1812 as it debated the enactment of a constitution that would restrain the powers of the monarchy, nobility, and church upon the return of Ferdinand VII. Conservative *criollos* that had once feared the unreliable boundaries that separated political reform from social and economic reform began to question why they should support a relationship with Spain that did not serve their interests. Liberal *criollos* found energy in a constitution that reflected the enlightened ideas of the American and French revolutions, and some went further, calling for the pursuit of these ideas separately in their own state. The thought of independence was now clearly on the table, but what independence meant— the preservation of the conservative order or the creation of a new liberal regime—was still a matter of debate. In much of Latin America, the response replayed what had happened in Spain. Juntas, often led by the councilors of the *cabildos*, sprung up throughout the region to proclaim provisional authority and loyalty to Ferdinand VII. But many took the oath to the crown with a grain of salt—the uncertain status of the king provided a cover for those seeking independence, and persuaded them to join the juntas. The announcements pit the juntas against the viceroyalties and *audiencias* that represented the throne now occupied by Joseph Bonaparte, and initiated battles between hastily organized militia groups and royalist forces.

Where independence first began is a matter of debate, and pride, among Latin Americans. Francisco de Miranda made one of the more daring military moves early on, in 1806. With financial support from the United States and Great Britain, he landed an expedition in Venezuela hoping to stir a rebellion. Royalist forces soundly denied him, but de Miranda's story would inspire later rebellions. Buenos Aires has its own tale of rebellion. Great Britain attempted to capitalize on the vulnerabilities of Spain after the Battle of Trafalgar with attacks on Buenos Aires in 1806 and 1807. British troops landed in the second offensive, but were famously turned back in the narrow streets of Buenos Aires due in no small part to the courageous actions of citizens who threw stones and poured boiling water from their residency balconies. Afterward, *porteños* (people from Buenos Aires) knew they could not count on Spain for defense, but could depend on their on their own resolve. On the other side of the continent, several prominent elites in Quito, Ecuador, declared their right to self-government in the name of Ferdinand VII in August 1809. Within a year, the viceroy had them placed in prison, where royal guards killed them during an attempted escape. The junta in Buenos Aires had more success when it declared independence on May 25, 1810. In 1812 they called on General José de San Martin, who had experience fighting the French in Spain, to lead their quest for autonomy. But the junta also lobbed the opening salvos of the civil strife that would plague the country when it associated independence with free trade, and thereby threatened the economic oligarchies of the interior. Two priests, Miguel Hidalgo and José María Morelos, mobilized the indigenous and brought Mexico to the verge of revolution from 1810 to 1815. Both would be executed for their valiant efforts. In 1811, Simón Bolívar joined with Francisco de Miranda in Caracas to declare the independence of New Granada. Unlike his contemporaries in Mexico, Bolívar represented the wealthy *criollos*, and as a member of one of the largest families of cacao growers he saw independence as a means to guarantee trade with the United States and Great Britain. It is no surprise that his call for separation did not resonate with the *mulattos*, indigenous, or mestizos, some of whom supported the royalist forces. After his retreat to Jamaica in 1815, Bolívar would rethink his relationship with the nonwhites of New Granada.

The disarray in Latin America came to a presumable end in 1814, after Napoleon's defeat and the restoration of Ferdinand VII to the Spanish throne. Rebellion in the name of Ferdinand VII was no longer an option.

Now, rebellion could mean only one thing—treason. Fear once again played its crucial role in the calculus of the *criollos* and many withdrew their support for independence. Besides, the rebellious movements never really agreed on what independence would mean. The elites of Quito favored an oligarchy to protect their interests, Buenos Aires showed sympathy with the Jacobins of the French Revolution, and Morelos wanted nothing short of a social revolution. Loyalty to the crown had its costs for the *criollos*, but independence still represented a jump into the void. In short order, Ferdinand VII quashed liberal hopes by invalidating the Constitution of Cádiz and reestablishing absolutist rule. For the next six years, it seemed that all would return to normal for Spain. Bolívar and San Martin continued their fight, but they deliberately avoided large-scale confrontations with royal forces, and instead concentrated on taking peripheral areas in the colonies. These lands may have held less military or economic significance, but politically, the strategy would demonstrate that the fight was still alive. Previously, San Martin attempted to make his way directly through Bolivia on the way to the royalist stronghold of Peru. Now he set his sights on the Andes and Chile before moving north. And when Bolívar returned to South America from Jamaica, he did not brazenly challenge the royalist forces in Caracas, but instead turned inward toward the plains and Bogotá. And most importantly, he also developed alliances with nonwhites to initiate a more popular appeal.

The rebellious forces were biding their time, and they were lucky that they did so. Victories through the interior of New Granada by Bolívar and up the coast of Chile by San Martin provided moral inspiration, but the regiments remained no match for the Spanish forces. Still, once again, events in Spain would create a new wrinkle in the sentiments of colonial elites, and tip the balance toward independence. In 1820, King Ferdinand capitulated to reformist demands at home, and agreed to reinstate the Constitution of Cádiz. The shift virtually turned the argument for independence on its head. The tie with Spain now meant an association with a constitutional monarchy open to liberal ideas. This was too much for the conservative peninsulares and criollos in Latin America. They had witnessed the erosion of church authority under the Bourbon Reforms, and now they saw a monarch willing to entertain principles of liberty, fraternity, and equality. Even the most tolerant conservatives held that such ideas, even if bearable in Europe, could never be put into practice in the Americas. The steep social hierarchy on which they sat could only be justified by tagging the masses of nonwhites as unfit for rule. But liberalism questioned this gratuitous claim, and directly threatened their status.

So it happened that the clarion call for independence became a conservative cause for some. The effects were felt almost immediately in Mexico. In 1820, General Agustín de Iturbide, commander of the royalist forces in New Spain, received word of Ferdinand's submission while mopping up remnants of the rebellion initiated by Hidalgo and Morelos. Despite his advantage, he so disapproved of the reform that he called on his adversary, Vicente

Guerrero, to negotiate. If conservative principles were to be compromised, Iturbide preferred to manage the concessions himself. Under the Plan of Iguala, issued February 24, 1821, Mexico would become independent and guarantee equal rights for all, but as a constitutional monarchy with vast protections for the Church. After an unsuccessful attempt to lure a Spanish prince to the throne, Iturbide made himself emperor, and declared the independence of Mexico on September 28, 1821. Meanwhile, in New Granada, Spain responded to the growing revolt led by Bolívar with a truce in the spring of 1821. The hope was that the armistice would give the monarchy time to adapt to the reforms at home and get back on its feet. But the plan backfired. The uncertainty caused disarray in colonial offices and the military ranks, and allowed Bolívar to reinforce his troops. Bolívar marched on Caracas on June 24, 1821, finally gaining a foothold on the strategically important coast and setting the stage for the independence of all New Granada. And for San Martin, the news could not have come more quickly. His campaign had come to a standstill outside the conservative bastion of Lima. The elites of this viceregal capital were far too devoted to Spain to break ties. Moreover, San Martin's Army of the Andes drew on *mestizo* and *mulatto* conscripts. The sight of nonwhites bearing arms in Peru all too easily stirred memories of the Túpac Amaru II rebellion. But Ferdinand's reforms caused just enough dissension to give San Martin the advantage. The royalists retreated to strongholds in the highlands where they held out until reinforcements came from Bolívar's forces. The Spanish had their last stand in the interior of Peru at the Battle of Ayacucho on December 9, 1824. Afterward, the islands of Cuba and Puerto Rico were all that remained of the empire that had once spread from the southwest of North America to Tierra del Fuego.

COUNTRY IN THE SPOTLIGHT

Explaining the Exceptionalism of Colonial Legacies in the United States

It is ironic: Central and South America were the first choices for European colonization, and yet the less favored region of North America would experience far greater economic growth and political stability after the advent of independent states. Certainly, ocean currents directed Columbus south, but the Spanish were not unaware of the lands to the north. From 1540 to 1541, the conquistador Hernando de Soto trudged the southern Appalachian Mountains, crossed the Mississippi near Memphis, and bathed in the thermal waters at Hot Springs, Arkansas. Juan de Fuca sailed the Pacific from Acapulco to

(continued)

Vancouver in 1542. Much of the southwestern United States fell under the viceroy of New Spain throughout the colonial period. Present-day visitors to Jackson Square in New Orleans might notice a plaque that reads, "When New Orleans was the capital of the Spanish Province of Luisiana (1762–1803), this square bore the name 'Plaza de Armas.'" The French and the British wrested away some territories, but for the most part, Spain neglected these presumably second-rate lands due to their lack of precious metals.

Basic matters of land and people provide initial clues to the different fates of Latin America and the United States. The climate and soil of areas colonized for farming purposes in Latin America were ideal for sugar, coffee, tobacco, and other highly valued products that suited large-scale production and slave labor (especially in the Caribbean and Brazil). Conditions in the northern areas of British settlement favored more mixed farming focused on grains and livestock—where slave labor was not as efficient and smaller farms could survive. The mining areas of Spanish and Portuguese America replayed this drive toward large-scale production. Layering extensive farming estates and mining operations on the relatively larger indigenous populations found in Latin America meant one thing for the economics of the region— inequality. Sugar, coffee, silver, and other goods offered tremendous profits, but the indigenous and African slaves would be shut out of these opportunities. Indeed, most studies contend that the wealth in Latin America at the time of independence was about equal to, and in some cases surpassed, that found in North America. But that wealth mostly stayed in the hands of hacienda owners and mining operators (Engerman and Sokoloff, 2002). Still, natural resource endowments do not tell the entire story. The American South had its share of tobacco-growing, slave-dependent plantations, and Argentina has always been suitable for grains and livestock—yet their fortunes would be reversed.

A further look at differences in people provides further explanation. The larger indigenous population of Latin America did not just set the stage for economic inequality, it also affected political organization. The indigenous represented a threat to the British, French, Spanish, and Dutch alike. But only Spain confronted large-scale civilizations, and residual populations capable of rebellions such as the one stirred by Túpac Amaru II. Likewise, the indigenous societies of the south were more likely to be warlike theocracies. North American settlers did not face empires, and therefore could protect themselves with decentralized militias. Spanish colonizers required large standing armies, which all too often took on government positions in the name of security, and thereby set a precedent for the entry of the military into politics. Population size, in addition to the drive to evangelize, also meant that Spanish authorities had no choice but to integrate the indigenous. But their "barbarian" status meant that incorporation would be accomplished through subjugation. The English were content (and able) to exclude the indigenous as they settled and organized their politics. A more homogeneous population provided more comfort for competitive politics—even if it took merciless displacements such as the Trail of Tears to maintain that homogeneity (Lipset and Larkin, 2004, pp. 286–288).

Culture also played a role. England had a long history of constitutional, limited monarchy reaching back to the Magna Carta (1215) and the Glorious Revolution (1688). Its settlers were liberal, in the traditional sense. They valued pluralism, free markets, individualism, and representative government. Colonists in Latin America lived under a traditional monarchy, one that grew more absolute over time. For them, it was natural and proper to grant the Catholic Church and aristocratic elites considerable influence, and militarism seemed a normal thing due to the long wars against the Moors. The monarchy appointed political officials who in turn represented not the people, but the crown. Hierarchy and corporatism, not individualism and pluralism, guided Iberian thinking. To put it plainly,

> The North American colonies were largely settled by persons fleeing the feudal restraints, royal absolutism, clerical oppression, of the Old World. In Latin America, in contrast, the conquistadores sought to re-create in the New World the feudal society, political authoritarianism, and religious orthodoxy they had carried over from medieval Europe. (Wiarda, 2001, p. 3)

And despite the confrontation between the Spanish and indigenous civilizations such as the Aztecs, Mayans, and Incans, there was one area in which their thinking dovetailed. Both groups embraced a political culture that validated hierarchical rule and a stratified society. This is precisely what allowed the Spanish to essentially lop off the top layer of these civilizations, and rule with the lower levels of indigenous organization intact (Wiarda, 2001, pp. 104–107).

(*continued*)

But political decisions and institutional design had the most immediate impact on the post-independent futures of Latin America and North America. The firm mercantilist push of the Spanish monarchy had an almost determinative impact on colonial settlement. Restrictions on intercolonial trade were not lifted until 1789, and the fleet system that channeled trade from just a few major ports—from Acapulco to the Philippines, from Lima and across Panama to Havana, from Veracruz to Havana, and from Havana to Spain—stymied the growth of harbor cities. The much smaller coastline of British America had Boston, New York, Philadelphia, and Charleston handle much of the seafaring commerce. And in addition, Baltimore, Williamsburg, Savannah, and other port areas offered ample trading opportunities. Similarly, population was more widely distributed in North America. In 1760, about 19 percent lived in Virginia, 12 percent in Pennsylvania, 9 percent in Massachusetts, 9 percent in Maryland, and so on. The result was a dispersed commercial network primed for economic development at independence. Spanish mercantilism also sapped the profits of agricultural or mining producers because it granted monopolies to merchants and transporters, who of course exploited their positions. This dulled the ability and desire of producers to develop or incorporate new technologies (Burkholder and Johnson, 1990, p. 139). Free trade and less restrictive markets (political decisions) would have prompted long-term growth, but mercantilism served the short-term interests of the monarchy—the speedy flow of bullion.

The fundamental nature of feudal relations in colonial Latin America tinged political institutions. Loyalty to the crown and elite status determined access to economic rights such as landownership, the use of labor, access to markets, and investment licensing. In North America, a third party—the courts—protected and mediated economic rights. This not only instilled more confidence in the contracts drafted by entrepreneurs, but it also provided space for an independent judiciary to emerge as a defender of the rule of law. And finally, the centralized nature of Spanish and Portuguese colonial institutions foiled the rise of representative institutions. The cabildo was the only institution that approached a representative government, but it sat at the local level and only in the urban centers—it hardly served as an institution that could unify large regions. Cabildos in Buenos Aires, Quito, Caracas, and elsewhere may have made the historic declarations of independence, but they did so largely as representatives of their cities. Towns in the countryside received word of the declarations and some supported but others fought against the move. In North America, colonial assemblies had long enjoyed broad policymaking powers over political, economic, and religious liberties within the more decentralized British colonial system. They served as a forum to debate relations with Great Britain, and ultimately to rally support for self-government. Upon independence, they essentially just changed their names to state legislatures. The populations within their territories had long grown accustomed to viewing the assemblies as the legitimate venues for resolving issues and drafting laws. And for political elites, the assemblies provided a lengthy experience with representative government— a sort of training ground for democratic rule (North et al., 2000).

Diffuse colonial boundaries and institutions provided much less direction in Latin America. Immediately, the newly independent states had to address one of their most fundamental features—territorial demarcation. Most looked to colonial administrative divisions, but quickly realized just how counterfeit they were. The overlapping jurisdictions and powers held by viceroys, audiencias, captains-general, and intendants, the large swaths of unoccupied lands, and the existence of huge haciendas with the manpower to affiliate with the emerging government of their choice virtually guaranteed territorial conflict (Mares, 2001, pp. 28–54). Reliance on the armed forces to decide such matters furthered military involvement in politics. It also allowed the armed forces to presume a role as state builders. A second enduring impact followed from the practice of colonial administration in Latin America, which would infect the development of governance. As noted, financial troubles meant that Spain had to maintain its empire on the cheap. It auctioned government offices to the highest bidder and turned a blind eye as officials exploited their positions—after all, tales of a lucrative experience could only increase the value of the office. The fusion of public service and private gain bred a culture of corruption that still exists in Latin America today. Similarly, the impossible expectations of royal dictates that spawned *"obedezco pero no cumplo"* and the rampant evasion of unrealistic trade restrictions helped create an instrumental and conditional approach to politics. Government was to be followed not because it was legitimate, but when it was convenient and practical.

National identity proved to be another crucial difference between the United States and Latin America. Typically, a fight for independence can unify a people. The recognition of a common enemy and

(*continued*)

the intensity of warfare bring disparate groups together. But what really matters is what a rebellion is fighting for, not what it is fighting against. These goals become ingrained in the collective consciousness and create founding myths for a people. By myth, we do not mean a concocted story, but rather shared historical narratives that express deep-seated, common values and form a basis for nationalism. Many celebrated quotes capture the ideals of the American Revolution and evoke loaded anecdotes—"Give Me Liberty or Give Me Death" and "No Taxation without Representation," for example. But such is not the case in Latin America, where what the rebellion was fighting for was a contested matter. More often than not, expediency rather than principle motivated the independence heroes of Latin America. Over time, Bolívar concluded that Spanish tyranny left Latin America unprepared for democracy, such that he favored "not the best system of government, but the one that is most likely to succeed"—even if it came with a dose of authoritarianism. San Martin documented the constant quarreling of elites in Buenos Aires, and charged that they "aspired solely to an emancipation from Spain, and the establishment of some solid form of government whatever that may be." San Martin favored monarchy under a Spanish prince when he faced off against royalist forces because it was most likely to succeed in negotiations with Spain. For San Martin, monarchy may not have been ideal, but it was practical and that was what mattered (Millington, 1996, pp. 14–18).

Of course, the United States had its share of instability—most prominently in the form of the Civil War. With well over 600,000 casualties, it was one of the deadliest conflicts of the nineteenth century. But the Civil War really just highlights factors that more profoundly affected Latin America. As in Latin America, geography geared the South toward large-scale agricultural economies and the use of slave labor, and the impact on demography was similar—inequality. But the extent of inequality and its impact on the position of the white political elite were very different. At the outset of the Civil War in 1860, whites represented 61.7 percent of the population in the South. There was a substantial nonwhite, impoverished, and oppressed population, but its relative size pales in comparison to that seen in Latin America. In 1825, just after independence and at the outset of many civil wars to come, Spanish America had an isolated European elite that comprised only 18 percent of the population, and in Brazil Europeans represented just 23.4 percent of society. Political decisions determined these demographics. Great Britain, in fact, permitted migration from neighboring European countries to its colonies, whereas both Spain and Portugal maintained much tighter restrictions on colonial settlements. A second distinction highlighted by the Civil War was that the rebellion initiated to preserve this inequality in the South took place within the confines of state institutions. It was Georgia, South Carolina, and others that made the decision, raised the armies, fought the battles, and ultimately negotiated the surrender. This also meant that there was a structure in place for the reconstruction of the South after its defeat at the hands of the North. The impressive restoration of political order in the South (albeit at the cost of continued legally sanctioned racism in the form of Jim Crow policies) was in part the result of institutional factors that favored political and economic development in the United States, just as the Civil War was in part the result of factors that tore much more deeply into the social fabric of Latin America.

A host of factors, then, gave the United States the upper hand relative to Latin America as it endeavored to consolidate a new state and nation. No doubt, the route taken by the United States had its less-than-admirable qualities. All ethnic minorities, not just the indigenous and Africans, but also Asians and Latin Americans who remained after the U.S.-Mexico War or migrated, found themselves largely excluded as whites debated and crafted the rules for competitive politics. Participation followed contestation, and this evolution of the regime has spurred new debates in the United States over national identity over the past 50 or so years. Even in the stable United States, we see interactions among the state, nation, and regime. Most countries in Latin America, saddled with a less favorable colonial history, find themselves pressed to construct states, nations, and regimes all at the same time. And exclusion is no longer an option for contemporary democratic regimes.

Discussion Questions

1 Discuss how differences in state and nation in Latin America and North America led to differences in regime. How can regimes, in turn, affect states and nations?
2 After independence, Latin America incorporated but subjugated its indigenous populations, whereas the United States excluded its minority population. Is one route more just than the other?

Conclusion

The feeble foundations of state and nation provided a visionary opportunity to craft sizable political unions—as when elites in Central America joined Iturbide's conservative regime, and then attempted to unify on their own when it failed; when Bolívar endeavored to preserve Ecuador, Colombia, and Venezuela under the umbrella of New Granada; and when Peru and Bolivia united from 1836 to 1839. But ultimately it was a pull in the other direction, the local level, that provided the longer-lasting check on the consolidation of states and nations. This occurred essentially by default. The expansive unions were impractical. Colonialism had structured economic and political affairs toward the motherland, and did little to encourage integration from region to region. Roadways and townships were lined up to support the transport of goods from the interior of the country to the coast, where they would be sent to Spain. Cities in the colonies just were not designed to trade or communicate with each other. Besides, nationalism and the modern state were too abstract to be used as ideas that could pull distant peoples together. They could not compete with the visceral bonds that emerged from intimate interactions at the village level or the personal authority wielded by a village chief, regional strongman, or hacienda owner. This local affinity would be all the more strongly felt by the indigenous—their decimated civilizations no longer provided a source of unity, if they did speak Spanish they were usually illiterate, and they often did not care to grasp the European concepts of nation and state. Latin American countries faced an uphill battle to craft states and nations. Attempting to forge a regime, let alone a democratic one, simultaneously ensured that the journey would be all the more difficult.

Key Terms

state   38
nation   38
regime   39
government   39
mestizo   45
mulatto   45
Line of Tordesillas   49
encomienda   51
mercantilism   52
corregidor   52
repartimiento   52
reduccion   53
hacienda   53

Council of the Indies   54
viceroy   54
audiencia   55
obedezco pero no cumplo   56
cabildo   56
Requerimiento   56
patronato real   57
secular clergy   57
religious order   57
criollo   59
peninsular   59
Bourbon Reforms   60

Discussion Questions

1 How did fundamental features of geography and demography affect colonialism in the Americas?
2 How did colonial institutions accommodate interests in God, glory, and gold?
3 Discuss the pivotal role played by *criollos* in the period leading up to independence.
4 How did the institutions of colonialism undermine the emergence of nations and states in Latin America?

Suggested Readings

De Las Casas, Bartolomé. 1999. *A Short Account of the Destruction of the Indies.* **New York: Penguin Classics.** This firsthand account and critique of Spanish treatment of the indigenous in the earliest years of colonialism offers an authentic description of events. De Las Casas's writings were so influential at the time that he initiated (and participated in) a great debate over the proper treatment of the indigenous. De Las Casas personally advised the crown, although he did not always win over the monarchy.

Kenneth Mills, William B. Taylor, and Sandra Lauderdale Graham. 2002. *Colonial Latin America: A Documentary History.* **Lanham, MD: SR Books.** This text has collected a diverse set of historical documents from the colonial period. It includes government communications, letters and reflections by significant individuals, testimonies and religious sermons, and official decrees and documents. There are also maps and illustrations from the period.

Walker, Charles. 2008. *Shaky Colonialism: The 1746 Earthquake-Tsunami in Lima Peru and Its Long Aftermath.* **Durham, NC: Duke University Press.** Charles Walker skillfully uses the devastating earthquake-tsunami that wiped out Lima, Peru, to examine power relations in colonial Peru. He documents how efforts by the viceroy to rebuild the city initiated debates over church-state relations, as well as issues of race and gender. Because the catastrophe took place when the Bourbon Reforms were first being discussed, the examination of the period also looks into widespread debates on such proposed changes.

Howard Wiarda, with Esther M. Skelley. 2005. *Dilemmas of Democracy in Latin America: Crisis and Opportunity.* **New York: Oxford University Press.** Wiarda and Skelley claim that the different history, culture, and traditions of Latin America render it unfit for the U.S. model of democracy. It is a provocative argument, but one that must be addressed as we assess the suitability of certain political institutions.

Notes

1　Rustow (1970), p. 363.
2　Some scholars argue that individuals traveled across the seas from islands in the South Pacific. Some indigenous groups claim that their origins rest in the Americas.

References

Adelman, Jeremy. 2006. *Sovereignty and Revolution in the Iberian Atlantic*. Princeton, NJ: Princeton University Press.

Burkholder, Mark A., and Lyman L. Johnson. 1990. *Colonial Latin America*. New York: Oxford University Press.

Denevan, William M., ed. 1992. *The Native Population of the Americas in 1942*. Madison, WI: University of Wisconsin Press.

Diamond, Jared M. 1999. *Guns, Germs, and Steel: The Fates of Human Societies*. New York: W. W. Norton.

Engerman, Stanley L., and Kenneth L. Sokoloff. 2002. "Factor Endowments, Inequality, and Paths of Development among New World Economies." *Economia* 3:1, pp. 41–109.

Fiedel, Stuart J. 1992. *Prehistory of the Americas*. New York: Cambridge University Press.

Klein, Herbert S. 2003. *A Concise History of Bolivia*. New York: Cambridge University Press.

Linz, Juan J., and Alfred Stepan. 1996. *Problems of Democratic Transition and Consolidation*. Baltimore, MD: Johns Hopkins University Press.

Lipset, Seymour Martin, and Jason M. Larkin. 2004. *The Democratic Century*. Norman, OK: University of Oklahoma Press.

Loveman, Brian. 1999. *For la Patria: Politics and the Armed Forces in Latin America*. Wilmington, DE: SR Books.

Mahoney, James. 2010. *Colonialism and Postcolonial Development: Spain in Comparative Perspective*. New York: Cambridge University Press.

Mares, David R. 2001. *Violent Peace: Militarized Interstate Bargaining in Latin America*. New York: Columbia University Press.

Millington, Thomas. 1996. *Colombia's Military and Brazil's Monarchy: Undermining the Republican Foundations of South American Independence*. Westport, MI: Greenwood Press.

North, Douglass C., William Summerhill, and Barry R. Weingast. 2000. "Order, Disorder, and Economic Change: Latin America Versus North America," in Bruce Bueno de Mesquita and Hilton L. Root, eds., *Governing for Prosperity*, pp. 17–58. New Haven, CT: Yale University Press.

Pérez-Brignoli, Héctor. 1989. *A Brief History of Central America*. Berkeley: University of California Press.

Rustow, Dankwart. 1970. "Transitions to Democracy: Toward a Dynamic Model." *Comparative Politics* 2:3, pp. 337–63.

Sánchez-Albornoz, Nicolás. 1984. "The Population of Colonial Spanish America," in Leslie Bethell, ed., *The Cambridge History of Latin America*, Vol. 2, pp. 3–35. New York: Cambridge University Press.

Smith, Donald E. 1913. *The Viceroy of New Spain*. Berkeley: University of California.
Stein, Stanley J., and Barbara H. Stein. 1970. *The Colonial Heritage of Latin America: Essays on Economic Dependence in Perspective*. New York: Oxford.
Townsend, Camilla. 2003. "Burying the White Gods: New Perspectives on the Conquest of Mexico." *American Historical Review* 108:3, pp. 659–87.
Wang, Sijia et al. 2007. "Genetic Variation and Population Structure in Native Americans." *PLoS Genetics* 3:11. Available at plosgenetic.org.
Weber, Max. 1964. "The Fundamental Concepts of Sociology," in Talcott Parsons, ed., *The Theory of Social and Economic Organization*. New York: Free Press.
Wiarda, Howard J. 2001. *The Soul of Latin America*. New Haven, CT: Yale University Press.

3 Constitutions

From States and Nations to Regimes, and Back Again

Photo 3.1 Ecuador was placed under a state of siege after the October 2010 police mutiny. Here, police stand guard on a city street in the capital of Quito.

Source: © Shutterstock

> Para os amigos tudo, para os indiferentes nada, e para os inimigos a lei! (For my friends, everything; for strangers, nothing; and for my enemies, the law!)
> —A Brazilian proverb, attributed by some to President Getulio Vargas (1930–1945, 1951–1954)

Celebrating the results of an April 2007 referendum to convene a constitutional assembly, Ecuadorian president Rafael Correa proudly proclaimed, "Fear has been left behind. The future was at stake, the country was at stake, and Ecuadorans have said yes to that future." With support running at over 70 percent, Correa believed he had a mandate to instill his populist goals in a new constitution, and to overhaul an unsympathetic congress and judiciary that had fallen from public favor. And few could argue that Ecuadorian democracy was trouble-free. Congress had used suspect measures to remove three presidents in the past decade, and mounting social protests attested to the growing gulf between government and the populace. But others saw ulterior motives. Former President Osvaldo Hurtado (1981–1984) rebutted, "It's not a project for a better democracy. It's a project to accumulate power. All dictators always have had constitutions made to fit them."[1]

Hurtado's concern is not a new one. Scholars as far back as Aristotle have touted the importance of a "nation of laws, not men," and have looked with suspicion upon those calling for constitutional change, even when backed by tremendous popular support. But Correa's position is no less valid. If political institutions are defective and their legitimacy is questioned, constitutional change can be a suitable route for repair. As it turns out, Correa got his wish when voters approved the new constitution in September 2008. Hurtado must have been disturbed when he heard of the new clauses allowing presidential reelection, and granting presidents powers to dissolve congress within three years of their election. Nonetheless, Correa was reelected by a wide margin in the 2009 election, effectively "refreshing" his term and making him eligible for the next campaign in 2013. The opposition contends that Correa now rules with a confrontational style, and point to further constitutional changes in 2011, which allowed him to overhaul the judiciary and implement sweeping media regulations. Their protests over his revisions to a civil service law that received majority support in congress led to a police mutiny in October 2010. The unrest saw the president tear-gassed and forced him to hole up in a hospital for 12 hours. Some analysts viewed the strife as an attempted coup d'état. Even so, Correa celebrated another electoral victory with 57 percent of the vote in 2013, besting the runner up in the fragmented opposition by 34 points.

The Ecuadoran dispute is not unique within Latin America. This is a region that has seen more than 200 constitutions since the independence era, let alone the near constant efforts to amend or edit standing constitutions. Why has Latin America experienced so much constitutional change? Constitutions provide a sweeping profile of a regime. They represent that great compromise which is supposed to address the interests of all politically significant groups in a country so that they buy in to the rules of the game. As such, they rest midway between the state and nation at one level, and regime institutions at the next. Ultimately, constitutions are as stable as their states, nations, and institutions. This chapter examines the role of a constitution in a regime, and the dynamics of constitutional change. To set the stage for this discussion, we first return to the search for nation and state in Latin American history to assess the foundations for constitutional development in Latin America.

Constitutional Foundations: The Consolidation of Independent States and the Search for National Identity in Latin America

After independence, countries in Latin America did not all follow the same path lockstep in the journey to craft stable states and nations. Nonetheless, they all worked their way through certain historical eras to one extent or another. As states and nations consolidated, the institutional rules of the game took on a stronger meaning, and the constitutions that outlined these regimes gradually took their position as the law of the land.

The Caudillo Period (1820s–1870s)

The caudillo period followed on the heels of independence. It was a time of civil conflict, felt more strongly in some countries than others, but ultimately endured by all. Regional elites riddled the countryside and wielded near complete authority in their domains. Undersized national armies often could not compete with these regional strongmen. The word *caudillo* can be translated as "military leader." Nonetheless, the caudillo was in many ways the opposite of a professional military officer. A professional officer works his way through the ranks by scrupulously following the rules for promotion and completing assignments without question, and views the military as at the service of the national state. But the caudillo gains his position through personal charisma and a ruthless reputation. The caudillo has no real sense of nationalism. His devotion and support base rests at the regional level. Those caudillos who strove for the presidency did not do so to unify their countries, but to satisfy their appetites for power and prestige.

Problems created during the wars for independence and from colonial legacies triggered the caudillo period. The wars themselves upset the social balance as *peninsulares* fled, or had their estates confiscated. Most importantly, new opportunities opened for *mestizos* in the emerging military forces. *Criollos*, concerned first with military victory, did not mind supporting a *mestizo* commander if he could get the job done. Thus military talent became a means by which the marginalized *mestizo* group could make a living and even gain some status. And after independence had been won, the hacienda-based economic structure left behind by colonialism made it easy for *criollos* to withdraw to their nearly self-sufficient estates far off in the countryside, and to leave the presidency for the caudillos to fight over. Taxation could rarely be enforced in the hinterlands, so hacienda owners quickly formed the impression that politics in the capital was distant and unimportant.

It is also important to recognize the impact of the severe economic toll taken by the wars for independence. The fighting lasted about 15 years. Conflict devastated the civilian labor force and reduced livestock populations. Farmlands sat fallow and vacated mines flooded. Criminal bands took full advantage of the opportunity to pillage communities and attack those who dared to travel or trade. Upon independence, governments found themselves saddled with debt from loans (often from the British) used to fund the war effort. Independence also left the countries with large disparate forces, headed by *mestizos* with no alternative careers. As the *criollos* retreated to their haciendas, these caudillos were left to contest the presidency through the only means they knew—military force. The result was **caudillo politics**, which entailed the following cycle: A caudillo would take the presidential palace by force with fanfare from his troops because he had achieved the ultimate power quest. But the caudillo would find more debt than booty in the national treasury. His troops, denied the ultimate reward, would withdraw support, weakening him just enough for the next unsuspecting caudillo to take power and begin the process anew.

The most infamous caudillo may have been Antonio López de Santa Anna of Mexico. He started his career in the Spanish Royalist Army and took responsibility for areas near Veracruz. He was known to be overly harsh with rebels, but as he scored victories he redistributed land to those same rebels to gain their allegiance. He also took full advantage of the port at Veracruz, confiscating funds from its customs house with regularity. All this afforded Santa Anna a significant support base for his aims. True to the caudillo character, these aims were always more personal than political. Santa Anna switched sides as independence grew more likely. He rallied support for decentralization to oppose Mexico's first leader, Agustin Iturbide, but would concentrate power when he himself became president—and even take the title "His Serene Highness." He gained fame in 1829 after turning back a Spanish attempt to retake Mexico, and again in 1838 after fending off French forces seeking to support property losses suffered by French citizens during the war for independence. But Santa Anna was no nationalist. While president, he made off with monies in 1844 meant to fund an expeditionary force to reclaim Texas, and in 1854 he accepted $10 million from the United States to hand over what would become southern Arizona (the Gadsden Purchase). Taking full advantage of the unstable state in Mexico, Santa Anna would take the presidency at ten different times for his own benefit.

The Export Economy (1860s–1930s)

A number of factors stifled early economic development in Latin America. For almost 300 years, mercantilism placed a check on industrial growth, and geared agriculture toward exotic goods such as spices or dyes. Independence could have provided an opportunity to catch up, but the lengthy wars and caudillo politics restrained economies for much of the nineteenth century. The timing could not have been worse. While Latin America languished, industrialization rolled on at breakneck paces in Europe and the United States. Quickly, Latin America found that it could not compete with the productive, enormous businesses abroad. Still, industrialization overseas offered a role for Latin America not as a competitor, but as a source for raw materials and agriculture. The region gained an opportunity to develop, but from a position of dependency. The lack of a diverse entrepreneurial class or developed capital markets narrowed investment activity in each country, and pushed economic activity toward just a few or even a single commodity. El Salvador became almost synonymous with coffee, Bolivia with tin, Venezuela with oil, and so on. The exports brought newfound wealth to the region, but they also brought inequality. Only those with access to foreign markets or able to secure employment in the export sector prospered.

The rise of the **export economy** dealt a fatal blow to the caudillos. Hacienda owners, once comfortable in their isolated estates, found cause to support law and order throughout the country to guarantee the delivery of their goods to foreign markets. Railways, roads, and telephone lines designed to move exports spurred national integration. Export taxes furnished state coffers with the resources to build this infrastructure, and to fund a stronger national military to confront regional militias. The armed forces gained further ground as interstate battles compelled governments to think more seriously about the professional development of the military. During this period, relatively strong states emerged in most countries of Latin America for the first time.

But the search for nation remained difficult. The newfound stability provided a boon to liberal thought, which had long supported open markets as the road to prosperity. Much of the region would see liberals take the most important positions of political power during this time. But the stigma of underdevelopment affected liberal thinking about the nation in a unique way. Latin American liberals laid blame for the region's ills on the *mestizo* caudillos, and scorned the thought of extending equal rights to the illiterate, impoverished indigenous masses. To draw a clean break with the difficult past, they embraced **positivism**, which looks to science and empirical knowledge and away from tradition or religious values to guide government. Positivism provides a patronal road map to a prosperous, civilized country, one that places elites at the forefront of decision making because of their presumed insight. The theory allowed Latin American elites to hold on to liberal values, and at the same time exclude the lower classes until they too became duly educated and acculturated. In 1845, Domingo Sarmiento (president of Argentina from 1868 to 1874) penned *Civilization and Barbarism: The Life of Juan Facundo Quiroga*, which not only took aim at Argentina's legendary caudillo, Juan Manuel de Rosas, but also the gauchos (cowboys) and all those who lived in the country's interior. He portrayed them as dim-witted and graceless, driven by carnal desires. In contrast, inhabitants of Buenos Aires were enlightened and dignified, due to their access to education and contact with the thought and culture of Europe. The message was clear: To develop, Argentina cannot look inward, but must look outward— to the enlightened thinking in Europe.

The export economy period saw democratic institutions gain a foothold, but participation remained minimal. As in the rest of the world, women were denied the right to vote. Many indigenous struggled to gain citizenship status, and literacy or income requirements denied suffrage for most citizens—positivist thought justified the exclusion of the unrefined masses. Nonetheless, in many countries the period did see the rise of competitive party systems at an elite level, among men. Normally, a conservative party looked to preserve the interests of the traditional agricultural classes and the Church, a liberal party catered to commercial interests and the budding middle classes, and a socialist party fought to extend suffrage to working classes and the peasantry. Over time, the social mobilization associated with mounting urbanization and industrialization challenged this competitive structure. Conservative parties became increasingly irrelevant or unable to compete at the ballot box because of their narrow agricultural base. Liberal parties did best, but just barely. They promised a future of equality and prosperity, but their condescending tone resonated poorly outside the cities. Rural inhabitants found it difficult to associate with a positivist ideology that portrayed them as backward and barbarian. Socialist parties catered directly to the economic interests of the masses, but they also inspired unrealistic hopes for redistribution and egalitarianism. Most often, a strong president would preside over the limited competition, and rule in a semi-authoritarian manner.

The Opening of the U.S. Umbrella (1898)

The United States had an uneven impact on Latin America in the nineteenth century. The Monroe Doctrine (1823) warned European powers not to interfere in the western hemisphere, but it was largely a symbolic gesture. The doctrine actually grew out of a proposal from Great Britain, which was concerned that France would take advantage of Spain's withdrawal from the region. In fact, two months before the doctrine was issued, France and England agreed under the Polignac Memorandum that neither country would move to fill the vacuum created by Spain's retreat. Hence, the Monroe Doctrine largely fell on deaf ears. Moreover, European powers did intervene in Latin America at will during this time. Great Britain stationed troops in Nicaragua during the 1850s as it considered plans to carve a transoceanic route. From 1864 to 1866, Spain occupied the Chincha Islands off Peru and shelled coastal cities in Chile in a vengeful effort to support reparation claims associated with the independence wars. The Mexican holiday of Cinco de Mayo celebrates the Battle of Puebla in 1862, when Mexican forces turned back French troops that had landed to support debt payments. Nonetheless, the French reestablished their influence by installing an Austrian Archduke, Maximilian I, as emperor of Mexico from 1864 to 1867. Of course, the United States was not absent from Latin America during the nineteenth century. It gobbled up almost one-half of Mexico's territory after the 1846–1848 U.S.-Mexico War.

But things changed dramatically beginning with the Spanish-American War in 1898, when the United States took Cuba and Puerto Rico (as well as The Philippines and Guam) from Spain. This was a time when Alfred Mahan's writings on the significance of sea power and the use of distant military bases as force multipliers held great sway among military strategists. As such, the acquisition of these island territories marked the rise of the United States as a global power. From this point forward, U.S. interests would increasingly affect state building throughout Latin America. Still, brazen moves by European powers into the hemisphere challenged the newfound stature of the United States. A blockade on Venezuela by British forces—supported with ships from Germany and Italy—to collect debts in 1902–1903 was the last straw for the United States. President Theodore Roosevelt had no qualms with the use of force to ensure debt payments, but the movement of European forces into the hemisphere perturbed him. The **Roosevelt Corollary** (an addition to the Monroe Doctrine) came to terms with this thought by establishing the United States as the regional policeman. From here on out, the United States would enforce debt repayments on behalf of the Europeans. At its root, the Roosevelt Corollary was a political move, designed to send a signal to Europe regarding the rise of the United States as a contender on the world stage. But U.S. relations directly with Latin America took a decidedly economic turn under **Dollar Diplomacy**, which placed U.S. foreign policy and military forces at the behest of U.S. business interests.

Dollar Diplomacy appeared to be such an easy proposition. After all, U.S. forces dwarfed those found in Latin America, and there was much money to be made in the hemisphere. But in lessons that are all too quickly forgotten, it took time for the country to appreciate the errors of substituting naked force for diplomacy, or the consequences of focusing so squarely on short-term economic interests. Between 1909 and 1933, U.S. troops marched on Nicaraguan soil every year save one (1911), largely due to Japanese and British intrigue over a possible transoceanic canal in the country. Support for the dependable, but corrupt, Conservative Party gave rise to a guerrilla insurgency led by César Augusto Sandino, whose name would be embraced later in the century by another anti-imperialist movement—the Sandinista Party. Support for the Conservative Party now meant doing battle against the guerrillas. United States marines battled, at the cost of some 130 troops and to no avail, and their involvement brought attacks on U.S. business interests. Over time, the intervention became an embarrassment and tore at the moral authority of the United States in all its world affairs. The country could hardly take the high ground as it endeavored to criticize the growing military involvement of Japan in China. In all, the Nicaraguan case illustrates the costliness of Dollar Diplomacy.

The case of Cuba, on the other hand, highlights the ethical dilemmas associated with the Dollar Diplomacy. As a condition of independence, the United States imposed the Platt Amendment on Cuba in 1903. It allowed U.S. intervention "for the preservation of Cuban independence, for the maintenance of a government adequate for the protection of life, property, and individual liberty." The amendment justified interventions in 1906–1909, 1912, and 1917–1922, but the rise of the dictator Gerardo Machado posed a problem in the 1920s. Machado increased repression and blatantly violated constitutional guarantees, but he did bring stability and protected foreign investors. The United States strained to remain true to the Platt Amendment by insisting that it in fact applied only to foreigners, not Cubans.

The Great Depression (1929)

The U.S. stock market crashed October 29, 1929, initiating a global economic crisis. Governments worldwide reacted impulsively with protectionist measures. This had a crippling effect on international trade, as did the dwindling demand for goods and services. These conditions made the export economy unsustainable for Latin American countries. Economies geared toward feeding industrial growth in the United States and Europe struggled to sell their supplies. What was sold fell subject to falling prices. From 1928 to 1932, export prices fell 63 cents on the dollar in Argentina and Guatemala, 49 cents on the dollar in Ecuador, and 46 cents on the dollar in Costa Rica. Keep in mind that most states depended heavily on export taxes for their revenues. By way of example, in 1928 Brazil's government collected 42.4 percent of revenues from exports (largely coffee). Dependency on a waning stream led to a 25 percent cut in total government revenue in Brazil by 1930 (Bulmer-Thomas, 1994, pp. 69).

The export sectors, largely based in agriculture, had played the electoral game under the stead of conservative parties. They had lost significant ground to liberal and even socialist parties leading up to 1930, but profits from exports had allowed them to protect their interests with aggressive lobbying, and more often, corruption and bribery. With their books in the red, electoral politics now held little promise. Democracy, even limited democracy, could not protect their interests and had to be overthrown. They found a willing ally in the armed forces, which had grown anxious as competitive politics brought radical politicians closer to government, and as the depression gave rise to growing strike activity and street protests. Profits from the export economy had nourished professional development in the military, and instilled a sense of duty to protect the state at all costs. Officers viewed communist thought, with its call for international solidarity among all workers, as a threat to the state, and concluded that if elected governments could not hold off this menace, it would be up to the armed forces. Argentina, Bolivia, Brazil, and the Dominican Republic fell to military coups in 1930. El Salvador, Guatemala, and Peru followed in 1931. By 1935, eight more countries would succumb to at least one coup. In Ecuador, nineteen presidents took the presidential sash in 18 years. None completed their term (Loveman, 1999, p. 102).

The Great Depression was not the first, and certainly would not be the last economic crisis to shock Latin America, but it did have one fairly unique characteristic. The depth of the crisis abroad sapped worldwide demand, undercutting not just export, but import prices as well. It also reduced foreign investment and led to shortages in manufactured goods from abroad. Even the traditional export sectors based in agriculture and mining knew that their economies had to diversify and move toward manufacturing for the good of the entire economy. The lack of inflationary pressures made it easier for government to initiate investment in industry, as did the withdrawal of competitive pressures from abroad. Hence, after the 1930 coup in Argentina, the military, with support from agricultural interests in the Conservative Party, created the National Commission for Industrial Development (1931). Unsurprisingly, the commission promoted foodstuffs, textiles, and leather—those industries most closely tied to Argentina's powerful ranching industry. Still, this was the start of government-initiated industrial development in the country. In Argentina and elsewhere in Latin America, economic recovery from the Great Depression came earlier than in the United States and Europe, allowing for a modest base of light industry to develop and set the foundations for a more forceful push toward industrial development in the populist era.

Social mobilization during the export economy era and the dislocation caused by the Great Depression stirred Latin American intellectuals to again rethink the basis for national identity. Economic change provided new opportunities for *mestizos*, who quickly came to dominate the emergent middle classes. Important thinkers such as Manuel González Prada (1844–1918) and José Carlos Mariátegui (1894–1930) in Peru, José Vasconcelos (1882–1959) in Mexico, and others in Bolivia, Ecuador, and Guatemala looked to come to terms with the large indigenous populations that surrounded them. They celebrated indigenous history and culture, but still found it difficult to spotlight a people that continued to live in squalor. Such conditions hardly appeared to offer a foundation for modern nationalism. Still, indigenous identity could motivate national identity. **Indigenismo** denied the biological basis for race, and argued that the practice of culture was what really mattered. These *mestizo* intellectuals argued that colonization and dislocation had so disrupted lifestyles and traditions, that the indigenous were not really authentic indigenous peoples anymore. But not all was lost. Indigenous culture survived not in bloodlines, but in cultural celebrations, traditions, and the arts—activities that *mestizo* intellectuals could preserve and promote, and reintroduce to the indigenous. In effect, *indigenismo* contended, "we are all mestizos now." The thinking created fluidity in racial identities, and facilitated social mobility. But its critics charged that it did so at the cost of depriving the indigenous of control over their own identity. Whereas the indigenous saw their identity excluded from the nation in the past, they now feared it would be hijacked.

The Populist Era (1930s–1960s)

World War II lengthened the economic rupture with Europe and the United States first triggered by the Great Depression, and created a stronger incentive for industrialization. The economic policy designed to guide this movement was **import-substitution industrialization** (ISI). ISI calls for the temporary use of protectionism to create a domestic market for industrial goods. It is designed to give the infant industries of a country some breathing room, so that they can grow and one day compete in the global marketplace. To support industry, governments placed import taxes on foreign goods to raise their prices. They also placed export taxes on the traditional exports in agriculture and raw materials for revenue that would be used to finance cheap loans for industry. Typically, the plan was to start small—in light industries such as textiles, soft drinks, or small household appliances—then gradually move on to heavy industry such as chemicals, rolled steel, machinery, or automobiles. The economic crisis of the 1930s had spurred piecemeal moves by governments to support industry, as with the National Commission for Industrial Development in Argentina, but ISI offered a comprehensive plan of action.

Intellectual support for ISI came from the Economic Commission for Latin America (ECLA), a part of the United Nations located in Santiago, Chile, since its founding in 1948. The policy emerged primarily from the thinking of Latin American economists at ECLA, such as the Argentine economist Raúl Prebisch. ISI gained greater scholarly appeal as it was placed in the context of **Dependency Theory**. This theory rejected classical economics, which argued that free trade would lead to economic gains for all in the long run as countries moved toward their respective comparative advantages. Dependency Theory held that certain goods—primary products such as agriculture or raw materials—were inherently less profitable because their prices did not rise in tandem with industrial goods as economies grew. Hence, the export-import economy doomed Latin America to a future of underdevelopment because it placed the countries on the wrong side of an imbalance in the terms of trade. The solution was to break economic ties with the industrial countries. Fernando Henrique Cardoso would capture some of these thoughts in his 1971 book, *Dependency and Development in Latin America*. He would later go on to be elected President of Brazil (1995–2003). Dependency Theory is important because it expanded the recognition of external influences on state building—such as overt U.S. military intervention—to include economic pressures as well.

Import-substitution industrialization was an economic policy, but it also had a political dimension, and that was populism. Because the policy looked to the domestic market to support the early stages of industrial growth, it offered a favorable role for the working classes, who after all represented the masses and were expected to purchase goods from the protected industries. This gave government a stake in the economic standing of the lower classes. Wage supports, unemployment insurance, pension programs, assistance for trade unions, and price controls on foodstuffs all became part of the ISI formula. And the middle classes also benefited as they secured jobs in state bureaucracies created to manage these programs. Most importantly, because ISI served the immediate economic interests of the majority of the population, it was compatible with electoral politics. For the first time, many in the urban lower classes felt included as part of the nation. Populist politicians catered to the needs of the masses for electoral support, and they often did so with a heavy dose of nationalism as they promoted the idea that the country could industrialize on its own. But populism did not appeal to all sectors. Import-substitution industrialization shouldered agriculture and the traditional export sectors with heavy taxes. Many were prohibited from placing their goods on the open market, and were instead compelled to sell to state boards at depressed prices. The government would then turn around, peddle the items at market rates, and pocket the difference to fund state policies for the working classes and industry. Larger businesses enjoyed the protection from foreign competition, but over time international businesses simply jumped the tariff wall and invested in the country to avoid the import taxes. Most businesses still found favor in the industrial policies of government, but for many it was not worth the fiery labor unions that were also part of the populist formula or the inflation that followed government spending on social programs. Populism catered to the majority, but encumbered the minority and thus inevitably took on a divisive character. It also introduced patronage as central political strategy—this would have an enduring impact on political parties in Latin America. The nationalism of populism often appealed to the armed forces, but they remained wary of trade union mobilization and the divisiveness that threatened social stability.

Because ISI counted on a domestic market to drive industrial growth, larger countries found it most appealing. Juan Perón in Argentina may be the most celebrated populist. From 1945 to 1955 he made industry a priority, and his wife Evita indulged the *descamisadas* ("shirtless ones"—the name given to the impoverished working classes) to rally their support at the polls. When agribusiness fussed over taxes or big business howled about rising wages, Perón would call on the unions to hit the streets with protest activity as a show of strength. The policy produced tremendous gains at the outset. The economy grew 8.6 percent in 1946, and 12.6 percent the following year. From 1946 to 1950, labor's share of national income increased 25 percent. But ISI contained a hidden presumption that would ultimately be its undoing—the belief that subsidized industries would not only grow, but also become productive enough to export and compete in the global marketplace. They did grow, but lacking competition, they did not grow productive. By the early 1950s, Argentina had developed an industrial base, but one dependent upon government subsidies. This was troubling news because ISI had taken its toll on agriculture—from 1934 to 1954, the agricultural sector declined 11 percent. At one point it may have literally been a cash cow, but those days were gone. And populism made any move away from the now inefficient ISI policies nearly impossible. Any proposal to change the policies would initiate intense lobbying from protected businesses and massive protest activity from labor unions. The Argentine government saw its once lucrative agricultural sector declined precipitously, and found itself saddled with a large, noncompetitive industrial base. Whereas exports represented 25 percent of GDP in 1932, they made up only 13 percent of GDP by 1950.

Bureaucratic Authoritarianism and the Cold War (1960s–1980s)

The armed forces have always been a relevant actor in Latin American politics. Throughout the nineteenth century, and well into the twentieth, militaries tossed civilians at will, and often placed one of their own in power. But they typically portrayed their political involvement as transitory—there to remove an ineffective president, install a dependable ruler, and perhaps to stay on just long enough to restore stability. The distinction of this earlier era was that when an officer did remain in the presidency, the rest of the armed forces played only a subsidiary role. Troops might be called on to enforce threats or coerce rivals, but civilians remained in most government positions. Beginning in the 1960s, however, things changed considerably. Militaries intervened as an institution, placing officers in positions throughout government, and outlined long-term goals to restructure the economic or political order. Unlike the past, when the armed forces intervened in favor of one civilian faction or another, this time the military was intervening on its own behalf and with its own designs. Scholars referred to this form of rule as **bureaucratic authoritarianism**.

The bureaucratic-authoritarian regimes stemmed from the intense security environment created by Cold War politics, and the economic crisis caused by ISI and sustained by populist politics. Contact through training programs and military exercises allowed the United States to instill its own Cold War concerns into the military thought of the region. **National Security Doctrine** held that the threat of nuclear war locked the United States and Soviet Union in a stalemate, and meant that the real battle between capitalism and communism—between freedom and oppression—would take place in the developing world. The armed forces of Latin America thus had a central role to play in world politics, and the stakes could not be greater. But this thinking led Latin American militaries to perceive almost any type of instability—from labor strikes to support higher wages to congressional deadlocks created by dogged politicians—as opportunities for communist subversion. Unfortunately, such difficulties were commonly associated with the economic crises that followed ISI policies, and calls by populist politicians to rally the masses only provoked more military anxiety.

Beginning with the 1964 coup d'état in Brazil, Latin America suffered a wave of military interventions. The United States had attempted to forestall communist activity under the Kennedy Administration with the **Alliance for Progress**. This program dramatically increased foreign aid to Latin America in an effort to alleviate the socioeconomic ills associated with rebellion. And it had a political carrot that required countries to enact political reforms to remain eligible. But bureaucratic authoritarianism offered its own solution to those driven to protest—repression. The United States, with its first priority set on containing communist expansion, sacrificed its support of democracy for political order. Under the Johnson administration, foreign aid was no longer tied to political reform. The costs of this policy change were appalling and shameful. In country after country, military governments conducted "dirty wars" that rounded up suspects and subjected them to torture and death. The Guatemalan military conducted a "scorched-earth" campaign against its own people that displaced more than one million, and killed tens of thousands. In Chile, the military corralled thousands in soccer stadiums after the 1973 coup, and subjected them to electric shocks and water boarding. Detained female suspects in Argentina who were pregnant had labor induced so that their children could be handed over to military families for a "proper" upbringing, and they were murdered after delivery. Throughout the region, political opponents "disappeared." In the past, detention, torture, and murder left a paper trail in police records. To avoid detection, the military kidnapped individuals—often on city streets in unmarked cars—and brought them to secret detention centers for interrogation. Many never made it out, and had their bodies placed in mass or otherwise unmarked graves. When family members inquired on their whereabouts in police stations, they would receive the same kind of answer: "They must have joined the subversives" or "Perhaps they left the country." The disappearances gave the military governments the deniability to engage in massive human rights abuses. The most systematic violations occurred in Argentina, where more than 20,000 people disappeared.

The history of abuse under the military still plagues democracies in the region. Many militaries received amnesties to draw them out of government (others drafted their own). But civilian leaders have rethought the justness of the concession, typically conducted under duress. The push for human rights trials thus remains a topic of conversation in Latin America. Still, the abuse varied through the region, and some sectors welcomed and look back fondly upon military rule. The armed forces took power in Peru and Ecuador, but took on a populist tone and catered to the developmental needs of the masses with land reform and other redistributive policies. And even in countries where the military conducted horrific abuses, some groups excused the violations as necessary costs in the battle against socialism and instability. The topic of civil-military relations remains important in Latin America, as noted in Chapter 10.

Ultimately, most of the militaries failed to consolidate new political orders. Popular sovereignty remained the only legitimate basis for rule. A growing debt crisis in the 1980s, caused in part by the inability of military leaders to dismantle the old ISI policies of the past, helped to drive many from power. Sectors within the military also called for a withdrawal from government, which they viewed as a drag on military professionalism. And finally, with the end of the Cold War, the armed forces could no longer justify communist threats as a reason to reenter government.

From the Washington Consensus to the "Pink Tide" (1980s to Present)

As bureaucratic authoritarianism crumbled in Latin America, dramatic forces from and changes in the global arena moved in to leave their mark. First, the debt crisis had strapped the new democracies. Shouldered with massive debts, the fledgling civilian governments were compelled to follow the neoliberal dictates of international financial institutions. The International Monetary Fund sent a firm message to deregulate the economy, free up trade, sell off state enterprises, open financial markets, and reduce government subsidies and spending. To not do so would guarantee isolation in international credit markets and bankruptcy. The United States echoed this message, and followed up with a presumable carrot—insofar as Latin American countries embraced neoliberal reform, the United States would endeavor to open its own markets to the region and create a hemisphere-wide free trade area (excluding Cuba). As if the sticks and carrots that followed alongside the neoliberal push were not enough, against the backdrop of the fall of the Soviet Union, state-based economic formulas had lost all weight as an alternative. Neoliberalism emerged as virtually the only game in town in the 1990s.

Because neoliberal reform was so embraced (even if forcibly so) through the region, and because the United States so stridently supported the effort, it became known as the **Washington Consensus**. As a first step, the North American Free Trade Agreement (NAFTA) opened commercial and investment flows between Canada, the United States, and Mexico in January 1994. Later that year, 34 leaders representing every democracy in the region met in Santiago, Chile, in the first Summit of the Americas to initiate work on a Free Trade Area of the Americas (FTAA). The location of the meeting in Chile was symbolic—this country was to be the first of a succession that would slowly but surely join NAFTA. But a monetary crisis in Mexico, alongside the sudden emergence of the Zapatista guerrilla movement in Chiapas, gave the U.S. Congress cold feet. Subsequent Summits of the Americas came and went—in 1996, 1998, 2001, and 2004. By 2005, if not well before, it became clear that the United States was unlikely to concede access to its markets without exacting substantial reforms in Latin American economies, even as the U.S. Congress stood pat in its refusal to lower farming subsidies in products that mattered most to Latin American economies, such as oranges, sugar, soybeans, and dairy items.

At the outset of the Washington Consensus, economies in Latin America did quite well. Privatization swelled state accounts, deregulation spurred business activity, and optimistic investors flocked to the region. After the "lost decade" of the 1980s, when growth stagnated, Latin American economies grew an impressive 3.95 percent from 1991 to 1994. Some of the most faithful adherents to the neoliberal line achieved staggering gains, such as Argentina under Carlos Menem, which grew 12.7 percent in 1991 and 11.9 percent in 1992. But over time, austerity proved too much for the lowest economic sectors. Economies grew, but inequality and unemployment remained. In addition, neoliberal reforms that opened financial markets introduced new vulnerabilities. Hopeful investors can easily turn skittish, and with less controls on capital markets, their withdrawals can quickly force economies into a tailspin. Currency crises replaced debt crises as the new economic malaise as governments struggled to stabilize their exchange rates in the face of capital flight. This happened in Mexico in 1995, in Brazil in 1999, and in Argentina from 2001 to 2002. Growth, as uneven as it was, had decreased considerably by the end of the 1990s, and had become much more unreliable. Growth fell from 2.5 percent in 1998 to 0.4 percent in 1999. After a brief commodity boom in 2000 pushed the regional rate to 4.0 percent, it fell to 0.5 percent in 2001, and then finally crossed to negative territory at –0.3 percent in 2002. In Argentina, unemployment topped off at 18.3 percent in 2001, and the economy shrank 10.9 percent in 2002.[2]

Parties on the right in Latin America that had pleaded for patience while the FTAA developed lost credibility. United States intransigence on free trade confirmed the growing skepticism and undermined confidence in U.S. leadership. More importantly, the neoliberal model just did not appear to be working. Most Latin Americans were not better off, and many were worse off, well over a decade into the Washington Consensus. President Néstor Kirchner of Argentina hosted the 2005 Summit of the Americas. In his opening address, he asserted that the United States has the "inescapable and inexcusable responsibility" for economic policies that caused poverty and undermined democratic rule. Venezuelan president Hugo Chávez met with protestors who had filled the streets to voice their grievances and proclaimed, "The FTAA is dead and we are attending a funeral here." United States actions soon thereafter all but verified Chávez's pronouncement, as the country set its sights on narrower economic agreements—first with CAFTA (Central America Free Trade Agreement), a treaty that excluded the more vociferous middle-income countries in South America, and then with a push to craft bilateral free trade agreements (FTAs) with Chile, Colombia, Panama, and Peru.

Indignation over the Washington Consensus fueled support for a growing field of progressive politicians and parties critical of U.S. leadership. Hugo Chávez, elected in 1999, represented the most stridently critical of these new leaders. But the field of leaders expressing greater independence from U.S. policy was diverse. Ricardo Lagos (2000) in Chile, Luiz Inácio Lula da Silva (2003) of Brazil, and Nestor Kirchner (2003) in Argentina all set the pace for a more moderate, but still critical, approach by their countries to Washington. Some later leaders settled more squarely within the Chávez camp, including Evo Morales (2006) of Bolivia, Rafael Correa (2007) of Ecuador, and Daniel Ortega (2007) of Nicaragua. To capture the range of progressive political leaders who favored economic equality over economic growth, and sovereignty over unquestioned devotion to U.S. policy, analysts have referred to a **pink tide**. The reference to "pink" is used to distinguish these leftist politicians from the more radical ("red") communist movements of the past, though as noted, Latin American leaders embraced different shades of pink.

The pink tide swept through Latin America well into the second decade of the millennium. In the early 2000s the United States could usually muster some support from El Salvador, Mexico, Peru, and Colombia. But the election of Mauricio Funes in El Salvador (2009) and Ollanta Humala in Peru (2011) placed these countries further away from Washington at the time. But it bears repeating that the pink tide was an ideologically diverse group. In addition, although exasperation over neoliberalism spurred the political change, free markets are hardly endangered in Latin America. The ultra-conservative Fraser Institute measures neoliberal policy commitments on a scale of 1–10, and it charted a rise in Latin America from 5.37 in 1990 to 6.56 in 2000 and 6.67 in 2008, shadowing a global average that ran from 5.87 to 6.58 and 6.67 in those same years (Gwartney et al., 2010). In so far as one might portray the years after 2008 as the heyday of the pink tide, according to the Fraser Institute, by 2013 the countries under study here had actually raised their average score to 6.74. And although the global average reached 6.86 at this time, if we exclude the draining score of Venezuela (lowest in the world at 3.23), the countries reach an aggregate score of 6.94 (Gwartney et al., 2015). Pink as it was, most all members of the tide worked to address social welfare concerns within the general confines of market mechanisms.

Indeed, the pink tide reacted just as much to economic concerns as to the continued bluster of U.S. foreign policy, which continued to treat the region as a backyard rather than a neighborhood. Chile and Mexico sat on the UN Security Council when the United States sought support for its invasion of Iraq in 2003. They refused to comply, and the invasion itself created tensions for the United States with governments throughout the region. Further grievances emerged as Latin American states signed on to the International Criminal Court (ICC), a welcome advance in international law for countries that had suffered from dictatorial rule. In 2003, fears that its soldiers might be prosecuted led the United States to threaten a withdrawal of military aid for states that refused to sign on to a so-called Article 98 agreement—a commitment not to cooperate with the ICC in cases involving U.S. citizens.[3] To the surprise of the United States, several Latin American states, including Bolivia, Brazil, Costa Rica, Ecuador, Mexico, Paraguay, Peru, and Venezuela, refused, and responded that they would do without U.S. military assistance. The rebuff caused a stir between the U.S. Congress, which was accustomed to asserting its priorities on Latin America, and the U.S. military, which wanted to preserve its only means of influence in the region. The Bush administration proceeded to backtrack on the threat by allowing partial exemptions. Members of the pink tide generally welcomed the election of Barack Obama, but remained generally unsatisfied with the continued lack of multilateralism in U.S. policy. They led a near unanimous vote (opposed only by the United States and Canada) at the 2012 Summit of the Americas to invite Cuba to the following summit in a move clearly designed to pressure Washington. Cuba did indeed attend the 2015 summit, the same year that the U.S. restored diplomatic relations.

But the pink tide was not just about U.S. policy. Many of its leaders railed against the "corrupt practices of the past" and pointed to an entrenched economic elite within their own countries as a roadblock to social and economic reforms that would benefit the vast majority in the middle and lower classes. They control media outlets, hold long tenures in the judiciary, sway politicians with bribes, and mediate access to financial markets. Faced with such opposition, some of the more radical members of the pink tide—such as Chávez (and his successor Nicolás Maduro), Morales, and Correa—expressed doubts over the capacity of traditional liberal democratic institutions as tools sufficient to empower common people. Instead, they called for a greater concentration of authority in the executive and move to completely overhaul politicians and bureaucrats throughout government. Their opponents characterized the changes as power grabs by would-be authoritarians. Other members of the pink tide appeared to grow too comfortable, and allowed corruption to seep into their own administrations. Allegations of malfeasance quickly corroded the once venerated reputations of Cristina Fernández in Argentina, Dilma Rousseff in Brazil, and Michelle Bachelet in Chile. Many proclaimed an end to the pink tide in 2015 as right-wing oppositions rolled up electoral victories in Argentina and Venezuela, denied constitutional changes in Bolivia, and initiated impeachment proceedings against the president in Brazil.

One can debate whether the pink tide has receded, but one might also celebrate the rise of competitive politics and strident efforts against corruption to end impunity. To be sure, some changes have transpired on suspect terms as corruption charges emerge as a political tactic that strain due process. In June 2012, it took just two days for Paraguay's congress to impeach its progressive president, Fernando Lugo, after offering him two hours of testimony. The 2016 impeachment and removal of President Dilma Rousseff of Brazil was led by congresspersons themselves embroiled in corruption scandals, and who proceeded to swiftly reverse her progressive policies. Then U.S. presidential candidate Bernie Sanders captured the sentiments of many international observers when he charged that "the effort to remove President Dilma Rousseff is not a legal trial but rather a political one," involving a process "that more closely resembles a coup d'état."[4]

The controversies surrounding the pink tide represent another layer of history in the challenges Latin Americans must face as they continue to craft and revive democratic institutions. State building, nation building, and regime building continue to take place, all at once. In the following section, we return to some of this history with an eye on the document meant to lay out the institutional arrangements of a country—the constitution.

Constitutions: The Rules of the Game and More

Constitutional development cannot be divorced from the rise of the state or nation. Nor can the difficulties of constitutional development be separated from failures by states or nations to consolidate themselves. Constitutions depend on the stability delivered by political order and a unified sense of national identity. But constitutions return the favor by deepening the order and identity of a country. The constitutional scholar Ivo Duchacek (1973) aptly tagged constitutions as "**power maps**" to capture their relationship to the state. At their core, constitutions diagram the formal distribution of power within the state. In this sense, constitutions set the rules of the game for the politics of a country. Generally, there are two sets of rules in any constitution. One assigns authority and certain duties among the different branches of government, while the other spells out the relationship between these government authorities and the public (Finer, 1988). But constitutions are also about nation building. Differences in dominant political values and historical experiences lead constitutional rules to develop uniquely from country to country. Furthermore, the acceptance of these rules is a sign that the nation has come into being. How did the development of states and nations through the historical eras outlined above affect constitutions in Latin American countries?

Constitutional Development in Latin America

In much of the region, constitutions emerged from a maelstrom of political thought, and evolved in an environment of political violence and economic disorder (Brazil is the most obvious exception; colonial rule under Portugal placed it on a different path to independence). As we saw, many **conservatives** formed independence movements in 1808 as a mark of loyalty after Napoleon's troops deposed King Ferdinand VII of Spain. And after Ferdinand VII regained the throne in 1814, but appeased his adversaries by embracing a liberal constitution, these same movements shifted their efforts to creating independent, conservative governments in Latin America.

They sought to retain privileges for the Church and military, draft laws in accord with Catholic moral codes, institutionalize aristocratic rule in congress, and centralize power in the executive. Other independence groups, the **radicals**, embraced the ideas of the French Revolution and hoped to inject a stalwart sense of majoritarian activism into government by creating strong parliaments. And a third group, the **liberals**, looked to the principles expressed in the U.S. Constitution. They favored a presidential system girded by a balance of powers among government branches, and sought to limit government while providing vast protections for individual rights. Over time, the radicals lost influence—the instability of post-Napoleonic France undercut the model's appeal. Nonetheless, the French left their mark on the judiciaries of the region (see Chapter 6). The constitutions that finally emerged appeared to be liberal documents. They called for checks and balances, presidentialism, and guarantees for political rights and civil liberties. But there were obvious compromises with conservative thought (Gargarella, 2005).

In particular, the liberal blueprint for presidentialism easily gave way to the conservative desire for executive power. This occurred as political elites in the region reacted to the long period of lawless *caudillismo* that followed independence, and as they realized the magnitude of nation building in a new country. Moreover, the legacy of Spanish colonial rule, in which government by decree and military involvement in politics were common, tilted the region toward strong presidencies and away from a balance of powers. This tilt manifested itself most egregiously in constitutional provisions that allowed presidents to declare **states of exception** which granted the president extraordinary powers to decree laws, suspend rights and liberties, intervene in provincial and local affairs, and act beyond formal constitutional limitations (Loveman, 1993). The necessary rationales for these declarations were always vague and easily exploited. Typical of constitutions throughout the region that had preceded it, the 1958 Venezuelan Constitution allowed the president to proclaim a state of emergency "in case of emergency, commotion that disturbs the peace of the Republic, or grave circumstances that affect economic or social life" (Article 244).

Constitutionalism and Democracy

The ease with which a state of exception could be abused illustrates the point that constitutional government is not synonymous with democratic government. The codification of government authority reaches far back into time, to Babylonian empires and Chinese dynasties, but the struggle for democracy is a far more recent phenomenon. And as illustrated by wide-open provisions for states of exception, constitutions can be blatantly rigged against democratic procedures. General Alfredo Stroessner of Paraguay governed under the Constitutions of 1940 and 1967 during his 34-year dictatorship. Both constitutions allowed the president to declare a state of siege, but only for 90 days. Not to be impeded and in full formal compliance with his legal obligations, Stroessner simply renewed the declaration every 90 days for 15 years (and for 33 years in a measure applied to the capital region). With a similar snub of legality, military governments in Argentina, Brazil, Chile, and Uruguay, like so many others during the 1960s to 1980s decades of bureaucratic authoritarianism, made it a priority to implement constitutions with "**protected democracies**." They proposed (but ultimately failed to enact) political arrangements that would institutionalize military involvement in policymaking, ban certain political parties, offer extensive amnesties to military forces scarred by human rights abuses, and circumscribe political liberties (Arceneaux, 2001).

And states of exception are not mere historical footnotes in Latin America. Even after the period of authoritarianism and return to civilian rule, "every new Latin American constitution adopted from 1978 to 1993 reaffirmed and/or broadened such regimes of exception" (Loveman, 1994, p. 69). But many countries have acted in the decades since to hem in these extraordinary policies through constitutional reforms. The range of civil liberties open to suspension has been curtailed, stricter guidelines for congressional approval have been mandated, stern time limits have been set, and prohibitions have been placed on the enactment of new laws during the state of exception. While states of exception offered a "loophole" for authoritarianism in the past, the gradual closing of that loophole is one indicator of democratic consolidation—as well as the work that remains.

Iberian legacies and conservative principles produced other constitutional permutations of the classic liberal constitutional thought found in the United States. In particular, Howard Wiarda (2001) notes that while the United States developed under the influence of settlers from England and Holland who had largely severed their feudal pasts, Latin America embraced a conservative corporatist culture that thought more in terms of rank and status. **Corporatism** envisions society in terms of hierarchically arranged groups that secure privileges and associate on the basis of duties and obligations. In contrast, liberalism visualizes atomistic individuals who are guaranteed rights and full freedoms to interact. According to Wiarda, liberal constitutions may have blanketed the region, but they could not fully conceal the contours of the conservative, corporatist terrain that lay beneath them.

Two especially significant groups, the Catholic Church and the military, acquired legal privileges known as *fueros* that were often enshrined in constitutions at independence. The Church assumed a near monopoly over education and marriage, received tax exemptions, was allowed to run its own court system, and could even deny political rights (in many countries individuals were required to register for citizenship through local parishes). Soldiers were not subject to civilian courts, and other legal exemptions meant that their garrisons had the effective status of foreign embassies. Though liberal reforms removed many Church *fueros* throughout the nineteenth century (often only after brutal civil wars), the Church retained considerable influence in the politics of many countries. Divorce remained illegal in Chile until 2004, and the 1994 constitutional reforms in Argentina finally removed the requirement that the president be a Catholic. Repeated military interventions would give the military *fueros* greater lasting power. Most constitutions still have separate sections devoted to military affairs, but their *fueros* have been a central target in democratization efforts over the past few decades (see Chapter 10).

Though *fueros* are becoming a thing of the past, there remains a strong inclination to envision society and discuss politics in terms of groups. Constitutions of the region devote considerable space to workers, consumers, senior citizens, children, businesses, students, and indigenous communities. Often, there are two separate sections for civil and political rights—one titled individual rights and the other titled social rights. Though this emphasis on groups may have emerged from the corporatist thinking of long ago, subsequent political movements reinforced this perspective. The latter half of the twentieth century saw many progressive Christian Democratic parties and more radical socialist parties make electoral gains, and they both shared the emphasis on collective over individual rights. In the twenty-first century, many indigenous groups mobilized in part to replace the individualism of liberal democracy with the collective nature of traditional decision making. For example, Aymara and Quechua groups in Bolivia promote "ayllu democracy," which emphasizes communal consensus over majoritarian rule, direct democracy over representative democracy, traditional leaders over elected politicians, and prioritizes the equitable distribution of resources (Rivera Cusicanqui, 1990, pp. 69).

The emphasis on privilege over rights can be seen in the controversy surrounding "**insult laws**." Few rights are more fundamental to democracy than that of freedom of expression. But although the constitution of El Salvador guarantees "all persons can express and broadcast their thoughts," it qualifies the right. Such expressions cannot "subvert the public order, nor harm the morale, honor, or the private life of others" (Article 6). To ensure the enforcement of this principle, Article 2 directs the government to safeguard the "right to honor, to personal and family intimacy, and to a proper image" and requires that it "establish compensation, in conformity with the law, for damages to moral character." The penal code (article 179) backs up the "protections," allowing those who offend the "dignity or decorum" of another to be jailed from six months to two years, and to be fined the equivalent of 50–100 days' wages. Should the suspect repeat the affront, up to 240 days' wages may be garnished. In Ecuador, defamation laws have turned into blatant political tools. Title VII of its criminal code is entitled "Crimes Against Honor." It outlines penalties for "expressions made to discredit, disparage, or dishonor … an authority." Powerful individuals can use insult laws to bring civil suits against their critics, and thus deter would-be whistle-blowing employees or social activists concerned with their business dealings. Government officials have long used defamation laws to stifle or castigate investigative journalists or protestors. President Rafael Correa in Ecuador filed a lawsuit for $10 million for "pain and suffering" after the publication of a book that criticized him. He also filed a criminal complaint after a protestor shouted "fascist" at him in February 2011.[5] Other countries with particularly strong defamation laws include Bolivia, Brazil, Colombia, Ecuador, Guatemala, and Venezuela. In Chile and Colombia, courts ruled that defamation laws were constitutional, arguing that citizens ought to trust the capacity of judges to balance a person's right to expression with another's right to honor. There have been some reforms in the region. Most notably, Argentina, Brazil, El Salvador, and Brazil all made significant moves to limit the application of defamation laws to members of the press.

Constitutions and Political Pacts

The addition of conservative ingredients to liberal constitutional recipes reminds us that constitutions do more than just outline the political rules of the game. As the basis for nations, they also represent settlements between contending political forces and their attendant values and concerns. Hence the U.S. Constitution grants extra representation for small states to ensure their support—though most small states today did not exist in 1789. The Japanese Constitution prohibits the establishment of a military—even as the country recognizes its regional threats and reassesses the dependence it must place on U.S. military interests. And the German Constitution places high thresholds on party representation to limit the entrance of extremist groups and discourage fragmentation—all in response to the long-passed fear of a Nazi resurgence. The persistence of bygone settlements is almost inevitable for any constitution, and over time they are often embraced as they take on new meaning (today, the overrepresentation of small states in the United States is championed as yet another mechanism of checks and balances). Nonetheless, constitutions always present the danger of freezing political concerns from long ago and distorting contemporary politics.

Scholars have investigated the possibility of "freezing" bygone concerns in their studies of **political pacts** (also referred to as elite settlements). Political pacts are negotiated compromises wrought by political elites. They often involve power-sharing formulas, strict guidelines on policymaking, and not only a recognition of who will be granted favoritism in the political order but also an indication of which groups will be excluded (e.g., the communist party or labor unions). Political pacts are, in essence, double-edged swords. They can engender compromise among important groups in fledgling democracies and therefore provide needed stability, but by definition they lock in expectations and goals, regardless of how the character and number of politically significant actors—the nation itself—may change over time (Karl, 1986). In both Venezuela and Colombia, political pacts allowed these countries to avoid the instability other countries suffered during the populist era, and ultimately safeguarded them from bureaucratic authoritarianism.

In Venezuela, the pact outlined principles and general guidelines, though it was formalized in a written document. After the fall of authoritarian rule in 1958, a few prominent political parties gathered to sign the Pact of Punto Fijo. The pact bounded its signatories to respect electoral outcomes, create a more activist state, ensure access for each to state jobs and contracts, and accord certain rights and privileges to the Church and military. For almost 40 years, Venezuelan parties embraced these principles as they adapted to and interpreted their new constitution. In Colombia, the pact made its way more explicitly into the constitution as the National Front, the name given to the alliance of the Conservative and Liberal parties after authoritarian rule ended in 1957. Under the National Front, the new Colombian Constitution required the parties to equally divide up representation in the national congress, cabinet ministries (who would in turn earmark thousands of administrative positions for their respective party adherents), departmental assemblies, municipal councils, and the appointment of governors and mayors. The Constitution also required a two-thirds majority for all congressional decisions to ensure participation from both sides. The Constitution pledged the two parties to the National Front agreement until 1974, though some offices became competitive earlier due to constitutional reforms in 1968 and 1970.

Proponents of political pacts recognize that Venezuela and Colombia remained under civilian rule while much of the rest of Latin America fell to the brutal bureaucratic authoritarianism of the 1960s and 1970s. But critics of this political formula highlight the cronyism and exclusion that developed in each country even as the region entered the contemporary democratic period. By the 1990s, Venezuelan politics was described as a "partyarchy," where party elites controlled a spoils system that encouraged corruption and economic mismanagement (Coppedge, 1994). Alienation spread through the populace and the party system collapsed, leaving the country ripe for the personalistic politics of Hugo Chávez. And in Colombia, the National Front worked just as it was designed—to accommodate political elites from the Liberal and Conservative parties. But this excluded the interests of all those groups in the rural hinterlands, and left them open to influence from revolutionary guerrilla groups, such as the FARC (*Fuerzas Armadas Revolucionarias de Colombia*), which threatened the very existence of the government in the 1990s and still controls vast amounts of territory. Likewise, Colombia's traditional parties have suffered a swift decline in recent years as voters sought to distance themselves from the old guard. At least five major parties, and half a dozen smaller parties, now roam the congressional chambers in Bogotá.

Constitutions and National Identity

How else do constitutions affect national identity? Just as constitutions may look backward in time to past affairs and interests (and sometimes freeze them in time), they can also look forward. Constitutions can be used to project an image of the country, and more explicitly, to designate precise values and even goals as the basis of a new nation. For example, Article 3 of the Brazilian Constitution lists "to eradicate poverty" among the "fundamental objectives" of the state. In the Costa Rican Constitution, Article 78 prohibits government spending on education from falling below 6 percent of GDP. Article 107 of Venezuela's Constitution requires environmental education in the school system. Ecuador's Constitution has a section (Article 52) devoted to consumer protection and the responsibilities of producers, whereas Paraguay's Constitution devotes an entire section to agrarian reform. And a recent amendment to the Uruguayan Constitution defines access to water as a fundamental human right, mandates public ownership of all water resources, and requires government water policy to place a priority on sustainability. Though a corporatist culture may have instilled a sense of conservatism in Latin American constitutions, the incorporation of so many social, political, and economic rights gives them a progressive flair. In this sense, most of the constitutions go far beyond the **procedural democracy** we see in the U.S. Constitution, and instead promote **substantive democracy**.

Procedural democracy seeks to outline only the bare-bones rules of governance, and avoids references to outcomes—or what government ought to do. It defines the distribution of authority among government branches, and rather than demarcate specific goals, it focuses on spelling out what government cannot do. Hence the U.S. Bill of Rights does not commit the government *to promote* certain rights, but rather it prohibits government *from infringing* on individual rights. Substantive democracy goes far beyond the detail of government procedures, and instead presumes an activist government instilled with already-defined goals and values. Critics of substantive democracy note how it raises the bar for political opposition. To disagree with certain policies may not simply mean a dispute with government officials—it may mean opposition to the constitution itself and thus leave challengers vulnerable to charges of treason. Other critics argue that the inclusion of goals in the constitution is dangerous because it places greater lawmaking power in the hands of unelected judges (Gargarella, 1997). Alternatively, Linz and Stepan note, "If a democracy never produced policies that generated government-mandated public goods in the areas of education, health, transportation, some safety net for its citizens hurt by major market swings, and some alleviation of gross inequality, democracy would not be sustainable" (1996, pp. 69). If democracy requires certain policy goals, why not mandate them?

Though the emphasis on policy outcomes distinguishes Latin American constitutions from the procedural democracy of the U.S. Constitution, it does not distinguish the region from the rest of the world. Most constitutions worldwide do in fact go far beyond the skeletal outline of government found in the U.S. Constitution. Still, Latin American constitutions stand out in the world arena for other reasons, such as the dynamics of constitutional change. Latin America is unlike most developing regions in that it gained independence much earlier, and thus acquired the opportunity to accumulate constitutional traditions. But the head start failed to produce constitutional stability. The propensity for constitutional change in the region has long been recognized by scholars (e.g., Mecham, 1959), and this tendency shows no signs of abating. Eleven of the seventeen countries in this study enacted entirely new constitutions after 1980, and the pace of piecemeal change shows no signs of decrease.

The Politics of Constitutional Change

The transition to democracy in the late decades of the twentieth century offered many Latin American countries the opportunity to rethink their constitutional foundations. Six countries—Brazil, El Salvador, Guatemala, Honduras, Nicaragua, and Paraguay—decided to wipe the slate clean and draft entirely new constitutions. An additional five—Bolivia (2009), Colombia (1991), Ecuador (2008), Peru (1993), and Venezuela (1999)— enacted new constitutions well after they had completed the transition to democracy. Four other countries either restored constitutions that were in effect prior to military rule (Argentina and Uruguay), or worked to reform constitutions drafted under military duress or direct military rule (Chile and Panama). Only Mexico (1917) and Costa Rica (1948) can point to constitutions that predate the 1960s to 1980s period of authoritarianism.

Moves to enact new constitutions stir political drama and capture the headlines. But beneath the din of such excitement, constitutions do not necessarily stand idle. Constitutional change may still occur through more piecemeal formal means of reform whereby constitution articles are added, edited, or abrogated. And less formally, change can be achieved as in the United States, where judicial review is used to develop new interpretations of standing constitutional clauses (Ackerman, 1998). For their part, Latin American countries seem to hold a greater propensity for formal rather than informal constitutional reform. And this type of reform continues at a steady pace, indicating that political actors view formal changes to fundamental law as a legitimate and viable political technique. The following section documents these changes and discusses the consequences of such actions.

Types of Constitutional Reform

No country in the region has excused itself from the practice of constitutional reform. In fact, there have been several common reforms (Gargarella, 1997; Gil Lavedra, 2002). The most conspicuous has been the effort to delineate a full range of social rights, very often in an entirely new section devoted solely to this topic. As noted, this nod to substantive democracy is characteristic of the more global trend to enumerate solidarity rights. But there are pathbreaking examples in Latin America. In particular, in its 1994 reforms Argentina not only added a new chapter on "New Rights and Guarantees," but also gave constitutional rank to expressly listed international human rights treaties (Art. 75, sec. 22). Venezuela has gone one step further—it accords constitutional status to all human rights treaties ratified by the government (Art. 23). Other reforms have targeted the judiciary and rule of law. In an attempt to depoliticize this branch, several countries have created new institutions, such the Council of the Judicature in Colombia, to assume some of the judicial appointment powers previously held by the president and congress. Reforms targeting the rule of law have created or more fully empowered administrative bodies to act as watchdogs in the battle against corruption. These include Comptroller Generals, General Auditorships, and even, as in the cases of Ecuador (the Council for Public Participation and Social Control) and Venezuela (the Republican Moral Council), nongovernmental bodies charged with investigating suspected wrongdoing.

Reforms have also targeted presidential power, largely by adding to congressional powers (e.g., the power to censure or in rare instances force the resignation of executive officials, and the power to demand testimony or documents from executive personnel) or through moves to disperse executive administrative control with new positions such as Cabinet Head or Executive Vice President. But fragmented party systems and scarce resources continue to hamper congresses in the region, making it difficult for them to take advantage of the reforms. Moreover, seemingly endemic crises (political, economic, or natural disaster related) create a sense of urgency that all too often feeds executive power and justifies presidential moves to take on legislative capacities (see Chapter 4).

Additional reforms have sought to more generally decentralize state power and deepen democratic participation. As part of its 1994 reforms, Argentina declared Buenos Aires an "autonomous city" and mandated that the mayor be popularly elected rather than appointed by the president. Other countries instituted similar reforms to allow the direct election of mayors, governors, and local or regional councils. Brazil opted to weaken federal control over state and local government budgets in its 1988 Constitution. Many of these decentralizing reforms were economic in nature, and acted as part of a neoliberal strategy to disperse the financial power of the state. And a final set of reforms has introduced various types of **direct democracy**, including citizen's initiatives, recalls, referendums, and even the power to call for a constituent assembly. Venezuela's Constitution may hold the most ambitious provisions for popular input. Signature campaigns face fairly low thresholds to force referendums on international treaties (20 percent of registered voters) and "matters of national importance" (10 percent of registered voters), or to initiate a constitutional modification (15 percent of registered voters), and a legislative initiative requires only 0.1 percent of registered voters. Likewise, 20 percent of registered voters can force a recall vote for any public official (within their district), including the president.

Photo 3.2 Bolivians in the province of Santa Cruz sign a petition calling for a new constitution in July 2005. A new constitution would later be enacted in 2009.

The Source of Reform: The People or Congress?

In a democracy, the constitution protects the rights of the people. Does this mean that the people should be involved in the process of constitutional change, or does this open the prospects for change too widely to the winds of public opinion? Countries in Latin American have selected various procedures to work out the balance between stability and popular input.

Congress stands center stage in the constitutional reform process of most countries. Bolivia, Brazil, El Salvador, Honduras, and Nicaragua define processes exclusively controlled by congress. Argentina is unique, in that it allows constitutional change only through the convening of a constituent assembly (by congress). Mexico's provisions require passage in the state legislatures, as well as at the federal level. Beyond these seven countries, the remaining ten all reserve some room for participation by citizens. Chile and Panama have a qualified dependence on popular input. In the case of Chile, if the president vetoes a congressionally approved reform, the issue goes to a referendum to be settled. Panama requires reforms to be approved in two separate sessions of congress (as do many of the unicameral states), but if any alterations are made in the second session, a referendum must be called. Costa Rica, Ecuador, and Peru each have popular input as an option. In Costa Rica, only a two-thirds vote in congress is required, but the reform can then be put to a referendum for added legitimacy (and as a bargaining tool, as some representatives may vote for the proposal only on this condition). Ecuador allows a referendum at the request of 8 percent of the voting public, and this threshold is reduced to 1 percent if the constitutional change entails only a partial reform. Peru uses the popular option explicitly to ease congressional approval—a referendum reduces the requisite vote from the branch from two-thirds to a simple majority (but in Ecuador presidential approval is also required for the reduced vote). Colombia,

Guatemala, Paraguay, and Venezuela form a distinct group in that popular input is compulsory to some extent. Colombia demands a referendum for all reforms dealing with the constitution's sections on rights and guarantees, electoral participation, or congress, while the other three demand a referendum under all circumstances (though Guatemala and Paraguay allow reforms to certain core sections of the constitution only through a constituent assembly). Finally, Uruguay allows voters to both initiate and approve constitutional reforms, and though congress does hold the power to draft a reform, such a reform also must be put to a referendum.

Motives for Reform

Politicians change constitutions, so it makes sense to consider their motives if we want to explain why change takes place. Those politicians responding directly to, or hoping to appeal to, particular political interests enact what we could term **popular reforms**. These changes typically target single issues. Examples include the 2004 move in Uruguay to nationalize water resources, the 1999 El Salvadoran reform that protects the right to life from the moment of conception, and the 2012 Mexican reform that established Mexico as a "secular country." **Radical reforms** are more extensive, and often take place after previously excluded parties find their way into government. Having been on the outside while others drafted the constitution, they now feel that it is their turn, and seek to change rules they judge to be biased or otherwise unfair. Some obvious examples of radical reforms would be Nicaragua's 1995 reforms when Violeta Chamorro's UNO government sought to rework the constitution drafted under the Sandinista government (see "Country in the Spotlight" discussion below), and references to indigenous spirituality and methods of justice in the constitutions of Bolivia and Ecuador. But significant reforms also can be enacted by traditional, status quo powers hoping to appease critics and opposition parties. Examples of such **concessionary reforms** are Mexico's changes in 1997 and 1999, as the long-empowered PRI party recognized its vulnerabilities leading to the 2000 presidential elections, and the 2002 and 2004 Bolivian reforms where traditional parties attempted to deal with increasingly powerful indigenous movements. As evidenced by the fall of the PRI in Mexico and rise of indigenous movements under Evo Morales in Bolivia, concessionary reforms often represent the last gasp of traditional parties, or all too easily slip out of control and open the floodgates for the opposition.

A fourth type of reform, the **selfish reform**, takes place when status quo powers make changes that offer nothing to outsiders, and instead solidify their position or in some way protect their own interests. The most common examples of such manipulative reforms occur when presidents change constitutional provisions to remove restrictions on their reelection, as in Colombia, Ecuador, Honduras, Nicaragua, and Venezuela. Such reforms may also tilt the balance of power among government institutions.

Both Peru (1993) and Venezuela (1999) pushed through constitutional reforms to abolish their senates, in the expectation that the president could more easily work with just one chamber of congress. Similarly, Bolivia (2009) opened its judicial branch to electoral politics to pressure justices that had not kept pace with the political changes taking place in the congress and executive. The political pacts behind the older Colombian and Venezuela constitutions provide classic examples of selfish reforms that serve the interests of more than one actor. And the 2005 Nicaraguan reforms (see "Country in the Spotlight" discussion below) demonstrate that pacts still occur. A final type of reform occurs when a broad constellation of political parties simply recognize that constitutional change is required to further democratize or modernize government institutions. Consensus and cooperation distinguish these constitutional changes, known as **governance reforms**. Many of the constitutional changes legislated to empower local or regional governments and to allow for direct elections of officials at these levels could be considered governance reforms, insofar as centralized control became increasingly viewed as archaic and undemocratic. Some governance reforms led to the creation of new institutions, such as magistrate councils to professionalize the judiciary, or electoral councils to enhance the transparency of elections. Governance reforms often happened after military rule. In Chile, the *Alianza* and *Concertación* party coalitions agreed to scrap several provisions of the Constitution of 1980, which was drafted under the dictatorship of Augusto Pinochet. These included undemocratic rules that installed unelected senators, gave undue influence to the National Security Council, and prohibited the president from removing military commanders. Although the military handed power to civilians in 1990, many view these 2005 reforms as the step that solidified Chile's transition to democracy.

This typology of reforms illustrates the various motives that rest behind constitutional changes, but it does not completely explain why change takes place. An institutional explanation also asks us to survey the opportunity to act upon these motives for change, and looks to institutions to uncover the openings for, or barriers faced by, those who seek change—whatever their motive. To evidence the importance of institutions, one need look no further than the case of Paraguay and its lack of constitutional change since the ratification of the 1992 Constitution. One very powerful reason for this stability was the provision that prohibited any constitutional modifications for 10 years. Political leaders gained the opportunity to enact change in 2002, but the 10-year restriction may have influenced politicians to develop other strategies to pursue their interests.

Institutional Opportunities and Barriers

There are two means to formal constitutional change. A comprehensive overhaul, or even complete redrafting, is typically charged to a **constituent assembly**, expressly convened for this purpose by congress through a supermajority of at least two-thirds. Members of the body are popularly elected to instill legitimacy in the process. The calling of a constituent assembly can be risky business for a congress because it opens the fundamental rules of the political game to complete revision. Even the least represented can take comfort in the fact that the status quo rules offer them some role—would change make things worse? To reduce the uncertainty surrounding the work of a constituent assembly, some constitutions require congress to specifically define which articles or portions of the constitution are to be revised. Others will ban any alterations of certain fundamental portions of the constitution, such as the form of government or national territory. Still wary of caudillo-style rule, El Salvador and Guatemala prohibit any changes to the presidential term of office. In Brazil, the constitution establishes federalism as an irrevocable feature of its political system.

President Hugo Chávez of Venezuela used a constituent assembly to consolidate power in 1999. Though the 1961 Constitution contained no references to an assembly, the Supreme Court ruled that the summoning of one was not unconstitutional. Opponents to the controversial decision boycotted the elections to the assembly. Buoyed by the overrepresentation of his supporters, Chávez directed the body to draft a document to his liking, and then had it dismiss the congress (as well as the state legislatures), judiciary, and several important administrative positions such as the national electoral council and attorney general, all in preparation for a general replenishment of personnel under the new constitution. Still, the document was put to a referendum, where it won a resounding victory—aided by yet another opposition boycott. The convening of constituent assemblies is now a very politicized issue in Latin America. The suspicion is that they have emerged as a technique not for consensually reassessing fundamental law, but for accumulating personal power. Bolivia and Ecuador also convened constituent assemblies that redrafted their constitutions, and indigenous groups in Peru and Guatemala have promised a similar strategy.

COMPARING COUNTRIES

What Distinguishes the Structure and Content of Constitutions in Latin America?

Compared to other constitutions, the U.S. Constitution is unusually short, composed of just 4,585 words (7,712 including amendments). Constitutions in Latin America are much longer, though they do vary substantially in length, from Argentina's 12,517 words to Brazil's total of 64,082 words. The constitutions also diverge in the length of their transitory dispositions. Most transitory dispositions are technical in nature, and deal with the mechanics of implementing the new

(continued)

constitution or its reforms (e.g., the timeline to conduct a census for new congressional representation or the listing of precise dates for the establishment of new institutions), but they can also further elaborate constitutional provisions (e.g., specify how the budget of a new administrative office will be funded) or enumerate negotiated settlements among the signatories of the constitution (El Salvador drafted constitutional reforms in 1991 to help end its civil war and incorporated many of the terms of the cease-fire in its transitory dispositions). For most countries, constitutional reform adds to the stock of transitory dispositions—Brazil's transitory dispositions surpass the entire length of the Argentine Constitution!

Table 3.1 **Length of Latin American Constitutions**

Country	Total Words	(Words in Transitory Dispositions)	Articles
Brazil	64,082	13,348	250
Ecuador	54,843	5,400	444
Mexico	45,900	1,070	136
Colombia	40,660	5,000	380
Venezuela	37,001	2,364	350
Uruguay	29,576	2,639	332
Chile	29,034	5,215	120
Guatemala	27,740	2,063	280
Dominican Republic	27,655	1,149	277
Paraguay	25,810	1,182	291
Honduras	24,802	68	378
Panama	24,230	1,288	320
El Salvador	22,279	1,457	249
Peru	18,732	896	206
Nicaragua	17,798	410	202
Bolivia	16,344	none	234
Costa Rica	12,602	none	197
Argentina	12,517	1,271	129

Source: Constitutions accessed on Political Database of the Americas. Available at pdba.georgetown.edu/Constitutions/constudies.html.
*Total words in the U.S. Constitution: 4,585 (w/out amendments), 7,712 (w/amendments)

Latin American constitutions are distinguished by their embrace of substantive democracy, references to social rights and guarantees, sections devoted to the armed forces, extensive discussions of budgetary and financial matters, detailed notations on administrative offices, and provisions that allow for presidential decree powers and states of exception. The Guatemalan Constitution of 1985 provides one example. The extensive reference to human rights and constitutional guarantees is partially a product of the reforms drafted after the civil war of the 1980s and 1990s, but similar provisions are found in most other Latin American constitutions.

Title I: The Human Person, Purposes and Duties of the State
Title II: Human Rights
    Chap 1: Individual Rights
    Chap 2: Social Rights (the family, culture, indigenous communities, education, universities, sports, health and social assistance, labor, civil servants, economic and social regime)
    Chap 3: Civic and Political Duties and Rights
    Chap 4: Limitations on Constitutional Rights
Title III: The State
    Chap 1: The State and Its Form of Government
    Chap 2: Nationality and Citizenship
    Chap 3: International Relations of the State
Title IV: Public Power
    Chap 1: The Exercise of Public Power
    Chap 2: Legislative Branch
    Chap 3: Executive Branch
    Chap 4: Judicial Branch
Title V: Structure and Organization of the State
    Chap 1: Electoral Regime
    Chap 2: Administrative Regime (Regional-Local Relations)
    Chap 3: Comptroller and Auditing Regime
    Chap 4: Financial Regime
    Chap 5: Armed Forces
    Chap 6: Public Minister
    Chap 7: Municipal Regime
Title VI: Constitutional Guarantees and Defense of the Constitutional Order
    Chap 1: Habeas Corpus
    Chap 2: Amparo*

(continued)

Chap 3: Unconstitutionality of the Laws
Chap 4: Constitutional Court
Chap 5: Commission on Human Rights and Attorney for Human
        Rights
Chap 6: Law on Habeas Corpus, Amparo and Constitutionality
Title VII: Reforms to the Constitution
Title VIII: Transitory Dispositions

Discussion Questions

1   Discuss the advantages and disadvantages of having a lengthy
    constitution. Do detailed rules and procedures help to reduce con-
    flict, or do they encourage conflict?
2   How are Latin American constitutions a product of their own
    unique history and political development?

*Establishes broader protections than habeas corpus; common in many Latin
American countries (see Chapter 6).

The second type of formal constitutional change is **partial reform**, which
entails amendments, deletions, or alterations of portions of the current text.
Two opposing concerns tug at the rules for reform, and pull them toward
either greater flexibility or durability. On the one hand, constitutions should
be open to change so that they guard against freezing past interests or concerns, and so that they answer to popular demands as a matter of democratic
principle. But the argument for durability recognizes that constitutions represent the fundamental law of the land and should not be held hostage to
the political whims of the day. After all, today's majority is all too often
tomorrow's minority. Most states lean toward durability, and establish extra
hurdles for constitutional change. In his book *Patterns of Democracy* (1999),
Arend Lijphart devised a 4-point scale of **constitutional rigidity**. The scale
measures the ease of the decision rules surrounding constitutional reform.
Those countries with the weakest barriers receive a score of 4, and those
with the greatest hurdles receive a score of 1. In countries that hold different rules for different portions of the constitution (Chile, Colombia, and
Guatemala have such rules), the decision rule for the most "basic articles" of
the constitution is counted. And when different routes to reform are given,
the least-constraining threshold is used to score the country. For example,
Peru requires a two-thirds vote in congress for a reform, but this is reduced
to one-half if the vote is followed by a referendum. The scores for the Latin
American states under study here are as shown in Table 3.2.

Table 3.2 Constitutional Rigidity Scores in Latin America. It is easier to change constitutions in some Latin American countries than others

Score	Reform Rule	Countries
1	Supermajorities greater than two-thirds	*none*
2	Two-thirds majorities or equivalent	*Argentina, Bolivia, Chile, Costa Rica, Dominican Republic, El Salvador, Guatemala, Honduras, Mexico, Paraguay, Venezuela*
3	Between two-thirds and ordinary majorities	*Brazil, Nicaragua*
4	Ordinary majorities	*Colombia, Ecuador, Panama, Peru, Uruguay*

*Data collected from national constitutions by author.

Explaining Constitutional Change in Latin America

The procedures for constitutional change in Latin America are not unique. Some countries exhibit slightly greater levels of constitutional rigidity than others, but most regions of the world feature a similar range. What is unique in the region is the extent of constitutional change. Indeed, the alterations occur so often, *The Economist* felt compelled to declare, "Latin America's politicians fiddle far too much with their constitutions" (*The Economist*, 2014). And the magazine had the numbers to back up its claim. The region has seen over 200 constitutions since the independence period. The United States, with just one constitution since this time, may be exceptional. But European states, despite moves from monarchy and anguish in world wars, have also demonstrated greater stability. On average, European constitutions have lasted 77 years. In Latin America, they have folded every 16.5 years. While the average European state has made its way through 3.2 constitutions, Latin Americans on average have shuffled through 10.7. No country in the world has had more than the Dominican Republic, with 32 locked up in its national archives.

The range of constitutional rigidity (see Table 3.2) appears to make little difference here. When Latin American governments desire to change their constitutions, they are generally successful at doing so, whether it be through an entirely new constitution or amendment. One would be hard-pressed to conceive of unique, individual country characteristics that act as causal agents. Number of military interventions, intensity of partisan competition, level of socioeconomic development, and government ideology all do not seem to have much bearing on the course of reform. Constitutional change simply appears to be part of the political debate in everyday politics. More often than not, it happens when it is wanted. But the puzzle remains—how is it that the appetite for change is so easily fed? We are still lacking insight into the process that allows desires to be translated into outcomes.

If we cannot find a sufficient explanation tied to singular country characteristics, the next step is to consider some larger factor, common to all countries and strong enough to attenuate the obstacles raised in individual countries. A cultural explanation might note that historically, Latin American elites have embraced a form of jurisprudence known as **legal positivism**. This thinking holds that law does not come from some higher authority or from fixed ethical principles. Rather, it is formulated as a practical response to the pressing economic, political, or social needs of the day, or as novel values develop. Hence, Latin American leaders tend to react to urgent issues by amending or drafting entirely new constitutions (Hartlyn and Valenzuela, 1994, p. 109). And as we well know, history has offered Latin America no shortage of crises. Experience with the Constitution of Cádiz may have primed Latin America for legal positivism. The promulgation, suspension, restoration, and renovation of the document as the countries moved toward independence (see Chapter 2) "linked constitutions to political change and thus politicized constitutional law and constitutionalism" (Mirow, 2015, p. 3).

There is no doubt that legal positivism influenced thinking in the region, but an institutional approach provides a more comprehensive explanation for constitutional change. For example, we need to investigate why and how Latin American jurists and political elites latched on to this specific type of jurisprudence rather than some other. And there indeed are general institutional explanations for the penchant for constitutional change—the judiciary and the presidency.

Recall that informal change through judicial review represents an alternative to the formal constitutional change used by congress. It stands to reason that if we want to know why Latin American countries opt for formal change, we ought to understand why they do not favor informal change. And this means asking why the judiciary fails to significantly exert its judicial review authority. First and foremost, we need to recognize that Latin American states follow code law rather than case law, and code law is meant to remove the judiciary from lawmaking (see Chapter 6). But in reality, the legislated law is always incomplete and often ambiguous, allowing judges some room to interpret as they adjudicate no matter their system of law. Code law does abbreviate the judicial role in Latin American lawmaking, but other factors are also at play.

Chapter 6 discusses several obstacles faced by the judiciary in Latin America. Here, we highlight perhaps the most important factor when it comes to exerting the power of judicial review—credibility. Judiciaries in the region faced a tough road as defenders of fundamental law from the beginning. Latin America can point to constitutions drafted almost 200 years ago, but almost all have experienced significant and repeated ruptures in their political orders, making the life cycle of any constitution short indeed.

Moves by *de facto* authoritarian governments to redesign or completely substitute constitutions undermined the accumulation of traditional authority in constitutional provisions. Judges thus always faced a moving target as they asserted constitutional authority. And in more recent times, the political culture surrounding the rule of law languished as many judiciaries stood idle—or worse, colluded—while authoritarian governments ran roughshod over the rule of law and engaged in rampant human rights abuses (Popkin, 2004).

Still, a history of political unrest or authoritarian rule is not unique to Latin America. In the early twentieth century, many European countries seeking to build democratic institutions also found themselves with courts tied to autocratic regimes. To prohibit these courts from the important questions of constitutional adjudication, **constitutional tribunals** independent of the judiciary were established. Many Latin American countries looked to this model, even as they held fast to the more traditional U.S. model, which lodges judicial review in the judicial branch. The result is a "mixed system" whereby most countries have constitutional tribunals, but place them within the judiciary (the exceptions are Peru and, to an extent, Chile) (Navia and Rios-Figueroa, 2005). But even though the constitutional tribunals are found in the judiciary, politicians exert more significant appointment and even budgetary powers over these tribunals compared to supreme courts and their bodies. This has contributed to a relationship in which "Latin America's judiciaries have tended to be less functionally relevant and at the same time more politically penetrated than their European counterparts. While they have sometimes been manipulated by the powerful, they have just as often been ignored" (Hammergren, 2002).

It is then of little surprise that in Latin America, judiciaries—vanguards of the rule of law in a democratic society—fail to gain significant approval ratings in the eyes of a skeptical public. Writing almost two decades ago, Buscaglia and Dakolias (1996) argued that this public distrust of judicial institutions contributed to a "state of crisis." And recent polls have done little to change this impression. Data annually compiled by *Latinobarometro* regularly gauge public confidence in state institutions, and in the aggregate, only about 30 percent of Latin Americans express trust in their courts. The Inter-Parliamentary Union, which collects regional data, finds Latin American publics far behind Africa, East Asia, and Eastern Europe when queried on the confidence they place in their courts.[6]

Constitutional reform through the congress, rather than through the judiciary, does not just represent a different route of change; it also imbues different meaning into the process of reform. Judges, when held in high repute, tend to be viewed as apolitical. In this case, judicial review can be embraced by society as authentic reform—almost like a message from the village elders. But the public will always be skeptical of reform wrought by politicians. It is, after all, their job to cater to particular interests. And this skepticism is certainly shared by politicians outside the governing reform coalition, who, upon their own assumption of government, will certainly seek to implement further reforms to counter (or abrogate) those of the past. The result is a politically charged reform process that feeds upon itself.

And presidential power adds to dynamic. Congresses do face substantial voting thresholds when seeking reform, and party fragmentation can hamper their efforts. But strong presidents have the capacity to offset these hurdles. Colombia, Ecuador, Guatemala, Paraguay, Peru, Uruguay, and Venezuela all give the president the power to initiate a constitutional reform. Likewise, when some avenue for popular input is allowed (through initiation or referendum), the president can act as a mobilizing figure (only Argentina, Bolivia, Brazil, El Salvador, Honduras, Mexico, and Nicaragua do not offer popular input at any stage). And perhaps most importantly, the president exerts tremendous influence over congress as a party leader, prime legislator, or administrator of goods and services.

Hence, whereas a weak judiciary opens political space for congress, a strong presidency catalyzes that congress. And the result is not only more reform, but more politicized reform. It is not a single institution, but rather the interactions of institutions that determine the path of constitutional reform in Latin America.

COUNTRY IN THE SPOTLIGHT

Constitutional Reform in Nicaragua

Article 147 of the Constitution of Nicaragua appears to be clear enough: It prohibits the reelection of a president and does not allow any individual to hold the office for more than two terms. Daniel Ortega failed the test as a presidential candidate on both counts in 2011. Not only did he hold the office from 2006 to 2011, but he also served a previous term from 1995 to 2000. Nonetheless, a Supreme Court ruling in September 2010 rendered the article "inapplicable" to Ortega since the first term took place before Article 147 had been written, and violated his rights to "legal equality" with legislators, who can be reelected. However questionable, the reasoning is there, but what really irked the opposition was that the terms of two Supreme Court justices had expired, and without their votes, the ruling would not have stood. Likewise, when the electoral court also approved the ruling, they noted that an official whose term had also expired held its chair. As it turns out, the terms of these officials had been extended by a questionable presidential decree in January 2010 after the fractured national assembly proved unable to elect successors. And when a majority within the divided assembly attempted to overrule the decree, protests mobilized by Ortega's Sandinista Party prevented them from even meeting (*NotiCen*, 2011).

United States Senator John Kerry remarked that Ortega's moves "reeked of authoritarianism." Various U.S. media outlets echoed his sentiments. Still, the bigger story is that suspect political behavior is not new in Nicaragua, and certainly is not characteristic of just Daniel Ortega and his Sandinista Party. A deeper look into institutional developments and the struggle to achieve the rule of law in Nicaragua provides a more complete understanding of why Daniel Ortega and other Nicaraguan politicians so egregiously skirt constitutional guidelines.

When Violeta Chamorro won the Nicaraguan presidency in 1990, she and her UNO (Unión Nacional Opositora) coalition did so under a constitution drafted in 1987 by, and in many ways for, the opposing Sandinista Party and the commitment to socialist principles it had broadcast since the 1979 revolution. Her campaign had emphasized constitutional reforms to reduce state management of the economy, ensure civilian supremacy over the Sandinista-controlled armed forces, attenuate the social welfare commitments of government, and instill greater balance among the executive, legislative, and judicial branches (Anderson, 2006, pp. 69). But UNO's electoral gains in the National Assembly placed it below the threshold required to implement reforms on its own. Under the rules of the Nicaraguan Constitution, partial reforms need to be approved by a three-fifths majority in the National Assembly, in two sessions.[7] Though the president cannot veto a reform, the executive does holds the power of initiative. Absent such a move by the president, the assembly must marshal a two-thirds majority to initiate a reform on its own. With 52 of the assembly's 92 seats,[8] UNO could not meet the three-fifths requirement alone, making the party dependent on an embattled and now very defensive Sandinista Party.

Dealing with the Sandinistas would quickly fracture the fragile UNO coalition. Chamorro attempted to gain the upper hand with an early court-packing initiative that took advantage of the constitution's failure to designate a set membership for the Supreme Court. The Sandinistas mobilized widespread strikes in response. When the strikes subsided after two Sandinista judges resigned and Chamorro added two more to the body of seven, it became clear that a scheme had been arranged (the court now had four Sandinista loyalists, four appointed by Chamorro, and one Sandinista appointee viewed as

(*continued*)

a swing vote). Less clear was the fact that such dealing would be a harbinger of things to come (McConnell, 1997, pp. 69).

Many UNO supporters grew frustrated as Chamorro backtracked on her stalwart promises to reverse property confiscations enacted during the 1980s under the Sandinistas, others saw administrative ineptness as the economy unraveled, and still more grew disenchanted as Chamorro reacted to crises by asserting greater presidential powers and displacing legislative efforts. Chamorro's embracement of the very executive power she had vowed to curtail led dissident members of the disintegrating UNO coalition to draft their own constitutional reforms in 1993 (Close, 1999, pp. 69). When they passed in February 1995 (after a successful first vote during the previous session in November 1994), Chamorro refused to publish them, noting that the constitution required publication by the executive. But did the requirement mean that the president was obliged to publish, or that the reforms would not be authorized until they were published—giving the president an insurmountable veto?

The constitution provided a simple answer to this disagreement— the Supreme Court holds the power of judicial review. But political reality would prove far more complex. Unfortunately, the terms of three judges had just lapsed, leaving the court one short of its seven-member quorum. Chamorro pointed to the 1987 Constitution, which grants the executive exclusive appointment power. But the assembly, referencing the reformed constitution, pointed to the new appointment powers of the legislature, and in turn designated six new justices to ensure a compliant judiciary. Seeking to avoid the political fray, the six standing judges issued their own opinion—they held that the reforms were not valid until published by the executive. The court did order the president to publish the reforms, but did not set a date. The assembly dismissed the decision due to the lack of a quorum. International mediators coaxed the sides to an agreement in June, aided no doubt by a threat from international creditors to withhold debt renegotiations until the crisis was resolved. Chamorro published the reforms in return for a "framework law" passed by the assembly that suspended some of the reforms until after her term and committed the assembly to cooperate with her cabinet as it enacted fiscal policy and nominated individuals to the Supreme Court, Supreme Electoral Council, and Comptroller General (McConnell, 1997, pp. 69).

Though Sandinistas in the National Assembly supported the reform package, it had the markings of a radical reform insofar as it undid many of the substantive socioeconomic commitments of the 1987 draft, deleted some of the revolutionary language, and loosened Sandinista ties to the military. Executive power also characterized the original charter, but by this time the Sandinistas had come to appreciate their reservoir of strength in the assembly, and thus were more than happy to support reforms that fortified the legislature (Close, 1999, pp. 69). One seemingly curious reform not only prohibits presidential reelection, but also excludes relatives or former relatives of a standing president from the office in the subsequent term. But the provision is understandable—Nicaraguans retain the painful memory of the Somoza dynasty, which saw three family members pass the presidency from one to another. And more pressingly, Sandinista critics feared presidential handovers from Daniel Ortega to his brother Humberto (former commander of the army), while Sandinistas worried over the transfer of power from Violeta Chamorro to her son-in-law (and Minister of Government), Antonio Lacayo. As for the reference to "former relatives," this addressed the threats made by Lacayo in response to the reform—that he could divorce his wife and render it inapplicable! This is a good example of how unique, or even momentary, concerns often find their way into a country's fundamental law.

The deal making under Chamorro would take a turn for the worse under Nicaragua's next president, Arnoldo Alemán of the Liberal Alliance (1997–2002). His party controlled 42 seats in the assembly, just under the 46 required to pass ordinary legislation. To induce further support (and secure that within his own party), Alemán launched a corrupt campaign to bribe or otherwise press legislators. But the Sandinistas remained a formidable force both within the assembly, where they retained 36 seats, and in society due to their capacity to mobilize strikes and protests. Confrontation with the Sandinistas would occur immediately, as Alemán sought to again address the issue of property confiscations, as well as the whirlwind of seizures committed by Sandinista officials for their own enrichment as they departed from government in 1990 (Nicaraguans refer to the affair as the "piñata"). Street protests soon forced Alemán into a dialogue with Sandinista leader Daniel Ortega by mid-1997, and the short-term result was an agreement to largely accept the confiscations of the past in return for social stability (EcoCentral, 1997). But over the long term, this agreement would evolve into a wide-ranging power-sharing agreement between Alemán and Ortega, an agreement derisively tagged "El Pacto" by Nicaraguans.

(*continued*)

El Pacto blossomed in the 2000 constitutional reforms. Alemán and Ortega proceeded to expand and divvy up open positions in the Supreme Court, Supreme Electoral Council, General Comptroller's Office, and Attorney General's Office. Their influence was felt almost immediately. The General Comptroller (raised from one to five members under the reform) sat on its hands as corruption mushroomed. The courts sullied their own reputation with taciturn responses when Alemán targeted political rivals with various trumped up charges (*NotiCen*, 2001). And the electoral council took immediate action to quash smaller parties by changing the rules for public financing.[9] Though the Sandinistas and Liberals controlled 78 of the 93 seats in the 1997–2002 assembly (and thus could enact constitutional reform at will), each felt unable to reach a majority on its own due to the eight smaller parties in control of the remaining seats. The effects of the electoral reform were clear in the following assembly—the Sandinistas gained two seats, the Liberals acquired a majority of 52 seats, and only one small party, controlling two seats, remained. The electoral rule changes were also applied to municipal elections, and small parties suffered here too.

But the core elements of El Pacto fed the personal needs and aspirations of Alemán and Ortega. To save himself from future prosecution related to the blatant corruption under his administration, Alemán secured a reform that granted congressional representation to previous presidents. Membership in the National Assembly would allow him to enjoy the congressional immunity protections enshrined in the constitution. Ortega would also be guaranteed a seat under the reform (though his continuous involvement in presidential elections provided an already established route to membership), which was of great personal significance because of corruption charges levied against him as well as growing speculations over sexual abuse allegations. But more important to Ortega would be a change in the presidential electoral code. The 1987 Constitution held that a candidate must receive at least 45 percent of the vote, or a second round would be held for the top two vote-getters. Ortega, a candidate in every presidential election since the fall of Somoza, could always count on some 35 percent of the vote from staunch Sandinista loyalists. The problem was the other 60 percent or so of the population that deplored him. In a reform clearly tailored for his predicament, the new election rules set the threshold for a first-round victory at 40 percent, but added that a second round would still not be required if the leader tallied 35 percent and bested the runner-up by at least 5 percent.

Ortega would in fact gather 42 percent of the vote in the 2001 elections, but the total fell short of the 56 percent garnered by Alemán's vice president, Enrique Bolaños. Alemán, now President of the National Assembly due to his leadership of the majority Liberal Party, planned to control things from the newly empowered legislature until the following presidential elections. But Bolaños had grown weary of Alemán's domineering ways, and reached out to Ortega to assemble a legislative majority to strip Alemán of his immunity (Anderson, 2006, pp. 69). When Ortega saw the sexual abuse charges filed by his step-daughter dismissed in court, many speculated that a new pact with Bolaños was in the works. Their thinking appeared to be confirmed when Ortega supported the removal of Alemán's immunity (*NotiCen*, 2002). But with Alemán under house arrest by mid-2003, and the Liberal Party shattered by the Bolaños-Alemán feud, Ortega saw that he could play both sides to his advantage. The clash of interests would drive Nicaragua to a full-blown constitutional crisis.

Alemán still wielded considerable influence, and his supporters would not let his detention go unanswered. In late 2004, adherents in the Comptroller General's office opened an investigation into illicit campaign contributions to Bolaños, and by early 2005, partisans in the National Assembly contemplated impeachment—a threat that could only transpire with the support of the Sandinista Party. Bolaños came under yet more fire when the assembly passed a comprehensive set of constitutional reforms that would dramatically enhance its powers. The reforms granted the assembly the power to appoint cabinet officials, ambassadors, and other diplomats. The constitutional changes would also create two new administrative bodies to regulate services and property conflicts, and place them under the control of the legislature (such bodies are traditionally under the purview of executives). Bolaños quickly retorted that such changes were too fundamental— they changed the political system from a presidential to a parliamentary system—and thus could not be effected through the partial reform provisions of the constitution. Rather, a constituent assembly would have to be assembled and charged with such general reform.

To enforce his position, Bolaños could not count on the support of domestic political institutions tainted by the Alemán-Ortega pact, so he looked outside the country. He received a favorable ruling on his

(*continued*)

position from the Central American Court of Justice, appealed to the Organization of American States for support, and repeated warnings of foreign aid cuts from international financial organizations and the United States if the crisis were not resolved. The National Assembly condemned the acts as international meddling, and called attention to rulings in its favor from the Supreme Court. Confirming the involvement of Alemán, his supporters also made it clear that a presidential pardon for his crimes could resolve the crisis (*NotiCen*, 2005). The sides were at loggerheads for much of the year, but finally negotiated a compromise that dropped the impeachment proceedings, and promised a reappraisal of the reforms after Bolaños's presidential term ended in 2006.

Bolaños term did end in 2006, and so too did a chapter in Nicaraguan politics as he handed the presidential sash to Daniel Ortega. The electoral rule change negotiated under El Pacto finally paid off. Ortega won with 38 percent of the vote, surpassing Eduardo Montealegre from a faction in the Liberal Party by nine points, and thus avoiding a second-round runoff, which he would have surely lost. Still, though a chapter in Nicaraguan politics had passed, the similarity of the subsequent behavior by Ortega to that of Bolaños, Alemán, and Chamorro confirm that they are all characters in the same book.

For 16 years, opponents of the Sandinista Revolution had schemed and bickered among themselves, offering one opportunity after another for Ortega to make his way back into power. And now that he had returned, Ortega was not about to look back. In a final maneuver through El Pacto, he dropped charges against Alemán to curry favor with his congressional allies and garner the support necessary to retract the 2005 reforms. From the perspective of Ortega, they were solely designed to hobble Bolaños, not the presidency, and not now that he was in office. Still, his Sandinista Party failed to command a majority in the National Assembly, so Ortega did his best to sidestep it. He made extensive and questionable use of his decree powers, and created Citizen Power Councils to distribute government aid and win over support at the local level.

And as luck would have it, a growing economy sparked genuine support for Ortega from more of the population. Hence, as the 2011 elections approached, Ortega saw no reason to let a constitutional ban on reelection end his work, as noted above. Likewise, since 2012, he has seen no reason to allow other constitutional details spoil his plans.

Almost immediately, he overhauled electoral rules at the local level, expanding the number of city council seats throughout the country from 2,178 to 6,534. With elections just five months out, most parties scrambled to find candidates. But the Sandinistas simply looked to locally known individuals in the Citizens Power Councils, who had grown popular due to their work on anti-poverty programs. To further confuse the opposition, the rules to create a party and make the ballot were relaxed, resulting in a proliferation of parties. The Sandinistas would win 80 percent of all the city council and mayoral seats in municipal elections that saw deceased persons on the ballot and heretofore unheard-of parties. One opposition voice declared, "In the spirit of November 2 (the Day of the Dead), we could call this the zombie election" (*NotiCen*, 2012).

Ortega then looked directly to the constitution, proposing reforms that affected 20 percent of the document. Tellingly, he introduced his model of government as "evolving constitutionalism"—as if to validate constitutional change as a matter of convenience. The reforms, passed in 2014, withdraw the restriction on presidential reelection, broaden presidential decree power, allow appointments of active military officers to government positions, expand the role of the Citizens Power Councils, and end run-off elections for president—requiring only a plurality in a single round. When they were proposed, the reforms were widely condemned as selfish reforms, benefitting no one but Daniel Ortega (*NotiCen*, 2013).

To no one's surprise, Ortega announced his bid for a fourth presidential term in 2016. And predictably, a compliant Supreme Court used a technicality to disqualify Eduardo Montealegre, Ortega's 2006 foe and only viable opposition candidate. Montealegre promised to launch a "civic fight" outside the halls of government and announced, "We're going to honor this commitment to Nicaragua with the same firmness we've shown since 2005, when we said no to the pact, no to corruption" (*NotiCen*, 2016). The "pact" was of course a reference to El Pacto, but the comment was directed just as much to the Alemán faction in his party. And more broadly, the criticism might be directed to most any political leader in Nicaragua over the past several decades. Ortega is rightly criticized for his behaviors, but his actions, those of his predecessors, and El Pacto are all just symptoms of the lack of the rule of law in Nicaragua

(continued)

Discussion Questions

1   Who or what is to blame for the political crises in Nicaragua? Would "good leadership" be sufficient to resolve the country's problems?
2   Is it possible to create politically neutral procedures for constitutional change? Is there any hope for Nicaragua?

Conclusion

Constitutions stand on the twin pillars of state and nation, pillars that are often underdeveloped or contested in much of Latin America. This helps to explain the amount of constitutional change we see in Latin America, but so does the broader institutional context of Latin American regimes. In particular, weak judiciaries lead congress and especially executives to take the initiative for constitutional change through the only means they have—formal modifications or even new constitutions. And because politicians handle this change, it becomes more conflict-ridden and politicized. Institutions, then, offer a fundamental explanation not only for the political change but also for the politicized change we see in Latin America.

It is easy to point to Nicaragua's politicians as the source of its constitutional crises, just as it is easy to paint President Rafael Correa—noted at the start of the chapter—as a demagogue. But one is reminded of James Madison's famous line in *Federalist* No. 51, "If men were angels, no government would be necessary." History provides countless cases of shady politicians and corrupt dealings, and in most cases we can point to how institutional failures set the stage for such behavior. Nicaraguan politicians and Correa are no different from politicians in other countries, but what is different is the institutional setting: Presidents and legislatures face off under blurred lines of responsibility and authority, the judiciary lacks the credibility to adjudicate the rule of law, party discipline is a constant struggle, and partisanship rather than merit guides bureaucratic appointment, leading to a form of governance in which politics and self-interest trump prudence and the common good.

A constitution sets the rules of the game and comes to be accepted as definitive law as political institutions establish their authority and work together like a well-oiled machine. Lacking an underlying consensus on the division of authority and respect for the independence of different government branches, the constitution becomes no more than a convenient chart of the prevailing balance of political power—invariably recast with the ebb and flow of political interests. Nicaragua may be an extreme example, more so than Ecuador, but the political instability that has afflicted all of Latin America means that every country in the region faces a similar risk. The good news is that the same relationship that causes a spiral of disorder can also cause a spiral of order. Institutions and constitutions feed off each other, such that instability can lead to crisis, as in Nicaragua. But if consensus is there and institutions develop strong foundations, the rule of law will thrive and the constitution will assume its proper role—to guide politics rather than to be guided by politics. The following chapters will draw us more deeply into the makeup and dynamics of regime institutions. And in each, we will see how they operate alongside other regime institutions, and how even slight adjustments to their rules have dramatic consequences for political behavior.

Key Terms

caudillo politics   79
export economy   80
positivism   80
Roosevelt Corollary   82
Dollar Diplomacy   82
indigenismo   84
import-substitution
   industrialization   85
Dependency Theory   85
bureaucratic authoritarianism   87
National Security Doctrine   87
Alliance for Progress   88
Washington Consensus   89
pink tide   91
power maps   93
conservatives   93
radicals   94
liberals   94
states of exception   94

protected democracies   95
corporatism   95
fueros   95
insult laws   96
political pacts   97
procedural democracy   99
substantive democracy   99
direct democracy   101
popular reforms   103
radical reforms   103
concessionary reforms   103
selfish reforms   103
governance reforms   104
constituent assembly   104
partial reform   108
constitutional rigidity   108
legal positivism   110
constitutional tribunals   111

Discussion Questions

1   If a politician is elected by a wide margin, does that politician have the right to call for widespread constitutional change?
2   Compare and contrast the constitutions of Latin America and the U.S. Constitution. In your view, what are the advantages and disadvantages of each?
3   How can a country effect desired constitutional change and still ensure that it remains a "nation of laws, not men"? What role can institutions play here?
4   How do constitutions interact with states and nations? Can we describe this interaction as a never-ending process?

Suggested Readings

Benedict Anderson. 1991. *Imagined Communities: Reflections on the Origins and Spread of Nationalism.* **London: Verso.** Benedict Anderson refers to nations as "imagined communities" because of one fundamental fact—most members of a nation do not know each other. And yet there is a bond and people even die for their nation. Anderson's work is one of the most important studies on the emergence of nationalism. Though he devotes only a small section to Latin America, it is a necessary read for understanding nation building.

Brian Loveman. 1993. *The Constitution of Tyranny: Regimes of Exception in Spanish America.* **Pittsburgh: University of Pittsburgh Press.** Brian Loveman looks back to Iberian traditions to explain the use of constitutions in Latin America by military dictatorships. It is a reminder that constitutions can empower authoritarian rule. This comprehensive work covers countries throughout the region in historical detail.

Roberto Gargarella. 2013. *Latin American Constitutionalism, 1810–2010.* **New York: Oxford University Press.** Constitutions in Latin America took path breaking steps to incorporate social rights. Gargarella documents these moves, but then addresses the fundamental question of why the countries have not had such difficulty actually implementing these rights. He looks to the lack of complementary political reform such as excessive executive authority as the source of this inconsistency.

Florencia Mallon. 1995. *Peasant and Nation: The Making of Post-Colonial Mexico and Peru.* **Berkeley: University of California Press.** This book presents a rich social history of nationalist struggle and state building in Mexico and Peru, two countries that have some of the largest indigenous and rural populations in Latin America. Mallon details how citizenship is a contested goal.

Notes

1   "Ecuador: Voters Overwhelmingly Approve Forming Assembly to Rewrite Constitution," *NotiSur*, April 20, 2007.
2   All economic data is from the World Bank, *World Economic Indicators*, available at www.data.worldbank.org.
3   Article 98 is a reference to a specific article in the International Criminal Court Treaty (the Rome Statute) that exempts countries from complying with ICC requests if the act requires a state to act "inconsistently with its obligations under international agreements."
4   See "Sanders Condemns Efforts to Remove Brazil's Democratically Elected President." Press Statement issued August 8, 2016. Available at http://www.sanders.senate.gov/newsroom/press-releases/sanders-condemns-efforts-to-remove-brazils-democratically-elected-president.
5   "Office of the Special Rapporteur for Freedom of Expression Expresses Concern Regarding the Existence and Application of Criminal Defamation Laws Against Persons Who Have Criticized Public Officials in Ecuador." Press Release R32/11,

April 15, 2011. Inter-American Commission on Human Rights. Available online at: http://www.cidh.oas.org/relatoria/showarticle.asp?artID=837&lID=1.
6 Data published by United Nations Department of Economic and Social Affairs. Available online at: http://unpan1.un.org/intradoc/groups/public/documents/UN/UNPAN025132.pdf.
7 Many countries with unicameral legislatures require reforms to be voted upon in two legislative sessions. This is one way such countries can add a second step to reform—something that is more easily addressed in bicameral legislatures when reforms are required to pass through both chambers.
8 The National Assembly has an official membership of 90, and this number is used to compute quorum and voting rules. The actual membership often surpasses 90 because the constitution grants a concessionary seat to losing presidential candidates who gain a certain percentage of the vote. Under the 2000 reforms, it also grants a seat to past presidents.
9 Previously, parties needed to hold just one seat in the assembly to be eligible for financing. Now they would be required to garner over 4 percent of the national vote in the election. This also meant that financing could be acquired only after the election. For other rulings against smaller parties, see *NotiCen* (2000).

References

Ackerman, Bruce. 1998. *We the People: Transformations*. Cambridge: Harvard University Press.

Anderson, Leslie E. 2006. "The Authoritarian Executive: Horizontal and Vertical Accountability in Nicaragua." *Latin American Politics and Society* 48:2, pp. 149–61.

Arceneaux, Craig L. 2001. *Bounded Missions: Military Regimes and Democratization in the Southern Cone and Brazil*. University Park, PA: Penn State Press.

Bulmer-Thomas, Victor. 1994. *The Economic History of Latin America since Independence*. New York: Cambridge.

Buscaglia, Edgardo, and Maria Dakolias. 1996. "Judicial Reform in Latin American Courts." World Bank Technical Paper, 350. Washington, DC.

Close, David. 1999. *Nicaragua: The Chamorro Years*. Boulder, CO: Lynne Reinner.

Coppedge, Michael. 1994. *Strong Parties and Lame Ducks: Presidential Partyarchy and Factionalism in Venezuela*. Palo Alto, CA: Stanford University Press.

Duchacek, Ivo. 1973. *Power Maps: Comparative Politics of Constitutions*. Santa Barbara, CA: ABC-Clio.

EcoCentral. 1997, December 18. "Nicaragua: New Law on Property Goes into Effect."

The Economist. 2014, March 15. "Changing Constitutions: All Shall Have Rights."

Finer, S. E. 1988. "Notes Toward a History of Constitutions." In Vernon Bogdanor, ed., *Constitutions in Democratic Politics*, pp. 17–32. Brookfield, VT: Gower.

Gargarella, Roberto. 1997. "Recientes reformas constitucionales en América Latina: Una primera aproximación." *Desarrollo Económico* 36:144, pp. 971–90.

———. 2005. "The Constitution of Inequality: Constitutionalism in the Americas, 1776–1860." *International Journal of Constitutional Law* 3:1, pp. 1–23.

Gil Lavedra, Ricardo. 2002. "A Quick Look at Constitutional Reforms in Latin America." Paper presented at the 2002 *Seminario en Latinoamérica de Teoría Constitucional y Política*, June 6–9, Punta del Este, Uruguay.

Gwartney, James et al. 2010. *Economic Freedom of the World: Annual Report*. Vancouver: Fraser Institute. Available at www.freetheworld.com.

———. 2015. *Economic Freedom of the World: 2015 Annual Report*. Vancouver: Fraser Institute. Available at fraserinstitute.org.

Hammergren, Linn. 2002. "Fifteen Years of Judicial Reform in Latin America: Where We Are and Why We Haven't Made More Progress." Document published by UN Development Programme's Project on Governance in the Arab Region, March 2002. Available at http://www.undp-pogar.org/publications/judiciary/linn2/areas.html.

Hartlyn, Jonathan, and Arturo Valenzuela. 1994. "Democracy in Latin America since 1930." In L. Bethell, ed., *The Cambridge History of Latin America*, Vol. 6, part II: *Politics and Society*, pp. 99–162. Cambridge: Cambridge University Press.

Karl, Terry. 1986. "Petroleum and Political Pacts: The Transition to Democracy in Venezuela." In Guillermo O'Donnell, Philippe C. Schmitter, and Laurence Whitehead, eds., *Transitions from Authoritarian Rule: Latin America*. Baltimore, MD: Johns Hopkins University Press.

Lijphart, Arend. 1999. *Patterns of Democracy: Government Forms and Performance in Thirty-Six Countries*. New Haven, CT: Yale University Press.

Linz, Juan, and Alfred Stepan. 1996. *Problems of Democratic Consolidation*. Baltimore, MD: Johns Hopkins University Press.

Loveman, Brian. 1993. *The Constitution of Tyranny: Regimes of Exception in Spanish America*. Pittsburgh, PA: University of Pittsburgh Press.

———. 1994. "Protected Democracies and Military Guardianship: Political Transitions in Latin America, 1978–1994." *Journal of InterAmerican Studies and World Affairs* 36:2, pp. 105–89.

———. 1999. *For la Patria: Politics and the Armed Forces in Latin America*. Wilmington, DE: SR Books.

McConnell, Shelley A. 1997. "Institutional Development." In Thomas W. Walker, ed., *Nicaragua without Illusions*. Wilmington, DE: Scholarly Resources.

Mecham, J. Lloyd. 1959. "Latin America's Constitutions: Nominal and Real." *Journal of Politics* 21:2, pp. 258–75.

Mirow, Matthew C. 2015. *Latin American Constitutions: The Constitution of Cádiz and its Legacy in Spanish America*. New York: Cambridge University Press.

Navia, Patricio, and Julio Rios-Figueroa. 2005. "The Constitutional Adjudication Mosaic of Latin America." *Comparative Political Studies* 38:2, pp. 189–17.

NotiCen. 2000, July 27. "Nicaragua: Opposition Parties Shut Out of Municipal Elections Assail Electoral Council."

———. 2001, March 1. "Nicaragua: High Profile Legal Cases Hint at Political Motives and Bring Judicial System into Disrepute."

———. 2002, August 29. "Nicaragua: Country Near Unity on Alemán Indictment."

———. 2005, January 13. "Nicaragua's Congress Looks to Limit Presidential Powers; Alemán Could Rescue Bolaños."

———. 2011, February 3. "President Daniel Ortega Primed for Controversial Sixth Run at Nicaragua's Presidency."

———. 2012, November 15. "Sandinistas Dominate Municipal Elections in Nicaragua."

———. 2013, December 12. "Nicaraguan Legislature Ready to Ratify President Daniel Ortega's Constitutional Rewrite."

———. 2016, July 7. "Daniel Ortega, FSLN Draw Scant Opposition in Nicaraguan Elections."

Popkin, Margaret. 2004. "*Fortalecer la independencia judicial*." In Luis Pásara, ed., *La Experiencia Latinoamericana en la Reforma de la Justicia*. Lima, Perú: Instituto de Investigaciones Jurídicas, UNAM, México, and Instituto de Defensa Legal.

Rivera Cusicanqui, Silvia. 1990. "Liberal Democracy and Ayllu Democracy in Bolivia: The Case of Northern Potosí." *Journal of Development Studies* 26:4, pp. 97–121.

Wiarda, Howard John. 2001. *The Soul of Latin America: The Cultural and Political Tradition*. New Haven, CT: Yale University Press.

4 The Executive Branch

Latin American Style

Photo 4.1 In many ways, the sashes worn by presidents throughout Latin America reflect the same concern over tradition and continuity found in the coats of arms used by the monarchs of Europe. Here, President Rafael Correa of Ecuador proudly displays his sash while on parade to underscore his role as the head of state.

Source: © Shutterstock

> Do not adopt the best system of government, but the one that is most likely to succeed.
>
> —Simón Bolívar, "The Jamaica Letter" (1815, p. 119)

Presidentialism is a signature institution, and it is a familiar institution to most of us. Upon seeing presidencies in Latin America, many conclude that this is all they need know about government institutions in the region. But the label is misleading, for presidencies work very differently in Latin America than they do in many other countries. And why they work differently is in large part the result of history. To overlook the details of Latin American presidencies is to miss out on a window to past political developments that now have a significant impact on contemporary democratic institutions. Indeed, the very monopoly of presidentialism in contemporary Latin America belies the ferment of different ideas on executive design seen in the region at the time of independence. The liberals, conservatives, and radicals that fought it out over fundamental constitutional issues recognized the significance of executive configuration, and each one had an impact in the years after independence. Conservatives pushed for monarchy, and their ideas resonated with an elite seeking immediate stability. It should not be forgotten that both Brazil and Mexico (and recall that most Central American states united with Mexico at this time) emerged with emperors at their stead.[1] The hope that a European sovereign would sail to the Americas to assume the reins of government was not uncommon among conservative groups in the region. General José de San Martín unsuccessfully promoted monarchy for Peru after he helped secure its independence. This was, in fact, a central source of tension between him and Simón Bolívar. Manuel Belgrano, independence leader of Argentina, actually searched for an Incan "princess" in the hopes that a marriage between her and a European noble would produce a native, and thus more legitimate, monarchic formula.

And radical thought, with its penchant for parliamentary government, was far from absent in the early political systems of Latin America. After the first spark of independence, "setting up executive power vested in committees named by the legislative body was imitated in nearly all South American countries" (Belaúnde, 1967, p. 32). Peru's first constitution established a parliamentary form of government, and though it lasted only a short three years, the country retains a semi-presidential system. The currency of French revolutionary thought at the time of independence is of little surprise. After all, Latin American elites were more likely to speak French than English, and thus easily latched on to the Jacobin ideas of Voltaire, Rousseau, and Raynal, even as translations of both French and U.S. revolutionary thought made their way to Latin America. Likewise, the battle to restore the Spanish crown brought with it a renovated Spanish government under the Constitution of Cádiz. It attempted to assuage reformists with a limited (for its time) monarchic system that empowered parliament to form and remove government ministers. This blending of conservative and radical ideas had tremendous appeal in the years after independence (Belaúnde, 1967, p. 152).

But liberal thought, so prominently advertised in the newly independent United States and passionately backed by the fashionable writings of Franklin, Jefferson, Madison, Paine, and other U.S. forefathers, provided its own steady stream of influence. References to the U.S. model in political statements by Latin American leaders, obvious replications of the U.S. system in Latin American governing structures, and even visitations to U.S. cities by early Latin American statesmen and their impressions, have all been duly documented (Robertson, 1969, pp. 60–100). Nonetheless, it is all too easy to overemphasize the initial impact and lure of presidentialism as a foreign product. In fact, there were significant homegrown inspirations for the executive power granted by presidentialism. As the Spanish empire slowly crumbled through the eighteenth century, the crown enacted the Bourbon Reforms, which in part concentrated executive power in a last-ditch effort to save the colonies. The range of powers accorded to Latin American presidencies is more suggestive of these reforms than influences from the separation-of-powers principle seen in the North American model (Nohlen and Fernández, 1998, p. 112). Similarly, colonial rule had brought with it a blending of military and government roles, and military administrators were always more apt to rule by decree rather than through representative institutions (Loveman, 1993). Another influence comes from the corporatist political culture historically found in the region, which contributed to a more expansive, regulatory executive. Finally, one cannot ignore the practical appeal of strong presidentialism for a region facing economic and political crises at the onset of independence. These factors will all be discussed as we point out unique characteristics of presidentialism in the region.

All told, it is clear that homemade forces were at least as significant as foreign influences for the tilt toward presidentialism in Latin America. We should then recognize that what we have in the region is *Latin American* presidentialism. This point is important because, as documented below, many scholars have drafted sweeping condemnations of presidentialism based upon its record in Latin America. There is no doubt that presidentialism produces distinctive political dynamics, and not all of them are good. But the fact is that the perils of presidentialism (as one author has put it—see Linz, 1990) can also be attributed to certain aspects of Latin America politics and the institutional setting in which presidentialism sits in Latin America. To disentangle "Latin America" and "presidentialism," this chapter discusses presidentialism in its generic form, as one type of executive design distinct from parliamentary government. It then takes a look at how presidentialism has been instituted in Latin America to draw an accurate assessment of the criticisms associated with presidential government. A discussion on bureaucracy follows to capture the administrative aspects of the executive branch. To further illustrate the contours of executive design in Latin America, a case study of Argentina concludes the chapter.

The Executive Branch in Presidential and Parliamentary Forms of Government

In everyday conversation, we use the term *government* quite loosely to refer to the vast array of organizations that employ public servants—everything from the national or state congresses and local councils of elected officials, to the administrative organs that direct government services. But the term takes on a more definitive meaning in the study of politics. Namely, **government** refers to the group of people that hold ultimate executive power in a society. In democracies, this power is lodged within a **cabinet** and its presiding official, the head of government. The cabinet itself is divided into a number of policy-specific administrative divisions, such as the ministry of transportation, ministry of health, or ministry of defense. These ministers not only supervise policy implementation, but also serve to advise the head of government in their area of expertise. In the United Kingdom, the head of government is known as the prime minister, but this same role can take on a different name in different countries— chancellor in Germany, premier in Italy, or the Gaelic word *taoiseach* in Ireland. Both parliamentary and presidential systems have governments, but they primarily differ in how they originate and subsist (Shugart and Carey, 1992).

The Parliamentary System

In a **parliamentary system**, government emerges from and is dependent on the legislature for its very survival.[2] It emerges from the legislature in that the head of government and cabinet members are selected from the members of the majority party in the legislative assembly. The head of government is elected within a district like any other member of parliament. In the sense that there is a "national election" for the prime minister, it could only be described as indirect insofar as most voters know that supporting the local candidate of a given party raises the prospects that its party leader will become prime minister. And to survive, the government must retain the support of the legislature. At any time, the legislative assembly can pass a "motion of no confidence," and thereby force either the replacement of the government with another leader within the party, or the dissolution of parliament and a call for new elections. Importantly, a motion of no confidence can be, and most often is, based on purely political reasons. That is, the legislature can express its disapproval of government simply because it disagrees with its policy proposals. It does not have to document or otherwise make reference to legal wrongdoings. The high stakes that surround a motion of no confidence makes its appearance relatively rare in parliaments with a one-party majority and strong party discipline. But in the many countries with multiparty systems and/or less dependable party discipline, the threat is much greater.

Absent a no-confidence motion, a parliament may still not reach the end of its maximum term. These systems allow the prime minister to call for general elections at any time. Hence, though the British parliamentary system fixes the maximum tenure of a parliamentary session at five years, traditionally a prime minister could call early elections and effectively restart the five-year clock at any time. A crafty government facing a sudden surge in popularity could use this motion to its advantage. Margaret Thatcher did this after the 1982 Falklands-Malvinas conflict with Argentina produced a rally-around-the-flag effect and spiked her popularity, even in the midst of a severe economic downturn. The legacies of Thatcher's revolutionary changes in the British economic system are well known by many, but fewer recognize that the fortuitous combination of military confrontation with a distant, easily defeated foe and the rules of parliamentary procedure probably made these changes possible (Norpoth, 1987). To place a check on such scheming, in 2011 Britain reformed its rules such that an early election now requires support from two-thirds of parliament.

The Presidential System

In a **presidential system**, the executive emerges independently of the legislature through a national election and is guaranteed a fixed term of office. Here, a national constituency directly elects the head of government, who in turn appoints a cabinet whose members cannot simultaneously serve in the legislature. Rather, they serve at the pleasure of the head of government. Thus, whereas cabinet members in parliamentary systems take full responsibility for their area of administration and interact with the prime minister as coequals, cabinet members in a presidential system act in a subordinate position as mere advisers to the president. We may even go so far as to say that parliamentary systems have collegial executives whereas presidential systems have one-person executives (Lijphart, 1994). Also, in presidential systems the legislature may remove the executive only through the extraordinary procedure of an impeachment. The act is extraordinary because the motion for removal must have a legal, rather than political, justification. For example, in the United States, impeachment must be based upon "high crimes and misdemeanors." Hence in a presidential system, it is entirely possible to have the executive and legislative branches controlled by different parties, thereby producing a **minority president**. This situation is not uncommon in presidential systems. Many in the electorate may in fact prefer minority presidents as an additional check on political power. But a minority president is not necessarily a death knell for government activity. In an interesting contrast to parliamentary systems, here the presence of weak party discipline (usually assisted by more practical and less ideological parties) allows members of the legislature to cross party lines and form piecemeal majorities, thereby ensuring that the basic operations of government continue.

Origins of Parliamentarism and Presidentialism

The historical roots of parliamentary and presidential systems differ rather dramatically. Parliamentary government took a more evolutionary route as it paralleled the unfolding of popular sovereignty in Great Britain. Some 100 years before King John signed the Magna Carta in 1215, it had become commonplace for the king to consult informally with strong lords and archbishops. Soon afterward, regional nobles representing towns and villages also gained a regular audience with the monarch, forming a less prestigious body known as the House of Commons, which would sit underneath the House of Lords. Still, the monarch held full responsibility for the assignment of personnel in cabinet-like roles. In this time, the monarch not only played the role of the head of government, but also the **head of state**, a largely ceremonial position that is meant to represent the entire country irrespective of the political differences that might be found in it. Over time the two houses, collectively known as parliament, eroded the legitimacy of the monarch as more and more of the British population looked to them as the proper venue for political decision making. Civil war in 1688 settled the issue; henceforth, decision making would rest in the hands of parliament and government would derive only from it. The monarch retained its role as head of state, and was charged with the **investiture** and dissolution of government, but the legal binding of the crown's decisions with the preferences of parliament makes the monarch little more than a rubber stamp. That still left the unelected House of Lords with great influence, though it too would largely be relegated to a ceremonial position by reforms in the early twentieth century. Since then, the House of Commons has assumed full responsibility for the passage of laws.

Presidential government has a more recent history, one which developed not so much through the evolution of a political system, but more so from the calculations of political leaders seeking to build a state anew. Montesquieu provides the philosophical rational for presidentialism. He decried despotism, which inevitably grows corrupt due to the concentration of power. To maintain the rule of law in government, Montesquieu wrote, "power must check power by the arrangement of things" (Montesquieu, 1989, p. 155). The formula was not meant to criticize monarchies. In fact, Montesquieu lauded monarchies, so long as they amounted to what we would today call **constitutional monarchies**. In a constitutional monarchy, the rule of law strictly defines the role of the monarch, who shares power with other political bodies (most importantly, the parliament). Montesquieu argued that this more limited role for the crown could be ensured, and despotism avoided, so long as the country retained a strong court, clergy, nobility, and parliament. But what if a country lacked a monarch, as in the new countries of the Americas? Here we see the practical application of Montesquieu's thoughts. The founding fathers of the United States also wished to avoid despotism, and saw in Montesquieu a formula for what would become a signature feature of presidential government—the separation of powers in distinct executive, legislative, and judicial branches of government.

Still, the lack of a monarch saddled the constitutional framers with the task of finding a head of state. They answered this problem by combining the roles of head of government and head of state in the presidency. The fusion of these roles intensifies the one-person nature of the presidential executive, and makes impeachment proceedings all the more extraordinary. The removal of a prime minister rids government of a plain politician, one who holds the position as an agent of parliament and acts as no more than *primus inter pares* (first among equals) with the cabinet.[3] And because the head of state continues in office uninterrupted as a symbol of apolitical unity, parliamentary systems maintain a sense of continuity from one government to another. However, to remove a president is to challenge the will of the people, and the act itself not only disrupts government, but also shakes the very foundations of state authority because it represents an attack on the head of state. In yet another interesting divergence between parliamentary and presidential systems, we see that the symbolism surrounding the head of state role recedes to a largely ceremonial function when it stands alone in parliamentary systems, but this same symbolism empowers tremendously when combined with the head of government role in presidential systems (Figure 4.1).

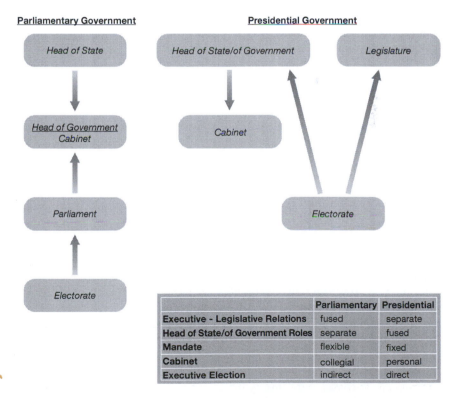

	Parliamentary	Presidential
Executive - Legislative Relations	fused	separate
Head of State/of Government Roles	separate	fused
Mandate	flexible	fixed
Cabinet	collegial	personal
Executive Election	indirect	direct

Figure 4.1 Presidential and parliamentary systems share the same actors, but those actors behave and interact differently in each.

Variations in Parliamentary and Presidential Systems

The aforementioned explanations of parliamentary and presidential systems describe the political systems of the United Kingdom and United States, respectively. Indeed, many look upon the systems of government found in these countries essentially as ideal types. They define the most fundamental features and dynamics of parliamentary and presidential government.[4] But when we look to other countries, we see many deviations. For example, the German parliamentary system allows only the chancellor to initiate a vote of no confidence, and offers the lower house of the German parliament—the Bundestag—the alternative **constructive vote of no confidence**. This motion allows the Bundestag to dissolve government only if an alternative government supported by a majority in the Bundestag can be identified. The provision attenuates the influence of extremist parties eager to disrupt government simply for the sake of disruption. It is no surprise that this motion originated in post-WWII Germany when the memory of Nazism and the prospects of communism tendered a constitution designed to safeguard moderate politics. More variations on Westminster-style parliamentarism include the investiture process—which may come through a vote of parliament rather than from a decision by the head of state, bicameral versus unicameral options (see Chapter 5), the opportunity to appoint cabinet members who are not members of parliament, and parliaments with fixed terms.

One of the more noticeable adaptations of "pure parliamentarism" occurs when a country lacks a monarch, but prefers not to fuse the head of state and head of government roles as in presidentialism. In this case, parliament can simply appoint a head of state in addition to the head of government, as in India, Greece, and Iraq. And to ensure a more consensus-based and theoretically less politicized office, the decision may require a supermajority and/or the term of the office may be longer than the term of parliament. In Italy, the head of state requires a two-thirds vote (but only a majority if the motion fails three times) and the head of state retains the position for seven years, whereas parliament can last a maximum of only five years. Some countries opt to have nationally elected heads of state who actually assume some of the policymaking power of the head of government (most often in defense and foreign policy), and who can even force the reconsideration of unsuccessful bills and dissolve parliament. In reference to these countries, Duverger (1980) coined the term **"semi-presidential"** (though they are just as much "semi-parliamentary") to distinguish a third executive system in addition to the presidential and parliamentary variants, and pointed to France as an ideal example. In reality, the balance of power between presidents and prime ministers in semi-presidential systems varies considerably. Finland and Poland have strong prime ministers and weak presidents, whereas South Korea has a strong president and weak prime minister, but all have semi-presidential forms of government (Elgie, 2005). But these systems do form an independent subspecies of executive design insofar as they require two executives—one nationally elected and another dependent on the legislature—to share decision-making power.

We do find one case of a semi-presidential system in Latin America. Peru has such a system, and in general it tilts power toward the president so that it is more like South Korea than Finland or Poland. The 1993 Constitution of Peru sets out separate elections for the executive and a unicameral legislature (each receive five-year terms). Once elected, the president appoints not only a cabinet (known as the Council of Ministers), but also a President of the Council of Ministers, who heads cabinet meetings just like a prime minister. The appointment procedures themselves veer from presidentialism because members of the legislature are allowed to sit on the cabinet. But more importantly, the role of the council borrows from parliamentary procedures in order to attenuate presidential power. In particular, all presidential acts must be signed by at least one minister (and certain decrees must be approved by a majority vote in the council). Upon approval, a minister becomes legally responsible for the act (and open to prosecution), and can be censured (thereby forcing a resignation) through a simple majority vote of the legislature. Not only does this force the minister to think very carefully about the legality of presidential action, but it also offers congress an opportunity to check executive power in a way that lowers the stakes compared to an accusation levied directly at the president. Congress can also dismiss the entire cabinet in a vote of no confidence, but the Council must initiate this motion.

The ability to censure and remove cabinet officials is not unique to Peru (though the country flaunts a more active record than most). Many Latin American states offer easier removal procedures than those found in the United States to counter the stronger, more independent cabinet appointment powers held by the president (see Chapter 5). But Peru's removal procedures add much more to the intertwining of executive-legislative relations. To guard against an overly antagonistic congress—perhaps in times of a minority president—if congress either uses its censure power or supports a vote of no confidence twice during a presidential term, the president gains the opportunity to dissolve congress and call new elections. Although most of the time Peru looks like a presidential system, it allows for some of the interdependencies found in parliamentarism (Schmidt, 1998).

The presidential systems in the remaining Latin American countries look more like the prototypical system we see in the United States, but still with significant twists. Just as deviations from British parliamentarism may represent improvements, adjustments to local traditions, or even misguided errors, a comprehensive evaluation of presidential options will expose a range of choices within this system of executive design. Knowledge of these options will allow us to make informed proposals on how and where institutional modifications could effect a desirable change in politics.

Latin American Presidencies

The whirlpool of radical, conservative, and liberal ideas at the time of independence may not have been strong enough to avert the presidential design favored by Spanish colonial traditions and the Bourbon Reforms, or to ward off the history of militarism and its appetite for centralized government, or to rebut what appeared to be a successful example of presidentialism in the United States to the north. But when historians seek to identify a symbolic turning point—the moment when a decisive argument for presidentialism was made—many look to Simón Bolívar's 1819 speech before the Assembly of Angostura, in Venezuela. The assembly acted as Venezuela's parliament (though it rarely met), but for this meeting representatives from the neighboring country of New Granada (present-day Colombia, Ecuador, and Panama) showed up to draft a new constitution to unite the two countries. Here Bolívar made his case for executive power as the best means for governing a Latin America that he saw as fraught with cultural divisions, lacking hereditary nobility, in need of an enlightened and moral education, and still fighting for liberty from Spain. For Bolívar, a strong presidency was an immanently practical thing: "We must never forget that the excellence of government lies not in its theories, not in its form or mechanism, but in its being suited to the nature and character of the nation for which it is instituted" (Bolívar, 1819, p. 184). This was straight from Montesquieu, who wrote of the need to consider first a country's geography, people, climate, population, religion, commerce, and other distinctive elements, before addressing the issue of governmental construction.

This practical line of reasoning gained currency as Latin America continued on its rugged road to independence (Lambert, 1974, pp. 263–271). More than a dozen years of war left the region in dire economic straits. Mines sat unattended and flooded, agricultural fields fell fallow as elites migrated to safety and the rural poor sought new opportunity, swollen defense budgets sapped the public treasury (and initiated a legacy of international debt), bandits disrupted trade routes, and the uncertainty of it all made investment an impossible decision. Social strife compounded the disorder as excluded groups—the indigenous, Africans, and the marginalized with mixed-blood—pressed for more revolutionary changes. The lack of order fed the appeal to expediency, rather than principle, as new political institutions came into being. "This meant that all constitution writers, conservative or liberal, federalist or unitarian, anticipated the possibility of disorder and violence—and the requisite authority for its suppression. In some cases, this anticipation manifested itself in vague assignments of authority to the executive to maintain peace and internal order. In other cases, it resulted in more explicit designs for constitutional regimes of exception" (Loveman, 1993, p. 54). And as we saw in Chapter 3, regimes of exception (or states of siege) hand power to the presidency.

Constitutional Powers

Given their histories, it is not surprising that Latin American executive institutions would point toward strong presidents and take their toll on the separation-of-powers principle. The most conspicuous element of strength held by Latin American presidents is their greater lawmaking power when compared to the U.S. president. In the United States, lawmaking is under the formal purview of Congress. Only a member of Congress can introduce a bill; if a president wishes to submit a bill, a sponsor must be found (though one always can be found). Still, Congress monopolizes the actual creation of law. The president's constructive role in lawmaking is limited to **executive orders**, which are directives used to guide federal agencies as they implement policy in accord with the laws passed by Congress. Executive orders come into play when a law requires more precision as it is applied in specific areas, or when Congress deliberately grants some discretionary decision-making authority to the president. But the key here is that executive orders can occur only under the umbrella of existing legislation. They cannot direct policy absent some linkage to an act of Congress and thus ultimately have more to do with "law-applying" than novel lawmaking. Outside the use of a sponsor to submit legislation or the enactment of executive orders, the U.S. president's only other formal role in lawmaking rests in the **block veto**, which is a reactive rather than constructive power. Under the U.S. Constitution, a block veto negates a bill in its entirety unless a two-thirds majority in each house votes to override the veto. Beyond these powers, it is a well-known fact that the U.S. president wields tremendous indirect influence over the lawmaking function by crafting public agendas and advising Congress, but the formal constitutionally defined rules stay true to the separation-of-powers principle which places Congress center stage and stations the president in a largely reactive role.

The veto appears straightforward on its surface, but there are in fact numerous factors to consider even under the block veto alone. The United States requires a veto override to pass through each house, but Bolivia and Brazil count votes in a joint session of congress, and the unicameral congresses of Latin America also offer just one vote. In Argentina, the legislature can dodge a potential veto by submitting the bill to a popular referendum. Ecuador stands out as an extreme case here. Under its constitution, congress must wait one full year before attempting to override a block veto. There are also variations on whether the rules call for an override vote that counts only members present or the total members of a chamber, which can make things tough if absentee rates are high. And then there is the actual voting threshold. Most countries use the two-thirds vote threshold, but Uruguay requires only a three-fifths majority override, and six countries demand only a simple majority (Brazil, Colombia, Nicaragua, Paraguay, Peru, and Venezuela). The simple majority may appear to be limited to delaying a final outcome (because it appears to simply replay the original vote). But studies have shown that under certain conditions the threat of a veto, even with a simple majority override, can change the legislative outcomes when stable majorities are lacking—a common scenario in Latin America (Schwartz, 2004).

But the block veto is but one weapon in the arsenal of executive powers found in Latin America. In fact, just three countries—the Dominican Republic, Guatemala, and Honduras—allow solely the block veto like the United States.[5] Twelve countries also allow the **partial veto**, whereby a president can delete portions of a bill.[6] And here, a majority override will never represent a simple replaying of the original vote. Bills typically make their way through congress as compromises—different legislators attach different levels of support to different sections of the bill. Once that bill is disassembled and repackaged through the partial veto, delicate majorities may fall apart. So while the Paraguayan president holds both a block veto and a partial veto, both of which can be overturned with a simple majority in each chamber of congress, the president may want to use the block veto to buy time if circumstances have changed (e.g., a sudden economic crisis, new security situation, or abrupt movement in public opinion) and some legislators appear willing to reconsider their stance in favor of a new proposal. And on the other hand, the partial veto opens a new strategy for a president facing an obstinate congress but hoping to hinder at least some portions of a bill.

The partial veto turns the president into something more than a reactive force because it forces a debate with congress and raises the prospects for an outcome different from either the bill originally proposed by congress or the status quo. That desire for a more activist president can be traced to the historic debates over presidential and parliamentary forms of government, and represents a slight victory in the midst of a more general defeat for parliamentary proponents. The writings of Bolívar celebrate the separation of powers as an antidote to despotic government, but he also showers praise on the programmatic efficiency of the British parliamentary system, a model he saw fit for the pressing needs confronting Latin America. Bolívar felt that one way to prevent the separation of powers from curbing expeditious governance would be to grant the executive in a presidential system actual lawmaking power, something more than the negative power of a block veto. The partial veto is a move in this direction, and a bolder move came from the innovation of another form of veto, the **amendatory observation**. This veto allows a president to return a bill to congress with remarks, be they substitutions, additions, or deletions (the amendatory observation effectively subsumes the power of the partial veto). The amendatory observation procedure first appeared in the 1826 Constitution of Bolivia, drafted by Bolívar himself, and then in the Constitution of Peru ratified that same year and prepared under Bolívar's direction. Other constitutions of the region soon adopted the procedure, and today it is still found in ten Latin American countries.

Another nod toward parliamentary governance comes in the executive power to introduce legislation, a strict forbiddance under the U.S. Constitution. Beyond this, many countries grant the president the *exclusive* right to initiate legislation in certain especially significant policy areas such as modifications of the bureaucracy, military affairs, tariff and credit regulations, and the budget (Mainwaring and Shugart, 1997, p. 48). The budgetary process is arguably the most important government activity on a year-to-year basis. Typically, Latin American presidents receive a distinct set of powers for use only in budgetary affairs. Several constitutions allow only the president to propose a budget and place strict limitations on congressional motions to make modifications. In Brazil, the Dominican Republic, El Salvador, Nicaragua, Peru, Uruguay, and Venezuela, congress can only decrease spending or raise revenue, and cannot increase spending or the deficit under any circumstances; in Brazil, Ecuador, Mexico, and Peru, the president has the power to shift monies within the budget after congressional approval; and in El Salvador and Paraguay, the president can impound spending on certain programs after congressional approval (UNDP, 2004).

Several Latin American presidents also possess the power to call for a **referendum**. The ability to make direct appeals to the electorate might be celebrated as an expansion of the democratic process, but as one researcher notes, "it seems naïve to assume that referendums exclusively serve genuine consultative purposes or are promoted by governments on the grounds of a participatory understanding of democracy" (Breuer, 2008). Referendums can be, and have been, used by presidents to circumvent opposition in congress. While this may allow the political system to avoid deadlock, there is concern that it leaves unresolved the underlying discord between the president and congress, and may even raise hostilities.

An additional initiative power afforded to many presidents is the ability to attach an **urgency petition** to a bill introduced in congress. In such cases, the executive can force congress to consider a bill either within a set period of time (usually 30–45 days) or immediately, in advance of all other proposals on the legislative agenda. And in the cases of Chile, Ecuador, Paraguay, and Uruguay, if congress does not expressly reject the bill in the time allotted for consideration, it becomes law. But each country does provide some limitations on urgency petitions. In Uruguay, budget bills can never be tagged urgent, and the president can never send more than one urgency petition at a time. In Paraguay, presidents can use the urgency petition only three times during each legislative session. In Ecuador, the urgency petition is limited to economic affairs. Chile's constitution furnishes the most generous urgency powers.[7] To offset some executive power here, those countries with broader exclusive initiative power also tend to be those with simple majority veto overrides (Mainwaring and Shugart, 1997, pp. 47–48). Generally speaking, the power of executive initiative is greatest in Brazil, Chile, and Colombia (UNDP, 2004, p. 80).

Partial vetoes, amendatory observations, and initiative powers give many Latin American presidents far more lawmaking powers than we find in the U.S. presidency. But the most glaring example of lawmaking power is found in the decree powers held by several Latin American presidents. Recall that executive orders take place under the umbrella of existing legislation. **Decree authority**, on the other hand, allows executives to draft and implement new laws. This decree authority can take one of two forms. Executives can gain **emergency decree authority** after declaring a state of exception in reaction to civil unrest or urgent situations. But the presumption here is that executive actions will be geared toward restoring order rather than some transformative agenda. Hence, emergency decree authority allows a president to expedite relief and reconstruction assistance when natural disasters strike, suspend civil liberties to address widespread street rioting, or enact price controls to check price gouging when food supplies run low. The authority is temporary, congress typically must consider all decrees at a later date, and often certain policy areas (e.g., changes in electoral procedures or budgetary rules) are off limits. Mindful of the abuse of emergency power under military regimes, many countries prohibit the declaration of new crimes

Photo 4.2 President Michelle Bachelet declared a "state of catastrophe" after a devastating earthquake hit Chile in February 2010. This lower-level emergency authority allows the president to impose measures such as curfews and to call on the military to support relief efforts. Distinguishing states of "siege," "exception," "catastrophe," and the like can help prevent executives from taking advantage of emergency authority.

Source: © Shutterstock

or penalties, moves to modify or otherwise interrupt the normal functions of the state (e.g., closing congress or reorganizing the judiciary), and/or the trial of civilians in military courts. Nonetheless, some presidents have taken it upon themselves to push the limits of emergency decree authority by introducing legislation that is in fact novel.[8] A second form of decree authority is **standard decree authority**. Here, executives hold the power to issue decrees outside the umbrella of existing legislation or to otherwise effect some change in the status quo.

In regard to the standard decree powers of presidents, Brazil stands alone. As originally inscribed in the Constitution of 1988 (Article 62), Brazilian presidents held the authority to issue provisional decrees when facing a situation of "urgency and relevance"—even in the absence of a state of exception declaration. The power was provisional because a decree would expire within 30 days if congress did not pass it as law. Still, the power proved to be far from negligible. Brazilian presidents embraced a permissive interpretation of an "urgent and relevant" situation, and skirted the 30-day expiration by simply reissuing the decree. By 2001, Brazilian executives had issued 619 original decrees, and reissued decrees another 1,611 times (President Henrique Cardoso's wide-ranging 1994 economic reform known as the *Real Plan* was decreed and re-decreed over an 80-month period)! A constitutional reform in 2001 revised the executive power so that (a) decrees could be reissued only once (though their provisional status was extended to 60 days); (b) there was a blanket prohibition on decrees in certain policy areas such as electoral rules, political rights, and budgetary matters; and (c) congress would be required to consider the provisional decrees within 45 days. The reform was supposed to rein in executive power, but a study of executive power in Brazil found that decrees actually increased after 2001, and that the percentage of provisional decrees converted into law by the legislature rose from 43 percent to 79 percent. What explains this unintended consequence? It seems that congress had unwittingly tied its own hands when it committed itself to considering presidential decrees. Legislators, always itching to address a plethora of policy initiatives on their agenda, could be easily overwhelmed by the number of provisional decrees sent by the executive. Rather than take the time to address the details of a provisional decree, more often than not enough legislators feel satisfied with the president's proposal or would rather not take the time to address it while their own agendas sit waiting (Pereira et al., 2006).

Partisan Powers

The Brazilian case is certainly an illustration of how the best-laid plans often go awry. But we should think twice before viewing it as evidence for the belief that Latin American presidents are increasingly seizing power from legislative bodies. The Brazilian congress still retains the power to reject provisional measures and can always go back to the drawing board and reform the constitution again (as noted in Chapter 3, Brazil is a leader in constitutional reform activity). This question of whether executive lawmaking actually indicates an antagonistic move on the part of a president to assume congressional powers is central to studies of executive authority. And to the surprise of many, research has shown that executive-legislative relations are more often characterized by a congressional delegation of power to the president than a presidential usurpation of authority from congress (Shugart and Carey, 1992). Often, the rules for delegation are outlined in the constitution. Congress will look to a particular issue area, say labor rights, and pass an act that allows the president to decree original laws in this area. Only Bolivia, Costa Rica, the Dominican Republic, El Salvador, Nicaragua, and Paraguay have constitutions that either deny or leave unaddressed the power of congress to delegate standard decree authority to the president.

But why would a congress relinquish such authority? This typically occurs when a president holds strong **partisan power**—which is largely measured by the size of the president's party in congress, how well the president is able to control that party (party discipline), and the mandate acquired by a president through direct popular election (no other politician in the country can point to a national constituency) (Lijphart, 1999, pp. 127–129; Mainwaring and Shugart, 1997). With partisan power in hand, a president can usually count on a more cooperative, if not compliant, congress. Hence, we have two ways to think about the influence of a president. On the one hand, we can look to formal legislative power (a form of constitutional power), and on the other, we can look to partisan power. Each adds to the political capacity of a president, but one especially important difference is the stability of formal legislative power (because it is largely encoded in the constitution) compared to the potential instability of partisan powers (which may fluctuate from one election to another, or even as presidential popularity swings) (Lijphart, 1999, pp. 127–129). This means that at different times—as partisan powers rise and fall—Latin American presidents may find themselves more or less dependent on their formal legislative powers. This creates a very different dynamic in Latin American presidencies compared to the U.S. presidential system. U.S. presidents can also experience shifts in partisan powers, but they cannot look to formal legislative powers as a substitute for declining partisan power. Instead, the U.S. president may simply fall into a deadlock with Congress. Shugart and Carey (1992) argue that the potential for deadlock is not necessarily a bad thing. After all, both Congress and the president represent the "will" of the electorate, and such "logjams" force cooperation and compromise. What is more democratic than that? But the strong presidents of Latin America can more easily seek recourse in their legislative powers when facing an unaccommodating congress, and effectively sideline democratically elected representatives.

COMPARING INSTITUTIONS

An Assessment of Presidentialism

Students are often surprised to learn that presidentialism holds a far weaker record than parliamentarism when it comes to political stability. And why shouldn't they be rattled? Most are familiar with U.S. history, and Montesquieu's balance-of-powers formula has served the country well. But the data send a clear message—from 1946 to 2002, parliamentary democracies lasted an average of 58 years, whereas presidential democracies survived an average of just 24 years (Cheibub, 2007, p. 2). Another study found that during the 1973–1989 period, only 5 of 25 (20 percent) presidential democracies lasted at least 10 years, whereas 17 of 28 (61 percent) of parliamentary democracies surpassed 10 years. Similarly, presidential systems were twice as likely to experience a military coup (Stepan and Skach, 1993, p. 10). Still, some take note that the vast majority of the world's presidencies rest in Latin America. Perhaps the short life spans of presidential systems have less to do with institutional dynamics, and more to do with certain facets of Latin America—be it economic underdevelopment, an illiberal political culture, or more politically charged militaries (Cheibub, 2007; Lipset and Lakin, 2004). But institutions may still hold the answer given the significant institutional differences between the U.S. presidency and presidencies in Latin America. We need to keep that in mind as we assess the promise and pitfalls of presidentialism.

Criticisms of Presidentialism

What are the arguments against presidentialism? First, parliamentary democracy offers a collegial executive, a setting that is more amenable to compromise when competing groups make their way into the legislature and find that none hold a majority. The collegial executive allows coalition governments to be formed as various political parties assume different ministerial positions. And in such cases of minority government, the prime minister—always wary of the vote of no confidence—is compelled to listen to parties beyond those of his or her own. On the other hand, presidentialism is a winner-take-all system. Only one party can control the executive. Ministerial positions may be

(continued)

offered to different parties, but all realize that real power rests in the president. Lacking the ability to offer a true coalition government, the politics of compromise can all too easily be replaced by the politics of exclusion, even when there is a minority government. Extensive lawmaking powers can entice a president to work around congress and thus upend a central appeal of presidentialism, that of the balance of powers. Guillermo O'Donnell (1994) warned of such presidents when he wrote of **delegative democracies**. These political systems may experience free and fair elections, but after the ballots have been counted and the offices awarded, the president emerges as a domineering force able to act with little to no interference from congress, the judiciary, or other government institutions. In the vernacular of political science, delegative democracies allow vertical accountability (public input through elections), but fail to foster horizontal accountability (a balance of government institutions).

The strong presidencies of the 1990s—from Carlos Menem in Argentina to Alberto Fujimori in Peru—appeared to signal the rise of delegative democracies. Although some examples remain—Hugo Chávez's Venezuela comes to mind—a number of factors have since emboldened the initiative of congresses when confronted with minority government. Growing civilian supremacy (see Chapter 10) means that congress no longer need fear how political infighting between it and the president might instigate a coup d'état by officers looking to break the logjam. A growing press corps now watches over presidential improprieties as never before; they often expose scandals that rally congressional action. And perhaps most importantly, expanded civil liberties allow for popular protest, which can undercut a president's claim to popular legitimacy. Given these factors, impeachment or the threat of impeachment has become much more common in the region (Pérez-Liñán, 2007). Though one cannot but applaud such moves to address malfeasance, critics of presidentialism emphasize just how difficult this system makes it to address these crimes or misdemeanors. It takes a heightened scandal and often violent social protest, rather than a simple vote of no confidence. In Argentina, two-week-long food riots in late 2001 left hundreds of stores looted and dozens dead as the country worked its way through five executives. In Bolivia, more than 100 died in the protests that pushed Gonzalo Sánchez de Lozada from office in 2003, and deaths also occurred when his successor faced the same fate in 2005. Impeachment crises represent an extreme logical consequence to the **immobilism** to which presidentialism is prone—given an executive and legislature with independent, fixed mandates, what happens when they do not get along? Deadlock may inhibit government activity, but clearly things can get much worse.

Responses to Criticisms of Presidentialism

But is presidentialism really a system that *inevitably* leads to either delegative democracy or immobilism? In principle, presidential democracy does offer a number of advantages. There is the classic liberal line—that presidentialism offers a safeguard against tyranny as it separates and diffuses power. This separation of powers begins with the independent election of presidents and legislatures, which gives each a prominent and counterbalancing claim to legitimacy. And proponents of presidentialism add that independent elections spin off another advantage—citizens have more than one opportunity to participate in elections. This can help to dull conflict, because a loss in one venue can be compensated by victory in another. Finally, it is not just the number, but also the type of participation that sets presidentialism aside from parliamentarism. In parliamentary democracies, different constituencies throughout the country elect representatives, but only presidential democracy allows the entire country to mobilize as a single constituency and express a collective will (von Mettenheim, 1997). And we do have the example of the United States, where presidentialism has worked just fine.

Recognizing variations within executive design allows us to move beyond the abstract and seemingly intractable debate over the liabilities or merits of presidentialism. As noted, Latin American presidencies do differ substantially from the U.S. presidency, especially in the lawmaking powers granted to the executive, and these differences can be the source of many ills associated with presidentialism. Simply put, the U.S. presidential democracy does not have the same opportunity to move toward a delegative democracy. A second explanation looks to the institutional setting of presidentialism. Parties are especially important here (Mainwaring, 1990). Presidentialism erects separate pillars for executive and legislative institutions, and as they reach up from the ground it becomes all too easy for each to forget that they share the same foundation of governance. But parties bridge this gap. More practical, and less ideological, parties ensure a channel of communication despite the formal separation of powers. And parties also

(continued)

help in the relationship between government and society. If parties effectively voice popular demands, groups may not feel the same need to mobilize in street protest, and immobilism is less likely to boil over to crisis. But the party *system* also matters. It is difficult for a president and legislature to achieve compromise when the legislature speaks with the manifold voices of a multiparty system. In Latin America, institutional designs tend to produce more disciplined, ideological parties than we find in the United States, and electoral laws guided by proportional representation open the field for more numerous and diverse parties. Regardless of our judgment on the desirability of these party features, here the point is that they do make governance more difficult for presidentialism.

Discussion Questions

1   Where do you stand on the debate over presidentialism? Give support for your answer.
2   How do presidential institutions create a trade-off between stability and efficiency? Which of these goals is more important to contemporary Latin America?

The Administrative Arm of the Executive: Bureaucracy

Efficiency and Bureaucracy

Politicians regularly bask in the fanfare of lawmaking, but laws mean nothing if left unimplemented. These laws should be administered efficiently, impartially, and in good faith, so that the original intent of the policymakers remains unblemished. The head of government and cabinet officials take the lead in this administrative effort, but they can hardly take on the task alone. They depend on a vast array of personnel to distribute services, assess results, and maintain records. Bureaucracy thus plays a critical role in democracy as a bridge between elected officials and the general public. In fact, consider that even in a democracy, the vast majority of government officials remain in the unelected positions of the bureaucracy, and our interaction with government occurs most often through these unelected officials. Still, what makes a democracy is the assurance that these individuals will be responsive to decisions crafted in democratic institutions—hence the term *civil servants*. The **accountability** of civil servants to elected policymakers, then, is a hallmark of bureaucracy in a democracy.

But oddly enough, **autonomy** is another feature important to public administration. In his classic writings on bureaucracy, Max Weber outlined a set of requirements for bureaucracy, one that was meant to lift the modern state out of patrimonial politics, where political elites enact policy with an eye toward private gain rather than the public good:

1 Hierarchy—An explicit chain of command links all individuals in the organization.
2 Specialization—Groups of experts on particular issues form distinct jurisdictions within the organization.
3 Meritocracy—Individuals acquire their positions by virtue of their proficiency in a specific set of skills.
4 Codification—Written rules to guide administrative behavior are exhaustive, rigid, and transparent in order to depersonalize decision making.
5 Job security—Fixed salaries and tenured employment safeguard individuals from political pressures; explicit procedures for promotion allow for career advancement. (Weber, 1964, pp. 329–336)

The Pathologies of Bureaucracy

Today we readily associate bureaucracy with incompetence and red tape, but to Weber, bureaucracy could refashion government so that it purred like a well-oiled machine. Only with a capable bureaucracy could government ensure the rational decision making required to address whatever social, economic, or political problems it might face. But Weber himself and generations of scholars since have noted that bureaucracy is fraught with unavoidable pathologies. Bureaucratic accountability and autonomy may be two desirable goals in a democracy, but they are also competing goals. Likewise, the protections required to shield bureaucrats from political influence can reduce the incentive to work. On the other hand, those who unremittingly focus on cost-effectiveness and propose the application of profit-based criteria to instill efficiency must come to terms with the fact that governments often pursue social goals which cannot be easily reduced to economic gains and losses—especially not in the short run. And then there is the possibility that bureaucracies might not just become unresponsive, but that these unelected officials might use their expertise to control policymaking.

The pathologies of bureaucracy are unnerving because they exist even in the ideal type form of bureaucracy identified by Weber. The sad news is that bureaucracy represents an inevitable feature of the modern state, and that bureaucracy will always be laden with complications. But the alternative to Weber's ideal bureaucracy—a politicized administration, one enmeshed in the patronage politics of governing officials—is much worse. Here bureaucrats dole out state services as rewards or punishments. In Mexico, where patronage politics reigned supreme from 1929 to the 1990s, if a small village failed to cast sufficient ballots for the hegemonic PRI party, inhabitants could expect federal funds to construct roads, build schools, or administer health care to dry up. Administration also becomes a breeding ground for corruption, as bureaucrats unbounded by meritocratic principles or codified rules seek to enrich themselves.

The Size of Bureaucracy

In Latin America, the public sector has experienced considerable change over the past two decades. For much of the twentieth century, scholars would uniformly and commonly point to bloated bureaucracies standing at the forefront of states hoping desperately to foster development under their own guidance and on their own terms. Many of them emerged as a result of ISI policies and remained even after the populist era. Regulatory agencies charged with setting prices, wages, or production levels presided over almost every economic sector, and banking usually fell under the arm of government. States exerted full ownership of the transport infrastructure (e.g., railways, bus systems, and port facilities) and public utilities such as water, gas, electricity, and telephones. States also created large parastatal industries such as oil refining, natural resource extraction, petrochemicals, or steel production with the rationale that only a state-led monopoly would allow industries large enough to compete in foreign markets. Reflecting on this period in 1990, Wiarda and Kline wrote, "If one asks who 'owns' Brazil … the answer is will not be Coca-Cola, General Motors, or International Telephone and Telegraph (ITT), but the Brazilian government." Assessing all of Latin America, they noted that the state corporations "are giant patronage agencies by which one rewards friends and cronies and finds places for (and hence secures the loyalty or at least neutrality of) the opposition. Depending on the country, 30–50 percent of the gainfully employed labor force now works for the government" (Wiarda and Kline, 1990, pp. 91–92). Though this portrayal was valid for its time, today it is only one-half accurate.

First, nowadays it is patently wrong to speak of huge bureaucracies in Latin America. Just 5 percent of employed Latin Americans find work in the public sector, compared to 7.4 percent in the United States, 10 percent in the United Kingdom, and an average of 9.4 percent in all western industrialized countries (World Bank, 2016). Pressure from the IMF and other lending authorities during the debt crisis of the 1980s and neoliberal reforms of the 1990s helped to compel these changes. However, the move to downsize government also had significant domestic support from groups critical of state-led models of economic development such as ISI. But smaller government should not be mistaken for more efficient government, and this is where Wiarda and Kline's observations remain valid. Patronage politics remains a core feature of public administration in Latin America. Only 6 of 18 Latin American countries rest above the global median in Transparency International's 2015 corruption perception index (see Table 4.1). One survey of Latin Americans found that about 20 percent reported that they had to pay a bribe in order to receive a government service in the past year. There are variances—from a high of over 40 percent in Bolivia to a low of

6 percent in Chile. And there are significant changes, such as in Ecuador, where 21 percent reported paying a bribe in 2010 and 40 percent reported the same in 2012 (*Miami Herald,* 2013). Also of note is that poorer people tend to be asked for bribes more often than wealthier people.

Corruption and Bureaucracy

Corruption can be defined as the abuse of a public position for private gain. It includes a broad range of illicit activities, including bribery, embezzlement, extortion, nepotism, and conflict of interest. Corruption is often described as a cancer on the body politic, a fitting image given its tendency to proliferate through all levels of government over time. Analysts distinguish between **petty corruption,** which involves relatively minor acts of bribery or favoritism at the lower levels of public administration, and **grand corruption,** which refers to malfeasance at the highest levels of governance. The former acts as scourge on the daily lives of citizens, while the latter erodes public confidence in government and tears at the legitimacy of a regime over time. According to the 2015 Latinobarometer survey, one in five Latin Americans either experienced or know of a family member who experienced an act of petty corruption within the past 12 months.[9] The box feature below evaluates the growing frustration of Latin Americans with grand corruption.

COMPARING COUNTRIES

Taking Action against Grand Corruption

2016 was not supposed to look like this for Brazil. Two years had passed since the country's beloved soccer team suffered an embarrassing defeat at the hands of the Germans in the World Cup, which was hosted by Brazil. But 2016 offered a chance at redemption. Once again all eyes would be upon the country as it now played host to the Olympics. Though denied victory in the World Cup, the Olympic spotlight would allow Brazil to capture the image it longed for—one that went beyond the label of an "emerging market" to that of an alluring country able to flaunt its cultural diversity, remarkable progress, and robust democracy, and take its stand as a prominent player in the world arena. But more than the denial of a World Cup had happened since 2014. A scandal that saw the state oil company, Petrobras, pay off bloated contracts, only to kick back bribes to politicians to look the other way, had grown to encompass over 100 contractors, executives, and politicians to the tune of some $3 billion. In March 2016, an estimated 6 million Brazilians took to the streets to register their

(continued)

disgust with government. The international media, turning their sights once again toward Brazil, found a story that would run well beyond the sports page. And Brazilians found their notability replaced by notoriety.

Grand corruption is not new to Brazil, nor to Latin America. The lawlessness of the caudillo era cast a long shadow. And the twentieth century had no shortage of depraved dictators. The Somoza family ran Nicaragua as their personal fiefdom from 1937 to 1979. Fulgencio Batista of Cuba worked with U.S. mobsters to attract U.S. businesspersons to Havana with prostitution and gambling. Rafael Trujillo ruled the Dominican Republic from 1930 to 1961, and according to the *Guinness Book of World Records* erected more statues of himself than any other world leader. Even after the transition to democracy, corruption scandals engulfed political leaders in Argentina (Carlos Menem), Peru (Alberto Fujimori), and Brazil (Fernando Color de Mello). In the 1990s, the U.S. State Department tagged Colombia as a "narco-state" due to the close connections between public officials, including the president, and drug cartels. Corruption might actually occur at lower levels today than in the past, but what is different is the willingness of Latin Americans to express their frustration, press for change, and even make a difference. What accounts for this change?

Generally speaking, the growth of the middle class has sparked some of this change throughout the region. In just under two decades, the size of the middle class has grown from about 20 percent to about 50 percent of the population. The commodities boom, in no small part associated with exports to the voracious appetite of the Chinese economy, generated the growth. But a variety of causes—the cooling of China's economy, declining prices in natural resources, reduced remittances from workers abroad, and poorly invested commodity profits—now threaten the status of the middle class. This has produced an explosive situation that social scientists call "the revolution of rising expectations." Individuals have grown accustomed to rising incomes, such that their frustration and likelihood to rebel is even greater than that of the impoverished, who may be more habituated with their more dire circumstances. Add to this, the new middle classes are more informed and more willing to hold public officials accountable for corrupt activities.

Technology has also played a role, but one that must be placed in perspective. In Guatemala, reports in early 2015 that government officials were skimming millions in customs revenues led a frustrated middle-class businessman to vent on his Facebook page. Eight other Guatemalans—none with experience in social activism—felt equally outraged and made contact through the social media site. One proposed the hashtag, #RenunciaYa ("Resign already"), and they posted an invitation for others to join them on Saturdays in the central plaza facing the presidential palace. They had hoped for dozens to show, but were met by thousands more—30,000 at the peak of the protest. Reports of the scandal soon implicated President Otto Pérez Molina, who would be placed under arrest within five months. Guatemala's story appears to substantiate the power of technology in the fight against corruption. Panama had similar hopes when a journalist launched the web site *Mi Panama Transparente* in 2010 (www.mipanamatransparente. org). The site used crowdsourcing to collect information on corruption for journalists. The information flowed in, but the lack of a vibrant, active media in the country meant that much of the information sat idle. The site stopped collecting reports in 2013, but remains online with a heading that disappointingly plugs the domain as a "testimony to the possibilities of an alliance between the media and the public."

Perhaps a more engaged media would have allowed the Panamanian experiment to succeed. But reflecting back on the Guatemalan case, one would be misled to believe that social media alone initiated greater government accountability. In Guatemala, the actions against President Pérez Molina could not have been possible without the participation of the International Commission against Impunity in Guatemala. The United Nations created the commission at the request of Guatemala in 2007 to compensate for its ineffective judicial institutions. Though the early going was rough, it was this body that conducted the investigations, collected the evidence, and ultimately ordered the arrests in the scandal. On the other hand, in Panama it is not that the courts have been inactive. The Supreme Court ordered the arrest of former president Ricardo Martinelli (2009–2014) for directing state security services to spy on his political opponents, and the attorney general has opened a series of investigations into wrongdoings by cabinet members in the current government of Juan Carlos Varela, who ironically enough ran on a campaign of anti-corruption. The greater effort directed toward the Martinelli administration, and the fact that Varela is uncomfortably close to several of the scandals in his cabinet—yet remains untouched—has led many critics to paint the corruption crusade as a political crusade.

(continued)

The fight for judicial independence and capacity is key to the success of anti-corruption campaigns in Latin America. Without such judicial fortitude, an anti-corruption offensive appears politicized. Activists in Honduras clamored to replicate the Guatemalan experience. Inspired by the protests in their neighboring country, they organized their own movement, which included torch-bearing marches through the capital each Friday night. President Juan Orlando Hernández hoped to mollify the movement by organizing an international commission, as in Guatemala. But the Honduran commission hails from the Organization of American States, which is likely to be more docile than a UN-sponsored organization, for many of its member fear throwing stones in glass houses. Likewise, the commission can only make recommendations, and they are not binding. Similar to Panama, Honduras may be at a tipping point. Important moves are being made to fight impunity, but time will tell whether they are but a smokescreen. In Brazil, the bold moves against corruption can be tied to 2004 judicial reforms, which created a more independent judiciary. And an important tool was added in 2013, when prosecutors gained the ability to plea-bargain, and therefore build larger cases as suspects provided further information in exchange for reduced sentences. We will return to the important of judicial change in Latin America in Chapter 6.

When seeking the cause of corruption, be it petty or grand, it is easy to point to underdevelopment. The reasoning would be that economic insecurity or depressed incomes lead public officials to use their positions to line their own pockets. Likewise, the lower education and socioeconomic standing of individuals in underdeveloped societies feeds a sense of powerlessness that officials are able to prey upon. But this explanation sheds little light on the wide variation in corruption found among less-developed states. Chile's ranking in the Corruption Perceptions Index (see Table 4.1 below) regularly outstrips that of Mexico's, and both countries sit at a generally similar level of development. Costa Rica appears to outshine its level of development, especially when compared to wealthier Argentina. And studies looking for an association between wealth and corruption have not only found very little evidence for a relationship between lower GNP per capita and corruption, but they do not even find evidence for a relationship between lower bureaucratic salaries and corruption.

But this does not mean that socioeconomic change or modernization does not have any impact on corruption. Corrupt officials may gain a motive to act due to their low salaries, and a disempowered public may provide an opportunity to act, but what ultimately allows them to act is the lack of

Table 4.1 **Competency, Meritocratic Practices, and Corruption in Latin American Bureaucracies.** Although they still have a long way to go, many countries have reduced corruption in the bureaucracy with reforms to professionalize the civil service

Country	Efficiency of Civil Service*	Meritocratic Practices*	Corruption Perceptions Index**	Global Ranking of Corruption Perception**
Chile	85 (2013)	67 (2013)	70	(23)
Uruguay	45 (2013)	73 (2013)	74	(21)
Costa Rica	50 (2012)	73 (2012)	55	(40)
El Salvador	25 (2012)	33 (2012)	39	(72)
Panama	35 (2012)	20 (2012)	39	(72)
Brazil	50 (2013)	93 (2013)	38	(76)
Colombia	55 (2013)	67 (2013)	37	(83)
Peru	40 (2015)	53 (2015)	36	(88)
Mexico	40 (2013)	40 (2013)	35	(95)
Bolivia	32 (2013)	7 (2013)	34	(99)
Dominican Rep	40 (2012)	27 (2012)	33	(103)
Argentina	—	—	32	(107)
Ecuador	40 (2015)	53 (2015)	32	(107)
Honduras	5 (2012)	7 (2012)	31	(112)
Guatemala	35 (2012)	20 (2012)	28	(123)
Nicaragua	35 (2012)	40 (2012)	27	(130)
Paraguay	15 (2013)	40 (2013)	27	(130)
Venezuela	—	—	17	(158)

*Scores: tabulated on the *Governance Indicators Database* available on the Web page of the Inter-American Development Bank (https://mydata.iadb.org/Reform-Modernization-of-the-State/Civil-Service-Development-Index/ddw5-db4y).
**Index and global ranking figures are from Transparency International, 2016. Available at www.transparency.org.

accountability. There may be rules that prohibit a local official from withholding a business license until satisfied with a bribe, but if they are not enforced and bribery can be conducted with impunity, the rules will mean nothing. How then, can accountability come about? The growth of a robust media is one aspect of socioeconomic change that can grow, or decline, independent of other socioeconomic changes. A vibrant media can act as a watchdog on government action, disperse information so individuals can make informed decisions, and provide a voice to those who might otherwise find themselves unable to influence politics.

It is understandable how media outlets in small markets, such as those in Honduras or Paraguay, would find it difficult to perform a watchdog role. They may lack resources and staffing to exert oversight over government activities. But socioeconomic growth does not guarantee that the media will contribute to government accountability. As much as the media may see its resources grow, so too might politicians use their own power to deflect media oversight. In Ecuador, President Rafael Correa has made brazen use of defamation and libel laws to threaten media and soften their coverage. In Argentina, Cristina Kirchner selectively applied licensing and regulatory provisions to punish critical outlets and reward complaint media. In Mexico, the PRI Party provided payouts and guarantees of mutual accommodation for the country's largest media conglomerate to support the presidential candidacy of Enrique Peña Nieto, who would be elected in 2012.

Hence, socioeconomic modernization alone is not sufficient for the growth of a media able to hold leaders accountable. Political competition sets politicians against each other and tapers their power, creating space for the media to thrive and press for government accountability. And from an institutional perspective, we can consider how electoral rules, party systems, executive power, lawmaking procedures, and other institutions might be designed to ensure the viability of opposition groups after elections have been held and the winners take office (Stein and Kellum, 2014). Other institutional designs matter as well. Tavits (2007) notes that politicians have less incentive to address corruption when they can shrug responsibility. Hence, institutions that promote greater "clarity of responsibility" lead to less corruption. The majority status of government, cabinet stability, minimal opportunities for the opposition to influence policy (such as through the control of one chamber in a bicameral system), and less party fragmentation all allow voters to identify who is responsible for policy, and punish or reward as they see fit.

In regard to the petty corruption that takes place specifically within the bureaucracy, research indicates that bureaucracies shed corruption as they implement merit-based procedures for the selection and promotion of personnel (Rauch and Evans, 2000). This is an important finding, because it shows how even a poorer country, given the prudent use of policy resources, might effectively address corruption. But implementing merit-based reforms is no easy task. Barbara Geddes looks to the interests of politicians to predict when they are most likely to implement civil service reforms. Unfortunately, she finds that their motivations may be mixed. Politicians see long-term benefits in civil service reform insofar as it enhances state capacity and generally reduces the predatory actions of civil servants on the general population. This cannot but increase the popularity of any politician. But in the short run, politicians recognize that administrative reform frustrates their own access to patronage politics, which allows them to ensure political support (and punish enemies). Geddes refers to the clash between long- and short-term interests as the **politician's dilemma**. But she highlights when politicians are most likely to surmount the dilemma, and the answer once again brings us back to political competition. According to Geddes, the politician's dilemma can be overcome when political leaders face an opposition of near equal strength with similar access to patronage politics. In this scenario, the relative advantage afforded by patronage is minimal, and politicians gain greater appeal in the electorate with campaign promises to address corruption. As evidence, she finds that civil service reform comes most often when competing parties hold near equal levels of representation in the legislature. Though Geddes's argument focuses on the electoral interests of politicians, we can see how certain institutional alignments that increase competitive politics can have an effect on corruption. Table 4.1 demonstrates that the relationship between professionalism and decreases in corruption appears to hold in Latin America, though exceptions (e.g., a higher-than-expected El Salvador and a lower-than-expected Brazil) do exist.

Bureaucratic Boundaries

Generally, democracies place decision making in the hands of elected officials, and leave it to bureaucrats to implement policy. To ensure supervision over administration, bureaucracies typically find a selection of **political appointees** at the apex of their hierarchy. For example, just below Chile's Ministry of Mining we find divisions devoted to public relations, law, environmental studies, administration and finance, and foreign relations (this division is testimony to the importance of exports and foreign investment). When a new government enters office, it deserves the opportunity to redesign mining policy as it sees fit—perhaps with an eye toward greater environmental protection, or with the intention to compete in different overseas markets. To pursue these goals, a particular minister will be selected, and this minister will in turn select individuals to lead the different divisions in the ministry. But just how deep should the political appointments reach, and at what level should we find bureaucrats with greater job protection? Good mining policy requires a corps of experts in environmental studies, geology, marketing, finance, and other fields, and these skills grow as individuals gain on-the-job experience. Hence, some sort of balance must be found between the desire to offer new governments a genuine opportunity to assume control over policy, and the need for an environment that cultivates expertise.

A tilt toward political appointees may appear to safeguard certain principles of democracy, but this is not always the case. At times, more insulated bureaucratic agencies may better serve democracy. How does this work? First, we have already recognized how a balance of powers between executive and legislative branches helps to ensure horizontal accountability in a regime. Bureaucratic agencies can augment this general balancing function insofar as they monitor, and even investigate or punish government for specific violations of power. The most prominent oversight agencies include auditing authorities and ombudsman's offices (see Chapter 5), electoral commissions (see Chapter 7), and public prosecutors (see Chapter 6). A second, albeit more controversial, way in which more insulated bureaucratic agencies can further democracy is when they assume control over a policy area to separate it from the volatility and myopia of "normal politics." For example, over the past few decades, many countries have established independent central banks to depoliticize some economic decision making. The banks receive general (often constitutionally) mandated goals such as reducing inflation, ensuring financial stability, promoting savings, acting as a lender of last resort, anchoring exchange rates, and in the case of Brazil, fostering economic growth. Some of the goals may be quite specific, as in the case of Nicaragua, whose state banks are constitutionally mandated to diversify credit with an "emphasis on small and medium size producers" (Nicaraguan Constitution, Article 99). But more often, the existence of several goals allows the banks some freedom to pick and choose as they set priorities. It is important to remember that independent agencies, whether they act as monitors or wholly monopolize policymaking, can vary in their level of autonomy from country to country. Factors that determine autonomy include the length of tenure granted to officeholders, the financial independence of the institution, and whether or not the agency answers and/ or reports to another governing institution (be it the president, legislature, or judiciary).

COUNTRY IN THE SPOTLIGHT

Presidential Politics in Argentina

The presidency is of tremendous importance in all of Latin America, but in Argentina the office takes on more sweeping significance. Argentines mark their political identities with reference to presidential figures of the past. Some look to Juan Manuel de Rosas (1829–1832, 1835–1852), who steered the country from the civil wars that followed independence and sowed the seeds of patriotism as he fought off British and French naval incursions seeking to impose free trade.[10] But his stabilizing efforts came with a cost, as he ruled with an iron fist and ran roughshod over the checks and balances of democratic politics. Still, those with a hunger for law and order see a principled man in Rosas. He once ordered himself to be placed in stocks after inadvertently violating his own decree against carrying a dagger on Sundays. Other Argentines look to Domingo Sarmiento, who championed liberal, cosmopolitan values and sought to engage other "civilized" nations through extensive commercial relations. To him, the caudillo rule of Rosas was barbaric, and the real path to development rested not in the unflinching commitment to order, but in civic education and the promotion of liberty. Sarmiento had joined a rebellion with groups frustrated by Rosas's dictatorial rule and favoritism of the agricultural sector. He would later assume the presidency from 1868 to 1874. To help erase the memory of Rosas's barbaric rule, Sarmiento had a zoo and botanical gardens constructed on his estate. Some years after his death in 1888, admirers hoping to complete the turn from caudillo politics dynamited Rosas's Roman villa and commissioned the famed artist Rodin to erect a statue of Sarmiento on the precise location of Rosas's bedroom. Argentina's booming economy at the turn of the century appeared to affirm the move toward a more open economy and the growth of a "civilized" society. But the Great Depression of the 1930s led many to reconsider the security of isolationist policies. Likewise, the growing demands of foreign creditors fanned nationalism, and the attendant social unrest stirred cravings for law and order—even if at the expense of liberty. Rosas thus gained renewed stature in political circles. And today, the debate continues. Are the difficulties faced by the country so dire that they require a strong, caudillo-like figure as president to rise above politics and rule with an iron fist? Or, should Argentina accept a president who accepts the checks and balances of democratic institutions, and works through consensus-building procedures to seek long-lasting solutions to Argentina's predicament?[11]

Argentina's current constitution dates to 1853, just after the overthrow of Rosas. Though modeled on the U.S. vision of a separation of powers, even Sarmiento's camp felt a need to tilt the balance toward executive power.[12] The president received state of siege powers, the right to intervene in provincial governments to "guarantee the republican form of government" or "repel external invasion," the power to initiate legislation, and the right to appoint cabinet members without confirmation from congress. But beyond constitutional provisions, history would do more to take its toll on the balance of powers and

(continued)

to touch off increases in presidential power. Economic and political instability led the military to intervene in 1930, 1943, 1955, 1962, 1966, and 1976. A total of 14 military officers seized the presidential sash during the 1930–1983 period. While in government, the armed forces would typically take aim at congress and the judiciary as troublesome hurdles to the efficient administration of government. Over time, these institutions weakened, so that in democratic periods, civilian presidents would find themselves much less encumbered by the balance of powers detailed in the constitution. Consequently, a number of executive powers evolved through practice over time. The first move came in the form of decree authority delegated by congress. The authority came to be standard practice by the 1920s after the Supreme Court decided that congress held an inherent right to delegate to ensure efficient government. Under the presidency of populist Juan Perón in the 1940s, the veto took on new powers. The constitution granted executive power to either fully or partially veto bills, but clearly specified that the entire bill would have to be sent to congress for reconsideration. But Perón initiated the practice of partial promulgation. He would implement some clauses in a bill, and force congress to muster an improbable two-thirds majority if it desired to see the remaining portions implemented. A 1967 Supreme Court ruling on the practice held that the partial promulgation could not alter the "unity" (or original legislative intent) of the bill. The inexplicit language did little to contain partial promulgation, and the decision itself actually legitimated the practice by failing to proscribe an executive power not found in the constitution (Llanos, 2002, pp. 16–24).

The expansion of executive power would continue under the democratic regime inaugurated in 1983. The stage was set as the first president, Raúl Alfonsín, fell victim to a degenerating economy brought on by the debt crisis that hit all of Latin America in the 1980s. In the next presidential election, his Radical Party gave way to the candidate of the Peronist party (Justicialist Party), Carlos Menem. After a few months in office, Menem made the stunning decision to repatriate the body of Juan Manuel de Rosas from Great Britain, where he had taken refuge after his ouster in 1853. Officially, the government publicized the move as a gesture to put the past behind, and as part of a broader effort of national reconciliation in the aftermath of the Dirty War unleashed by the 1976–1983 military dictatorship. But others saw a symbolic political maneuver—a sign of things to come. Liberals had long ago characterized Juan Perón's government as "the second tyranny," in an attempt to link his demagogic politics to the brutal dictatorship of Rosas. And Menem's election marked the return of the Peronists to power (Robben, 2000). Sure enough, Menem's own politics soon appeared to replay the imperious behavior of Rosas. Partial promulgation of vetoed bills became standard practice. Congress passed 625 bills from 1989 to 1993, only to find 37 of them fully vetoed, and 41 partially promulgated. But Menem's relationship with congress was not wholly antagonistic. With a near-majority of Peronists in the Chamber of Deputies, a simple majority in the Senate, and a general willingness of congress to comply in the face of economic crisis, Menem did hold a measure of partisan power, and he used this to acquire delegated decree authority. In late 1989, congress passed the Administrative Emergency Act and the Economic Emergency Act to furnish Menem with the power to decree laws in several policy areas such as taxation, privatization, administrative reorganization, public contracts, foreign investment regulations, and the dismissal of public-sector employees (Ferriera Rubio and Goretti, 1998).

Still, seeking revolutionary changes in the Argentine economy—from an ISI state-led model of development to one that embraced the dictates of the IMF and neoliberal policy prescriptions—Menem sought to further enhance executive power, but this time through outright unconstitutional means. He looked back upon his predecessors and saw instances in which presidents had fully monopolized the legislative process, issuing "need and urgency" decrees (NUDs) unilaterally. Fifteen times previous to the transition to democracy in 1983, civilian presidents had issued laws under the justification that an emergency situation warranted unilateral action. In fact, it was Alfonsín who had revived the tactic, issuing ten of his own from 1983 to 1989. But in 1986, the court held that NUDs would "require prior recognition by congress of the emergency" (Ferriera Rubio and Goretti, 1998, p. 37). Menem, hoping to use NUDs in policy areas not covered by the Administrative Emergency Act and the Economic Emergency Act (and after these acts expired), sought to overstep this minor check on executive power. To ensure that the Supreme Court would not impede his desire to legislate through NUDs, he pushed a court-packing scheme through congress to manufacture a compliant judiciary. Staffed with Menem appointees, in 1990 the court ruled that NUDs

(*continued*)

had legal grounding given the existence of a "serious social situation" that required immediate legislative activity, and under the condition that congress at least had the opportunity to override the NUD by passing its own bill on the matter. This meant that the determination of an emergency now fell to presidential discretion, and given executive veto power, Menem could issue decrees and prevent congressional action with support from a mere 33 percent + 1 of representatives. Menem would sign off on 336 NUDs by August 1994.

The crumbling of horizontal accountability in the Argentine government made it an ideal example of a delegative democracy (O'Donnell, 1994). In an attempt to reverse the decline, Alfonsín called on Menem to open negotiations on the expanding presidential powers. Menem, hoping to amend the constitutional provision that limited presidents to a single term, agreed to meet. The two leaders signed the Pact of Olivos (named after the location of the presidential residence) to set the stage for a vast package of constitutional reforms. As leaders of the two largest political parties, together they could rally the votes required for a constitutional reform. Alfonsin agreed to a second term for presidents, but in exchange for a reduction of the presidential term from six to four years. A number of reforms addressed the legislative powers of the president. Delegated decree authority, partial promulgation, and NUDs were now explicitly incorporated into the constitution. As argued by Jones (1997), though the changes represented an expansion in the legal powers of the president, at the same time they also represented a decrease in the *de facto* powers of the president. The reforms may have enshrined a stronger presidency, but they also provided clear boundaries as to the limits of presidential power. Congress could delegate policymaking, but only in the policy areas of administration and public emergency and for a specified period of time (Constitution of Argentina, Article 76). A constitutional amendment recognized partial promulgation, so long as the portions promulgated have "normative autonomy" and do not alter the "spirit or unity" of the original bill (Constitution of Argentina, Article 80). An additional amendment required that congress have the opportunity to reconsider any bill that is partially vetoed before a partial promulgation takes place (Constitution of Argentina, Article 83). Finally, though the reforms recognized NUDs, they required that all NUDs be rejected or ratified by a bicameral committee of congress within ten days. NUDs can be issued "only when exceptional circumstances make it impossible" to follow normal lawmaking procedures, and cannot be applied to criminal, fiscal, electoral, or political party matters (Constitution of Argentina, Article 99). Still, the language leaves some room for interpretation, such as who will decide when circumstances become "exceptional," and whether the "impossibility" of using normal lawmaking channels includes "political impossibility" (e.g., if the president lacks a supportive majority in congress) (Ferriera Rubio and Goretti, 1998, p. 57). Other constitutional reforms placed additional checks on presidential power. One reform created the Council of the Magistracy, a 20-member body of judges that administrates, disciplines, and trains judges. The council also selects candidates for federal judges; in the case of the Supreme Court, this limits presidential choices to a list presented by the council. In all, the council is meant to bolster judicial autonomy. Another reform created the position of Chief of Cabinet to head cabinet meetings and thereby diffuse presidential power. In a slight nod to parliamentary governance, Congress gained the power to remove the Chief of Cabinet through a majority vote.

Despite Alfonsín's honest efforts to stave off Menem's power grab, voters focused on the reform that allowed a second presidential term, and concluded that Alfonsín had buckled under pressure. With Alfonsín's Radical Party demoralized, Menem easily won a second term in 1995. But Menem's ambition would soon undermine his own party. As the 1999 elections approached, Menem claimed eligibility for yet another term. He argued that the 1994 constitutional reform effectively restarted his electoral clock, such that his 1995 term was in fact his first term under the new rules. Many in his Peronist party were growing weary of his neoliberal policies, and had turned their support toward the more populist politics embraced by Eduardo Duhalde, the governor of Buenos Aires. With the Peronist party split, the Radical Party reached out to a new political party, FREPASO (Front for a Country in Solidarity), to create an alliance that brought Fernando de la Rúa to the presidency in 1999. But things were not going well in the Argentine economy. An overvalued exchange rate put a drag on exports, and government debt was growing unmanageable. Inflexible revenue-sharing agreements between the federal and provincial governments drafted under Menem further aggravated de la Rúa's situation (Eaton, 2005). The compacts guaranteed that transfers would not fall below a set floor, but this grew problematic as the sagging economy

(continued)

sapped tax revenues. And with most provincial governors in the hands of the Peronist party, the provinces saw little reason to negotiate a more feasible transfer formula with their partisan foe. A full-blown economic crisis erupted in late 2001. De la Rúa resigned, only to be followed by three selected replacements, each of whom quickly concluded that the growing unrest was too much.[13] Congress finally agreed to support the appointment of Eduardo Duhalde as president. As a Peronist, Duhalde negotiated a new transfer agreement with the governors, and after dismissing any desires to seek another term as president, effectively situated himself as a caretaker government until the economic crisis passed.

With Menem blamed by many for neoliberal policies that contributed to the crisis, and with Duhalde officially out of the bidding, the stage was set for new blood in the Peronist party. The Radical and FREPASO parties had been tainted by the crisis, effectively leveling the opposition. Peronists came in three of the top four positions in the 2003 elections (garnering over 60 percent of the total vote), the Radical candidate received just under 2.5 percent of the vote, and FREPASO disintegrated. The ultimate victor was Peronist Néstor Kircher. His past experience as a little-known governor from the distant province of Santa Cruz resonated with the street protestors who had embraced the slogan, "*Que se vayan todos!*" ("Throw them all out"). Kirchner appointed a number of government officials from the Duhalde government to create a strong sense of continuity—a very important move given the recent economic instability. But as the economy slowly recovered, Kirchner took a more independent path. Peronists now dominated Argentine politics, but the Peronists were hardly a unified group. This gave Kirchner the opportunity to solidify and expand his own faction, and to launch the Kirchner era, which would last until 2015. Though the populist policies of this time contrasted sharply with the neoliberalism of the 1990s, the presidential power used to implement them would show surprising continuity with the Menem era and Argentine history more generally.

Kirchner looked to the October 2005 legislative elections as a plebiscite on his rule. The economic recovery, a defiant stance in the face of international creditors (Kirchner would negotiate a reduction of some 70 percent in foreign debt), and his commitment to seek justice for the human rights violations during the Dirty War produced a surge in popularity. Kirchner also tapped into the growing public fury directed at the Supreme Court due to its dismissal of corruption charges levied against former president Menem and various decisions that maintained severe economic austerity measures. Menem's court-packing scheme had produced an "automatic majority" that most Argentines viewed as politicized. Kirchner's threats to initiate impeachment proceedings led to the removal of six of the nine justices, and the public viewed his appointment of respected jurists as a move toward a more independent judiciary (*NotiSur*, 2003). To no one's surprise, Kirchner supporters won the congressional elections in a landslide. Kirchner lost little time to consolidate his gains. The following month, he overhauled the Economics Ministry to signal a clear break with the neoliberal policies of the past (*NotiSur*, 2006a). And despite his previous contribution to judicial independence, a 2006 law reduced the membership of the Magistrates' Council so as to increase the relative representation of members appointed from the Peronist-dominated congress. Perhaps most significantly, Kirchner expanded executive lawmaking authority. A July 2006 bill allows executive orders to become law unless they are opposed by both congressional chambers—a stark change from the previous procedure that required congressional *approval* for executive orders to become law. Another reform in 2006 expanded the budgetary power of the president so that after congress approves a budget, the president would gain full freedom to reassign funds. The Law of Economic Emergency, which allows executive intervention in financial and currency markets, greater regulation of unemployment payments, and full authority to negotiate contracts (and thus set prices) for public services, was extended each year since its enactment in early 2002 as a response to the erstwhile economic crisis (*NotiSur*, 2006b). Finally, Kirchner harnessed new resources for the state with considerable exports taxes to take advantage of surging agricultural prices in international markets. The export taxes do not fall under the extensive revenue-sharing arrangements negotiated with the provinces, and thus not only offer a lucrative revenue stream, but also empower the executive vis-à-vis the governors. Because governors play a significant role in the selection of senatorial candidates, the ability to dangle increased revenues over governors provided a back door to influence the composure and support of the senate (Manzetti 2014, p. 178).

Most Argentines saw little cause for concern as Kirchner expanded executive authority. This, despite the fact that he issued 294 DNUs

(*continued*)

during his term, paling the 176 laws passed by the legislature in the same period. Menem tallied a higher total—with 370 DNUs—but he did so through an entire decade. Nonetheless, Kirchner remained very popular toward the end of his term in 2007. Many were surprised to see him step down and endorse the election of his wife, Cristina Fernández de Kirchner, to the presidency. And in free and fair elections, Argentines expressed their support. Fernández won the election, and Kirchner allies won 160 of 257 seats in the Chamber of Deputies, 47 of 74 seats in the Senate, and 18 of 23 governorships. But others saw a scheming power-sharing arrangement at play, one that would allow the Kirchners to rotate and hold the presidency for 16 years (four terms). Protests on all fronts began to grow. On several occasions agricultural producers trekked to Buenos Aires to block traffic and protest the onerous export taxes. Increasingly, middle-class groups critical of the populist turn in government have joined them. In a move that deepened divisive politics in the country, Fernández met the protests by staging mass rallies to paint the protestors as greedy, self-centered farmers seeking to take advantage of international markets even as working-class groups in Argentina go hungry. At one rally, Néstor Kircher proclaimed, "They want to sell everything abroad because food prices are absolutely expensive.... They don't care about the stomachs or pocketbooks of Argentines." Distrust of government grew quickly under Fernández. There was a strong sense that the economic recovery and populist policies fed inflation, but that government has impinged on bureaucratic autonomy to conceal the problem. In February 2007, government partisans replaced top technocrats at the independent state statistical agency, INDEC. Creditors and investors alike accepted economic calculations from INDEC with a great deal of skepticism.

Fernández retained a considerable base of support, but saw it drop through her first term, especially as the economy began to sour. Similar to the political environment under Menem—Argentines appear willing to overlook the growth of executive authority while times are good. But as with the end of the Menem era, the country could again see a troublesome combination of strong executive power and weak partisan power. The protests against the agricultural taxes fueled dissension by formerly dependable Kirchner allies in congress that represented rural provinces (*NotiSur*, 2008), and in July 2009, Fernández's Peronist party lost its majorities in both chambers of congress.

Things were not going well for Fernández, and at a personal level they grew worse when Néstor Kirchner died in October 2010. But the tragedy created an upwell of sympathy, and probably proved critical when she won a second term in 2011. The economy did not recover, and soon the public once again focused on the growing allegations of corruption within the administration. Nonetheless, Fernández had little to fear from congress. Moves by her predecessors had already emasculated an institution that was weak to begin with. But allegations raised the specter of investigations, and to prevent this, Fernández took aim at the judiciary. Continuing a tactic first used by her husband, she delayed court appointments to slow judicial action and gain leverage over future appointments.[14] Then, in 2013 she proposed a judicial reform that would open members of the Council of the Magistracy to election (and partisan influence). The Supreme Court fought back, and ruled the reform unconstitutional. Still, Fernández's most important tool rested in her influence over the attorney general's office, who readily dismissed investigations looking into corruption under the Kirchners.

The media in Argentina is highly developed and capable of exerting a watchdog role over government. It did not dawdle as the Kirchners accumulated power and allegations of corruption grew. Favorable reporting on the agricultural protests ignited the tension between Fernández and the media. To avoid direct scrutiny, she rarely convened press conferences, opting to use social media to address the public. And to preempt media coverage, she made ample use of what are termed *cadenas*, presidential addresses that must be covered by all radio and television stations (though they are supposed to be used only in times of crisis). Claiming a desire to democratize the media, Fernández passed legislation to break up the largest media conglomerate, Clarín, which also happened to be one of her main critics.

Despite the attacks sustained by both, the oversight roles of the media and courts dovetailed in 2015. Alberto Nisman had been charged with investigating a 1994 bombing of a Jewish community center that killed 85. Because he had been appointed in 2004 under the Secretariat of Intelligence, his investigation could not be so easily dismissed by the attorney general's office. He found evidence that pointed to Iran, and claimed to have documents linking Fernández. Allegedly, she had conspired to cover up the Iranian role to secure a $7 billion grain-for-oil deal. On January 18, the day before he was scheduled to

(continued)

testify before congress, he was found dead of a self-inflicted wound under suspicious circumstances. A media frenzy followed, and few believed it was a suicide, nor that Fernández was not involved.

With a declining economy, growing corruption allegations, and the Nisman death, Fernández limped through the last year of her term. Her sullied reputation did little for her would-be successor, Daniel Scioli, who lost to a center-right candidate, Mauricio Macri, with 48.7 percent of the vote to Macri's 51.3 percent in the November 2015 elections. Macri has sworn to reverse the populist policies implemented under the Kirchners, and revive the economy with market-friendly reforms. He hardly has an overwhelming popular mandate. Most Argentines favored the Kirchners' populist policies, but grew disgusted with their abuse of power. Time will tell whether Macri will make use of the extensive powers accumulated by his predecessors to push his agenda. We might assume that Sarmiento would be pleased with the current democratic status of his country, but in Argentina, the specter of Rosas always looms large.

Discussion Questions

1   Identify the sources of presidential power in Argentina. What might be done to restore the balance of power in the country?
2   Is executive power a cause or consequence of political and economic crises? Use the case of Argentina to support your answer.

Conclusion

Latin America has a history of instability and strong rulers. This has in part led constitutional designers to instill significant powers in the executives of Latin America, and that institutional design now feeds expectations that presidents should resolve problems in earnest. This survey of executive designs illustrates some of the institutional bases to issues and concerns in Latin America. Whether presidentialism is a "good" system or a good "fit" for Latin America depends on the type of presidentialism. There are many varieties, and knowledge of this allows us to envision how modifications might support good governance in Latin America. Likewise, corruption is not just a matter of culture or economic underdevelopment. Institutional changes that support meritocratic practices have been shown to decrease corruption. Indeed, the very fact that such variation in corrupt practices exists across Latin American countries indicates that government malfeasance is not necessarily inherent to the region.

Key Terms

government   128
cabinet   128
parliamentary system   128
presidential system   129
minority president   129
head of state   130
investiture   130
constitutional monarchies   130
constructive vote of no
   confidence   132
semi-presidential   132
executive order   135
block veto   135
partial veto   136
amendatory observation   136

referendum   137
urgency petition   137
decree authority   138
emergency decree
   authority   138
standard decree authority   139
partisan power   140
delegative democracies   142
immobilism   142
accountability   144
autonomy   144
petty corruption   147
grand corruption   147
politician's dilemma   153
political appointee   153

Discussion Questions

1   Discuss the trade-offs that one must consider in the choice between presidentialism and parliamentarism. On what basis might one argue that one is more democratic than the other?
2   How do presidential systems in Latin America differ from what we find in the United States? How are Latin American presidencies more prone than the presidency in the United States to delegative democracy?
3   What is meant by the "pathology" of bureaucracy? How can we reduce the pathologies associated with bureaucracy?
4   Distinguish "constitutional power" from "partisan power." Which has played a stronger role in the development of executive power in contemporary Argentina?

Suggested Readings

Javier Corrales and Michael Penfold. 2011. *Dragon in the Tropics: Hugo Chávez and the Political Economy of Revolution in Venezuela.* **Washington, D.C.: Brookings Institution.** There is no lack of books on the rise of controversial president Hugo Chávez of Venezuela. This is one of the few that offers a grounded, nonpoliticized assessment. Corrales and Penfold pay special attention the use of institutions by Hugo Chávez to concentrate power.

Juan Linz and Arturo Valenzuela. 1994. *The Failure of Presidential Democracy.* **Baltimore: Johns Hopkins University Press.** This is a two-volume set of collected essays that offer some of the classic criticisms of presidential government. The first volume takes a more theoretical approach, whereas the second volume looks specifically at cases in Latin America. Linz and Valenzuela have since continued their critiques of presidentialism in multiple articles and books.

Mariana Llanos and Leiv Marsteintredet. 2010. *Presidential Breakdown in Latin America: Causes and Outcomes of Executive Instability in Developing Democracies.* **New York: Palgrave Macmillan.** Llanos and Marsteintredet reexamine Linz and Valenzuela's attack on presidentialism. They had associated presidentialism with the breakdown of democratic regimes, yet democracy has survived. Nonetheless, this edited book notes that presidentialism still causes government crises, and they assess the conditions under which it does so. Contributors offer a number of case studies.

Aníbal Pérez-Liñán. 2010. *Presidential Impeachment and the New Political Instability in Latin America.* **New York: Cambridge University Press.** This is one of the only comprehensive, theory-based studies of impeachment in Latin America. Pérez-Liñán provides a detailed description of the variety of impeachment proceedings in Latin America, and explains the increasing use of these proceedings as the result of a strategy shift by civilian elites who can no longer look to military intervention to remove adversaries.

Notes

1   Mexican conservatives would revive the idea that European royalty could best serve Mexican politics with the crowning of another emperor, the Austrian archduke Ferdinand Maximilian (1864–1867). Millington (1996) argues that the reluctance of South America's independence heroes to militarily confront the Brazilian monarchy allowed the idea of aristocratic rule and foreign influence to persist, and that this in turn undermined republican politics in South America.

2   This discussion of parliament is based on the ideal type as expressed in the British political system.

3   For a discussion on the range of power sharing found in parliamentary systems, see Sartori (1997). The expectation that prime ministers should act as no more than a first among equals is illustrated by the criticisms leveled upon Tony Blair, prime minister of Great Britain from 1997 to 2007. His moves to take a stronger leadership role in the government generated a tide of criticism among British political commentators, who spoke disapprovingly of the "presidentialization" of British politics. For example, see Foley (2000).

4   For a classic analysis of the U.S. and U.K. models as distinct prototypes, see Verney, 1959.

5   No Latin American country allows the pocket veto, whereby a bill dies if the U.S. president does not sign it within 10 days while Congress is out of session. Barring an explicit rejection of a bill by the president, Latin American constitutions typically require the president to publish legislation passed by Congress (at which point the bill becomes a law). If the bill is returned to congress for reconsideration, either the Congress is allowed to readdress the bill when it reconvenes, or in some cases of inaction on the part of Congress the president's version of the bill goes into law. But under no conditions does a bill die absent a presidential signature.

6 The partial veto should not be confused with the line-item veto in effect in many U.S. states. The partial veto is much more expansive in that it can be applied to any type of legislation, while the line-item veto is only applied to the allocations (line items) in budget bills.

7 In Chile, the president can make use of three urgency powers to expedite congressional consideration: "simple urgency" sets a time period of 30 days for each branch, "extreme urgency" allots 10 days each, and "immediate discussion" gives each chamber only 3 days.

8 Carey and Shugart (1998) term such acts "paraconstitutional initiative." Because such lawmaking pushes aside congressional deliberation, they typically have little legitimacy and easily become the targets of social protest. Still, that does not necessarily diminish their impact. Many of the neoliberal economic reforms passed during the 1990s were enacted as emergency decrees.

9 See 2015 data available at www.latinobarometro.org.

10 Rosas actually held the title of Governor of Buenos Aires when Argentina was known as the United Provinces of La Plata. As governor of the strongest province, he was able to dominate the confederacy and act as a *de facto* president.11

11 Larry Rohter, "A Street Battle Rages in Argentina's 150 Years War," *New York Times*. August 14, 2003, p. A4; Matt Moffett, "Shade of Difference: Getting Blue Right in Argentina's Flag," *Wall Street Journal*, June 26, 2006.

12 Likewise, Argentina's "enlightened elites" held fast to a guarded democracy. Democratic pressures would not really emerge until the Sáenz Peña Law (1912), which expanded suffrage to all adult males (women received the vote in 1947).

13 An earlier resignation by the vice president left congress scrambling to find a willing and able replacement.

14 The 1994 constitutional reforms had presumably empowered the magistrate council by placing responsibility for nominations in its hands. The council was to create a list of three, the president would select one, and the senate would confirm. But both Kirchners simply delayed, and stopped the entire appointment process when they did not see a nominee they favored. As evidence of this tactic, Manzetti (2014, p. 181) notes that in 2013, 20 percent of federal judges in the lower courts, and 30 percent in the appeals courts, were left vacant.

References

Belaúnde, Víctor Andrés. 1967. *Bolívar and the Political Thought of the Spanish American Revolution*. New York: Octagon Books.

Breuer, Anita. 2008. "The Problematic Relation between Direct Democracy and Accountability in Latin America: Evidence from the Bolivian Case." *Latin American Research Review* 27:1, pp. 1–23.

Carey, John and Matthew Soberg Shugart. 1998. "Calling Out the Tanks or Filling Out the Forms?" In John Carey and Matthew Soberg Shugart, eds. Executive Decree Authority. New York: Cambridge, pp. 1–29.

Cheibub, José Antonio. 2007. *Presidentialism, Parliamentarism, and Democracy*. New York: Cambridge.

Duverger, Maurice. 1980. "A New Political System Model: Semi-Presidential Government." *European Journal of Political Research* 8, pp. 165–187.

Eaton, Kent. 2005. "Menem and the Governors: Intergovernmental Relations in the 1990s," in Steven Levitsky and María Victoria Murillo, eds., *Argentine Democracy: The Politics of Institutional Weakness*. University Park, PA: Penn State Press.

Elgie, Robert. July 2005. "Variations on a Theme." *Journal of Democracy* 16:3, pp. 98–112.

Ferriera Rubio, Delia, and Matteo Goretti. 1998. "When the President Governs Alone: The Decretazo in Argentina, 1989–93," in John M. Carey and Matthew S. Shugart, eds., *Executive Decree Authority*. New York: Cambridge University Press.

Foley, Michael. 2000. *The British Presidency: Tony Blair and the Politics of Public Leadership*. Manchester: Manchester University Press.

Jones, Mark. 1997. "Evaluating Argentina's Presidential Democracy: 1983–1995," in Scott Mainwaring and Matthew S. Shugart, eds., *Presidentialism and Democracy in Latin America*, pp. 259–299. New York: Cambridge University Press.

Lambert, Jacques. 1974. *Latin America: Social Structures and Political Institutions*. Berkeley, CA: University of California Press.

Lijphart, Arend. 1994. "Presidentialism and Majoritarian Democracy: Theoretical Observations," in Juan J. Linz and Arturo Valenzuela, eds., *The Failure of Presidential Democracy: Comparative Perspectives*, pp. 91–105. Baltimore: Johns Hopkins University Press.

———. 1999. *Patterns of Democracy: Government and Performance in Thirty-Six Countries*. New Haven, CT: Yale University Press.

Linz, Juan. 1990. "The Perils of Presidentialism." *Journal of Democracy* 1:1, pp. 51–69.

Lipset, Seymour Martin, and Jason M. Lakin. 2004. *The Democratic Century*. Norman, OK: University of Oklahoma Press.

Llanos, Mariana. 2002. *Privatization and Democracy in Argentina: An Analysis of President-Congress Relations*. New York: Palgrave.

Loveman, Brian. 1993. *The Constitution of Tyranny: Regimes of Exception in Spanish America*. Pittsburgh, PA: University of Pittsburgh Press.

Mainwaring, Scott. 1990. "Presidentialism in Latin America." *Latin American Research Review* 25:1, pp. 157–79.

Mainwaring, Scott, and Matthew S. Shugart., eds. 1997. "Presidentialism and Democracy in Latin America: Rethinking the Terms of Debate," in *Presidentialism and Democracy in Latin America*. New York: Cambridge.

Manzetti, Luigi. 2014. "Accountability and Corruption During the Kirchners' Era." *Latin American Research Review* 49:2, pp. 173–95.

Miami Herald. 2013. "Latin America's Corruption Starts at Top." February 9. Available at www.miamiherald.com.

Millington, Thomas. 1996. *Colombia's Military and Brazil's Monarchy: Undermining the Republican Foundations of South American Independence*. Westport, CT: Greenwood Press.

Montesquieu, Charles de Secondat. 1989. *The Spirit of the Laws*. Anne M. Cohler, Basia Carolyn Miller, and Harold Samuel Stone, trans. and eds. New York: Cambridge.

Nohlen, Dieter, and Mario Fernández B. 1998. "*El presidencialismo latinoamericano: Evolución y perspectivas*," in Dieter Nohlen and Mario Fernández B., eds., *El presidencialismo renovado: Instituciones y cambio politico en América Latina*. Caracas: Editorial Nueva Sociedad.

Norpoth, Helmut. September 1987. "Guns and Butter and Government Popularity in Britain." *American Political Science Review* 81:3, pp. 949–959.

NotiSur. 2003, October 31. "Argentina: Overhaul of Supreme Court Continues."

———. 2006a, January 6. "Argentina: President Néstor Kirchner Replaces Economy Minister."

———. 2006b, July 28. "Argentina: President Néstor Kirchner and Opposition Figures Lay Groundwork for 2007 Presidential Race."

———. 2008, August 1. "Argentina: Senate Stalemate Forces President Cristina Fernandez to Cancel Contentious Agricultural Export Tax Hike."

O'Donnell, Guillermo. 1994. "Delegative Democracy." *Journal of Democracy* 5:1, pp. 55–69.

Pereira, Carlos, Timothy J. Power, and Lucio Rennó. 2006. "From Logrolling to Logjam: Agenda Power, Presidential Decrees, and the Unintended Consequences of Reform in the Brazilian Congress." Working Paper CBS-71-06. Centre for Brazil Studies, University of Oxford.

Pérez-Liñán, Aníbal. 2007. *Presidential Impeachment and the New Political Instability in Latin America*. New York: Cambridge University Press.

Rauch, James, and Peter Evans. 2000. "Bureaucratic Structure and Bureaucratic Performance in Less Developed Countries." *Journal of Public Economics* 75, pp. 49–71.

Robben, Antonius C. G. M. 2000. "State Terror in the Netherworld: Disappearance and Reburial in Argentina," in Jefferey A. Sluka, ed., *Death Squad: The Anthropology of State Terror*. Philadelphia, PA: University of Pennsylvania Press.

Robertson, William Spence. 1969. *Hispanic-American Relations with the United States*. New York: Oxford University Press.

Sartori, Giovanni. 1997. *Comparative Constitutional Engineering: An Inquiry into Structures, Incentives, and Outcomes*. New York: NYU Press.

Schmidt, Gregory. 1998. "Presidential Usurpation or Congressional Preference?: The Evolution of Executive Decree Authority in Peru," in John M. Carey and Matthew S. Shugart, eds., *Executive Decree Authority*, pp. 142–174. New York: Cambridge University Press.

Schwartz, Thomas. 2004. "Vetoes Overridable by Simple Majorities." *Constitutional Political Economy* 15:4, pp. 383–389.

Shugart, Matthew S., and John M. Carey. 1992. *Presidents and Assemblies: Constitutional Design and Electoral Dynamics*. New York: Cambridge University Press.

Stepan, Alfred, and Cindy Skach. 1993. "Constitutional Frameworks and Democratic Consolidation: Parliamentarism versus Presidentialism." *World Politics* 46: October, pp. 1–22.

Stein, Elizabeth A., and Marisa Kellam. 2014. "Programming Presidential Agendas: Partisan and Media Environments That Lead Presidents to Fight Corruption." *Political Communication* 31:1, pp. 25–52.

Tavits, Margit. 2007. "Clarity of Responsibility and Corruption." *American Journal of Political Science* 51:1, pp. 218–29.

United Nations Development Programme (UNDP). 2004. *Democracy in Latin America: Towards a Citizen's Democracy*. New York: UNDP.

Verney, D. V. 1959. *The Analysis of Political Systems*. London: Routledge & Kegan Paul.

Von Mettenheim, Kurt. 1997. "Presidential Institutions and Democratic Politics," in Kurt von Mettenheim, ed., *Presidential Institutions and Democratic Politics*, pp. 1–18. Baltimore, MD: Johns Hopkins University Press.

Weber, Max. 1964. *The Theory of Social and Economic Organization*. A. M. Henderson and Talcott Parsons, trans. New York: Free Press.

Wiarda, Howard J., and Harvey F. Kline. 1990. *Latin American Politics and Development*. Boulder, CO: Westview Press.

World Bank. 2016. "Brief: Size of the Public Sector: Government Wage Bill and Employment." February 17. Available at www.worldbank.org.

5   The Legislative Branch

The Centerpiece of Democracy Under Fire

Photo 5.1 A Bolivian representative meets with her constituents. In the historic 2014 elections, women won a majority of seats in the Chamber of Deputies.

Do you really believe that with that elephant-like congress we had before April 5th, it was feasible to effect a deep reform.... How many laws did that congress produce? You count how many laws congress produced. We can expect absolutely nothing. This is the reality all the people recognize.[1]

—President Alberto Fujimori of Peru, commenting on
his popularly supported April 5, 1992, dissolution of congress

In Latin America, congress is a familiar target for criticism and outrage. The region has a long history of congresses acting more like privileged clubs than responsive assemblies. Citizens, stung by seemingly endless streams of corruption scandals, routinely consider their representatives to be self-serving and unaccountable. When asked whether they feel represented by congress, only 23.4 percent of Latin Americans answered "yes" in a 2015 poll.[2] In that same poll, when respondents were asked about their confidence in various social and public institutions, congress ranked far below other institutions such as the Church, the armed forces, the media, and the president (see Table 5.1). Presidents add fuel to the fire, as they habitually fault the institution for gridlock. And the lack of confidence in congress cuts across ideological divides. To the right, President Alberto Fujimori of Peru dissolved congress in 1992 to expedite his efforts toward economic reform and military action against insurgents. A vast majority of Peruvians— polls showed some 70 percent—supported his move. And to the left, Hugo Chávez railed against the disreputable Venezuelan congress in his successful 1998 presidential campaign. The following year, he sidelined the institution

Table 5.1 **Confidence in Groups and Institutions in Latin America.** Latin Americans tend to place little confidence in their legislatures, even less so than other government institutions

Church	69.3
Radio	48.6
Armed forces	44.2
Television	46.6
President	46.0*
Newspapers	42.6
Private business	40.0
Police	36.5
Local government	33.0
Judiciary	29.6
Congress	26.7
Political parties	19.9

Source: Latinobarómetro, 2015, p. 92.
Question: How much confidence do you have in each of the groups/institutions or persons mentioned: a lot, some, little, or none? This chart combines all the "a lot" and "some" responses. The chart itself contains only a partial listing of all the groups/institutions and persons placed on the survey.
*2013 data. Question not asked on 2015 survey.

with a constitutional reform that dismissed the incumbents and replaced the traditional bicameral assembly with a streamlined, single-house legislature. Seventy-one percent of voters supported the reform in a referendum.

Dissatisfaction with legislative institutions is not unique to Latin America. Voters in democracies worldwide find it easy to admonish their legislature, even as they view their own representative in good light. The legislature is filled with so many politicians they have never heard of, and the long-winded debates and meticulous attention to the intricacies of parliamentary procedure feed perceptions of incompetence. But in Latin America, the disapproval is especially acute. In many cases the grumbling has triggered reforms to weaken the institution or has fed violent social protests that bully congress. The resentment directed toward legislatures is in some ways surprising because, after all, this institution is supposed to not only speak for the people, but also to embody the very core of democratic politics. No other political institution embraces the democratic values of representation and deliberation like legislatures. To assess why Latin Americans view their legislatures in such poor light, and what could be done to shore up support, we need to know all of the functions served by congress. In this way, we can gauge precisely where Latin American legislatures appear to be failing, and consider what types of reforms might strengthen the assemblies of the region.

Parliament and Congress

In democracies, we refer to the legislative institution as either **parliament** or **congress**. The labels indicate whether the legislature sits in a parliamentary system or a presidential system, respectively.[3] The distinction is meaningful, because while both play an indispensable role in legislative action, they appear at different stages of the lawmaking process. Parliaments first and foremost concern themselves with the formation and preservation of government. As we saw in Chapter 4, a parliamentary government looks to the assembly for cabinet members and depends upon it for its very survival. And because bills originate in this cabinet, parliament does not really enter the lawmaking process until the very end, when a vote is taken. Congresses, on the other hand, take the field at the very start of lawmaking, and continue their involvement until the very end. Any individual congressperson can initiate legislation and take the lead to lobby for its passage. Such behavior is unheard of in parliamentary systems, where members patiently wait for bills to arrive from government and look to their party leaders for direction on how to vote.

The different interplay with the lawmaking process means that congresses and parliaments work very differently. Given responsibility to initiate legislation, the ideal congress comes equipped with more capable and specialized committees than parliaments. This gives it more expertise and empowers individual members. And relationships within the two

types of assemblies also work differently. Members of parliaments answer
to their party leadership, on whom they typically depend for nomination
in the next election. On the other hand, members of congress answer to
their constituencies, and invariably support legislation that best serves
their own local interests. In congresses, the demand for **constituency service** all too commonly upends the unity forged by partisan ties. Party
leaders know this, and often allow their members to vote independent of
the party. The result is that conflict emerges differently in the two types of
legislatures. In parliaments, it is plainly structured along party lines. But
in congresses, representatives are just as likely to negotiate with, rather
than follow, their leaders. The opportunity for individual congresspersons
to reach across party lines or to follow their own conscience disperses
conflict. With each new issue, there is always the likelihood that a slightly
different coalition will arise. Uslaner and Zittel put it bluntly: "parliamentary legislative systems are orderly. Congressional legislative systems are
disorderly" (2006, p. 149).

In Latin America, congress has been the norm. The only real exception
comes from Chile, which experienced some aspects of parliamentary rule
from 1891 to 1925. Following years of hostility (even outright civil war) over
the balance of presidential-congressional power, a system emerged in 1891
that required the president to appoint a cabinet from members of congress.
The cabinet had to represent the distribution of parties in congress, received
significant policymaking powers, and was dependent upon legislative motions
of confidence. The president retained a fixed term of office, but had his policymaking powers severely curtailed. The absence of any provision allowing
the executive to dissolve congress in cases where a motion of confidence failed
ensured the tilt toward legislative power. Congress could dissolve the cabinet,
but the subsequent cabinet would invariably look very much like its predecessor and fall victim to the same criticisms. Instability plagued the system, which
averaged a new cabinet every four months. By 1925, Chilean leaders had had
enough, and wrote a new constitution that increased presidential power. But
one important aspect of legislative power remained. Namely, in presidential
elections where no candidate received a majority, it was up to congress to select
a president. Chile dropped this rule in its (current) 1980 Constitution, and a
similar provision was found in Bolivia until it enacted a new constitution in
2009. Peru's semi-presidential system is the only contemporary case that could
be considered an exception to congressional government (see Chapter 4). But
even here, the expectations placed upon the legislature and its behavior are
more akin to a congress than a parliament.

The Functions of Congress

We readily associate congresses with lawmaking, but they actually take on a
number of functions. Indeed, it may surprise some to learn that the British
parliament—the predecessor of all western democratic legislatures—did not

embrace lawmaking as a central function at its origin. Rather, the body first took on a number of judicial functions, acting as a high court and administrator of justice. Even later on, instead of making laws, early European parliaments of the thirteenth to fifteenth centuries more regularly served as advisory councils. Insofar as they did make policy, the vast majority of their decision making focused on the granting (or withholding) of taxes to the monarchy. Only very gradually did they engage lawmaking on a wide variety of fronts, operate as a check on royal authority, or assert their role as a representative of "the people," the very functions that we so readily associate with legislatures today.

Identifying the varied historical functions of congress demonstrates that legislatures can fulfill many functions, and that legislative functions are likely to continue their evolution. It also allows us to create a framework for comparing legislatures—for identifying where one particular congress might excel or fail. The presidential systems of Latin America place certain expectations on congress. By gauging where a congress fulfills its functions and where it does not, we gain some insight into how democracy is sustained, or how it could be enhanced from an institutional perspective. In this section the legislature is associated with four distinct functions in a modern democracy: representation, lawmaking, oversight, and education.

Representation

The representative function refers to how well congress corresponds with, speaks for, and answers to society. A representative congress mirrors society. The public should be able to see its most significant divisions replicated in the legislature, and should expect the body to reflect changes in political sentiments over time. Representation is critical to congress because it is here that congress most uniquely lays its claim to legitimacy as part of government. No other government institution is better equipped to embody the range of groups found in the population at any given time.

Of course, no congress can perfectly emulate the political divisions found in society. The electoral system may create some disproportionality (see Chapter 7), and the timing of elections means that congress always represents a portrait of society at a distinct moment in time—it can replicate societal divisions but it cannot move lockstep with these divisions between elections. Institutions inevitably modify how purely a congress represents its people. Moreover, there is debate over precisely *how* legislators should represent the people. Some hold fast to the **delegate model**, which holds that representatives should echo the concerns of their constituencies. Others counter with the **trustee model**, and propose that legislators consider how long-term, national interests might warrant decisions that veer from the immediate interests of their constituents.

Past Roadblocks to Representation

Historically, Latin American congresses did not have much success in the effort to represent their people. But all democracies reaching back to the nineteenth century limited popular input and expanded the vote only gradually. Latin America is no exception here. Like the United States, early restrictions were based on economic criteria such as property qualifications, income, or taxes paid, and prohibited women from participation. Constitutional reforms did away with many of the economic barriers in the middle to late nineteenth century, but a new hurdle, literacy requirements, effectively replaced them. The restriction affected the marginalized, indigenous peoples especially hard. Many countries retained literacy conditions well into the twentieth century. They were found in Chile's electoral laws until 1970, were dropped in Peru only under the 1979 Constitution, and remained in Brazil up to 1985. Most countries extended the franchise to women in the 1940s and 1950s, with Uruguay and Brazil (1932) leading the pack, and Paraguay (1961) following further behind.

But the right to vote is only an opportunity for political engagement. Political parties stand at the gateway to representation, and in Latin America, parties gradually came to safeguard the status quo, and impede representation of groups such as women and the indigenous. This partly resulted from the cycles of authoritarianism that plagued the region. In the uncertain times of a democratic opening, especially following military rule where officers look on from the barracks and threaten reentry at the first sign of trouble, the most vulnerable are least likely to organize. It is then little wonder that time and time again, the restoration of civilian rule would return familiar faces and parties to congress. The **politics of patronage**—the use of state resources to reward supporters and punish opponents—came to characterize almost every party, regardless of its ideological bend. Analysts labeled countries such as Venezuela in the 1980s "partyarchies" as it became clear that the region faced a crisis of representation (Coppedge, 1994).

More Recent Changes in Representation

Deepening socioeconomic inequality in the 1980s and 1990s led to a collapse of these stagnant party systems and set the stage for a complete overhaul of representation in congress. We should add to this the crumbling of the political left in the post–Cold War period, which meant that traditional working-class, union-based, urban parties no longer held a monopoly on progressive politics. A political space therefore opened for women and indigenous groups to voice concerns and political visions on their own terms. Furthermore, the growth of global social movements and human rights organizations contributed valuable support to these previously excluded groups. The Fourth UN Women's Conference in Beijing in 1995 raised greater awareness on women's issues, and served as a rallying point for Latin

American countries (Buvinic and Roza, 2004, pp. 149). One proposal from the conference called for the use of quotas in party lists for congressional elections. Argentina had already blazed its own trail, becoming the first democratic country in the world to adopt gender quotas in 1991. Today, all but Chile, Guatemala, and Venezuela require political parties to reserve some percentage of their candidates for women (see Table 5.2).

Table 5.2 **Gender Quota Minimums in Latin America.** Institutional rule changes have had a significant impact on the representation of women in Latin American legislatures

Country	Year First Reform Enacted	Legislative Body	Quota (%)	Actual Female Representation (%, 2016)
Argentina	1991	lower chamber	30	35.8
	2001	senate	30	41.7
Bolivia	1997	lower chamber	50	53.1
		senate	50	47.2
Brazil	1997	lower chamber	30	9.9
		senate	none	16.0
Chile*		lower chamber	none	15.8
		senate	none	15.8
Colombia	2011	lower chamber	30	19.9
		senate	30	22.6
Costa Rica	1996	unicameral	50	33.3
Dominican Republic	1997	lower chamber	33	26.8
Ecuador	1997	unicameral	50	41.6
El Salvador	2013	unicameral	30	32.1
Guatemala		unicameral	none	13.9
Honduras	2000	unicameral	50	25.8
Mexico	1996	lower chamber	50	42.4
		senate	40	33.6
Nicaragua	2000		50	42.4

Country	Year First Reform Enacted	Legislative Body	Quota (%)	Actual Female Representation (%, 2016)
Panama	1997	unicameral	50	18.3
Paraguay	1996	lower chamber	20	15.0
		senate	20	20.0
Peru	1997	unicameral	30	27.7
Venezuela		unicameral	none	14.4

Source: "Women in National Parliaments," accessed on the Inter-Parliamentary Union website: http://www.ipu.org/wmn-e/classif.htm.
*Chile will implement a provisional quota of 40 percent starting in 2017 and ending in 2029.

The quotas have made a difference. In the 2010's Latin America surpassed Europe as the region with the highest level of female representation in the legislature. Only the Nordic countries, when considered separate from Europe, can boast a higher percentage. In 2016, 12 Latin American countries could claim legislative female representation that surpassed the 19.4 percent total found in the US House of Representatives or 20 percent mark in the U.S. Senate. Still, Latin American countries vary dramatically in their rates, from 9.9 percent in the Brazilian Chamber of Deputies to 53.1 percent in the Bolivian Chamber of Deputies, and this is not simply due to differences in quotas. Compliance remains an issue in many cases, even with formal quota mandates. For example, though Brazil mandates a 30 percent quota, the law stipulates no penalties, allowing many parties to nominate more men with impunity. Honduras does impose a penalty, but the fine of just 5 percent of government-allocated party campaign finances is a small deterrent. Panama advertises an admirable gender parity quota of 50 percent, but the law only stipulates that parties make an effort to reach the quota. And some rules fail to mandate the placement of women in every other spot on party lists (as is the case in El Salvador, Brazil, Colombia, Honduras, Panama, and Peru), allowing party leaders to observe the rule by placing women at the bottom of their list. Finally, the electoral system can upend quota goals. Open-list proportional representation systems (see Chapter 7) allow voters to rank candidates on their own, and possibly scramble the quota effort.

Once in office, women have been known to rise above partisan politics through the creation of **caucus groups** that unite women from different parties. In Brazil, the women's caucus played a leading role to ensure that the constitution included sections on women's rights when it was rewritten in 1988. Success often breeds resentment, and in Brazil's case, critics derisively tagged the group "the lipstick caucus." In Uruguay, the women's caucus combines not only members of the Chamber of Representatives and Senate, but also women from academia and social movements. Among their greatest achievements, the caucus points to 2003 legislation creating restriction orders in domestic violence cases, and a law that allows all women the right to take a day off from work for their annual gynecological exam. To reinforce their connection with all Uruguayan women, the caucus collaborates with female city councilors to organize training courses on participation. In El Salvador, the women's caucus draws together members of the leftist Farabundo Martí National Liberation Front (FMLN) and the right-wing Nationalist Republican Alliance (ARENA)—parties linked to groups that fought a civil war against each other in the 1980s and early 1990s (Inter Press Service, 2006). In general, research shows that greater women's representation has increased the prominence of gender issues on the legislative agenda (Htun and Jones, 2002; Schwindt-Bayer, 2006).

Caucus groups allow women to forge informal bonds and press their initiatives. A stronger indicator of a *legislature*'s commitment to gender empowerment is the existence of a formal committee devoted to gender issues, and here again there is diversity. Mexico has the Committee on Gender Equality in its lower chamber, and it has the power to initiate and revise legislation, conduct hearings, and study selected topics. Brazil has the Committee on the Status of Women, but it is not a standing committee. Although created in 2003 and in existence since then, it is officially a temporary committee holding only the power to propose legislation. Chile places responsibility for gender issues in its Committee on the Family and the Elderly. Although it has all the powers of a standing committee, it arguably constrains and even subverts gender issues by framing them as domestic issues—as if the interests of women revolve solely around the rearing of children and marriage.[4]

Indigenous peoples have also seen some gains in legislative representation, but most countries fall short. The indigenous represent about 13 percent of the entire population in Latin America, but their numbers differ dramatically from country to country. Estimates vary, but the largest concentrations, some 30–60 percent of the population, rest in Bolivia, Guatemala, and Peru. The indigenous comprise about 20–30 percent of the population in Ecuador, and although Mexico's indigenous population holds a relatively smaller percentage at about 15–20 percent, the country does have the largest absolute number of indigenous peoples (about 8 million). The indigenous have lived through a long history of exploitation and marginalization, one that continues today. Indigenous persons in Latin America are 2.7 times more likely to live in extreme poverty than the non-indigenous population. They are more likely to live in rural areas, and thus lack access to basic services in health, education, and legal support. Rural living also reduces economic opportunities. Political representation therefore offers an important first step to social inclusion and economic betterment, but it remains a matter of concern. In Ecuador, indigenous peoples comprise only 5 percent of congress. These numbers are 2.8 percent for Mexico, 7 percent for Peru, 12.5 percent for Guatemala, and 25 percent for Bolivia (Hoffay and Rivas, 2016; World Bank, 2015).

Nonetheless, even these meager numbers signify important gains over the past few decades. A legacy of repression and exclusion meant that indigenous groups had long been hampered by a dulled political consciousness—that is, a dulled sense of common identity and political efficacy. But three decades of democracy have made a difference. And unlike the strategies employed by women's groups, indigenous peoples have not worked through caucus groups. Rather, they have sought to organize their own political parties to ensure representation. In 1996, the Pachakutik Plurinational Unity Movement (created in 1995) made history in Ecuador when it elected eight members to congress. Patchakutik was instrumental to the election of Lucio Guitiérrez to the presidency in 2002, though disagreements led the party to call for his removal soon afterward. In Bolivia, indigenous groups have worked with the political party of President Evo Morales (the first indigenous president in the country's history), Movement for Socialism (MAS), to secure greater representation.

Still, several hurdles remain. "The indigenous" may be 45 million strong, but this number masks important divisions among the roughly 500 indigenous groups in the region, each of whom have distinct interests. The evangelical movement cuts across many indigenous groups in Guatemala, creating links with the non-indigenous population, but barriers with other indigenous groups. Indigenous mobilization appeared to reach a crescendo in the 2000s. Latching on to "pink tide" movements (see Chapter 3), many scored important gains. Bolivia, Colombia, Ecuador, Mexico, Nicaragua, Paraguay, and Peru changed their constitutions to recognize, and celebrate, the multiethnic nature of their societies. Real policy changes, such as bilingual education, the collective ownership of land, stronger self-governance, and the recognition of customary legal procedures, occurred across the region. But further legislative gains in representation appear remote. Ironically, in countries where indigenous groups fail to achieve a critical mass, institutional designs to support them may have backfired. Colombia and Panama both offer "reserve seats," that guarantee representation for the indigenous, but that guarantee also means that larger parties view the indigenous vote as captured and no longer see a need to cater to their interests (Agrawal, 2012).

Lawmaking

Legislatures have the creation of law as a central function. Indeed, lawmaking is embodied within their very name. Presidents may decree laws, but it is problematic to view this action as something other than extraordinary. The winner-take-all nature of the office reduces the legitimacy of such laws. But legislatures, insofar as they represent society, offer the entire public an opportunity to see all significant opinions and preferences operate on policy-making. Because legislatures are deliberative bodies, even minority parties have at least the occasion to express themselves in debate and to gain a fair chance to persuade. In a democratic regime, the process of lawmaking is just as important as the law itself.

Initiation

How does a bill become a law? The first stage involves the power of initiative, which is not fully controlled by legislatures in Latin America. As we saw in Chapter 4, the president may share the power of initiative, and may even monopolize this power on particular issues, as in the budget, or in certain policy areas such as trade and tariff agreements, defense, or public employment. In fact, in every country save Mexico and Nicaragua, the president holds the power to call a special session of congress to deal with issues of his or her own choosing. In addition, several countries allow citizens to introduce bills through signature campaigns, and many grant initiative power to the courts or autonomous public agencies (e.g., electoral commissions, regulatory commissions, and the comptroller general) in matters related to their responsibilities. In Peru, regional and local governments, and even private-sector professional associations, hold initiative power in their own affairs. The involvement of so many actors is significant because congress must expend valuable time on bills emerging from outside its chambers.

Debate

After a bill is introduced, the president of the chamber typically sends it to an editing board to ensure that the bill is properly organized into distinct articles, which are numbered to facilitate debate. Bills then may receive a first reading before a **plenary session** (a session composed of all members of congress). Historically, first readings served an important purpose when the lack of modern copying equipment or illiteracy necessitated oral presentations. Some countries, such as Guatemala, retain the tradition, and use the occasion to allow members to make basic comments on the bill, request clarifications, or ask general questions; however, no motions for amendments are ever allowed at this stage. The bill then moves on to a **committee**. To some extent or another, all legislatures incorporate a division of labor with the use of committees both to handle the sheer volume of bills, as well as to develop expertise as certain members and staff address bills of a similar nature over time. Committees may be either permanent or temporary. (A third type of committee—the oversight committee—is designed to check on other branches of government. It is addressed later on.) In more advanced western democracies, permanent committees essentially replicate the president's cabinet (agriculture, education, defense, finance, etc.) to shadow government, but in Latin America all committee systems fall short in their coverage. Temporary committees deal with more specific issues, such as trade agreements under negotiation, human rights abuses related to a previous government, electoral reform, or proposals to privatize state industries. Within the committees an effort is made to reflect the partisan composition of congress. Here bills receive their most careful scrutiny—committees are efficient because their small membership size facilitates partisan compromises.

Committees can be powerful actors in congress. Within their specialized policy areas, they have more time and resources than other members of congress to refashion bills. Committees can convene hearings to invite testimony from outside specialists or interested groups and individuals, or to query other members of government. In much of Latin America, committees are also expected to call on the constitutional tribunal (see Chapter 6) to comment on the legality of the bill. This is unlike the more reactive process seen in the United States, where courts will take action only after a bill has been made into law. Committees also influence lawmaking by submitting a report with each bill. The report summarizes the main findings of the committee, notes the positions of different members, and articulates approval or disapproval. Committee reports thus provide valuable information to other members of congress on how to vote. By changing and reporting bills, committees exert significant agenda-setting powers. And committees may also exert a form of negative power by placing bills at the bottom of their docket to delay or even "kill" the bill. But this power varies across countries. With some variations, Brazil, Chile, Colombia, Ecuador, Paraguay, and Uruguay authorize the executive to demand a plenary vote. In 11 countries, committees face deadlines in their review of bills.[5] These range from 90 days in Uruguay to just 10 days in Panama. Another limitation on committees is the **discharge petition**, by which the plenary can demand that a bill move from committee and to the floor for a vote. But when the discharge requires a two-thirds majority, committees can more easily control legislation[6] (Alemán, 2006).

More broadly speaking, committees are a key element to the power of the legislature itself, insofar as power varies along with the level of expertise found in the committee system. Unfortunately, most Latin American countries have weak committee systems, for a number of reasons. First and foremost—effective committees require knowledge, and knowledge costs money. Policy experts from a variety of fields must be consulted, studies must be commissioned, and legislators must have a sufficient staff to organize their workload. In the United States, the House of Representatives spends more than $200 million on its committee system alone, and employs about 1,500 staff members. In addition, each representative receives funding for 18 full-time and 4 part-time personal staff. In the U.S. Senate, each individual member receives an average of $3 million for personnel and office expenses, and committees employ some 1,000 individuals. Does the U.S. Congress spend too much? Perhaps. But consider that congress plays an indispensable role in a presidential system. For the system to work, it must check the power of the executive, and it cannot do this without sufficient resources. In Latin

America, personal and committee staffs are meager. Parties may contribute staff, but this injects greater partisanship into staff research. At times, an executive may "lend" staff support, a move that clearly compromises legislative autonomy.

The lack of financing plagues the expertise and breadth of all Latin American committee systems. But institutional variations also explain committee weaknesses. Costa Rica does not allow legislators to seek reelection, whereas Ecuador limits representatives to just two terms. These term limits can place a drag on the development of experience and the expertise of politicians in specialized committees. Other times, the career choices of representatives can have the same impact. Though U.S. legislators tend to see congress as a career, many Latin American legislators view congress as little more than a jumping point to more lucrative positions at the local or regional level, or in the national bureaucracy. Federal institutions increase these motivations, as in Brazil, where one in every five members of the Chamber of Deputies takes a leave of absence to join government at the state level (Samuels, 2003). Electoral turnover, weak parties, and party system fragmentation, partial by-products of electoral system design (see Chapter 7), also trigger personnel change and encumber expertise in the committee system.

After committee, bills move to the plenary, but how they move is of great consequence. With so many bills under consideration in any given session, some will inevitably be left behind. Almost all countries specify a select committee that reflects the partisan composition of the assembly to set the order of the day. In most cases, this stage grants the majority party yet another edge, but Costa Rica illustrates a possibility for more consensual procedures. For each business day, every party has the right to submit a number of bills from committee in proportion to its assembly representation (and each holds the right to place at least one item on the agenda). Parties then go through several rounds in which each has the right to place an item on the agenda until all of their items are exhausted. Of course, who goes first in each round must still be negotiated, and if the order of the day is not agreed upon by party leaders representing at least two-thirds of the assembly, the agenda is then set by a prearranged formula that ranks items by policy area and their phase of debate (first, second, or third).[7]

When under consideration by the plenary, a bill will typically go through phases of debate to help organize deliberation. In Nicaragua, bills first face **general debate**, which grants deputies two opportunities to speak for ten minutes on why they support or oppose a bill. A vote is then taken to move the bill to **specific debate**, where it is considered article by article and deputies can offer motions to eliminate, modify, or add material within each article. For each motion under consideration, a deputy has the right to speak three times—first for 10 minutes, then only for 5 minutes on the second and third occasions. In other countries, there may be three phases of debates, and there may also be variation in the speaking time allotted to legislators.

And in some cases, executive privileges to declare a bill urgent may limit the time of debate and/or the opportunity to propose changes.[8]

In the final vote, members have the option to vote in favor or against, or to abstain. Almost every legislature in the world follows recommendations from the classic text on parliamentary procedure, *Robert's Rules of Order*, and requires that bills receive an affirmative vote from over one-half of all members present and voting. The phrase *present and voting* is of utmost importance here. Legislatures do not need to have all of their members present to conduct business. They require only a **quorum**, which is typically set at one-half plus one of the membership. The rule is important because often some representatives cannot make it to a session. The "voting" requirement is also significant because abstentions are not considered to be votes. Hence, if only 51 members of a 100-member congress attend a session and vote 11 in favor and 10 against, with 30 abstentions, the motion passes.

After a measure passes in the plenary, it does not automatically become law. In Guatemala, if five deputies question the constitutionality of the resolution, it is sent to the Court of Constitutionality, which has 60 days to review the matter (if the time expires, the legislature can continue its work on the resolution). And whether a review occurs or not, every passed resolution must wait five days during which deputies have the chance to make minor editorial or stylistic changes (but not amendments or any changes that affect the spirit of the measure). Any motion to revise requires the support of fifteen deputies and must be supported by a majority. Whether changes are made or not, the constitution requires the law to reach the president's office within 10 days. The president then has 15 days to sign or veto the law. The veto is a formidable hurdle for the Guatemalan Congress. Passing a resolution requires only a vote by a simple majority of those present and voting. But the overturn of a veto requires a vote equal to two-thirds of the *total of its members*.[9] With 158 representatives, this means that congress must amass 106 votes, no matter the number present or the number of abstentions. If the president vetoes a law while congress is out of session, the measure must be returned to congress within the first eight days of its subsequent session. If congress successfully overturns the veto, the law returns to the president who must sign it within eight days and have it printed in the *Diario Oficial*, or Official Journal, which records all national laws. The law takes effect eight days after its publication. The Guatemalan case illustrates both how meticulous the rules of parliamentary procedure must be, as well as how many opportunities are available to those who wish to delay or block the enactment of a law.[10]

Oversight

Accountability is a defining aspect of democratic governance. The signature feature of democracy, elections, ensures the **vertical accountability** of a government to its citizenry.[11] Presidential governance places a priority on accountability by supplementing vertical accountability with an institutional design that obligates interaction among independent branches of government. This interaction provides a source of **horizontal accountability**. Cooperation is built into the system as congresses make laws, presidents execute laws, and judiciaries adjudicate laws. But there is also a disciplinary side to horizontal accountability that allows (and in some cases requires) different branches of government to question, punish, or even dismiss members of each other. John Adams saw these checks as fundamental to democratic government in the United States: "Without three divisions of power, stationed to watch each other, and compare each other's conduct with the laws, it will be impossible that the laws should at all times preserve their authority and govern all men."[12] As Latin American countries seized upon these ideas and constructed their own presidential systems, the question became, "Could legislatures do their part?" This question is especially important in regard to legislative-executive relations, given the power of the presidency in Latin American countries.

Direct Oversight

Nonpunitive checks wielded by congress emerge in the form of reports or hearings. Reporting refers to the regular, often legally mandated, information sent to congress by individual government agencies. For example, a Ministry of Transportation may be required to detail in writing how it used money allocated to it in the budget, and to explain the progress of important projects authorized by congress. Hearings are more conspicuously public events. They center on testimony from and questioning of individuals by members of congress, typically within a committee. Committees most often use them to gather information on a proposed law, but they also can take on an investigatory role. When they do, an important consideration is whether or not the committee is authorized to subpoena official documents or witness testimony. Most congresses in Latin America possess subpoena power, but it is often limited in matters of national security, which executives sometimes extend to include economic policy. Moreover, frequently the power is not—or cannot be— extended to committees. Even when a committee does acquire subpoena power, meager staff and resources hamper their investigative abilities. Hence, for a variety of reasons, the daily workings of legislatures in Latin America are very different from what we see in the U.S. Congress, where ample resources allow the committee system to spend time sifting through volumes of reports and to open hearings freely on almost any matter.

Strapped in their efforts to assess reports and conduct hearings, most Latin American legislatures must rely on **interpellation** to confront the executive. Interpellation is not found in the U.S. Congress, but it is common in much of the world. It refers to the right of a legislature to question executive branch officials before the plenary. Legislatures can use interpellations to denounce executive policy decisions, and the interpellated official can be subject to a motion of censure, though what this means varies from one country to another.[13] In Costa Rica, El Salvador, and Panama, a motion to censure is nothing more than a moral reprimand. In Colombia and Peru, a censure requires ministers to resign from office. The censure motion in Uruguay triggers a high-stakes interplay between the president and congress. Here congress can censure a minister with a simple majority, but if less than two-thirds endorse the motion, the president can refuse to remove the official. In turn, a second vote must be taken, and if it fails to receive a three-fifths majority, the president can dissolve congress. Interestingly, interpellation and censure can be initiated not only because of suspected legal wrongdoing, but also for purely political purposes, which is suggestive of a parliamentary system.

Congresses can also set their sights on the executive through the process of **impeachment**. Impeachment refers to the decision to authorize a trial of the chief executive. In presidential systems, this process is always initiated by the legislature. But not all systems follow the U.S. model, whereby the lower chamber impeaches and the upper chamber conducts the trial. Most obviously, the model poses a problem for countries with only one chamber. Here, a common solution is to have the judiciary take responsibility for the trial, though the unicameral legislatures of Ecuador and Peru retain control of both impeachment and the trial. Brazil and Colombia use a mixed model—if the accusation is a criminal offense, the supreme court conducts the trial, and if it is a high crime or misdemeanor, the senate takes charge.

Censures and impeachment proceedings, or threats thereof, have become common by-products of political crises in Latin America of late. This stands in stark contrast to past decades, where crises all too easily led to the fall of democracy. It may be that punitive measures by legislatures now act as a safety valve that sacrifices the government for the regime. Avoiding a turn to authoritarianism is good news, but the fact that legislatures are resorting to punitive measures more often begs the question of what might be done to avoid crises in the first place. Pérez Liñán notes that contemporary Latin American legislatures display "a proven capacity to punish presidential wrongdoing, but with almost no capacity to prevent it" (2007, p. 149). One answer may come from the lack of nonpunitive oversight such as hearings and reports. Though burdensome, such formal interactions reduce chances for misunderstanding between the executive and legislature, and they also help to prevent executives from developing a sense of impunity. Absent hearings and reports, minor issues can fester and expand, and may only garner congressional attention after they reach the crisis point.

Indirect Oversight

The development of effective legislative oversight is more problematic than it might seem on the surface. Partisanship can undercut the will to supervise, especially in regard to executive actions. For many legislators, the president is not only the head of the executive branch, but also their party leader. Clearly, one should expect less legislative oversight when the president's party controls congress (or when supportive parties control the majority). One way to ensure oversight in times of both unified and divided government is for congress to create formal, autonomous agencies to oversee executive action. Ideally, these agencies are technocratic—that is, expertise and experience rather than partisanship form the central criteria for appointment. Often there is a tremendous public outcry for legislatures to create such agencies in order to boost public confidence in government. But representatives have a hard time relinquishing political power, even when they are in the minority (after the next election, they may be the majority). The interplay of partisanship, popular pressures, and the self-interests of politicians produces oversight processes that range from the more political to the more technocratic (Morgenstern and Manzetti, 2003, pp. 149).

Audit agencies illustrate this range across different countries. These agencies supervise the allocation of public monies as specified in the annual budget. Congress passes a budget as a matter of law, but it is up to the president to carry out the use of funds—a task that congress certainly wants to see fulfilled faithfully. A number of factors related to institutional design determine whether an auditing agency takes on a more political or technocratic tone. A single director heads some, whereas others have more collective leadership. Their terms range from just three years in El Salvador or four years in Ecuador, to eight years in Argentina or the lifelong term offered in Chile. In most countries the legislature holds complete power over appointments, but in some the selection is limited to a list provided by some outside authority. In Venezuela this list comes from a group of citizens, in Colombia the judiciary submits a list, and in Peru the president submits a nomination. In Bolivia, Chile, and Ecuador, it is the president who appoints, subject to a proposal from the legislature. Although most audit agencies are dependent upon the legislature, they are formally independent in Chile, Colombia, Ecuador, Panama, and Peru. Bolivia and the Dominican Republic are distinguished as the only countries in the region with audit agencies tied to the executive (Carrillo Flórez, 2007, p. 149). Beyond the links created in the appointment process, the most important indicators of autonomy for an auditing agency are constitutional guarantees of independence, guarantees of access to financial information, and budgetary independence (Santiso, 2009).

Audit agencies in Latin America also vary in the extent of their power. Most countries follow the Anglo-American model that concentrates on recommendations and nonbinding reports. In its weakest form, this approach can take the form of an Auditor General (*auditoria general*) who simply reviews expenditures. Stronger versions take on a more proactive position that allows the public official to look into the feasibility of financial requests as they are made. In such cases, the office usually takes on the name of Comptroller General (*controlaría general*). Other countries in the region follow a judicial model influenced by Napoleonic Law and use courts of accounts (*corte de cuentas* or *tribunal de cuentas*). These bodies are always collegial, are staffed by judges, and assume powers to impose penalties. A central consequence of this institutional choice is that judicial models tend to focus on compliance with the detailed rules governing how public funds are to be used, whereas the Anglo-American model (staffed more by accountants and financial analysts than by lawyers and judges) is more apt to examine the "big picture" of financial management and focus on the efficient use of public funds. Illustrating the blend of Anglo-American and French influence, some countries (Chile, Colombia, Guatemala, and Panama) follow the comptroller model, but allow the office to initiate legal action through indictments (DFID, 2004; Carrillo Flórez, 2007).

Another oversight agency is the **ombudsman**, which offers citizens a channel to initiate investigations of unlawful behavior by public officials. The link to society contributes to vertical accountability, but the ombudsman also imparts horizontal accountability. As a forum for public grievances tied to the legislature, the office offers a service that partially complements the judiciary, and that allows a legislature to prod the courts into action. Historically, many states have made use of such mediating institutions— from ancient Greeks, Romans, and Chinese, to more modern designs in the Scandinavian countries. But it was the Spanish model that most influenced Latin American countries. Spain worked through its own transition to democracy in 1978, and as part of its new constitution created an office called the *Defender of the People* (*Defensor del Pueblo*) to protect the fundamental rights of citizens. The focus on human rights, rather than unlawful behavior more generally, had tremendous resonance in Latin American countries attempting to move on from repressive regimes. In 1985 Guatemala first embraced the idea, and today only Brazil lacks a national ombudsman's office dedicated to human rights.

To address human rights issues, the ombudsman drafts resolutions in one of two forms. A resolution may carry forward an individual complaint from a citizen, or it may address a broader concern (in this form, the resolution is initiated *ex officio* by the ombudsman). The resolution documents alleged abuse by a government authority, but lacks binding authority. At most, government officials may be required to reply to the allegation, but in many cases they are not so required. The ombudsman office can also support aggrieved citizens by initiating court action against state authorities, submitting *amicus curiae* (friend of the court) briefs to persuade judicial decisions, and offering education on how to defend individual rights. It can also influence public opinion through an annual report, which is submitted to congress and required of all ombudsman offices. The annual report documents the complaints received through the year, assesses government institutions, and offers proposals for the advancement of human rights issues. Though the ombudsman lacks compelling power, it does exert a form of "moral" power (Uggla, 2004, pp. 149). This may not appear to be much, but given the lack of confidence most Latin Americans show toward their judicial institutions (see Chapter 6), the supportive role played by the ombudsman can be crucial to the development of trust in government and long term democratic consolidation.

In Peru, the ombudsman has played just such a role, though it has fought hard to achieve a position of prominence. The 1993 Constitution created the *Defensoría del Pueblo* as an autonomous agency in the government of Peru. Its legal responsibility is to "to defend the fundamental and constitutional rights of individuals and the community, and to supervise the obligations of public administration and the execution of public services."[14] Its primary goal is "to be an institution that leads the transformation of the country as it overcomes existing social divisions, and that contributes to the elimination of exclusion, racism, and all forms of discrimination."[15] Initially, the agency was little more than window dressing under the autocratic government of Alberto Fujimori (1990–2000), created basically to placate those interested in real democratic reform. But the stunt backfired. The Defender at the time, Jorge Santistevan, remarked:

> Normally, an ombudsman deals with individual cases. But that only functions if the institutional framework functions, if the district attorney's office functions, if the courts function. [If] all of that has been undermined, the framework for protecting individual human rights does not exist.

Santistevan thus felt obliged to tackle broader questions of democracy. In the 2000 presidential elections, when Fujimori resorted to fraud to ensure a constitutionally suspect third term, Santistevan's office was the only organization in the country willing to investigate voting irregularities. The public approval rating for the *Defensoría del Pueblo* soared, surpassed only by the Catholic Church.[16] Thanks in part to efforts by the office, Fujimori later fled the country, fearing prosecution for misdeeds while in office. Santistevan's term ended in 2000, but his successor, Walter Albán, built upon his work with the creation of the Commission on Truth and Reconciliation to explore human right abuses during the Fujimori period. This body collected testimonies from victims of abuse and published an official report on the period in 2003. Statements that affirmed government involvement in torture, illegal imprisonment, displacement, and kidnappings exposed the heinous nature of the Fujimori regime, though it claimed it was forced to harsh measures in the midst of civil war. The conclusions of the Commission, which found government forces responsible for just over 40 percent of the 69,240 killed during the conflict, discredited such claims. The vast majority of victims were indigenous rural villagers living in poverty.

Walter Gutiérrez assumed leadership of the *Defensoría* in 2016 after gaining the required two-thirds vote in congress. He will serve a five-year term. Headquartered in the capital of Lima, the agency has 28 regional offices, and several agencies with specialized themes, such as the rights of the disabled, indigenous peoples, and children and adolescents, the protection of one's identity, the prevention of social conflicts, and access to health and education. The office also has a small corps of teams that travel to the more inaccessible areas of the country and communities struck by natural disasters. In 2015, the agency received 29,736 complaints (allegations of government abuse or failures to protect fundamental rights), 16,691 petitions (requests for the *Defensoría* to mediate disputes between citizens and government), and 64,626 consultations (advice on legal questions or basic information on citizen rights). It was able to close 72.4 percent of the cases by the end of the year. Its 2016 annual report indicates that the office saw a disconcerting rise in cases of corruption and infringements on the rights of indigenous groups by corporations that fail to properly consult them as they extract resources from their historical lands. As part of its educational function, the *Defensoría* also publishes periodic reports on a wide range of issues. About 150 in total have been published thus far. Recent reports have addressed the issue of government reparations for human rights abuses under the Fujimori regime, access to maternal health, urban transit in Lima, the quality of pension plans, air pollution, and public education.[17]

But Gutiérrez did not arrive at his post without controversy. The two-thirds vote is a high hurdle for Peru's fractious congress. In fact, the legislature's inability to muster a supermajority had left an interim *defensoría* in office for five years. What was different about 2016? Pedro Pablo Kuczynski had eked out a presidential victory over none other than Keiko Fujimori, daughter of Alberto Fujimori. But Keiko's party, Popular Force, won 73 out of 130 congressional seats. As a minority president, Kuczynski will have to work with the Fujimoristas, and he pressured his party in congress to support Gutiérrez, who was favored by Popular Force. Walter Albán criticized the lack of transparency in the selection process for his old post, and others highlighted Gutiérrez's lack of experience in human rights. Where Gutiérrez takes the *Defensoría* will be of tremendous interest to Peruvians. After his selection, Gutiérrez promised to focus on government efficiency and transparency (*NotiSur,* 2016). While few Peruvians would reject efforts to reduce corruption, others see unfinished work surrounding the Commission on Truth and Reconciliation, such as the calls for reparations and trials. But this would once again spotlight the abuses of the Fujimori period—something Popular Force would rather not see.

Education

Legislatures rest at the crux of democratic politics. They offer a forum for divergent views, and a readily observable process for conflict resolution. And their members offer the most immediate contact with national politics for citizens. As such, legislatures can play an educational role as they trumpet the consensual values required in a democratic society, and inform voters on national political matters. Legislators do this most formally as they debate and hold public hearings. But the quality of these activities is directly related to the level of expertise found in the legislature. As noted, this expertise is often lacking due to underdeveloped committee systems. Moreover, although only Costa Rica, Ecuador, and Mexico impose term limits on their representatives, the political lives of all Latin American representatives tend to be limited by volatile voting practices, or by the lure of public-sector employment or opportunities in state and local governments.

One remedy to the shortcomings of individual politicians is for the representative institution as a whole to take on the task of civic education and to thoroughly document legislative activities. Internet resources have proved invaluable here. The Inter-Parliamentary Union (IPU), an organization created in 1889 to support national parliaments and their collaborative efforts, has published a guide for the web pages of legislative institutions. According to it, a home page should disseminate information in six areas: (1) general information on parliament, including its history and functions, a schedule of activities, a list of elected leaders and members of parliament, a description of the partisan composition of parliament, an explanation of the electoral system, and an organizational chart; (2) a section on content that offers information about pending legislation, the legislative process, the budget, and oversight activities, and committees; (3) tools that allow citizens to search archives of past legislation and access webcasts of current proceedings; (4) methods to offer feedback on the web site itself, and to contact current legislators and committees regarding pending legislation; (5) a design that is user friendly, offered in relevant language formats, and with accessibility features to address the needs of persons with disabilities; and (6) a clear identification of the staff charged with website maintenance (IPU, 2009).

Latin American countries have made important strides in the effort to disseminate information about their legislative institutions with information technology. One study showed regional compliance with IPU standards resting at 47.8 percent in 2008.[18] Since then, Latin American legislatures have done reasonably well from a comparative perspective. The 2012 World e-Parliament Report, which collects data on the use of information and communication technologies (ICT) by legislatures, found Latin America to be a close second to Europe, which led the world. The region made use of 53.3 percent of possible ICT, compared to 55.6 percent by Europe (Global Centre for ICT in Parliament, 2012). Admirably, since 2009 the Brazilian Chamber of Deputies has made use of a portal called e-Democracia, which allows citizens to not only watch but also query legislators in real time as they debate legislation. But significant differences remain in the region. One comparative study looked at the documentation of legislative work, and found Uruguay at 67 percent compliance and Peru at 60 percent, but Bolivia and Venezuela far behind at 24 percent and 12 percent, respectively (Red Latinoamericana por la Transparency Legislative, 2014).

Of course, as a medium of communication, Internet resources can run not only from the legislature to society, but in reverse as well. Unwilling to accept a passive role as prospective receptors of information, many Latin American groups have taken the initiative and created websites of their own to document legislative activities. They are a new breed of social movements known as parliamentary monitoring organizations, or PMOs. Several have organized collectively under the wing of the Latin American Network for Legislative Transparency.[19] One such group is WebCitizen, a Brazilian non-governmental organization that created "Vote na Web" ("Vote on the Web") in 2009. The site allows users to search basic information on politicians, including their voting records; review congressional bills (which are conveniently simplified and summarized); and, most interestingly, symbolically vote on bills themselves. Users can then compare the support or opposition expressed toward a particular bill in a given constituency to the vote of their representative. Ideally, the site could dramatically strengthen the accountability of the Brazilian congress. But like many PMOs, the group struggles to remain up-to-date and thoroughly sift through legislation, and for good reason—legislative activity is extensive and complex. Consider the following description:

> From 2000–2010 ... the 513 deputies in (Brazil's) lower house introduced over 700 initiatives per year, of which only 14% became law. If the government's legislative project's are added to those of the lower house, there are over 100 legislative projects being presented per month. Assuming that the average bill is approximately 3,000 words, 100 initiatives means approximately 1,200 pages of legislative production per month. On top of legislation, there are 41 different committees to keep track of, 20 permanent committees, 15 special committees, 4 external committees and 2 mixed committees. Assuming each committee meets an average of once a week, that's over 80 meetings per month. (Michener, 2012)

And, of course, Brazil has a senate as well. The effort to document legislative activity, whether undertaken by a group in society or the legislature itself, requires a tremendous commitment of time and resources. Still, some records—such as individual voting and attendance—are easier to collect and more important to civic engagement. Here, the issue is often not resources constraints, but political concerns. Web pages could provide an ideal medium for citizens to search voting records and learn more about their representatives. But the precarious positions of many legislators often give them second thoughts. Uncertain of their prospects in the next election, many would rather not advertise votes that rebuff the president, other veteran politicians, or business elites in fear of curtailing future career options. It is therefore of little surprise that most Latin American legislative bodies do not even conduct formal roll calls that catalog individual votes—despite the fact that most do have electronic voting systems in their chambers and could easily place the data on the Internet for public perusal. Again, there have been advances, but still only Argentina, Brazil,

Chile, Colombia, Mexico, and Peru post the voting records of individual politicians (Arnold, 2013, p. 187). Politicians argue that the secrecy protects them from the undue influence of lobbyists or the president. It is done, they claim, to defend the autonomy and integrity of the legislature as a whole. But as noted by Peter Smith, "The underlying reason of course, is protection of the legislators. It eliminates accountability, promotes duplicity, and fosters opportunism" (2005, p. 149). The transparency required by the educational function of congress may enhance the collective accountability and integrity of an assembly, but, from the perspective of many politicians, it comes at the expense of their individual self-interests.

COMPARING COUNTRIES

Legislative Strength

Presidential systems require engaged, capable legislatures to help maintain a balance of power among the branches of government, the central tenet upon which they are based. Legislative strength also supports democracy insofar as it helps to develop strong political parties. When a legislature holds meaningful power, individual politicians find that they need to work together to mobilize votes and pass laws, and this calls for just the organization provided by a political party. Strong political parties in turn heighten competitiveness and deepen linkages with society (see Chapter 8) (Fish, 2006).

There is a general consensus that strong legislatures are good for democracy, but there is much less agreement over just how to measure legislative power (Barkan, 2008). One might begin by examining the legal powers formally wielded by congress. This largely describes the approach taken in the Parliamentary Powers Index developed by Fish and Kroenig (2009), which uses a total of 32 indicators of legislative strength. The index includes the following measures:

1   Exclusive control over the impeachment process.
2   Members of the legislatures cannot also work in the executive branch.
3   Oversight powers over the agencies of coercion (e.g., the military and intelligence services).
4   Legislative approval required for the appointment of individual cabinet members.
5   The executive cannot dissolve the legislature.
6   Limitations on executive decree power.
7   The ease with which an executive veto can be overridden.

8 The legislature's laws are supreme and not subject to judicial review.

9 The right to initiate laws in any policy area.

10 The legislature has an independent budget that it fully controls.

11 Members of the legislature are immune from arrest and/or criminal prosecution.

12 The legislature's approval is required for a declaration of war, or for the ratification of international treaties.

13 The legislature has the power to grant amnesty, and the power of pardon.

14 Oversight over appointments to the judiciary and the board of the central bank.

15 Each legislator has a personal secretary, and at least one nonsecretarial staff member with policy expertise.

Applied to legislatures in Latin America, the Parliamentary Powers Index broadly illustrates the differences in capabilities held by Latin American legislatures:

Table 5.3 The Parliamentary Powers Index (2009)

Nicaragua	.69
Peru	.66
Uruguay	.66
El Salvador	.59
Brazil	.56
Colombia	.56
Costa Rica	.53
Ecuador	.53
Honduras	.53
Venezuela	.53
Argentina	.50
Guatemala	.50
Panama	.50

(*continued*)

Bolivia	.44
Mexico	.44
Dominican Republic	.41
United Kingdom	.78
Canada	.72
United States	.63

Source: Fish, M. Steven, and Matthew Kroenig. 2009. The Handbook of National Legislatures: A Global Survey. New York: Cambridge University Press.

A list of indicators such as that provided by the Parliamentary Powers Index gives us a sense of just what a legislature is capable of doing. But whether or not a legislature uses its powers is another question. Especially in presidential systems, where legislatures must face off against executives and judiciaries, the legitimacy of the institution plays an important role. If the public questions the authority of the legislature, representatives find it difficult to act. The Latinobarometro poll referenced at the beginning of this chapter is one indicator of the reputation of congress. The World Economic Forum conducts a similar poll, though it takes an elite perspective with queries of business elites. Another way to assess whether or not a legislature is able to use the powers accorded to it is to examine certain characteristics of the legislators themselves. Education and experience are central variables here. One could also examine the number of committee assignments imposed upon each representative, with the presumption that more assignments tax the energies of a representative and impair policy specialization. And finally, one could simply ask the legislatures themselves to describe their influence, opinions, and concerns to get an insider's view. Since 1994, researchers at the University of Salamanca in Spain have collected data from surveys distributed to Latin American legislators. Their "Observatory of Parliamentary Elites in Latin America" publishes analysis, and researchers from around the world use their data, which is available by request on the Internet. But in all of these surveys, one must consider the role of the subjective, as well as the fact that surveys capture just one point in time—the impressions they convey may be fleeting. A final way to assess the power of a legislature is to weigh the number of bills it initiates relative to the number initiated by the president, and to compute the number of vetoes it is able to override. But these figures must be considered in the context of whether or not the president holds majority support in congress. A reduced number of initiated bills may be an indicator of partisan power and thus simply illustrate affinity with, rather than debility toward, the executive. Analysts all agree that estimates of legislative strength must make use of several measures, but debate continues over how those measures should be weighted. Still, the evidence generally places legislative strength in Latin America below western democracies but well above most less-developed countries in Africa, Asia, and the Middle East.

Discussion Questions

1   Can a legislature grow too powerful? Which measures would best indicate that a legislature has overstepped its bounds?
2   Countries that rank highest on the Parliamentary Powers Index are not necessarily the most stable. What other factors must be considered to better assess how legislative powers affect democracy?

Legislative Structure

Size

A number of considerations affect the design of a legislature. One of the more fundamental is the question of size. Costa Rica's Legislative Assembly convenes just 57 representatives. They meet in a room about the size of a basketball court, and arrange their desks along the walls so that they face each other. This allows members to maintain visual contact, and to speak comfortably from their seats. The obligation to fill some 16 committees with roughly seven to nine members each affords each deputy multiple settings for collaborative work, though it does stretch their talents. Compare this to Brazil's Chamber of Deputies, which places 513 members in a stadium setting. The deputies lounge within long rows of seats that form a semicircle around the chamber president and his or her assistants, who sit at a dais on a roughly 10-foot platform. For the benefit of those in the farthest reaches of the cavernous room, large-screen televisions flank the platform. Deputies hoping to address the body must make their way down the aisle to speak at one of the podiums alongside the dais. If the anonymity afforded by this atmosphere is not enough, consider also that the deputies share their legislative work with the Federal Senate, which has 81 members of its own working in an entirely different building. Still, the large size allows the deputies to develop specializations in certain issue areas. In fact, the standing rules of the chamber prohibit a deputy from serving on more than one committee (and a committee may hold up to 61 deputies—more than the entire membership of Costa Rica's Legislative Assembly). Similarly, the large size allows a greater range of the country's population to be represented.

The trade-off is clear—Costa Rica's Legislative Assembly offers an intimate, consensual environment, whereas Brazil's Chamber of Deputies affords more specialized skills and diversity. But it would be misleading to discuss the size of a legislature as a deliberate choice. Population plays an almost determinative role here. With just over 4 million inhabitants in Costa Rica, its 57-member assembly represents an average of 70,600 persons each.[20] In contrast, Brazil's assembly faces the monumental task of representing more than 170 million persons. Even with 513 members, this still means that each member must represent an average of 331,000 persons. To match Costa Rica's average, Brazil's Chamber of Deputies would have to mushroom to more than 2,400 members! If a congenial atmosphere is the preference, it appears to be more of a luxury for small countries than an option for all countries.

Sessions

When a legislature meets is another fundamental consideration. Constitutions typically specify the precise starting date of a congressional session. If they did not, the functioning of congress would depend upon (and thus be open to manipulation by) a single official or government body. Length is one variable here. The National Congress of Bolivia begins its sessions August 5 and continues for 90 days (though this can be increased to 120 days). The National Congress of Honduras trebles the minimum imposed on Bolivia's assembly, requiring a session that runs from January 25 to October 30. Generally, most legislatures meet between 120 and 270 days per year. Frequency is a second variable. Argentina, Bolivia, Chile, Honduras, Mexico, Nicaragua, Peru, and Uruguay have constitutions that specify one single session through the legislative year. Other countries mandate recesses and typically designate two calendar periods, such as in Guatemala where the dates run from January 14 to May 15, and August 1 to November 30. The session holds tremendous importance to the livelihood of bills. Faced with a shorter session, bills placed toward the bottom of the agenda may never find their way to the floor for a vote. The session also determines second chances for bills. In most cases, bills that fail cannot be reintroduced until the following session. El Salvador departs from the norm by stipulating a straightforward six-month moratorium before a bill can be reintroduced.[21] Outside the ordinary sessions noted in the constitutions, legislatures may also decide to convene under emergency sessions. In a nod to the executive power found in Latin American political systems, in most cases the president shares the authority to convene an emergency session. When an emergency session takes place, the legislature is typically limited to debating the issue(s) that prompted the emergency.

Table 5. 4 Legislative Structure in Latin America

Country	Chamber Name	Size	Avg. Pop. Per Member	Term	Age	District Residency	Impeachment Model	Bicameral Resolution	Electoral Calendar
Argentina	Chamber of Deputies	257	144,100	4	25	2 yrs*	Congressional	*navette* only	mixed
	Senate	72	514,300	6	30	2 yrs*	–	–	–
Bolivia	Chamber of Deputies	130	64,100	5	18	2 yrs	Judicial	joint session	–
	Chamber of Senators	36		5	18	2 yrs	–	–	–
Brazil	Chamber of Deputies	513	332,200	4	21	current	Mixed	joint session	concurrent
	Federal Senate	81	2,103,800	8	35	current	–	–	–
Chile	Chamber of Deputies	120	126,800	4	21	2 yrs	Congressional	committee	–
	Senate of the Republic	38	400,300	8	35	None	–	–	–
Colombia	House of Representatives	166	253,600	4	25	None	Mixed	committee	–
	Senate of the Republic	102	412,800	4	30	None	–	–	–

(continued)

Table 5. 4 Legislative Structure in Latin America (continued)

Country	Chamber Name	Size	Avg. Pop. Per Member	Term	Age	District Residency	Impeachment Model	Bicameral Resolution	Electoral Calendar
Costa Rica	Legislative Assembly	57	70,600	4	21	None	Judicial	–	concurrent
Dominican Republic	House of Deputies	178	56,700	4	25	5 yrs*	Congressional	*navette* only	nonconcurrent
	Senate	32	315,300	4	25	5 yrs*	–	–	–
Ecuador	National Assembly	124	102,000	4	30	None	Congressional	–	concurrent
El Salvador	Legislative Assembly	84	74,700	3	25	None	Judicial	–	nonconcurrent
Guatemala	Congress of the Republic	158	72,044	4	–	None	Judicial	–	concurrent
Honduras	National Congress	128	50,100	4	21	5 yrs*	Judicial	–	concurrent
Mexico	Chamber of Deputies	500	197,700	3	21	6 mos	Congressional	*navette* only	mixed
	Chamber of Senators	128	772,400	6	25	6 mos**	–	–	–

Country	Chamber Name	Size	Avg. Pop. Per Member	Term	Age	District Residency	Impeachment Model	Bicameral Resolution	Electoral Calendar
Nicaragua	National Assembly	90*	56,300	5	21	None	Judicial	–	concurrent
Panama	Legislative Assembly	71	40,200	5	21	1 yr	Congressional	–	concurrent
Paraguay	Chamber of Deputies	80	68,700	5	25	None	Congressional	*navette* only	concurrent
	Chamber of Senators	45	122,100	5	40	None	–	–	–
Peru	Congress of the Republic	120	213,850	5	25	None	Congressional	*navette* only	concurrent
Uruguay	House of Representatives	99	33,707	5	25	None	Congressional	joint session	concurrent
	Chamber of Senators	30*		5	30	None	–	–	–
Venezuela	National Assembly	167	144,700	5	21	4 yrs	Judicial	–	nonconcurrent

* or birth in district
** or 6 mos. residency in neighboring state

Terms and Alternates

Legislatures also vary by the length of the terms served by their members. No country matches the brief two-year term given to House members in the U.S. Congress, but the three-year terms given in El Salvador and Mexico (in the Chamber of Deputies) come closest. Proponents of shorter term lengths contend that brevity ensures responsiveness to the electorate. Critics argue that shorter terms make it more difficult for representatives to accumulate experience and expertise. Moreover, with elections always on the horizon, legislators feel pressured to support only those policies that bring about short-term gains, and to avoid important policies that require long-term investments.

A final feature of legislative structures in Latin America is the use of alternates. When elections for congressional offices are held in most Latin American countries, the rules require parties to list both a proprietary candidate (*propietario*) and an alternate (*suplente*). In theory, the *suplente* acts as a ready substitute should the *propietario* be unable to attend a session and cast a vote, for whatever reason. More significantly, the *suplente* assumes the position in the event that the *propietario* resigns or is removed from office. But beyond its practical rationale, the *suplente* system generates a number of political side effects. It has been known to facilitate the movement of legislators into the executive (there is no need for special elections, or quarrels over appointment power), which is another indicator of the weak separation of power that we find in the presidential systems of Latin America. In fact, Cox and Morgenstern (2001, p. 149) report that in Brazil "ministers (initially elected as *propietarios* but then appointed to the cabinet) will occasionally resign their ministerial positions just before an important vote in the assembly, resume their legislative seats, vote, then resign their legislative seats and resume their ministerial posts again."

The *suplente* system also adds a negotiating tool, such as when a party allows another party to nominate some of their *suplentes* in return for their coalition support (Montero, 2005, p. 149). And on a disquieting note, the *suplente* system opens a door for subversion. In Mexico, parties have been known to bypass gender quotas by assigning female representatives to *suplente* positions. During recent contentious constitutional reforms in Bolivia and Ecuador favored by the government, opposition *propietarios* attempted to block the process by refusing to join congressional sessions, thereby denying the body a quorum. When they saw their *suplentes* all too willing to take their place, charges of bribery inevitably followed.

Bicameralism

The structure of congresses can differ in many ways, but perhaps the most overarching structural difference among legislatures in Latin America is bicameralism, which refers to the use of two representative chambers to fulfill the legislative role (a unicameral system has just one representative chamber). Today, nine states in the region employ a bicameral legislature: Argentina, Bolivia, Brazil, Chile, Colombia, the Dominican Republic, Mexico, Paraguay, and Uruguay. In the past, bicameral systems were also found in Cuba (to 1959), Ecuador (to 1978), Nicaragua (to 1979), Peru (to 1994), and Venezuela (to 1999).

The classic rationale behind bicameralism is that it allows different interests to be represented. Great Britain pioneered the design as its House of Commons, representative of the people as a whole, assumed powers from the House of Lords, which stood for the interests of the nobility. The United States took a less class-based approach as it sought to balance the interests of large states and small states. According to the Great Compromise, the House of Representatives would be based on population size, whereas the Senate would safeguard small-state affairs by according all states equal status. Today, a class-based formula for representation would not hold legitimacy in any country. But offering separate representation to regional interests would be justifiable, and could be useful for assuaging localized fears or apprehensions directed toward the central government. For example, while the indigenous majority in the highland areas of Bolivia celebrated the presidential inauguration of Evo Morales in 2006, *mestizo* elites in the low-lying jungle regions reacted with trepidation. They feared he would confiscate their landholdings and their massive natural gas deposits to redistribute wealth in favor of indigenous peoples, and they made it clear that they would resist—with arms, if necessary. But Bolivia's bicameral system gave their political party, Plan Progress, an institutional alternative. The Bolivian Senate divides the country into nine departments and grants equal representation to each. This means that the tiny department of Pando (population 110,436) sends the same number of representatives as the largest department, La Paz (population 2,706,351). The formula favored Plan Progress because although its stronghold sat in the large department of Santa Cruz, the party received support from the three smallest departments in the country. This allowed the party to retain a disproportionate advantage in the Senate, and to safeguard many of its interests, especially as the country worked through a constitutional change in 2008–2009. Although extremist groups affiliated with the party resorted to violence and sabotage to oppose Morales, the Senate allowed moderate opposition members to work effectively within the system and in this way helps to defuse their fears. Plan Progress splintered in 2013, but one could argue that its role in the senate helped the country adjust to the significant political changes pushed by Morales.

Another justification for bicameralism looks to the quality of legislation. In fact, according to Tsebelis and Money (1997, p. 149), it is not just the fact that asking two sets of eyes to review legislation creates a process for quality control, but also that the simple expectation of some other actor reviewing the same issue creates a strong incentive to act with more diligence at the outset. This view finds virtue in redundancy. Another argument is that bicameralism improves legislation insofar as the senate acts as a "council of elders." And legislatures can use a number of institutional rules to produce a more experienced, "wiser" upper house. Compared to lower legislative chambers, senates typically have more stringent eligibility requisites (e.g., higher ages and more demanding citizenship requirements). They also offer extended terms of

Photo 5.2 Famed architect Oscar Niemeyer designed the Brazilian congress building with bicameralism in mind. The concave bowl represents the Chamber of Deputies, which is large, diverse, and thus more open to ideas. The convex bowl represents the Senate, which is smaller, measured, and more predictable in its decision making.

Source: © Shutterstock

office and only partially renew their memberships during elections to buffer themselves from vacillating public passions. And finally, senates are invariably smaller than lower legislative chambers, and this design presumably creates a more collegial body. It also means that senators must answer to larger constituencies, which both creates higher campaign costs for them than for their lower-chamber colleagues (another restrictive entry cost), and theoretically allows them to stand above particular interests and to forge broad alliances. Ideally, senates are institutionally designed to create an atmosphere where seasoned lawmakers can deliberate with greater regard for prudence than politics (Llanos and Sánchez, 2006).

But not all bicameral systems are alike. First, some can be described as symmetrical and others as asymmetrical. Symmetrical bicameral systems confer on each chamber formally equal powers, whereas asymmetrical systems tilt the balance of power toward one house. Second, the chambers of a bicameral system may be congruent or incongruent. Congruent systems shun the "council of elders" model and instead create chambers that are more similar than different in their composition. These distinctions are important. Institutional designs that produce symmetrical, incongruent chambers make for **strong bicameralism**. Here, chambers answer to different constituencies and contend on an equal footing. Political theorists view strong bicameralism as another ingredient in the system of checks and balances espoused by presidential systems—one that creates checks within congress itself. Weak bicameralism, on the other hand, eschews the representational alternative offered by a second chamber, and provides a second level of review that is little more than advisory in form (Lijphart, 1999, pp. 149). Generally speaking, Latin American bicameral systems are symmetrical, but they exhibit diversity in their levels of congruence. Argentina, Brazil, and Chile come closest to the "ideal" type of strong bicameralism seen in the United States. The remaining bicameral systems depart from this model by creating more congruent chambers while retaining symmetry. For example, in the Dominican Republic, senators and deputies face the same age restrictions (minimum of 25 years) as well as similar eligibility qualifications. And in Bolivia, Colombia, the Dominican Republic, Paraguay, and Uruguay, *all* members of the two chambers share the same electoral calendar.

Perhaps the most important practical consideration all bicameral systems face is how to resolve intercameral differences. What happens when the two chambers desire different versions of the same bill? In Latin America, bicameral legislatures employ the *navette* (the French word for "shuttle"). The *navette* calls for bills to originate in one chamber, then to be sent to the other chamber—and to be "shuttled" back and forth to work out differences. In some instances, such as when the Brazilian legislature considers constitutional amendments, the shuttling continues until agreement is reached. But in most cases legislatures make use of a stopping rule. The classic *navette* differentiates the **initiating chamber** from the **reviewing chamber**, and advantages the former to create a stopping rule. In Argentina, if the reviewing chamber modifies the bill it receives from the initiating chamber, the initiating chamber can insist on the original version with a simple majority vote. And if the reviewing chamber responds with a two-thirds majority in favor of its version, this obligates the initiating chamber to muster its own two-thirds majority if its version is to prevail. The Dominican Republic, Mexico, Paraguay, and Peru also exercise classic forms of the *navette*. Ideally, the *navette* helps to balance power between the chambers because either can play the role of initiator. But often the constitution grants the lower house exclusive charge over certain policy areas (e.g., tax increases) or requires executive measures to be considered first by the lower house. Such provisions attenuate bicameral symmetry.

Other Latin American countries resort to two other stopping rules that either increase or decrease symmetry. Chile and Colombia supplement the classic *navette* with the **conference committee** to resolve differences. This measure preserves symmetry because although each chamber can send as many members as it pleases to the committee, each chamber receives just one vote. Still, Chile's commitment to symmetry is weakened by a provision that allows the initiating chamber to insist on its version with a two-thirds vote in the event that the conference committee fails to reach an agreement. Bolivia and Uruguay resolve legislative discord by calling a **joint session** of both chambers. This inserts a dose of asymmetry due to the larger number of votes that the lower chamber brings to the session. Uruguay mitigates the imbalance slightly by requiring a two-thirds vote in the joint session.

COUNTRY IN THE SPOTLIGHT

The National Congress of Chile: A Barometer of Chilean Democracy

The National Congress of Chile proudly portrays itself as "among the oldest in the world ... preceded only by the United Kingdom, France, and the United States."[22] Political instability did lead to periods of suspension early on—in 1811, 1891, and 1924—but through it all and by the twentieth century, Chile could easily lay claim to one of the most vibrant democracies in the western hemisphere. An array of political parties—from communists to rural conservatives—butted heads and crafted national policies in the halls of the legislature. Bargaining, persuasion, and the free exchange of ideas in the legislature tapered the political divides found in society, divides that grew deeper during the Cold War. But congress had its critics, most of whom centered on the constant drive for special interests and pork barrel spending by politicians. In the 1950s and 1960s, reforms shifted budgetary control to the executive and curtailed the ability of congresspersons to add amendments to legislation. Furthermore, executives embraced a more liberal interpretation of their line-item veto authority. Despite their intention, these changes weakened the ability of congress to act as a forum for bargaining and compromise, and thereby allowed differences among political groups in Chile to fester, and deepen. Though many factors would contribute to the fall of democracy in 1973, the diminished role of congress was certainly one of them (Valenzuela, 1978). Congress would return with the transition to democracy in 1989, and just as before, the institution can be viewed as a barometer of Chilean democracy. Democratic consolidation would not have occurred without significant changes to congress. On the other hand, more recent political unrest and the growing frustration of Chileans with politics can be tied to lingering institutional deficiencies that have contributed to a crisis of representation in congress.

Chile has a bicameral legislature. Both chambers meet in ordinary sessions from May 21 to September 18. There are 120 members in the Chamber of Deputies. Deputies emerge from 60 two-member districts and serve four-year terms. The 38 members of the Senate represent 19 regions. They too emerge from two-member districts, but their terms last eight years, with one-half of the Senate renewed every four years. The two branches are incongruent. Aside from the differences in size, constituencies, term lengths, and the partial renewal of the

Senate, deputies need be only 21 years of age, whereas senators must be at least 35 years old. The legislature can also be described as symmetrical, but with some qualifications. The Chamber retains exclusive initiative authority in several important areas (taxes, budget, military recruitment), but faces a Senate with its own exclusive controls over amnesties and pardons. Likewise, as noted, Chile supplements the symmetry of the *navette* system with a conference committee process that, should it fail, tilts the balance toward the initiating chamber (Llanos and Nolte, 2003).

Surprisingly, congress is not located in the capital city of Santiago, but rather some 80 miles away in the coastal city of Valparaiso. The location encumbers a congress that already faces resource limitations in staff and advising (most representatives make do with one secretary and one or two advisors). Not only must legislators travel to Santiago to consult and negotiate with the executive and various ministers, but they also have to visit their home constituencies to maintain contact. And keep in mind the tremendous geographic length of Chile. This means that legislators must follow a rigorous travel schedule while in session. During the first three weeks of each month, members of the Chamber of Deputies work in Valparaiso on Tuesdays, Wednesdays, and Thursdays. On Fridays and Mondays they travel to Santiago to conduct more specialized work in their respective committees, and to meet with members of the executive cabinet. The final week of the month is reserved for district visits. The schedule is grueling, but Chileans demand due diligence. Unexcused absences from congressional sessions are addressed with a fine equivalent to 1 percent of the representative's salary.

The military government planned the location of the legislature in 1987, under the rationale that the Valparaiso setting would guard against a concentration of power in the capital. A more genuine explanation would recognize that this was but one move in a larger plan by the military government to create a restricted democracy with a sidelined congress. As noted by one analyst, "In the view of the military reformers, a strong presidency would better guarantee the economic legacy of the authoritarian regime by squelching the personalism, populism, and party politicking that had led to the corruption of democratic institutions" (Siavelis, 2000, p. 149). This economic legacy came in the form of a commitment to neoliberal economics, which espoused the free market and tagged government involvement in education,

(*continued*)

health, welfare, pensions, and other social policies as impositions on individual freedom. Social policies were to prioritize efficiency, not equality. The military would allow the transition to democracy in 1989, but only on their terms. Early on, military officials, including Pinochet himself, shadowed the government and even threatened military intervention to safeguard their interests. As their influence waned over time, opportunities emerged to reform institutions, and politics.

Since the transition, the legislature has functioned under the Constitution of 1980, a document drafted by the military government to protect its interests. Democratic consolidation has been a gradual, piecemeal process, one chaperoned as congress enacted constitutional reforms to dismantle the legacies of authoritarianism. Many of the most important of these reforms affected congress itself. Under the original constitution, the president held the right to dissolve the Chamber of Deputies, and the Constitutional Tribunal possessed the power to censure legislators—an act that would trigger a dismissal from office. A package of reforms passed in 1989 removed these powers. It also increased the number of elected senators from 26 (elected from 13 regions) to 38 (elected from 18 regions) in order to offset the influence of the nine senators appointed by the president, Supreme Court, and National Security Council. Over the years, further constitutional reforms eroded many other "authoritarian legacies" of the constitution. These included stronger protections for free expression, explicit references to gender rights, the direct election of municipal leaders, and an overhaul of the criminal justice system. In 2005, however, another large package of reforms moved congress to the spotlight. One reform slightly increased the congruency of the chambers by reducing the minimum age of senators from 40 to 35. But this same reform also removed the stipulation that required senators to be residents of their districts for at least two years previous to the election (deputies still face this constraint). A more substantial reform affecting congruency and the general democratic quality of the country abolished the system of designated senators; hereon forth, all senators would be elected by the people. And a number of reforms shifted authority from the president and toward congress. For the first time, the president was obliged to visit congress and deliver an annual "state of the nation" address. The president also lost the ability to convene congress under extraordinary conditions, thereby leaving the legislature with complete control over its sessions. Congress gained stronger advisory and approval powers during the states of emergency declared by the president. And finally, congress saw its investigatory tools expanded. The Chamber of Deputies now not only holds the constitutional power to create investigatory committees, but also to arm them with subpoena authority. And whereas previously, requests for information from executive officials could be answered in writing, the Chamber's interpellation capability now allows it to question ministers of the government in person before the plenary.

With these institutional changes, Chile's legislative branch became a much more relevant player than that envisioned under the original designs of the 1980 Constitution. And for outsiders, Chile appeared to have all the markings of a successful democratic transition by 2005. There was a diverse range of political parties, corruption had not infected the public sector, the military had learned to accept civilian rule, the courts emerged as robust defenders of the rule of law, and economic growth surpassed rates found in much the rest of the world. Freedom House rated the country a "2" from the time of transition to 2003. Since then, Chile has received a score of "1," which places it on par with the most stable democratic countries in the world. But despite the accolades, the years since 2005 have been far from trouble-free. As significant as the institutional changes had been, there remained work to be done. Moreover, the bridled institutions imposed by the military left a stain on Chilean political culture, one that made it wary of political change. The military government had lasted almost two decades, and the battle to democratize institutions another two decades. Chileans were grateful, and proud, of the changes they had accomplished. But today's generation, one born under democratic rule, is not so risk-averse, and much more willing to push recalcitrant political elites for further change. Difficulties in congress in the years after 2005 gave hints of these problems, and more recently Chile has seen a full-blown collision between the desires of its society and the designs of its institutions.

After the democratic transition, the Socialist Party, Christian Democratic Party, Party for Democracy, and Radical Social-Democratic Party combined to form the Coalition for Democracy (*Concertación*). To oppose them from the right, the National Renovation Party and Independent Democratic Union formed the Alliance for Chile (*Alianza*). The *Concertación* won the presidency four times over, and could typically count on a majority or near-majority in each chamber of congress. With the 2006 election of Socialist Party

(*continued*)

member Michelle Bachelet to the presidency, they were in an enviable position with majorities in both chamber of congress. But expansive coalitions have a tendency to fragment as members question power-sharing arrangements. Likewise, the comfort of electoral victory often leads politicians to neglect the very voters who placed them in office. In August 2007, the *Concertación* suffered a historic blow when one of its own—longtime leader of the conservative wing of the Christian Democrats, Adolfo Zaldívar—mobilized opposition to a massive transportation bill in the Senate. Outraged by this breach of party loyalty, party leaders ousted Zaldívar from the party. The harsh reprisal generated widespread criticism from Chileans who felt that their political leaders had lost touch and were concerned only with maintaining their positions. Many inside and outside the party defended Zaldívar's right to vote his conscience. Several senators and deputies professed their allegiance to Zaldívar, and pronounced themselves *colorines*, or "redheads," in recognition of Zaldívar's red hair. Quickly, the *colorine* movement transformed political power in the closely divided Chamber and Senate. Party leaders from *Alianza* reached out to the *colorines* and wrested control of the President of the Senate from the *Concertación*. *Alianza* members in the Chamber found *colorine* support in April 2008 when they investigated into the government's education minister on charges of misappropriating funds. Four *colorines* sided with the 55 members of *Alianza* to produce a 59–55 vote in favor of accusing the minister, an accusation that was later accepted in the Senate and represented the first removal of a government minister by congress in more than four decades.

For the first time, the *Concertación* looked vulnerable. Growing media attention to the dissension spurred criticisms that the coalition was elitist. With the 2009 elections on the horizon, such criticisms resonated with members of the party. Under Chile's binomial electoral system, parties can run up to two candidates in each two-member district. If the winning party doubles the votes received by the second-place party, it gains both seats. The Pinochet regime had designed the system supposedly in the name of stability. Doubling the vote of a competitor sets a very high bar for victory, such that the second-place party need secure only 33 percent of the vote to gain a seat (giving it 50 percent of representation in the district). In reality, analysts knew that the electoral system was rigged to favor the political right, which had traditionally appealed to about 33 percent of the electorate (Polga-Hecimovich and Siavelis, 2015). And whether a voter supported the *Concertación* or *Alianza*, the binomial system failed to create strong ties between representatives and voters. The incentive to gather 66 percent of the vote pressured parties to form coalitions, and left little room for independents. Coalitions may help to create consensus, but for many Chileans this came at the cost of a more dynamic and responsive party system. Members of the lower rungs in each coalition also increasingly felt that they faced the brunt of the electoral system. Because parties did not often sweep districts, a candidate placed second on the party list faced an especially anxious campaign. The electoral rule thus gave party leaders a powerful weapon to reward or punish their members (Navia, 2004).

Frustrated by elite-centered politics, several *Concertación* members picked up on the growing sense of alienation in the public, and announced that they would run as independents in the 2009 elections. Five senators and eight deputies from the *Concertación* made this choice in September 2009. Their leader was Marco Enríquez-Ominami, who had gained a reputation for criticizing and often refusing to support *Concertación* initiatives as a deputy. The press gave him the name "el díscolo," which roughly translates as "the disobedient one." He and other disgruntled members of the *Concertación* latched on to the name, and referred to themselves as "los díscolos." Ominami took things one step further, and announced an independent campaign for the presidency.

Concertación appeared oblivious to the calls for change surrounding it. For its presidential candidate, it nominated Eduardo Frei, former president from 1994 to 2000 and clearly a member of the inner circle (electoral rules prohibit presidents from serving consecutive terms, denying the party the obvious choice of the still-popular Bachelet). Ominami split the center-left vote, forcing a runoff that saw the right take the presidency under Sebastián Piñera for the very first time. For analysts, the transfer of power to the opposition after a democratic transition was a momentous occasion. It showed that former victors could play the democratic game and accept defeat. But Chileans were far more discouraged than delighted by their democracy. Voter turnout among eligible voters had plunged over 20 points since the transition to democracy. And only one in nine could identify with a political party—one of the lowest figures in all of Latin America. Chile could point to an array of political parties, but the coalitions muddled their appeal.

(continued)

Piñera (2010–14) plodded through his term. The country weathered the 2008 global crisis much better than most countries: Piñera could point to an annual economic growth rate of about 5 percent under his term, and the country had an inflation rate under 3 percent and unemployment at just under 6 percent at end of his term. But it was growing crystal clear that Chileans were more concerned with politics than with economics. The country could flaunt the most admirable indicators of economic growth and efficiency in all of Latin America, but it could not hide the most disconcerting levels of economic inequality. Twenty years of *Concertación* had left a fairly extensive web of health, housing, employment, social security, education, and other social policies, but they were all pocketed by neoliberalism. Party leaders, mindful of how polarization over government involvement in the economy preceded the 1973 military coup, compromised by extending social policy through contracts with private investors. With the market dictating policy design and implementation, access grew uneven and contributed to inequality. In addition, blind faith in market solutions led many politicians to balk at oversight duties and oppose any level of regulation in principle. Devious contractors could skimp on quality as they took charge of government services.

Nowhere were these problems more apparent than in education. By 2010, over half of all elementary and postsecondary students were in state-subsidized private schools, where teacher accreditation and the quality of the curriculum suffered. Private universities, charging the most expensive tuition in the world (at 40 percent of family income), also took hold of a majority of the enrollment by this time (Larrabure and Torchia, 2015). This turning point may have sparked the wave of university protests that hit the country in 2011. But perhaps most important, this was a generation born under democracy. They were "*la generación sin miedo*" (the fearless generation). They were not dissuaded from action by the specter of military intervention (Cummings, 2015). But the government responded harshly to their protests, with water cannons atop military vehicles spraying marchers and Piñera admonishing the students by proclaiming, "We all want education, healthcare, and many more things for free, but I want to remind them that nothing is free is this life. Someone has to pay" (*Al-Jazeera*, 2011). The rebuff did not resonate with the students, who could rightly note that the reliance on private contractors allowed the Chilean government to spend less on education (as a percentage of GDP) than any other country in the world (Larrabure and Torchia, 2015). Nor did it appeal to the rest of Chilean society, which saw the link between educational opportunities and their shared concern with inequality. Later in the year, labor unions joined students in protest.

The gulf between society and the state had only grown greater by the time of the 2013 elections. If *Alianza* was faulted for not addressing inequality, voters also knew that *Concertación* shared the blame. Eager to refresh its image, *Concertación* incorporated a few parties further to the left that ran student candidates (including the Communist Party), and changed its name to *Nueva Mayoría* (New Majority). Michelle Bachelet returned to the presidency under its candidacy, but there was little wind behind the sails of this electoral victory. Over 7 million voted in the 2009 elections; this time, just over 5.5 million bothered to show. And, to signal protest, 10 percent of all voters marked their ballots "AC" to convey their desire for a constitutional assembly (*asamblea constitucional*) to completely overhaul the political system. Few could doubt that Chile faced a true crisis of representation.

Bachelet was keenly aware of the crisis, and knew that education reform had to be a priority. But once again the strictures of the Pinochet era came into play. The Chilean Constitution enshrines many neoliberal policy commitments in "organic laws," which require supermajorities of 4/7 to change, rather than in ordinary law. Unsurprisingly, education falls under an organic law. With only slim majorities, Bachelet and her party will need to compromise. But *Nueva Mayoría* and *Alianza* alike recognize that something has to be done to address the crisis of representation. It did not help in 2014 when members within both coalitions were implicated in corruption scandals involving kickbacks and illicit contributions to campaigns by major businesses. Bachelet has in many ways set the calculus for political change. In her 2014 annual address to the country, she called for a new constitution, and by the following year laid out plans for a constitutional assembly to possibly do so. Fully aware that a constitutional assembly might leave them completely out of the process, *Alianza* members agreed to cooperate on significant congressional reforms.

Perhaps most significantly, in 2015 congress agreed to scrap the binomial electoral system in favor of proportional representation. Under the new rules, the chamber will emerge from 28 districts with three to eight representatives each, and the senate will have 15 districts with two to five representatives. Thirty-five more seats will be

(*continued*)

added to the chamber, and 12 to the senate to better accommodate a proportional allotment of seats. The increased numbers also helped to soften the blow for individual members of the *Alianza*. The binomial system favored the coalition, and the new one will probably reduce its share of congress. But with more seats, the same absolute number of *Alianza* members might still retain their positions. In another move to address the crisis of representation, congress enacted a gender quota for the first time. But the goal of gender equality in Chile interestingly illustrates the difficulty of institutional crafting when multiple goals come into play. In particular, to increase transparency in politics and broaden voter choice, Chile's parties had implemented primary elections for the very first time in 2013. To balance voter input and the gender quota, the 2015 reform allows up to 40 percent of a party's candidates to be selected through primaries, so that the remainder can be selected with an eye toward the quota. But another facet of the electoral law also competes with the gender quota. Chile will institute an open-list form of proportional representation (see Chapter 7), allowing voters to rank representatives on their own. Like primaries, this reform offers voters more influence and helps to address charges of elitism in political parties. But it also undermines the ability of party leaders to ensure that a minimum of 40 percent of *elected* representatives are women.

The changes to the electoral system and congress will take place for the first time in the 2017 elections. Whether they help to address the crisis of representation has yet to be seen. But one thing is doubtless: As the barometer of Chilean democracy, changes in congress will pace changes in Chilean democracy—for good or for worse.

Discussion Questions

1   Describe how changes in the Congress of Chile have paralleled greater democratization in Chile. What does this case tell us about the relationship between legislatures and democratization?

2   How can the Congress of Chile best maintain its legitimacy and popular support: By ensuring the representation of a diverse range of groups in society? By upholding its ability to balance off presidential power? Or by encouraging independent initiatives by legislators? How do these goals conflict with each other?

Conclusion

In Latin America, congress takes the brunt of the criticism when the people grow dissatisfied with government—despite the fact that no democracy could survive without a congress. But this may be why congress is such a target of criticism. In Latin America, congresses must make do with meager budgets, weakly institutionalized party systems ensure a constant turnover of offices and constrain the growth of experience, electoral rules add to the proliferation of parties and difficulty of creating majorities, and constitutional provisions hand over many lawmaking powers to the executive. Congresses in Latin America do have room to improve so that they can take their due place in democratic politics. Many have begun to shed their elitist reputation as previously disenfranchised or excluded groups such as women and the indigenous have made their way into office, in no small part due to important institutional changes. As illustrated by the case of Chile, the more a congress embraces the competitive politics that rest at the core of democratic politics, the more it helps to enrich democracy. The less it does so, the less it does for the prospects for democracy.

Key Terms

parliament   172
congress   172
constituency service   173
delegate model   174
trustee model   174
politics of patronage   175
caucus groups   177
plenary session   180
committee   180
discharge petition   181
general debate   182
specific debate   182
quorum   183

vertical accountability   183
horizontal accountability   184
interpellation   184
impeachment   185
audit agencies   186
ombudsman   187
strong bicameralism   202
navette   203
initiating chamber   203
reviewing chamber   203
conference committee   203
joint session   203

Discussion Questions

1   What is the difference between a parliament and a congress? Is one more democratic than the other?
2   Consider all the steps required for a bill to become a law, and create your own procedures. What considerations guide your design (consensus, efficiency, accountability, etc.)?
3   What prevents congresses from effectively balancing off the power of an executive or judiciary? What are the most practical and immediate steps available to empower a congress?
4   Why are congresses the target of such intense criticism? Is this criticism warranted, or is it the result of ignorance?

Notes

1 "Interview with Peruvian President Alberto Fujimori." *NotiSur*, November 17, 1992.
2 Data accessed at www.latinobarometro.org.
3 Semi-presidential systems use either designation. France uses the term *parliament*, and Peru uses *congress*. Both are semi-presidential systems.
4 For information on legislative committees devoted to women's issues, see Parline Database: Specialized Parliamentary Bodies, located on the web site of the InterParliamentary Union, at www.ipu.org.
5 Argentina, Chile, the Dominican Republic, Ecuador, El Salvador, Honduras, and Mexico do not impose deadlines.
6 This is the case under certain conditions in Argentina, Bolivia, Costa Rica, the Dominican Republic, Guatemala, Panama, and Paraguay.
7 On variations in scheduling procedures, see Alemán (2006), pp. 32–33. For the precise formula used by the Assembly of Costa Rica, see Article 35 of Rules of the Legislative Assembly, available at www.asamblea.go.cr/reglamnt/regla000 .htm.
8 Members of the U.S. Senate do not face debate limitations, and can therefore permanently delay bills with the use of the filibuster. The filibuster is not found in Latin America, even though the term has Latin American origins (U.S. citizens who traveled to Latin America in the nineteenth century to foment rebellion or otherwise cause trouble for personal gain were known as *filibusteros*, or freebooters).
9 Constitution of Guatemala, Article 179.
10 Many of the details on the rules for parliamentary procedure are found in legal documents outside the constitution. In Latin America, these supplementary texts are often referred to as organic laws. For Guatemala, see "Ley orgánica del organismo legislativo, decreto número 63-94 del Congreso de la República," available at www.congreso.gob.gt/Pdf/Normativa/DECRETO63-94Ley_Organica.pdf.
11 Other aspects of vertical accountability include recall, referendum, and initiative opportunities, as well as the ability of the media and civil society to assess and report on the performance of public officials. On both vertical and horizontal accountability, see O'Donnell, 1994.
12 Here Adams was specifically referring to relations between the House, Senate, and president. See Adams 1851, p. 462.
13 Brazil, Chile, the Dominican Republic, Ecuador, Honduras, Mexico, and Nicaragua have no constitutional provisions that allow for censure motions.
14 Ley N° 26520, Diario Oficial. Lima. August 8, 1995.
15 Web page of the Defender of the People in Peru: www.defensoria.gob.pe/mision-vision.php.
16 "Ombudsman Rewriting Peru's History." *Los Angeles Times*. November 7, 2000, p. A-4.
17 The 2015 Annual Report can be found on the website of the Defender of the People in Peru. See Decimonoveno Informe Annual de la Defensoría del Pueblo. Lima: Defensoría del Pueblo. January–December 2015.
18 See "Internet 2.0: Avances de los Sitios Web de los Poderes Legislativos de las Américas." RED-FTiP Américas (Red de Funcionarios de Tecnología de la Información en los Parlamentos de las Américas). Study available at: www.ictparliament.org/worldeparliamentconference2008/documentation/INTERNET%20 2.0%20Sitios%20Web%20America%20Latina.pdf.
19 See www.transparencialegislativa.org.
20 The actual number varies significantly from one representative to another because of differences in district sizes and the use of multimember districts, but this figure is useful for comparative purposes.

21 Chile is more complex. A failed bill in the originating chamber must wait one full year before it is reintroduced. However, if the president introduced the bill, the president can demand a vote in the reviewing chamber. If the bill receives a two-thirds majority, the initiating chamber can then kill the bill only with its own two-thirds vote.

22 See description on the Web page of the Chamber of Deputies: www.camara.cl/camara/historia_congreso.aspx.

Suggested Readings

John Carey. 2009. *Legislative Voting and Accountability.* **New York: Cambridge University Press.** John Carey takes a careful look at how the voting behavior of legislatures is affected by issues of accountability. He identifies how accountability is not a straightforward process. It depends on the transparency of policymaking, and accountability toward citizens often competes with a legislator's accountability toward party leaders and the effort to be decisive. This is a broadly comparative study—rich in theory—but Latin America comprises a significant portion of the casework.

Eduardo Alemán and George Tsebelis. 2016. *Legislative Institutions and Lawmaking in Latin America.* **New York: Oxford University Press.** This edited volume takes a detailed look at the constitutional and congressional rules covering the proposal, amendment, and vetoing of legislation in Argentina, Brazil, Chile, Colombia, Mexico, Peru, and Uruguay. It uses a framework to illustrate how the strictures of institutional rules channel the policy positions and strategies of relevant political actors. Understanding the composure of legislative institutions is shown to offer insight into the relative strength and influence of the executive as well.

Scott Morgenstern and Benito Nacif. 2002. *Legislative Politics in Latin America.* **New York: Cambridge University Press.** This book delivers an authoritative overview of the theory and concepts relevant to legislative studies of Latin America. In a series of case studies, it examines the relationship of legislatures to executives, political parties, and the policy process. Rather than offering a sweeping criticism of legislatures in presidential systems, the studies highlight the institutional details that either support or work against continued democratic consolidation.

Leslie A. Schwindt-Bayer. 2010. *Political Power and Women's Representation in Latin America.* **New York: Oxford University Press.** The growth of women's representation in Latin America has been dramatic, and the subject is finally gaining more attention as a central line of study. Schwindt-Bayer explains the variations in representation across countries, and also provides a detailed study of how representation works—from voting to constituency service. The study illustrates how institutions play a central role in women's representation in its many forms.

References

Adams, John. 1851. "A Defence of the Constitutions of Government of the United States of America, volume I," in Charles Francis Adams, ed., *The Works of John Adams*, Vol. 4. Boston, MA: Charles C. Little and James Brown.

Agrawal, Nina, Richard André, Ryan Berger, and Wilda Escarfuller. 2012. *Political Representation, Policy and Inclusion: A Comparative Study of Bolivia, Colombia, Ecuador, and Guatemala*. New York: Americas Society.

Al-Jazeera. 2011. "Chilean President Berates Students over Protest." August 11. Available at www.aljazeera.com.

Alemán, Eduardo. 2006. "Policy Gatekeepers in Latin American Legislatures." *Latin American Politics and Society* 48:3, pp. 125–55.

Arnold, Jason Ross. 2013. "Parliaments and Citizens in Latin America," in Cristina Leston-Bandeira, ed., *Parliaments and Citizens*, pp. 177–98. New York: Routledge.

Barkan, Joel D. 2008. "Legislatures on the Rise?" *Journal of Democracy* 19:2, pp. 124–37.

Buvinic, Mayra, and Vivian Roza. 2004. "Women in Latin American Politics: Trends and Prospects," in Karen Mokate, ed., *Women's Participation in Social Development: Experiences from Asia, Latin America, and the Caribbean*, pp. 193–210. Washington, DC: Inter-American Development Bank.

Carrillo Flórez, Fernando. 2007. "Institutions of Democratic Accountability in Latin America: Legal Design versus Actual Performance," in J. Mark Payne, Daniel Zovatto G., and Mercedes Mateo Díaz, eds., *Democracies in Development: Politics and Reform in Latin America*, pp. 117–48. Washington, DC: Inter-American Development Bank.

Coppedge, Michael. 1994. *Strong Parties and Lame Ducks: Presidential Partyarchy and Factionalism in Venezuela*. Palo Alto, CA: Stanford University Press.

Cox, Gary W., and Scott Morgenstern. 2001. "Latin America's Reactive Assemblies and Proactive Presidents." *Comparative Politics* 33:2 (January), pp. 171–189.

Cummings, Peter M. M. 2015. "Democracy and Student Discontent: Chilean Student Protest in the Post-Pinochet Era." *Journal of Politics in Latin America* 7:3, pp. 49–84.

Department for International Development (DFID). 2004. "Characteristics of Different External Audit Systems." Policy Division Info series. PD Info 21. Available at www.dfid.gov.uk/aboutdfid/organisation/pfma/pfma-externalaudit-briefing.pdf.

Fish, M. Steven. 2006. "Stronger Legislatures, Stronger Democracies." *Journal of Democracy* 17:1 (January), pp. 5–20.

Fish, M. Steven, and Matthew Kroenig. 2009. *The Handbook of National Legislatures: A Global Survey*. New York: Cambridge University Press.

Global Centre for ICT in Parliament. 2012. *World e-Parliament Report 2012*. New York: United Nations. Available at www.ictparliament.org.

Hoffay, Mercedes, and Sofía Rivas. 2016. "The Indigenous in Latin America: 45 million with Little Voice." *Latin America Goes Global*. Available at latinamericagoesglobal.org.

Htun, Mala N., and Mark P. Jones. 2002. "Engendering the Right to Participate in Decision-Making: Electoral Quotas and Women's Leadership in Latin America," in K. Craske and M. Molyneux, eds., *Gender and the Politics of Rights and Democracy in Latin America*. New York: Palgrave.

Inter-Parliamentary Union (IPU). 2009. "Guidelines for Parliamentary Web Sites." Available at www.ipu.org/PDF/publications/web-e.pdf.

Inter Press Service. 2006, September 23. Angela Castellanos. "Latin America: Women Lawmakers Find Strength in Unity."

Larrabure, Manuel, and Carlos Torchia. 2015. "The 2011 Chilean Student Movement and the Struggle for a New Left." *Latin American Perspectives* 42:5, pp. 248–268.

Latinobarómetro. 2015. Informe Latinobarómetro 2015. Available online at latinobarómetro.org

Lijphart, Arend. 1999. *Patterns of Democracy: Government Forms and Performance in Thirty-Six Countries.* New Haven, CT: Yale University Press.

Llanos, Mariana, and Detlef Nolte. 2003. "Bicameralism in the Americas: Around the Extremes of Symmetry and Incongruence." *Journal of Legislative Studies* 9:3, pp. 54–86.

Llanos, Mariana, and Francisco Sánchez. 2006. "Council of Elders: The Senate and Its Members in the Southern Cone." *Latin American Research Review* 41:1, pp. 133–52.

Michener, Greg. 2012. *Parliamentary Power to the People: Analyzing Online and Offline Strategies in Latin America.* New York: Open Society Foundations. Available at www.opensocietyfoundations.org.

Montero, Alfred P. 2005. *Brazilian Politics: Reforming a Democratic State in a Changing World.* Cambridge, UK: Polity.

Morgenstern, Scott, and Luigi Manzetti. 2003. "Legislative Oversight: Interests and Institutions in the United States and Argentina," in Scott Mainwaring and Christopher Welna, eds., *Democratic Accountability in Latin America*, pp. 132–69. New York: Oxford University Press.

Navia, Patricio. 2004. "Legislative Candidate Selection in Chile." Paper prepared for the Pathways to Power: Political Recruitment and Democracy in Latin America symposium, April 3–4, 2004, Graylyn International Conference Center, Wake Forest University, Winston-Salem, NC.

NotiSur. 2016. "Questions Swirl after Peru's Congress Chooses New Ombudsman." September 30, 25: 37.

O'Donnell, Guillermo. 1994. "Delegative Democracy." *Journal of Democracy* 5:1, pp. 55–69.

Pérez Liñán, Aníbal. 2007. *Presidential Impeachment and the New Political Instability in Latin America.* New York: Cambridge University Press.

Polga-Hecimovich, John and Peter Siavelis. 2015. "Here's the Bias! A (Re-) Reassessment of the Chilean Electoral System." Electoral Studies 40, pp. 268–79.

Red Latinoamericana por la Transparencia Legislativa. 2014. *Indice Latinoamericano de Transparencia Legislative.* Available at www.indice2014.transparencialegislativa.org.

Samuels, David. 2003. *Ambition, Federalism, and Legislative Politics in Brazil.* New York: Cambridge University Press.

Santiso, Carlos. 2009. *The Political Economy of Government Auditing: Financial Governance and the Rule of Law in Latin America and Beyond.* New York: Routledge.

Schwindt-Bayer, Leslie A. 2006. "Still Supermadres? Gender and the Policy Priorities of Latin American Legislators." *American Journal of Political Science* 50:3, pp. 570–85.

Siavelis, Peter M. 2000. *The President and Congress in Post-Authoritarian Chile.* University Park, PA: Penn State University Press.

Smith, Peter. 2005. *Democracy in Latin America: Political Change in Comparative Perspective.* New York: Oxford University Press.

Tsebelis, George, and Jeannette Money. 1997. *Bicameralism.* New York: Cambridge.

Uggla, Frederik. 2004. "The Ombudsman in Latin America." *Journal of Latin American Studies* 36:3, pp. 423–60.

Uslaner, Eric, and Thomas Zittel. 2006. "Comparative Legislative Behavior," in R. A. W. Rhodes, Sarah A. Binder, and Bert A. Rockman, eds., *The Oxford Handbook of Political Institutions*, pp. 455–73. New York: Oxford University Press.

Valenzuela, Arturo. 1978. *The Breakdown of Democratic Regimes: Chile*. Baltimore, MD: Johns Hopkins University Press.

World Bank. 2015. *Indigenous Latin America in the Twenty-First Century: The First Decade*. Washington, DC: World Bank Group.

6 The Judiciary in Latin America
Separate but Unequal

Photo 6.1 A statue of Lady Justice sits in front of the Supreme Federal Court building in Brasília, Brazil.

Source: © Alamy

> The judiciary, and particularly the Supreme Court, must ensure that the Constitution and the laws are upheld. If they succeed, they will win the respect and following of the citizenry. If they fail, they will lose their prestige and power; moreover, this failure will open the doors to anarchy or oppression.
> —Raúl Alfonsín, President of Argentina, 1983–1987[1]

The judiciary is a pivotal and vulnerable institution. The congress makes laws and the president executes laws, but what of the settlement of disputes that emerge as the law is interpreted and/or applied? Such settlement, known as **adjudication**, is the primary responsibility of the judiciary. When the judiciary adjudicates fairly, it supports the rule of law and thereby plays an essential role for democracy. But curiously, the significance of this role is not matched with muscle. The judicial branch has the power of neither the purse nor military forces to compel obedience. It has only a reservoir of legitimacy to draw on to ensure that others will abide. The courts grow more powerful only as people *believe* that they are powerful. And should the judiciary fail to gain esteem, it is not just that this institution will then lose authority and lay idle as other political institutions grow more powerful. Rather, a decrepit judiciary will put the entire country at risk as the rule of law grows vulnerable to manipulation and abuse. As noted by Raúl Alfonsín, this is the situation that "opens the doors to anarchy or oppression."

But if the role of the judiciary is both pivotal and vulnerable, it is also puzzling. It can gain legitimacy only as it upholds the law, but in order to uphold the law it must brandish this legitimacy at the outset. The clout of a judiciary feeds upon itself. Unfortunately, in Latin America it has been difficult for the courts to position themselves as defenders of the rule of law. Historically, the legal tradition in the region discouraged judges from assuming an activist role to promote the rule of law. Even as militaries moved in to overthrow governments and rewrite constitutions, judges often carried on and simply adjudicated under the new, *de facto* rules enforced by authoritarian rule. The courts, then, did not enter the most recent democratic period with strong credentials. Even today, many look upon them as incompetent, or even untrustworthy. Lacking a favorable opinion to nourish their legitimacy, the courts find it difficult to play their part as potent adjudicators of the law, and democracy suffers.

This chapter examines the role of the judiciary and its contribution to democratic rule in Latin America. European influences affected the development of Latin American judiciaries more extensively than its congresses or executives. This has created unique challenges for Latin American democracies because the European influence, in the form of code law, is skeptical of empowered courts. Such suspicion, when placed within presidential systems that call for independent branches of government, means that in practice Latin American countries tend to have judiciaries that are formally separate but functionally unequal as branches of government. This has made it all the more difficult for the courts to support the rule of law. Of late, many have rightly portrayed judicial reform as crucial to continued democratic consolidation. To assess the role of the court and the challenges of judicial reform, this chapter will compare and contrast the legal traditions of common law and code law; review measures of judicial independence, power, access, and efficiency; and discuss the relevance of courts in contemporary Latin America. The chapter concludes with a case study of the judicial branch in Mexico.

Approaches to Judicial Organization

What is the source of law? What is the function of a judge? What sort of powers should a judge wield? Should the judiciary act as a check on the executive and legislative branches of government? How should courts be organized? Adjudication appears to be a straightforward process, but as with other institutions, the judiciary is open to a range of designs. In western political thought, two principal legal traditions have guided judicial design. The **common law** tradition emerged in Great Britain, and took root in many of its colonies, most significantly in the United States. **Code law** has a deeper history reaching back to the Roman Empire, though the French Revolution would fashion its approach to public and administrative law. As we shall see, most Latin American states fell sway to code law, but proximity to the United States and its political ideas opened a door of influence from common law thought. Still, this influence remained incomplete and affected some countries more than others. In Latin America, code law became the norm, with some mixtures from common law.

Common Law and Code Law Traditions

Common law presumes that the legal order emerges over time through the interplay of the legislature and the courts. Legislatures are expected to work under the rubric of natural law. They assess dominant customs and habits in society, and then enact statutes that reflect these traditions. Nonetheless, their statutes may be ambiguous, contradictory, or incomplete. Worse yet, they may conflict with the ultimate legal expression of dominant values in the country—the constitution. The judiciary, charged with the duty to supervise the rendition of law, acts as a sort of traffic cop. It is supposed to right the legislature when it strays from the course of natural law or pathways charted by existing statutes, or when it fails to plainly spell out the direction and scope of legislation. To do so, judges inevitably assume a lawmaking function as they interpret existing law to resolve inconsistencies or fill gaps in legislative action. Their interpretations occur as cases are heard and decisions are made in all the courts of the land, and thus it is very important that these decisions remain consistent and build upon one another. Judges ensure this steadiness and strengthen the legal order as they follow precedent, a practice known as *stare decisis*.

Judges thus add certainty to the law, but common law practices shoulder them with additional responsibilities. Common law recognizes that the legal order should be adjusted over time as circumstances change, or even recalibrated to accommodate a unique case. In addition, common law systems concede that statutes may be unduly harsh under certain circumstances, so they allow judges some discretion to moderate the application of law. Hence, in the end, common laws systems embrace not only certainty, but also flexibility and equity, and confer upon judges the duty to balance these often-competing values (Merryman and Pérez-Perdomo, 2007, p. 49).

When it comes to actual disputes between litigants, under common law judges play the role of a referee in three arenas. The first pits citizens against each other (civil law), the second matches the government against citizens (criminal law), while the third sees different government branches or agencies confront each other (constitutional law). In each, a judge interprets and applies the law to mediate disputes. To ensure an equal playing field in the first arena, citizens receive a number of protections such as the right against self-incrimination, *habeas corpus*, and a presumption of innocence. These safeguards remind us that the government itself is beholden to the law. The understanding that law stands above the state makes common law systems much more agreeable to granting courts the power of **judicial review**, a function that originated in the United States. Alexis de Tocqueville noted in the nineteenth century, "this power is the only one which is peculiar to the American magistrate," and defined judicial review as "the right of judges to found their decisions on the constitution rather than the laws" (1900, p. 98). Ultimately, the prerogative allows a judge to nullify acts of government.

It is not surprising that common law emerged in Great Britain. Its gradual and relatively uninterrupted political development nourished a deep sense of reverence for customary law and the idea that natural law rested above the state. Likewise, common law reflects the country's admiration for commercial liberalism insofar as the judiciary acts as a restraint on government. But few countries have shared a similar history. Most worked their way through turbulent rebellious and revolutionary periods, and did not necessarily share the adoration for limited government. Seeking political stability and the founding of a new political order, many looked to the state for a wholesale codification of the law. The tradition reaches back to Roman times, but the French Revolution provided the most famous inspiration for such thought. Its advocates sought a clean break with the *ancien régime*, which included the institutions of monarchy and feudalism, as well as the Catholic Church. Judges, who had long protected and legitimated these institutions, immediately became the object of scorn. According to French revolutionaries, a true democracy requires that the people be placed firmly in control of the law. And as a practical measure, because parliament represents the people, it should gain full command of the law. The nationalism of the French Revolution also influenced the development of code law. It galvanized the view that law should emerge not from murky traditions that cut across state boundaries or from foreign institutions such as the Catholic Church, but only from popularly elected government officials.

So what of the role of judges? They are common administrators. Their application of the law as they mediate disputes is tightly controlled by the detailed codes of the legislature that clarify the basis and breadth of every decision. In the end, they are mere bureaucrats with no authority to shape the law. In fact, to this day French jurists are known to remark, "*la loi est la loi*" ("the law is the law"), as they adjudicate. The phrase could not more clearly embrace the values of code law—the law is that which is written by legislators; there is no room for judicial interpretation. Far from the task granted to judges in common laws systems to balance flexibility, equity, and certainty, code law charges the legislature alone to safeguard flexibility and equity, and views judicial interpretation as a threat to the certainty provided by legislative codes (Merryman and Pérez-Perdomo, 2007, p. 82).

Common law and code law deliver unmistakable consequences for the role that courts play in the everyday lives of citizens. In a common law system, the law stands above the state, and given disputes between citizens and the state, it is up to the courts to mediate as they adjudicate. In code law systems, the law is an instrument of the state, and the courts are in turn agents of the government. Faced with a dispute between a citizen and the state, judges act as delegates of the state. They often initiate investigations and personally question witnesses. Such differences illustrate the very different proceedings that we find in common law and code law courts. One might identify the trial as the heart and soul of a common law proceeding. Here, a plaintiff and defendant square off in the presence of a jury. They are represented by lawyers, who take center stage in what often appears to be a theatrical production. Lawyers carefully craft the presentation of evidence and witnesses, all with an eye toward persuading a jury. The proceedings are "concentrated" into a trial event, interrupted only by recesses. But no such "theatrical concentration" takes place in a judicial proceeding under the code law tradition. Instead, the process takes places in a series of meetings, and largely through written correspondence between the counsels and judge. The affair is hardly public. Indeed, due to the presumption of an exhaustive, unambiguous code, as well as a diligent judge, a jury is considered irrelevant, if not inappropriate. After all, to hand over the ruling to a jury of one's peers is to introduce opportunities for manipulation and error in what should otherwise be a straightforward application of the law. "*La loi est la loi.*"

Mixed Judicial Systems in Latin America

Continental Europe had embraced code law well before the colonial period, and so it is of little surprise that the legal thought made its way to the colonies of Spain and Portugal. Add to this the appeal of the French Revolution at the time of independence and the shared sense that a new political order had to be constructed, and we can understand the influence of code law in the region. But as we have seen, the ideas surrounding the American Revolution and its constitution also gained a foothold in Latin America. Why was influence from the north weaker when it came to judicial design?

At the outset, we should not confuse the U.S. judiciary of today with the U.S. judiciary during the independence period in Latin America. The hallmark of the court's power, judicial review, was not even found in the 1789 Constitution, but rather emerged after the 1803 *Marbury v. Madison* decision by the Supreme Court. And thereafter, through much of the nineteenth century, the high court attenuated its newfound power, exercising it primarily in cases that addressed disputes over the relative powers of states and the federal government. It is not surprising, then, that the U.S. influence on courts would be felt chiefly in the federal states of Latin America— Mexico in its 1857 Constitution, Argentina in the 1860 amendments to its 1853 Constitution, and in Brazil after it moved from monarchy to republic under the 1891 Constitution (Kommers, 1976, pp. 55–56). Judicial review and other common law ideas would gain more traction in the entire region over time, but would have to come to terms with established code law norms. An interesting blend of the two legal traditions evolved.

For example, the thought of granting the judiciary power to evaluate acts of government resonated in Latin America. But it produced a unique form of judicial review, the *amparo*, which emerged as a by-product to the then-novel idea of listing fundamental rights. The move to list basic human rights first appeared in the "Declaration of Rights" drafted by the Convention of Virginia in 1776. The U.S. Bill of Rights repeated the effort in 1791, as did the "Declaration of the Rights of Man and of the Citizen," found in the first French Constitution (1791). But the third declaration of rights by an independent state in world history occurred in Venezuela in 1811, after the Supreme Congress of Venezuela adopted the "Declaration of Rights of the People" and later added it to the country's first constitution. The trend caught fire and soon countries throughout Latin America included lists of civil liberties and political rights in their constitutions. But it is one thing to list rights, and it is another to safeguard them. *Caudillo* rule in the early nineteenth century hollowed out these declarative lists, and unfortunately meant that the state itself was the usual suspect when violations occurred. One of the countries hardest hit by *caudillo* rule was Mexico. Prompted to act, and influenced by judicial thought in the United States due to its proximity (not to mention the 1845–1848 war between the two), the Mexican Constitution of 1857 introduced the *amparo* form of judicial review by charging the judicial branch with the protection of those civil and political rights declared in the constitution (Kommers, 1976, p. 57).

How does the power work in practice? As originally designed, the writ of *amparo* (from the Spanish *amparar*—to protect) defines an explicit procedure that grants all citizens the right to file suit against the state, should it violate any of the fundamental rights guaranteed in the constitution. It is broader than the more conventional idea of *habeas corpus*, which protects citizens specifically against unlawful arrests and detentions. It is a form of judicial review in that it empowers the courts to guarantee the conformity of government actions to the constitution. Despite this nod to common law thought, *amparo* also suggests the thinking of code law, in that *amparo* court decisions have only *inter partes* effects—that is, they can affect only the case at hand (as compared to a case with *erga omnes* effects, which is applicable to everyone). Also, although the *amparo* might appear to be similar to the "injunction" a U.S. court uses to cease government action under threat of contempt, to this day most Latin American judges lack any contempt power to back their decisions. Similarly, a successful *amparo* decision rarely produces any type of compensation for the plaintiff. Reflective of the value that code law places on judicial restraint, the decision is meant to protect rights rather than to condemn defendants, and in general the proceeding is supposed to be protective and restorative rather than compensatory (Merryman and Pérez-Perdomo, 2007, pp. 377–396). Judges in Latin America are thus both empowered and restricted in their *amparo* faculties. Soon after Mexico pioneered the proceeding, El Salvador, Honduras, and Nicaragua added *amparo* procedures to their constitutions, and through the twentieth century, the rest of the region (except for Cuba) followed suit.[2] Several code law countries in Europe also adopted the proceeding.

Constitutional law in Latin America also reflects this blending of code and common law. As noted, code law traditionally stood averse to the notion of any sort of judicial review, but this position became increasingly difficult to sustain through the nineteenth century. Over time, democratic rule became synonymous with a written constitution, and this called for some institution to ensure that all acts of government complied with the rule of law. The judiciary seemed a natural choice, but code law purists still eyed the branch with suspicion. Others feared that any form of constitutional review would politicize the judiciary. Austrian legal theorists Hans Kelsen and Adolf Merkl developed a compromise solution that handed exclusive authority of constitutional review to a tribunal, which would sit independent of the judiciary. In its ideal form, the tribunal would be staffed not only by judges, but more so by lawyers, legal scholars, or even eminent politicians— all individuals thought to be more attuned to the political currents of the day. And to further ensure the political responsiveness of the institution, members would hold limited terms and the legislature would retain appointment powers. The concentrated nature of this form of constitutional review stands in contrast to the diffuse **U.S. model**, where a court at any level can exert the power. There are two other distinctions between the U.S. model and what could be considered the **European model**. Under the U.S. formula, adjudication is concrete (it requires an actual case) and, by logical extension, it is also *a posteriori* (a decision is made only after the enactment of a law). Under the European model, adjudication can be either concrete or abstract (a ruling can be made as part of a hypothetical inquiry), and it can be either *a posteriori* or *a priori* (conducted before the actual enactment of a law).

Kelsen and Merkl's ideas quickly found their way into the Austrian Constitution of 1920, but were picked up by several other European countries after WWII. For many code law adherents, the atrocities associated with Nazi rule in Germany confirmed that the legislature could not be blindly trusted to protect the law from political manipulation. Others, still suspicious of judicial ties to the old guard or doubtful of their commitment to democracy, firmly advised against U.S.-style form of judicial review.

The constitutional tribunal appeared to accommodate all concerns. In Latin America, some of these same anxieties plagued constitutional designers in the aftermath of the brutal military regimes of the 1960s to 1980s. They were especially worried about judges who simply stood aside as authoritarian governments trampled over the rule of law, and about those who in some cases actually justified military rule.

It is difficult to place Latin American judiciaries squarely under the U.S. or European model. Common law practices have crept into the region, but they have had to compromise with standing code law traditions. For example, following code law traditions, most Latin American countries have adopted a judicial structure with multiple sets of courts, each with their own jurisdiction and rules. Ordinary courts address most matters of civil and criminal law, but there are also administrative courts to assess the conduct of government action, agrarian courts to mediate clashes over land tenure, electoral courts that collect allegations of voter fraud or campaign irregularities, labor courts for disputes in the workplace, and more controversially, military courts staffed by the armed forces themselves (see Chapter 10). Which of these courts look to the Supreme Court as a final court of appeal, and which retain final appeal rights, varies from country to country. In many countries, the constitutional tribunal also stands structurally separate—though in others the Supreme Court itself acts as the constitutional court. In sum, far from the singular pyramid configuration we see in the United States, where all courts look to the Supreme Court as a final court of appeal and most work according to similar rules, in most Latin American countries the judicial structure takes the form of multiple pyramids standing side by side. And within each—be they the administrative courts, ordinary courts, agrarian courts, or otherwise—the rules of adjudication can differ. They may allow centralized or diffuse review, decide cases *a posteriori* or *a priori*, take on concrete or abstract cases, have *erga omnes* or *inter partes* effects, and embrace *stare decisis* to different extents. For this reason, Latin American systems are best described as mixed systems (Navia and Ríos-Figueroa, 2005).

The Rule of Law

Defining the Rule of Law

The **rule of law** implies the existence of comprehensive, explicit legal guidelines to direct the decisions made by government. It is meant to guarantee that all are treated equally under the law, and to guard against arbitrary decisions or the manipulation of the law by powerful individuals or groups. References to the concept reach back to antiquity, perhaps most famously to Aristotle's deliberation over which is preferable—"the rule of the best man or the rule of the best law."[3] One of the more influential modern studies comes from Joseph Raz, who attempted to lay out preconditions for the rule of law:

1   The law should be unambiguous, publicized, and comprehensive.
2   The law should be relatively stable.
3   The process by which laws themselves are made should be open, stable, clear, and comprehensive.
4   The independence of the judiciary must be guaranteed.
5   Principles of natural justice (e.g., open and fair hearings and the absence of bias) must be observed.
6   The courts should have review powers over legislative and administrative actions to ensure conformity to the rule of law.
7   The courts should be easily accessible.
8   The discretion of crime-prevention authorities (the police and public prosecutors) should be bound by the law. (1983, pp. 214–218)

Raz recognizes that his list is incomplete. For example, it says nothing about the efficiency of the judiciary, and he concedes that the rule of law could be supported through constitutional review by an institution other than the judiciary. As an illustration, few would question the rule of law in Great Britain, yet there is no judicial review in the country; parliament holds the final say over the constitutionality of the law. Nonetheless, the list does demonstrate that it is possible to formulate standards to assess the rule of law. Moreover, it exposes the essential role of the judiciary. If one is to ensure equal protection and guard against capricious acts by government, it is difficult to envision how this might be done without a judiciary.

This connection between the rule of law and the judiciary is important because the rule of law is considered to be so fundamental to political development. Lacking a staunch judiciary, it is almost impossible for a country to achieve liberal democracy, with truly competitive elections and meaningful protections for civil liberties. Some scholars place doubt on the ability of a regime even to sustain an electoral democracy absent the rule of law, and refer to illiberal democracies to distinguish regimes that may advertise democratic proceedings on their legal parchment, but in fact exhibit widespread lawlessness and abuses of power.[4] In addition, analysts have tied the rule of law to economic development insofar as the predictability of government acts and the faithful regulation of contracts instill business confidence and attract investment (North, 1990). The World Bank annually compiles a database that ranks countries on the rule of law as a measure of development. Only four Latin American countries—Chile, Costa Rica, Panama and Uruguay—sit in the top one-half of all countries. And half of all countries examined languish in the bottom one-third of all countries (see Table 6.1).

Table 6.1 **World Bank Measures of the Rule of Law in Latin America.** Lack of adherence to the rule of law remains one of the most troubling features of democratic regimes in Latin America

Country	Rule of Law Score (2015)	Percentile Rank (2015)
Chile	+1.30	87.0
Uruguay	+0.70	74.5
Costa Rica	+0.50	69.2
Panama	–0.10	53.4
Brazil	–0.20	50.0
Colombia	–0.30	44.7
Dominican Republic	–0.50	38.0
Mexico	–0.50	37.5
Peru	–0.50	34.6
El Salvador	–0.60	31.7
Paraguay	–0.70	28.4
Nicaragua	–0.70	27.9
Argentina	–0.80	22.1
Honduras	–1.00	16.8
Guatemala	–1.00	15.4
Bolivia	–1.20	11.1
Ecuador	–1.00	13.9
Venezuela	–2.00	0.5

*The World Bank Rule scores range from 2.5 to –2.5. The percentile rank compares the governance score of a country globally. See http://info.worldbank.org/governance/wgi/mc_chart.asp#.

The Judiciary's Contribution to the Rule of Law

To evaluate the role of the courts in the rule of law, analysts have developed a number of concepts, but four stand out: **power, independence, access,** and **efficiency**. These concepts describe the judiciary along two dimensions. Judicial power and independence tell us something about the interplay between the courts and other government agencies (especially the executive and legislative branches). On the other hand, access and efficiency have more to do with the relationship between the judiciary and the people. In order for a judiciary to contribute to the rule of law, it must perform well on both of these dimensions.

The Judiciary and Other Government Institutions: Power and Independence

Judicial review is the principal indicator of judicial power. Courts can express this power in two ways. Ordinary judicial review determines whether government action complies with ordinary law, while constitutional judicial review gauges compliance with the constitution itself. Individuals are far more likely to come into contact with ordinary judicial review than with constitutional judicial review, for it is here that the most common complaints are directed toward government. These complaints may be related to government pensions, taxes, social welfare programs, business regulations, school administration, postal services, construction codes—in short, any of the ways in which government administration affects the everyday lives of individuals. It is of little surprise that the ability of a court to address these grievances determines, for many individuals, their assessment of the judiciary.

Unfortunately, Latin American judiciaries face several impediments to ordinary judicial review. Code law, so inclined to disconnect judicial activities from lawmaking, called for the creation of administrative courts separate from the judicial branch to adjudicate government actions in ordinary law. Most countries have not strictly followed this model, and allow individuals to either initiate administrative complaints in the judicial branch or make appeals to the judicial branch. Still, the general result is a hodgepodge of sector-specific courts for the different areas of government administration. Because each court maintains its own particular procedures on litigation, the structure hinders the development of a professional corps of administrative law specialists able to support a range of complaints. Moreover, the aversion to *erga omnes* effects hampers the courts' ability to address complaints from multiple individuals in a single case. For example, rather than emitting one sweeping decision on a government act that illegally reduced pension benefits, each retiree would have to initiate a claim in court and each case would have to be decided, one by one (Hammergren, 2007, pp. 192–195).

As noted above and as described in Table 6.2, Latin American countries cannot be easily distinguished by their use of different types of constitutional judicial review, because most incorporate more than one route and type of review. Argentina is the only exception. There, review takes place exclusively in a fashion similar to the United States—the power is open to any individual with standing; the process is diffuse, concrete, and

Table 6.2 **Institutional Variations in the Judicial Systems of Latin America.** Differences in institutions significantly affect the power and influence of Latin American courts

Country	A Priori Review of Gov't Statutes[a]	Concentrated or Diffuse Review[b]	Constitutional Tribunal[b]	Magistrate Council: Proportion of Judges	Magistrate Council: Power[a]	Public Prosecutor's Office: Location
Argentina	no	diffuse	no	25%	medium	autonomous
Bolivia	no	diffuse	yes	20%	medium	autonomous
Brazil	no	diffuse	(chamber)[c]	100%	weak	judiciary
Chile	yes	diffuse	yes	n/a	n/a	autonomous
Colombia	no	diffuse	yes	100%	powerful	autonomous
Costa Rica	yes	concentrated	(chamber)[c]	60%	medium	judiciary
Dom Rep	no	diffuse	no	no data	no data	executive
Ecuador	yes	diffuse	yes	13%	powerful	judiciary
El Salvador	no	concentrated	(chamber)[c]	0	medium	autonomous
Guatemala	yes	concentrated	yes	60%	medium	autonomous
Honduras	no	concentrated	(chamber)[c]	no data	no data	autonomous
Mexico	no	concentrated	no	100%	powerful	executive
Nicaragua	no	concentrated	no	n/a	n/a	independent

Country	A Priori Review of Gov't Statutes[a]	Concentrated or Diffuse Review[b]	Constitutional Tribunal[b]	Magistrate Council: Proportion of Judges	Magistrate Council: Power[d]	Public Prosecutor's Office: Location
Panama	no	diffuse	no	63%	weak	judiciary
Paraguay	no	concentrated	no	13%	medium	executive
Peru	yes	diffuse	yes	14%	medium	autonomous
Uruguay	no	concentrated	no	43%	powerful	executive
Venezuela	yes	diffuse	(chamber)[c]	50%	powerful	executive

[a] Data from www.concourts.net.

[b] Data from Hammergren (2007), pp. 196–197.

[c] A chamber of the Supreme Court holds constitutional review power.

[d] Data from Garoupa and Ginsburg, 2008. "Power" is scored on the following basis: weak—purely administrative functions; medium—involvement in appointments; powerful—roles in appointments, discipline, removal, and promotion.

a posteriori; and depending on the procedure the decision may have either *erga omnes* or *inter partes* effects. Perhaps due to the complexity of Latin American court systems, few analysts have attempted to apply comparative measures of judicial power to the region. Most studies focus on single countries, or comparisons of a few cases. Nevertheless, there is some agreement that Brazil, Colombia, Costa Rica, and Mexico have the strongest courts in the region. Scholars have also noted the extensive formal powers granted to judiciaries in Argentina and Chile, but recognize that judges in both countries tend to be reluctant to assert those powers (Kapiszewski and Taylor, 2008).

The question of judicial power is closely linked to that of judicial independence (Cameron, 2002). In theory, one can note how little it means to be empowered if some other actor controls the exertion of that power. For this reason, many indicators of judicial independence also provide some insight into the possibilities for judicial power. Locating the highest court of appeal for constitutional questions provides a rather blunt indicator of independence. The constitutional tribunals in Bolivia, Chile, Colombia, Ecuador, Guatemala, and Peru rest outside of the judicial branch. In theory, there is a clear division of jurisdiction insofar as the tribunals deal exclusively with constitutional questions and the regular courts deal with questions of ordinary law, but in practice overlaps inevitably arise. Constitutional tribunals create an inroad to the Supreme Court's custody of ordinary legislation when they hold the power of concrete review, and the expansive listings of rights in constitutions have driven the regular courts to consider constitutional provisions when deciding civil or criminal cases (Garlicki, 2007). Having two "high courts"—let alone the other independent courts that exist in code law systems—can produce confusion or tensions, and can open the door to political meddling by other members of government. Chile has successfully avoided overt conflicts with a strict division of labor between its two courts. The Constitutional Tribunal holds the exclusive authority to exert *a priori* review, while the Supreme Court can assert only *a posteriori* review.

If the Supreme Court alone acts as the constitutional arbiter, another question to consider is whether the entire court of Supreme Court justices decides constitutional cases, or only a select group of magistrates does, as in Brazil, Costa Rica, and Venezuela. Such organization can create a layer of insulation to help guard the autonomy of the court as politicians appoint members to the court as a whole. In addition, a smaller number of justices can more easily foster a sense of camaraderie to feed the sense of empowerment.

Since the 1990s, nongovernmental organizations (NGOs) and foreign aid providers have increasingly focused on the supportive role of the courts in new or fragile democracies. Constitutional courts have received special attention under the presumption that they can galvanize judicial efforts to shore up the rule of law. The International Foundation for Electoral Systems, a U.S.-based NGO, offers the following list of "best practices" in one of its studies:

1 *Right of constitutional review*: Most democracies around the world recognize some power to review the compatibility of legal norms to the constitution and the principles enshrined therein to the courts. Two dominant models of this core, democratic check on the power of the legislative and executive branches of government exist: (i) diffuse constitutional review by courts under the control of the Supreme Court (American model); or (ii) concentrated constitutional review by a constitutional court or chamber (European model).

2 *Creation of specialized constitutional courts/chambers*: Many emerging democracies have chosen to create constitutional courts in order to strengthen their democratic institutional framework. While all constitutional courts have a power of constitutional review of legal norms, the way they exercise this power and any additional powers entrusted to them vary greatly from country to country.

3 *Independence of the judiciary*: Constitutional courts, as guarantors of the integrity of the constitution and of fundamental rights, have an important role to play in consolidating democracy and the rule of law and in promoting judicial independence. The structure, composition and powers of constitutional courts must therefore be carefully crafted in order to protect the underlying principles of democracy such as separation of powers and judicial independence.

4 *Institutional independence*: There is an emerging consensus that constitutional courts should be granted a certain number of guarantees likely to protect their independence, including organizational autonomy, budgetary autonomy, clear rules of conflict of interest, objective and transparent appointment procedures, clear powers, binding effect of decisions, and high qualification requirements.

5 *Transparent appointments*: While there is no consensus as to the number of members or the length of their term, most specialists and reformers agree that the constitutional court members should be eminent jurists or public figures, known for their honesty and respect for constitutional principles. Moreover, their terms in office should be sufficiently long to guarantee their independence.

6 *Transparent and accountable decision-making process*: The nature of constitutional courts calls for the attribution of jurisdiction over a variety of issues, ranging from elections to civil liberties. While there is virtually no common package of powers identifiable among the constitutional courts existing around the world, there is consensus that these powers must be clearly defined and exercised in a transparent and objective manner in order to safeguard the integrity and legitimacy of the court.

7 *Access to information*: Clear information mechanisms must be in place for the public to access information on constitutional court processes and decisions. Moreover, the public should be fully aware of existing complaint mechanisms and procedures for protecting their constitutional rights (Autheman, 2004).

Another consideration is the location of the prosecutor's office. Prosecutors act as gatekeepers to the judicial process because of their control over the investigation of alleged crimes. Previous to 1970, well over half of Latin American countries stationed the prosecutor's office in the executive branch. Today, less than one-quarter do so. Most countries have either created an autonomous prosecutor's office or moved the responsibility to the judicial branch. Either institutional design helps shelter the judicial process from manipulation by the executive branch (Pozas-Loyo and Ríos Figueroa, 2010).

A similar, more recent reform designed to improve judicial independence has been the creation of **magistrate councils**. Though significant variations exist, these bodies hold responsibilities that can include nominating or even appointing judges from the lowest levels to the highest court, evaluating the performance of judges and meting out disciplinary action, managing training programs, and even administering the budget for the entire judicial branch. But to assess judicial independence, the range of responsibilities must be viewed in the context of the composition of the council. For example, the magistrate council in the Dominican Republic holds complete control over the designation of Supreme Court members. Nonetheless, only two of its seven members are judges, ensuring that the Supreme Court justices remain political appointees.[5] Judges dominate Panama's magistrate council, but the council really only performs a consultative function on the selection of judges or prosecutors, as well as on administrative procedures and proposed laws. A few countries look to civil society for representation. Peru's council has seven members; one is selected by the Supreme Court and another by the public ministry, while the remaining five must include a lawyer, one professor from a public law school and one from a private law school, and two representatives from professional law associations. The five nongovernmental members are elected by their own peers. All countries of the region, save Brazil, Costa Rica, and Guatemala, have formally independent magistrate councils. Though situated outside the judiciary, magistrate councils still aid judicial independence insofar as they shield the branch from executive pressure (Hammergren, 2002).

The tenure and appointment procedures of Supreme Court justices provide a simple measure of judicial power and independence. True to code law thought, most countries offer limited tenure to ensure political oversight. Only Argentina, Brazil, Mexico, and Panama employ an appointment procedure similar to that found in the United States, whereby the president nominates and the senate confirms (in Panama the unicameral assembly confirms). Paraguay reverses the process—the senate elects, and the president exercises veto power. Generally, most countries grant the legislature primary control over the election of Supreme Court judges. Bolivia's new constitution offers a unique process for appointing not only members to its Supreme Court, but also to its Constitutional Court, Agrarian Court, and magistrates council. Namely, the legislature drafts a list of candidates, with quotas geared for women and indigenous representation, who then face a national election. To minimize politicization, campaigning is prohibited and voters receive official, one-page descriptions of the candidates and their qualifications. The first elections, held in 2011, had mixed results (see Driscoll and Nelson, 2015). The quotas addressed representative issues well by producing a diverse set of winners, with more than a majority women and more than a majority indigenous. But many criticized the selection process by the legislature for its lack of transparency, as well as the inability or unwillingness of voters to weigh the merits of the nominees. Indeed, some 60 percent cast blank or spoiled ballots in frustration. If the goal is qualified judges, Bolivia must ensure that politics does not engulf meritocratic considerations in the nomination process, and that confusion does not mar the selection process. National elections for judges makes Bolivia an exception in Latin America (and in the world) In the remainder of Latin America the procedures of appointment and tenure largely reverse what we see in the United States, where politics envelops the selection process, but lifelong tenures ostensibly shelter justices from political influences.

A final organizational variation of note is the size of Supreme Courts in Latin America. Only five justices sit on the Supreme Court in Uruguay, but 32 arbitrate on the Supreme Court in Venezuela. The large number of justices found in the courts of most countries arises from the use of **chambers**. Most courts (the exceptions are Argentina and Uruguay) divide themselves into specialized chambers to decide cases. For example, in El Salvador, there are 15 supreme court justices—five judges sit in the Constitutional Chamber, four sit in the Administrative Disputes Chamber, three sit in the Civil Chamber, and another three sit in the Criminal Chamber. Ecuador's high court (with its 31 members) tops the region with 10 chambers. Insofar as the court itself decides where to assign justices, chambers can provide another modest layer of insulation from political influence. Chile adds an element of unpredictability to its organization with the use of panels. To decide a case, a panel of five judges is created from among the 21 members of the court. Whether the court takes a conservative or liberal perspective is largely dependent on the composition of a panel.[6] Table 6.3 details several of the institutional variations of supreme courts in Latin America relevant to independence and power.

Table 6.3 **Supreme Courts in Latin America.*** Supreme courts can be designed in response to the needs and desires of the regime

Country	Number of Justices	Percentage of Female Justices	Tenure	Appointment Process	Number of Chambers
Argentina	5	20% (1)	to age 75[a]	President selects, 2/3 senate confirms	none
Bolivia	9	33% (3)	6 yrs, no reelection	2/3 legislature creates list, national election	4
Brazil	11	18% (2)	to age 70	President selects, senate confirms	2
Chile	20	25% (5)	life	Court creates list of 5, president selects one, 2/3 senate confirms	4
Colombia	22	14% (3)	8 yrs, no reelection	Magistrate Council creates list of 5, Court appoints	5
Costa Rica	22	27% (6)	8 yrs[b]	Legislature appoints	4
Dom Rep	16	25% (4)	life	Magistrate Council appoints	3
Ecuador	21	43% (9)	9 yrs, 1/3 staggered, no reelection	Magistrate Council appoints	9
El Salvador	15	33% (5)	9 yrs, 1/3 staggered	Magistrate Council creates list, 2/3 legislature appoints	4
Guatemala	13	46% (6)	5 yrs	Independent nominations board creates list of 26, legislature appoints 13	3
Honduras	15	20% (3)	7 yrs	Independent nominations board creates list of not less than 3 names per position, 2/3 legislature appoints	4

Country	Number of Justices	Percentage of Female Justices	Tenure	Appointment Process	Number of Chambers
Mexico	11	18% (2)	15 yrs	President creates list of 3 names, senate appoints[d]	2
Nicaragua	15	20% (3)	5 yrs	Legislature appoints	4
Panama	9	11% (1)	10 yrs	President (with cabinet agreement) selects, legislature confirms	4
Paraguay	9	33% (3)	5 yrs[c]	Magistrate Council drafts list of 3, senate selects one, president confirms	3
Peru	19	16% (3)		Magistrate Council appoints	3
Uruguay	5	20% (1)	10 yrs, no reelection	2/3 legislature appoints	none
Venezuela	32	50% (16)	12 yrs	Independent nominations board creates list, Citizen's Branch[e] confirms, legislature reconfirms	7

Source: Data collected from national Supreme Court websites of individual countries and national constitutions.

*As of December 2016.

[a]After age 75, justices may be reappointed for five-year terms.

[b]After 8 years, term is renewed unless 2/3 of the national assembly object.

[c]If members are reelected three consecutive times, they hold the position until age 75.

[d]If the senate rejects all names, there is a second submission, and if the senate again rejects all names, the president designates the justice from the submitted list.

[e]This body consists of the Public Prosecutor, the Ombudsman, and the Comptroller General.

The Judiciary and the People: Access and Efficiency

After the transitions to democracy in the 1980s, judicial reforms in most Latin American states focused on the power and independence of the courts. This made sense. The move from authoritarianism to democracy required the courts to hold their own, and to no longer bend to the aims of powerful executives—even those elected democratically. Also, one should not overlook the influence of U.S.-based foreign aid agencies, which reflected upon the common law system in the United States and encouraged governments to bolster the separation of powers. Indeed, some one billion dollars in aid poured into government coffers to support capacity-building in the judicial branch. Larger budgets, new training programs, expanded staffs, computer technologies, as well as organizational reinforcements such as magistrate councils, independent prosecutors, and constitutional tribunals buoyed Latin American judiciaries. Undoubtedly, the courts are much stronger today when compared to the past. But questions of competence continue to hound the branch, leading to calls for a second generation of reforms that focus on outputs (Hammergren, 2006). Delays in court proceedings, corruption, misuse of funds, cronyism, and the lack of responsiveness to the concerns of the impoverished or otherwise marginalized groups remain as almost intractable problems. These sorts of issues have more to do with relations between the courts and the people, than with relations between the courts and other government institutions.

One study of judicial reform argues that piecemeal reform is in fact the core of the problem (Prillaman, 2000). In particular, gains in judicial power and independence toward other government institutions can actually tarnish accountability toward the public. Several studies note that this is precisely the case in Brazil, where "judicial independence has proven excessive in many respects, creating an insulated, unresponsive, and, at times, irresponsible judiciary" (Santiso, 2004, p. 163). The Brazilian courts, faced with congressional inquiries or executive proposals looking to address the large backloads of cases, to introduce greater transparency in the budgetary process and in appointment and promotion decisions, or seeking to discipline indolent or corrupt justices, have successfully shielded themselves and are able to work with tremendous autonomy. A counterexample is found in Chile, where reformers successfully addressed issues of independence and power alongside access and efficiency. They did so in spite of international aid agencies that advised an incremental, piecemeal approach focusing first on power and independence (Prillaman, 2000). Such studies underscore the importance of exploring not only power and independence, but also efficiency and access in the judicial branch—and recognizing interdependencies.

Courts in Latin America are notoriously lethargic. Litigants face a labyrinth-like judicial system, often receive inadequate counsel, and face lengthy delays before their cases even begin. Many of these problems can be traced to the ill-fated blend of code law procedures and economic underdevelopment. The inquisitorial style of justice requires an extensive pretrial investigation to ensure that no innocent person is indicted (because there is no presumption of innocence), and relies on written communication and reporting rather than oral proceedings. These responsibilities rest almost exclusively with the judge, who is expected to gather evidence, lead the questioning of witnesses, adjudicate on behalf of both the prosecution and the defense, and ultimately decide cases. Public prosecutors and defense counsels traditionally do little more than ask follow-up questions and offer suggestions, and juries are rarely used (Hafetz, 2003). Add to this workload the managerial duties that code law systems ask of judges, who are, after all, supposed to be bureaucrats rather than craftsmen in the field of law. One study reported that Supreme Court justices in Ecuador spent about four days per week on administrative matters, which included the disbursement of funds to pay for gasoline so that prosecutors could travel to crime scenes, and the consideration of leave requests for judicial employees. Consider this heavy workload in the context of underdevelopment. Deficiencies in higher education and training programs for the workplace strain the human capital of the region, poor salaries and benefits combined with generous tenure protections create incentives for cronyism and corruption, and basic resource scarcities—from office space to computer equipment and telephones—add to the frustration (Prillaman, 2000, pp. 21–26).

The consequences of overworked, understaffed, and unprepared courts cannot be reduced to simple productivity concerns. Beyond the economics of judicial inefficiency, there are clear-cut implications for fundamental human rights. Delays in judicial proceedings deny individuals basic rights to a speedy trial, and in fact lead to extensive periods of pretrial detention. The accused commonly have to wait it out in prison, often alongside and thereby under the influence of convicted criminals. Indeed, there are many cases in which the judicial delay surpasses the sentence of the alleged crime. More than one-half of the prison populations in Argentina, Bolivia, the Dominican Republic, Guatemala, Honduras Panama, Paraguay, Peru, Uruguay, and Venezuela have not been convicted of a crime. And as if pretrial detention is not enough, others remain behind bars after their sentences have been completed simply because judges have yet to issue their release orders. Some 2,500 Colombians faced this predicament in 2008.

All this has created an overcrowded, overburdened prison system. From 2000 to 2015, the number of Latin Americans behind bars doubled, with Central America charting an 80 percent increase and South America plotting a 145 percent rise (Walmsley, 2016). Brazil alone experienced a net increase of about 375,000 prisoners, just over the total population of New Orleans, Louisiana. Although several factors—such as higher crime rates, more severe laws, and longer sentencing guidelines—contribute to growing prison populations, delays in judicial proceedings also play a role. The congestion acts as a tinderbox for violence and prison riots, and fosters a variety of mental and physical health problems (Dammert and Zúñiga, 2009). The opening lines describing prison conditions in El Salvador from a 2012 article in the *New York Times* offer testimony to the grueling conditions:

> In a prison called Hope, there is little of it to go around. Inmates at La Esperanza penitentiary here cram into "the caves," their name for the suffocating spaces underneath bunk beds, desperate for a place to sleep. Others sprawl out on every inch of floor under a thicket of exposed

electrical wires in sweltering, dirty cells, until they can come up with the $35 or more they will need to buy space on a bunk from fellow prisoners. In these tights quarters, it has become a flourishing trade. The 19 prisons in this country were built to hold 8,000 people. These days, 24,000 are stuffed into them ...

A despondent inmate quoted in the article summed it all up: "I'd rather be dead than in here" (*New York Times*, 2012).

Some of the inefficiencies in the courts can be attributed to simple labor shortages. For example, the United Nations recommends that countries employ about 25 judges for every 100,000 inhabitants. Most developed countries surpass this target with 30 or more judges, but in Latin America, only Costa Rica and Uruguay have a record of doing so. In 2014, Argentina had to make due with just 5.1 judges per 100,000, Guatemala leaned on an average of 4.5, and Peru placed the burden of adjudication on just 2.9 for every 100,000 (UNODC, 2016). Notably, the heavy workload creates disconcerting opportunities for corruption. In Mexico, overworked judges look to the lower levels of their secretarial staff (*secretarios*) to review cases and write decisions, and they are often more prone to corrupt influences (Calleros, 2009, p. 170). In addition to the scarcity of judges, there are similar shortfalls in the number of prosecutors and public defenders throughout the region.

Other inefficiencies are directly related to the legal code. Absent the presumption of innocence, many countries of the region lack bail statutes to allow for release pending prosecution. The use of written correspondence, rather than oral proceedings, encumbers communication. Unable to assert *erga omnes* authority, courts often find themselves ruling on cases with similar circumstances over and over again, rather than issuing decisions that can be applied to other cases (Hammergren, 2007, pp. 188, 192). Another facet of code law is the inadmissibility of the guilty plea, because it is up to the state alone to decide guilt or innocence. This omission drags many cases into the courtroom, even when a defendant is fully prepared to offer a full confession. Similarly, the strict adherence to codes for sentencing decisions prohibits plea-bargaining, which might otherwise draw a case to completion more quickly. But perhaps the most significant difficulty created by the code law tradition emerges from the overwhelming role that judges are expected to play as an agent of the state. Situating the judge as a referee, as in common law systems, would allow prosecutors and defendants to assume more of the workload in matters of investigation and questioning. In response to the difficulties created by code law practices, Chile overhauled its criminal justice system with a series of reforms between 2000 and 2005. Some of the highlights of the reforms included oral proceedings, a greater role for prosecutors in the evidence-gathering stage, and expanded opportunities for plea-bargaining and case dismissals. The modifications have scored successes. For example, the percentage of the unconvicted population in prisons dropped from about 60 percent in the early 1990s to under 30 percent by 2007 (Riego, 2008).

Efficiency failures can directly affect issues of access, as when those looking to the courts for support grow frustrated by delays and abandon their efforts. But beyond concerns over timeliness, some individuals find it difficult simply to approach the courts. Sometimes it is a simple matter of location. Often, courts and legal assistance can be found only in urban areas, necessitating long trips for those living in rural areas. When they do make it to the city, many indigenous rural inhabitants encounter administrators who do not speak their language, and then must face legal proceedings with the same predicament. Consider that among the indigenous in Ecuador, only 58.5 percent identify themselves as bilingual (Spanish and "indigenous"— most often Quichua), meaning that about 40 percent cannot understand Spanish. And this measure undoubtedly overstates the actual number of those who are able to speak proficient Spanish. Ecuadorian law requires courts to provide a translator, but often they do not for lack of resources, or they require payment by the litigants. When translators are used, they often lack proper training. "Court-appointed translators" may be volunteers from the community, staff members of the court (even a receptionist or a custodian), or a member of a litigant's family. Bilingualism among indigenous women is lower than among indigenous men, which adds a gender disparity to the problem (Berk-Seligson, 2008). Beyond language difficulties, individuals may be denied service altogether if they lack proper identity documents, as is the case with many poor, rural inhabitants.

One reform meant to extend access has been the creation of "one-stop service centers" that house officials from relevant public offices (e.g., the ministry of justice, the public prosecutor, and the police), as well as legal assistance, counseling services, forensic doctors, and human rights specialists. Peru initiated the experiment in the mid-1980s, but the idea is now widely supported and ardently funded by foreign aid providers, especially the U.S. Agency for International Development (USAID) and the Inter-American Development Bank. In Colombia, these centers are known as *Casas de Justicia*. About 40 operate throughout the country, and some are fashioned to meet the particular needs of the Afro-Colombian and indigenous populations. Although many *Casas* lack the full array of services that they would ideally offer, they remain central to the government's efforts to extend justice to the more vulnerable portions of the population. In 2014 alone, about 400,000 Colombians made use of the *Casas de Justicia* (*El País*, 2016).

Another reform designed to expand access, and often used in the one-stop service centers, has been the development of mechanisms for **alternative dispute resolution** (ADR). Typically, these take the form of mediation services so that disputants can directly communicate with each other and formulate their own settlement. Other forms of ADR introduce plea-bargaining to code law systems, so that the accused can negotiate their sentences. The process lightens the load on the judiciary as it skirts formal judicial proceedings and the extensive use of written correspondence and documentation. Decisions are not based upon extensive casework or the search through applicable government statutes, but rather upon what settlement best leads the disputants to reconcile their differences. ADRs cast aside the value that code law places on certainty in the legal process in favor of expediency and, in the case of civil proceedings long-lasting solutions to reconcile differences. Ideally ADRs can kindle greater trust in government as citizens make use of more functional judicial institutions. But ADRs can also pose a risk when implemented in a setting where the rule of law remains suspect. The affluent and well-connected—from elite sectors within business to politicians and drug traffickers—are able to bring more legal resources to bear on processes of plea bargaining and motions to dismiss cases. Bribery, coercion, and other forms of corruption may also come into play. ADRs may make for a more efficient judiciary, but it may also lead to one that addresses cases unevenly, creates new barriers for the middle and working classes, and ultimately further undermines confidence in government (Alkon, 2011). The strictures of code law may contribute to inefficiencies, but the reform of code law where the rule of law has yet to embed itself brings its own risks.

COMPARING COUNTRIES

Courts Versus Politicians in Guatemala and Colombia

Article 186 of the 1985 Constitution of Guatemala prohibits participants in a coup d'état from assuming the office of the presidency. It would appear applicable to the case of Efraín Ríos Montt, who took the presidency from 1982 to 1983 through a military coup. In fact many claim that the clause was designed with him in mind. Ríos Montt unsuccessfully challenged the article during his 1990 and 1995 bids for the presidency, but this did not dissuade him from a third try, in 2003, when the Supreme Court once again rejected his claim. In fact, up to this point, in proceedings conducted by the Registrar of Citizens, Federal Electoral Tribunal, and Supreme Court, a total of 52 justices rebuffed Ríos Montt, and only five sided with him. But this time, Ríos Montt decided to take his case to the Court of Constitutionality. And in July 2003, the court decided 4–3 in his favor, ruling that the 1985 article could not be applied retroactively.

One may wonder how Ríos Montt could restart case his multiple times. The code law tradition does not embrace a strict adherence to the legal principle of *res judicata* (Latin for "a thing already judged"). Under common law, the rules are typically clear—a final court of appeal is designated, and after a judgment from this court, the same case cannot be relitigated. *Res judicata* exists in code law, but in a much weaker form due to the reluctance to empower the courts with authority. A second relevant institutional factor is the appointment and staffing procedures in the courts. In Guatemala, an independent body vets appointments to the Supreme Court to preclude political appointees, but members of the Court of Constitutionality are appointed directly by different government and professional bodies, increasing the likelihood of political appointees.[7] And in addition to the five court members, five alternates are designated. Importantly, when the court addresses a constitutional question already litigated in the Supreme Court, a panel of seven justices must be convened. The President of the Court of Constitutionality is responsible for designating the additional panelists from among the alternates. Only two of the five judges had political ties to Ríos Montt, but one happened to be the President of the Court (the position rotates annually), and he selected two alternate judges with partisan ties to Ríos Montt.

The decision led to massive protests throughout Guatemala. Protestors and legal analysts called on the electoral tribunal to maintain its position, on the grounds that the decision by the Court of Constitutionality contravened the constitution. Soon afterward, the Supreme Court suspended the Ríos Montt campaign to hear a complaint from an opposing political party, but backed off after violent demonstrations by Ríos Montt supporters. Guatemala fell into a constitutional crisis that dissipated only as activists realized that Ríos Montt held little electoral support. He collected only 11 percent of the vote in the November 2003 elections (*NotiCen*, 2003a, 2003b).

The case of Guatemala could not be more different from that of Colombia. Alvaro Uribe was elected President of Colombia in 2002, at a time when a guerrilla war, rampant drug trafficking, and ceaseless violence had brought the country to the brink of collapse. Fortified by a surge in military aid from the United States, Uribe presided over a massive military campaign that largely succeeded in quelling the guerrilla threat. He also induced many of the paramilitary groups organized to combat the guerrillas (and often involved in criminal activities of their own) to lay down their arms. Riding his wave of success, Uribe convinced congress in October 2004 to reform the constitutional prohibition on reelection, and allow him a second term. He retained his hold on the presidency in the 2006 elections, but a series of scandals soon threatened to undermine his popularity. The so-called para-politics scandal exposed close connections between politicians allied with the Uribe government and the paramilitaries. Soon afterward, there

(*continued*)

emerged allegations that Uribe had offered bribes to congresspersons in advance of the constitutional reform vote. And finally, a series of reports detailed how military units, egged on by Uribe's policies to show "results" in the guerrilla war, killed innocent civilians and dressed them up as combatants or drug traffickers. Despite all this, polls consistently indicated that over 60 percent of Colombians continued to support Uribe. Most, it seems, were willing to put aside the scandals in favor of the newfound security under Uribe.

And so it appeared that Uribe had a good chance to secure a third term in office in when some 4 million Colombians signed a petition to allow his reelection. Although the constitution allows congress alone to pass constitutional reforms, in this case congress decided that a referendum would add legitimacy to change, and passed a law calling for a referendum in September 2009. But a procedural problem immediately hounded the legality of the law. The original signature campaign was poorly worded, with language that simply expressed support for the right of a president who has served two terms to serve another. It did not refer to a sitting president, or call for the annulment of the term limits set in the constitution. The House of Representatives decided to play it safe, and passed a bill calling for a referendum to allow the president a run at the presidency in 2014. But the Senate felt much more confident. It changed the wording to allow immediate reelection in 2010. The Constitutional Court took up the matter, and ruled against it in February 2010 for a number of reasons. First, it noted that the Senate erred by changing the wording. This meant that in effect, two different bills had been debated. Second, the court identified gross violations of campaign spending limits during the signature campaign. Third, the justices questioned an emergency decree passed by the president that had allowed the House to extend its regular session so that it had time to debate and pass the referendum bill. As it turned out, the decree had not been published in the *Diario Oficial*, which is required for it to have legal standing. And perhaps most importantly, the court questioned the very constitutionality of a third term, because it threatened the principle of the balance of power enshrined in the constitution. Uribe accepted the decision, and sat out the 2010 elections.

In Guatemala, a widely shunned politician ran roughshod over the courts in pursuit of his electoral goals. Alvaro Uribe—whose principles hardly appeared untainted—had substantial support, yet he bent to the will of the Colombian justice system. The two cases highlight the significance of the rule of law and the intangible sources of judicial power. Reputation, prestige, and legitimacy made the difference here. Guatemalan courts struggle to maintain their independence and give force to their decisions. But in Colombia, the justice system has started to feed off its base of legitimacy.

Discussion Questions

1   How did the cases of confrontation in Guatemala and Colombia differ, and what institutional differences explain these differences? Are there other important noninstitutional factors that we need to consider?

2   Should a court be allowed to stop a politician from seeking political office, or should it just let the people decide in an election? Reflect on the cases of Guatemala and Colombia to support your answer.

The Judicialization of Politics in Contemporary Latin America

In Latin America, the rule of law has always operated against a backdrop of profound socioeconomic inequality. In the past, the law more blatantly reflected this inequality, and often worked to magnify it. This can be traced to the ambivalent attitudes of *criollo* elites, who embraced independence and espoused liberal ideas, but feared the ambitions of the impoverished masses and used the law to restrain them (see Chapters 2 and 3). Land tenure laws advocated individual ownership to dismantle traditional communal holdings, and debt peonage regulations legitimated the effective enslavement of the indigent by large landowners. Vagrancy laws required those unable to document employment to work on large haciendas. Some countries that conceded communal ownership obligated all indigenous peoples to pay a head tax, under the rationale that individual property taxes would be impossible to assess. Many of these laws remained on the books until the mid-twentieth century (Mirow, 2004). To back up these repressive laws, constitutions incorporated "regimes of exception" that allowed presidents to suspend constitutional guarantees given a (generously defined) "state of emergency." In essence, the constitutions themselves legalized oppressive behavior by political leaders (Loveman, 1993).

Socioeconomic inequality still torments the region, but there is hope that the newly rooted democracies will instill a genuine respect for the rule of law. Whether this occurs depends in large part on the ability of the judiciary to preserve its independence and power, and through increases in efficiency and access to become a more relevant actor in the lives of individuals. Analysts refer to the "increased presence of judicial processes and court rulings in political and social life, and the increasing resolution of political, social, or state-society conflicts in the courts" as the **judicialization of politics** (Sieder et al., 2005, p. 3). If the courts sustain the rule of law, the democratic rules of the game can shape legitimate and long-lasting strategies to address confrontational issues. The history of Latin America shows how law can reflect socioeconomic inequality. In theory, the relationship can be changed so that the law acts as a means to address socioeconomic inequality itself. So when and how can the courts assume a footing that would allow them to protect and strengthen the rule of law?

Motives and Opportunities to Judicialize Politics

Because political power has historically rested outside the judiciary, and typically in the executive, it is reasonable to begin by investigating what prompts politicians to hand over power to the courts. Beyond the incentives or pressures from foreign aid agencies, some analysts look to domestic politics and draw a tie between judicial empowerment and the electoral uncertainty politicians often face. In particular, when politicians fear electoral defeat, they may view judicial empowerment as an insurance policy to deny their political opponents power should they assume office. As discussed below, this is what happened in Mexico in the 1990s, as the PRI party gradually came to realize that it could no longer sustain its authoritarian control of the government (Finkel, 2005). But other analysts emphasize that courts are not entirely passive actors and examine the conditions under which justices engineer their own capabilities. In particular, the judiciary can better assert its power when faced with a divided government. The Argentine Constitution of 1994 called for a court-dominated magistrate council and impeachment jury to control judicial appointments and removals. Nonetheless, President Carlos Menem was able to sideline these bodies so long as his Peronist party held a majority in congress. Only after his party lost its majority in the 1997 elections were these bodies able to assume the authority originally prescribed to them (Chávez, 2007). Similarly, Helmke (2002) finds evidence that courts are more likely to rule against the government when it is divided, and thereby weakened. Clearly, judicial empowerment can occur either as politicians delegate power or as judges assert themselves. And in either scenario, institutions play a critical role given their impact on electoral competition, party discipline, and executive-legislative relations.

International Actors and the Judicialization of Politics

Despite modest gains in the judicialization of politics, the relevancy of the courts remains a distant goal in most Latin American countries. Perhaps as a compromise, other means for constitutional protection and dispute resolution have surfaced to share or even assume duties otherwise performed by national courts in the region. Some of these avenues have emerged in the international arena. The 1969 *American Convention on Human Rights* proclaimed *amparo* and *habeas corpus* to be not just judicial remedies meriting due respect in domestic courts, but fundamental human rights of concern to the international community. The **Inter-American Court of Human Rights** was created in 1979 to decide cases material to the Convention, and by the late 1980s it began to assert its jurisdiction over the protection of *amparo* and *habeas corpus* rights (Brewer-Carías, 2009, pp. 27–61). Citizens of signatory states do not have standing, but their cases can still reach the court if they are referred either by the implicated state itself, or more likely, by the **Inter-American Commission on Human Rights**. This body was created in 1959 to investigate alleged violations of the *American Declaration of the Rights and Duties of Man* (1948), and it later assumed jurisdiction over the more comprehensive 1969 convention. Located in San José, Costa Rica, the Inter-American Court of Human Rights has decided more than 200 cases since 1987.

The inability or unwillingness of some courts in Latin America to address certain issues has spurred individuals to look to avenues of international justice. From 1996 to 2000, more than 300,000 women were part of a sterilization program implemented under the authoritarian government of Alberto Fujimori in Peru. Most were poor, rural, indigenous women. A special government commission in the Ministry of Health, formed after the fall of the Fujimori government, investigated the program and concluded, "Those people were rounded up using pressure, extortion, or threats, or by offers of food, and without being given an adequate explanation of the procedure, which prevented them from making an informed decision." Doctors received numerical goals, and many met those goals by deceiving their patients. Such was the case of Yonny Quellop, who at age 23 delivered her fourth baby. After the birth, the doctor put her under anesthesia and performed a tubal ligation. In a recent interview, Quellop recounted her experience:

> When I woke up, I realized they'd operated on me and I asked the doctor what they had done. And he told me: "I fixed you up so you wouldn't have any more babies. Now you won't be like all those other women who have babies like bunnies." But I never asked him to operate. I didn't sign anything. Nobody asked me if I wanted it done.

At least 16 women died from the procedure.

The family of one victim, Maria Mestanza, took her case to the Inter-American Commission on Human Rights in 2000, and in a case advised by the Inter-American Court on Human Rights, secured an agreement with the Peruvian government in 2003. It would compensate the Mestanza family, and conduct an investigation both to compensate others and to prosecute those responsible for the program. The family received its compensation, but was less than satisfied with the investigation. In 2009, the government prosecutor determined that the crimes at play were instances of medical negligence, and beyond the statute of limitation. The decision contradicted the position of the Commission and human rights activists, which classify the affair as a crime against humanity, which has no statute of limitation. The Inter-American Commission on Human Rights criticized the government decision as a breach of the 2003 agreement, and renewed the possibility that the Inter-American Court would revisit the case. The warning provided a spotlight, and made it a campaign issue in the 2011 elections. When Ollanta Humala won the election, he did reopen an investigation, but it was closed in 2014 after the prosecutor found no evidence of a systematic state policy, and blamed the sterilizations on rogue doctors. The international court did not provide the justice sought by the victims of the program, but it did help to keep the issue alive. Perhaps it provided the time required to stir consciences and activate the wheels of justice within Peru. In late 2015, three doctors came forward to offer evidence of a systemic policy. One reported he was given a quota of 250 sterilizations within four days. Peruvian activists continue to document cases and fight for appeals, emboldened in part by the supportive decisions of the Inter-American Court.[8]

National courts in Europe have played a critical role in the fight against impunity in Latin America. In many countries, the transition to democracy came with a twist—either a written amnesty or informal understanding hindered moves to prosecute former government officials suspected of human rights abuses. In some cases, blatant threats stifled efforts. But many of those persecuted had citizenship in Europe, and therefore access to European courts. As Argentina backtracked on early efforts to try military officers in 1987, Italian courts opened their own cases against the military on behalf of eight Italians killed in the dirty war. Spain, France, and Germany also initiated high-profile cases on behalf of their citizens.

Photo 6.2 For many Latin Americans, the ability and willingness of judiciaries to address the human rights abuses under the military regimes of the 1970s and 1980s remain a central measure of their legitimacy. Here, Chileans recognize the anniversary of the 1973 coup with reminders of those who disappeared under the dictatorship.
Source: © Alamy

But the real impact from Europe would begin in the 1990s as its courts gradually incorporated the principle of **universal jurisdiction**, which grants access to courts not based on the nationality of the victim or suspect, but rather on the nature of the crime. The idea is that some offenses—such as crimes against humanity, torture, and genocide—are so contemptible that all courts have an obligation to address them. Spain took the lead here. This was due not only to its historical and cultural connections in the region, but perhaps more so to the drive and resourcefulness of one judge, Baltazar Garzón. In 1998, Garzón set his sights on Augusto Pinochet of Chile, and issued an arrest warrant while the former dictator underwent back surgery in London. Britain litigated the extradition for 16 months, and ultimately denied the request based on, ironically enough, humanitarian reasons—the government deemed him unfit to stand trial due to "moderate dementia."

Although unsuccessful, the Pinochet case sparked judicial action in Chile, and signaled to all Latin American courts that they too would in essence be "shamed" into action if they did not act on their own (Arceneaux and Pion-Berlin, 2005, pp. 124–155). Another international dynamic—this one largely within Latin America itself—came into play essentially by chance. In late 1992, a Paraguayan judge visited a police station in the capital of Asunción to examine documents related to a pending case. There he came across records that detailed the cooperative efforts of secret intelligence branches under past military regimes in Argentina, Bolivia, Brazil, Chile, Paraguay, and Uruguay to kidnap, torture, and disappear each other's citizens. Gradually, each government released military files implicating its own services in what was termed Operation Condor.[9] In doing so, victims of abuses or their family members—some place the total number at more than 50,000—gained evidence to file charges in neighboring countries. The documents have proved to be a boon to those who faced more resistant judicial channels in their own countries. In 2016, a court in Argentina used the documents to try 18 former military officers for the murder of over 100 Bolivians, Chileans, Paraguayans, and Uruguayans who died in the country.[10]

Courts in the United States have also played a role in Latin America. Perhaps the most famous instance occurred when a U.S. court issued a warrant for Manuel Noriega, then President of Panama, on federal drug and money laundering charges. Enforcing the indictment set the stage for the 1989 U.S. invasion of the country. More commonly, Colombia has long looked to U.S. courts to process powerful suspects that its courts appear unable or unwilling to process. This first applied to drug lords in the 1980s, and later applied to members of the guerrilla FARC group and right-wing paramilitaries. In these cases, Colombian government authorities recognized the vulnerability of their own courts to corruption or intimidation, and expressed greater confidence in U.S. courts. After the rapid expansion of drug trafficking through Mexico in the early twentieth century, the Calderón government (2006–2012) extradited a record number of suspects to the United States to shelter the judicial proceedings from the intimidation of criminal organizations. But extraditions have tumbled under the Peña Nieto government (2012–2018)—from 115 in 2012 to 54 in 2013—reflecting growing doubts in Mexico over the effectiveness of Calderón's U.S.-supported war on drugs (see "Mexico: Country in the Spotlight" section below) (*Washington Post*, 2014).

The Judicialization of Politics at the Local Level

On the other hand, at the local level of many countries indigenous law has moved in to fill the void of judicial authority. The recognition of **indigenous justice** is not novel—colonial authorities often deferred to such customary law in civil matters at the local level, and instances of acknowledgment can be found throughout Latin American history (Yrigoyen, 2000). But indigenous law has gained much more traction in recent decades, in part due to the ratification of the *International Labor Organization Convention 169* of 1989, which requires signatory states to preserve and respect indigenous legal customs, and to seek "free, prior, and informed consent" when social or economic policies affect indigenous peoples.[11] But ratifying the treaty is not enough. Governments also need to pass legislation to implement the principles of the treaty. When they do not, the provisions of the treaty can do more to inflame than to alleviate tensions. For example, indigenous groups in Guatemala have conducted over 60 plebiscites to reject investment activities by oil, mining, and hydroelectric projects, but the government has dismissed all of them as nonbinding due to the lack of implementing legislation (*NotiCen*, 2012). Peru did pass a "prior consultation" law in 2012, but it has caused some confusion and debate. In particular, Does prior consent simply require dialogue, or does it imply a form of veto power over a developmental project? Many activists point to a troubling correlation between lucrative hydrocarbon exploration projects and mining operations in the Andes and a greater reluctance of the government to accept a strict interpretation of "consent" (*InterPress Service*, 2012).

In response to the "prior consent" obligation and the growing power of indigenous groups more generally, the constitutions of several countries have explicitly incorporated indigenous justice as a lawful alternative to government courts. Article 260 of the 1999 Constitution of Venezuela reads: "The legitimate authorities of the indigenous peoples may apply in their habitat instances of justice based on their ancestral traditions," under the condition that said justice "only affects their own members" and is not "contrary to the Constitution, to the law, and to public order." Similar provisions can be found in the constitutions of Bolivia, Brazil, Colombia, Ecuador, Mexico, Nicaragua, Paraguay, and Peru. Chile, Guatemala, and Panama recognize indigenous justice in their ordinary law.

Although such provisions represent triumphs for the self-determination of marginalized indigenous groups, they are not without controversy. Indigenous justice often skirts celebrated liberal protections for the accused, punitive judgments may include banishment or corporal punishments such as flogging, and customary traditions may allow men to be treated differently than women. Such criticisms aside, Faundez notes, "However unsavory some of the activities of these community organizations might be, it is necessary to bear in mind that their very existence is often a consequence of the weakness or corruption of state institutions at national or local levels" (2005, p. 189).

Despite supplements from abroad and at the local level, judicial processes remain far from relevant or instrumental to the daily lives of many Latin Americans. Lacking official channels to settle disputes or harboring severe distrust of those channels, many have looked to **vigilantism**, a chilling indicator of the absence of the rule of law. In recent decades, reports of lynchings have grown more frequent. In Guatemala, 47 people were killed and 441 hurt as a result of vigilante actions in 2013—a tenfold increase since 2004. Bolivia, Mexico, and Peru also experience high levels of vigilantism. It is no surprise that these countries also hold some of the largest indigenous populations of the region, but it is not that indigenous beliefs or customs encourage lynchings. Traditionally, indigenous justice focuses on righting wrongs, often through manual labor. But vigilantism is prevalent in indigenous communities because of their isolation and exclusion from the courts and local police (*PRI*, 2014). In 2012, Bolivia had just seven public defenders per 100,000 persons (compared to 305 per 100,000 in Argentina), and 45 percent of Bolivian provinces lacked a judge (*International Business Times*, 2014). Of course, the endemic corruption within the courts and police only adds to the problem. Middle-class groups and the wealthy react to shortcomings in the rule of law by withdrawing to gated communities and enlisting support from licensed security firms. Both communal mob activity by the marginalized and individual efforts to privatize security demonstrate a lack of faith in official judicial avenues and a lack of trust in government more generally.

COUNTRY IN THE SPOTLIGHT

The Judicial Branch in Mexico: Seeking Reform

December 2000 marked a momentous change in Mexico. For the first time in 70 years, the presidential sash moved from one political party, the long-dominant PRI (*Partido Revolucionario Institucional*) to another, the PAN (*Partido Acción Nacional*). The transition brought a formal end to what the Peruvian writer Mario Vargas Llosa called "the perfect dictatorship." The judicial branch, a subservient institution while the PRI wielded power, played a fundamental role as the winds of democratic change swept across the country during the 1990s. It plays a no less important role at present, as serious problems

(*continued*)

surrounding the rule of law continue to chafe at the process of democratic consolidation.

The Constitution of 1917 created a guise of democracy under the PRI. It outlined a presidential system with an independent judiciary, but in reality, the PRI dominated all parts of the regime. The constitution itself hardly constrained the authoritarian government. It was amended almost 400 times to suit the needs of the PRI. Insofar as the courts sought authority in their interpretation of the constitution, the PRI presented them with a moving target. The president exerted more direct control over the courts through appointments and dismissals. Officially, members of the Supreme Court acquired lifetime tenure after appointment by the president, and the Supreme Court managed all decisions on assignments, promotions, and dismissals in the lower courts. But the Supreme Court was not a particularly prestigious body, so presidents could always lure its justices to more lucrative government positions. And because most gained their positions precisely because of their willingness to curry favor among the PRI elite, justices could be counted upon to retire when solicited.[12] Hence, despite the lifetime tenures, most executives could expect to appoint a majority of justices during their own six-year term. And a compliant Supreme Court meant that personnel decisions in the lower courts really just reflected the interests of the PRI. These factors discouraged the court from ever moving to expand its judicial review authority, and to instead embrace a doctrine of judicial restraint (Magaloni, 2003).

As with all parts of the regime, the judicial branch ultimately worked to support the authoritarian policies of the PRI. The courts did take on *amparo* proceedings, which allowed them to address grievances brought by citizens against government officials. But these were typically municipal- and state-level officials. So as *amparo* decisions made their way through the appeal process, the entire system reinforced the hierarchy of the PRI, especially as rival parties gained control over lower-level governments. And if an *amparo* did involve federal officials, the *inter partes* nature of the decision limited its effects (Magaloni, 2003). More generally, the courts buttressed the authoritarian regime as their compliance imparted a sense of legality, and legitimacy, to the PRI government.

The authority of the PRI rested fundamentally on the government's ability to distribute state resources to supporters and to deny such benefits to would-be opponents, all under the cloak of populist discourse. It had successfully "purchased" popular consent for decades, but a severe debt crisis in the 1980s and the move toward neoliberal policies sabotaged the traditional PRI formula. By the 1990s, few doubted that the PRI would have to face real competition at the polls, and could even lose control of government. The only alternative would be brute repression—unthinkable while a wave of democratization was making its way through Latin America. As part of the democratic opening, the PRI arranged for a slate of reforms that increased the power and independence of the judiciary. Some analysts saw the move as political insurance by the PRI—unsure of their hold on government, PRI elites hoped that a more independent judiciary would inhibit, or at least stall changes proposed by an alternative government (Finkel, 2005). Other analysts saw the judicial reforms as a move by the PRI to restore its own legitimacy—a move to convince voters that a new PRI would accept competitive democracy (Inclán Oseguera, 2009). Either way, Mexico's judiciary emerged as a relevant player in the politics of the country.

The constitution identifies four bodies under the judicial branch: district courts; unitary (i.e., single-judge) and collegial circuit courts; the Federal Electoral Tribunal; and the Supreme Court. There are 354 district and auxiliary district courts. The 297 circuit and auxiliary circuit courts receive appeals of district court decisions, and they also resolve jurisdictional disputes among district courts. The Federal Electoral Tribunal consists of a superior chamber and five regional chambers. The superior chamber has seven members. They are elected to 10-year, nonrenewable terms in a process that asks the president of the Supreme Court to submit a list of three names to the Senate, which in turn elects an individual with a two-thirds vote. The superior chamber hears cases related to disputes in national congressional and presidential elections, as well as complaints from voters. Its decisions can be appealed to the Supreme Court only if the case involves a constitutional question. The Supreme Court is an 11-member body. It is divided into two chambers of five justices each. One addresses civil and penal matters, while the other handles administrative and labor issues. The chief justice of the court participates in decisions only when the court meets in plenary session to decide *amparo* cases, to address appeals from the two chambers, or to resolve constitutional controversies and unconstitutional actions (see below, p. 255). A 1994 reform removed lifetime tenures and slashed the court from 26 to 11 justices in the hope that a renovation would sever connections between

(*continued*)

the court and the *ancien régime*. To free Supreme Court members from the preferences of any single president, the justices now serve staggered 15-year terms. In addition, to appoint a judge the president now submits a list of three candidates to the Senate, which selects one by a two-thirds vote.

Mexico also has a magistrate council. It has vast responsibilities over administrative matters, personnel decisions, and the budget, and it even decides the number of district and circuit courts (only the Supreme Court is exempt from its oversight). The President of the Supreme Court presides over the council, and the Supreme Court as a whole appoints three of the remaining six magistrates. The senate appoints two others, and the president appoints one member. They serve four-year, nonrenewable terms. It is an independent institution, but still rests in the judicial branch; its members are not supposed to represent those who appoint them.

The 1917 Constitution is the ultimate source of law in Mexico. But as a code law country, Mexico also looks to the detailed regulations drafted by the legislature since the nineteenth century—though with major revisions after the 1920 Revolution. The Civil Code has 3,074 articles, and is divided into four books. One covers the rights of individuals, another addresses property, a third details inheritance rules, and the fourth specifies contract regulations. State governments and Mexico City largely duplicate the federal codes, but they can make adjustments to suit their own needs or desires. Testimony to its progressive politics, Mexico City amended its civil code in 2004 to allow transgender individuals to change their name and gender in their birth certificates, and in 2009 lawmakers enacted changes to legalize same-sex marriage. There is also a Commercial Code, Criminal Code, Civil Procedure Code, and Criminal Procedure Code. In theory, the codes are comprehensive and provide explicit directions for all judicial decisions. Code law strives to achieve this predictability in the law, but in practice, countries must develop strategies to update the law or to address situations where existing law appears to be incomplete or inapplicable. In Mexico, this is done through *jurisprudencia*, a weak counterpart to the common law tradition of *stare decisis*. *Jurisprudencia* refers to the written commentaries that judges may add to their decisions when the law appears incomplete or in need of interpretation. A *jurisprudencia* can be applied only to an *amparo* decision, and it becomes binding on all courts (state and federal) if the interpretation is upheld in five consecutive decisions in the collegiate circuit courts, Federal Electoral Tribunal, or Supreme

Court. True to the code law tradition, such *jurisprudencia* is binding only on the courts, and not on the executive or legislative branches. For example, stirred by the changes in Mexico City, gay rights activists in other states filed *amparo* suits for the right to marry. In 2015, the Supreme Court issued a *jurisprudencia* declaring prohibitions of same-sex marriage in state-level civil codes to be unconstitutional. The ruling did not overturn the provisions of the code as one would expect in a common law system—municipal clerks can still deny marriage licenses. But a prospective couple can now appeal to a district court to force the clerk to issue the license. Seeing the writing on the wall, most Mexican states have revised their codes to allow same-sex marriage.

To supplement the *amparo*, the pathbreaking 1994 judicial reforms activated two additional types of judicial review. The "action of unconstitutionality" empowers the court to overturn acts of government if they contradict the constitution. The "constitutional controversy" is a separate provision that allows the court to address disputes between different branches or levels of government. These are powerful new tools, but they face significant limitations. First, both review procedures are concentrated—only the Supreme Court can make use of these instruments. Second, each review confronts a formidable voting threshold. The "action of unconstitutionality" calls for a supermajority of 8 of the 11 justices. A "constitutional controversy" decision can pass with a simple majority, but achieves only *inter partes* effects. A supermajority of 8 justices must be reached if the decision is to have *erga omnes* effects. Third, only certain public officials, and never private citizens, can initiate these types of judicial review. The aggrieved government official must trigger a "constitutional controversy." The "action of unconstitutionality" is available only to the attorney general, one-third of deputies or senators, one-third of any state legislature, and political parties (in cases dealing with electoral laws). Moreover, the call for review must be declared within 30 days after passage of the law in question. An interesting distinction between the two processes of judicial review is that the "action of unconstitutionality" potentially represents an abstract form of review—it does not require an actual dispute. On the other hand, a "constitutional controversy" can only be a concrete form of review, requiring an actual altercation between two government bodies.

The judicial reforms of the 1990s inspired the court to act even before the 2000 transition (Domingo, 2000; Finkel, 2003). In 1996,

(*continued*)

the Supreme Court ruled against compulsory union membership for state workers and obligatory affiliation in chambers of commerce and industry—clear blows to the time-honored corporatist formula of the PRI. And in 1998 the court overturned an electoral code in the state of Quintana Roo, declaring that it would disproportionately favor the PRI party. But in the end, and despite its contribution to LGBT rights, the newfound resolve of the Supreme Court has really only affected intergovernmental relations. For most citizens, the judicial branch remains an inefficient, distant, and corrupt institution. In fact, a 2015 poll found that just 27 percent of Mexicans expressed "a lot" or "some" confidence in the judiciary. The Supreme Court alone did not fare much better, instilling confidence in just 30 percent of Mexicans.[13]

Changes to the Supreme Court have no doubt increased the general power and independence of the judiciary. But what matters to most citizens is the access and efficiency of the courts, where few gains have been made. The country recently received a grim reminder of this in 2009, when the Inter-American Court of Human Rights chastised government officials for failing to properly investigate the 2001 murders of three women in Ciudad Juarez. The decision highlighted the abject dereliction of duties on the part of law enforcement and prosecutors during the infamous wave of *femicides* that saw about 400 murders over a decade. To accentuate their displeasure, the international court even ordered the Mexican government to erect a monument to the victims. In a second case that further exposed shortcomings in the rule of law, in April 2010 the Inter-American Court of Human Rights agreed to hear a case on behalf of two indigenous women from small villages in Guerrero who had accused military officers of rape in 2002. In both cases, civilian authorities had refused to investigate due to the involvement of military officers, holding that the military courts had exclusive jurisdiction. The military investigations that followed issued summary exonerations. The outreach to international courts illustrates the lack of confidence in the courts. Indeed, a study by the National Commission on Human Rights found that citizens report only 10 percent of all crimes in the country. Yet more disturbing is the finding that among those reported crimes, only 1 in 100 leads to a criminal conviction.[14]

Growing corruption has also tarnished the reputation of the courts, given their presumed role as stewards of the rule of law. When reports that a construction company that had just secured lucrative contract for a bullet train through Mexico City had essentially gifted a multimillion dollar luxury home to the wife of President Enrique Peña Nieto, the media covered every angle. Faced with denials and evasions as Peña Nieto struggled to explain his proprietorship, the media investigated and spotlighted the scandal for two years until the president felt compelled to apologize in 2016. The apology rang hollow for most Mexicans, whose attention turned to another scandal involving the president's use of a luxury condominium in Florida owned by a company that had just obtained a contract to manage seaports in Mexico. Even as the media again extended its coverage, the courts remained idle. But perhaps the deepest discontent emerged in 2014, after 43 college students en route to a protest went missing on a road outside the city of Iguala. Many suspected collaboration between corrupt police officers and local drug traffickers, and saw validation when local, state, and federal investigations floundered. Families of the victims appealed to the Inter-American Commission on Human Rights, which found the explanations offered by official government investigations to be "scientifically impossible" (*The New Yorker*, 2016).

Trust in the courts, so fundamental to the rule of law, remains crippled in Mexico. It is not that the groundwork for change has not been laid. Constitutional reforms targeting the judiciary passed in 2008. Generally speaking, the reforms introduced a number of common law practices such as oral proceedings, public trials, a presumption of innocence, and a stronger division of labor between investigators, prosecutors, and judges. New procedures that allow for plea-bargaining, and alternative dispute mechanisms will help address the backlog of cases. But the reforms will take time. Lawyers must be schooled in adversarial methods to build cross-examination skills. Guidelines need to be drafted to instruct those police officers and public prosecutors asked to take on new investigatory responsibilities. New methods for the documentation of proceedings have to be developed. Standardization in criminal procedures, offenses, and sentencing needs to occur across Mexico's 31 states and the federal judiciary. New facilities have to be constructed to accommodate public trials. The extent of these practical hurdles led the government to set a deadline of 2016 to complete the reforms. While about one-quarter of all municipalities had still not fully implemented the reforms by the time of the deadline, the magnitude of the change that had taken place was impressive. Nonetheless, the impact of the reform will take time as officials tune their skills and citizens evaluate the significance of the changes.

(*continued*)

The reforms are laudable, but the very process of change may prove to be too difficult for Mexico. Some critics bring up the drug war that has claimed more than 20,000 lives since 2006, and question the capability of common law procedures. They paint the reforms as "soft on crime," pointing to new protections for the accused such as the right to a speedy trial and enhanced discovery rights. In Ciudad Juarez, where several reforms were first implemented, some citizens expressed concern over new rules allowing the release of suspects pending trial. After the reforms took effect in January 2008, critics noted that only 14 of the first 100 suspects found themselves in preventative detention. This created some anxiety in a community accustomed to an average of 92 suspects detained out of every 100 under the old rules.[15] But other groups argue that adjustments to allow for more aggressive action against drug traffickers strain international human rights norms. One provision allows individuals suspected of participating in organized crime to be held up to 80 days without a formal charge. Another forbids judges from releasing prisoners pending trial if they are suspected of a crime on a prescribed list (Human Rights Watch, 2010, p. 239). Today, Mexico faces a dilemma and the rule of law hangs in the balance. Serious concerns over the rise in violent crime have prompted many to accept a heavy-handed approach to law enforcement, even at the expense of access and efficiency in the courts. But there is good reason to recognize how this very lack of access and efficiency contributed to criminal activity in the first place.

Discussion Questions

1   Discuss how the case of Mexico illustrates some of the tensions between power and independence on one hand, and access and efficiency on the other.
2   Identify the elements of code law and common law in the Mexican judicial system. Would Mexico benefit from a complete move to a common law system? Would this move create new problems?

Conclusion

Courts are meant to settle disputes. But their ability to do so effectively hinges on their level of legitimacy. Lacking force of arms or budgetary power, the judiciary holds a critical responsibility but lacks the muscle to see its decisions through. This, though, is how it should be in a democracy—where just decisions need not be backed by coercive measures. Judiciaries that are competent, independent, and enjoy the public trust have all the power they need to play the role required of them in a democracy. The problem is that judiciaries in Latin America tend to lack these features. Latin America has certainly not reached the point of anarchy or oppression forewarned by Raúl Alfonsín at the outset of this chapter. But the hesitance to use the courts, the surge in mob activity, and steady recourse to vigilantism suggest that the doors to such a state now sit unlatched.

There are signs of hope, however. Magistrate councils along with term and appointment reforms have helped the courts to gain their own footing. Sensitivity to local and indigenous traditions has improved the authenticity of the judicial process. New judicial review powers have opened new opportunities for justices to contribute to democratic politics. Such institutional changes can change people's perceptions of the judiciary. This is a crucial step in the judicialization of politics, which can occur only as people view the courts as relevant. As this happens, judicial prestige can energize the rule of law, and within government the courts can take their place as an effective player in the balance of power.

Key Terms

adjudication   220
common law   221
code law   221
stare decisis   221
judicial review   222
amparo   224
U.S. model of constitutional review   225
European model of constitutional review   225
rule of law   226
power   228
independence   228
access   228

efficiency   228
magistrate councils   234
chambers   235
alternative dispute resolution   241
judicialization of politics   246
Inter-American Court of Human Rights   247
Inter-American Commission on Human Rights   247
universal jurisdiction   249
indigenous justice   250
vigilantism   251
jurisprudencia   254

Discussion Questions

1   Which is more democratic, code law or common law?
2   Define the rule of law. How does a judiciary contribute to the rule of law?
3   Discuss the different ways that judicial review can be implemented in a regime. What are the political consequences of these variations?
4   How can institutions be designed to balance the independence and responsiveness of the judiciary?

Suggested Readings

Wayne A. Cornelius and David A. Shirk. 2007. *Reforming the Administration of Justice in Mexico.* **Notre Dame, IN: University of Notre Dame Press.** With a raging drug war in Mexico, the study of criminal affairs has never been so important. Twenty-one essays from leading scholars look at topics that include the history and sociology of crime, the militarization of the police, border issues, judicial and local institutions, and indigenous rights. Several chapters discuss best practices and offer policy recommendations.

Gretchen Helmke and Julio Ríos-Figueroa, eds. 2011. *Courts in Latin America.* **New York: Cambridge University Press.** This collection of case studies assesses the recent growth of Latin American courts as a check on government power and protector of individual rights. Chapters examine Argentina, Bolivia, Brazil, Chile, Colombia, Costa Rica, Mexico, and the United States. Several chapters take a close look at how the separation of powers has opened opportunities or otherwise influenced judicial decision making.

M. C. Mirow. 2004. *Latin American Law: A History of Private Law and Institutions in Spanish America.* **Austin, TX: University of Texas Press.** Mirow surveys the development of private law in Latin America from the colonial period to the twentieth century. If there is one underlying theme to the book, it is the tension that developed and the modifications that followed as Latin American governments adopted legal traditions from abroad, and attempted to apply them to the socioeconomic conditions of Latin America.

Ezequiel A. Gonzàlez-Ocantos. 2016. *Shifting Legal Visions: Judicial Change and Human Rights Trials in Latin America.* **New York: Cambridge University Press.** Most Latin American judiciaries were complacent or even complicit during the period of repressive authoritarian rule. Yet, in many countries, national courts later took the lead and meted out justice through human rights trials. Gonzàlez-Ocantos documents changes in the norms and beliefs of judges and prosecutors to explain this turn of events.

Notes

1   Raúl Alfonsín, "The Function of Judicial Power," in Irwin P. Stotzky, ed., *Transition to Democracy in Latin America: The Role of the Judiciary.* Boulder, CO: Westview Press, 1993.
2   One exception is that the Dominican Republic does not mention the power in the constitution, though the power is recognized. The countries do exhibit some differences in the scope of rights protected by *amparo* (some exclude social rights) and in the procedures for effecting an *amparo* (e.g., most importantly, which court(s) hold this power). There are also some differences in terms—the proceeding is known as the *mandado de securança* in Brazil, the *acción de protección* in Chile, and the *acción de tutela* in Colombia.

3 See Aristotle, *The Politics*, Book 3: Chapters XV and XVI.

4 See the October 2004 edition of the *Journal of Democracy*, "The Quality of Democracy," 15:4. Also see Zakaria (2003).

5 The President of the Republic, Presidents of the Senate and Chamber of Deputies, and one senator and one deputy compose the political members of the council, while the President of the Supreme Court and one ordinary judge compose the judicial members.

6 The use of panels, alongside the *inter partes* effects of the court's decisions, has frustrated human rights groups working through the courts. Charges of torture or abuse that occurred under the military dictatorship often face the general amnesty on such acts passed under the regime and still in effect. Human rights groups have successfully stripped the immunity from some alleged abusers, but the lack of *erga omnes* denies the application of those decisions to similar cases. And given the changing composure of panels, the consistency of decisions from one case to another is not ensured. See *World Report Chapter: Chile*, January 2009, Human Rights Watch. Available at: www.hrw.org/en/world-report-2009-country-chapters.

7 The Supreme Court, congress, president, a university council, and a lawyers' organization each appoint a member to a five-year term.

8 "Peru: IACHR Calls for Justice for Victims of Forced Sterilization," Inter Press Service, November 26, 2009, Lexis-Nexus. "Forced Sterilization Victims Demand Justice in Peru." *NotiSur*, Latin American Database, July 24, 2015.

9 Released files have implicated the United States, and some declassified U.S. documents also indicate U.S. participation in Operation Condor. See "Operation Condor: Cable Suggests U.S. Role." National Security Archive, March 6, 2001. Available at: www.gwu.edu/~nsarchiv/news/20010306/.

10 "Operation Condor Conspiracy Faces Day of Judgment in Argentina Court." *The Guardian*. May 26, 2016.

11 The requirement is found in articles 8 and 9 of the convention. Only the Dominican Republic, El Salvador, Panama, and Uruguay have not ratified ILO 169.

12 Domingo (2000), notes that between 1933 and 1995, 47 percent of Supreme Court justices occupied a political position prior to appointment, whereas just 29 percent emerged from within the judicial branch. Background data could not be found for the remaining 24 percent.

13 Parametría: *Encuesta Nacional en Vivienda*. July/August 2015. Available at www.parametria.com.mx.

14 "*CNDH ve impunidad en 99% de delitos*," *El Universal*, December 15, 2008.

15 "Rough Border Town Leads Reform of Mexico's Legal System," *Christian Science Monitor*, April 3, 2008.

References

Alkon, Cynthia. 2011. "Lost in Translation: Can Exporting ADR Harm Rule of Law Development?" *Journal of Dispute Resolution* 165, pp. 165–87.

Arceneaux, Craig, and David Pion-Berlin. 2005. *Transforming Latin America: The International and Domestic Sources of Change*. Pittsburgh, PA: University of Pittsburgh Press.

Autheman, Violaine. 2004. *Global Lessons Learned: Constitutional Courts, Judicial Independence, and the Rule of Law*. IFES Rule of Law White Paper Series. Available at www.ifes.org/publication/b16a9e8de58c95b427b29472b1eca130/WhitePaper_4_FINAL.pdf.

Berk-Seligson, Susan. 2008. "Judicial Systems in Contact: Access to Justice and the Right to Interpreting/Translating Services among the Quichua or Ecuador." *Interpreting* 10:1, pp. 9–33.

Brewer-Carías, Allan R. 2009. *Constitutional Protection of Human Rights in Latin America: A Comparative Study of Amparo Proceedings*. New York: Cambridge.

Calleros, Juan Carlos. 2009. *The Unfinished Transition to Democracy in Latin America*. New York: Routledge.

Cameron, Charles M. 2002. "Judicial Independence: How Can You Tell It When You See It? And, Who Cares?," in Steven B. Burbank and Barry Friedman, eds., *Judicial Independence at the Crossroads: An Interdisciplinary Approach*, pp. 134–47. New York: Sage.

Chávez, Rebecca Bill. 2007. "The Appointment and Removal Process for Judges in Argentina: The Role of Judicial Councils and Impeachment Juries in Promoting Judicial Independence." *Latin American Politics and Society* 49:2, pp. 33–58.

Dammert, Lucía, and Liza Zúñiga. 2009. *Prison: Problems and Challenges for the Americas*. Santiago: FLACSO-Chile.

De Tocqueville, Alexis. 1900. *Democracy in America: Volume 1*. Henry Reeve, trans. New York: Colonial Press.

Domingo, Pilar. 2000. "Judicial Independence: The Politics of the Supreme Court in Mexico." *Journal of Latin American Studies* 32, pp. 705–35.

Driscoll, Amanda, and Michael J. Nelson. 2015. "Judicial Selection and the Democratization of Justice: Lessons from the Bolivian Judicial Elections." *Journal of Law and Courts* 3:1, pp. 115–48.

El País. 2016, October 14. "Viente años 'agridulces' de las Casas de Justicia en el país." Available at www.elpais.com.co.

Faundez, Julio. 2005. "Community Justice Institutions and Judicialization: Lessons from Rural Peru," in Rachel Sieder, Line Schjolden, and Alan Angel, eds., *The Judicialization of Politics in Latin America*, pp. 187–209. New York: Palgrave Press.

Finkel, Jodi. 2003. "Supreme Court Decisions on Electoral Rules After Mexico's 1994 Judicial Reform: An Empowered Court." *Journal of Latin American Studies* 35:4, pp. 777–99.

———. 2005. "Judicial Reform as Insurance Policy: Mexico in the 1990s." *Latin American Politics and Society* 47:1, pp. 87–113.

Garlicki, Lech. 2007. "Constitutional Courts Versus Supreme Courts." *International Journal of Constitutional Law* 5:1, pp. 44–68.

Garoupa, Nuno, and Tom Ginsburg. 2008. "Guarding the Guardians: Judicial Councils and Judicial Independence." *American Journal of Comparative Law* 57, pp. 201–32.

Hafetz, Jonathan L. 2003. "Pretrial Detention, Human Rights and Judicial Reform in Latin America." *Fordham International Law Journal* 26, pp. 1754–77.

Hammergren, Linn. 2002. "Do Judicial Councils Further Judicial Reform? Lessons from Latin America." Working Paper 28: Rule of Law Series. New York: Carnegie Endowment for International Peace.

———. 2006. "Toward a More Results-Focused Approach to Judicial Reform." XI International Congress in the Reform of the State and Public Administration, November 7–10, 2006, Guatemala City.

———. 2007. *Envisioning Reform: Improving Judicial Performance in Latin America*. University Park, PA: Penn State University Press.

Helmke, Gretchen. 2002. "The Logic of Strategic Defection: Court-Executive Relations in Argentina under Dictatorship and Democracy." *American Political Science Review* 96:2, pp. 305–20.

Human Rights Watch. 2010. "World Report." New York: Human Rights Watch.

Inclán Oseguera, Silvia. 2009. "Judicial Reform in Mexico: Political Insurance or the Search for Political Legitimacy?" *Political Research Quarterly* 62:4, pp. 753–66.

International Business Times. 2014, April 19. "As Mexico Cracks Down, Vigilantism Is on the Rise in Latin America." Available at www.ibtimes.com.

InterPress Service. 2012, February 8. "Native Peruvians See Loopholes in Prior Consultation Law." Available at www.ipsnews.net.

Kapiszewski, Diana, and Matthew M. Taylor. 2008. "Doing Courts Justice? Studying Judicial Politics in Latin America." *Perspectives on Politics* 6:4 (December), pp. 741–67.

Kommers, Donald P. 1976. "Judicial Review: Its Influence Abroad." *Annals of the American Academy of Political and Social Science 428: The American Revolution Abroad*, pp. 52–64.

Loveman, Brian. 1993. *Constitutions of Tyranny: Regimes of Exception in Spanish America*. Pittsburgh, PA: University of Pittsburgh Press.

Magaloni, Beatriz. 2003. "Authoritarianism, Democracy and the Supreme Court: Horizontal Exchange and the Rule of Law in Mexico," in Scott Mainwaring and Christopher Welna, eds., *Democratic Accountability in Latin America*. New York: Oxford University Press.

Merryman, John Henry, and Rogelio Pérez-Perdomo. 2007. *The Civil Law Tradition: An Introduction to the Legal Systems of Europe and Latin America*. Palo Alto, CA: Stanford University Press.

Mirow, Matthew C. 2004. *Latin American Law: A History of Private Law and Institutions in Spanish America*. Austin, TX: University of Texas Press.

Navia, Patricio, and Julio Ríos-Figueroa. 2005. "The Constitutional Adjudication Mosaic of Latin America." *Comparative Political Studies* 38:2, pp. 189–217.

New York Times. 2012, March 14. "Inmate's Lament: 'Rather Be Dead Than Here.'"

The New Yorker. 2016, April 22. "The Missing Forty-Three: The Mexican Government Sabotages Its Own Independent Investigation."

North, Douglass. 1990. *Institutions, Institutional Change and Economic Performance*. New York: Cambridge.

NotiCen. 2003a, July 17. "Guatemala's Highest Court Shreds Constitution to Let Gen. Efraín Ríos Montt Run." University of New Mexico: Latin America Data Base.

———. 2003b, August 7. "Guatemala: Signs of a New Solidarity Against F.R.G. and Efraín Ríos Montt." University of New Mexico: Latin America Data Base.

———. 2012, December 6, 2012. "Civil Society Organizations Brand Guatemalan Government's Report to U.N. Superficial." University of New Mexico: Latin America Data Base.

Pozas-Loyo, Andrea, and Julio Ríos Figueroa. 2010. "Enacting Constitutionalism: The Origins of Independent Judicial Institutions in Latin America." *Comparative Politics* 42:3, pp. 293–311.

PRI (Public Radio International). 2014, January 24. "Lynching Is Still a Common Practice Across Latin America." Available at www.pri.org.

Prillaman, William. 2000. *The Judiciary and Democratic Decay in Latin America*. Westport, CN: Praeger.

Raz, Joseph. 1983. *The Authority of Law: Essays on Law and Morality*. New York: Oxford University Press.

Riego, Cristian. 2008. "Oral Procedures and Case Management: The Innovations of Chile's Reform." *Southwestern Journal of Law and Trade in the Americas* 14, pp. 339–56.

Sieder, Rachel, Line Schjolden, and Alan Angell. 2005. *The Judicialization of Politics in Latin America*. New York: Palgrave Macmillan.

UNODC (United Nations Office on Drugs and Crime) 2016. Data and Indicators: Crime and Criminal Justice. Available at www.data.unodc.org.

Walmsley, Roy. 2016. *World Prison Population List, 11th ed*. London: Institute for Criminal Policy Research. Available at www.prisonstudies.org.

Washington Post. 2014, February 18. "A Different U.S.-Mexico Partnership Under President Peña-Nieto."

Yrigoyen, Raquel. 2000. "The Constitutional Recognition of Indigenous Law in Andean Countries," in Willem Assies et al., eds., *The Challenge of Diversity. Indigenous Peoples and Reform of the State in Latin America*, pp. 197–222. Amsterdam: Thela Thesis.

Zakaria, Fareed. 2003. *The Future of Freedom: Illiberal Democracy at Home and Abroad*. New York: W. W. Norton.

7 Electoral Systems
The Core of Democratic Politics

Photo 7.1 Electoral campaigns, like this one in Argentina, can be colorful events, but the elections themselves are quite technical.

Source: © Shutterstock

"Bolivia: President's Hunger Strike Ends" President Evo Morales ended a hunger strike on Tuesday after Congress approved a measure setting rules for general elections this year. Mr. Morales began fasting last Thursday to protest delays in voting on the measure, which guarantees some representation for indigenous groups in Congress and could allow Gran Chaco, a gas-rich area, to seek administrative autonomy. The measure also opens the way for him to run for re-election.

—*New York Times*—World Briefing: The Americas, April 15, 2009

Elections highlight some of the most exciting and memorable features of democratic politics. Consider the images that come to mind when we think of an election: motivational speeches, colorful campaign events, cheering crowds, vigorous debates, the rise of underdog candidates, the surge in nationalism, and perhaps most of all, the anxiety of election day itself. It is this element of surprise—the sense that every candidate has a chance and anything is possible—that makes an election so exciting. And so it is hard to believe that at their core, elections are rote, technical affairs. In fact, the drama of democratic elections requires explicit, exhaustive rules to cover everything from the registration of voters and candidates to the counting of votes and certification of results. Democratic elections are captivating precisely because they are embedded in a predictable setting of rules and procedures.

Adam Przeworski tackled this odd combination by describing democracy as the "institutionalization of uncertainty" (1986, p. 58). Specifically, he argued that democratic rule allows uncertainty in outcomes, but demands regularity in procedures. Democracy lets adversaries play out their differences and vigorously pursue changes in public policies, but obliges them to agree upon *how* they are to resolve their differences. No other institution in a democratic regime so dramatically captures this delicate balance between uncertainty and certainty than the electoral system. This is why the electoral system is often identified as the most critical piece of a democratic regime. Put simply, one cannot have a democratic regime without elections. And if electoral outcomes are to be deemed legitimate, the rules that govern those elections must be known and approved in advance.

But electoral design is not as easy as it seems once we realize the array of alternatives and how different electoral laws cater to different, often incompatible, values such as representation, stability, effectiveness, party discipline, responsiveness, or consensus. The fact that electoral systems condition the calculations, expectations, and behavior of political actors is not unique to electoral institutions—indeed, we see such consequences associated with every political institution discussed in this book. But of all the major institutions in a democratic regime, electoral institutions are often more likely to become the target of change. This is because whereas most other institutions find their details in the rigid confines of constitutional documents, electoral rules more commonly reside in statutory law, and often take little more than a majority vote in the legislature to change. Moreover, electoral laws are so closely and obviously tied to the careers of politicians. President Evo Morales of Bolivia may be an extreme example, but he has seen enough at stake in electoral laws to submit to a hunger strike in the hope of rallying support for his desired changes.

This chapter provides an overview of the different parts of and options available to an electoral system. It also introduces the reader to some of the consequences of electoral design for party systems and discusses how countries can create electoral monitoring boards and use foreign observers to foster confidence in election returns. The chapter closes with a look at recent electoral changes in Bolivia.

Voting

Voting is meant to make equals of us all, and this appears to be affirmed on election day as poll workers collect and count ballots one by one. But behind the act of voting is the fundamental question, "Who votes?" Age is one consideration. Though there is a near-global standard of 18 years old, Latin America holds most of the exceptions found throughout the world. Argentina, Brazil, Ecuador, and Nicaragua allow individuals to vote at the age of 16. Citizens of the Dominican Republic can also vote below age 18, but only if they are married. Even after passing the age threshold, several restrictions still hold. Many countries restrict the suffrage of felons, or place specific constitutional restrictions on those convicted of fomenting rebellion, treason, or the misuse of public funds. In a clear reaction to past interference by the military, Colombia, the Dominican Republic, Guatemala, Honduras, Paraguay, and Peru prohibit soldiers from voting (most other countries use constitutional provisions to restrict political activities or "deliberation" by members of the military). Brazil shelters only its enlisted troops, allowing those at the rank of sergeant or above to vote.

Of late, one of the more interesting changes in Latin American elections has been the expansion of suffrage to expatriates. Many countries have long had laws on the books to allow for external voting, but have limited its use due to logistical difficulties and costs. But recent decades have seen helpful gains in technology and more Latin Americans living abroad. In addition, several countries have grown dependent upon remittances from those citizens, making it difficult to deny this constituency the vote. In general, countries can allow overseas citizens to vote either in person at a consulate, by mail, or in the model used in Panama, through the Internet. The issue is particularly spirited in Mexico, which has some 11 million citizens residing permanently in the United States. These citizens received the right to vote for the first time in the 2006 presidential elections, but the country is still working through its system. To protect the integrity of the voting process, initially Mexicans abroad were required to hold a photographic voting card that could be acquired only in Mexico, had to register for the July 2006 elections within a specified three-month period in late 2005, and needed to mail their ballots to the electoral board in Mexico City such that they arrived by the day before the election. The government spent almost $28 million on the program to run educational campaigns, pay for postal fees, and offer supportive services at consulates throughout the United States and in other countries. But in the end, only 40,876 Mexicans registered, and of those, only 32,632 returned properly completed ballots by the deadline—with 70 percent from the United States. Despite further outreach leading to the 2012 election, votes from abroad barely nudged upward, to just 40,714. Recognizing the difficulty of traveling home to obtain a voting ID card, in 2016 the Mexican Congress changed the electoral law so that Mexicans abroad could receive a voting card at their local consulate. Given that some 50 million vote in national elections, it will be interesting to see if the vote from abroad tilts the 2018 presidential elections.[1] Despite the difficulties faced by external voting, several countries have gone further than simply extending suffrage, and have reserved legislative seats for the representation of expatriates. Ecuador and Panama reserve six seats, and Colombia sets aside one seat.

Generally speaking, Latin America has an average voter turnout, typically sitting below that of Western Europe, but above that of the United States and Canada. The region does display significant variation. In their most recent presidential elections, some countries rallied impressive turnout numbers (Uruguay: 97.1 percent, Ecuador: 94.6 percent, and Bolivia: 90.5 percent, and Peru 87.7 percent), whereas others languished at the 50 percent mark or well below (e.g., Colombia: 37.7 percent, Guatemala: 44.1 percent, and El Salvador: 46.9 percent). Some of the lower turnout is explained by the legacy civil conflict, which tends to dull political mobilization. Some of the higher turnout is explained by the widespread use of compulsory voting; however, only Bolivia, Ecuador, Peru, and Uruguay impose penalties for abstention *and* enforce those penalties, which probably explains their higher rankings. The penalties usually consist of a small monetary fine, but may include the denial of access to public funds or restrictions from holding public office. Bolivia's high turnout rate may in no small part be due to the ban on making bank transactions for nonvoters. Other explanations for voter turnout look to public satisfaction with government, the general sense of efficacy, attitudes toward the legitimacy of government, and the salience of competition. Basically, people are more likely to use government (i.e., vote) when they are optimistic that government is willing and able to respond to their ambitions. This was the mood after the transitions to democracy almost 30 years ago, but since that time, economic stagnation or instability, political corruption, criminal activity, and inequity in the rule of law have led many to rethink the usefulness of government. This explains the downward trend in voter turnout that has occurred in much of the region over time. Hence, although Latin America still averages higher turnout than the United States or Canada, differences in the reasons for abstention are important. People may avoid the polls if they are satisfied with the status quo, as is often the case in the United States and Canada. But if they stay home on election day because they feel ineffectual and consider the government unresponsive, the legitimacy of government suffers and political instability grows more likely. This is an explanation that concerns many Latin American governments.

The Electoral System

An electoral system uses voting to measure preferences and make decisions. It does so by accumulating individual preferences, and translating them into a single, collective preference. Most voting is done to elect representatives to public office, but countries can also use direct democracy to allow voting on specific policies. There are five main components to any electoral system: electoral formula, district magnitude, electoral threshold, ballot structure, and districting/apportionment. Table 7.1 illustrates the wide range of electoral systems found in Latin America.

Electoral Formula

Given a legislature with seats to be filled, individuals of all political stripes would agree that we ought to call the public to the polls, and have them fill out ballots to indicate their preferences. On that—the very principle of voting—few would disagree. But what do we do after the ballots are collected? How do we decide who won? The answer seems simple enough—we count the ballots. But things are not really that easy, because there are in fact multiple, perfectly acceptable ways to count votes and translate those votes into seats.

Majoritarian Systems

As a start, we can distinguish two basic formulas for the counting of votes and allocation of seats. **Majoritarian systems** divide the country into districts, and pit individual candidates against each other in "winner-take-all" contests. In its most basic form, whoever receives the most votes—a simple majority (or, plurality)—gains the right to represent the entire district. The rules are simple and intuitive, and this probably explains why most countries, in Latin America and throughout the world, historically employed the majoritarian electoral formula. But majoritarianism finds less favor in contemporary Latin America. Indeed, of the Latin American legislatures examined in this book, only the Senate of the Dominican Republican retains a classic majoritarian electoral formula. The country is divided into 30 districts, and each district holds an election to send one representative to the 30-member Senate. The Argentine Senate also uses a majoritarian formula, but awards seats to three representatives in each district. Voters select a party rather than an individual, and the party that receives the most votes gains two seats whereas the second-place party receives one seat. The Brazilian Senate adjusts its majoritarian formula to accommodate staggered eight-year terms. Each of the 27 states in the country has three representatives, and in alternating elections every four years, either one seat or two seats need to be filled. When the prize is one seat, the election proceeds in classic majoritarian style—the candidate with the most votes wins. But when there are two seats, voters receive two votes and seats go to the first- and second-place candidates.

Proportional Representation

Majoritarian elections in Latin America dwindled in number from the 1920s to 1950s. It is no coincidence that this time period saw suffrage expand as many governments reduced or eliminated property and literacy restrictions,

Table 7.1 **Electoral Systems in Latin America**

Country	Chamber	Voting	Ballot Structure	Electoral Formula	District Magnitude Range	Number of Districts	Electoral Threshold	Reserved seats
Argentina	Chamber of Deputies	Compulsory (punishable by fine and 3-yr prohibition from public office or employment), 18 yrs	Closed and blocked	PR: d'Hondt	5–70	24 (provinces and BA)	3% of registered voters at the constituency level	None
	Senate	Compulsory (punishable by fine and 3-yr prohibition from public office or employment), 18 yrs	Closed and blocked	Majoritarian: winner receives 2 seats, second place receives 3rd seat*	3	24 (provinces and BA)	n/a	None
Bolivia	Chamber of Deputies	Compulsory	Closed and blocked (two votes: one for S M D P, and fused party vote for PR, and president)	Tiered, mixed independent:70 SMDP seats, 7 reserved indigenous SMDP seats, and 53 closed list seats allocated to the provinces according to population and distributed according to party's presidential vote share	1–13	79	3%	7 reserved indigenous S M DP seats

Country	Chamber	Voting	Ballot Structure	Electoral Formula	District Magnitude Range	Number of Districts	Electoral Threshold	Reserved seats
	Chamber of Senators	Compulsory	Closed and blocked	PR: d'Hondt	4	9 (provinces)	3%	None
Brazil	Chamber of Deputies	16–17 yrs, voluntary registration, 18 yrs, compulsory (punishable by fine)	Closed and unblocked	PR: Hare quota, then d'Hondt method to distribute remainders	8–70	27 (provinces and capital)	Electoral quotient (number of seats divided by number of votes)	None
	Federal Senate	16–17 yrs, voluntary registration, 18 yrs, compulsory (punishable by fine)		Majoritarian: FPTP when one seat, block vote when 2 seats	3	27 (provinces and capital)	n/a	None
Chile**	Chamber of Deputies	18 yrs, compulsory (punishable by fine)	Open list	Majoritarian: party list must double number of votes of runner-up party to gain both seats	2	60	n/a	None
	Senate of the Republic	18 yrs, compulsory (punishable by fine)		Majoritarian: party list must double number of votes of runner-up party to gain both seats	2	19	n/a	None

(continued)

Table 7.1 **Electoral Systems in Latin America** (*continued*)

Country	Chamber	Voting	Ballot Structure	Electoral Formula	District Magnitude Range	Number of Districts	Electoral Threshold	Reserved seats
Colombia	House of Representatives	18 yrs, voluntary	Closed, some blocked and some unblocked	PR: in 2-member constituencies, Hare quota; in others, d'Hondt	2–19s	33	In 2 member constituencies—30% of electoral quota; others—50% of the electoral quotient (number of seats divided by the number of votes)	4 minority seat (2 for Afro-Colombians, 1 for indigenous, and 1 for other minorities); 1 for Colombians living abroad
	Senate of the Republic	18 yrs, voluntary	Closed, party choice if blocked or unblocked	PR: Hare quota in first round, remaining seats allocated through d'Hondt	100	1	2%	2 seats for indigenous from a national constituency
Costa Rica	Legislative Assembly	18 yrs, compulsory (no sanctions)	Closed and blocked	PR–Hare quota, sub-quotient threshold for remainders	4–21	7	None	
Dom Rep	House of Deputies	18 yrs or married, compulsory (no sanctions)	Closed and unblocked; preferential vote	P R–d'Hondt	1–8	30	1%	None

Country	Chamber	Voting	Ballot Structure	Electoral Formula	District Magnitude Range	Number of Districts	Electoral Threshold	Reserved seats
	Senate	18 yrs or married, compulsory (no sanctions)	Voters have only one vote for House and Senate, and thus cannot vote for different parties	Majoritarian	1	30	n/a	None
Ecuador	National Assembly	16 yrs, compulsory	Panachage system: voters have as many votes as seats	Tiered independent: PR: open list, Saint Lague in districts with 2 seats, lurality	2–17, with one 15-member nationwide district	27, plus the nationwide district	None	The 3 MMcs with 2 seats each are reserved for three sets of Ecuadorians abroad: those in the U.S. and Canada; in Europe; in Asia, and Oceana, and in Latin America
El Salvador	Legislative Assembly	18 yrs, compulsory (no sanctions)	Closed and blocked list; voters have one vote applied to regional and nationwide districts	PR: Hare quota	3–16, and one 20-member nationwide district	14, plus the nationwide district	None	None

(continued)

Table 7.1 **Electoral Systems in Latin America** (*continued*)

Country	Chamber	Voting	Ballot Structure	Electoral Formula	District Magnitude Range	Number of Districts	Electoral Threshold	Reserved seats
Guatemala	Congress of the Republic	18 yrs, compulsory (punishable by fine)	Closed and blocked list; voters have two votes (regional and national, which is tied to presidential vote)	PR: d'Hondt	1–19, and one 31-member nationwide district	23, plus the nation-wide district	None	None
Honduras	National Congress	18 yrs, compulsory (no sanctions)	Closed and unblocked list for PR constituen-cies	Mixed independent: plurality system with 2 SMCs, and 16 MMCs with Hare quota	1–23	18	None	None
Mexico	Chamber of Deputies	18 yrs, com-pulsory (no sanctions)	Voters have one vote for SMC and regional MMC (closed and blocked)	Tiered, mixed dependent: 300 SMCs, 5 MMC with 40 seats each	1–40	305	2% nationwide	None

Country	Chamber	Voting	Ballot Structure	Electoral Formula	District Magnitude Range	Number of Districts	Electoral Threshold	Reserved seats
	Chamber of Senators	18 yrs, compulsory (no sanctions)	Voters have two votes for regional MMC and nationwide MMC (closed and blocked)	Tiered, mixed independent: in 32 regional MMCs, winning party receives 2 seats and runner-up receives one seat; in nationwide MMC, PR Hare quota	3 and 32	33	None	None
Nicaragua	National Assembly	16 yrs, voluntary	Two votes—one for department list and one for national list (closed and blocked)	Tiered, PR: department and nationwide districts use Hare quota or largest remainder	1–20	18	4%	Seats given to out-going president and runner-up
Panama	Legislative Assembly	18 yrs, compulsory (no sanctions)	MMCs use closed and unblocked lists	Mixed, independent: 26 SMCs and 14 MMCs; MMCs are PR and allocate seats using different formulas in three stages (initially with simple electoral quotient)	1–6	40	None	None

(continued)

Table 7.1 Electoral Systems in Latin America (continued)

Country	Chamber	Voting	Ballot Structure	Electoral Formula	District Magnitude Range	Number of Districts	Electoral Threshold	Reserved seats
Paraguay	Chamber of Deputies	18 yrs, voluntary	Closed and blocked lists in MMCs	Mixed, independent: 2 SMCs and 16 MMCs	1–19	18	None	None
	Chamber of Senators	18 yrs, voluntary	Closed and blocked	PR: d'Hondt	45	1	None	None
Peru	Congress of the Republic	18 yrs, compulsory	Closed and unblocked; voters may either choose a party list, or opt for two preferential votes to select two candidates on the list	Mixed, independent: one majoritarian SMC, and 24 PR MMCs	1–35		5%	None
Uruguay	House of Representatives	18 yrs, compulsory	Closed and blocked	PR: d'Hondt	2–45	19	None	None

Country	Chamber	Voting	Ballot Structure	Electoral Formula	District Magnitude Range	Number of Districts	Electoral Threshold	Reserved seats
	Chamber of Senators	18 yrs, compulsory	Closed and unblocked; voters must vote for same party as president, but allowed to select from competing lists from that party	PR: d'Hondt, in two rounds; seats first allocated to parties, then parties allocate their seats to different lists	30	1	None	None
Venezuela	National Assembly	18 yrs	Voters receive two votes; closed and blocked for PR vote	Tiered, mixed independent: 68 seats in single- and 42 seats in two to three multimember majoritarian districts; 52 seats under PR in four three-member districts and 20 two-member districts. PR seats allocated under d'Hondt	1–4	111	None	3 seats reserved for indigenous groups

Source: Data collected by author from the Inter-Parliamentary Union (www.ipu.org), ACE Electoral Network (www.ACEProject.org), Political Database of the Americas (pdba.georgetown.edu), and national electoral documents.
Provinces decide precise electoral rules. Some use double simultaneous vote.
Chile will use its new electoral system beginning in the 2017 congressional elections (see Country in the Spotlight, Chapter 5).

and implemented the secret ballot. Before these changes, majoritarian systems ensured the interests of the wealthy because they faced a truncated and sympathetic electorate. So long as they mustered the most votes in a district, they would win a seat and gain 100 percent control over representation in the district. But the newly enfranchised working and middle classes clouded these prospects by the start of the twentieth century. Unsurprisingly, elite politicians of the time introduced electoral reforms that moved away from winner-take-all systems, and toward an electoral formula that would ensure representation for minority parties—a status that they soon expected (Wills-Otero, 2009). This electoral formula, **proportional representation** (PR), works very differently than majoritarian systems. In a PR system, the allocation of seats reflects the distribution of votes across competing political parties in a district. Ideally, if a party receives 20 percent of the vote, it receives 20 percent of the legislative seats in play. Though PR systems may have found their origins in the self-interest of upper-class elites, today a range of minority parties that would otherwise be excluded in a winner-take-all system values them.

Allocating seats in proportion to votes received requires precise mathematical formulas to be established in advance of the election. There are numerous procedures for achieving proportionality, but most can be placed under **largest remainder** methods or **highest average** methods. Largest remainder methods begin by using a quota to distribute seats. The Hare quota is the most common, and it is calculated by dividing the number of seats by the total number of votes in the district. For example, Table 7.2 shows the results of the January 2009 elections to the Legislative

Table 7.2 **The Hare Quota—La Libertad, El Salvador: January 2009 Legislative Elections.** The Hare quota is the most common form of the largest remainder approach under proportional representation. It tends to produce the lowest rates of disproportionality among proportional representation systems

Party	Votes	% Votes	Quota Deputies	Votes Used	Remainder	Remainder Deputies	Total Deputies	% Seats
ARENA	104,400	42%	3	92,682	11,718	0	3	38%
CD	4,952	2%	0	0	4,952	0	0	0%
FDR	2,020	1%	0	0	2,020	0	0	0%
FMLN	102,437	41%	3	92,682	9,755	0	3	38%
PCN	19,526	8%	0	0	19,526	1	1	12%
PDC	13,816	6%	0	0	13,816	1	1	12%
	247,151		6					2%

Source: Data from the website of the *Tribunal Supremo Electoral* of El Salvador: www.tse .gob.sv.

*El Salvador moved to its current panachage system (see below, p. 284) in 2015.

Assembly of El Salvador, in which 247,151 voters in the district of La Libertad cast ballots for eight seats. If we divide that vote total by the number of seats contested (247,151/8) we establish a Hare quota of 30,894. The votes received by two parties, ARENA and FMLN, surpass this quota three times and therefore each received an initial allocation of three seats each. With two seats left still to be claimed, a second round of distribution was conducted based upon which parties had the largest remaining number of votes after subtracting the votes used to secure seats under the quota. In La Libertad, this stage allowed PCN and PDC to secure the final two seats. Consider the effects of PR in this case. Assuming similar results under a majoritarian system and with each party fielding individual candidates, ARENA would emerge as the sole winner, despite the fact that 58 percent of the electorate voted for some other party's candidate. And FMLN would leave the contest especially embittered, with nearly as much support as ARENA but nothing to show for it. Indeed, under majoritarian rules, FMLN would receive as much representation as FDR, which received just 1 percent of the vote. The 42 percent of the La Libertad residents who voted for ARENA would be ecstatic over the outcome, but the remaining would feel left out, possibly creating a recipe for political apathy or even rebellion.

The highest average method distributes seats in a series of rounds. It uses a sequence of numbers to divide a party's initial vote total in each round that awards it a seat. The numbers in the sequence increase so that the winning party's vote total drops in the subsequent round, giving parties with fewer votes a chance to pick up a seat. The d'Hondt formula is the most common highest average method. It uses a sequence of divisors equal to the total number of seats won plus one. Because all parties start with zero seats and accrue them individually, this produces a simple sequence of 1, 2, 3, 4, 5, 6, 7, …. To illustrate how the method works, we can examine electoral results from Paraguay, which uses the d'Hondt method to allocate seats in its 80-member Chamber of Deputies. Table 7.3 shows results from the April 2008 elections in the district of Asunción, the capital, which is represented in the Chamber by nine seats. ANR enters round 1 with the highest vote total. Awarded its first seat, the party then has its vote total divided by 2 for the second round. The reduction of ANR's vote is deep enough to allow two other parties, PPQ and UNACE, to gain seats in the following two rounds, though each of them also have their votes divided by 2. By round 4, ANR is once again poised to take a seat, but as a result its initial vote total of 65,049 now faces a divisor of three, and falls to 21,683. The adjustment leaves PLRA with the highest vote total in round 5. The process continues until all nine seats are filled. In the end, P-MAS fails to gain a seat. It comes close in round 9, and would have won a seat had there been a tenth to fill.

Though both are considered "proportional," largest remainder methods tend to favor smaller parties and highest average methods tend to favor larger parties. This is seen in the examples. In La Libertad, the Hare quota awards PCN and PDC a percentage of the seats above their percentages

Table 7.3 **The d'Hondt Method—Asunción, Paraguay: April 2008 Elections for the Chamber of Deputies.** The d'Hondt formula is the most common of the highest average approaches under proportional representation. It tends to produce the highest rates of disproportionality among proportional representation systems

	ANR	PPQ	UNACE	PLRA	PDP	P-MAS
Round 1	**65,049**	44,503	40,761	32,390	22,473	19,146
Round 2	32,525	**44,503**	40,761	32,390	22,473	19,146
Round 3	32,525	22,252	**40,761**	32,390	22,473	19,146
Round 4	**32,525**	22,252	20,381	32,390	22,473	19,146
Round 5	21,683	22,252	20,381	**32,390**	22,473	19,146
Round 6	21,683	22,252	20,381	16,195	**22,473**	19,146
Round 7	21,683	**22,252**	20,381	16,195	11,237	19,146
Round 8	**21,683**	14,834	20,381	16,195	11,237	19,146
Round 9	16,262	14,834	**20,381**	16,195	11,237	19,146
Total seats	3	2	2	1	1	0
Vote %*	25%	17%	16%	12%	9%	7%
Seat %	33%	22%	22%	11%	11%	0%

Source: Data from Memoria y Estadísticas Electorales: Elecciones Generales y Departamentales 2008. Justicia Electoral, 2008. Available on the website of the Justicia Electoral de Paraguay: www.tsje.gov.py.
Twenty-one percent of the vote was distributed across 13 parties that received no representation (including P-MAS).

of the vote, and offers the dominant FMLN and ARENA a percentage of seats slightly below their vote percentages. In Asunción, the d'Hondt formula "over-rewards" ANR, giving it one-third of the seats even though it accumulated one-quarter of the vote. The discrepancy between the percentage of votes received and seats awarded is nowhere near as great as those found in majoritarian systems, and in fact each type of electoral method can be adjusted. Some countries (outside of Latin America) use the Droop quota in the largest remainder approach, which divides the total votes by number of seats *plus one*. The larger denominator produces a smaller quota, allowing large parties to accumulate more quota deputies before the remainders are compared. Costa Rica attenuates its Hare quota by using a subquotient equal to one-half the quota as a threshold for parties to contend for the residual seats. If La Libertad used the method, a subquotient of 15,447 would have excluded PDC from the second round and its seat would have gone to ARENA. Highest average methods can be modified to accommodate smaller parties if a different sequence of numbers is used. The Sainte-Lagüe method uses an odd sequence of numbers (1, 3, 5, 7, ...) to reduce the vote totals of winning parties more quickly and give those with lower totals a chance. In Latin America, it is used only in Ecuador.

Hybrid Systems

Majoritarian and PR electoral formulas have several political consequences. First, one readily recognizes the very different opportunities for small parties. Majoritarian formulas offer them little chance of victory. Indeed, the hurdle is so great that most would-be parties decide not to waste time and resources on the effort and fail to form. Smaller parties seeking influence must join larger parties, which readily absorb them to retain their relative majority. In a PR system a sprightly party can at least win a few seats, and hope to build support from there. The relative electoral prospects largely explain why majoritarian formulas typically lead to two-party systems, whereas PR formulas tend to allow for multiparty systems. Moreover, electoral formulas also affect the way parties behave. The incentive to merge under majoritarian rules leads to parties with broad-based appeal. On the other hand, PR systems allow parties that cater to narrow interests to survive—indeed, finding a niche in the political spectrum is the key to survival under PR. Critics of majoritarian systems argue that the effort to appeal to all leads to parties that appeal to none. Critics of PR systems point out the troubles created when so many disparate voices with narrow interests find their way into government. Their spirited debate may appear to be the epitome of democracy, but **party system fragmentation** makes it difficult to gather the simple majorities required for government to work. Another important difference arises from the fact that individuals run in majoritarian systems, whereas parties appear on the ticket in PR systems. Voters under majoritarian formulas know who their representatives are, and can hold them accountable. Voters in PR systems have multiple representatives, making it difficult to lay blame if they fail to effectively represent the district. This difference also creates much stronger incentives for constituency service in majoritarian systems.

Due to the advantages of both electoral formulas, many countries attempt to get the best of both worlds. One simple way to do this is with **mixed systems**. These allocate seats through some combination of single-member and multimember districts, using both majoritarian and PR formulas. For example, Panama divides itself into 26 majoritarian single-member districts, and 14 multimember PR districts. Some countries also make use of **tiered districts** to mix electoral formulas. In Mexico, each of the 31 states and the capital send three representatives to the Senate. They are elected under the same majoritarian formula used by the Argentine Senate—the winning party receives two seats and the runner-up receives one seat. But layered upon these districts is one large national district of 32 seats. The allocation of these seats is determined by summing the votes received by each party in the 32 regional districts, and assigning representation according to a Hare quota. Not all countries, however, use different electoral formulas in their tiers. Nicaragua has both regional districts and one large nationwide district, but both tiers use PR (under a Hare quota). The examples from Mexico and Nicaragua illustrate another variation in tiered systems. Specifically, under the Mexican system, voters receive just one vote—their district votes directly determine the seat distribution in the national tier. In Nicaragua, voters receive two ballots—one for the regional district and a second for the nationwide district. Hence, we would describe the Mexican system as one with dependent tiers, whereas Nicaragua has independent tiers.

District Magnitude

District magnitude refers to the number of representatives in a district. Globally, majoritarian systems usually have just one representative. Latin America is unusual in that its majoritarian districts more often contain two or three seats. These include the senates of Argentina, Brazil, and Mexico, and some assembly districts in Ecuador (those with two representatives). Though PR systems always have more than one representative per district, the number can vary tremendously. In fact, almost all countries with PR systems have districts of different sizes. In Brazil's Chamber of Deputies, multimember constituencies range from eight to seventy representatives. Ultimately, the average district magnitude largely defines the proportionality of a proportional system. Simply put, it is easier to approximate the vote distribution when there are more seats to allocate. And generally speaking, analysts have calculated that a district requires at least five seats to effectively address disproportionality.

Hence, it is not enough to identify the electoral formula of a country to assess how the electoral system of the country affects the proportional translation of seats into votes. Proportional representation may be pervasive in Latin America, but it is undercut not only by mixed systems that add majoritarian districts, but also by low district magnitudes. Panama has a mixed system, but 97.5 percent of its districts contain five or fewer seats. Primarily PR systems with particularly low average district magnitudes include Colombia's lower house (4.8), El Salvador's assembly (4.6), Paraguay's lower house (4.4), the Dominican Republic's lower house (3.2), and Panama's assembly (3.2) (Nohlen, 2005, vol. 2, pp. 31–32). Ecuador may appear to have a proportional system in its 124-member national assembly, but within its 28 districts, 20 seats emerge from majoritarian two-member districts, and an additional 42 emerge from PR districts with only three or four members.

Electoral Thresholds

One criticism of PR systems is that they allow too many small parties to survive. Thresholds, which require a party to receive some minimum portion of the vote to be eligible for seats, can help guard against such party system fragmentation. All parties face an **effective threshold** that emerges from some combination of district magnitude and the number of competing parties. So long as there are fewer parties than the number of available seats, the effective threshold is easily calculated by dividing 100 percent by the number of seats in a district. For example, if four parties were competing in a district with five seats, any party would only have to collect at least 20 percent of the vote to guarantee itself a seat. But countries can also create a **legal threshold** by mandating some minimum amount of the vote—though again, there are several variations on how this can be done. Nicaragua requires its parties to obtain at least 4 percent of the nationwide vote to be eligible for seats in any of its districts. Hence, if a Nicaraguan party does very well in one district—even if it amasses over 50 percent—but does very poorly in the remainder of the country, it may be denied representation in that district. Peru slightly attenuates its nationwide threshold of 4 percent with an exception for parties that win five seats or more across at least two districts. Unlike in Nicaragua, this gives regional parties in Peru a chance. Argentina goes further to accommodate regional parties in its Chamber of Deputies by placing its 3 percent threshold only at the district level.

Mexico's Chamber of Deputies makes use of several thresholds to distribute its 500 seats. The chamber uses a mixed, tiered system, with 300 seats elected in majoritarian single-member districts, and the other 200 elected in five multimember PR districts of 40 seats each. Although seats in the multimember districts are distributed proportionally, the allocation is also dependent on outcomes in the single-member districts. First, to be eligible for seats in the multimember districts, a party must collect at least 2 percent of the vote in each multimember district. Second, it also must run candidates in at least 200 of the 300 single-member districts. Third, all parties face a total seat ceiling of 300, with single-member district seats distributed first. Finally, to guard against disproportionality in the majoritarian single-member districts, the electoral law holds that a party's total share of seats may not outstrip its total share of the vote by more than eight percentage points. Any adjustments required by this rule are done with the PR seats.

Ballot Structure

Before a country determines how votes will be counted (the electoral formula), it must first decide how voters will be asked to vote. The **categorical ballot** is the most simple. It asks voters to vote for just one candidate or party. It is an obvious choice for majoritarian single-member districts, where the candidate with the most votes wins. It can also work in a majoritarian system with multimember districts, as in every other election for the Brazilian Senate, when two-thirds of the seats are filled. In this case, Brazilian voters receive two votes for the two offices, and the two candidates with the most votes win (the vote is categorical in this case because there are two votes for two seats). But the categorical ballot is also common in PR systems. Argentina (Chamber of Deputies), Bolivia, Costa Rica,

El Salvador, Guatemala, Mexico, Nicaragua, Paraguay, Uruguay (House of Representatives), and Venezuela all use this ballot structure in their PR multimember districts. In such cases each party must submit a numbered list of candidates before the election, and if a party wins seats, it then assigns the seats in order to the highest-listed candidates. These lists are referred to as **closed**, because voters must select just one party, and **blocked**, because voters have no sway over the order of the list. Closed and blocked ballots contribute to party discipline, because when party members veer from the party line, party leaders can retaliate by dropping them farther down the list.

A second type of ballot is the **ordinal ballot**, which comes in many forms. This ballot allows voters to express their preferences more completely and to influence the order of party lists. Because it requires multiple winners in a district, it is much more common to PR than to majoritarian systems. Chile was one of the few majoritarian systems that used an ordinal ballot before its 2015 reform. Brazil (Chamber of Deputies), Dominican Republic (House of Deputies), Honduras, Panama, and Uruguay (Senate) give voters a single vote to select a preferred candidate on party lists. Votes for all the candidates of individual parties are accumulated to determine the allocation of seats to parties, but the parties are then required to offer the seats to those candidates with the most votes. Such party lists are labeled closed and unblocked. Peru gives its voters a choice between a categorical ballot to select closed and blocked party lists, or an ordinal ballot with two votes that can be assigned to two favored candidates within the list. Colombia's ballot varies across districts and legislative chambers. Party lists are always closed, but whether they are blocked or not depends on the district in the House of Representatives, whereas in the Senate parties have the choice to block or unblock their seats. Ecuador, El Salvador, and Honduras offer voters the greatest range of choice with open (and by definition unblocked) party lists in what is called the "panachage" system. Voters receive as many votes as seats up for election in the district. If a voter strongly supports a given candidate, the system allows voters to vote multiple times for a single candidate. Voters can also distribute votes across different party lists, effectively creating their own lists. Outside Latin America the panachage system is used only in the national elections of Switzerland, Monaco, Luxembourg, and Liechtenstein. It is the most extreme example of the ordinal ballot. And like all ordinal ballots, by moving control of candidate placement from of the hands of party elites to the hands of voters, it tends to weaken party discipline. Still, proponents of ordinal ballots note that they create stronger ties between voters and politicians. A slothful, even corrupt, politician can survive under a categorical ballot in a PR system if he or she curries favor with party elites. But that same politician is likely to be punished by voters equipped with an ordinal ballot.

Another consideration of ballot structure is the use of **fused voting**, which refers to the practice of tying different offices to a single vote. In the

Photo 7.2 A well-constructed voting system expands the sense of empowerment and dignity in a democracy.

Source: © Alamy

Dominican Republic voters must vote under the same party in the House of Deputies and Senate. And in Bolivia, seats are apportioned to senate members and to deputies in PR districts according to their parties' vote in the presidential election. Critics of fused voting recognize that it limits voter choices, but advocates argue that it counters party system fragmentation.

Districting and Apportionment

Districting refers to the drawing of constituency lines. Apportionment is the allocation of seats to these districts. Majoritarian systems require districting, and as we have seen, although these systems classically have one representative per district, Latin American majoritarian systems more often have two or three representatives apportioned to each district. In PR systems, districting is a choice. The Senates of Colombia, Paraguay, and Uruguay each arise from a single, nationwide district. This allows the countries to create more proportional representation. The trade-off is that they typically fail to create very strong ties between voters and individual politicians. Colombian voters can look to a highly representative Senate, with 100 seats distributed to some one dozen various parties, but cannot readily distinguish who "their" representative is. Little surprise that Colombia, Paraguay, and Uruguay are all bicameral system. All have smaller districts in their lower chambers and this allows voters to better identify with these individual politicians. Indeed, most PR systems divide the country into districts to forge a bond between voters and politicians. The bond cannot be as strong as that of the majoritarian single-member district, but it will certainly be greater than that found in a nationwide district.

Districting and apportionment are not mere administrative tasks. They are political processes that can affect the translation of votes into seats to the same extent as the electoral formula. Generally, districting is more open to abuse in majoritarian systems, whereas apportionment can undermine representation in a PR system as district magnitudes veer from relative population totals (e.g., one district with a population of 100,000 receives six representatives, while another similarly populated district receives only four representatives). The most egregious abuse of districting, known as **gerrymandering**, occurs when constituency lines are drawn so as to spread the votes of one party thinly across a number of districts, and to concentrate the votes of another party in relative majorities across as many districts as possible. Some analysts contend that the military dictator of Chile, Augusto Pinochet, used electoral data from a plebiscite to assess the geographical voting distribution of his opposition, and then to gerrymander district lines against it before the transition to democracy in 1990 (Londregan, 2000, pp. 87–93). The 2015 electoral reform has allowed the Chilean legislature to free itself from this authoritarian legacy (see "Country in the Spotlight," Chapter 5).

Malapportionment refers to imbalances in representation across districts. Legislatures in Latin America have greater levels of malapportionment compared to other regions of the world. More often than not, such disproportionality advantages conservative, rural areas. This is largely the result of two factors. The use of senates to ensure representation to specific regions (especially in federal systems) has offered constitutional guarantees to geographic areas with populations that have grown sparser as individuals move to the more liberal, urban areas. Argentina has the most malapportioned senate in the world. Twenty-three provinces and the capital of Buenos Aires send three representatives each to the Senate. That equality in district magnitude is belied by the vast differences in population, which run from 13.8 million in Buenos Aires Province to just 101,000 in tiny Tierra del Fuego Province. Over 45 percent of the population lives in the capital or Buenos Aires Province, yet they are represented by just 6 of the 72 senators in the chamber. On the other hand, the four most lightly populated provinces, with just over one million inhabitants—or 2.8 percent of the total population, control 12 of the 72 senators. A second source of malapportionment has come from the explicit strategies of outgoing military dictators, who targeted the lower chambers of congress. These military dictators sought to overrepresent rural conservative areas, which had some sympathy for military rule. In Argentina, lower chamber districts with 31 percent of the population control 44 percent of representation. In Brazil, lower chamber districts with 42 percent of the population hold 51 percent of the seats. And in the Chilean post-authoritarian electoral system, just 35 percent of the population controlled 50 percent of representation in the lower chamber (Snyder and Samuels, 2004).

The Electoral System and Political Change

Once we break down the electoral system into its components, we can gauge how different parts might work together or how they might offset each other to affect questions of proportionality, party system fragmentation, or the behavior of parties and politicians. A country may use a Hare quota to distribute its seats in proportion to the vote, but low district magnitudes, high thresholds, and malapportionment could offset this effort. Disaggregating the electoral system also allows us to recognize which parts play a more or less crucial difference depending on the composure of an electoral system. We know that majoritarian systems create incentives for politicians to engage in constituency service, but whether or not PR systems do is dependent upon the ballot structure (specifically, the use of an ordinal ballot).

It is no secret that the parts of an electoral system have such significant political consequences. They have long been a magnet for political intrigue and abuse. The possibility for such manipulation poses a dire threat to democracy. A country may enjoy all the laurels of political competition and proudly showcase free and fair elections, but the process may still be warped by rules explicitly devised to reward some and to punish others. This is not to claim that built-in biases are always signs of a democracy gone astray. At times, such predispositions are part of the founding compromises of a country, embraced as sacred parts of the constitutional fabric. Malapportionment may be inequitable, but it also may be ingrained in the federal identity of a country and in this way reinforce the traditional legitimacy of the political system. Gerrymandering may unfairly prop up representation for some groups, but if it is used to boost historically underrepresented indigenous groups, the move could bolster prospects for democratic consolidation. And although thresholds shut out smaller political factions, the fact that they also may enhance governability proves that there are often competing justifiable political values at play.

Hence, what is important is not the incidence of bias, but rather unilateral moves by one group to advantage itself and to suppress the would-be gains of another group. This is why electoral rules must be transparent and agreed upon in advance by all significant political groups. This point is important, because of all the political institutions in a regime, electoral rules are usually the easiest to change. Some elements may be enshrined in the constitution, but more often than not, they are vaguely defined. For example, Article 132 of the Nicaraguan Constitution establishes a National Assembly comprised of 90 deputies, with 20 elected in a national district and 70 from local and regional districts. Furthermore, it explicitly calls for proportional representation. But that still leaves unanswered questions over districting, apportionment, the use of thresholds, and the precise electoral formula. Table 7.4

Table 7.4 **Electoral Rules and the Constitution.** A country can protect its electoral rules from potential manipulations by placing them in the constitution

Country	Electoral Formula in Constitution	Size of Chamber Fixed in Constitution	Apportionment Rules in Constitution
Argentina—Deputies	no	no	no
Argentina—Senate	yes	yes	yes
Bolivia—Deputies	yes	yes	no
Bolivia—Senate	yes	yes	yes
Brazil—Deputies	yes	no	yes
Brazil—Senate	yes	yes	yes
Chile—Deputies	no	yes	organic law*
Chile—Senate	no	no	organic law*
Colombia—House	no	yes	yes
Colombia—Senate	yes	yes	yes
Costa Rica	no	yes	no
Dom Rep—Deputies	no	no	yes
Dom Rep—Senate	yes	yes	yes
Ecuador	yes	no	yes
El Salvador	yes	no	no
Guatemala	yes	no	yes
Honduras	yes	yes	no
Mexico—Deputies	yes	yes	no
Mexico—Senate	yes	yes	yes
Nicaragua	yes	no	no
Panama	yes	yes	no
Paraguay—Deputies	no	no	no
Paraguay—Senate	yes	no	yes
Peru	yes	yes	no

Country	Electoral Formula in Constitution	Size of Chamber Fixed in Constitution	Apportionment Rules in Constitution
Uruguay—Deputies	yes	no	no
Uruguay—Senate	yes	yes	yes
Venezuela	yes	no	yes

* In Chile an organic law is a piece of legislation typically designed to elaborate on a feature of the constitution. Although an organic law does not have constitutional status, it requires a supermajority to change it.

illustrates the relative malleability of electoral rules in Latin American countries. It charts just a few variables relevant to the electoral system and notes which rules rest in the constitution, making them most resistant to change. For most countries, the details of electoral rules rest in statutory law, which is more open to change.

Presidential Elections in Latin America

Because presidential elections are such high-stakes affairs, it should come as no surprise that they radiate political effects across a regime, including the broader electoral system and party system. A couple of variables are important here. First, it matters whether presidential elections run concurrently with legislative elections or not. If they do, the presidential campaign tends to overshadow legislative races. Presidential candidates receive the lion's share of the media spotlight, and this allows them to set the agenda for political debate, and draw attention to the platforms of their own political parties. Voters know that if they want their favored presidential candidate to rule effectively, they had better support their candidate's party in the legislature. This is not good news for small parties, which usually lack the resources to fund a competitive presidential candidate, and generally find themselves shut out as media outlets focus on just a few of the top presidential contenders. The result is that presidential elections, when enacted concurrently with legislative elections, tend to reduce the number of parties in a country (Shugart and Carey, 1992).

A second variable is the precise method of presidential election. Only Honduras, Mexico, Nicaragua, Panama, Paraguay, and Venezuela use the simple plurality rule, whereby the candidate with the most votes wins. All other countries allow for a runoff election between the two top candidates under certain conditions. Brazil, Chile, Colombia, the Dominican Republic, El Salvador, Guatemala, Peru, and Uruguay require the winner to surpass 50 percent of the vote to avoid a runoff. Advocates of the majority runoff argue that it enhances stability and consensus because it ensures that the winner collects an endorsement from over 50 percent of the electorate.

Such advocates would likely point to Mexico's 2012 election, which saw Enrique Peña Nieto take the presidential sash with just 38.15 percent of the vote. Under such plurality rules, the opposition can always argue that a majority of the population voted for someone else, and thus question the popular mandate of the president. Supporters of the plurality rule counter that runoffs make matters worse as they contribute to party fragmentation. Plurality contests allow smaller parties to follow on the coattails of the greater number of candidates who perceive a chance at making it to the second round than they would have in a single-round plurality contest. In addition, even those who expect to gather only a small percentage of the vote in the first round still see reason to run in the hope that they can negotiate their support with one of the two top contenders in the second round. Hence, the legitimacy afforded to runoff winners by virtue of their majority mandate is mitigated by a fragmented legislature that challenges governability (Mainwaring and Shugart, 1997).

Some countries attempt to split the difference between plurality and majority runoff rules by calling for qualified majorities. Costa Rica suffered from a bitterly contested election in 1932, which saw no candidate win a majority. In response, a 1936 reform required presidential winners to accrue at least 40 percent of the vote to avoid a runoff. The country has experienced only one runoff (in 2002), but the rule provides some comfort to those who fear for the legitimacy of presidents elected with a minimal amount of the vote. Bolivia raises the bar, calling for 45 percent with at least a 10 percent margin of victory to avoid a runoff. Other countries offer two routes to the presidency in the first round. In Ecuador, a candidate can avoid a runoff by gathering 50 percent of the vote, or by gaining 40 percent with a 10 percent margin of victory. Argentina requires 45 percent, or 40 percent with a 10 percent margin of victory. Table 7.5 lists recent presidential election outcomes in Latin America, and identifies those countries that use a second-round runoff election.

The impact of presidential elections should not be underestimated. **Duverger's Law** underscores the strong relationship between electoral systems and party systems. But as is always the case in regimes, the entire institutional setting matters. A PR system will create pressures for a multiparty system, but these same pressures will be undercut by concurrent presidential-legislative elections, and a plurality presidential election. Even if a regime does not have concurrent elections and uses a runoff in the race for executive office, presidentialism itself has a winnowing effect on the number of parties due to the winner-take-all nature of the executive office (Lijphart, 1994, p. 131).

Another important variation in presidential elections is whether an incumbent is allowed to stand for reelection. Mexico spearheaded the effort to institute term limits in reaction to the abusive moves made by President Porfirio Díaz to stay in office from 1876 to 1911. *"No re-elección"* became a rallying cry of his opponents, and to this day the phrase is essentially

Table 7.5 **Recent Presidential Elections in Latin America.** Latin American presidents have entered office with different electoral mandates—some of which have been increased by a runoff election

Country	President	Term	Percentage of Vote	
			1st Round	*2nd Round*
Argentina	Mauricio Macri	2015–2019	34.2	51.3
Bolivia	Evo Morales	2005–2009	53.7	–
		2009–2014	63.0	–
		2014–2019	61.0	
Brazil	Dilma Rousseff	2011–2015	46.9	56.1
		2015–2016[a]	41.6	51.6
Chile	Michelle Bachelet	2014–2018	46.7	62.2
Colombia	Juan Manuel Santos	2010–2014	46.7	69.0
		2014–2018	25.7	53.1
Costa Rica	Luis Guillermo Solis	2014–2018	30.64	77.81
Dominican Republic	Danilo Medina Sánchez	2016–2020	61.8	–
Ecuador	Rafael Correa	2007–2009[b]	23.0	56.7
		2009–2013	52.0	–
		2013–2017	57.2	
El Salvador	Salvador Sánchez Cerén	2014–2019	48.9	50.1
Guatemala	Jimmy Morales	2015–2019	23.9	67.4
Honduras	Juan Orlando Hernández	2014–2018	36.9	–
Mexico	Enrique Peña Nieto	2012–2018	38.2	–
Nicaragua	Daniel Ortega	2007–2012	38.0	–

(*continued*)

Table 7.5 **Recent Presidential Elections in Latin America.** Latin American presidents have entered office with different electoral mandates—some of which have been increased by a runoff election (*continued*)

Country	President	Term	Percentage of Vote	
			1st Round	*2nd Round*
		2012–2017	62.4	
		2017–2021	72.4	
Panama	Juan Carlos Varela	2014–2019	39.1	–
Paraguay	Horacio Cartes	2013–2018	45.8	–
Peru	Pedro Kuczynski	2016–2021	21.1	50.1
Uruguay	Tabaré Vázquez	2015–2020	49.5	56.6
Venezuela	Nicolás Maduro	2013–2019	50.0	–

Source: Data from "Adam Carr's Election Archive." Available at sephos.adam-carr.net.
In 2016, Dilma Rousseff was impeached and replaced by Michel Temer.
Presidential term reinitiated after the passing of a new constitution, and new elections.

synonymous with the guarantee of democratic rule for Mexicans. The limit applied to legislators as well until it was nullified in 2014. The thinking spread to several Latin American countries as they reacted to their own experiences with *caudillo* rule. But today, only Guatemala, Mexico, and Paraguay prohibit immediate reelection. Nicaragua and Venezuela allow indefinite reelection. Chile, Costa Rica, Ecuador, El Salvador, Nicaragua, Panama, Peru, and Uruguay ask incumbent presidents to sit out at least one term before running again. Latin American countries also show variation in the length of presidential terms. Mexico and Venezuela offer the longest terms, at six years. Bolivia, El Salvador, Nicaragua, Panama, Paraguay, Peru, and Uruguay set five-year terms, and the remaining countries have four-year terms.

With a history that has seen presidents cling to power through repressive or fraudulent measures, one can understand the constitutional limits that were placed upon presidential terms in Latin America. But what has allowed countries to move away from such restrictions over the past 20 years? The argument to do away with limits usually takes on a similar form—limits made sense when democracy was fragile, but today the country is on much more solid footing; and, to retain limits is to restrict the will of the people. The argument forces those hoping to preserve limits to take a position that is easily portrayed as cynical, pessimistic, and even antidemocratic.

Alberto Fujimori of Peru and Carlos Menem of Argentina ushered in the strategy to extend presidential rule—either through longer terms or by dropping term limits—in the 1990s. Hugo Chavez of Venezuela followed in 2000. Alvaro Uribe pushed through a constitutional change to allow his own reelection in 2005. Rafael Correa of Ecuador and Evo Morales of Bolivia made their moves in 2009. Nicaragua's Daniel Ortega, barred from reelection by two constitutional provisions, one that prohibits immediate reelection and another that allows only two terms at any point in time, tried a different tack. He had the Supreme Court declare the constitutional articles "inapplicable" before the 2011 elections, then changed the constitution in 2014. The record indicates that neither the political right nor left claims a monopoly on presidential term reform efforts.

The idea of term reform stood at the center of the constitutional crisis that hit Honduras in 2009. The Constitution of Honduras not only prohibits presidential reelection, but it also states that this portion of the constitution cannot be reformed. President Manuel Zelaya appeared to sidetrack this stipulation when he called for a referendum to assess public opinion on constitutional reform, including a provision to lift presidential term limits. The Supreme Court ruled the referendum illegal, and with support from congress and the public prosecutor, issued a warrant for Zelaya's arrest when he attempted to organize a vote on constitutional reform. The military carried out the arrest warrant, but then on its own initiative decided to exile Zelaya to Costa Rica. Hastily organized elections allowed Zelaya's opponent, Juan Orlando Hernandez, to then take the presidency. The entire event was widely condemned in diplomatic circles, and characterized throughout international media as a coup d'état. The rule of law is clearly frail in Honduras, but the story does not stop there. In 2016, the Supreme Court issued a ruling to disable the constitutional articles that prohibit reelection so that Hernandez could seek reelection in 2017.

Presidential term reform has emerged as the new battleground for political powerholders in Latin America. The crisis in Honduras may have been exceptional, but the debate over term reform was not.

The Management and Observation of Elections

Consider the dilemma that elections pose to a democratic regime: How can a government be trusted to organize an event that may lead to its own downfall? Also keep in mind that elections create quite a logistical

COMPARING COUNTRIES

Direct Democracy in Latin America

Direct democracy refers to the active involvement of citizens in government decision-making. For practical reasons, countries throughout the world have opted for representative democracy rather than direct democracy. Nonetheless, many countries allow opportunities for direct democracy alongside representative democracy. The distinction of direct democracy is that voters take an active role in decision-making, rather than delegating matters to a representative. Direct democracy involves either decisions on actual policy, or the removal of elected officials from office, as in recall campaigns.

Direct democracy comes in many shapes and sizes. One type, the recall, allows voters to remove an elected official from office. Other types of direct democracy allow voters to participate in the legislative process, though at different stages. Citizens' initiatives involve the public at the very outset of the lawmaking process. Legislative proposals can be drafted outside the halls of government by private citizens, and a popular vote will decide whether they become law or not. Citizens' initiatives can also take the form of a petition for government to legislate in a given policy area. In other instances, the public can have the final say on a piece of legislation working its way through government. The *consulta*, or consultation, is required under some conditions (mandated *consulta*), but it can also be triggered by popular demand (optional popular *consulta*) or by decision within the executive or legislature (optional government *consulta*). Finally, citizens can also hold repeal authority, so that they are able to revoke a piece of legislation even after it has become law.

Forms of Direct Democracy in Latin America

Several countries make use of mandated *consultas*. Guatemala, Paraguay, Uruguay, and Venezuela require a popular vote to approve any constitutional change. Chile, Panama, and Peru also oblige a public vote, but only when the normal procedure for constitutional change is interrupted. In Chile this happens when the president and congress disagree, in Peru when the congressional vote surpasses a simple majority but fails to meet the required two-thirds majority needed for approval, and in Panama when the legislature decides to modify a constitutional proposal during the reform process (which requires approval of the change by three consecutive legislatures).

Table 7.6 **Forms of Direct Democracy in Latin America**

Country	Citizen's Initiative	Optional Popular Consulta	Optional Government Consulta	Mandated Consulta	Recall
Argentina	Y	N	Y	N	N
Bolivia	Y	Y	Y	Y	Y
Brazil	Y	N	Y	Y	N
Chile	N	N	N	Y	N
Colombia	Y	Y	Y	Y	N
Costa Rica	Y	Y	Y	Y	N
Dominican Republic	Y	Y	Y	N	N
Ecuador	Y	Y	Y	Y	Y
El Salvador	N	N	N	Y	N
Guatemala	Y	N	Y	Y	N
Honduras	Y	Y	Y	N	N
Mexico	Y	Y	Y	N	N
Nicaragua	Y	Y	Y	N	N
Panama	Y	Y	Y	Y	Y
Paraguay	Y	N	Y	Y	N
Peru	Y	Y	Y	Y	N
Uruguay	Y	Y	N	N	N
Venezuela	Y	Y	Y	Y	Y

Source: Data compiled from Zovatto Garetto 2015.

Other countries have mandated *consultas* for specific issues. In Bolivia any international treaty that entails border changes, economic integration, or the handover of decision-making authority to international or supranational organizations must be put to a popular vote. El Salvador requires a vote of support on issues that involve regional unification in Central America. Guatemala instructs its government to request public approval on decisions related to its border with Belize.

(continued)

And the people of Panama have the final say over policies related to the future of the Panama Canal.

Optional consultas come into play more often. More important, governments in the region in fact do initiate more referenda than citizens. Since 1978, there have been 51 *consultas*, and governments have initiated 38 (74 percent) of them. Moreover, of the 13 initiated by the public, 10 took place in just one country—Uruguay. One can interpret this disparity in initiation as a hint that direct democracy is not really used to reinforce government accountability, as the conventional wisdom would hold. Rather, it may have more to do with discord between the executive and legislative branches. That is, government officials resort to direct democracy in an effort to sidestep the normal legislative process when they fail to get their way on a policy initiative. In this sense, direct democracy is not a complement to representative democracy, but instead a subversion of representative democracy (Breuer, 2011). Viewing direct democracy in this way also exposes an opportune institutional context for the long-standing Latin American tradition of populism. Populism looks to a strong, charismatic individual for leadership, and regards standing government policy-making channels, such as the legislature, bureaucracy, and the courts, as obstacles to the popular will and true democracy. Direct democracy thus provides the perfect cloak for demagogues to run roughshod over normal policy-making channels and to skirt the protections offered by the balance of powers in a presidential system. Of course, whether a leader who makes use of direct democracy is a demagogue or genuine spokesperson for the general will is typically a matter of intense debate. Presidents Evo Morales of Bolivia, Rafael Correa of Ecuador, and Hugo Chávez of Venezuela all used referenda to convene constituent assemblies that then drafted new constitutions to their liking. Critics charged that they were simply playing upon the passions of the day, but the leaders had the ultimate defense—a popular mandate.

Discussion Questions

1   Is direct democracy inherently democratic, or does it subvert democracy? How do institutional details shape the ultimate impact of direct democracy?
2   Are there some questions that should never be subject to direct democracy? Why or why not?

challenge. They do not consist only of the counting of votes, but also of the supervision of campaigns, education of voters, development of registration rolls, enforcement of candidacy requirements, design and delivery of ballots, placement of poll stations, procurement of voting supplies, provision of security arrangements, adjudication of disputes, documentation of results, and more. Inevitably, technical glitches and human error will come into play. If a government fails to demonstrate a good faith effort to minimize logistical lapses, it runs the risk that voters will suspect foul play. Sometimes a purely logistical oversight will lead to unfair charges of political impropriety. Of course, at other times governments may actually use "administrative errors" to disguise their true, malicious intentions.

To reassure the skeptical, governments in Latin America and elsewhere have created independent **electoral management bodies** (EMBs) to administrate elections. The body is typically given some level of administrative and financial autonomy, and some countries, such as Costa Rica, Uruguay, and Venezuela, go further by establishing their EMBs as separate bodies in the constitution. Typically some half-dozen individuals staff the board for four- to six-year terms. They can be appointed by the legislature or judiciary, or through a process that involves both branches. Only Argentina, Bolivia, Brazil, and Chile involve the president in the appointment of members to their EMBs. Most commonly, countries use merit-based and professional criteria to decide appointments. Colombia and Honduras are the only countries that use exclusively partisan-based criteria. Staffing an EMB with party affiliates is not uncommon elsewhere throughout the world, and it is a defensible arrangement (about one-third of countries worldwide apply partisan criteria for EMB membership). So long as there is a balance among competing political parties, the members can act as watchdogs on each other. And in countries working their way through conflict-ridden transitions from authoritarianism, many administrative experts lack credibility because they have associations with the old regime, whereas party affiliates stir greater participation in the electoral process due to their closer connections in society. El Salvador employs a mixed-recruitment model, with experts and partisans, an arrangement well suited to its needs as the country implemented peace accords to end a civil war. The lessons for EMB design are relatively straightforward— EMBs ought to receive sufficient autonomy from the standing government to offset suspicions of foul play, and the precise mix of merit or partisan-based criteria for membership can move toward expertise as voters grow more confident in the electoral process (Hartlyn et al., 2008; IDEA, 2006).

To further advance confidence in elections, more and more countries are making use of electoral observation by both domestic and foreign organizations. Within the country, civil society groups and political parties may receive permission to place observers at the polls or at vote-counting locations, and to monitor the delivery of ballots. But many of these groups lack the resources or skills to mount a national, professional monitoring program, and they may be subject to government pressure. International organizations and nongovernmental organizations (NGOs) from abroad may have these resources and skills, but they often lack local knowledge or sensitivity to particular issues and arrive with their own interests. Observation groups from international organizations must ultimately answer to the member states of their organization, and states are often reluctant to take actions that might destabilize another state. Hence, they may set the bar for declaring electoral fraud rather high. Many foreign NGOs arrive with an activist agenda, and pose the opposite problem. And then there are the larger, more mainstream NGOs that profess independence but are resource-rich precisely because they are well-funded by a foreign state agency or private group with its own interests. In the case of Latin America, the Organization of American States offers electoral monitoring services. The European Union has also sent teams to the region. The United Nations, through the UN Development Program, has geared its efforts more toward technical assistance rather than monitoring. Some important NGOs from the United States include the National Democratic Institute, International Republican Institute, Carter Center, and Washington Office on Latin America.

Clearly, electoral management and observation is best done through the cooperative efforts of several groups. And although each organization brings its own assets and biases, they all must answer to a similar predicament faced by all involved in an election. Namely, that an election is a deceptively concentrated event. In most cases, it appears to take place on a single day, and this feeds the fantasy that so long as all goes well on that day, the election can be dubbed clean and fair. But as our understanding of electoral systems shows, the structure of the elections themselves can be a serious matter of debate. In addition, registration drives and the campaign open myriad opportunities for abuse. Election day is but a staged snapshot in a process that takes place over several months. Election analysts have coined the term **"electoral cycle"** to capture the true labor that electoral management and observation entails, and to educate all on areas of concern beyond the day of the vote (see Figure 7.1). To adequately address all portions of the electoral cycle, agencies that manage and observe elections employ both long-term and short-term staff. For the EMBs, the short-term staff supervises the poll booth, offers assistance to voters, and helps count the ballots. For observers, the short-term staff arrives just a few days before election day to watch the vote, whereas the long-term staff visits for at least few weeks to evaluate the electoral cycle more completely. The reliance on short-term staff is a necessity, but it also means that individuals who may only receive minimal or moderate training will conduct a large portion of the work.

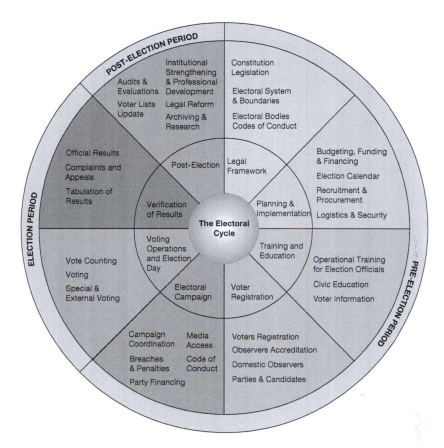

Figure 7.1 The electoral cycle.

The electoral cycle shows how voting involves a much more extensive process than just the voting that takes place on election day.

Source: Diagram from The European Commission—UN Development Program Partnership on Electoral Assistance (Image courtesy of the ACE Project at aceproject.com).

COUNTRY IN THE SPOTLIGHT

The Electoral System in Bolivia

If elections are meant to reflect the will of the people in government, then it would seem that they have only started to function properly in Bolivia. This is a country with an indigenous populace that composes at least two-thirds of the total population, and yet they have just recently seen real representation in government. Their rise has

(continued)

occurred alongside significant reforms of the electoral system meant to solidify the turn toward more democratic politics. Nonetheless, the recent electoral changes may have overstated the gains and unity of the indigenous movement. Bolivia presents an interesting case study that illustrates how the craftsmanship of electoral design must ultimately answer to real political divisions in society.

The very first constitution of Bolivia, enacted in 1826, obliged the country to have a "representative popular government" in which sovereignty "emanated from the people."[2] But the country soon experienced instability, and over the course of some 150 years saw the ratification of 15 other constitutions, commonly during the fleeting rule of the many *caudillos* that made it to the presidential palace. All of the constitutions proclaimed some commitment to democracy—even if limited by positivist thought—and committed the country to free and fair elections, but the indigenous were consistently shut out from representative politics. A 1952 revolution gave indigenous peoples the right to vote for the very first time, but a series of military interventions soon ended any real hope for social change. The most recent transition from military dictatorship, in 1982, occurred under the 1967 Constitution, which again declared the country a "representative democracy," with "sovereignty residing in the people."[3] The country moved toward liberal democracy through the 1980s and 1990s, placing few constraints on political activities. But the efficacy of the indigenous population had been wounded by centuries of repression. They had only gained access to educational institutions in the 1950s. Most lived in poverty far from urban centers where national politics were decided. Things grew worse in the 1980s and 1990s, when Bolivia's embrace of neoliberal reform removed the agricultural subsidies, price supports, and access to credit that had allowed them to eke out a living. Those that worked the tin mines saw their jobs disappear as the industry declined under the competitive pressures of globalization. The economic despair initiated an exodus to the city fringes, where the destitute erected brick shantytowns with population sizes that soon rivaled that of the urban core. The concentrated population facilitated mobilization, especially as the indigenous sought access to land, or protested government moves to privatize gas, water, and other utilities.

Instability was the norm by the 2000s. Protests against the neoliberalism of the Washington Consensus had grown so commonplace that the capital of La Paz would close its main street every Thursday afternoon to facilitate demonstrations. The institutionalization of the party system had fallen apart, leaving an unmistakable disconnect between Bolivian society and the Bolivian government. Evo Morales, an Aymara Indian who had "cut his teeth" organizing trade unions and protests against U.S.-sponsored efforts to eradicate coca, emerged as a symbol of this rift. Morales had a humble background as a llama herder and coca farmer. Spanish was not even his first language, and he did not finish high school. This was a background familiar to most of the indigenous. He won a seat in congress in 1997, when indigenous faces made up little more than a small minority in the legislature. In 2002, congress expelled him after he declared that indigenous *cocaleros* had the right to armed resistance in the face of military efforts to eliminate their livelihood through coca eradication. An impressive, albeit unsuccessful, bid for the presidency later that year cinched his stature as a national figure. The instability continued from 2002 to 2005 as three presidents resigned their posts in three years. Morales rallied his supporters in a 2005 presidential campaign, and in January 2006, Bolivia inaugurated him as its first indigenous president in history. Evo Morales assigned indigenous representatives throughout his cabinet, and consolidated the growth of indigenous representation in congress.[4] Importantly, although indigenous political representation had already increased precipitously (from 1 percent of congress in 1998 to 27 percent of congress in 2001), indigenous representation in public employment remained minimal. To re-found the country with an eye toward incorporating all ethnicities, Morales almost immediately called for a new constitution, including a completely refashioned electoral system. A constituent assembly was elected the following year. It drafted a constitution, which was approved in a January 2009 referendum.

The first national elections under the new constitution took place on December 6, 2009, and put the presidency and all the seats in both legislative chambers up for voting. By this time, Bolivian politics had polarized into factions that either supported, or did not support, Evo Morales. Morales supporters—indigenous, left-leaning, nationalist, and anti-imperialist—organized under the Movement Toward Socialism (MAS) party. His opponents found their stronghold in the department of Santa Cruz, Bolivia's wealthiest region due to its vast natural gas and agricultural resources. Other resource-rich, lowland departments—Beni, Pando, and Tarija—housed vibrant oppositions

(*continued*)

to Morales. The four departments cradle the highland regions of the country and are thus known as the *media luna* (half-moon) departments. There is also a clear ethnic split. A white, economic elite leads the *media luna* departments, whereas indigenous populations dominate the highland regions. Several parties make up the opposition to MAS, and they usually form coalitions to increase their electoral chances. In the 2009 elections they unified as the National Convergence party, and in the most recent elections (2014) they ran as the Democratic Unity Coalition. The following discussion documents the first elections under the new constitution, and then evaluates how Bolivian politics have since evolved.

The 2009 Constitution established a general outline for the December elections. Law 4021, "Transitory Electoral Regime," of April 14, 2009, provided the details.[5] Bolivian citizens 18 or above are obliged to vote; those over 70 have the option to vote. Those abroad have the right to vote in all elections for president and vice-president. To accommodate the complexity of a new biometric registration system, Law 4021 stated that for this election only, registration from abroad would not be allowed to exceed 6 percent of the total registered voters nationally.[6] In addition, no single country could register over 50 percent of the total registered voters abroad. The registration rolls remained open until November 22, and collected a total of 5,138,583 registrants—a 28 percent increase over the number registered for the January 2009 constitutional referendum. The electoral law required candidates to declare membership in a political party, citizen's association, or indigenous organization. A group receives official status and becomes eligible to field candidates only after it collects signatures in excess of 2 percent of the total votes in the last election. Candidates may register up to 90 days before election day, and must submit all required documents within 40 days. Under the electoral law, the campaign begins 60 days before the election, and must end two days beforehand, allowing for a 48-hour "silent" period.

Bolivia's legislative chamber is officially named the Plurinational Legislative Assembly, and has a Senate and a Chamber of Deputies. There are a total of 36 Senate seats, with four apportioned to each of the nine departments and elected by proportional representation. The Chamber has 130 seats. In the 2009 elections, seventy "uninominal" seats emerged from single-member majoritarian districts, and 53 "plurinominal" seats were distributed to the nine departments of the country based on their population. In addition, 7 seats were reserved for indigenous representatives and distributed to relevant departments. Under the electoral law, the uninominal districts must have territorial continuity and cannot cross department lines. The indigenous reserved seats also cannot cross department lines and can only be placed in rural areas. The electoral law requires all political parties to rotate men and women in their party lists for the plurinominal and Senate seats, and to identify the opposite gender in the substitutes (*suplentes*) under the uninominal candidates.[7] The lists themselves are closed and blocked. The National Electoral Court controls districting and apportionment. The court is to be comprised of five members with four-year terms. The president appoints one, and the legislature appoints the remaining in a two-thirds majority vote.[8] The presidential race requires the victor to receive a simple majority, or to gain 40 percent of the vote with an advantage of at least 10 percent over the second-place candidate. If this does not happen, a second round between the top two vote-getters must occur within 70 days.

As indicated in the following Table, apportionment in the Chamber of Deputies stays fairly true to the principle of proportionality, and in fact advantages the smaller departments. The *media luna* departments control 36.8 percent of the seats with 33.6 percent of the population. But there is obvious malapportionment in the Senate, where tiny Pando and colossal La Paz meet as equals, with four senators each. And here, the *media luna* controls 44 percent of the seats. On the issue of legislative approval of constitutional reform, the malapportionment is slightly attenuated by the rule that requires reforms to receive a two-thirds vote from the legislature sitting jointly, thus allowing the larger, more proportional Chamber of Deputies to have more effect. This means that a reform would require 110 of the total 166 legislators. The *media luna* departments control a total of 64 representatives, though one should keep in mind that the opposition would be unlikely to win all of the *media luna* seats (but on the other hand, the opposition could win some seats in the highland departments).

Apportionment in Bolivia's Chamber of Deputies

Smaller departments in Bolivia can take some comfort in an electoral system than provides some representational advantage for them.

(*continued*)

Table 7.7 **Apportionment in Bolivia's Chamber of Deputies**

Department	Total Seats	Uni- nominal Seats	Pluri- nominal Seats	Indigenous Reserved Seats	Percentage of Assembly Seats	Percentage of Population
La Paz	29	15	13	1	22.3%	28.4%
Santa Cruz	25	13	11	1	19.2%	24.5%
Cochabamba	19	10	8	1	14.6%	17.6%
Potosí	14	8	6	–	10.7%	8.6%
Chuquisaca	11	6	5	–	8.5%	6.4%
Oruro	9	5	3	1	6.9%	4.7%
Tarija	9	5	3	1	6.9%	4.7%
Beni	9	5	3	1	6.9%	4.4%
Pando	5	3	1	1	3.8%	.006%
Totals	**130**	**70**	**53**	**7**		

Source: 2001 Census: *Instituto Nacional de Estadística*, Bolivia. Available at: www.ine .gov.bo.

Several parts of the electoral system advantaged larger parties, and thus worked in the favor of MAS as the foremost political party. The Constitution leaves room for interpretation in the assignment of seats to the different districts in the Chamber of Deputies. It specifies 130 members with one-half distributed to uninominal districts and the other half to plurinominal districts, but then it requires reserved seats without establishing a set amount or reconciling their assignment with the rule to divide the seats between the uninominal and plurinominal districts. As it turns out, in the 2009 elections the number of uninominal districts exceeded the one-half mark (there were 70), and the seven indigenous seats were taken from the plurinomial districts, thereby reducing some of their district sizes. Because the indigenous districts have only one representative, this meant that in fact 77 of the 130 seats in the Chamber emerged from single-member, majoritarian districts. The Constitution does call for proportional representation in the allocation of the plurinominal seats, but Law 4021 specifies the large party favoring d'Hondt system as the method of choice. A 3 percent national threshold was placed on the assignment of plurinational seats, and this further disadvantaged small parties. In yet another hurdle of the 2009 elections, the requirement that all candidates declare affiliation with a political group effectively proscribed independents. And upstart parties, civic groups, or indigenous groups had to face an onerous certification process that obligated them to collect signatures in excess of 2 percent of the total votes in the last election (more than 90,000 signatures). All this meant that many would-be independents or emergent political groups had to join an existing party to secure eligibility for office.

Other elements of the electoral system worked to the benefit of MAS by funneling voters to the party. First, the presidential term parallels the Chamber and Senate terms of office—all are set at five years. Evo Morales entered the election with strong popularity ratings, and this concurrent setup ensured that his coattails would have an effect on the voting for legislative seats. But a more dependable coattail effect was built into the system by the ballot structure, which used fused voting. The ballot consisted of two sections on one piece of paper. On the top, the colors, symbols, and names of the contending political parties along with a photo of the presidential candidate were placed in evenly sized rectangular banners. Voters marked a box within each banner to signify their choice for president. But that same selection for president also determined their vote for the plurinominal and Senate seats. A bottom row of similarly designed banners asked voters to choose a candidate for the uninominal seat, and replaced the presidential candidate photo with a photo of the party's respective candidate in the district. Morales vigorously lobbied for fused voting to take full advantage of his coattails, recognizing that several impending constitutional reforms would require supermajorities of two-thirds in the congress, and hoping that he could count on such a supermajority to control the process (MercoPress, 2009). All the rules that grew the MAS party would come as a double-edged sword, as the party absorbed candidates with suspect party discipline, and voters of unreliable loyalty.

Turnout for the elections was excellent, reaching 94.5 percent of all registered voters. Only 2.5 percent of the ballots had to be nullified (typically because they were completed incorrectly), signifying that the ballot was designed well and did not confuse voters; and 3.2 percent of votes were blank (some voters submit blank votes as a form of protest). A total of 120,375 votes (2.5 percent of all votes) came from abroad—most from Argentina, but others from polls set up in Brazil, Spain, and the United States. Ten parties, citizen groups, or alliances competed on the ballot, though MAS and National Convergence received by far the biggest share of the vote. Evo Morales's MAS came

(*continued*)

out on top, with 64.2 percent of the vote for president. This vote also awarded the party 26 Senate seats (72 percent of seats) and 33 plurinominal seats (62 percent of seats). The Senate races indicate how the effects of small district size over-rewarded MAS as the largest party. National Convergence ran second, with 26.5 percent of the vote. While this total failed to secure the party the presidential seat, it did award it 10 Senate seats (28 percent of seats) and 17 plurinominal seats (32 percent). In the uninominal races, MAS won 49 districts (70 percent) and National Convergence took 19 districts (27 percent). Just two other parties scored victories. The Alliance for Consensus and National Unity gained two plurinominal seats and Social Alliance won two uninominal districts. In the reserved indigenous districts, most candidates could not muster a sufficient number of signatures to run as independents in these lightly populated, rural areas, and thus had to affiliate with a political party. The hurdle benefited MAS, given its indigenous credentials, and it picked up six of the seven seats (National Convergence took the remaining seat) (*Corte Nacional Electoral—Bolivia*, 2009).

Three major foreign organizations observed the election. The Organization of the American States sent 119 observers. A small team arrived November 2, but the vast majority began their work November 30, and the entire team left by December 13. The European Union sent a team for a longer period, from October 26 until January 9. It ultimately had 130 observers. The Carter Center sent a modest team of just six observers from mid-August to October 15 to concentrate on the new biometric registration system and to visit registration centers abroad. They were joined by about two-dozen short-term observers near election day. All of the teams reported a generally clean and fair election, but there were interesting differences. Recommendations from the OAS team focused on institutional strengthening and professional development. It called for more resources for the registration process, better training for poll workers, more systemic and prompt communication of electoral results, and expressed its concern over vacancies on the National Electoral Court and several departmental electoral courts (OAS, 2010). Comments from the EU were a bit more severe. Its report devoted more space to the campaign, and called for more detailed monitoring of campaign financing and stricter observation of stated prohibitions on the use of public funds for campaigns, especially in the use of the media. It also tagged as excessive a rule that strips voters of their registration status if they fail to vote, recommended eliminating the 6 percent roof on voting from abroad to expand suffrage, and noted that the allocation of seats by population may not be accurate because it was based on the outdated 2001 census. In all, the EU report was forthrightly critical of the governing MAS party, especially as it highlighted concerns over the use of public funds and state media outlets to support MAS (MOE-UE, 2010). The Carter Center team offered technical advice to assist what it viewed as a largely successful registration process. Its report did express some concern over the lack of enforcement of the new gender quotas on the party candidate lists, but praised government efforts to support the role of women in Bolivian elections (Carter Center, 2009a, b).

The final results of the election consolidated and pushed further the gains made over the past four years by Evo Morales and MAS. When the results came in, the party controlled 26 of the 36 Senate seats, and 88 of the 130 Chamber seats. With 114 seats overall, MAS secured the two-thirds vote to pass reforms of the constitution through congress. But the MAS majorities crafted by the electoral system were far from rock-solid. Tying the senate and plurinominal seats to the presidential vote allowed Morales to extend his coattails and increase the MAS vote, and the registration requirements for candidates compelled many to join MAS more out of necessity than out of devotion to party principles—this was especially the case for the six representatives of the reserved indigenous districts. The allegiance of party members would be tested soon enough. In 2010, the government tackled the last major constitutional reform mandated by the new constitution. The reform was to address the issue of regional and local autonomy, an issue dear to the hearts of the *media luna* departments, which viewed it as a potential shield from the governing authority of the central government. But autonomy was also critical to the interests of indigenous groups, and the issue challenged the loyalty of MAS members with indigenous ties. In fact, in mid-2010 Morales saw eight indigenous members of his party (all six of the MAS members elected in the reserved districts) cross party lines and refuse to support his proposed reform, thereby denying Morales the two-thirds vote he needed.[9] Additionally, in the April 2010 local and governor elections, MAS saw a splinter group emerge—the Movement without Fear (*Movimiento sin Miedo*—MSM). The April 4 elections were reported to be a "blow to the MAS militancy," but in reality, they simply exposed the artificial nature of the overly large majority constructed in the December 2009 elections (*NotiSur*, 2010).

There is no doubt that Evo Morales and the MAS party can claim a legitimate mandate to govern Bolivia—then and now. Take note that

(*continued*)

Morales was initially elected with 54 percent of the vote in 2005, staved off a recall drive with 60 percent of the vote, took 62 percent in the December 2009 elections, and most recently retained the presidency with 62 percent of the vote in 2014. But whether Morales also holds a mandate to preside over wholesale constitutional reforms is a more complicated question. The electoral rules first used in 2009 pushed his party above the numbers required to pass such reforms, but they did so by incorporating some less devoted candidates and voters. 2014 was no different, when MAS took 88 (67.6 percent) seats in the Chamber and 25 (69.4 percent) in the Senate. But the stable MAS total from 2009 to 2014 masked significant changes. Morales irked his indigenous support base in 2011 when he removed fuel subsidies and funded a controversial road project through a national park and ancestral lands. Food shortages and wage demands from labor unions created further tensions. Morales has not backed from his socialist designs—indeed he has nationalized the country's lucrative gas and natural resources. But he has moved toward what he calls "pragmatic socialism," with an eye toward supporting private business and trade opportunities. As a result, MAS actually gained support in the *media luna* departments, though this was undercut by losses in the traditional indigenous highlands. Likewise, whereas the party retains strong support in rural areas, it has seen losses in some urban areas (Centellas, 2015). Overall, most Bolivians appear pleased with Morales. Economic growth has been stable, and poverty has fallen significantly. But even MAS supporters have made it clear that they will not be taken for granted. Hoping to pursue a fourth term in office, in 2015 Morales pushed a constitutional reform through congress to remove the restriction on reelection. But this triggered a mandated *consulta*—in Bolivia, constitutional reforms require the endorsement of voters. Electoral rules assured the two-thirds support required in congress, but the public proved not so willing, and rejected the reform, albeit narrowly, 48.7 percent to 51.3 percent. The lesson from Bolivia is that though electoral rules can be designed to benefit some groups, in a democracy they ultimately cannot veer too far astray from the tracks of popular expectations and the real divisions in society.

Discussion Questions

1   Explain how electoral reforms in Bolivia have overrepresented MAS. What sort of changes could grant more representation to smaller parties?

2 Evo Morales represents an indigenous majority that has long been repressed and shut out of national politics. Does he have the right to craft electoral rules that safeguard indigenous representation to ensure that the indigenous are never again excluded? What else can be done to preserve the rights of nonindigenous groups?

Conclusion

Elections sit at the heart of democratic politics. If a people lose faith in electoral procedures, it is nearly the same as losing confidence in the democratic system as a whole. For this reason, it is vitally important for electoral rules to be worked out and agreed upon by all significant political actors in a country well in advance of an election. The procedures of an election are the most essential element that must remain predictable in a democracy. This makes things difficult for countries still working their way through the phase of democratic consolidation. Changes in electoral rules may be just the thing that is required to instill greater confidence in government. But the move to make such changes is often looked upon with suspicion by those outside of government. Hence, electoral reform must always be done transparently, and extra efforts must be made to properly educate the population on the need for such reform.

We all realize that democracy entails the collection and counting of votes, but it is vital to recognize that how these votes are collected and counted is just as important. All the features of an electoral system offer choices that can have a determinative impact on who wins and who loses, the party system, and the general pattern of politics in a country. For this reason, it is imperative to understand fully the mechanics behind elections. In addition, the electoral cycle reminds us that elections are packaged within a longer process that also can affect outcomes. International actors can play a crucial role and help individuals gain greater confidence in elections, so long as they too remain mindful of the electoral cycle.

Key Terms

majoritarian system   269
proportional representation   278
largest remainder   278
highest average   278
party system fragmentation   281
mixed electoral systems   281
tiered districts   281
district magnitude   282
effective threshold   283
legal threshold   283
categorical ballot   283

closed party list   284
blocked party list   284
ordinal ballot   284
fused voting   284
gerrymandering   286
malapportionment   286
Duverger's Law   290
direct democracy   294
electoral management bodies   297
electoral cycle   298

Discussion Questions

1 What are the key differences between majoritarian and proportional systems? Discuss how these electoral formulas work better in some institutional settings compared to others.
2 How do the institutional rules that surround electoral systems affect the behavior of politicians?
3 Discuss how the identification of an electoral cycle allows us to more accurately evaluate the "free and fair" character of an election.
4 Is Bolivia more democratic today? How has institutional change affected democracy in the country?

Suggested Readings

Ryan E. Carlin, Matthew M. Singer, and Elizabeth J. Zechmeister, eds. 2015. *The Latin American Voter: Pursuing Representation and Accountability in Challenging Contexts.* **Ann Arbor: University of Michigan Press.** In 1960, a group of scholars published a book entitled *The American Voter*, providing one of the first authoritative studies on the psychology behind voting decisions and launching what became known as "The Michigan School." This text takes that same approach to Latin America, but adds updated, rigorous methodologies. It concludes that Latin American voters are like most voters, but act differently due to the significant challenges of governance, economic disparity and growth, crime, and corruption in the region. It is one of the most important books on Latin American voting behavior in recent years.

Thomas Legler, Sharon F. Lean, and Dexter S. Boniface, eds. 2007. *Promoting Democracy in the Americas.* **Baltimore: Johns Hopkins University Press.** International support for democracy has blossomed over the past two decades. This book notes that such support comes from several quarters—regional organizations such as the Organization of American States, nongovernmental organizations, and state-based support. In a series of case studies, the authors chart how these actors influence democratization differently and often carry distinct interests in and visions of democracy.

Arend Lijphart. 1998. *Electoral Systems and Party Systems: A Study of Twenty-Seven Democracies.* **New York: Oxford University Press.** Although Costa Rica is the only Latin American country in this comparative study, the text provides a comprehensive introduction to the technical makeup of electoral systems and analysis of their impact on party systems. The book takes a careful look at the limits of electoral engineering, and ultimately argues that electoral systems have their greatest impact on the level of disproportionality between votes and seats.

Stephen L. Taylor. 2009. *Voting Amid Violence: Electoral Democracy in Colombia.* **Boston: Northeastern University Press.** Colombia makes for an interesting case study of electoral systems and behavior, given the violence that has raged there for so long. Taylor carefully charts detailed reforms in the Colombian electoral system and shows how they made a difference, despite the environment of violence, especially in the movement of Colombia from a two-party to a multiparty system.

Notes

1 Data for Mexico can be accessed on the web page of the country's electoral institute, *Instituto Nacional Electoral*, at: www.ine.mx/archivos3/portal/historico/contenido/Historico_de_Resultados_Electorales/
2 Constitution of Bolivia, 1826, Articles 7 and 8. Keep in mind that positivist thought (see Chapter 3) gave only a very limited meaning to "the people."
3 Constitution of Bolivia, 1967, Articles 1 and 2.
4 Electoral reforms in 1994 replaced many PR seats with majoritarian representation, and this provided a foothold for upstart, locally concentrated indigenous groups to challenge traditional parties. The neoliberal protests further energized indigenous groups to take seats in congress. But at the time, there were several contending parties and leaders. By 2006, Morales had solidified his position as the leader of the indigenous movement, and MAS as its primary party.
5 Law 4021, *"Regimen electoral transitorio," Gaceta Oficial de Bolivia* n. 18, April 14, 2009.
6 About 2.5 million Bolivians live abroad. This number represents about 25 percent of the entire population in the country.
7 The law also requires parties to submit lists of substitutes (*suplentes*) for the plurinominal and Senate seats. These too must rotate male and female names.
8 Due to the inability of the legislature to elect two members, at the time of the December elections the CNE had only three members. In a reform mandated by the new Constitution, in June 2010, the Plurinational Electoral Court replaced the CNE. The new court has seven members, with one appointed by the president and six by a two-thirds vote in the legislature. They hold six-year terms and cannot be reelected. The Constitution requires two of the members to be of indigenous origin.
9 *"El MAS se queda sin 2/3 para aprobar la ley de autonomías." La Razón* (La Paz). June 29, 2010. Available at: www.la-razon.com.

References

Breuer, Anita. 2011. "Obstacles to Citizen Participation by Direct Democracy in Latin America: A Comparative Regional Analysis of Legal Frameworks and Evidence from the Costa Rican Case." *Democratization* 18:1, pp. 100–34.

Carter Center. 2009a, December 1. "Carter Center Election Observation Mission in Bolivia: Public Report." Available at http://cartercenter.org/resources/pdfs/news/pr/pr-bolivia-120109.pdf.

———. 2009b, December 7. "Carter Center Commends Bolivians on Peaceful Election Day." Available at http://cartercenter.org/news/pr/bolivia-120709.html.

Centellas, Miguel. 2015. "The 2014 Presidential and Legislative Elections in Bolivia." *Electoral Studies* 37, pp. 94–97.

Corte Nacional Electoral—Bolivia. 2009. *Acta de cómputo nacional elecciones generales y referendos 2009.* La Paz: Corte Nacional Electoral. Available at www.cne.org.bo/PadronBiometrico/COMUNICACION/ACTADECOMPUTO NACIONALGENERALES 2009.pdf.

Hartlyn, Jonathan, Jennifer McCoy, and Thomas M. Mustillo. 2008. "Electoral Governance Matters: Explaining the Quality of Elections in Contemporary Latin America." *Comparative Political Studies* 41:1, pp. 73–98.

Institute for Democracy and Electoral Assistance (IDEA). 2006. *Electoral Management Design: The International IDEA Handbook.* Stockholm, Sweden: International IDEA.

Lijphart, Arend. 1994. *Electoral Systems and Party Systems: A Study of Twenty-Seven Democracies, 1945–1990.* New York: Oxford University Press.

Londregan, John B. 2000. *Legislative Institutions and Ideology in Chile.* New York: Cambridge.

Mainwaring, Scott, and Matthew Shugart, eds. 1997. "Conclusion: Presidentialism and the Party System," in *Presidentialism and Democracy in Latin America,* pp. 394–439. New York: Cambridge University Press.

MercoPress. 2009, November 26. "Morales after a Two-Thirds Majority in Congress in Bolivia's December Elections." Available at www.en.mercopress.com.

MOE-UE (*Misión de Observación Electoral de la Unión Europea en Bolivia*). 2010. *Informe Final: Elecciones Generales y Referendos Autonómicos, 6 de Diciembre de 2009.* Available at www.eueombolivia.eu.

Nohlen, Dieter, ed. 2005. *Elections in the Americas,* Vols. 1 and 2. New York: Oxford.

NotiSur. 2010, April 16. "Bolivia: Local Elections Bring Surprises, Opposition from Left."

OAS. 2010. *Informe Final del la Misión de Observación Electoral de la OEA sobre las elecciones generales y referendums autonómicos celebrados en el estado plurinacional de Bolivia el 6 de Diciembre de 2009.*

Przeworski, Adam. 1986. "Some Problems in the Study of the Transition to Democracy," in Guilermo O'Donnell, Phillippe C. Schmitter, and Laurence Whitehead, eds., *Transitions from Authoritarian Rule: Comparative Perspectives.* Baltimore, MD: Johns Hopkins.

Shugart, Matthew, and John Carey. 1992. *Presidents and Assemblies: Constitutional Design and Electoral Dynamics.* New York: Cambridge.

Snyder, Richard, and David Samuels. 2004. "Legislative Malapportionment in Latin America: Historical and Comparative Perspectives," in Edward L. Gibson, ed., *Federalism and Democracy in Latin America.* Baltimore, MD: Johns Hopkins.

Wills-Otero, Laura. 2009. "Electoral Systems in Latin America: Explaining the Adoption of Proportional Representation Systems during the Twentieth Century." *Latin American Politics and Society* 51:3, pp. 33–58.

Zovatto Garetto, Daniel. 2015. "Las instituciones de democracia directa." *Revista de Derecho Electoral* 20, pp. 35–75.

8 From Civil Society to Political Parties

Putting Democracy into Practice

Photo 8.1 If political parties do not channel the political expressions of the people, they will take to the streets. Here, Brazilians call for the removal of President Dilma Rousseff.

> "Imagine if (the opposition) dominated the National Assembly ... I wouldn't allow it, I swear. I won't let my hands be tied by anyone. I'd take to the streets with the people!"
>
> —Nicolás Maduro, President of Venezuela, December 2015[1]

Nicolás Maduro issued his warning in advance of national elections that would in fact see the opposition gain a super majority in the National Assembly. When the legislature convened the following spring with its new members, Maduro faced an opposition that now had the votes to initiate substantial constitutional reforms and even to force a recall vote on his presidency. These moves had been threatened by an opposition that Maduro had ignored and berated since his election in 2013. At first glance, his comments appeared to follow in the footsteps of his predecessor, Hugo Chávez, whose blunt and blustery populist politics regularly led him to demonize his enemies and portray himself as righteous and conscientious. But the passions they capture are not so unique. Though calls to reject electoral outcomes and push aside the rule of law are indicative of the deeply polarized nature of contemporary Venezuelan politics, the sentiments actually capture an extreme version what is felt and what is required of every politician and political party.

Democracy is all about the confrontation of interests and values, and political parties sit at the front lines of this contest. A good party is a contentious party, one that vigorously protects and promotes the tenets of its platform. When politicians act on behalf of their parties and face off against other parties, antagonism is usually part of the game. While this may not lead to the contempt expressed by Maduro, it would be unnatural not to harbor some antagonism. But spiteful confrontation cannot define democracy. Democracy is meant to provide a forum for the mediation of differences, not for the promotion of hostilities. To offset the feelings of bitterness that often surround electoral campaigns, democracy requires that we respect the vote and celebrate the right of all to take office.

Democracy thus asks a lot of us. And more precisely, it asks a lot of political parties. They take center stage in the contentious consensus-building politics of democracy. Parties must both butt heads to stir debate, and bow heads to ensure civility. But parties are just the last link in a chain that connects society to the state. Before them comes civil society, and to fully understand the behavior of parties, one must also consider civil society. Many Latin American countries have seen their traditional party systems fall apart in recent decades, only to be replaced by a diverse range of small, fleeting parties. And fewer Latin Americans than in the past strongly identify with political parties. Indeed, in some sectors there are even calls to do away with political parties, and to rely only on civil society groups and social movements to express their interests. If parties are so important, but they are not effective in government or used by citizens, what does that mean for democracy? This chapter focuses on political parties, but it does so with an eye on the critical role played by civil society. It also takes a broader look at party systems in the region. In the final section, the chapter spotlights the case of Venezuela to illustrate how changes in civil society, political parties, and party systems offer insight into the dynamics of democracy.

Civil Society and Democracy

Civil society refers to "the realm of organized social life that is voluntary, self-generating, (largely) self-supporting, autonomous from the state, and bound by a legal order or shared set of rules" (Diamond, 1994). It is distinct from society more generally, in that civil society groups together all those private organizations with interests that direct them toward the state. Somehow, some way, these groups view communication with the state as central to their objectives. They may have interests in a certain public policy, want to share ideas on how to make the state more efficient or accountable, or they may hope to secure support from the state for their own collective goals. Civil society potentially consists of interest groups, cultural and religious organizations, civic and developmental associations, issue-oriented movements, media, research groups, educational institutions, and so on. Those societal groups that see little to no connections between their own values or goals and public policy—such as some sporting clubs or religious organizations—are not part of civil society. These groups embrace private, not public, goals. In addition, civil society excludes insurgent movements and other groups seeking to take control of the state or otherwise influence it through violent means.

Civil society has a fundamental impact on the quality of democracy. One argument holds that the more individuals get to know each other through mutual memberships in voluntary associations, the more they will trust each other. This trust is important, because democracy is dependent on trust—electoral losers must trust that winners will not abuse their power, and that they will have a fair chance the next time around. Researchers have also documented how civil society produces skills necessary to a healthy democracy. Democracy requires a pool of individuals skilled in leadership and bargaining, and who are able to hammer out compromises. Many voluntary associations require these same skills, so a society with a vibrant civil society has a large pool of individuals groomed for political leadership. Relatedly, individuals who regularly interact with such a civil society come to expect the same consensus-building behaviors in government (Lipset and Lakin, 2004, pp. 92–138).

Beyond the diffusion of trust and development of leadership skills, civil society plays an indispensable role as a mediating force within society. Democracy thrives as a battleground of ideas, and civil society abounds in the production of ideas. Think tanks, cultural exhibits, media outlets, and university groups all add to the storehouse of public thought. But how can we ensure that such diversity does not descend into headstrong differences and simply reinforce divisions? Part of the answer rests within civil society itself, and the relationship is a bit counterintuitive. A perfectly homogenous society, essentially by definition, will not produce much conflict. But there really are no "perfectly" homogenous societies. There are societies with few divisions, and societies with many divisions, and those with few divisions are actually more prone to conflict.

For example, in Bolivia the indigenous in the highlands eke out a living in agricultural or mining activities, whereas a *mestizo* population lives off the fruits of natural gas resources in the jungle lowlands. Unsurprisingly, whether or how to redistribute gas profits remains a primary issue of contention, and the debate has often descended into violence. One contributing factor is that the two groups are simply too different (they differ primarily by race, region, and economic class) and too overarching (they define the major division in Bolivia). What Bolivia lacks are the **cross-cutting divisions** (Lipset and Rokkan, 1967) associated with civil society. A vibrant civil society means that there are professional groups, unions, gender groups, student groups, religious groups, environmental groups—so that no one single division defines society. This undercuts conflict because although you may differ with your neighbor on religious grounds, you may be in the same income level or hold similar membership in an environmental group.

And finally, civil society plays a mediating role between society and the state. This occurs as voluntary associations develop their own policy expertise, and abilities to challenge government policy. Business councils can conduct their own economic surveys, and environmental groups can evaluate habitats independent of government reports. The media is especially important here, as it emerges to play a watchdog role. As noted in Chapter 3, insult laws have hindered the capacity of media outlets to play this role in many Latin American countries. More ominously, a curious media can also become the target for violent attacks in countries where crime has crippled the rule of law. It may be little surprise to learn that reporters on the beat in conflict-ridden countries, such as Iraq and Syria, are at greatest risk. But reporters pursuing stories on corruption face a nearly equal risk, and Latin America faces no shortage of potential bylines on this topic. Brazil, Honduras, and Mexico have proved particularly dangerous for journalists in recent years (*Al Día News*, 2015).

Civil society thus stands at the frontlines as groups in society mobilize for political influence. Nonetheless, we shall see that civil society alone cannot act as an effective line of communication with the state. Political parties also play a crucial role. Neither can live without the other in a democracy.

Protests and Social Movements

Ideally, democracy provides individuals with a forum to express their preferences and a set of mechanisms to work out their differences, typically through some sort of voting based on majority rule. With every decision, there are losers, but many of the defeated remain supportive of the democratic process because basic protections of civil liberties allow new opportunities to persuade others so that one day they might stand in the majority. Others may feel that they will always be outside the majority, but are comforted by the protections democracies give to minority groups. If the political system fails to fulfill these functions, people will view it as exclusionary.

They will then see no option but to press their interests against government authorities outside formal institutional channels, often in the form of armed insurrection. Insurgency, then, is the product of a defunct democracy, just as democracy is the antidote to insurgency.

But democracy never works according to its ideal form. Democracy is a constellation of institutions that must be pieced together just right, and refashioned as dominant values change or new challenges arise. And poor leadership or a sudden drop in revenues can set it awry at any given time. Still, though people may grow outraged, frustrated, or alienated, they rarely resort to armed insurrection even as their confidence in government dips. More often they look to protest. Protest offers another outlet for political expression that rests between formal, legal channels of political influence and violent, subversive methods—though its midway position creates some overlap on both sides. And because no democracy is ever likely to be ideal, protest is in fact part of the very fabric of democracy. Indeed, often it is a sign of a healthy democracy. The prime actors behind protests are social movements, which also play important educational roles and act as an important source of political identity for their members. A social movement can be defined as "collective efforts, of some duration and organization, (that use) noninstitutionalized methods to bring about social change" (Flacks, 2005). A key characteristic of social movements is that they are challengers and rest outside the established political power structure (Tilly, 1978). This is what most prominently separates them from the more conventional voluntary associations of civil society.

The protests used by social movements come in many forms. Petitions, street marches, boycotts, blockades, demonstrations, strikes, occupations of buildings or public places, and the destruction of property or graffiti are all examples. Reacting to the continued impunity surrounding gendered violence in Argentina, members of several women's groups called for a national protest after the horrific murder of 16-year-old girl who was drugged, raped, and tortured in October 2016. Using the hashtag #NiUnaMenos ("Not One Less"), they messaged, "ENOUGH! ... Strike for an hour outside of our workplaces to make ourselves visible. Strike then march. Wear black." One hundred and fifty thousand crowded the central streets of Buenos Aires in what was quickly tagged "Black Wednesday." The subways echoed with the voices of women as some shouted, "Ni uno menos!" (Not one less!), while those on opposite platforms responded, "Vivas nos queremos!" (We want us alive!). From 1 to 2:00 P.M. on October 19, 2016, things came to a standstill. Neighborhood kiosks, workplace assembly lines, universities, and even the National Congress dared not conduct business (NACLA, 2016). Unlike the #NiUnaMenos case in Argentina, some forms of protest are not disruptive and occur wholly through legal channels, as when a group secures a permit to march through downtown sidewalks and even stops at traffic lights. Nonetheless, even these typically signal that some groups feel like outsiders and have grown dissatisfied with conventional methods of political expression (i.e., voting). Other forms of protest can be violent, as when a street march becomes a riot. But violence is typically a transitory feature of protest and social movement activity. On the other hand, violence is the signature feature of an insurgency. Despite its myriad forms, most individuals approach all types of protest activity as an extraordinary decision. Involvement interrupts one's daily work, school, or personal schedule, requires travel to a location that may be distant or unfamiliar, and most of all, can entail significant risk. One might be fined, arrested, or beaten by counter-protesters.

The hazards of protesting led many analysts to associate it with the aggrieved. Intractable poverty, economic inequality, social exclusion, racial discrimination, or the denial of justice lead people to take to the streets. But protest occurs over too wide a range of countries to support a simple correlation. From 2008 to 2012, an average of 10.4 percent of Latin Americans answered in the affirmative when polled on whether they had participated in a protest over the course of the past year. Bolivia (19.5 percent), one of the most underdeveloped countries with a history of indigenous repression, topped the charts. But one of the most wealthy and homogeneous countries, Argentina (16.8 percent), also ranked high. And Peru (18.4 percent), which has a large, historically excluded indigenous population like Bolivia, but experienced some of the highest economic growth rates in the region during this time, stood in between. In addition, Brazil (7.2 percent) ranked rather low during this time, but in 2016 the country would experience some of the largest protests in the history of the entire region as individuals took to the streets to express either their support for, or indignation of, President Dilma Rousseff while impeachment proceedings loomed. Chile also fell below the average at 7.9 percent, but it would see a surge in protest actions as university students flooded the streets demanding education reform. Their unique protests included kiss-a-thons to illustrate their passion for education in 2013, but also erupted into violence in 2016 as stones were thrown at police, water cannons blasted demonstrators, and tear gas produced injuries, including the death of one security official.

The uneven relationship between various hardships—be they economic distress, political exclusion, social marginalization, or racial discrimination—and protest, led many researchers to turn their focus from grievances and toward what it takes to create a social movement. Focusing on the motivations behind protest is not enough. People need to be drawn together to make a protest happen, and this requires leadership skills, organization, fundraising and recruitment strategies, communications, funding, transportation, and other resources. Such commodities become more available with socioeconomic development, so it is not surprising that many analysts have linked the growth of the middle class with a rise in protest. This would appear to be part of the story in Latin America, where the middle class grew from about 100 million in 2000, to about 150 million in 2010 (Ferreira et al., 2013). By 2014, the middle class was larger than the number of poor in Latin America for the first time. The growth of cities also feeds the ability of social movements to mobilize and coordinate large gatherings. In 1950, just 40 percent of Latin Americans lived in cities, but the number shot up to 70 percent by 1990. Today, 80 percent of the population lives in cities, making Latin America the most urbanized region in the world (by comparison, urbanization rests at 74 percent in the European Union).[2] Today, social media is another important resource, and here too Latin Americans largely outpace the rest of the world, spending roughly 10 hours per month on Facebook, Twitter, and related media (twice the global average). Indeed, five of the countries rank in the top ten worldwide for "engagement" on social platforms (*The Economist*, 2013). But as social media grows as a resource for social protest activity, it does raise an important question: Will it create organizational disparities between those with less access—the poor working class, rural indigenous, or senior citizens—and those with more: the urban, young, educated, and upper middle classes (Valenzuela et al., 2016)?

Beyond the material resources required to craft and energize a social movement, there are also cultural and moral resources that tie protest to identity politics. Here we see a close connection between democracy itself and protest activity. Identity politics refers to the recognition that a group shares common political interests. At the time of democratic transition, many groups in Latin America faced an uphill battle in their first step toward self-recognition. For example, colonialism, religious missionaries, and socioeconomic changes that upended traditional societies trampled on indigenous consciousness, *machismo* (an exaggerated sense of masculine pride) stifled feminist thought and repressed the recognition of gays and lesbians, and the pressing concerns of underdevelopment overshadowed environmental activists and animal rights groups. But the gradual extension of civil liberties and political rights provided the space required for ideas and concerns to be shared and acted upon. Even more important, such space allowed individuals to recognize that they were part of a larger group.

In Bolivia and Ecuador, the indigenous were severely affected by neoliberal reforms and austerity measures throughout the 1980s and 1990s, and unsurprisingly, protest activity spiked. But the protests were as much a cause as consequence of identity politics. In 1997, the indigenous movement proved critical to the removal of President Abdalá Bucaram. In 2003, indigenous groups in Bolivia did the same. The proportion of indigenous people in Ecuador and Bolivia was roughly the same before these events as after. Nonetheless, the sense of empowerment meant that afterwards, more people felt indigenous. Their awareness of and pride in who they were had been raised. In 2008, when Panama and Nicaragua were the last countries to decriminalize same-sex relations, the tide finally began to turn for the LGBT movement throughout Latin America. A 2012 article noted "What was a taboo subject 20 years ago is today open to public discussion and debate. LGBT rights are central topics of concern, not just in academic circles, but even in presidential debates." As evidence of growing recognition, in 2008

Ecuador became just the third country in the world with a constitutional provision that prohibits discrimination based on sexual orientation, in 2009 Uruguay approved civil unions, and in 2010 Argentina legalized gay marriage and adoption (Corrales, 2012). Whereas hate crimes remain alarmingly high and tens of thousands marched in a September 2016 protest against same-sex marriage in Mexico City, there is no doubt that democratic politics have energized the LGBT movement.

The passage of democracy itself also stimulates greater protest activity. Under authoritarianism, Latin Americans lived each day under the fear of repression and knowledge of brutality against those that dared speak out. Restraint and caution were very much a legacy of dictatorship. But that memory is fading. Today, almost one in three Latin Americans were born after the transition to democracy in their country. No wonder that the Chilean student protest movement calls itself *"la generación sin miedo"* (the generation without fear). All together, it is little surprise that protest activity has surged in Latin America in recent years. The commodity boom that pulled the countries from the global recession of 2008 has cooled considerably. Corruption scandals have entangled government throughout the region. And in too many instances, polarizing politicians have demonized their opponents. With a rising middle class, growth in identity politics, and generational change, the stage is set for social movements to thrive and take their place in the democracies of Latin America.

Parties as Political Institutions

A political party is an organization bound by common political beliefs, linked to groups in society, and designed to recruit candidates for elected positions in government. Parties are institutions. They have formal organization with offices dedicated to specific functions such as fundraising, platform development, campaign strategies, recruitment, youth groups, education, and a hierarchy that ties leaders in the capital to functionaries in local districts. They have rules to outline the duties of officers, the procedures for conducting meetings, the distribution and use of funds, the qualifications and responsibilities of members, the steps in the nomination process, and the like. And they are definitely embedded with meanings that fashion political identities. Many individuals summarize their political beliefs with a simple reference to a party. Chileans who want to communicate conservative attitudes toward the role of the Church, confidence in the free market, concern over law and order, and fondness for the Pinochet era can simply identity themselves with the right-wing party of the country, the Independent Democratic Union (UDI—*Unión Demócrata Independiente*). In common parlance, Chileans package all that information in one simple expression, *"Soy udi"* ("I am an UDI"). Others might signal their opposition to these beliefs with a vociferous, *"No soy udi."* Either way, all Chileans know what it means to be an *"udi."* And on a day-to-day basis, like all parties the UDI provides a benchmark of appropriate behavior and thinking for its members.

But in the sense that parties are political institutions, they differ from the other institutions discussed in this book. Executives, federal arrangements, electoral rules, judiciaries, and the other regime institutions are firmly lodged within the state as legal, public entities. As noted, all these institutions are no doubt influenced by the history and culture of society. But political parties stand much more deliberately with one foot in the state and the other in society. Their primary goal—election to government office—sits within the state, but they emerge from society. On a day-to-day basis, they must conform to rules and regulations set by the state, but at the same time cater to their constituents in society if they are to survive.

Parties as Regime Institutions

All parties share the ambition to place their members in elected government offices. To achieve their goals, they must gain recognition as a political party and eligibility to run candidates, nominate candidates for offices, raise funds to compete in elections, and campaign in elections. A democratic regime creates rules for all of these steps because it has a responsibility to create and maintain competitive, free, and fair elections. Election day is simply the culmination of an electoral cycle (see Chapter 7) that begins with the mobilization of a party, its selection of candidates, and a campaign to persuade voters. Hence, the electoral process, the heartbeat of democratic politics, consists of a series of steps that work their way from society to the state. To ensure the legitimacy of the process, regime rules must reach out to society and deal with the primary actor in the electoral process—the political party.

Things were not always this way in Latin America. In the past, party organization, the nomination of candidates, the campaign, and even voting, rested much more in the hands of political parties as private and exclusive organizations. Parties reached into the regime, rather than vice versa. Throughout Latin America in the nineteenth century, there were Liberal and Conservative parties, but they hardly embraced a mission to educate voters on ideological commitments or even to aggressively recruit new members. Keep in mind that through the nineteenth century, gender, literacy, property, and marriage requirements meant that few countries had voting rates that surpassed 5 percent of adults. Even into the twentieth century voting rates exceeded 10 percent in only a few countries. Traditionally, parties—irrespective of their ideological labels—were elite clubs designed to protect and further the interests of local strongmen, and they were part and parcel of the personal ties that bound public office and private interests.

In Colombia, party elites would signal their preferences by endorsing a candidate in a local newspaper. These *"adhesiones,"* as they were known, clarified who would win the election. Once they hit the press, a candidate had no real need to campaign—local elites would use pressure, fraud, and violence to ensure outcomes in their districts (Delpar, 1981, pp. 102–103). And in Colombia and beyond, well into the twentieth century political parties took the responsibility (and authority) to print and distribute their own ballots. Especially in rural areas, this allowed large landowners to supervise and control the votes of their employees and smaller communities over which they held sway. As added insurance, most parties formed paramilitary organizations to intimidate voters, coerce purges of voter registries, or even to confiscate ballot boxes if need be. An election was in many ways a private affair.

Today the regulation of parties is generally covered in several government documents—the constitution, the electoral code, a statute on political parties, and various supplemental pieces of legislation. The constitution usually provides sweeping references to the role and operations of parties. The Constitution of El Salvador offers some of the clearest language. It identifies parties as the "only instrument for the exercise of the representation of the people in government" (Article 85). On the other hand, Chile's constitution expressly recognizes the rights of independent candidates. And in a growing trend, constitutions in Bolivia, Colombia, the Dominican Republic, Ecuador, and Paraguay allow social movement groups to field candidates in elections. Echoing the personalist politics of Hugo Chávez, Venezuela's constitution is the only one lacking any reference to political parties. It guarantees the right of individuals to form "organizations with political goals" (which could include political parties) for the purpose of contesting elections (Article 67). The U.S. Constitution also omits references to political parties (or even "organizations with political goals"), but worldwide, most modern constitutions do contain clauses on political parties.

COMPARING COUNTRIES

The Rules for Party Funding in Latin America

Throughout the world individuals are less likely than in the past to be associated with a political party. Latin Americans are no different. With fewer opportunities to raise funds through membership dues or individual contributions, parties increasingly must look to corporate donations or support from the state. Venezuela, with its constitutional ban on public funding, is the only state lacking a public financing system. The rules for party funding have never been more important not only to the survival of parties, but to the quality of democracy. But these rules can vary significantly. Consider the following questions and alternatives:

* *Should a limit be placed on the amount of a private contribution?* The U.S. Supreme Court characterizes such limitations as a limitation on free speech. In Latin America, there is greater concern over corruption and the funneling of monies from drug trafficking. For this reason, many countries also prohibit anonymous donations.

* *If parties are so important to democracy, should countries offering foreign aid be allowed to target them?*
Most Latin American countries have a greater fear of foreign meddling. Only Colombia and Nicaragua allow party contributions from foreign governments, institutions, or individuals.

* *Which parties are eligible for public funding and how should funding be allocated?*
An equal distribution of funding levels the playing field, but it may also mean that monies are going to unpopular parties. Equity also gives individuals and groups an incentive to create new parties, contributing to party fragmentation. On the other hand, a distribution proportionate to current representation simply enforces the status quo. Countries balance these concerns by (1) establishing a minimum threshold for eligibility based on votes received (ranging from 0.04 percent in Ecuador to 5 percent in Guatemala); and (2) allocating funds based on the votes received—although many countries use a formula to distribute a portion of the funding equally.

* *When should public funding be distributed?*
Colombia, Costa Rica, Ecuador, Nicaragua, Paraguay, and Uruguay distribute funding after the elections and have no special facilities for new parties. This clearly advantages existing parties. Other countries distribute funding before and after an election. Only Argentina allocates funding before the campaign (eligibility is gained simply by participating in the previous elections for national deputies), and the country does offer special facilities for new parties.

* *Are there limitations on the uses of public funding?*
Bolivia, El Salvador, Honduras, Nicaragua, and Uruguay allow parties to use their funding on the campaign and nothing else. This helps to keep down costs. Other countries allow monies to be used for basic operations, research, institutional development, and civic education to aid the institutional strengthening of political parties. But does this allow parties to crowd out the research and development activities of private foundations and civil society groups?

* *How much public money should be distributed?*
A public can quickly grow disenchanted with a system that appears to lavish political parties with financial support. Costa Rica

(continued)

follows a strict formula that allows for decreases in funding during an economic downturn or when public finances are strained. (Zovatto, 2003)

Discussion Questions

1   Does state funding of political parties contribute to democratization? What sorts of rules need to be in place to ensure that it does?
2   The financing of political parties involves a number of goals, including representation, party system institutionalization, and free speech. Discuss how different financing rules favor some of these goals more than others.

The constitutions also place conditions on political parties. Most commonly, constitutions require parties to be organized and to function democratically, and to respect the constitutional order. Some also require national organization by obliging party offices in a certain number of regions, membership throughout the country, by or demanding minimal levels of votes in national elections across several regions. **Nationalization requirements** tend to foster more integrative parties, and thus appear a natural fit for promoting consensual politics (Jones and Mainwaring, 2003). They are also meant to thwart the rise of a governing party that would favor some regions more than others. But they can have a repressive effect on minority groups. In 2000 Nicaragua passed an electoral law that required its parties to collect signatures from 3 percent of registered voters in a region, and to run candidates in 80 percent of that region's municipalities. The conditions proved prohibitive for YATAMA, an organization created to represent the indigenous Miskito peoples concentrated in just one small portion of the large Atlantic Coast Region of the country. The YATAMA filed suit in the Inter-American Court of Human Rights, and won its case in 2005 (Campbell, 2007). Nicaragua accepted the decision, and since that time has attempted to balance nationalization and the protection of indigenous rights through an uneasy alliance between YATAMA and the dominant Sandinista (FSLN) party.

Other countries walk this line by reserving congressional seats for indigenous groups, or exempting indigenous groups from nationalization requirements. Alongside these conditions, constitutions establish various restrictions on party activity. Chile bans cooperative arrangements between political parties and trade unions (Article 23). In Ecuador, a constitutional clause bars men from composing more than one-half of a party's governing board (Article 108). Parties in Panama cannot be created on the basis of gender, race, or religion (Article 139). Brazil's constitution prohibits parties from forming paramilitary organizations (Article 17). Beyond the constitution, the details on party organization usually rest in a comprehensive "Law on Political Parties."

The Law on Political Parties (Law 30.414) in Peru is fairly typical of the party statutes found in most countries. It is just over a dozen pages long, and is divided into six parts with 42 total articles. The first section defines the importance of political parties and lays out their goals and objectives—such as to develop **party platforms**, participate in elections, support democratic values, and contribute to governability. A second section defines how parties are recognized. For example, a party must collect signatures in excess of 4 percent of the total number of voters in the last election, designate leaders and publicize bylaws and the formal organization of the party, draft a party platform, and select a party symbol. The section also outlines how a party loses recognition. This occurs when it fails to gain at least six seats in the national assembly or receives less than 5 percent of the vote in a national election (for party alliances, this number rises 1 percent with each additional party), or if the Supreme Court declares the party undemocratic. In such cases the party would have to reapply for recognition. Other articles specify when parties must select their candidates, allow party leaders to nominate up to 25 percent of all candidates (less those for president and vice president), and require that women compose at least 30 percent of all candidates. All candidates not nominated by the leadership must be selected by the secret vote of party members in a party convention. One section is devoted to direct public party financing, and sets fines for candidates who offer gifts to voters in excess of 20 *soles* (about 6 U.S.$). It also sets the campaign at 60 days, with a two-day blackout period before the election, and specifies how much media time parties may purchase (or be offered at no cost by the state).

State regulations are meant to ensure the democratic credentials of political parties, and to even out the competitive pressures among parties. Nonetheless, the regulations must strike a careful balance between respecting the freedom of individuals to organize and protecting the integrity of the democratic electoral process. Take, for example, the drive to ensure a democratic nomination process. A **primary election** pits various party candidates against each other in a competitive vote rather than allowing party leaders to unilaterally select who will run. Uruguay and Argentina go furthest in their presidential primaries by requiring parties to have open primaries, which means that even nonparty members can participate (a closed primary restricts the vote to party members).

Such provisions allow greater popular input, but should parties be compelled to hold primary elections? Does this requirement infringe on the basic right to free assembly? Shouldn't party leaders have the right to select those they feel best represent the party platform? When applied to indigenous movements, does a competitive primary undercut indigenous traditions, which often rely on consensus-based nomination procedures? In the case of legislative elections, one could argue that primaries are impractical in proportional representation systems (or that an open list system could somewhat substitute for a primary). Most importantly, one might also contend that primaries undermine party discipline because leaders lose the power to reward or punish potential candidates based on their loyalty. Hence, there is a clear trade-off in the mechanics of democracy: Cohesive parties give voters greater confidence in the platforms they support, but a primary meant to offer more popular input to party decisions undoes this cohesion. In the end, national party leaders in Latin America tend to dominate candidate selection for legislative races. Only Brazil and Colombia have distinguished themselves with legislative candidate nomination processes that rest largely outside the hands of party leaders (Jones, 2010, pp. 27–29).

And what of presidential primaries? Only Argentina, the Dominican Republic, Ecuador Honduras, Panama, Peru, and Uruguay, and Venezuela require parties to hold presidential primaries. Several other countries lay out regulations for primaries, but make them voluntary (Estuan, 2015). Nonetheless, most countries in this study had at least one party opt to hold primaries in recent elections. This is something new for Latin America, where presidential primaries were almost unheard of before the 1990s. Why have so many parties made the switch? Part of the explanation has to do with the growing concern over transparency and accountability. Many parties in Latin America lost wholesale support in the 1990s as voters grew frustrated with the inability of political leaders to resolve deepening economic problems, and as a more inquisitive media drew attention to corruption scandals. Those parties that wanted to survive and those that emerged on a platform calling for greater openness in politics saw primaries as a way to signal their resolve. One study showed that parties holding primaries in Latin America received a "bounce" of three to six points in the general election—an amount that can clearly make the difference between winning and losing (Carey and PolgaHecimovich, 2006). Primaries also helped many of the parties fractured by voting swings to settle leadership battles. This was the case in Argentina, where the diverse FREPASO coalition distinguished itself with primaries in 1994, and then again in 1999 when the UCR party joined it in an alliance. The Peronist party, undercut by factions with dominant personalities, took this strategy one step further by supporting an electoral change in 2003 that allowed parties to field multiple candidates in the general election (thereby in effect consolidating the primary and general election). But by 2011, Cristina Fernández felt she had consolidated control over the party, and pushed through a reform that mandates primary elections for all parties in advance of the general election (Table 8.1).

Table 8.1 **Party Regulations in Latin America.** Parties may emerge from society, but institutional rules ensure that the regime affects which parties will survive and prosper

Country	Recognition Requirements	Nationality Requirements	Presidential Primary Required	Presidential Primary in Practice	Party Monopoly on Nationally Elected Offices
Argentina	4% of registered voters	Active in 5 districts	Yes	Yes	Yes
Bolivia	2% of votes in last presidential election	(–)	No	No	No
Brazil	0.5% of votes in last chamber election	0.1% of votes in 1/3 of states in last chamber election	No	No	Yes
Chile	.05% of votes in last chamber elections	Active in 8 regions or 3 contiguous regions	No	Yes	No
Colombia	2% of votes in last congressional elections	(–)	No	Yes	No
Costa Rica	3,000 registered voters	(–)	Yes	Yes	Yes
Dominican Republic	2% of votes in last presidential elections	(–)	Yes	Yes	No
Ecuador	1.5% of registered voters in last general elections	Active in 50% of provinces, including 2 of 3 most populous provinces	Yes	Yes	No
El Salvador	3% of votes in last presidential election	(–)	No	Yes	Yes

(continued)

Table 8.1 **Party Regulations in Latin America.** Parties may emerge from society, but institutional rules ensure that the regime affects which parties will survive and prosper *(continued)*

Country	Recognition Requirements	Nationality Requirements	Presidential Primary Required	Presidential Primary in Practice	Party Monopoly on Nationally Elected Offices
Guatemala	0.3% of registered voters in last general elections	Active in 50 municipalities or 12 departments	No	No	No
Honduras	2% of votes in last presidential elections	Active in at least ½ of municipalities and departments	Yes	Yes	No
Mexico	0.26% of registered voters	3,000 members across minimum 20 states, or 300 across minimum 200 congressional districts	No	Yes	No
Nicaragua	3% votes cast in last national election*	Active in all levels of government, to district level*	No	Yes	Yes
Panama	4% of votes cast in last presidential elections	1,000 members, with at least 50 in each province and 20 in each indigenous territory (comarca)	Yes	Yes	Yes
Paraguay	0.5% of votes cast in last senate elections	Active in the capital and at least 4 department capitals	Yes	Yes	No
Peru	5% of votes in last national elections	Active in at least 2/3 of departments of 1/3 of provinces	Yes	Yes	Yes
Uruguay	None	(–)	Yes	Yes	Yes
Venezuela	None	(–)	Yes	Yes	No

Source: Author's compilation based on electoral laws, party laws, and national constitutions.
*Both of these regulations have been declared inapplicable by the Supreme Court of Justice in Nicaragua.

Parties as Social Institutions

The historical roots of parties rest in the halls of legislatures, far from voters. The first parties developed in the United States and France as informal caucus groups among like-minded politicians. And as noted in Latin America of the nineteenth century, parties could best be described as elite political clubs—a reputation they would find difficult to shed in the late twentieth century. Today, parties cannot ignore the broader society that surrounds them. Democratic politics oblige parties to forge widespread connections in society and to develop a dependable support base. Doing so is not only more important today compared to the past due to the expansion of suffrage, but it has also grown more difficult as alternative forms of political organization in civil society have emerged to challenge the role of political parties, and voters in general show a greater reluctance to associate themselves with a single party.

Parties can use several types of linkages to create a connection with society. Mexico has three parties that run from the right-wing National Action Party (PAN) to the centrist Institutional Revolutionary Party (PRI) and on to the left-wing Democratic Revolutionary Party (PRD). The parties have developed distinct party platforms, take pains to educate voters on their beliefs, and commit themselves to stand by their policy proposals if elected to office. From one election to the next, each party pins its hopes on a swing in popular beliefs toward its ideological orientations. Democratic theorists favor this model for party linkages.[3] They have tagged it the **"responsible party model"** because under it, a party commits to certain policy proposals, adopts those policies when elected, and this then allow voters to evaluate party performance in the next election based upon the implementation of the party platforms. The model is meant to ensure that elections serve as a means of communication between parties and voters, and it also promotes ideological diversity as parties carve out their own niches to distinguish themselves (Kitschelt et al., 2010, pp. 14–29). But there are costs to the model. A "responsible" party can lose flexibility if it locks itself into a particular ideological orientation. This happened to both the Radical Party in Argentina and APRA (American Popular Revolutionary Alliance) in Peru. Both parties faced the debt crisis of the 1980s. They reacted by recommitting themselves to traditional ISI-based policies, and rebuffed international creditors suggesting economic reforms. Their intransigence only worsened the economic crisis, and voters deserted them in later elections.

Assuming parties take care to learn and adapt over time, the responsible party model offers a good argument. But whether parties actually adopt the model in practice is another question. Studies of political parties show that the drive to win office is so great that parties often cast off their ideological garb and follow public opinion, however far that may take them from expressed principles. The **"rational party model"** sees parties as pragmatic organizations that do what it takes to win votes (Downs, 1957). Hence, parties do not set anchor in ideology; they ride the currents of public opinion toward voters. Often this means compromising initial policy commitments and adopting more centrist positions to appeal to the most voters. Under the rational party model, parties are not responsible to ideology. They are responsive to the public—if they are to survive. In contemporary Mexican politics, the PAN has struggled to portray itself as a center-right party, the PRI has benefited from its placement as a centrist party, and the PRD has suffered the consequences of remaining true to its leftist principles. The 2015 Chamber of Deputies elections saw PAN retain just 108 seats (down from 206 in 2006), and the PRD held on to only 56 (a fall from 127 in 2006). Meanwhile, the PRI shot up from 106 to 241 seats from 2006 to 2009, and suffered a smaller decline to 203 seats in 2015. Despite its connection to Mexico's authoritarian past, the PRI has found that the center has its benefits. And more generally, Mexico has seen less ideological and more issue-oriented parties such as the Green Party, National Regeneration Movement, and Social Encounter Party do better. The share of seats held by the three traditional, ideological parties has fallen from 92 percent in 2009 to 86 percent in 2012, and just 73 percent in 2015.

Theorists may advocate a responsible party and studies may expose the pressures that lead to responsive parties, but the culture and history of a region also affect party linkages. The colonial experience of Latin America meshed public service and private gain, and contributed to an instrumental approach to government. And because underdevelopment made for a weak civil society in much of the region, parties took the initiative to create connections with various groups as suffrage expanded, and came to dominate them. This was unlike the experience in Europe or the United States, where more developed and vibrant social organizations took on the task of lobbying government, and grew alongside parties over time. Hence, although patronage occurs in party systems throughout the world, it is very common in Latin America. The responsible and rational party models have in common the articulation of comprehensive policy goals that apply to all of society. But parties can also develop more narrow **clientelistic linkages** as they promise specific rewards to certain groups. Before the transition to democracy in 2000, the PRI party had a history of rewarding supportive voting districts with new schools, road repair, medical extension programs, and other public policy expenditures. Today, it is still no secret that certain groups will benefit more from the success of one party than another. The PAN caters to business interests, the PRD to workers, and the PRI receives support from many small farming groups and public unions.

Yet another linkage can emerge from the personal appeal of individual leaders. This sort of **charismatic linkage** is, again, found throughout the world, but it resonates more strongly in Latin America due to the *caudillo* past. Disruptive and destructive as it was, *caudillo* politics contributed to the romantic notion that when times get bad, a man on horseback rides in to save the day. The continued use of presidential institutions also helps to personalize politics. With a charismatic linkage, a leader tends to downplay ideological currents in favor of presenting himself as a problem solver who stands above politics for the benefit of all. Vicente Fox of the PAN party took on the look of a cowboy with leather boots and a large shiny belt buckle to convince Mexicans that he would guide them from authoritarian rule during his 2000–2006 tenure as president (Kitschelt, 2000). More recently in 2012, Mexican voters looked to the youthful Enrique Peña Nieto (PRI), with his telenovela star wife, as a fresh face in the presidency who symbolized the country's move toward a modern economy.

The responsible party model and the rational party model are not necessarily incompatible. In fact, the pressures of public opinion can work to ensure that ideological commitments adapt and evolve over time, even as a party articulates a distinct platform for voters. But clientelistic and charismatic linkages tend to have more perverse effects. Clientelism commits parties to rewarding voters. This makes them responsive, but the rewards tend to be narrow and directed toward specific groups, such that clientelistic politics easily leads to divisive politics. The Peronist party in Argentina has long had success in its appeal to urban working-class groups, but it has catered to their interests with price ceilings on foodstuffs and social programs funded by agricultural export taxes—all to the dismay of the farming and ranching industries who feel increasingly alienated from Argentine politics. In addition, clientelism leads voters to expect immediate rewards and to abandon parties that fail to satisfy their expectations. Instability often results as voters move from one party to another. Charisma can be a powerful tool to ensure loyalty, and it helps party leaders to create long-lasting bonds with the public. But it also stymies the rule of law as charismatic leaders set aside rules and regulations that they portray as constraints on their ability to quickly solve problems. In 2007 and 2010 President Hugo Chàvez of Venezuela made use of "enabling laws" giving him decree authority to bypass the legislature so that he could, as he would have it, attend to the pressing economic needs of the people. His successor, Nicolas Maduro, made the same argument in 2015—this time to defend the country from U.S. imperialism. But by this time it was clear to Venezuelans that the move was more of a power grab, especially as unemployment deepened and store shelves sat bare of basic household necessities. Opposition leader Henrique Capriles countered, "Nicolas, are you requesting the Enabling Law to make soap, nappies and medicines appear, to lower inflation? … It's just another smokescreen" (Reuters, 2015).

In Latin America, Chile and Uruguay have parties that most closely follow the responsible party model. Argentina, Mexico, and Venezuela also come close (Rosas, 2010). But generally speaking, parties in the region are not defined by a strident devotion to ideology or a commitment to a comprehensive party platform. Clientelism and charisma tend to tailor party linkages in the region. This has undermined the ability of parties to initiate clear policy distinctions and debates, to appeal to all voters, and to create bonds that are not dependent on the whims of an individual leader. But no matter the character of the linkage, one other thing is clear—parties in Latin America have not maintained strong ties to society. A survey conducted out of Vanderbilt University found a sense of **party identification** that averaged only 35 percent among Latin American countries (see Table 8.2). The same survey found a 63.3 percent average in the United States (2012 data), where pundits and scholars alike have long charted the growth of independent voters. Does this low level of party identification mean that Latin Americans are disengaged from politics?

Table 8.2 **Party Identification in Latin America, 2014**. Partisan affiliations tend to be very weak in Latin America. In several countries, this is because they experienced a collapse of their party systems in recent years

Costa Rica	67.4%
Uruguay	60.0%
Dominican Republic	54.3%
Nicaragua	46.9%
Panama	45.6%
Ecuador	45.2%
El Salvador	44.8%
Venezuela	44.5%
Paraguay	40.3%
Honduras	40.0%
Colombia	28.2%
Mexico	27.8%
Argentina	26.7%
Bolivia	25.7%
Brazil	23.0%
Peru	19.2%
Chile	13.1%
Guatemala	11.4%
Average	**35.1%**

Source: AmericasBarometer, Latin American Public Opinion Project, Vanderbilt University. Data available at www.AmericasBarometer.org. Survey asked, "Do you currently identify with a political party?"

To the contrary, evidence suggests that Latin Americans are looking away from parties and developing alternative mechanisms for mobilizing and expressing political beliefs and values. Some now look first to social movements and voluntary associations in civil society as sources of political identity and channels for mobilization. Social movements tend to focus on a narrow range of issues, in distinction to the wide-ranging platforms devised by political parties. The landless movement in Brazil (MST—*Movimento dos Trabalhadores Rurais sem Terra*) fights for the rights of squatters. The *piqueteros* ("picketers") in Argentina emerged in response to the economic crisis of 2001–2002, and still represent the urban unemployed. And the Zapatista movement (EZLN—*Ejército Zapatista de Liberación Nacional*), created in 1994, centers on globalization as a threat to indigenous culture and welfare in southern Mexico. Indigenous customs and traditional forms of organization offer another alternative to political parties. As part of the move to decentralize politics, some countries allow indigenous groups to use time-honored procedures for selecting local leaders, allocating state resources, and meting out justice. And finally, an increasing number of voters are looking to the individual qualities of politicians who identify themselves as independents rather than partisans. The following section examines the political consequences that follow as parties increasingly share the field with civil society.

How Parties and Civil Society Must Work Together in Democratic Latin America

Does it matter if parties bow out of—or find themselves dismissed from—democratic politics? What is it precisely that parties contribute to democratic politics? More importantly, what is it that they *uniquely* contribute? Given the surge in social movements, indigenous organizations, and independent candidates—as well as changes in some state constitutions to allow these groups to participate in elections—we need to seriously consider whether parties matter, and whether alternative forms of organization from civil society can substitute for parties.

So what is it that parties do? Political parties can, in theory, take on a number of responsibilities in a democracy. In particular, in an authoritative study, Diamond and Gunther (2001, pp. 7–9) identify seven primary functions:

1 *Candidate nomination*—Parties design specific processes for selecting candidates to government offices, such as primary elections. The process itself offers an opportunity for candidates to gain publicity, and for prospective members of government to be vetted as they are scrutinized even before the official campaign begins.

2 *Electoral mobilization*—Party members take the initiative to get out the vote through telephone calls, door-to-door visits, rallies, and even

transportation to the polls. They also enliven political interest during the campaign by promoting engaging initiatives.

3 *Issue structuring* parties—Political may latch on to different policy priorities from campaign to campaign, but over the long run they offer durable, ideologically coherent party platforms that tie together positions on various issues.

4 *Societal representation*—Parties make connections with groups in society, and offer assurances that their interests will be heard in government.

5 *Interest aggregation*—Parties act like funnels that consolidate the numerous and diverse interests of social groups. While parties do develop strong associations with some social groups and vouch to represent them, they also clarify that all groups must be willing to compromise as the party crafts a collective platform.

6 *Forming and sustaining governments*—Parties bind together politicians and serve as building blocks as governments seek out majorities to support legislation and other government initiatives.

7 *Social integration*—The more effectively parties fulfill their social representation function, the more citizens will identify with the regime and accept it as legitimate.

Different political parties may concentrate on some of these functions more than others. The responsible party will pay close attention to issue structuring, whereas the rational party will prioritize societal representation and regularly appraise its relationships with groups in society. And groups in civil society can serve some of these functions, especially in the mobilization of voters and the recruitment of leaders to be nominated for public office. But the most significant distinction between the character and abilities of civil society groups compared to political parties relates to **interest aggregation**. Groups in civil society tend to be concerned with a narrow set of interests, or even a single interest—environmental degradation, economic policy, the distribution of wealth, indigenous rights, religious issues, and so on. Long ago, Gabriel Almond (1958) distinguished these groups from political parties by labeling them **interest articulators**. But parties have the capability to draw together a range of issues and meld them together under an ideological label. As such, they play a fundamental role in the move from contention to consensus in a democracy.

Highlighting the interest aggregation function not only identifies a unique contribution of political parties, it also exposes the interdependence between civil society groups and political parties in a democracy. Civil society plays an indispensable role in the articulation of interests. Labor unions, environmental organizations, business councils, women's associations, indigenous movements, church groups, and others enliven political debate and offer a voice for the people. Without them, a government would grow isolated and unaware of sentiments and desires in society. But with only them, government would be overwhelmed by their varied and distinct demands. Only political parties can ensure that the voice of the people does not descend into the shouts of a mob.

But parties in Latin America have suffered from a crisis of legitimacy of late. They received the blame—often justifiably—as economic inequality and corruption tore at Latin American politics since the transition from authoritarian rule. In the past, parties could more easily preserve their hold as representatives. Media and communication services were much more limited and parties were integral to the gathering of information. The vast organizational resources of parties were even used at the local level as parties created sports leagues, held picnics, printed newsletters, and staged musical festivals. But today, communications technologies allow groups in civil society to fulfill those same functions and appeal to individuals as their primary source of political identification. If the private, club-like political parties of the past were too dominant and hindered the growth of civil society, today Latin America suffers from an imbalance in the opposite direction. In Bolivia, Ecuador, Venezuela, and elsewhere, opposition groups in civil society have effectively mobilized individuals and stridently expressed their interests—even to the extent of overturning governments. But these same disparate opposition groups have had less success as would-be governors. Social movements excel at the politics of protest, and thereby enrich politics, but too often it is only their opposition that unites them. Political parties are built for consensus-based governance, and thereby offer their own indispensable role in democratic politics.

From the Party to the Party System

A political party performs vital roles in a democracy. But democracy calls for more than one party to channel political participation, so we need to consider how parties work together in a **party system**, which simply refers to characteristics and interactions of the viable parties that regularly contest elections in a country. With interest aggregation as our point of entry, we can identify several concepts that describe the effectiveness of a party system. Party system fragmentation essentially points out the number of political parties. Party system institutionalization describes the stability of the system, especially in regard to whether parties enjoy durable linkages to society and whether individuals view political parties as legitimate and viable instruments for the voicing of their demands. And party system polarization expresses the intensity of ideological divisiveness among parties. There is an enterprising literature on how party systems evolve and operate. Basically, most analysts view the depth and range of societal divisions, and electoral rules as prime determinants of party system dynamics (Lipset and Rokkan, 1967). Here, the focus is on electoral rules because of this study's emphasis on regime institutions.

Party System Fragmentation

The classic statement connecting electoral systems and **party system fragmentation** came from a 1951 study by the French sociologist Maurice Duverger, who plainly noted, "the simple majority single-ballot system favors the two-party system" (1954, p. 217). He associated PR systems with multi-party systems, but recognized the variability in just how many parties different PR systems produce, largely as a result of district magnitude.[4] As he delved into the details of the connection, he noted that electoral systems affect party systems as they exert both a mechanical and a psychological factor.

Mechanically, an electoral system defines a precise method for counting votes and allocating seats, and psychologically, both parties and voters make decisions based upon these mechanics. For instance, a single-member district can only reward one candidate—the one that receives the largest amount of votes. No matter the willpower of smaller contenders, they will be denied representation in this winner-take-all system. Psychologically, smaller parties recognize this and will typically drop out of a race, join a larger party, or seek to combine forces with other small parties. Additionally, voters know this and usually choose not to waste their vote on a small party with little chance of victory. The electoral mechanics create a structure, and the psychology of parties and voters adapt in such a way that two parties evolve over time. Those that decide not to adapt face an unforgiving environment that either ensures their demise or stunts their growth (in cases where regional parties find refuge in a few districts). A PR system offers its own rules for survival. The mechanics offer opportunities for smaller parties, but that does not mean any party can succeed. The corresponding psychology leads voters to expect narrowly based parties that match their interests. Parties that assume a catch-all orientation or dilute their ideology as they combine will be unattractive in this climate. The connection between majoritarian systems and two-party systems, and PR systems and multiparty systems is known as **Duverger's Law**.

Duverger's Law provides a basis for predicting the number of parties in a country. We look to the electoral formula, and then we count the number of parties. But things are not as easy as they seem. We have already seen that the electoral formula can only act as a rough proxy for the electoral rules of the country because other factors also come into play (e.g., district magnitude). Moreover, counting the number of parties is not as simple as it appears to be. After the 2014 elections in Brazil, a total of 28 parties won seats in the Chamber of Deputies. But the number masks the fact that many of these parties worked together closely in alliances. Working within an alliance size affects the distribution of committee seats, the prioritization of agenda items, and commitments to support legislation so parties have a strong incentive to participate. In Brazil, the Workers' Party gained only 70 of the 543 seats in 2014, but it was the largest party and crafted a 304-seat alliance of 13 parties. Alliances are part of the fabric of most legislatures in Latin America, so counting them often provides an accurate indicator of party system fragmentation. Nonetheless, cohesion can vary across countries and alliances, and at the end of the day, alliances are but combinations of individual parties. Brazil learned this in 2015 when the second largest party of the governing alliance defected to support impeachment proceedings against President Dilma Rousseff, a member of the Workers' Party.

The imbalance in party sizes creates another problem for measurements of fragmentation. For example, even if we count alliances as parties in Argentina, we still see that the 2015 elections left it with a total of 20 parties. But 8 of them had just one seat in the 257-seat chamber, and another 4 had just 2 or 3 seats. The two largest parties (alliances) had 87 and 72 seats If we described this as a 20-party system, that would not capture the dynamics of a system in which some parties clearly wield more influence than others. To resolve this difficulty, political scientists measure the **effective number of parties** (ENP) when they compare party systems. The ENP weighs the sizes of parties in a summary calculation, which is computed with the following formula:

$$\text{ENP} = \frac{1}{\sum s_i^{\,2}}$$

In the formula, s^i represents the percentage of seats held by the i-th party. The Greek symbol sigma (Σ) is used to indicate summation. Hence, the formula has three steps to it: (1) the share of seats held by each party is squared; (2) those numbers are summed; (3) and the total is then divided by one. For example, if a legislature has seats equally divided between three parties (.33 of seats each), the ENP is $1/(.33^2 + .33^2 + .33^2) = 3$. If a legislature has one party with .5 of the seats, and two others with .25 each, the ENP is $1/(.5^2 + .25^2 + .25^2) = 2.67$. And if a legislature has one party with .7 of the seats, and two others with .15 each, the ENP is $1/(.7^2 + .15^2 + .15^2) = 1.87$. In each of the examples, three parties vie for influence in the legislature, but the ENP measure captures their relative impact. If we apply the formula to the 20 party coalitions in the Chamber of Deputies in Argentina, we compute an ENP of 4.54, which better depicts the dynamics of a legislature where only four parties held more than 10 seats in 2015. Table 8.3 lists the electoral formulas of Latin American countries and presents data on the number of parties (calculations of the ENP would require a judgment on the strength of party alliances, should they exist).

Countries with majoritarian systems average a 3.3 ENP, whereas those with PR systems average a 3.9 ENP. The difference is not tremendous. In fact, mixed systems have the lowest average ENP at 2.8. The limited data do not refute Duverger's Law, which has been corroborated in countless political studies. Rather, the data illustrate what is so common in politics—causal connections rarely occur in isolation. Rather, they must make do in a sea of often-disparate forces. Alternative factors—some noninstitutional and others institutional—act like currents that may divert, reverse, or even intensify their effects.

Table 8.3 **Electoral Formulas and the Number of Parties in Latin America**. Electoral rules are one determinant of the number of parties that emerge in a regime

Country	Latest Elections	Electoral Formula	Largest Party	Largest Party (% Seats)	Actual Number of Parties
Argentina— Chamber	2015	PR	Victory Front— Peronists	27%	37
Argentina— Senate	2011	Majoritarian	Victory Front— Peronists	54%	19
Bolivia— Chamber	2014	Mixed	Movement for Socialism	69%	3
Bolivia— Senate	2014	PR	Movement for Socialism	68%	3
Brazil— Chamber	2014	PR	Brazilian Democratic Movement Party	13%	27
Brazil— Senate	2014	Majoritarian	Brazilian Democratic Movement Party	23%	19
Chile— Chamber	2013	Majoritarian	Independent Democratic Union	23%	16
Chile— Senate	2013	Majoritarian	Independent Democratic Union and Christian Democrats (tie)	18%	11
Colombia— Chamber	2014	PR	Liberal Party	23%	14
Colombia— Senate	2014	PR	Social Party and Conservatives (tie)	20%	9
Costa Rica	2014	PR	National Liberation Party	32%	9
Dom Rep— Chamber	2016	PR	Dominican Liberation	56%	10

Country	Latest Elections	Electoral Formula	Largest Party	Largest Party (% Seats)	Actual Number of Parties
Dom Rep—Senate	2016	Majoritarian	Dominican Liberation	81%	6
Ecuador	2013	PR	PAIS	73%	11
El Salvador	2012	PR	ARENA	42%	5
Guatemala	2015	PR	Renewed Democratic Liberty	28%	13
Honduras*	2013	PR	National Party	39%	8
Mexico— Deputies	2015	Mixed	Institutional Revolutionary Party	42%	9
Mexico— Senate	2015	Mixed	Institutional Revolutionary Party	43%	7
Nicaragua	2016	PR	Sandinista National Liberation Front	77%	3
Panama	2014	Mixed	Democratic Revolutionary Party	37%	6
Paraguay— Chamber*	2013	PR	National Republican Association	58%	6
Paraguay— Senate	2013	PR	National Republican Association	42%	7
Peru*	2016	PR	Popular Force	55%	7
Uruguay— Chamber	2014	PR	Broad Front	51%	5
Uruguay— Senate	2014	PR	Broad Front	53%	3
Venezuela	2015	Mixed	MUD	66%	15

Source: Data accessed on the Inter-Parliamentary Union website: www.ipu.org.
*Honduras, Paraguay, and Peru have mixed systems, but with a very small majoritarian component. They are labeled PR here because of this dramatic imbalance in PR and majoritarian districts.

El Salvador and Nicaragua not only have PR systems, but they also share a history of bitter civil war, with combatants who now fight it out in the electoral arena. Old antagonisms still serve to rally the populace to one side or the other of the political spectrum. This galvanizes standing parties and limits the emergence of new parties. Guatemala had its own horrific conflict, but its guerrillas proved more adept at military than political organization. They now rarely score over 5 percent of the vote. Seeing less of a threat from the former rebels, those who stood opposed to them have been more willing to break into factions. The details of electoral rules also matter. Brazil has an unblocked list PR system, but a rule that allows parties to present party lists that surpass the number of seats by up to 1.5 further energizes intra-party competition. The ballot structure leads politicians to curry personal favor with voters, and lax campaign financing regulations allow special interest groups to reciprocate on an individual basis. Hence, elected politicians develop strong incentives to break from established parties and create their own, and the financing furnishes the capacity to act on these motivations. The federal structure also comes into play in Brazil. Governors wield considerable influence over spending, and many politicians actually look at the national legislature as but a stepping-stone to the state assemblies, which place them closer to the distribution of pork barrel spending. The desire to think regionally undermines the development of strong, cohesive national parties (Samuels, 2003).

Party System Institutionalization

Part of the story behind party system fragmentation in Latin America rests in the related concept of **party system institutionalization**. A party system can be considered institutionalized when it can boast a number of parties that (a) maintain a relatively stable base of electoral support over time, (b) have solid linkages to society, and (c) are perceived as legitimate and important components to the politics of the country (Mainwaring and Scully, 1995). History has not been kind to the development of party systems in Latin America. Although many countries in the region can reflect on party competition that reaches back to the nineteenth century, this is a checkered history. Military rule, political instability, social exclusion and rebellion, and economic malaise have all created problems for parties hoping to establish roots. One study examined the 1,200 different parties that competed in the 166 legislative elections held in Latin America through the twentieth century. Only 15 parties competed in every election held in their country, and only three had their name on the ballot in at least 20. Over 80 percent participated in just one election. To say the least, the survival rates of Latin American political parties have not been very high (Coppedge, 2001).

More recently, military rule through the 1960s and 1980s forced many parties to start anew. When democratization did occur, a massive debt crisis in the 1980s, and then growing inequality associated with the neoliberal reforms of the 1990s strained the legitimacy of governing authorities, as did the corruption issues of the twenty-first century. All this upended many party systems in the region. **Pedersen's index of electoral volatility** offers one way to measure party system institutionalization. It takes the amount of seats gained or lost by each party in subsequent elections, and then divides this total by two to capture the amount of seats that changed hands (Pedersen, 1983).[5]

Table 8.4 applies the Pedersen index to the 2001 and 2006 elections in Peru for the national legislature. The index score of 67 shows that over half of the seats changed partisan hands in the 120-member chamber. (The scale of the index depends on the size of the legislature. In Peru a high score of 120 would indicate that every seat changed hands). Peru has a reputation for some of highest levels of electoral volatility in the region. By the 2016 elections, only two of the parties that contested seats in 2006 remained, and they won less than 10 percent of the vote. And Latin America as a whole is recognized for its unstable electoral politics. One analyst notes that over two-thirds of the countries in the region recorded higher levels of electoral volatility from the 1980s to 2000s than the most volatile country, in its most volatile period, in all Western Europe from 1880 to 1980 (Payne, 2007, p. 155).

Photo 8.2 Social movements use a variety of nonconventional techniques to gather attention and press their interests. Here, protestors "occupy" the main plaza (*zocalo*) in Mexico City.

Source: © Shutterstock

Table 8.4 **Electoral Volatility in Peru**. Voters in Peru have some of the weakest linkages to parties in all of Latin America

Party	2001	2006	Difference
Perú Posible	47	2	45
American Popular Revolutionary Alliance	28	36	8
National Unity	17	17	0
Independent Moralizing Front	11	0	11
Union for Peru	6	45	39
Somos Perú	4	0	4
Popular Action	3	0	3
Independents	4	0	4
Alliance for the Future	0	13	13
Centre Front	0	5	5
National Restoration	0	2	2
		Total: 134	**Electoral volatility:** $134/2 = 67$

Source: Data accessed on the Inter-Parliamentary Union website: www.ipu.org.

A second way to measure party system volatility is with survey data. Voters can be queried on what they think of political parties to evaluate their attachment. The 2015 Latinobarómetro survey asked Latin Americans to indicate their level of confidence in political parties—a lot, some, little, or no confidence. Only Uruguay (35 percent) had over one-third of their respondents mark "a lot" or "some." The average across all countries was just 20 percent, indicating that on average 80 percent of Latin Americans express little to no confidence in their political parties. Another question in the 2013 survey asked individuals whether they agreed with the statement "without political parties, one cannot have democracy." The average across all countries was a dismal 51 percent. The Latinobarómetro survey, with data reaching back to 1996, shows fairly consistent levels of disapproval directed toward political parties, with the nadir resting at the turn of the century when frustration with neoliberal reform reached its peak and several countries took a turn to the political left.[6] The data helps to explain the low levels of party identification in Latin America.

Party System Polarization

A final measure of the party system examines the distribution and intensity of ideological sentiments. **Party system polarization** can create an insurmountable obstacle as governments seek to craft consensus-based policies. What issues divide political parties in Latin America? The role of the state in the economy is the most common cleavage. Given the historic influence of the Catholic Church in the region, it is not surprising that social issues also rest at the forefront of political disagreement. Access to abortion, ease of divorce, and policies on sexual orientation remain heated areas of debate. The experience with military rule, which some viewed as a despicable period, whereas others saw as a regrettable but necessary reaction to communist influences, also resonates in legislative halls. Finally, some parties exhibit authoritarian tendencies with doubts over the benefits of democracy and elections, whereas others profess unconditional support for democracy (Rivas-Pérez, 2008). One analysis of polarization found the deepest ideological gulfs in the legislatures of Chile, Mexico, and Uruguay (Kitschelt et al., 2010).[7]

Despite these ruptures, moderation appears to be far more the norm today compared to the past. Even after an economic slide in the late 1990s spurred a turn to the left in the early twentieth century, commentators characterized the change as a "pink tide" to distinguish it from the more radical leftist movements of the 1960s and 1970s. Leaders throughout the region may have denounced the rigors of neoliberalism, but most still acceded that the market economy remained the only game in town. As if to signal their own moderation, voters in "pink tide" countries such as Argentina and Brazil supported right-wing candidates in their most recent elections.

The Interaction of Fragmentation, Institutionalization, and Polarization

Democracy requires more than one party to ensure competitive politics. But what is the ideal number of parties for a democracy? At what point does the addition of one more competitive party make for a fragmented party system and cause other problems? Proponents of the two-party system place the bar low. They argue that fewer parties helps politicians overcome polarization as they compete for votes in the political center. Those who favor a multiparty system respond that such moderation comes at the cost of voter choices, and dampens political debate as politicians veer from distinct ideological commitments whether they are on the left or the right of the political spectrum. Hence, with less polarization comes less institutionalization. Two-party supporters also tout the ability of two-party systems to produce majority parties, claiming that this stabilizes government and allows voters to place responsibility for policy on a single party—which goes a long way toward institutionalizing a party in society. Multiparty advocates respond that having a majority party is not so important. A two-party system may make for greater government stability, but it also can undermine regime stability as voters grow alienated from a system lacking in party choices.

Neither side is wrong. Rather, the debate itself needs to be placed in the context of other political institutions. In particular, Scott Mainwaring called multipartism and presidentialism a "difficult combination" in 1993 because of the likelihood that a legislature fractured by many parties would create political vacuum and allow a president to assume yet more control. But he tapered his criticism in a 1997 publication (Mainwaring and Shugart, 1997), noting that party discipline could help create reliable coalitions in a multiparty system and that the extent of constitutional powers also determines the emergence of a domineering president. In a case study of Brazil, a country known for its plethora of parties in a presidential system, Armijo et al. (2006) added two more factors. They noted that the limited power of executive decree authority (decrees expire in two months if congress does not approved them), and the regular sunset legislation (which creates expiration dates in one or three years) create a framework that compels legislators and the executive not just to negotiate laws, but to constantly reevaluate and renegotiate. Institutions in Brazil in essence teach political leaders to cooperate despite their numerous partisan affiliations, lest they become irrelevant to the policy process. A 2012 essay by Carlos Pereira and Marcus André Melo underscored the importance of the rule of law, noting how it provides assurances that presidents will not overstep their bounds as they negotiate multipartism by doling out meaningful cabinet posts and enticing pork barrel projects. In complete contrast to the view taken in 1993, they argued that the multiparty presidential systems of Brazil and Chile "have emerged as *the* successful models for governance in Latin America" (2012). Of course, Chile would soon experience suffocating street protests that would compel electoral reform (see Chapter 4), and in 2016 Brazil would remove its president—a move dubbed a coup by its opponents (see Chapter 9). The debate over whether two-party or multiparty systems are best will undoubtedly continue, but some headway can be made if one places the debate in the context of other institutions.

COUNTRY IN THE SPOTLIGHT

Venezuela: Changes in Parties, Changes in Politics

Parties have played different roles at different times in the political history of Venezuela. Moreover, each change in their role can be associated with dramatic changes in the politics of the country more generally. This underscores the point that parties are indeed a central component of politics. In the case of Venezuela, history tells us that if we want to understand political developments, we can look to the action, or inaction, of parties. As such, the current status of parties in the country offers a barometer to contemporary politics and a signal of what we should expect in the near future of this important country.

Like many countries in Latin America during the nineteenth century, Venezuela had two major parties that took the names "Liberal Party" and "Conservative Party." But perhaps even more than most other countries, the ideological labels did not mean very much. In practice both parties acted similarly as agents of the landed elite and *caudillo* rule. Venezuela was a terribly fractionalized country at the time, and the parties did more to organize political violence than to contest elections. Militias from the parties formed the front lines in the Federal War (1859–1863), an internal conflict that displaced hundreds of thousands as *caudillo*-led guerrilla units attempted to consolidate regional control. Almost 200,000—which meant almost 10 percent of the entire population—died in this civil war. Antonio Guzmán Blanco helped to engineer a compromise through federal institutions under the 1854 Constitution. In essence, under the new regime 20 *caudillos* carved out and agreed to respect each other's authority in 20 federal states. As president for much of the period from 1870 to 1888, Guzmán Blanco sidelined political parties by interacting directly with the *caudillos* through the Federal Council. The institution was used to decide political positions and dole out spending on government programs (especially infrastructure development) (Díaz Cayeros, 2006, pp. 159–160).

Guzmán Blanco came to political terms with the *caudillos*. In many ways he represented the first "national *caudillo*" for Venezuela as he geared the country toward an export economy focused on ranching, cacao, and coffee. Later national *caudillos*, first under Cipriano Castro (1899–1908), and then much more so under Juan Vicente Gómez (1908–1935), would rely less on skillful negotiation and more on brute force to maintain, and ultimately centralize power. The discovery of massive oil deposits helped Gómez marshal the resources needed to quash his opponents. And as fate would have it, the oil economy also brought an end to the landed oligarchy, because the largest oil fields rested in many of the traditional agricultural valleys. Rural elites sold off their lands in what historians call "the dance of the concessions" and invested their profits in the emerging commercial and financial services linked to the oil sector (Karl, 1997). It was a gradual fade, but

(*continued*)

by this time the Conservative and Liberal parties had ceased to exist. Their blatant association with the landed oligarchy meant that they never developed real connections, or legitimacy, outside a small rural elite. The Federal Council illustrated their expendability. Then repression checked any thought of mobilization. And finally the decline of the agricultural sector eliminated their only real roots.

With the slate wiped clean, a unique opportunity for completely new political parties opened for Venezuela. But the story of their development serves as a reminder that political parties stand as the final gateway on the path from society to government. Ideally, they aggregate interests, but this function presumes a vibrant civil society, which in turn presumes a modest level of socioeconomic modernization and diversity.

In the case of Venezuela, the country had historically been lightly populated, rural, and beginning with the Guzmán Blanco period, dominated by Caracas. This was not a fertile setting for civil society. The oil economy also stunted the growth of voluntary associations. First and foremost, oil proceeds fed the repressive apparatus of the state, and allowed it to restrict civil liberties quite effectively. Budgeted state income shot up from 59.6 million *bolivares* in 1920–1921 to 202.6 million *bolivares* in 1930–1931 (Levine, 1973, p. 15). The country also lacked the traditional rural-urban divide between elite groups— a divide that prompted political mobilization in most other Latin American countries.

If the "dance of the concessions" did not induce agriculturalists to sell, the economic distortions of oil exports made things difficult for those who opted to till their land. Foreign demand for Venezuelan oil placed upward pressure on the national currency, and thereby raised the prices of all exports including those in agriculture. This made them less competitive in world markets. Oil profits also checked industrial growth. The 1939 Treaty of Reciprocity promised reduced tariff rates for U.S.-manufactured goods—which easily outcompeted Venezuelan manufacturers—in exchange for privileged access in the U.S. market for Venezuela oil. And finally, the oil industry itself did not offer a springboard for political organization. Though huge, its capital-intensive nature meant that it rarely employed more than 26,000 before the 1950s. Moreover, employment was concentrated in the petroleum areas, far from the urban centers of the country (Karl, 1986, pp. 202–203).

The universities provided the only real arena for social mobilization. In fact, many of the country's future party leaders "cut their teeth" in the university protests of the late 1920s. They would take on the name "The Generation of 1928." The Gómez government quashed the would-be rebellion, but sending the students underground or into exile had a pivotal impact on their strategic thinking. As noted by Levine,

> Students realized that to defeat Gómez, it was not enough to kill him and hope for the best. To change Venezuela, the system had to be changed, and this required a reorientation in thinking about politics and the redirection of all efforts into the formation of mass organizations. (1973, p. 22)

And because the work took place underground, it hastened the movement to forge durable bonds at the grassroots level, and generated a strong commitment to party discipline. Absent a meaningful civil society with which to work, the party took on activities of both parties and civil society groups. The activity also placed the Generation of 1928 in direct competition with communist organizers.

Juan Vicente Gómez died in 1935. Military rulers followed, but the level of repression declined and many exiles began to return. One prominent member of the Generation of 1928, Rómulo Betancourt, followed up on the underground work of the student movement and took the initiative to form a political party—Democratic Action (AD, *Acción Democrática*)—in 1941. The party gained a chance to rule in 1945 after infighting in the armed forces over political positions led a group of junior officers to rebel. They viewed governance as outside the professional duties of their institution, and supported the move to free elections and civilian rule. The AD party quickly dominated the political landscape, taking the highest government offices in the 1945 elections. Pent up by decades of repression, the party aggressively pushed the progressive political changes it had long debated, hoping to unite the nascent urban middle classes with peasant groups freed by the decline of the agricultural sector and the militant oil unions that had shifted loyalty from the communist organizers. The political alliance was broad, but it was also delicate. It was based on groups that had not really developed a solid base in the economy or strong sense of self-identity (Karl, 1986, pp. 203–206).

And the dominance of AD was illusive, created in part because it was the party that had made the first moves to organize in a country

(continued)

that lacked a strong civil society. But the political opening now allowed others to challenge what the AD had already decided. Ironically enough initial opposition emerged once again in the universities. But this time it was in the Catholic universities, where students protested secular educational reforms that gave the state greater regulatory power. Further confrontations over church-state relations led to the creation of a Christian Democratic party, COPEI, in 1946. Once bereft of political activity, Venezuela soon found itself drowned by partisan politics. And the electoral calendar did not help. To make the move to democracy, elections were held not only for the presidency, but also for congress, state positions, municipal offices, and for a constituent assembly to debate a new constitution. The country experienced a near nonstop campaign from 1946 to 1948, and it only served to heighten political tensions (Levine, 1973, pp. 37–38). Foreign oil investors and remnants of the traditional agricultural sector rallied their own opposition after AD pushed through a nationalization program in the oil sector and land reform in the countryside.

Disturbed by the bickering of party elites, and persuaded by Cold War concerns over communist influence in government, the military returned to rule in November 1948. An oil boom in the 1950s fortified the new authoritarian government under General Marcos Pérez Jiménez. A new security agency, the *Seguridad Nacional*, rounded up political adversaries and subjected many to torture. The boom also offered ample opportunities for corruption, which over time dampened support for the regime by military officers still concerned with the professional standing of the armed forces. Military units deposed Pérez Jiménez in 1958 so that civilians could return to the presidential palace.

The AD once again found itself in a position of power. But the 1945–1948 period had taught it the value of compromise, and repression during the 1950s instilled a powerful motive to do whatever was needed to keep the military in the barracks. In addition, Cold War pressures taught political leaders in AD to moderate their politics— the 1954 U.S. intervention in Guatemala served as a reminder of how the United States would react if reform looked like revolution. Thus AD reached out to COPEI and a leftist party known as the URD (*Unión Republicana Democrática*) in what became known as the **Pact of Punto Fijo**. The COPEI agreed to an expansive state, in exchange for a commitment by AD to respect private property and to attenuate secular reforms in education. All parties agreed to share access to state contracts and offices. In a clear response to Cold War pressures and as a signal to foreign oil investors, the pact excluded the Communist Party.

The pact brought a level of stability to Venezuela that allowed it to withstand the wave of military interventions that swept across the region in the 1960s and 1970s. But the elitist nature of the pact and its foundation in clientelistic linkages planted the seeds of its own destruction. The signing of the agreement at Punto Fijo had symbolic meaning by itself. Punto Fijo is a resort area in Venezuela, and the pact was signed there at the estate of Rafael Caldera, then leader of COPEI. It was hardly a popular affair.

Institutionally, a new constitution was enacted in 1961 that granted the president substantial power in budgetary actions, tax and tariff policies, appointments to governors and state enterprises, and even to declare states of emergency—all this to assure the power-sharing principles agreed to under the Pact of Punto Fijo. Because AD had been so intimately involved in the creation of the two major unions— the CTV (*Confederación de Trabajadores Venezolanas*) and the FCV (*Federación Campesina Venezolana*)—it was able to control labor relations rather effectively. There was an independent business association, FEDECAMARAS, but the Venezuelan government also had advantages in dealing with business associations. First, because industrialization had been delayed for so long, most manufacturing interests emerged as a result and under the influence of the ISI policies embraced by AD after 1958. This allowed the state to reward supporters through tax breaks and subsidies as industry expanded. Second, the state remained firmly in control of oil resources, and thus directly managed the most important economic sector of the country.

Democracy thus came to Venezuela, but it did so in a concentrated form, one firmly in the hands of political parties. Some scholars referred to the regime as a "partyarchy" (Coppedge, 1994). The 1958–1993 period could not have been more different from the time that had preceded it, when political parties were largely absent. But important changes took place during the time that parties monopolized politics. As Venezuela continued to modernize and urbanize, civil society finally started to sprout independent of party structures. In the 1960s and 1970s, civil society went through a "formative stage," with growth largely concentrated at the local level in middle-class neighborhoods. Communities organized in reaction to social and environmental ills associated with urban growth, in support of opportunities

(*continued*)

for women, or to offer vocational education. The 1980s would see a dramatic upsurge in civil society, when the debt crisis spurred inflation and forced government to slash social programs. Now more than ever, communities saw the need to act on their own for basic services (Salamanca, 2004).

But if there was a turning point in the relationship between political parties and civil society, it came during the social uprising known as the *Caracazo* on February 27–28, 1989. The Pact of Punto Fijo had brought stability and growth to Venezuela, but in the long run the web of clientelism and dearth of competition made for an unresponsive government, one that catered only to a select group of business associations, activist groups, and labor unions that had sworn loyalty to the traditional political parties. After the rioting, the message was clear—much of Venezuelan society was beginning to see the party-dominated regime as illegitimate. More independent groups emerged as human rights organizations looked into abuses surrounding the Caracazo. The Caracazo also led many soldiers to rethink their relationship with the government. They resented how the government depended on them to end the rioting with force that led to the deaths of more than 400 citizens. In their view, they had been asked to do the dirty work, and repress a population that was rightfully rebelling against a scandalous government. One mid-ranking officer, Lieutenant Colonel Hugo Chávez, tapped into this resentment to lead an attempted coup d'état on February 4, 1992. It failed, but the effort gained him fame. Motives behind the coup itself appeared to be vindicated in March 1993, when congress removed President Carlos Andrés Pérez from office after he was found guilty of corruption charges.

With the AD in disarray, COPEI had a chance to restore confidence in the regime. But the party splintered between its old guard, which simply wanted to take the reins of government from AD and continue as before, and a new generation that hoped to rethink party organization and policy alternatives. The preeminent leader of COPEI, Rafael Caldera, abandoned the party altogether and ran as an independent candidate in the December 1993 special election for a successor to Andrés Pérez. In the final tally, AD and COPEI collected less than 50 percent of the vote for the first time since the Pact of Punto Fijo. Caldera eked out a victory with just 30.5 percent of the vote, running on a platform that all but endorsed the coup attempt. The party system in place since 1958 had suffered a complete collapse (Dietz and Myers, 2007).

Caldera cemented the collapse when he turned on his campaign promises, and decided to embrace the same neoliberal agenda first promoted by Andrés Pérez. Oil prices had recently taken a dive, and Caldera concluded that economics left him no choice but to impose austerity. He made some amends with COPEI, and began to cooperate with AD, but the moves backfired—Venezuelans concluded that he was not the maverick he proclaimed to be. His history with COPEI made it easy to associate him with the old guard, and surmise that real change had yet to take place. That change would occur in the 1998 presidential elections. The AD and COPEI did not even run candidates, but instead supported the candidate of an upstart party. Hugo Chávez, released from prison by Caldera in 1994 as a gesture of national reconciliation, won the presidency with 59.6 percent of the vote.

Hugo Chávez ran as a candidate of the Fifth Republic Movement. Chávez had headed a clandestine political organization in the army, the Bolivarian Revolutionary Movement-200, in the lead-up to the 1992 coup attempt (Arceneaux, 1996). The Fifth Republic Movement was meant to expand his constituency to the general population. Normally, it would be difficult, if not impossible, to build a party from scratch and rally voters in a nationwide election. But Venezuela had a number of leftist parties that had been excluded from partyarchy, and they were willing to offer their organizational resources to the cause of Chávez (Sylvia and Danopoulos, 2003, p. 67). Many later regretted the decision after they were denied promised positions in government, grew critical of the centralization of power under Chávez, or—in the case of several revolutionary leftist parties—decided that Chávez was too moderate.

After riding the backs of several nationwide party structures, Chávez marginalized parties in favor of a personal, charismatic linkage with the Venezuelan people. Eager to separate himself from the partyarchy of the past, and critical of the liberal democracies aligned with the United States and global capitalism, Chávez promoted what he referred to as "participatory democracy." Despite the name, in practice the idea had less to do with new forms of popular decision making, and more to do with forming direct administrative connections between the people and politics—links that would rearrange clientelistic linkages that previously worked their way through political parties. Neighborhood groups called Bolivarian Circles formed the first undertaking of participatory democracy. Each Circle

(*continued*)

consisted of about one dozen members, all of whom pledged to uphold the principles of the government (including campaigning activities), and to take a leading role in the disbursement of social programs at the local level (e.g., remedial education and health services). The Bolivarian Circles were to be the front lines of revolutionary change (Hawkins and Hansen, 2006).

Chávez fanned popular animosities toward political parties, and used those sentiments to reorganize political institutions he declared to be contaminated by the old order. A new constitution in 1999 abolished the senate in favor of a single chamber and gave the executive substantial policymaking powers, allowed the president to pack the Supreme Court, and placed the attorney general, comptroller-general, and electoral commission more directly under the supervision of the executive. Popular passions could not have been more convenient for Chávez. The constitutional provision to deny public funding for political parties was an easy sale to a public jaded by decades of partyarchy, but it also institutionalized a disadvantage for the opposition (Corrales and Penfold, 2007, pp. 100–102).

In the early 2000s, Venezuela essentially became a country without political parties. The Fifth Republic Movement broadened its appeal and organization through an alliance—The Patriotic Pole—with several leftist parties when the new constitution was drafted. But the coalition fell apart due to disagreements over candidate selections in the 2000 elections. Those opposed to Chávez turned away from parties simply because they viewed the new regime as illegitimate—and to compete would only affirm its validity. The opposition found its new base in civil society. Chávez had hoped the Bolivarian Circles would allow him to reorganize civil society. But he soon discovered that Venezuela already had in place an energetic array of social organizations, and many were upper- and middle-class groups averse to his redistributive policies. From 2002 to 2004 Venezuela because a hotbed of protest activity, and violence—including an attempted coup d'état in April 2002. Politics was pushed from the halls of government to the plazas and side streets; it was all conflict and no consensus. This was a mirror image of the 1945–1948 period, when conflict was just as divisive, but rested at the elite rather than the mass level. While political parties would not have ensured the peace in 2002–2004, they clearly had to form part of the solution in a country that had become all interest articulation, and no interest aggregation.

The opposition made little headway. After a failed attempt to remove Chávez through a recall in 2004, they became dispirited and refused to participate in the 2005 congressional elections. Since 2005, both sides appear to have worked through a period of learning about the importance of political parties. Reacting to charges of centralization, the Fifth Republic Movement held primary elections for candidates to run in the 2005 municipal elections, and Chávez has since committed his party to further primaries. In an attempt to merge the parties that had supported the Fifth Republic Movement, Chávez dissolved the party and invited previous supporters to join a new party, the United Socialist Party of Venezuela (PSUV) in late 2007. On the other hand, the opposition surmised that electoral politics were in fact the only route to challenging Chávez. Some 50 parties joined together to create the Coalition for Democratic Unity (*Mesa de la Unidad Democrática*—MUD) and contest the 2010 elections to the National Assembly. They did quite well, taking 48 percent of the vote. Like AD after 1945, Chávez may have been discovering that his appeal was not as broad as he had thought.

The changes to the Venezuelan party system may be too little, too late. After 1998, Venezuelan politics were all about Hugo Chávez. But 2011 offered the first signs that things were about to change. Speculation mounted as the ever-present Chávez began to disappear from public view for weeks at a time. Commentators scanned photos and video footage for evidence of declining health. Then, mid-year, Chávez answered the speculation by disclosing that he had been diagnosed with cancer. Even so, he reassured Venezuelans that his treatments (typically conducted during trips to Cuba) were progressing, and that he had every intention to run in the 2012 presidential elections. A vast array of social programs kept Chávez popular with many Venezuelans, and his declining health may have added a sympathetic element to his voting base as the October 2012 elections approached. He would win, but after gaining 45 percent of the vote, the opposition showed that it was now a force to be reckoned with.

The tide shifted significantly after the death of Hugo Chávez in March 2013. His successor, Vice President Nicolás Maduro, lacked the charisma of Chávez, and perhaps more importantly, the economy began to sag under the weight of populist spending and entrenched corruption. After respectable growth rates of 4.2 percent in 2011 and 5.6 percent in 2012 offered some recovery from the 2008

(*continued*)

global economic crisis, 2013 saw a rate of just 1.3 percent, only to be followed by negative rates in 2014 (−3.9 percent) and 2015 (−5.7 percent). In this time, inflation rose from about 25 percent to well over 125 percent. Unemployment spiked; shortages of basic services such as gas, water, and electricity became commonplace; and crime grew rampant. Massive protests rocked Caracas beginning in early 2014. The charm of Chávez and a resource-rich economy allowed him to push the limits of democracy with court-packing, executive overreach, and the manipulation of electoral law. But when Maduro responded to the economic crisis by expanding his executive decree authority, and jailed opposition leaders for involvement in the protests, more and more Venezuelans saw the moves as blatantly autocratic. Under these conditions, Maduro saw his PSUV supermajority crumble in the 2015 legislative elections. The MUD coalition won a decisive majority, but now faces an isolated, but entrenched executive who is not up for reelection until 2019. Should MUD attain the presidency, it will face the difficulty that challenges all coalitions united by their opposition to a governing party—what binds them when it comes time to govern? The PSUV may disintegrate, but the masses of the working class and popular sectors who so strongly supported Chávez but grew alienated under Maduro would be left behind, awaiting mobilization by a new or reformed political party. On the other hand, the legacy of Chávez, through appointments in the courts and military, impact on the rule of law, and contortions of the electoral system, means that the Venezuelan political system is unlikely to face a clean slate any time in the near future. Tracing the change in political parties provides insight into the political development of Venezuela, but how its future unfolds will be dependent on other institutions.

Discussion Questions

1   Describe how parties have behaved and formed linkages over the course of history in Venezuela. How did changes in civil society affect party developments? How have things changed over time? How have they stayed the same?
2   How did changes in the party system open opportunities for Hugo Chávez? How did these same circumstances create challenges for Hugo Chávez as a political leader? How did Maduro illustrate the importance of leadership?

Conclusion

Political parties act as a gateway of participation from society to the state. As interest aggregators, they help to funnel the disparate demands of civil society, and thereby play an essential role in democratic politics. In theory, parties can best contribute to democracy by acting as responsible parties and sticking to their expressed party platforms. In practice, scholars note that parties act rationally and follow public opinion. This can help them adapt, but it can also disappoint those who elected a party with the expectation that they follow through on established campaign commitments. Beyond responsible or rational action, most political parties in Latin America seek to develop clientelistic or charismatic ties with voters. Party systems throughout Latin America can be compared on the bases of their fragmentation, institutionalization, and polarization.

Political parties provide a great deal of insight to the instability in some Latin American countries. During the authoritarian era of the 1960s to 1980s, parties in Colombia and Venezuela staved off military intervention with political pacts. Mexico was not a democracy during this time, but it too held the military at bay with the deft and patronage-based organization of the PRI party. In Costa Rica, the Party of National Liberation and Social Christian Unity Party institutionalized themselves during this time and helped the country retain its democracy. Once we realize the essential role of parties as interest aggregators, we can identify how they and civil society must work together to ensure that society is heard in government.

A number of other institutions influence parties. Majoritarian electoral rules tend to create two-party systems that behave as catch-all parties, whereas PR electoral rules allow for multiparty systems with parties that pursue more narrowly defined constituents. Federalism can undercut the nationalization of parties. One of the more interesting debates asks whether presidentialism is compatible with a multiparty system given the likelihood that more parties means greater difficulty forming majorities in congress, which in turn allows executives to take on a stronger role in government. Given the preponderance of PR electoral rules, multiparty systems, and presidential designs in Latin America, this would be troubling news for the region—but the debate does illustrate how political institutions can be crafted to address political concerns.

Key Terms

Discussion Questions

1   Is it better for a party to remain responsible to its party platform and campaign commitments, or responsive to public opinion? Which best serves democracy?

2   Are social movements and protest activities a sign that democracy is failing, or succeeding? How and why?

3   Which do you prefer, a two-party or a multiparty system? How would you arrange other political institutions to accommodate your preference?

4   Select a political party in Latin America. How nationalized and institutionalized is the party? How would you describe its ideological commitments? What role is the party currently playing in the politics of its country?

Suggested Readings

Alcántara Sáez, Manuel. 2007. *Politicians and Politics in Latin America.* **Boulder, CO: Lynne Reinner.** This edited book provides insight into political parties with careful examinations of the perspectives of politicians. It makes use of survey data from the Parliamentary Elites in Latin America (PELA) project at the University of Salamanca, Spain. Few studies offer such an intimate analysis of politicians in Latin America, with chapters that look into politicians' thoughts on trust, ideology, polarization, and career backgrounds.

Karen L. Remmer. 1984. *Party Competition in Argentina and Chile, 1890–1930.* **Lincoln, NE: University of Nebraska Press.** Remmer captures Argentina and Chile at a critical juncture in their political development—the move from oligarchic rule to competitive party politics. Beyond the simple argument that parties matter, Remmer identifies how the timing and sequence of their development matter more. The abrupt expansion of suffrage in Argentina, sudden emergence of distinct parties, and changes in the party system created greater anxiety among socioeconomic elites, and made them more willing than their counterparts in Chile to support military intervention.

Peter M. Siavelis and Scott Morgenstern. 2008. *Pathways to Power: Political Recruitment and Candidate Selection in Latin America.* **University Park, PA: Penn State University Press.** This book includes a number of case studies by prominent scholars on the recruitment and selection of candidates to both legislative and executive offices. The subject does not receive much attention, in part because the data are difficult to collect. This makes the work all the more valuable. In essence, the studies go "behind the curtain" of presumed relationships between electoral systems, party discipline, and the general nature of the party system to illustrate how the details of recruitment and selection matter.

Donna Lee Van Cott. 2005. *From Movements to Parties in Latin America: The Evolution of Ethnic Politics.* **New York: Cambridge.** Van Cott looks at differences in constitutional structures and party systems to assess opportunities for ethnic movements to transform into political parties. Special attention is given to the cases of Bolivia, Ecuador, and Peru. The study is especially significant, given the historical suppression of indigenous groups, and questions over how the consensus-oriented approach to politics practiced by indigenous groups will affect—or be affected by—competitive democratic politics.

Notes

1 "Venezuela Braces for Momentous Vote that Could Curb Chávez 'Revolution.'" *Washington Post.* December 5, 2015.
2 See "Urbanization in Latin America," February 5, 2014. Available at www .atlanticcouncil.org.
3 In its first comprehensive statement on political parties in 1950, the American Political Science Association issued a report calling on parties to adopt the responsible parties model. The organization still offers the same advice. See "APSA Responsible Parties Project, 1950–2000," available at: www.apsanet .org/~pop/APSA_Report. htm# REPORT.
4 Taagepera and Shugart (1993) would focus more intently on the impact of district magnitude.
5 The index can also be applied to the percentage of votes received by parties from one election to the next to illustrate the percentage of voters who changed their votes.
6 See the online analysis of the data available at www.latinobarometro.org.
7 This study included all the South American countries examined in this book, but only Costa Rica and the Dominican Republic from the Central America and Caribbean region.

References

Al Día News. 2015. "A Deadly Year for Journalists in Latin America and the Middle East." December 29. Available at aldianews.com.
Almond, Gabriel. 1958. "Research Note: A Comparative Study of Interest Groups and the Political Process." *American Political Science Review* 52:1, pp. 270–82.
Arceneaux, Craig. 1996. "Democratic Consolidation or Deconsolidation?: Military Doctrine and the 1992 Venezuelan Military Unrest." *Journal of Political and Military Sociology* 24, pp. 57–82.
Armijo, Leslie Elliot, Philippe Faucher, and Magdelena Dembinska. 2006. "Compared to What?: Assessing Brazil's Political Institutions." *Comparative Political Studies* 39:6, pp. 759–86.
Campbell, Maia Sophia. 2007. "The Right of Indigenous Peoples to Political Participation and the Case of Yatama v. Nicaragua." *Arizona Journal of International and Comparative Law* 24:2, pp. 499–540.

Carey, John, and John Polga-Hecimovich. 2006. "Primary Elections and Candidate Strength in Latin America." *Journal of Politics* 68:3, pp. 530–43.

Coppedge, Michael. 1994. *Strong Parties and Lame Ducks: Presidential Partyarchy and Factionalism in Venezuela*. Stanford: Stanford University Press.

———. 2001. "Political Darwinism in Latin America's Lost Decade," in Larry Diamond and Richard Gunther, eds., *Political Parties and Democracy*, pp. 173–205. Baltimore, MD: Johns Hopkins University Press.

Corrales, Javier. 2012. "LGBT Rights in the Americas." *Americas Quarterly*. Spring. Available at www.americasquarterly.org.

Corrales, Javier, and Michael Penfold. 2007. "Venezuela: Crowding Out the Opposition." *Journal of Democracy* 18:2, pp. 99–113.

Delpar, Helen. 1981. *Red Against Blue: The Liberal Party in Colombian Politics, 1863–99*. Tuscaloosa, AL: University of Alabama Press.

Diamond, Larry. 1994. "Rethinking Civil Society: Toward Democratic Consolidation." *Journal of Democracy* 5:3, pp. 4–17.

Diamond, Larry, and Richard Gunther, eds. 2001. "Types and Functions of Parties," in *Political Parties and Democracy*, pp. 3–49. Baltimore, MD: Johns Hopkins University Press.

Díaz Cayeros, Alberto. 2006. *Federalism, Fiscal Authority, and Centralization in Latin America*. New York: Cambridge University Press.

Dietz, Henry A. and David J. Myers. 2007. "From Thaw to Deluge: Party System Collapse in Venezuela and Peru." *Latin American Politics and Society* 49:2, pp. 59–86.

Downs, Anthony. 1957. *An Economic Theory of Democracy*. New York: Harper.

Duverger, Maurice. 1954. *Political Parties: Their Organization and Activity in the Modern State*. New York: Wiley.

The Economist. 2013. "Follow the Leader: Social Networking in Latin America." August 10. Available at www.economist.com.

Estuan, Eva. 2015. "Primary Elections in Latin America." Available at aceproject.org.

Ferreira, Francisco H. G. et al. 2013. *Economic Mobility and the Rise of the Latin American Middle Class*. Washington, DC: The World Bank Group.

Flacks, Richard. 2005. "The Question of Relevance in Social Movement Studies," in D. Croteau et al., eds., *Rhyming Hope and History*, pp. 3–19. Minneapolis: University of Minnesota Press.

Gunther, Richard, and Larry Diamond. 2001. "Types and Functions of Parties," in Larry Diamond and Richard Gunther, eds., *Political Parties and Democracy*, pp. 3–39. Baltimore, MD: Johns Hopkins University Press.

Hawkins, Kirk Andrew, and David R. Hansen. 2006. "Dependent Civil Society: The *Círculos Bolivarianos* in Venezuela." *Latin American Research Review* 41:1, pp. 102–32.

Jones, Mark P. 2010. "Beyond the Electoral Connection: The Effect of Political Parties on the Policymaking Process," in Carlos Scartascini, Ernesto Stein, and Mariano Tommasi, eds., *How Democracy Works: Political Institutions, Actors, and Arenas in Latin American Policymaking*, pp. 19–46. Washington, DC: Inter-American Development Bank.

Jones, Mark P., and Scott Mainwaring. 2003. "The Nationalization of Parties and Party Systems: An Empirical Measure and Application to the Americas." *Political Parties* 9:2, pp. 139–66.

Karl, Terry. 1997. The Paradox of Plenty. Berkeley: California.

Kitschelt, Herbert. 2000. "Linkages between Citizens and Politicians in Democratic Polities." *Comparative Political Studies* 33:6/7, pp. 845–79.

Kitschelt, Herbert, Kirk A. Hawkins, Guillermo Rosas, and Elizabeth J. Zechmeister. 2010. "Patterns of Programmatic Party Competition in Latin America," in

Herbert Kitschelt, Kirk A. Hawkins, and Juan Pablo Luna, eds., *Latin American Party Systems*, pp. 14–58. New York: Cambridge University Press.

Levine, Daniel H. 1973. *Conflict and Political Change in Venezuela*. Princeton, NJ: Princeton University Press.

Lipset, Seymour Martin, and Jason M. Lakin. 2004. *The Democratic Century*. Norman, OK: University of Oklahoma Press.

Lipset, Seymour Martin, and Stein Rokkan, eds. 1967. *Party Systems and Voter Alignments: Cross-National Perspectives*. New York: Free Press.

Mainwaring, Scott. 1993. "Presidentialism, Multipartism, and Democracy: A Difficult Combination." *Comparative Political Studies* 26:2, pp. 198–228.

Mainwaring, Scott, and Timothy R. Scully, eds. 1995. *Building Democratic Institutions: Party Systems in Latin America*. Stanford: Stanford University Press.

Mainwaring, Scott, and Matthew Shugart, eds. 1997. *Presidentialism and Democracy in Latin America*. New York: Cambridge University Press.

NACLA (North American Congress on Latin America). 2016. "#NiUnaMenos: Not One Woman Less, Not One More Death!" November 1. Available at www.nacla.org.

Payne, J. Mark. 2007. "Party Systems and Democratic Governability," in J. Mark Payne, Daniel Zovatto G., and Mercedes Mateo Díaz, eds., *Democracies in Development: Politics and Reform in Latin America*, pp. 149–78. Washington, DC: Inter-American Development Bank.

Pedersen, Mogens. 1983. "Changing Patterns of Electoral Volatility in European Party Systems, 1948–1977," in Hans Daalderand and Peter Mair, eds., *Western European Party Systems: Continuity and Change*, pp. 29–66. Beverly Hills, CA: Sage.

Pereira, Carlos, and Marcus André Melo. 2012. "The Surprising Success of Multiparty Presidentialism." *Journal of Democracy* 23:3, pp. 156–70.

Reuters. 2015. "Venezuela's Maduro Seeks Decree Powers to Face US 'Imperialism.'" March 10. Avaable at www.reuters.com.

Rivas-Pérez, Cristina. 2008. "The Dimensions of Polarization in Parliaments," in Manuel Alcántara Sáez, ed., *Politicians and Politics in Latin America*, pp. 87–112. Boulder, CO: Lynne Reinner.

Rosas, Guillermo. 2010. "Issues, Ideologies, and Partisan Divides: Imprints of Programmatic Structure on Latin American Legislatures," in Herbert Kitschelt, Kirk A. Hawkins, and Juan Pablo Luna, eds., *Latin American Party Systems*, pp. 70–95. New York: Cambridge University Press.

Salamanca, Luis. 2004. "Civil Society: Late Bloomers," in Jennifer McCoy and David J. Myers, eds., *The Unraveling of Representative Democracy in Venezuela*, pp. 93–114. Baltimore, MD: Johns Hopkins University Press.

Samuels, David. 2003. *Ambition, Federalism, and Legislative Politics in Brazil*. New York: Cambridge.

Sylvia, Ronald D., and Constantine P. Danopoulos. 2003. "The Chávez Phenomenon: Political Change in Venezuela." *Third World Quarterly* 24:1, pp. 63–76.

Taagepera, Rein, and Matthew Shugart. 1993. *Seats and Votes: The Effects and Determinants of Electoral Systems*. New Haven, CT: Yale University Press.

Tilly, Charles. 1978. *From Mobilization to Revolution*. Reading, MA: Addison-Wesley.

Valenzuela, Sebastián, Nicolás M. Sommo, and Arturo Andrés Arriagada. 2016. "Social Media in Latin America: Deepening or Bridging Gaps in Protest Participation?" *Online Information Review* 40:5, pp. 695–711.

Zovatto, Daniel. 2003. "The Legal and Practical Characteristics of the Funding of Political Parties and Election Campaigns in Latin America," in Reginald Austin and Maja Tjernström, eds., *Funding of Political Parties and Election Campaigns: International IDEA Handbook Series*, pp. 95–116. Stockholm, Sweden: International IDEA.

9 Federalism and Unitarism
Learning to Share

Photo 9.1 Federalism allows governments at lower levels to tailor policies such as education toward their specific needs.

Source: © Shutterstock

Haremos la unidad a palos. [We shall make unity with sticks.]

—Julián Segundo Agüero[1]

Julián Segundo Agüero was an adviser to Bernardino Rivadavia, the first president of Argentina—or more accurately, of the United Provinces of the River Plate, as the country was known in the 1820s. The country had just gone to war with Brazil to settle control over the neighboring region of Uruguay. Rivadavia's adviser saw an opportunity in the conflict, one that would provide justification for the raising of a large army, which could then be used to quell calls for autonomy from *caudillo* strongholds in the interior provinces, and to impose a new constitution that centralized power in Buenos Aires. But the scheme quickly foundered. The war effort took its toll on agricultural production, and stoked the *caudillo* opposition. Rivadavia resigned and went into exile. Civil war ensued, and in the aftermath, General Juan Manuel de Rosas stood supreme. He had fought for the cause of autonomy, but once in power he took on dictatorial powers. He catered to the economic interests of the cattlemen in the interior, but set aside politics as his own preserve. His rhetoric was confederal, but his style was firmly rooted in centralized decision making. His rule lasted from 1829 to 1852. It was the longest period of stability experienced by the country, and it depended on a permanent military campaign to not only subdue rebellions in the periphery, but also justify despotic rule. Perhaps unwittingly, he had assumed the very strategy he had once fought against. He made unity with sticks.

In time, Rosas would see the same fate as Rivadavia. His quest for supremacy united his opponents, who took power and sent him into exile. Conditions seemed to point toward a complete breakdown of the country in 1852. The interior provinces simply did not trust the bustling, increasingly cosmopolitan port city of Buenos Aires. But 40 years of independence also allowed time for learning, and adjustment. The interior provinces surmised that they could live neither with, nor without Buenos Aires. Global markets prized their exports of hides and salted beef, but accessing those markets proved problematic—the port at Buenos Aires was the only way out of the country. And Buenos Aires reached a similar conclusion on its relationship with the hinterland provinces. Without them, it would have nothing to export. It would be a port in name only. The revelation on both sides came slowly. Political elites drafted a new constitution in 1853, but disagreements led to civil strife and delayed its ratification and full implementation until 1862. The institution that finally drew the country together was federalism—a midway point between centralized rule and the generous regional autonomy afforded by confederate rule.

Federalism offers institutions geared toward the accommodation of diverse interests, but it requires a delicate balance as it disperses authority. Too much dispersion can feed calls for independence, and too little makes a mockery of the federal arrangement. And federalism is not without its costs. Policymaking at lower levels creates redundancies, increases the need for coordination, and spawns new arenas and opportunities for political conflicts. Despite this, proponents of the institution highlight how federalism allows policy experimentation in different government districts and lets politicians gain experience as they pursue higher offices. Moreover, federalism may be the only feasible option for large countries with diverse populations. Only four countries in Latin America use federal arrangements—Argentina, Brazil, Mexico, and Venezuela. But together, these countries make up the vast majority of the region's population and landmass. And although other countries do not share federal institutions, they too must confront questions of governance at lower levels. This chapter evaluates the various constitutional designs that link national and subnational politics, and concludes with a case study of Brazil.

Federalism and Unitarism, and the Range of Centralization

For practical reasons, most governments split their work between a single central government and lower-level governments. But federal regimes reinforce this division of labor with constitutional provisions that *guarantee* each level of government the final say over a set of policy responsibilities. Ideally then, **federalism** promotes both self-rule and shared rule. It offers distinct groups a level of autonomy in the making of certain decisions, but it also asks these groups to collaborate on other decisions (Elazar, 1987, pp. 5–6). In a **unitary** regime, final authority in all policy areas rests in the national government. A unitary regime may allocate power to a regional government, but unlike in the federal regime, such authority can be legally retracted.

The Division of Power in a Federal System

Federalism entails a rather common division of labor in most countries. Foremost, only the national government holds international sovereignty and the unqualified right to enter into international agreements with other countries. Subnational units enjoy sovereignty, but only in respect to each other and the central government (Gibson, 2004, pp. 5–6). To support its role in the global arena, national governments usually retain primary competencies over matters of defense, and take charge of economic planning. Lower levels of government typically focus on social affairs such as health, education, welfare, and cultural programs, as well as the maintenance of law and order.

Normally, the constitution will specify these exclusive competencies, but it may also recognize inevitable overlaps by detailing **concurrent powers**. Sometimes the constitution sets out concurrent powers such that the national government drafts general guidelines, and leaves it to the subnational governments to accommodate their own interests as they fill in the details. Article 24 of the Constitution of Brazil lists a number of concurrent powers, such as the protection of historical and cultural monuments, court procedures, social security, and education, and then notes, "within the confines of concurrent legislation, the power of the federal government is limited to establishing general guidelines."

And to ensure an exhaustive allocation of powers, constitutions will normally refer to **residual powers**, or those powers not expressly mentioned. Most countries assign residual powers to the subnational governments. However, the development of **implied powers** at the federal level can curtail the assignment of residual powers at the subnational level. Implied powers are those powers that are not explicitly mentioned in the constitution, but that are considered to be necessary and proper to the pursuit of their enumerated powers. The balance of residual powers resting at the subnational level, and implied powers expressed at the national level, are typically worked out in the court system.

The Balance of Centralization and Decentralization

Whether or not there exists a constitutional basis for the division of power between the central and regional government makes the difference between federalism and unitarism. This point is critical, because in practice a unitary regime may look like a federal regime if its central government decides to delegate authority to regional governments. Hence, both federal and unitary regimes rest on a continuum of **centralization–decentralization** that measures the extent of relative *de facto* authority exercised by central and regional governments. A centralized federal regime may appear to have a stronger national government than a decentralized unitary regime, but no matter the level of centralization in a federal regime, its regional governments always retain final authority over some matters. Still, it is undeniable that federal regimes can take only so much centralization before the federal nature of the regime loses its meaning.

The push to decentralize, even in unitary states, has played a pivotal role in the contemporary struggle to democratize, as illustrated by the case of Bolivia. At the time of democratic transition in 1982, the country reverted to its traditional unitary form of government. Prefects of the nine departments served at the pleasure of the president, and only the largest cities held elections for mayors and councilors—and they controlled few financial resources. The 1994 Popular Participation Law instituted popular elections for mayor and councilors in all cities, gave these officials real policymaking and revenue-raising powers, and guaranteed transfers from national coffers. A call to devolve authority to the department level gradually emerged, and was even backed up by street protests and strikes beginning in 2004. By 2005, popular elections were held for governor and legislative assemblies for the first time. The new constitution passed in 2009 makes references not only to departmental autonomy, but also to regional, municipal, rural and indigenous autonomy. The 2010 Framework Law of Autonomies and Decentralization references control over taxation, regulation, policy implementation, and appointment of local officials, and indigenous groups and rural localities have conducted elections to request autonomy. Nonetheless, it will take time to sort out the precise balance of powers. But in the end, Bolivia is not a federal state. Decentralization will vary and will be negotiated with the different subnational units, and changes in the balance of powers will result from statutory rather than constitutional law.

What explains the dramatic changes in intergovernmental relations? Bolivia had been one of the more centralized states in the region. A revolutionary government came to power in 1952 and concentrated power as it pushed for land reform and reforms to empower the working classes, but by 1964 it fell to factional conflict and gave way to a series of military governments that centralized rule to ensure stability. Hence, decentralization can be viewed as a backlash to this recent history. In addition, after the economic crisis of the 1980s, the country embraced neoliberal reforms— including decentralization—pushed by international financial institutions and U.S. officials. But the changes also reflect domestic developments in Bolivian politics. The 1994 decision to devolve power to cities, rather than departments, was taken in part because the MNR, which controlled the presidency at the time, saw electoral opportunities at the local level that it did not see at the departmental level (O'Neill, 2004). But like in Venezuela (see the Comparing Countries box), decentralization ultimately had the unintended consequence of upending the traditional party system as new actors competed for offices. This was especially the case under the Carlos Mesa government (2003–2005). In an effort to answer criticisms directed at the unresponsive party system, he opened competition beyond political parties to "civic groups" and "indigenous peoples." The number of groups participating in elections skyrocketed from 18 in 1999 to 425 in 2004 (Centellas, 2010). Traditional economic elites, especially those in the resource-rich province of Santa Cruz, felt threatened by the mobilization of new political actors. Recognizing that the stage was set for the progressive indigenous leader, Evo Morales, to win the presidency, these regional elites looked to the departmental level to shield themselves from political changes

COMPARING COUNTRIES

Centralization in Federal Venezuela and Decentralization in Unitary Peru

The cases of Venezuela and Peru illustrate how centralization can vary independent of the federal–unitary distinction. Historically, Venezuela's constitutions have expounded federal principles. But repeated military interventions and instability through the nineteenth century and first half of the twentieth century meant that most governments relied on emergency powers and centralized rule. And the transition to democracy in 1958 did not change much. The restoration of civilian rule was dependent upon a pact by dominant political parties that divided up government appointments and revenues.

The stability wrought by the pact did allow Venezuela to survive the wave of dictatorships that struck Latin America in the 1960s to 1980s, but over time the public grew alienated from national politics due to the lack of true electoral competition. Things grew much worse in the 1980s, when a severe debt crisis prompted Venezuelans to question the competency of their government, and to recognize how the pact and lack of accountability had contributed to corruption. As a response, the government decided to decentralize, in part by allowing direct elections for mayors and governors in 1989, and then following with a devolution of fiscal powers. The decision had long-ranging consequences as lower- and mid-level party officials shifted their allegiances from national party leaders to local constituents. The traditional political parties soon fragmented, and finally crumbled in the 1990s. This opened political opportunities for enterprising, new political figures such as Lt. Colonel Hugo Chávez, who had emerged as a prominent critic of the old regime and the crony politics of pacting after leading an unsuccessful coup d'état in 1992 (he would be jailed, but pardoned in 1994). Despite the long experience with centralized rule, federalism mattered in Venezuela because when the regime faced a legitimacy crisis in the 1980s, the dormant federal structure provided a ready-made blueprint for action (Penfold Becerra, 2004).

And federalism continues to matter in Venezuela, even though the country has seen a return of centralization since the election of Hugo Chávez in 1998. Chávez concentrated economic planning and investment strategies in the executive office, and created community councils—neighborhood associations that receive federal funding to distribute public services such as food subsidies, health and child care, housing, and transportation—that parallel state assistance programs (Ellner, 2009). His successor, President Nicolás Maduro, continued the policies, but these moves to consolidate authority must ultimately answer to the federal framework outlined in the 1999 Constitution. It specifies (in Article 164) a host of policies that fall under the discretion of the states, including the organization of municipalities, management of highways, governance of public services, and the right to raise revenue through taxation. In addition, the constitution (Article 167) guarantees a system of revenue sharing that sends 20 percent of all national proceeds to the states. City and state level offices emerged as the front lines for those opposed to moves by Chávez and Maduro to centralize power in the executive—a scenario largely made possible by federalism. The opposition rallied—*albeit* unsuccessfully—around

(*continued*)

the candidacy of Henrique Capriles in the 2012 and 2013 presidential elections. Capriles had gained national prominence as governor of the state of Miranda.

Peru provides an example of how unitary institutions matter independent of changes in centralization. Article 43 of the Constitution of Peru defines the government as "unitary, representative, and decentralized." Chapter XIV of the document, "On Decentralization, Regions, and Municipalities," describes decentralization as a process to be "carried out in stages" in "an orderly manner" (Article 188). It also identifies the "region" as the administrative level resting just beneath the central government, and charges the regions with planning and promoting regional development. But to ascertain what this means in practice, one must examine two pieces of legislation passed by congress in 2002—Law no. 27783, "Bases of Decentralization," and Law 27867 "Organic Law on Regional Governments." These laws detail the objectives of decentralization and specify the competencies of the different levels of government. Exactly what decentralization entails remains under the purview of the national government and ordinary legislation open to modification by simple majority vote. In fact, as it stands the regions of Peru still do not have taxation rights and thus remain dependent on the national government to fund their own initiatives. The country even held a referendum in 2005 that would have merged several of the regions had it passed—illustrating the insecure standing of the subnational units as administrative entities. Likewise, in 2014 the national government passed legislation to prohibit the reelection of regional leaders and mayors, despite some opposition at the subnational level. The unitary structure means that the national government retains full authority to push, stall, or reverse decentralization. The lack of a comprehensive constitutional framework for a defining, guaranteeing, and dividing authority makes for a precarious process that feeds anxieties and the potential for political conflict.

Peru is a unitary state with an expressed commitment to decentralization. But the lack of clear constitutional guarantees that specify policy and revenue-raising powers at the different levels of government has generated expectations that the central government has had trouble meeting. This has created uncertainty over the process of decentralization, as illustrated by mining and land-use policies.

Privatization of the mining sector in the 1990s created a new role for the state. It was no longer an owner, but a regulator and tax authority. After the authoritarian experience under Alberto Fujimori (1990–2000), Peru saw an opportunity to use mining resources to empower decentralization, and create a safeguard against the rise of another Fujimori. The central government's taxing authority was thus spelled out in the *"canon minero"* (the mining canon), a 2001 legal document that requires 50 percent of all taxes to be distributed to the regional and local governments with mining activity. A mining boom in the 2000s inflated the revenue stream and placed the *canon minero* at the center of national debate. Many impoverished districts see few proceeds from mining, even though they sit in mining regions, because the mining activity happens to take place in a neighboring district. For a country that gains some 60 percent of all its export profits from mining, the distribution of earnings from mining remains highly unequal. Each year, 7 or 8 (depending on annual production) of the 22 regions receive no funding whatsoever. And the resource flow to mining areas has had unintended and deleterious consequences. Some mining areas are more isolated, and lack the capacity to efficiently spend the funds. Though many suffer from poverty and various developmental needs that could be better addressed with investments in education and health care, such programs require more comprehensive initiatives from the national government. The result is that many localities see the funding geared toward community enhancement projects (e.g., plazas, public pools, and parks) and basic infrastructure rather than social programs that more directly address basic needs. In addition, the surge in funds has proved a recipe for corruption, undermining the intent to decentralize as a method of deepening democracy (Boland, 2013). Unsurprisingly, the *canon minero* has stirred a number of protests, some of which have turned violent.

In the Amazon territory of Peru, land use is another conflict-ridden area of policy-making. Over the course of decades, indigenous groups worked hard to have the state recognize and safeguard communal ownership, and nongovernmental organizations (NGOs) lobbied intensely to secure environmental protections. But the signing the Free Trade Agreement with the United States in 2006 led the central government to undermine these efforts. To comply with investment guarantees under the treaty, the government declared the palm oil industry a "national interest" and promptly rescinded regulations designed at the regional level, and another act opened previously protected lands to investors and allowed private interests to purchase indigenous lands. Violent protests followed, including one demonstration in Bagua that left at least 33 dead and 200 injured in June 2009. The violence led the congress to suspend some of the land-use regulations (NACLA, 2009). In response to decades of pollution and the lack of compensation, in 2015

(*continued*)

hundreds of indigenous people set cables across Amazon tributaries to prevent oil company boats from reaching their wells (*The Guardian*, 2015). Exactly what consultation, compensation, environmental protection, and social responsibility means differs among indigenous leaders, corporate leaders, and government officials at different levels. Continued uncertainty will only prolong the frustrations and protests.

Discussion Questions

1   How has federalism in Venezuela and decentralization in Peru affected political dynamics in these countries?
2   Would Venezuela be better off if it did not have federalism? Would Peru be better off if it did have a federal system?

in national politics (Eaton, 2007). After reaching the presidency in 2006, Morales had his own autonomy calls to answer. Many indigenous groups that had supported him desired greater self-rule, especially in land-use policies and justice. The incidental pressure from indigenous groups and regional economic elites cinched the inclusion of autonomy provisions in the 2009 Constitution, though what autonomy means in practice is still developing.

The Origins of Intergovernmental Relations in Latin America

The practice of federalism in Latin America mirrors what we find at the global level. Just 24 of the 193 countries in the world have adopted federalism, but these countries represent 40 percent of the world's population. Unsurprisingly, many large countries have federalism for practical purposes, or because they are more likely than small countries to incorporate diverse populations with claims to self-rule. Things are largely the same in Latin America. Four of the 18 countries in this study have federal systems—Argentina, Brazil, Mexico, and Venezuela. They all have large land masses and represent four of the six countries in the region with populations of over 25 million. The other two are Colombia and Peru, both of which have experienced significant decentralizing trends in recent years. But geography and demography alone do not determine the arrangement of governmental relations in Latin America, especially in regard to the extent of centralization underlying federal rule. Where federalism did emerge, it had to come to terms with a history of centralized colonial governance and long periods of militarism after independence.

Centralization was the order of the day during the period leading to independence in Latin America. The Bourbon Reforms of the later eighteenth century sought to reverse the decline of an overextended empire with a stronger presence of the Spanish monarchy in colonial administration. Borrowing from the French, Charles III (1759–1788) looked to streamline administrative control with the intendancy system. This system divided each of the viceroyalties into some 8–12 dominions headed by intendants who answered directly to the crown. With a more manageable workload than the viceroys, they were able to assert control over corrupt lower-level officials, ensure the effective receipt of tax revenue, and extend the due administration of justice. Brazil saw a similar change in its later colonial period. Early on, Portugal found its colonial holding to be a difficult sell because of the lack of wealth or labor. To induce settlements, the monarchy divided the region into districts (*capitanías*) and granted their leaders substantial economic privileges and local autonomy. But the country backtracked on this arrangement in the mid-eighteenth century in an effort to push industrialization through a centralized program of national development. For the first time, a single board took charge of all tax collection, and the crown moved aggressively to repurchase land grants assigned long ago (Véliz, 1980, pp. 70–115).

Militarism also geared the region toward more centralized rule. The military had always played an important role in colonial administration. After all, it was military men—the *conquistadores*—that had carved out the earliest settlements. Revolts by the indigenous and incursions by other European powers left the Spanish and Portuguese governments dependent on military force. Moves like the Bourbon Reforms meant to centralize administration riled local officials and regional strongmen, and only deepened this dependency. It was not uncommon to see military officers assume government positions. The long wars for independence further contributed to the expansive military role in government. Moreover, the social upheavals surrounding the independence wars created a vacuum of power as wealthy elites fled or were sent into exile. *Mestizo* groups, long shut out from power by *peninsular* and *criollo* elites, found the military to be a new route to prestige in the newly independent states, and they often used their positions to seize government under *caudillo* rule (Loveman, 1999, pp. 1–26).

Federalism and the Protection of Regional Caudillos

The experience with centralized colonial administration and militarism created a unique approach to federalism in Latin America, when it did appear. Customarily, we tend to think of federalism as the product of tensions between the national government and regions seeking greater autonomy, largely to protect ethnic identities. But in Latin America, the lines of conflict were set among the regions themselves, as *caudillos* sought to defend relative spheres of influence. Also, though there is no lack of diversity in the hemisphere, at the time of independence indigenous groups remained repressed, such that regional conflicts did not manifest themselves as ethnic or language based cleavages.

The Central American states, first with Mexico and then on their own, attempted to form a federal union before breaking into independent countries, largely along the lines of the intendant divisions created under the Bourbon Reforms. In Argentina, the former intendancies also constituted the basis for regional power struggles that pit the agriculturally based interior provinces against the bustling commercial province of Buenos Aires. After some 50 years of tense relations and sporadic civil war, a regime finally consolidated under federal arrangements. Mexico first emerged with a strong, centralized unitary regime under Agustín Iturbide, who declared himself emperor. Mexican states pushed for greater autonomy more as a strategy to declare and mobilize their opposition to Iturbide that as a principled commitment to the idea of federalism as a system of government (Mecham, 1938). Venezuela was once part of Gran Colombia, a short-lived federation that included it with Ecuador and Colombia, and which fell apart as regional leaders rebelled against Simón Bolívar's push for more centralized rule. Once independent, the Liberal Party in Venezuela championed federalism in the nineteenth century, but it did so for strategic reasons—to ensure support from local *caudillos* (Plaza, 2000). Brazil had a strong tradition of regional rule reaching back to the *capitanías*, but it opted for unitarism at independence to take advantage of the stabilizing impact of monarchic rule under Dom Pedro I. The infighting that plagued Spanish America at the time eased this decision for the political and economic elites of Brazil. Federalist sentiments would reappear when the country moved to a republic in 1891, but would suffer a reversal in the 1930s when President Getúlio Vargas centralized national development under the *Estado Novo*.

Because federalism in Latin America had more to do with interregional divisions than splits between the national and regional governments, it became an easy cover for avaricious regional oligarchs. Federalism had less to do with the protection of individual liberty against a menacing central government, than with the protection of local strongmen and their privileges. This allowed national populist leaders, such as Vargas, to call for a centralization of power in the name of the common people. Ironically, then, federalist ideas in Latin America were rebutted with a political narrative that conflated a strong central government with democratic rule. Hence, the commitment to federalism rarely took popular hold even where it was instituted. And when it was used, it came in a centralized federal form. Moreover, for much of Latin America in most of its history, persistent military interventions made the debate over federalism or centralization a moot point. With democratic regimes now in place throughout the area, federalism and decentralization have emerged as central topics in debates over political reforms.

Contemporary Moves to Recognize Indigenous Territories

Federalism would appear to be the ideal instrument for the representation of politically significant minorities, such as the indigenous in Latin America. But Latin America's federal countries did not consider the indigenous when they created their subnational units in the nineteenth century—a time when governments did more to exclude, than include, peoples they often openly viewed as uncivilized. Ironically, this means that today's federal borders do more to hinder indigenous representation. In 2001, Mexico attempted to accommodate indigenous groups that had rallied around the insurgent EZLN group in its southern region with constitutional reforms. But the provisions fell far short of the self-determination hoped for by indigenous groups. The Mexican Senate, fearing that a grant of autonomy would open the door to secession or otherwise fragment the country, amended the reforms such that the grant of autonomy would emerge at the behest of the state governments. The autonomous areas would thus hold the same status as cities (*municipios*), and their status could be modified or even repealed at any moment. The EZLN and eighteen state governments with indigenous majorities rejected the reform (Aída Hernández and Ortiz Elizondo, 2007).

Unitary systems offer more flexibility to implement territorial reconfigurations, but they lack the constitutional guarantees that would accompany federalism. In 1987 Nicaragua created two large autonomous regions along its Atlantic coast to accommodate indigenous groups that had long been isolated from Managua and the more populous Pacific region. Unfortunately, the majority of the population in each region is not indigenous, but *mestizo*, a situation likely to intensify as opportunities for resource exploitation draw more *mestizos* from the west. Most elected officials are *mestizo*, and although they answer to stipulations to protect and foster indigenous practices and culture, the details of autonomy are spelled out in statutory law. Moreover, the regions themselves only demarcate areas in which communities may be granted some form of autonomy, and these grants have been minimal. Fed up with the lack of "real" autonomy, leaders of the Miskito tribe declared an independent state in 2009 (Brunnegger, 2007; *New York Times*, 2009). But tensions continue to mount as mestizos encroach upon indigenous territories to exploit hardwood forests, ranch, and even establish drug trafficking outposts. Incidents of armed conflict left dozens dead in 2015–2016, and forced hundreds of Miskitos to seek refuge in neighboring Honduras (*NotiCen*, 2016). Panama has five autonomous regions, or "*comarcas*," the first of which was created in 1930. Still, only about one-half of the indigenous population lives in the *comarcas*, and a number of indigenous groups have not been granted a *comarca*. Moreover, because the *comarcas* remain state property, the government can decide to use the land for other purposes at any moment. Recent moves to build a hydroelectric dam and highway through a *comarca* without consulting the local population elicited violent protests (*NotiCen*, 2013).

Federal and Unitary Design in Contemporary Latin America

Institutions That Complement Federalism: Bicameralism, Strong Judiciary, Rigid Constitutions

Bicameralism, a strong judiciary, and rigid constitutions are associated with, though not exclusive to, federalism. As Lijphart put it, "they are guarantors of federalism rather than components of federalism itself" (1999, p. 188).

Ultimately, they do help to support its central function—that of dividing authority between the central government and regional government. The fact that Latin American federal states fail to staunchly embrace all these institutions illustrates the erosive legacy of centralization.

Bicameralism allows federalism to fully express its unique contribution to democratic representation. Our traditional understanding of democratic politics revolves around the idea of equality and "one person, one vote," or **popular representation**. But federalism places a premium on **territorial representation**. It envisions the political community not as a collection of individuals, as in popular representation, but as a union of regionally based communities. After all, the proper name of Mexico is "The United States of Mexico." But how can a regime incorporate both popular and territorial representation? Federal systems come to terms with these competing communal identities with the use of bicameral legislatures. The lower house, often called the Chamber of Deputies in Latin America, represents "the people," whereas the upper house, or Senate, represents the territorial divisions of the country. While even a unitary regime might opt for bicameralism for reasons other than territorial representation (e.g., to offer a second line of review over legislation—see Chapter 5), it is difficult to imagine federalism without bicameralism. Nonetheless, Venezuela joins just Ethiopia, Micronesia, and the United Arab Emirates as one of the few federal regimes with a unicameral legislature. And it is no surprise that Venezuela is the most centralized federal state in Latin America.

A strong judiciary is another characteristic of federal regimes. The rationale here is simple—a federal system requires a referee to mediate disputes between the national government and its constituent units. A competent, sufficiently empowered judiciary will decide exactly how to divide the labor of concurrent powers or to interpret the balance between residual and implied powers. The judicial branches of Brazil and Mexico are among the strongest in Latin America (see Chapter 6), and the two countries also brandish resilient federal institutions. It is telling that Argentina, Brazil, Mexico, and Venezuela do not employ constitutional tribunals, and instead concentrate all existing judicial review power in the Supreme Court. Even so, we saw in Chapter 6 how the code law tradition has encumbered the region's judiciaries.

A rigid constitution complements a strong judiciary because it ultimately forms a basis for its decision making. Malleable constitutions allow governments to undermine judicial authority by, in essence, presenting it with a moving target. As discussed in Chapter 3, constitutions in Latin America tend to be flexible, and governments tend to take full advantage of this flexibility. Only Mexico makes full use of its federal system in the constitutional reform process by requiring the amendment procedure to pass not only through the Senate, but also to gain approval at the state level.

The Contemporary Effort to Decentralize

Latin America may rest on a history of centralized rule, but of late both unitary and federal regimes in the region have come under the influence of a decentralization trend. Decentralization can occur in the political, fiscal, and administrative realms. Political decentralization is marked by the direct election of government and municipal officials. Fiscal decentralization ensues as regional or lower-level officials gain more rights to raise revenue, or receive guaranteed unconditional transfers from the national government. And administrative decentralization comes about as lower officials gain policy responsibilities, usually in areas such as education, health care, regional economic planning, and welfare.

Directly elected mayors are now the norm throughout the region. Chile, Costa Rica, Dominican Republic, El Salvador, Guatemala, Honduras, and Panama still have appointed governors (or their equivalent), but this does not really indicate a democratic shortcoming. These are all unitary states, where governors are meant to execute faithfully policies devised at the national, executive level. The governors are supposed to be administrators rather than decision makers. Fiscal decentralization is difficult to gauge because of the unreliability of subnational data, but numerous studies have documented growing levels of control over revenues and expenditures at regional and municipal levels after significant reforms in the late twentieth century.[2] One estimate charted an increase in the regional average of subnational expenditures as a percentage of national expenditures that moved from 13.1 percent in 1985 to 19.3 percent in 2004, a modest but notable movement closer to the 29.1 percent average among western developed countries (Daughters and Harper, 2007, p. 214). Today, subnational governments in Latin America on average spend a proportion of total government expenditures that is about equal to that seen in western developed countries (~30 percent), but they are far more dependent on federal transfers due to their difficulty in raising their own revenue (Fretes Cibils and Ter-Minassian, 2015). The reliance on federal transfers is important because it makes revenues more unpredictable and it also sheds some light on how much authority the central government hands over to subnational units. But in this measure of dependence, one must take care to distinguish between **conditional transfers**, which mandate specific activities, and **unconditional transfers**, which come with no strings attached. Unconditional transfers allow regional government to have a say in administrative decentralization (Table 9.1).

The move to decentralize is partly a reaction to the authoritarian period of the 1960s and 1980s. One argument is that dispersing authority to lower levels of government creates a barrier to imperious inclinations at the national level. And many contend that local officials are more responsive to the concerns of citizens than are politicians who work and answer to leaders in distant capital regions. Decentralization is also a product of the staggering levels of urbanization since the 1960s. The concentrated populations

Table 9.1 **Subdivisions of Latin American States.** Latin American states have various numbers of lower-level governments, but not all of them enjoy the privileges granted under federalism, and some of them do not even have separate representative institutions

Country	First Subdivision	Governor (or equivalent)	Assembly	Constitutionally Autonomous Administrative Divisions
Argentina	22 provinces	elected governor	elected legislature	Autonomous city of Buenos Aires (autonomous from BA Province)
Bolivia	9 departments	elected governor	elected legislature	n/a
Brazil	26 states	elected governor	elected legislature	Federal District of Brasília
Chile	15 regions	intendente (president appoints)	regional council, elected by municipal councils	n/a
Colombia	32 departments	elected governor	elected department assembly	Capital District of Bogotá
Costa Rica	7 provinces	governor (president appoints)	n/a	n/a
Dominican Republic	31 provinces	governor (president appoints)	n/a	National District (Santo Domingo)
Ecuador	24 provinces	elected provincial prefect	elected provincial council	n/a
El Salvador	14 departments	governor (president appoints)	n/a	n/a
Guatemala	22 departments	governor (president appoints)	departmental council composed of all department mayors	n/a
Honduras	18 departments	governor (president appoints)	n/a	n/a

Country	First Subdivision	Governor (or equivalent)	Assembly	Constitutionally Autonomous Administrative Divisions
Mexico	31 states	elected governor	elected legislature	Mexico City
Nicaragua	15 departments	no administrative authorities	n/a	2 autonomous indigenous regions
Panama	9 provinces	governor (president appoints)	departmental council composed of all department mayors	5 semiautonomous indigenous regions
Paraguay	17 departments	elected governor	elected departmental junta	Capital District of Asunción
Peru	25 regions	elected regional presidents	elected regional council	n/a
Uruguay	19 departments	elected intendentes	n/a	n/a
Venezuela	23 states	elected governor	elected legislature	Federal Dependencies' Metropolitan District of Caracas

in cities allow individuals to mobilize for more control over basic services, and their size means that decentralization often makes economic sense. And one cannot ignore the international pressures for decentralization. The idea gained favor in the research divisions of international financial institutions such as the World Bank, International Monetary Fund (IMF), and Inter-American Development Bank, and in a number of U.S.-based foreign policy think tanks for its purported economic benefits. According to this view, having multiple arenas of government work on policy replicates market competition and spurs the efficient allocation of resources. But recent studies are more sanguine over whether decentralization contributes to democracy and economic efficiency. Lower-level officials may turn out to be just as corrupt as national politicians, and in fact more vulnerable to parochial interests. And in many policy areas, decentralization may simply lead to duplications that add costs and confuse constituents, and that also ask too much of local officials with little capacity (Gibson, 2004; Rodden and Wibbels, 2002). For decentralization to achieve the promises posited by its proponents, it must take place within a context that supports professionalism and capacity-enhancement at all levels of government.

Variation in Federal Institutions

Dealing with Differences

Federalism offers constitutional designers the tools to spotlight regional differences. A country may hold within its borders a variety of ethnic, linguistic, economic, and political groups, but federalism can grant these groups measures of sovereignty in separate territorial confines. Of course, the federal architects might also opt to dilute differences by drawing borders that cut across the myriad groups of the country and mixing them together. Analysts capture this variation in territorial representation by distinguishing between congruent and incongruent federalism. With **incongruent federalism**, state boundaries are drawn so as to separate the different groups. With **congruent federalism**, boundaries cut across regional groupings so that the demographics of the subnational units look like that of the nation as a whole. As recognized by Lijphart, this is a powerful constitutional tool—"incongruent federalism can make a plural society less plural by creating relatively homogeneous smaller areas" (1999, p. 196).

As noted, the state borders in the federal countries of Latin America were not drafted with racial or ethnic diversity in mind. In most cases they either accommodated the interests of provincial strongmen or of regional economic interests. Unique cultures emerged over time, but most politically significant communal groups—the indigenous—were left out of federal arrangements. As it stands today, the divisions wrought by state lines and echoed in the senates largely reflect urban-rural differences and economic interests. Federal divisions in fact left Latin American states ill-equipped to deal with the resurgence of indigenous identity that began in the late twentieth century. With territorial representation denied to the indigenous, and popular representation of little use to a group with minority status, some governments have looked to the idea of **personal federalism** to target groups that are not geographically concentrated. Personal federalism directs government policies and services to distinct groups, regardless of their location. In the case of indigenous groups, this has involved the devolution of educational services, land ownership rights (especially communal ownership), justice regulations, and the extension of financial support to cultural promotion groups.

At times, the devolution of authority is done not only to empower local communities, but also just as much to compensate for deficient abilities of the national government. Peru enacted an extensive land reform in the early 1970s that effectively dismantled the authority structure long enforced under large landowners, especially in the northern highland region. In response to

Photo 9.2 A farmer in Parana, Brazil checks the feed in his grain silo. Federalism allows Brazil's interior states to concentrate on their primary concern, agriculture, rather than tourism, manufacturing, or financial services as in the bustling coastal states.

Source: © Shutterstock

the vacuum of authority, local community members created *rondas campesinas* (peasant patrols) to dispense local justice:

> Three or four cases are heard each night. Villagers—mostly men— gather and sit or stand in a circle, with *ronda* authorities sitting at a table together within the circle.... All attendees are encouraged to speak, which is important in a culture where state authorities had imposed centuries of silence. The circle implies that no one is placed before or above anyone else. Proceedings typically begin with the *ronda* president presenting a case. The main accusing witness and the accused then state their positions. Next, anyone may offer an opinion.... Over time, the crowd pressures (the accused and the accuser) to be more conciliatory, ultimately demanding that they find agreement. Rather than impose a verdict, the *ronda* president attempts to find the sense of the crowd and to impose this as a solution. Proceedings may continue until dawn or until a resolution is found. (Van Cott, 2006, p. 256)

Bolivia also devolved authority to compensate for deficiencies in government administration. Migrants from the hinterlands seeking employment have encircled the larger cities of the country with makeshift shantytowns, which typically lack not only basic services such as public utilities, but also police and judicial resources. Community members have responded by creating *juntas vecinales* (neighborhood groups), which incorporate indigenous cultural practices:

> In the Cochabamba barrio of Alto Sebastián Pagador, it is common for the aggrieved party to consult a *yatiri* (seer) to ascertain the truth of the matter, the person responsible (if unknown), or the appropriate sanction. In El Alto (near the capital, La Paz), aggrieved parties may also privately seek the advice of a *yatiri*, and junta authorities will invoke the norms of their ancestors as they begin the task of conflict resolution. Sanctioning takes place in the rural fashion, before a crucifix and a bible, which are set upon a block of salt. The accused apologizes, promises not to make the same mistake again, and asks forgiveness.... The oldest community member presides ... over the sanctioning phase. (Van Cott, 2006, p. 260)

In both Peru and Bolivia, these indigenous justice organizations keep detailed records and report decisions to public authorities. This indicates that they do not so much conflict with as complement the state—and ultimately help address voids in public authority. But that opportunity allows them to tailor institutions in fold with local customs.

Offsetting Regional Power Differences

Beyond the demographic composure of the regions within a federal regime, another question regards their relative power. Compare two provinces in Argentina—Córdoba and Chaco. Although Buenos Aires Province stands alone as the metropolitan center of the country and in terms of population and economic weight, Córdoba has been able to hold its own in national political debates. The province lays claim to the original capital of the country, and it has always rallied the agricultural-based interior provinces in their opposition to Buenos Aires. The province experienced an industrial boom in the 1950s and 1960s, and today its 3 million residents live at higher standards than the national average. Things are very different in Chaco, an underdeveloped northern province that has never been well integrated into the national economy. The Toba, one of the few indigenous groups in Argentina, eke out a living in mud and thatched huts, usually in a separated part of the province's major cities. The group received media spotlight in 2008, when the country was booming economically. Argentines in other provinces were stunned to hear of their abject poverty, and how many of them were dying of malnutrition and disease. The 600,000 residents of Chaco, living in a poor province with few resources, seem to gain attention only for the plight of their most desperate.

The contrast between Córdoba and Chaco illustrates **political asymmetry**, which refers to the economic, political, social, and cultural conditions that affect the relative power of subnational units with each other and the national government. Differences in affluence and influence inevitably emerge when provincial borders are set, but we can appreciate how some countries may exhibit more or less disparity across their regional boundaries. To offset political asymmetry, federal designers can use **constitutional asymmetry**, which refers to imbalances in the allocation of authority and constitutional powers to the subnational units, or in how they are treated by the central government. No Latin American federal state incorporates constitutional asymmetry to the extent of a country like Canada, where the province of Quebec receives greater autonomy than other provinces not only in social and cultural affairs, but also in tax policies and state-issued pension plans. But as noted in Chapter 5, Latin American states exhibit high levels of malapportionment. The political consequences of this design have been felt in Argentina, where the interior, agricultural provinces regularly use their representation in the Senate to defend agricultural subsidies, and to protest policies that favor urban interests (e.g., price controls on food products).

Countries throughout the region hold potentially dominant capital cities, which concentrate political and economic power. To guard against them, many countries have created federal or capital districts that fall under the direct authority of the central government. In fact, most of these districts emerged after elites from the interior, agricultural regions took hold of government. By paring out a district, these elites hoped to reduce the ability of their urban opponents to influence the central government (Myers, 2002, pp. 17–18). **Equalization transfers** represent another significant form of constitutional asymmetry. These monetary allocations are meant to compensate poorer regions with the more robust tax bases afforded by wealthier regions. The rationale behind equalization transfers is to assure all citizens within a federal country the same access to government services without exposing them to vastly different tax rates (Watts, 1999, p. 50).

COUNTRY IN THE SPOTLIGHT

Federalism in Brazil

Beneath its layer of national government, Brazil is composed of 26 states and a federal district, and below that, 5,563 municipal districts. The Constitution imposes a fairly uniform institutional structure at the subnational level. It requires that all states and the federal district have a popularly elected governor and unicameral legislature elected under proportional representation in a single district. They serve four-year terms that run concurrently with national elections for the president, Chamber of Deputies, and a portion of the Senate (one-third and two-thirds in alternating election years). Each state has an independent judiciary that exercises original jurisdiction in civil and criminal matters. The Constitution also delivers specific instructions on the organization and powers of municipal governments. They are required to have a mayor and unicameral council, elected in the second year

(*continued*)

between national elections. The Constitution even stipulates specific monetary limitations on the salaries of mayors and councilpersons (Article 29).

The Constitution is detailed, but it hardly hinders subnational autonomy. To be a governor in Brazil is to wield vast budgetary power and mayors act as a central arbiter in many policy areas. Both are appealing positions, and in fact represent ultimate career goals for many politicians. This is because Brazil is, in fact, one of the most decentralized states in the world, even at the municipal level. The extent of fiscal decentralization equals that of developed countries—subnational governments control about 40 percent of government spending, and raise about 30 percent of the country's taxes. And whereas in Argentina (as in the United States), provinces wield generous authority to create, reassemble, or abolish municipalities all on their own, cities in Brazil have their autonomy protected by the national constitution. In addition they are guaranteed exclusive or concurrent powers in several policy areas, and are also guaranteed extensive transfers of federal funding.

Federalism traditionally describes the balance of power between a national government and regional governments, but in Brazil federalism involves a tripartite distinction between national, regional, and municipal levels. Municipalities take the lead in primary education, public infrastructure and transportation, some areas of health care, sanitation, and urban planning initiatives in the larger cities. Equalization transfers send 90 percent of central government outlays designated for municipalities to the non-state capital municipalities, which find it more difficult than the vibrant capital cities to raise their own revenues. The fact that 60 percent of the population lives outside the capital cities underscores the equalizing impact of these transfers (Rodrigues Afonso and Amorim Araújo, 2006, pp. 396–397).

Brazil's expanse assures diversity in the socioeconomic makeup, demography, and cultural identity of its states. Its incongruent federalism partly captures significant political asymmetries. Three states hold burgeoning populations: São Paulo has 40 million people, 19 million live in Minas Gerias, and 15 million occupy Rio de Janeiro. On the other hand, six states hold populations of less than 2 million, including relatively tiny Roraima with just 400,000 residents. Economic interests have long distinguished the states. During the colonial period and for a time thereafter, sugar production and slave labor drove the interests of Pernambuco and neighboring states in the northeast. By the late nineteenth century, they were opposed by coffee producers in São Paulo (which, ironically, hosts the majority of sugar production today) unable to access the captured labor up north. Cattle ranchers in Minas Gerias joined the coffee oligarchs of São Paulo after the move to a republic in 1891. They forged a *café con liete* (coffee with milk) alliance that effectively controlled the presidency to 1930. Industrial development in the southeastern states—São Paulo, Bahia, Rio de Janeiro, Minas Gerias, and Rio Grande do Sul—created the impression of a "modern" Brazil, in contrast to the "backward" Brazil of the northeast and interior. Brazil's founding fathers presciently recognized the regional splits, and called for the movement of the capital from Rio de Janeiro to a more neutral region. Finally, in 1960, a special autonomous district was carved out of the interior state of Goiás to make way for the new capital of Brasilia.

The military government that ruled from 1964 to 1985 had hoped to end regional rivalries, but it just could not develop an alternative, and in fact eventually facilitated decentralization and reinforced it with significant constitutional asymmetries. The armed forces believed that a gradual transition would allow it to control the handover of power, but procrastination had its costs. Unwilling to jeopardize control of the national executive, but committed to introducing elections methodically, the military staged gubernatorial contests first, in 1982. The regional stage was thus set before national elections for the presidency, and this directed political parties and lobbyists to once again think and organize first under state politics. Elections also endowed governors with a level of legitimacy that the military could not match, and thereby strengthened their position as the democratization process continued (Montero, 2000). The military government further exacerbated regional distinctions as it set aside its intent to unify in favor of shoring up the political power of its civilian allies—largely the rural oligarchs of the northeast and other agricultural areas. In a clear effort to manipulate Senate representation, in 1975 it merged the states of Guanabara and Rio de Janeiro, which tended to support the opposition movement; and in 1977 it divided the supportive state of Mato Grosso into two, creating Mato Grosso do Sul. The military also engineered overrepresentation for the northeastern and agricultural states in the Chamber of Deputies.

Because the congress designed by the armed forces was in place during the transition to democracy, self-interests geared it toward maintaining malapportionment, which was maintained even as the constitution

(*continued*)

was rewritten under civilian rule in 1988. The constitution requires seats in the Chamber of Deputies to be distributed proportionally across the states, but it also sets a minimum of eight seats per state and maximum of 70 seats per state—a range that fails to adequately capture population differences and ends up advantaging smaller states (São Paulo has a population 100 times that of Roraima, but the representative formula allows it only 9.75 times the representation of its smaller counterpart). In fact, congress bolstered decentralization with strong guarantees for municipal autonomy in the 1988 Constitution. It may seem unusual that the congress in 1988 handed power to the municipal level, until one realizes that many representatives had their own career objectives in mind. Many Brazilian politicians tend to use the national congress as a stepping-stone to positions in state legislatures, city government, or the governorships because they realize that this is where patronage politics, and opportunities for personal influence, rest (Samuels, 2004). Keep in mind how the electoral calendar especially facilitates career movements to the municipal level. Deputies in their second year will often transfer the seat to their alternate (*suplente*) when municipal elections take place. In 2008, 85 federal deputies ran for the office of mayor (16 were successful) (Fleischer, 2008).Table 9.2

States of Brazil

Table 9.2 **States of Brazil.** Latin American states have various numbers of lower-level governments, but not all of them enjoy the privileges granted under federalism, and some of them do not even have separate representative institutions.

	2009 population	*2007 % national GDP*	*2007 GDP per capita ($)**
North Region		5.0	
Rondônia	1,503,928	0.6	5,831
Acre	691,132	0.2	4,943
Amazonas	3,393,369	1.6	7,328
Roraima	421,499	0.2	5,918
Pará	7,431,020	1.9	3,937
Amapá	626,609	0.2	5,761

	2009 population	2007 % national GDP	2007 GDP per capita ($)*
Tocantins	1,292,051	0.4	5,012
Northeast Region		13.1	
Maranhão	6,367,138	1.2	2,901
Piauí	3,145,325	0.5	2,619
Ceará	8,547,809	1.9	3,454
Rio Grande do Norte	3,137,541	0.9	4,274
Paraíba	3,769,977	0.8	3,425
Pernambuco	8,810,256	2.3	4,122
Alagoas	3,156,108	0.7	3,291
Sergipe	2,019,679	0.6	4,894
Bahia	14,637,364	4.1	4,375
Southeast Region		56.4	
Minas Gerias	20,033,665	9.1	7,033
Espírito Santo	3,487,199	2.3	10,114
Rio de Janeiro	16,010,429	11.2	10,812
São Paulo	41,384,039	33.9	12,734
South Region		16.6	
Paraná	10,686,247	6.1	8,826
Santa Catarina	6,118,743	3.9	10,019
Rio Grande do Sul	10,914,128	6.6	9,376
Central West Region		8.9	
Mato Grosso do Sul	2,360,498	1.1	6,972
Mato Grosso	3,001,692	1.6	8,401

(*continued*)

Table 9.2 (continued)

	2009 population	*2007 % national GDP*	*2007 GDP per capita ($)**
Goiás	5,926,300	2.5	6,488
Brasilia	2,606,885	3.8	22,863

Source: Brazilian Institute of Geography and Statistics. Available online at: www.ibge .gov.br.

*2007 GDP per capita presented in the national currency of reals converted into dollars using the December 2007 exchange rate of 1.78 reals to the dollar.

In all, the federal structure of Brazil has a determinative effect on the behavior of all politicians and politics generally. Political parties organize at the state level, creating 27 subnational party organizations, and 27 teams of party bosses that control nominations. This means that Brazil's already overpopulated party system—which regularly fields more than 20 parties in the Chamber of Deputies—is in fact more diverse than it appears. Indeed, local party leaders have significant leeway to initiate their own platforms and strategies, leading to some bizarre decisions. It may not be surprising to learn that the agro-industrial magnate Blairo Maggi, the self-proclaimed "King of Soy," was governor of Matto Grosso from 2003–10. It may not even rattle one to hear that he held the position despite his receipt of the 2006 Greenpeace "Golden Chainsaw Award" for the destruction of Amazon rainforests wrought by his vast farmlands. But what is perplexing is that he ran (in two successful campaigns) as the candidate of the People's Socialist Party, the former Communist Party of Brazil. And, indicative of the career moves by Brazilian politicians, Maggi moved on to take a seat in the Senate in 2011. In Brazil, party ideologies bend to pragmatic concerns at the regional level. Federalism has further effects due to the overrepresentation of the center-west, north, and northeastern areas. In these poor, rural states, patrimonial and clientelistic politics are as strong as ever. This forces politicians, especially presidents, to take on a more personalistic, patronage-based style of politics to garner support in these regions (Mainwaring, 1999, pp. 264–273).

Today, federalism is as strong as ever. The southeastern states remain the vibrant economic powerhouses that house bustling cosmopolitan cities. The northeastern states, once the crown of the Portuguese colonial empire, long ago fell into decline and many areas continue to be subject to the archaic, dominating influence of large landowners. Ranching interests are found throughout the country, but especially in the Brazilian Highlands that butt up against the Amazon region. The Amazon region itself contains diverse interests centered on the rainforest—indigenous tribes, environmental groups, tourist agencies, and a host of economic interests seeking to exploit resources in the area. Federal institutions allow states in these regions to focus upon their own particular affairs and reinforce the cultural, economic, and political tapestry of Brazil. Federalism also ensures that Brazilian politics at the national level remain fragmented and personalistic.

Discussion Questions

1   How do Brazil's federal institutions reflect historical interests and concerns of past political actors?
2   Weigh the relative costs and benefits of Brazil's federal institutions. Could Brazil survive without federal institutions?

Conclusion

Federalism is an institutional option. It is not found in all countries. We tend to find it in the largest countries, essentially for practical purposes. Nonetheless, all countries must come to terms with the balance of power between the national government and regional governments. The level of centralization or decentralization varies independent of federalism, and unlike federalism it is not constitutionally set.

Federalism cannot stand alone as an institution. Strong judiciaries, bicameralism, and rigid constitutions all help to buttress it. In addition, once a country selects federal institutions, a number of other considerations come into play. In particular, a country must attempt to balance the artificial political asymmetries created by federal lines with constitutional asymmetries.

There has been a strong push toward decentralization in recent years, largely as part of the move to democratize government at all levels, but also as a result of urbanization and pressures from international financial institutions. The presumed economic gains of these reforms should not be viewed as automatic, and they may even create new problems of their own. Notably, political decentralization to regional territories has not helped Latin American governments empower indigenous groups to the extent desired because existing regional lines were not drawn with cultural or linguistic groups in mind, and because many of the indigenous have dispersed across the country, and demographic shifts have brought more non-indigenous peoples to traditional lands.

Key Terms

federalism   362
unitarism   362
concurrent powers   362
residual powers   363
implied powers   363
centralization-decentralization   363
popular representation   372
territorial representation   372

conditional and unconditional transfers   373
congruent and incongruent federalism   376
personal federalism   376
political asymmetry   378
constitutional asymmetry   378
equalization transfers   379

Discussion Questions

1   Can a country lacking significant ethnic or cultural divisions benefit from federal institutions?
2   Does decentralization help democratization?
3   How can a regime ensure that federal institutions do not magnify differences and inequality?
4   Which other political institutions accommodate federalism? Which institutions appear to clash with federalism?

Suggested Readings

Tulia G. Falleti. 2010. *Decentralization and Subnational Politics in Latin America.* **New York: Cambridge University Press.** Decentralization can take place through administrative, fiscal, and political reforms. Falleti constructs a theory of decentralization that shows how the sequencing of these reforms, and the power of actors more supportive of some of these reforms than others, significantly affects the ultimate efficiency and extent of decentralization. The study includes an extensive theoretical discussion, and applies the theory to Argentina, Brazil, Colombia, and Mexico.

Edward L. Gibson, ed. 2004. *Federalism and Democracy in Latin America.* **Baltimore, MD: Johns Hopkins University Press.** This collection of articles looks at the impact of federalism on democratic rule in Latin America. It is wide ranging in its analysis, with examinations of public policy, political parties, the authority of subnational polities, the efficacy of government, consensual politics, and even theoretical assessments on the origins of federalism. Several chapters identify an interesting puzzle: that federalism may contribute to democratic transition, but also may pose problems for democratic consolidation.

Merilee S. Grindle. 2000. *Audacious Reforms: Institutional Invention and Democracy in Latin America.* **Baltimore, MD: Johns Hopkins University Press.** Merilee Grindle tackles a curious puzzle in this study: Why would politicians hand over power and resources in reforms that decentralize government? She answers this question basically by recognizing that the question itself simplifies a more complex process. In the decision to decentralize, politicians reacted not just to narrow, short-term self-interests, but also to considerations of their legacies, goals to unify the country, or strategies to isolate opponents. Further, it is not just politicians, but also technocrats and political advisors who make these decisions. Beyond the motive to decentralize, Grindle also looks at different methods of decentralization and their consequences. The book includes case studies of reforms in Argentina, Bolivia, and Venezuela.

Alberto Diaz-Cayeros. 2016. *Federalism, Fiscal Authority, and Centralization in Latin America.* **New York: Cambridge University Press.** Alberto Diaz-Cayeros approaches fiscal authority—the power to raise revenue—as a point of compromise between regional and national politicians, and thus offers some insight into how and why fiscal authority varies across different countries and over time. His focus on the case of Mexico illustrates how fiscal authority can vary even within federal states. In addition, his recognition of how current balances of fiscal authority are tied to bargains wrought long ago in history demonstrates the value of examining institutions as historical artifacts. His study includes comparisons with the other federal states of the region—Argentina, Brazil, and Venezuela.

Notes

1 Quoted in Rock (1985), p. 102.2
2 For reviews of this literature, see Smoke, Gómez, and Peterson, 2006, and Falleti, 2010.

References

Aída Hernández, Rosalva, and Héctor Ortiz Elizondo. 2007. "Different but Equal: Access to Justice for Mexico's Indigenous Peoples," in Wayne Cornelius and David A. Shirk, eds., *Reforming the Administration of Justice in Mexico*, pp. 369–92. Notre Dame, IN: Notre Dame University Press.

Boland, Margaret. 2013. "Corporate Conquistadores: Peru's Mineral Extraction Industry Boosts Economy While Rural Poor Continue to Suffer." Council on Hemispheric Affairs, July 12. Available at www.coha.org.

Brunnegger, Sandra. 2007. *From Conflict to Autonomy in Nicaragua: Lessons Learnt.* London: Minority Rights Group International. Available at http://www2.ohchr.org/english/bodies/cescr/docs/info-ngos/mrginicaragua39wg.pdf.

Centellas, Miguel. 2010. "Bolivia's Radical Decentralization." *Americas Quarterly* 4:3 (Summer), pp. 34–38.

Daughters, Robert, and Leslie Harper. 2007. "Fiscal and Political Decentralization Reforms," in Eduardo Lora, ed., *The State of State Reform in Latin America*, pp. 213–62. Washington, DC: Inter-American Development Bank.

Eaton, Kent. 2007. "Backlash in Bolivia: Regional Autonomy as a Reaction against Indigenous Mobilization." *Politics and Society* 35:1, pp. 71–102.

Elazar, Daniel J. 1987. *Exploring Federalism*. Tuscaloosa, AL: University of Alabama Press.

Ellner, Steve. 2009, May/June. "A New Model with Rough Edges: Venezuela's Community Councils." *NACLA Report on the Americas* 42:3, pp. 11–14.

Falleti, Tulia G. 2010. *Decentralization and Subnational Politics in Latin America*. New York: Cambridge.

Fleischer, David. 2008. "Political Outlook in Brazil in the Wake of Municipal Elections: 2009–2010," Working Paper. Washington, DC: Brazil Institute, Woodrow Wilson International Center for Scholars. Available at www.drclas .harvard.edu/files/2008novFleischer.pdf.

Fretes Cibils, Vicente, and Teresa Ter-Minassian, eds. 2015. *Decentralizing Revenue in Latin America: Why and How?* Washington, DC: InterAmerican Development Bank.

Gibson, Edward L., ed. 2004. *Federalism and Democracy in Latin America*. Baltimore, MD: Johns Hopkins.

The Guardian. 2015. "Peru's Indigenous People Protest Against Relicensing of Oil Concession." February 2. Available at www.theguardian.com.

Lijphart, Arend. 1999. *Patterns of Democracy: Government Forms and Performance in Thirty-Six Countries*. New Haven, CT: Yale University Press.

Loveman, Brian. 1999. *For la Patria: Politics and the Armed Forces in Latin America*. Wilmington, DE: SR Books.

Mainwaring, Scott. 1999. *Rethinking Party Systems in the Third Wave of Democratization: The Case of Brazil*. Palo Alto, CA: Stanford University Press.

Mecham, J. Lloyd. 1938. "The Origins of Federalism in Mexico." *Hispanic American Historical Review* 18:2, pp. 164–82.

Montero, Alfred P. 2000. "Devolving Democracy?: Political Decentralization and the New Brazilian Federalism," in Peter Kingstone and Timothy Power, eds., *Democratic Brazil: Actors, Institutions, and Processes*, pp. 58–76. Pittsburgh, PA: University of Pittsburgh Press.

Myers, David J. 2002. "The Dynamics of Local Empowerment: An Overview," in David J. Myers and Henry A. Dietz, eds., *Capital City Politics in Latin America: Democratization and Empowerment*, pp. 1–28. Boulder, CO: Lynne Rienner.

New York Times. 2009, June 10. "List of Grievances Grows into Independence Claim."

North American Congress on Latin America (NACLA). 2009, January/February. "Against the Law of the Jungle: Peru's Amazonian Uprising." *Report on the Americas* 42:1, pp. 5–8.

NotiCen. 2013, February 21. "Indigenous Communities in Panama Commemorate March Against Open-Pit Mining in which Two Protestors Were Killed." Latin American Database.

———. 2016, September 15. "Government Leaves Indigenous Residents Unprotected in Northeastern Nicaragua Land Dispute." Latin American Database.

O'Neill, Kathleen M. 2004. "Decentralization in Bolivia: Electoral Incentives," in Alfred P. Montero and David J. Samuels, eds., *Decentralization and Democracy in Latin America*, pp. 35–66. Notre Dame, IN: University of Notre Dame Press.

Penfold-Becerra, Michael. 2004. "Federalism and Institutional Change in Venezuela." In Edward L. Gibson, ed., Federalism and Democracy in Latin America, pp. 197–225. Baltimore: Johns Hopkins.

Plaza, Elena. 2000. "God and Federation: The Uses and Abuses of the Idea of 'Federation' during the Federal Wars in Venezuela, 1859–63," in Rebecca Earle, ed., *Rumours of Wars: Civil Conflict in Nineteenth-Century Latin America*, pp. 135–49. London: Institute of Latin American Studies.

Rock, David. 1985. *Argentina, 1516–1982: From Spanish Colonization to the Falklands War*. Berkeley, CA: University of California Press.

Rodden, Jonathan, and Erik Wibbels. 2002. "Beyond the Fiction of Federalism: Macroeconomic Management in Multitiered Systems." *World Politics* 54, pp. 494–531.

Rodrigues Afonso, José Roberto, and Erika Amorim Araújo. 2006. "Local Government Organization and Finance: Brazil," in Anwar Shah, ed., *Local Governance in Developing Countries*, pp. 381–418. Washington, DC: The World Bank.

Samuels, David J. 2004. "The Political Logic of Decentralization in Brazil," in Alfred P. Montero and David J. Samuels, eds., *Decentralization and Democracy in Latin America*, pp. 67–93. Notre Dame, IN: University of Notre Dame Press.

Smoke, Paul, Eduardo Gómez, and George E. Peterson. 2006. *Decentralization in Asia and Latin America*. Northampton, MA: Edward Elgar Publishing.

Van Cott, Donna Lee. 2006. "Dispensing Justice and the Margins of Formality: The Informal Rule of Law in Latin America," in Gretchen Helmke and Steven Levitsky, eds., *Informal Institutions and Democracy: Lessons from Latin America*, pp. 249–73. Baltimore, MD: Johns Hopkins.

Véliz, Claudio. 1980. *The Centralist Tradition in Latin America*. Princeton, NJ: Princeton University Press.

Watts, Ronald L. 1999. *Comparing Federal Systems*. Montreal: McGill-Queen's University Press.

10 The Armed Forces
Bridging the Civil-Military Divide

Photo 10.1 Military rule is a thing of the past in Latin America. But political tensions, criminal activities, and developmental needs ensure that the military presence remains. Two soldiers on patrol in Medellin, Colombia.

Source: © Shutterstock

At 5:30 A.M. we started hearing the first shots. My father woke up and said: "they're deposing me." There had already been shooting in front of the residence. They beat up my father but he got away and went up on the roof. My security guard entered, closed the windows and told me to shut the door. Four troopers entered the residence. When they opened the door to my room, with their weapons loaded, my security guard shouted "don't shoot."

They didn't find me because I had hidden under the bed. They broke down all the doors to my house. According to the record, they took my father away at 6:00 A.M. Approximately 200 soldiers were involved in his abduction. They did not have a search warrant.... There was no district attorney. When my father tried to straighten things out, one of the presidential escorts told him, "Shut up, you're a nobody now." They took him away in his pajamas, with his feet and hands bound; they boarded him on an aircraft with three heavily armed men wearing hoods. They abducted him without observing constitutional guarantees. There was never any trial.

—Testimony from a daughter of Manuel Zelaya,
President of Honduras (2006–2009)

When we detained President Zelaya, we were just carrying out an order of the Supreme Court because of a serious violation of the Constitution. There was no coup d'état. The Constitution says that the Armed Forces should ensure that the law is fulfilled. Once the order was fulfilled, we withdrew from the public arena and returned to our barracks. Moreover, no member of the military holds a position in the government.

—General Romeo Vasquez,
Chief of the Honduran Armed Forces[1]

The democratically elected president of Honduras, Manuel Zelaya, was arrested at his home and expelled from the country in the quiet morning hours of June 28, 2009. The Supreme Court, acting in secret, had issued the warrant. But heavily armed troops did the bidding, and they admitted that the decision to expel was all their own, done benevolently to save the country from violent protests. For Latin Americans, the military role in the event revived memories of a sordid past shared by so many countries of the region.

This was a past that saw military officers act with impunity as they removed elected officials from office, often took up the posts of government themselves, denied those who protested due process, and most horribly, relied on kidnapping, torture, and murder to enforce their decisions. General Romeo Vasquez, Chief of the Honduran Armed Forces, correctly notes that things were different this time—the military returned to their quarters promptly, and did not usurp authority, but rather facilitated the movement of authority from one civilian to another.

But the general failed to acknowledge what was the same, and what was so apparent to Latin Americans throughout the region—namely, the decisive role of the military. The armed forces had acted as an arbiter, and what happened would not have happened without its involvement. The incident was a grim reminder that whereas the military may play a different role than in the past, it would nonetheless still play a decisive role in the politics of many countries of the region. And make no mistake about it, this was a coup d'état, and it was widely condemned as such in the international community.[2]

The Armed Forces in Contemporary Latin America: Global Comparisons

Military Expenditures

A cursory examination of the armed forces in Latin America presents a puzzle. The political influence of the military in this region is well known. None of the countries were able to maintain a consistent record of civilian rule after independence, and very few avoided military rule within the past 50 years. In the history of Peru, a total of 20 presidents made their way to power through a military coup d'état, and many more relied on military force to sustain dictatorial forms of rule. Despite such cases, this is also a region with levels of military spending that have traditionally sat well below global averages—a status the region has retained in recent years (see Table 10.1). Of course, one might consider whether civilian rule over the past few decades is responsible for this relatively low level of spending. But another surprising finding is that military spending has increased in absolute terms even while the military has stayed in the barracks. One indicator in Table 10.1 shows military spending as a percentage of the economy, and the measure has not grown dramatically (especially for South America). But Latin American economies have grown over the past decade, and civilians in government have in fact directed some of that economic growth toward the armed forces. Military expenditures in constant 2014 U.S. dollars for the region as a whole were at $46.3 billion in 2000, $52.6 billion in 2005, $69.8 billion in 2010, and $76 billion in 2015 (SIPRI, 2016). As indicated by the per capita measure in Table 10.1, Latin American governments spend more per person on the military than in the past.

As these trends under democratic rule occurred, some analysts worried that the region was on the verge of an arms race, one fueled by outside weapons producers. Arms imports to the region increased 150 percent from 2000–2004 to 2005–2009 (worldwide, arms imports increased 22 percent over this time). The countries addressed the growth in spending at the 2010 General Assembly meeting of the Organization of American States, but could only muster mutual declarations on the importance of peaceful relations rather than concrete commitments to disarmament initiatives or greater transparency in weapons acquisitions (Inter Press Service, 2010). The economic boom created by natural resource exports allowed governments to spend more lavishly during this time, and it has started to subside. But even as arms imports cooled, actually falling 6 percent from 2006 to 2010 compared to 2011–2015, many ongoing tensions remained heated, justifying the overall rise in military spending. Colombia's campaign against the FARC insurgent group often crossed borders, and raised tensions with Ecuador and Venezuela. No doubt all participants will remain guarded even as the country pursues peace accords. Territorial disagreements between Chile, Peru, and Bolivia reach back to the War of the

Pacific (1879–1884), when Chile took away Bolivia's access to the ocean and incorporated land from the south of Peru. More recently, the discovery of offshore oil deposits has revived disagreements over territorial lines. Nicaragua expresses territorial claims on the San Andres Islands in the Caribbean, which are occupied by Colombia, and disagrees with Costa Rica on the demarcation of their border. President Jimmy Morales of Guatemala has aggravated relations with neighboring Belize by reviving historical claims on the country. For Mexico, the threat lies within its border. A declared war on drug trafficking spurred a 331 percent increase in arms imports from 2006 to 2010 compared to 2011–2015. And Brazil has escalated its spending on imports by roughly 35 percent between 2006 and 2010 and 2011–2015 as part of a broader attempt to situate itself as a regional power (Fleurant et al., 2016).

Table 10.1 **Military Expenditures as a Percentage of GDP and Per Capita.** Latin America has traditionally had lower levels of military spending compared with other regions of the world

	Spending as % of GDP			*Spending per capita*	
	2005	*2010*	*2015*	*2005*	*2015*
United States	3.8	4.7	3.3	1700	1854
Middle East	4.7	4.5	6.4	620	987
Western Europe	1.5	1.4	1.3	541	501
Russia	3.6	3.8	4.0	191	454
Oceana	1.3	1.2	1.2	260	374
South and Southeast Asia	1.8	1.9	1.9	142	223
North Africa	2.2	2.7	3.7	82	148
South America	1.9	1.8	1.8	70	145
Central and Eastern Europe	1.9	1.7	1.7	105	138
Central America	0.6	0.7	0.9	25	54
Sub-Saharan Africa	1.6	1.8	1.9	26	41

Source: *SIPRI Military Expenditure Database, 2016.* Available at www.sipri.org/databases/milex. Per capita amounts listed in current US$.

Military Spending and Development

Expenditures in Brazil far exceed those of any other country (see Table 10.2), but Brazil's economy is much larger than that of most countries in the region. When spending is measured as a percentage of the economy, smaller countries such as Ecuador and Panama take the lead.

Brazil joins Venezuela, Mexico, Colombia, Chile, and Argentina to compose a group of higher-spending countries. Examinations of military expenditures have traditionally raised concerns over the impact they have on development, especially as government spending is diverted from health and education programs. But careful studies question the supposed trade-off. It is truly a leap of faith to presume that money saved from reductions in military spending would be used for social programs (Perlo-Freeman and Perdomo, 2008). And the countries of Latin America fail to provide any empirical evidence for the trade-off, as indicated by their rankings on the human development index (HDI).[3] Countries with relatively generous spending, such as Chile and Argentina, exhibit high developmental rankings, whereas those with lower spending—Guatemala, Honduras, El Salvador, and Nicaragua—struggle with development.

Table 10.2 **Military Expenditures in Latin American Countries.** Some countries in Latin America spend much more than others on the military. This has raised debates over whether such spending takes away from development and spending on general social welfare needs

	2015 Defense Budget (U.S.$)	2015 Defense Spending/GDP	HDI: 2014 Regional Rank
Brazil	19.9b	1.30	9
Venezuela	8.5b	4.6	7
Mexico	6.0b	0.55	8
Colombia	4.9b	1.94	12
Chile	4.6b	1.94	2
Argentina	4.3b	0.98	1
Ecuador	2.5b	2.67	11
Peru	2.2b	1.25	10
Panama	1.3b	2.29	4
Costa Rica	949m	1.67	6
Uruguay	770m	1.45	3
Bolivia	568m	1.67	16
Dominican Republic	455m	0.64	13
Paraguay	357m	1.33	14
Guatemala	264m	0.39	18

	2015 Defense Budget (U.S.$)	2015 Defense Spending/GDP	HDI: 2014 Regional Rank
Honduras	332m	1.61	18
El Salvador	146m	0.53	15
Nicaragua	72.6m	0.56	17

Source: Donadio 2016; HDI rankings from the *Human Development Report 2015* (New York: United Nations Development Program).

Still, it would be wrong to flatly dismiss the impact of military expenditures. Oscar Arias, former president of Costa Rica, notes that incentives could be created to ensure that monies are shifted from military to social expenditures. The **"Costa Rica Consensus"** calls on the international community to provide debt relief and economic aid to developing countries that spend more on education, health care, housing, and environmental conservation, than on military expenditures (Arias, 2009). The generally low spending found in Latin America probably places these countries below the threshold at which defense expenditures begin to crowd out social spending priorities, but one must carefully examine the composure of military spending. Studies show that arms imports, as a specific portion of defense expenditures, tend to produce greater negative effects than defense expenditures generally. This is because they are associated with increases in foreign debt (used to pay for these imports), and they do not produce the positive economic spin-off effects generated by domestic arms production or defense spending directed toward military personnel. As noted, the general trend has seen imports decline, but that does not dismiss the debt from past imports and the prospects that a new surge in imports will accompany an economic revival. Finally, spending increases can contribute to interstate tensions and the likelihood for conflict, which would clearly have a deleterious impact on development. Military expenditures in Latin America are never going to disappear, so it is important to remain aware of their consequences.

Regional Distinctions

The armed forces in Latin America exhibit some important variations, and some similarities. First, one cannot overlook the two countries that have abolished their militaries—Costa Rica in 1949 and Panama in 1990. But most other countries hold on to prototypical models of the armed forces and strive to maintain ground, sea, and air forces. Indeed, at first glance one might be surprised to see naval branches in landlocked Bolivia and Paraguay, but these forces assume important missions on river systems. In Bolivia, drug traffickers and smugglers use rivers to travel through expansive jungle terrain, and in Paraguay, rivers compose nearly all of the country's territorial lines and thus require the border patrol to take on a naval function (in addition, Paraguay does have access to the Atlantic through the Paraná River). Honduras holds the most effective air force in Central America, a legacy of equipment and training furnished by the United States during the 1980s when it feared an invasion from the leftist Sandinista government in Nicaragua.

Throughout much of the region, paramilitary forces supplement the armed forces. These range from national police forces with direct chains of command and representation in the military institution, such as the *carabineros* in Chile, to the semiautonomous "self-defense forces" found in rural Colombia, Mexico, and Peru. The armed forces of the region also exhibit ideological differences. During the Cold War, the military regimes of Argentina, Brazil, Chile, and most of the Central American countries assumed a stalwart anticommunist, conservative character, but those in Ecuador and Peru professed a more progressive approach to politics, enacting land reform and calling for alliances with labor groups. The bloody battle against the insurgent group *Sendero Luminoso* in the 1980s undid the popular appeal gained by the Peruvian military. But in Ecuador, the military joined indigenous mobilizations to unseat neoliberal presidents in 1997, 2000, and 2005. In Nicaragua, the Sandinistas indoctrinated the armed forces with a populist, revolutionary orientation. Hugo Chávez undertook similar efforts to politicize the armed forces in Venezuela.

The military institution itself can serve an important function as a socializing agent, especially in those countries where military service remains mandatory. Bolivia, Brazil, Colombia, El Salvador, Guatemala, Mexico, and Paraguay all require their citizens to don a military uniform for at least one year. Of course, military institutions must also adapt to changes within society, and as gender and LGBT issues have gained greater prominence, so too has the pressure to reform traditional rules within the armed forces. The right for women to serve as officers in every branch gained ground at the turn of the century, with Brazil (2012), Bolivia (2010), Mexico (2010) as the last holdouts. Nonetheless, women are still prohibited from serving as noncommissioned officers in El Salvador and Paraguay (Donadio 2016). The list of countries lacking explicit legislation to allow LGBT persons to serve openly, or which outright prohibit LGBT persons, has shortened in recent decades, but remains lengthy, with Bolivia, Ecuador, the Dominican Republic, Guatemala, Honduras, Nicaragua, Paraguay, and Venezuela still lagging.

Table 10.3 **The Armed Forces in Latin America.** Latin America exhibits significant variations in the size of the armed forces across countries

	Active Armed Forces	Army	Navy	Air Force	per 10,000 inhabitants
Argentina	79,845	48,367	17,957	13,521	18
Bolivia	34,078	22,565	4,983	6,530	31

	Active Armed Forces	Army	Navy	Air Force	per 10,000 inhabitants
Brazil	214,941	190,000	85,605	66,068	18
Chile	67,683	40,417	18,973	8,293	37
Colombia	265,050	220,537	30,917	13,596	54
Dom Rep	58,281	28,815	11,320	18,146	55
Ecuador	41,403	*	*	*	25
El Salvador	24,023	*	*	*	38
Guatemala	18,181	15,797	1,452	932	11
Honduras	15,216	10,269	2,830	2,117	19
Mexico	267,565	205,689	54,179	7,788	21
Nicaragua	12,793	*	*	*	21
Paraguay	16,087	10,962	2,958	2,167	24
Peru	78,296	47,106	21,665	9,525	25
Uruguay	22,316	14,948	4,756	2,612	65
Venezuela	365,315	*	*	*	18

Source: Donadio 2016. * no data reported

The Military Perspective of Latin American History

The European settlers of Latin America were not fleeing religious persecution from a faraway state or seeking individual economic opportunities, as in much of North America. Rather, they were part of an organized effort to extract precious metals to benefit the Spanish and Portuguese monarchies—an effort accompanied and some would say masked by a mission to spread Christianity. And whereas the North American settlers had their own confrontations with indigenous populations, usually these were relatively small, nomadic communities that could be addressed with locally organized militias. But vast civilizations populated large areas of Central and South America, such that confrontation required massive, lasting military campaigns. This, as well as the need to protect the movement of gold and silver through the empire, to fortify storage areas in ports, and to defend shipments across the Atlantic in jam-packed convoys of galleons, further assured the military a prominent role during the colonial period.

Independence did little to reduce military influence. In fact, it magnified it. The length and turmoil of the independence wars contributed to the use of force in politics. From about 1810 to 1826 disparate troops fought against the Spanish monarchy, and often against each other. The fact that royalist troops could not easily march back to Spain stiffened their resolve. Mexico gained its independence in 1821, but up to 1825 Spanish troops remained holed up and planned attacks from the island garrison of San Juan de Ulua, off the port city of Veracruz. Many others settled in the Spanish colony of Cuba, and plotted to restore Spanish rule in Mexico. During the fight for independence, economic resources were diverted to the military effort, agricultural lands lay fallow, mines flooded, and trade routes became too dangerous to travel. The havoc unearthed racial divides long repressed in colonial society. As noted by Loveman, "Loss of the political legitimacy and 'social peace' imposed by Spain made post-independence political leaders and economic elites much more dependent on the armed forces for maintaining internal order than had been the colonial regime" (1999, p. 37).

Violent cycles of *caudillo* politics followed in most countries. Avaricious officers eyed the presidential palace, and thought little of taking up arms to feed their appetites for power. Mariano Melgarejo, a soldier with a reputation as a drunkard and womanizer, literally seized the presidential sash of Bolivia in 1865 when he confronted and murdered its dictator, Manuel Belzú, in the presidential palace. He then displayed Belzú's body on the balcony for those who had gathered in the plaza to see. Melgarejo would do no better as a leader—he would even sell large swaths of Bolivian territory to Brazil for personal gain. It was not just greed and incompetence that did in the *caudillos*. Debt from the war, rampant corruption, and persistent rebellions made governance all but impossible. This period of instability would last until the later nineteenth century, when demand for various raw materials and agricultural goods in the United States and Europe gave Latin American governments both the incentive and ability to impose order. These export economies required security throughout their lands to draw investments in roads, railways, communications, and port facilities. And the profits from exports permitted governments not only to bolster their administrative structures, but also to strengthen national armies and finally put an end to insurrections and defiance by local strongmen in the hinterlands.

The export economy brought a period of growth and stability to Latin America. But these changes concealed troubling deficiencies in political development. Economic gains flowed largely to the wealthy, and did little to foster a middle class. Moreover, a new working-class segment of the population that developed alongside the growth of cities and industries found themselves shut out of the political system due to restrictions on voting or political party and labor union organizations. President Porfirio Díaz (1876–1880, 1884–1911) of Mexico closed off representative government to ensure stability, and offered generous concessions to foreign investment as a formula to fuel economic growth—but not distribution. The success of opposition movements to his rule in 1911 set the stage for the Mexican Revolution. Elsewhere, the worldwide depression of the 1930s stoked protests by working-class groups and led to widespread unrest. Nearly every country experienced some level of military intervention. Each time, the armed forces appeared to follow the same script—working-class or reformist parties were tossed (or rebuffed) from power in favor of conservative interests that shared the military concern with order.

World War II and the postwar boom invigorated economies devastated by the Great Depression. Working-class groups slowly worked their way into the political system, and the middle classes began to diversify. But this was the period of the Cold War, when the battle between communism and capitalism defined politics. From the military point of view, democracy opened inroads for communist subversion—especially as socialist and communist parties saw their registration rolls grow. Such concerns triggered a wave of military interventions in the 1960s. But unlike the interventions of the 1930s, this time the militaries took the reins of power on their own and created bureaucratic-authoritarian regimes. And the military regimes ruled with brute force. More than 20,000 were kidnapped and disappeared in Argentina. In Guatemala, a scorched earth counterinsurgency campaign targeted Mayan indigenous communities, and killed thousands. In Chile, a presidential commission identified 28,000 individuals tortured by the military, and duly noted the reluctance of many others to come forward. Only Colombia, Costa Rica, and Venezuela held competitive elections and withstood military rule during this time period (Mexico maintained its civilian, single-party authoritarian regime). The era of military rule ended only after the debt crisis of the 1980s and growing outrage over human rights violations drove the armed forces from power.[4] Whether the repression ought to be investigated and the perpetrators prosecuted, or conveniently forgotten remains a matter of debate in many countries.

The armed forces in Latin America look upon this history from their own perspective. Beginning with the colonial government, they recognize how the Bourbon Reforms placed Spanish-borne elites (*peninsulares*) deemed most trustworthy by the crown in positions previously held by elites born in Latin America (*criollos*). Such changes did not occur in the military. In fact, *mestizos* often rose to higher positions in the officer corps, and all sectors of society had service opportunities in the lower ranks. Hence, at the time of independence, the armed forces represented the only true *Latin American* national institution. By all accounts, the military has a point here. But soldiers in the region go on to portray themselves as indispensable state builders. Militaries tell stories of how they consolidated countries as they spread authority across thick jungle terrain, rugged sierras, or open plains (in Argentina, the expansion of the state southward through Patagonia is known as the Conquest of the Desert). They also herald their historic defense of territorial boundaries. And they portray themselves as victims of political circumstance—as if time and time again, it was only the failures of civilian politicians that compelled them to intervene in government.

COMPARING COUNTRIES

Justice and the "Dirty Wars" in Argentina and Brazil

The military that governed Argentina from 1976 to 1983 used barbarous tactics in its ruthless effort to quell dissent to its rule. So many were kidnapped in this "dirty war," never to be seen again, that Argentines began to refer to these people as "the disappeared" (*los desaparecidos*). A study commissioned immediately after the transition to civilian rule listed the names of 8,961 disappeared, but most now agree that the actual total easily doubles that number. The disappeared were subject to forms of torture that included electric shocks, beatings, simulated drownings in sewage, sexual abuse, and asphyxiation. Some were forced to watch the torture of family members. Abetting doctors induced labor in pregnant women, so that military families could adopt their babies. Many of the disappeared were tossed from airplanes into the ocean to conceal their remains.

In a bold move after the resumption of democratic government, President Raúl Alfonsín put the nine military commanders who had led the regime on trial. Only five of the nine were found guilty, but the act was unprecedented. This was the first time a Latin American government had held commanding officers accountable for human rights abuses committed during military rule. But in 1987, as the trials reached into the mid-level ranks of the officer corps, the military rebelled and quartered themselves in an army base near the capital. In response, Alfonsín limited the trials to officers above the rank of colonel. Three more rebellions followed. Alfonsín's successor, Carlos Menem, decided to subdue military tensions so that he could fully concentrate on a growing economic crisis, which had quickly overshadowed the public's concern with military justice. By 1990, he stopped the trials and issued pardons for all those who had been convicted.

But the issue never really went away. Human rights activists continued their fight in the courts, and developed novel strategies in the pursuit of justice. Through the 1990s, evidence of collaboration in repressive activities between military regimes in Argentina, Bolivia, Brazil, Chile, Paraguay, and Uruguay gradually came to light. In what was known as "Operation Condor," the regimes detained, tortured, and killed one another's political suspects. The cross-national character of the repression opened additional judicial venues for human rights lawyers. In addition, activists noted the estimated 400 babies taken from their mothers, and successfully argued that the pardons did not cover the kidnapping of children. The first military president, Rafael Videla, was found guilty of this crime in 1998, and soon trials opened against other leaders. Activists also looked overseas for support. Beginning in the late 1990s, judges in France, Germany, Italy, and Spain opened investigations into cases that involved victims with citizenship in their countries.

But a landmark decision took place in 2001, when a federal court argued that the crimes against the disappeared were of such a scale that they were in fact "crimes against humanity," and thus not just the criminal code, but international human rights treaties applied. The reasoning was critical, because Article 118 of the Argentine Constitution expressly commits government to uphold international human rights law. The logic followed that the amnesties and pardons passed under Alfonsín and Menem were unconstitutional. But for the ruling to have effect beyond the case at hand, it would have to be decided by the Supreme Court. Congress reacted positively, and annulled the pardons and amnesties in 2003, but their power to do so was challenged in court. In the meantime, activists pursued justice on a case-by-case basis. By 2004, almost 100 officers had been detained for human rights crimes. The court finally issued its decision in June 2005, finding by a 7–1 majority that the pardons and amnesties were in fact unconstitutional. To date, some 600 military and police officers have been charged with abuses committed under the regime.

Brazil had its own dirty war under the military regime that ruled from 1964 to 1985, but the civilian governments since that time have made it clear that they would rather not pursue prosecution. To be sure, the human rights abuses in Brazil were not as extensive as in Argentina. Still, it is difficult to claim that the military regime killed and disappeared *only* 479. In addition, a report by the Archdiocese São Paulo drafted secretly during the period of military rule and published in 1985 documented 17,000 incidents of torture and abuse. Finally, the regime holds some responsibility for abuses in neighboring countries. The armed forces established a center in Manaus to train officers from throughout the region on torture methods, and the military also aided

(continued)

repression abroad through a collaborative effort known as Operation Condor, whereby South American military regimes shared intelligence and transferred political prisoners (Robin, 2005).

Why then, has so little been done in Brazil? One explanation looks to the transition to democracy. In Argentina, the military regime collapsed, allowing civilians to make a clean break with the past. In Brazil, the military withdrew from government gradually, and civilians participated in the highest levels of government. Most notably, the military retained the legislature. Though it was little more than a rubber stamp, civilian involvement did grant the regime some legitimacy. As in Argentina, the Brazilian armed forces drafted an amnesty (in 1979), but it was approved by a civilian legislature. Unexpected events also hampered attempts at justice. A member of the opposition, Tancredo Neves, won the first presidential election following military rule, but to ease apprehensive military officers, he selected a running mate who had been an active supporter of military rule. Unfortunately, Neves would die before taking office. His selection, Josè Sarney, took office and unsurprisingly showed little interest in past military abuses.

The first president clearly recognized as an active opponent to military rule was Fernando Henrique Cardoso, elected in 1995. A continuing economic crisis lowered human rights issues as a priority for many Brazilians. Nonetheless, Cardoso created a fund to compensate the families of 136 victims, and established a Special Commission on Deaths and Disappearances, which documented an additional 343 victims in a final report issued in 2007. Another body, the Amnesty Commission, looked into cases of torture not involving death, and has provided compensation to more than 12,000 victims. But the measures fall far short of the demands by human rights activists. The government refused to publish the investigatory notes of the Special Commission documenting details of the cases, including the names of perpetrators. In fact, in May 2005, President Luiz Inácio Lula da Silva signed a law that classified documents related to abuses under the military regime.

The actions by Lula were somewhat surprising. As a trade union leader under the authoritarian regime, he had been a vocal member of the opposition, and his left-wing Worker's Party places him ideologically far from the military regime. Even as congress considered a truth commission in 2010, Lula made it clear that he would not support such a move. And the thought of prosecution remained untenable in the government. Lula's Defense Minister Nelson Jobim all but portrayed the idea as subversive, arguing, "The right to memory is one thing and revenge is another."[5] The Chief Justice of the Supreme Court shared his opposition, and his court upheld the Amnesty Law in an April 2010 ruling. Curiously, Lula's opposition can be related to his stewardship of the country as a rising regional power. Even as the Inter-American Court of Human Rights ruled against the amnesty in December 2010, Lula criticized the body for infringing on national sovereignty. For Lula, international prominence is closely related to the emergence of Brazil as a military power, and this means further development of the Brazilian military industry. The armed forces already control civilian aviation, developed the Tucano air fighter for export to several countries worldwide, and even have ambitious plans to develop a nuclear submarine. Brazil's armed forces have clearly positioned themselves as a pivotal contributor to the country's stature—so long as moral issues are set aside.[6] Brazil's next president, Dilma Rousseff, was incarcerated under the military regime, but she never had the popular appeal and political capital of Lula. She commissioned a truth commission in 2014, but did not seek to overturn the amnesty. In Argentina, prosecution of human rights perpetrators followed the political interests of politicians, and the same is true in Brazil. Only in Brazil, presidents thus far have catered to the armed forces in the interest of other political goals.

Discussion Questions

1   Reflecting on the different experiences with dirty wars in Argentina and Brazil, would you say that it is better to forgive, forget, or punish human rights violators? Should the correct answer depend on the particular experience of the country in question?
2   Discuss how human rights policy in Argentina and Brazil has followed the political interests of politicians. Are Argentina's politicians more righteous?

The problem is that the military perspective veers dramatically from the reality of history. It reflects and contributes to the lack of communication and understanding in civil-military relations. Despite the military lore of nation and state building, the armed forces directed more of their energy inward, where they consistently involved themselves in struggles among regional strongmen or in defense of particular economic or political interests (Pion-Berlin, 2005). And their efforts did more to destabilize politics than spread law and order, or engender a national identity. Even today many countries cannot claim control of their hinterlands (Centeno, 2002). Though interstate war did occur—in the War of the Pacific, the War of the Triple Alliance, and the Chaco War, it was uncommon and became almost arcane by the middle of the twentieth century. But it is the justification of political violence—the unspeakable human rights abuses of the 1960s to the 1980s— that epitomizes the differences in civil-military perspectives. No level of "subversion" could have warranted the atrocities that took place.

The 2006 funeral of Augusto Pinochet, who ruled Chile from 1973 to 1990, roundly exposed the distance between military and civilian views. The president of Chile, Michele Bachelet (2006–2010)—herself a victim of repression under the military dictatorship—denied him a state funeral. The service was instead held in a military academy, where Pinochet's supporters gave eulogies that reflected on his battle against subversion, and praised him for saving the country from Marxism. His son, Captain Augusto Pinochet Molina, characterized the judges investigating human rights abuses as individuals who sought "notoriety rather than justice." A public viewing took place over several days, and more than 30,000 paid their respects. But outside the academy, street marches reminded all of the brutality that took place under Pinochet, and the popular investigations into human rights abuses of the period continued unabated. Later on, Captain Pinochet would be dismissed from the armed forces for making political statements while on active duty.

The gulf in civil-military relations cannot be attributed solely to the distorted attitudes of certain military officers. There were many civilians among the 30,000 that viewed Pinochet's corpse and celebrated his rule. And officers have come forward to issue apologies for the abuses under military rule. Although it took 12 years after the end of military rule, in 1995, General Martin Balza, the Army Chief of Staff in Argentina, finally admitted that soldiers "employed illegitimate methods, including the suppression of life, to obtain information" (*Los Angeles Times*, 1995). An institutional explanation for the discrepancy requires us to look into the mechanics and dynamics of civil-military relations. We need to understand the institutions of civil-military relations, and how they can be designed to work in a democratic regime. With such an ideal model in mind, we can reexamine civil-military relations in Latin America to discern what might be missing, and what might explain the civil-military discord.

Civil-Military Relations

To understand the differences in civilian and military perspectives, we can begin by looking into military thought and behavior. Because professionalization is so fundamental to the identity and development of the armed forces, it offers a sensible starting point. According to Samuel Huntington, **professionalization** of the armed forces occurs in three areas: expertise, responsibility, and corporateness. Expertise refers to the development of knowledge and skills related to the direction, operation, and control of an organization designed for the application of violence. Responsibility entails the growing sense of a social obligation to perform an essential service, that of preserving national security. And corporate solidarity involves the emergence of a distinct, common identity among officers, one that develops due to their common expertise and sense of responsibility.[7]

Huntington argues that the intense nature of military professionalization enhances the likelihood for civilian control. The maintenance of expertise, responsibility, and corporateness so fully commits the energy of the armed forces that it reduces their interests in political affairs. Professional officers become far too interested in being good soldiers, and fear that any involvement in politics would diminish the time devoted to the enhancement of expertise, pull them outside their sphere of social responsibility, and undermine their corporate unity with political debate. In Huntington's view, civilians can best assert control over the armed forces by recognizing and respecting an independent sphere of military action.

The Latin American experience does not support Huntington's theory. We saw that the export economies of the 1870s to 1930s allowed countries to strengthen their national armies. Part of that effort involved visits by various European military advisors, especially from France and Germany, to professionalize military forces. The advisors instituted regular training procedures, the development of military law, the organization of military schools and curricula, the refinement of strategic doctrine, and modifications in the chain of command and general staff arrangements. And yet, by the 1930s, the armed forces were as politicized as ever. What is Huntington's argument missing?

One problem with Huntington's argument is that he views professionalization as a uniform process, when in actuality it can take many forms. This can be better understood once we envision professionalization "as an institutional attribute ... in terms of the technical development and complexity of the military career." In this sense "the distinguishing characteristic of the professionalized military is the existence of a specialized military education and training system" (Fitch, 1998, p. 4). This leads us to look inside and assess the political content of military instruction. For as it turns out, French and German soldiers may have modernized military academies in Latin America, but they also shared their suspicions of civilians. These suspicions made their way into the curricula and military doctrines of the region and confirmed the acceptance of **"antipolitics"** in the armed forces. This view—that politicians are incapable of modernizing the country, and cannot be trusted to put aside their self-interest for the good of the nation—had developed since the colonial period, but professionalization institutionalized these ideas.

As an alternative to the unreliable nature of representative democracy, antipolitics extolled a different set of institutional values: the centralization of authority, the use of states of exception to suspend formal restrictions on government actions, the rejection of opposition or criticism of government as a legitimate undertaking, and the use of repression to quell active or would-be opponents of the regime (Loveman and Davies, 1997). Of course, the irony of antipolitics is that the scorn directed toward all things political is itself a political act. Nonetheless, officers embraced the myth that they could enter government and set politics aside.

Military attitudes sharpened after WWII, when **National Security Doctrine** (NSD) found its way into military academies and offered the armed forces a central role in the Cold War. On its surface, the Cold War was all about the struggle between communist Soviet Union and capitalist United States. But this war was a stalemate, maintained by the mutual threat of nuclear war. This meant that gains and losses in the Cold War would occur only incrementally, in the Third World, as countries shifted sides. United States military advisors encouraged this military mind-set, and with it, a division of labor that put the United States in charge of foreign threats and asked Latin American militaries to concentrate on internal security to quell suspected communist subversion. The NSD was fully compatible with antipolitics. After all, if the stakes of the Cold War were the future of the free world, why trust the civilians? But NSD sharpened the military concern with government because of the diffuse nature of the threat. Communist subversion was not some conventional military force, but rather a set of ideas that could infect everyday citizens anytime, anywhere, anyplace. It is not surprising that the military interventions of the Cold War period were so much more complete than in the 1930s, when officers often worked alongside civilian accomplices.

A second problem with Huntington's theory is that it focuses too narrowly on professionalization to define civil-military relations, without paying much attention to the civilian side of this equation. It is telling that many of the French and German officers who visited Latin America in the late nineteenth century agreed with the tenets of antipolitics. Yet we did not see military interventions in France and Germany during this time because strong, legitimate civilian institutions created a barrier to military encroachments. Given Latin America's underdeveloped economic and political structures, some civilian groups concurred with antipolitics and welcomed military intervention, whereas such sentiments were uncommon in the French and German societies. Moreover, politicians in France and Germany constructed institutions to manage the relations between civilians and soldiers—everything from ministries of defense in the executive and parliamentary committees on defense issues to civilian-based schools and research centers that focused on security affairs. These institutions fortified civilian credentials and allowed them to both set the terms for civil-military interaction, and to work with soldiers on a more equal footing. As one seminal study of democratization and military intervention notes:

> Typically ... military role expansion is induced by the corruption, stagnation, and malfunctioning of democratic institutions to the point at which the military is increasingly called upon to maintain order and comes to see itself as the country's only salvation. ... [T]he single most important requirement for keeping the military at bay is to make democracy work, to develop its institutional capacities so it accrues broad and unquestioned legitimacy. (Diamond et al., 1995, pp. 46–47)

To conclude, soldiers and civilians in Latin America have developed such different perspectives on history and politics, and such distinct sets of values, largely because they have failed to communicate and interact with each other. This, in turn, has made intervention more likely when tensions have mounted. And this is a story of institutional shortcomings. Professionalization occurred with little input from civilians, so that any misperceptions, presumptions, or anxieties on the part of the military were never really challenged or addressed. Rather, they were allowed to fester and become entrenched as they made their way into educational curricula and military doctrine. And civilians failed to build adequate governing institutions to bridge the civil-military divide. Now that the countries have made the transition to democracy, what have they done, and what can they do to address these deficiencies?

Civil-Military Relations Under Democracy

Civilian Supremacy or Political Management?

Democracy requires military subordination—that much is clear. But what exactly do we mean by subordination in practice, and how is it achieved? Analysts continue to grapple with these questions. Some place the bar quite high and require elected officials to not only control, but also to closely supervise, educate themselves on, and even participate in military affairs. **Civilian supremacy** refers to "the ability of a civilian, democratically elected government to conduct general policy without interference from the military, to define the goals and general organization of national defense, to formulate and conduct defense policy, and to monitor the implementation of military policy" (Agüero, 1995, p. 19). This measure is an ideal type, for even in advanced democracies, civilians may offer soldiers tremendous leeway to implement policy, and they may even invite military officers to take an active role as policies are designed. Other analysts argue that civilian supremacy is unreachable in most developing countries, and if we use it as the standard for military subordination, we could be setting up countries for failure and frustration. We just cannot expect civilians, especially in the short run, to gain the expertise required to monitor, let alone design, security and defense policies.

And perhaps civilian supremacy is not a requisite for military subordination. Notwithstanding some important exceptions, the past 20 years have seen Latin American governments exert a level of civilian control unseen in previous decades, despite glaring deficiencies in military expertise held by civilians. Perhaps civilians need only concentrate on their **political management** of the military—on their ability to maintain open channels of communication, and on the effort to command compliance by instilling respect for civilian authority and democracy rather than by improbable attempts to impress the military command with their stock of knowledge in defense and security affairs (Pion-Berlin, 2005). We will return to the question of whether civilian supremacy is achievable or required to ensure military subordination in Latin America after we take a closer look at developments in civil-military relations since the transition to democracy.

New Security Norms under Democracy

The closing of the Cold War in 1990 compelled the armed forces to rethink their doctrines and their role in national security. The new democratic governments welcomed this opportunity and sought to remove the vestiges of NSD from military academies. They introduced coursework on international law, democracy, and human rights, and they also worked to develop alternative security norms. The principle of **democratic security** draws from liberal thinking reaching back to Immanuel Kant (1724–1804), which holds that democracies do not fight democracies. Hence, it makes sense for countries to have an interest in the preservation of democracy not only at home, but among neighbors as well. President Raúl Alfonsín of Argentina (1983–1989) headed one of the first countries to democratize, and as civilian counterparts emerged in neighboring countries, he acted quickly to support them and forge cooperative treaties to undermine stubborn military suspicions. The watershed event occurred in 1985 at Iguaçu Falls at the border of long-time rival Brazil, when Alfonsín and the new civilian president of Brazil, José Sarney, met to discuss bilateral cooperation. They initiated agreements on nuclear and aeronautical cooperation—topics of tremendous sensitivity to the armed forces, and on trade and investment regulations. Alfonsín would also extend his diplomatic support to fledgling democracies in Bolivia, Paraguay, and Uruguay (Fournier, 1999). In 1991, these countries and Brazil would join with Argentina to create MERCOSUR, an economic cooperative community that also requires its members to remain democratic.[8]

Central America followed suit, but also attempted to further develop new security norms. In 1987, political leaders of the region created the Central American Security Commission. The organization drafted the Framework Treaty on Democratic Security in 1995, and it included references to **human security**. This idea links national security to basic human needs and human rights. For a region mired in poverty, beset by medical emergencies such as the AIDS crisis and regular waves of influenza epidemics, hammered by natural catastrophes such as earthquakes and hurricanes, and concerned with rising crime rates, the notion that security needed to be addressed first at the personal level had great appeal. Article 10 of the treaty reads, "Respect for the essential dignity of individuals, improvement of their quality of life and full development of their potential are prerequisites for security in all it aspects." The article commits governments to "consideration of poverty and extreme poverty as threats to the security of people and the democratic security of Central American societies."[9]

In addition, countries throughout the hemisphere put aside old suspicions and embraced the notion of **cooperative security**. This security norm asks the armed forces to take more of a defensive than offensive position, and encourages the widespread use of **confidence building measures** (CBMs) to allay interstate tensions. Some examples of CBMs include joint training exercises, exchange programs at military academies, notification protocols for the mobilization or movement of troops, and promoting transparency in the reporting of deployments, arms procurement, and weaponry inventories. Cooperative security also calls for regular multilateral forums on security issues, and participation in international peacekeeping missions. Though such arrangements have emerged throughout the hemisphere and often at the bilateral level, the most encompassing effort to promote cooperative security occurs at the biennial meetings of the Conference of Ministers of Defense of the Americas, which includes nearly every nation from Latin America and the Caribbean, as well Canada and the United States. The first conference was held in 1995 in Williamsburg, Virginia, and Trinidad and Tobago hosted the 2016 meeting.

Photo 10.2 Military trucks carry tourists on an eco-tour in Nicaragua. The armed forces have the most dependable transportation in rural areas.

Source: © Shutterstock

So have these new security norms taken root? The gains have been substantial, but few would deny that concerns remain. In 2001, the Organization of American States enshrined democratic security in the Inter-American Democratic Charter.[10] Article 19 of this document obligates regional responses when a democracy is under threat of a coup or other attempt to sideline normal constitutional practices. Nonetheless, countries of the region appear reluctant to apply sanctions outside the most egregious cases (Arceneaux and Pion-Berlin, 2007). Honduras's membership was suspended by the Organization of American States (OAS) after the 2009 coup referenced at the start of this chapter, but it also received very supportive guidelines on how it could reestablish membership. Also, the economic sanctions placed on the country applied only to nonhumanitarian aid and some loaning activity, leaving out far more painful measures encompassing trade and investment. Though the United States joined other OAS countries in the vote to oust Honduras, after the election of a new president the following year, the Obama administration joined Canada, Colombia, the Dominican Republic, Peru, and most of the Central American countries in an effort to reinstate the country (*New York Times*, 2010). The endeavor succeeded in 2011. Proponents argued that the reinstatement of Honduras allowed the country to put the past behind it, but that also meant putting aside questions of justice.

The notion of human security never gained much traction outside official pronouncements or as window dressing for traditional military involvement in civic action operations such as medical extension programs, emergency relief, road construction, and the building of schools—operations the military often takes on due to the inability of the civilian sector to sufficiently address these needs. Moreover, only those issues of human security with close relations to traditional security concerns have received any real attention by the military. Hence, although human trafficking and small-arms proliferation represent clear threats to dignity or personal security, they have received greater consideration in recent years primarily because of their relationship to criminal organizations. For the most part, the principal concerns of most Latin American militaries are drug trafficking, gangs, and terrorism, and as in the past, these are issues that have a strong domestic component. Insofar as the United States retains its hegemonic position over international affairs throughout the hemisphere, one wonders how much has changed in regard to the military division of labor since the Cold War.

In the area of cooperative security, the region has seen much more progress. Confidence building measures abound, and several armed forces have regularized their interaction in special units or peacekeeping operations. In 1997, El Salvador, Guatemala, Honduras, and Nicaragua created the Conference of Central American Armies (CFAC—*Conferencia de las Fuerzas Armadas Centroamericanas*). One of their first achievements was the creation of the Humanitarian and Rescue Unit for use in emergency relief operations. The unit saw action soon after its creation when it was deployed to address a dengue epidemic in Honduras (2000), and it also coordinated emergency assistance after a massive earthquake struck El Salvador (2001), and again when a destructive hurricane hit Nicaragua (2007). In 2014, CFAC launched a training program to support the deployment of member forces in UN peace operations (Manuela Estrada, 2014). Such a unit has already been created by Argentina and Chile. In 2008, these two historic rivals created the "Southern Cross" Combined Joint Peace Force to train and deploy troops for United Nations peacekeeping missions. Brazil saw peacekeeping as a method of displaying its regional leadership early on, and created a peace-keeping division in its military in 2001. By 2010, the unit would evolve into the Brazilian Peacekeeping Operations Joint Training Center and regularly invite the militaries of other countries to train for and collaborate in UN peacekeeping operations. Even when countries independently contribute troops to peacekeeping missions, the multilateral nature of these operations acts as a CBM as troops from different countries learn to work together. And the armed forces of the region increasingly embrace peacekeeping as a significant mission. From 2001 to 2016, contributions from the region increased 477 percent, outpacing the growth of contributions from the rest of the world, which rose 204 percent (Donadio, 2016). As illustrated in Table 10.4, the UN peacekeeping mission in Haiti, currently under Brazilian com-mand, draws together a number of Latin American countries. In 2016, Latin American militaries composed 46 percent of the UN mission in Haiti, and 30 percent of the mission in the Democratic Republic of the Congo.

Table 10.4 **Personnel Deployments to UN Peacekeeping Missions.*** UN peacekeeping is playing an increasingly important part of the security missions of many Latin American militaries

	Arg	Bol	Brz	Chl	Col	Ecu	ES	Gua	Hon	Mex	Par	Per	Urg
Western Sahara	3	–	10	–	–	–	3	–	12	4	–	–	–
Central African Republic	–	5	6	4	–	–	–	4	–	–	4	210	–
Mali	–	–	–	–	–	–	92	–	–	–	–	–	–
Haiti	85	–	986	403	39	1	65	54	47	6	84	161	257
DR Congo	–	8	–	–	–	–	–	152	–	–	15	12	1,188
Darfur	–	–	–	–	–	4	–	–	–	–	–	2	–
Golan Heights	–	–	–	–	–	–	–	–	–	–	–	–	–

(*continued*)

Table 10.4 (continued) **Personnel Deployments to UN Peacekeeping Missions.*** UN peacekeeping is playing an increasingly important part of the security missions of many Latin American militaries

	Arg	Bol	Brz	Chl	Col	Ecu	ES	Gua	Hon	Mex	Par	Per	Urg
Cyprus	362		3	14	–	–	–	–	–	–	14	–	–
Millennium Campaign	14	10	–	11	–	–	10	5	–	11	11	–	8
Lebanon	–	–	279	–	–	–	52	2	–	2	–	–	–
Abyei (Sudan)	–	–	2	–	–	3	1	3	–	–	–	1	–
Kosovo	–	–	–	–	–	–	–	–	–	–	–	–	–
Liberia	–	1	2	–	–	–	–	–	–	–	–	–	–
South Sudan	4	4	11	–	–	–	2	7	–	–	2	2	–
India-Pakistan	–	–	–	2	–	–	–	–	–	–	–	–	2
Cote d'Ivoire	–	1	4	–	–	2	–	4	–	–	2	1	2
Middle East	3	–	–	2	–	–	–	–	–	–	–	–	–
TOTAL	**471**	**29**	**1,303**	**436**	**39**	**10**	**225**	**231**	**59**	**23**	**132**	**389**	**1,457**

Source: *Country Contributions Detailed by Mission*. Available at www.un.org/en/peacekeeping Current as of August 2016.
**No deployments:* Costa Rica, Dominican Republic, Panama, Venezuela

Institutional Checks and Balances under Democracy

Aside from the push to instill new security norms, civil-military relations in Latin America have also been affected by institutional reforms designed to bolster civilian expertise.

The Legislature

All of the same issues that encumber legislative strength recognized in Chapter 5—limited sessions, a shortage of staff and research resources, executive decree power, and so on—also affect the legislature's ability to influence military policy (Giraldo, 2006). Every country has legislative committees devoted to defense, but only Argentina, Chile, El Salvador, Guatemala, Honduras, Mexico, and Uruguay have committees charged solely with defense. In other countries, these same committees must also deal with police affairs, human rights, and/or international affairs more broadly speaking. Moreover, only Argentina, Bolivia, Colombia, Honduras, Mexico, Paraguay, and Uruguay require legislative approval for nominations of superior military officers. And only Chile and El Salvador allow their legislators to file accusations against soldiers for crimes or misdemeanors.[11] In many countries, it is easy for the armed forces to look upon congress as an institution with little relevance to their affairs.

And apart from the actual powers and capabilities of the legislature, one might also question the incentive of legislators to develop expertise in military affairs and exert what oversight they hold. The lack of interstate conflict has in many ways convinced Latin American politicians that defense policy can be set aside so that issues of presumably greater importance— education, health, economic development—can be addressed. Furthermore, in contrast to the United States, the insignificant size of the defense sector in Latin America means that few voters depend on defense expenditures for employment or see the benefits of military spending in their local communities. In Latin America, a show of expertise in defense issues is not likely to increase the appeal of a politician at the polls. Finally, the low level of party institutionalization in the region curbs reelection rates, such that even those unlikely politicians who do take an interest in defense affairs do not find themselves in office for long (Pion-Berlin and Trinkunas, 2007).

The Courts

One measure of civilian supremacy is the level of authority civilians hold over the military justice system. Military courts have a long history of autonomy from and authority over civilian courts in Latin America. Traditionally, the military *fuero* guaranteed not only soldiers, but also their immediate families, access to military courts, even in cases that involved civilians. And military courts sidelined civilian oversight in certain crimes against the national security, such as sedition. The experience with military rule allowed military courts to further expand their jurisdiction, especially in the simple maintenance of public order. At present, some countries have had more success than others in reducing the jurisdiction of military justice. The collapse of military rule in Argentina has allowed for extensive reforms in military justice. Civilians have gained widespread appeal authority over military court decisions, and both civilians and police are now excluded from military courts. In Uruguay the military has retained some prerogatives. The Supreme Court holds final appeal authority over all the courts in the land. But when a case involves a military matter, the five-member body must add two military justices. Chile, a country often cited as a success story in the move toward democratic consolidation, still has not enacted substantial reforms to its military justice code. Because the police force (the *Carabineros*) is considered part of the armed forces, alleged assaults by civilians on officers work their way through military courts, where judges tend to be more sympathetic toward the police. Likewise, when soldiers or police officers are found guilty of a crime, military courts tend to levy lighter sentences than would be the case in the civilian courts (Pereira and Zaverucha, 2005).

Military justice recently emerged as a central issue in Mexico due to the use of the armed forces to combat drug trafficking. Between 2006 and 2008, charges of abuse by civilians against soldiers increased from 182 per year to 1,230 as the Calderón administration launched the drug war. From December 2012 to April 2014, citizens filed 1,050 complaints against soldiers with the country's National Human Rights Commission.[12] The Mexican Military Justice Code gave military courts jurisdiction when a case involved "military discipline," but the term was broadly applied to everything from insubordination to rape, so that nearly all allegations against soldiers worked their way through military courts. Reformers hope to introduce language to guarantee the trial of human rights violations solely in civilian courts (Inter Press Service, 2010). In 2014, both chamber of the Mexican congress unanimously passed a reform to require all allegations of abuse by soldiers against civilians to be heard in civilian courts.

Military justice is a necessary part of the armed forces to ensure discipline. But military courts raise significant problems when there are allegations of abuse from civilians. Most importantly, the use of military courts allows the military to judge itself. The impartiality of the military judges is suspect because the courts are not independent—they are part of the military hierarchy. The courts answer to the Ministry of Defense, and ultimately to the president. Most military judges serve short tenures, which leads them to be more responsive to the concerns of the military hierarchy.

The Executive

The placement of the president at the top of the chain of command is an indispensable feature of civilian control. But how that chain weaves its way to the executive office is critical to the long-term maintenance of civilian control. All presidents must cope with shortcomings in information and expertise when dealing with an organization as large and complex as the armed forces. If allowed to linger, such deficiencies will feed antipolitics in the military as officers question why civilians hold the final say over matters they do not understand. And insofar as civilians cede decision making to officers due to their own incompetence in expertise, and fail to maintain clear channels of communication, civilian control can deteriorate.

A **ministry of defense** (MOD) can counteract these shortcomings and their adverse effects by acting as a central forum for civil-military interaction in government (Bruneau and Goetze, 2006a). This is the place where the policy preferences of government should meet up with the advice and recommendations of the armed forces, and where civilian directives should be translated into operational assignments for the military. Ideally, the chain of command should run from the president, through the MOD, to the service commanders. There are two other relevant institutions, both of which ideally sit outside the chain of command and instead take on an advisory role. The **national security council** advises the president, and may include military officers but should retain a civilian majority. The second institution is the **joint military staff**, which bands the service commanders in a council so that together they can share information and offer suggestions to the MOD as it implements and assesses the policy prescriptions from the president.

The chain of command offers a number of institutional variables that can affect civilian control. First and foremost, if the MOD is to be a forum where civilians formulate, administrate, and assess policy, it should be abundantly staffed with capable civilians. Most Latin American countries did not even have an MOD until the 1930s or 1940s (see Table 10.5). In Brazil, previous to 1999 the chain of command went directly from the president to the service commanders. Moreover, throughout the entire region civilians have only started to take on more significant positions within the ministries. A MOD is meant to deliver policy priorities and administrative instructions

Table 10.5 **The Ministry of Defense in Latin America.*** The Ministry of Defense is a central institution for assuring civilian control over the military

	Year Created	*% Civilian Ministers (creation to 2013)*
Argentina	1958	90%
Bolivia	1933	51%
Brazil	1999	100%
Chile	1932	66%
Colombia	1965	56%
Dominican Republic [1]	1930 / 2013	8% / 0%
Ecuador	1935	41%
El Salvador	1939	0%
Guatemala	1945	0%[2]
Honduras	1954	100%[3]
Mexico	1937	0%
Mexico—Navy [4]	1940	15%
Nicaragua	1979	83%
Paraguay	1943	22%
Peru	1987	45%
Uruguay	1935	62%
Venezuela	1946	2%

Source: Data from RESDAL (Network of Security and Defense in Latin America), 2014 *Atlas of Defense in Latin America and the Caribbean*. http://atlas.resdal.org.ar/.
*Costa Rica and Panama are not included in the table due to the absence of a military in these countries.
(1) Previous to a 2013 reform, the ministry was known as the Ministry of the Armed Forces.
(2) According to the constitution, civilians cannot be ministers of defense.
(3) Since 1998, year of constitutional reform.
(4) Mexico has a separate ministry for its navy.

from government to the service branches. But if it is staffed by officers, the flow of information is reversed, and the agency becomes a platform for soldiers to push their preferences at the highest decision-making levels of government. In this sense, it is troubling to note the constitutional provisions in Guatemala and Mexico that require their ministers to be military officers.

Beyond staffing, placement in the chain of command also matters. In Argentina, El Salvador, and Guatemala, the joint military staff rests not alongside the MOD as an advisory structure, but rather directly below it as part of the chain of command. The MODs in these countries cannot deal with the service sectors independently. This structure allows the services to better coordinate their interaction with government, and can thereby increase military influence. A much worse arrangement is found in Bolivia, Colombia, Ecuador, Honduras, Nicaragua, and Paraguay. These countries have a dual chain of command running from the presidential office. An administrative command to address matters such as training, education, veterans' affairs, and personnel management runs through the MOD to the service branches, whereas the chain of command dealing with operational matters runs from the president directly through the joint military staff and to the service branches. This structure not only relegates the MOD to less noteworthy duties, but also denies the MOD input from the joint military staff as an advisory board (Pion-Berlin, 2009).

Civil-Military Relations and New Challenges

Latin America has certainly made important strides in civil-military relations, but problems remain. It may well be that civilian supremacy is impractical in Latin America, and that politicians should focus instead on their political management of the military. But even though the largely positive gains in civil-military relations in the past two decades might substantiate this prescription, we should not lose sight of emerging security challenges that may prove too much for civilian leaders wagering that political prowess can compensate for shortcomings in military expertise.

Crime has swelled to excruciating levels, and many countries are looking to their military forces because of long-standing corruption in the police forces. For many countries, a military approach to crime appears fitting because the scale of criminal organization can almost be likened to a military force, especially in Central America and Mexico. Gang membership approaches 36,000 in Honduras, 14,000 in Guatemala, and 11,000 in El Salvador. Each of these countries have deployed either elite military brigades or joint police-military units to combat crime. Latin America as a whole accounts for one-third of all homicides in the world, although the region holds only 8 percent of the world's population. Profits from drug trafficking enrich criminal organizations, and attempts to control the lines of supply and demand (most of which ultimately connect to the United States) give rise to dreadful levels of violence. From 2006 to 2012, almost 60,000 were killed by drug-related violence in Mexico, leading then-President Felipe Calderón to affirm, "It's a war." And because drug trafficking crosses interstate borders, it attracts military involvement in an issue that is also rooted deeply in the domestic arena. Although the use of heavy-handed repressive tactics to address crime, or *mano dura*, have grown popular in some sectors of the population, they have contributed to a rise in human rights abuses by security officials. Police in São Paulo state, Brazil, killed 11,358 people from 1995 to 2015, more than the total number of persons killed by police throughout the United States from 1983 to 2012. One study of the violence surrounding Mexico's drug war found that, had the military not deployed units to address trafficking, there would have been 7,000 fewer homicides from 2008 to 2009.[13]

Another security challenge is the growing number of environmental crises—from hurricanes, to floods, and earthquakes. In 1998, almost 20,000 died in Central America due to Hurricane Mitch. Flooding in Venezuela killed 5,000 in 2000, and the 2001 earthquake in El Salvador killed 800. An estimated 700 died after the February 2010 earthquake in Chile, and many citizens criticized the hesitance of the Bachelet government to call on the armed forces to deliver aid and combat the looting that followed. In a clear reaction, at the start of her second term in 2014, Bachelet called for "enhancing our armed forces" to deal with natural disasters, and authorized the navy to develop a tsunami early warning system and the air force to purchase new helicopters designed for search and rescue missions. In Brazil, the armed forces developed its first military doctrine focused exclusively on humanitarian assistance operations in 2014.[14] Runaway urban growth, dilapidated buildings and infrastructure, deforestation and poor land-use policies, and climate change have increased the suffering associated with such environmental crises. As the disasters have grown, so too has the role of the military in search and rescue operations, the provision of aid, crime control, and rebuilding efforts. As these complex missions continue to mount, and military involvement in domestic affairs grows, civilians may find that political management is not enough to ensure military subordination. And if soldiers grow frustrated with these seemingly intractable missions, the military disdain for the lack of civilian expertise may once again give rise to antipolitics (Bruneau and Goetze, 2006b).

COUNTRY IN THE SPOTLIGHT

The Armed Forces of El Salvador

Like many militaries in the world today, the armed forces of El Salvador have their own website. It includes the banner "*La institución mas antigua del estado*"—the oldest institution of the state. It would be wrong to dismiss this claim categorically, but it does feed the dubious

(*continued*)

lore that places the armed forces as the primary force behind the creation of the Salvadoran state and nation. This lore is plainly captured by a famous quote attributed to the independence hero and founder of the Salvadoran armed forces, General Manuel José Arce: "*El Ejército vivirá mientras viva la República*"—"The army will live as long as the republic lives." Unsurprisingly, this quote is frequently cited by Salvadoran soldiers and referenced extensively on the website.

The boldness of such statements begs an inquiry into just how integral the military was to the development of El Salvador, and whether it continues to be so today. The country gained its independence in 1821 as part of the Captaincy General of Guatemala, which also joined Costa Rica, Guatemala, Honduras, and Nicaragua. As in other areas of Latin America, many conservative sectors did not favor independence, for they feared the rise of liberal thought associated with the French Revolution. But conservatives in Central America had another option—annexation to Mexico under the emerging conservative regime of Agustín de Iturbide. Iturbide invaded to support the decision, but when he fell to his own domestic opponents in 1823, it became clear that Central America would have to form their own government.

The Captaincy General offered a semblance of unity, and the recent Mexican incursion alongside suspicions that Spain or Britain might invade spurred calls for unity. The region formed the United Provinces of Central America, but intense divisions between regional leaders and between conservative and liberal factions meant unity in name only. Such rivalries stalled the work of a constituent assembly charged to create a constitution. Unable to agree on the composure of a military—but feeling pressed to address defense affairs, the assembly called on each province to create its own forces. In El Salvador, a constituent assembly working on a provincial constitution took up the task with urgency, especially as tensions with other provinces (particularly Guatemala) emerged.[15] On May 7, 1824, several military units were combined to create the "Legion of Liberty of the State of El Salvador." Some of the delegates noted the peculiarity of making reference to a state that they had yet to officially create. They would follow with the provincial constitution in June, even before the regional assembly decreed its constitution in November.[16] But divisions wracked the United Provinces. Its complete crumbling was in fact delayed in large part because the divisiveness within the provinces forestalled attempts to wrest power from the central government. But by the late 1830s, one province after another declared independence. El Salvador announced its separation in January 1841.

Which came first, the state or the military? El Salvador recognizes September 15, 1821—when Spain relinquished control of the Captaincy General—as its independence date. The Mexican annexation and interlude with the United Provinces are regarded as passing aberrations to the self-rule that actually began in 1821. Still, the lack of a *de jure* sovereign government allows the military to tag itself as "the oldest institution of the state." And as a reminder that the military formally came into being one month before the provincial constitution, May 7 is celebrated as "Armed Forces Day" in El Salvador. But the date is hardly the birth date of a modern, professional force. The military never surpassed more than a few hundred regular troops in the first half of the nineteenth century, and relied heavily upon forced conscripts and local militias. Real power continued to rest in the multitude of ragtag military units devoted to regional *caudillos* and their haciendas.

The rise of a modern force is more accurately associated with the presidency of General Gerardo Barrios (1859–1863), and the ascent of coffee exports. Indigo, the primary export of the country, had fallen into a steep decline after the development of a synthetic alternative for the dye in the mid-nineteenth century. With the economy in a lurch, Barrios and his successors looked to coffee—and the social consequences were considerable. To increase production, the government moved aggressively to break up communal indigenous lands. In addition, coffee required much more of a permanent labor force than did indigo. The harvest came but once a year, but producers also dried, processed, and sacked the coffee. The newly dispossessed offered a convenient labor supply, and by the 1880s, the government had passed vagrancy laws to compel them to work. The upsurge in coffee production would be closely related to series of rural uprisings—in 1872, 1875, 1880, 1885, and 1898. El Salvador was growing wealthy on coffee exports, but it was also growing unstable (Burns, 1984).

Barrios initiated the development of a professional military force when he invited two modest foreign military missions—one from Colombia in 1859, and then another from France in 1862. Coffee exports provided both the resources and rationale for the further development of the armed forces. Coffee composed less than 1 percent of exports in 1860, then about one-third in the 1870s, and well over

(continued)

90 percent by 1930. Army garrisons were placed at key points at newly constructed ports, roadways, rail service, and communications. The rural unrest was too much for the still emerging military, so the government allowed large hacienda owners to form their own patrol units and enforce vagrancy laws, even as a new National Police force struggled to impose order on its own. The armed forces offered support, but were generally preoccupied with external threats. Relations with Guatemala remained tense, territorial disagreements with Honduras laid unsettled, and disputes over islands and maritime rights in the Gulf of Fonseca entangled El Salvador with Honduras and Nicaragua.

A Chilean mission arrived in 1905 to hone skills directed toward foreign threats. But the consolidation of U.S. hegemony in the region at the turn of the century would prove a turning point in the maturation of the Salvadoran armed forces. The United States moved aggressively to quell interstate discord—sponsoring annual peace conferences, mediating disputes, and supporting the creation of a Central American Court. The United States sent a clear message that it would no longer tolerate militarized interstate clashes. In doing so it deprived the armed forces of their external mission, and allowed them to look inward. Rural instability concerned the armed forces, and so did the growing power of the semiautonomous militias. A new military mission in 1907 from Spain marked a clean break from the externally oriented Chilean mission. It helped the country establish a National Guard in 1911 to patrol the countryside, which in turn allowed the National Police to focus on urban areas. Both forces drew their officers from the military schools (Elam, 1997a).

The growth of the military institution had indeed brought stability to the state, but this was a state thoroughly infiltrated and representative of a very narrow, elite sector of society—the coffee industry. In fact, power was so concentrated and nepotism so rampant that Salvadorans referred to the oligarchy as "The Fourteen Families." There was a direct, private relation between military personnel and large landowners. When labor strife threatened, especially during harvest time, members of the National Guard would contract out their services. The army took on a more extensive, institutionalized presence in the countryside. Obligatory service ensured that all male citizens did some time in uniform, but only for one year. More importantly, men remained on active reserve until age 50, allowing for a lifetime bond between citizens and the military. The army made use of the reserve rolls to co-opt rural inhabitants. Every village had community patrols (*patrullas cantonales*) made of reserve personnel who reported directly to a local military officer. Though participation was obligatory, it was also desirable. Benefits included special access to medical and economic assistance. And because the patrols sought out draft dodgers or those who failed to report for reserve training sessions, members felt empowered as they exerted control over others. Members of the patrols were far from the disciplined, educated personnel one might find in specialized military units, and because of this, the army took it upon itself to institute literacy and basic education classes, along with strict regimens of physical training. As such, the military soon saw itself as a nation builder, one that was bringing civilization to the countryside (Walter and Williams, 1993).

The National Guard and *patrullas cantonales* of El Salvador exemplify the paramilitary groups commonly found in Latin America, especially in rural areas. Historically, they have represented something of a compromise between militaries that cannot afford a large standing force, and large landowners who want to control their own militias. Because such groups blend private incentives with a patriotic sense of duty, and often lack the disciplined training of regular armed units, they tend to be belligerent and often play a central role when violence erupts.

Such was the case when the Great Depression hit El Salvador. President Pío Romero Bosque (1927–1931) had turned from tradition and instituted significant political reforms that allowed the country to hold its first free and fair elections in 1931. The armed forces were already growing anxious as open debate allowed several candidates to propose solutions to the economic crisis—and many pointed to the military budget as a drain on the economy. The unease spread to the coffee oligarchy when the Labor Party candidate, Arturo Araujo, won the election. Araujo called for social and economic change, including land reform, but once in office he found that the government coffers could not support such policy changes. A growing communist movement took advantage of the frustration and called for revolution. Military tensions intensified as the government suspended military salaries on several occasions. Attempts by an emergent communist movement to stir divisions within the military with calls to disobey superior officers and join the movement proved to be the final straw (Elam, 1997a). A military coup d'état removed Araujo from the presidency in December 1931. Now in power, the military directed its attention to the growing revolutionary movement, arrested its

(*continued*)

leader—Agustín Farabundo Martí, and executed him on February 1, 1932. Absent direction, bands of discontented peasants revolted throughout the countryside, directing much of their violence toward the large landowners. The paramilitaries represented the first lines of defense for the government in the rural areas, and they responded ferociously. Upward of 30,000 peasants were killed in under a week in what Salvadorans simply call *La Matanza*—The Massacre.

The military would retain direct control of government for the following 50 years. A new paramilitary group, the Civic Guard, recruited civilians in rural areas to collect intelligence on subversive activities. The countryside was completely militarized. Up to 1944, General Maximiliano Hernández Martínez, who had served as vice president under Araujo and took the presidency after the coup, dominated government. But now that the military had full control of government, they faced the dilemma that all military governments face: how to reconcile the role of the military as an institution with that of the military as a government. A professional military concerns itself with state security above all else, and values order, hierarchy, and unity within the military corps. But governance thrusts the military into the world of political debate, and threatens the corporate unity of the armed forces (Arceneaux, 2001, pp. 13–25).

El Salvador had already seen these tensions in 1922, when junior officers at the *Escuela Politécnica* rebelled against the crony connections they saw between senior officers and the coffee oligarchy. Many of the junior officers emerged from the lower classes and sympathized with the plight of the peasantry. Moreover, they saw a stark contrast between their own vision of a modern professional military that rewarded expertise, and that of senior officers who held their positions due to graft, in particular their service to the coffee oligarchy. The *Politécnica* was closed as a result of the rebellion, but the new *Escuela Militar* was opened in 1927 to satisfy educational needs, and the splits between junior and senior officers reappeared. In fact President Romero Bosque deftly played off these divisions to hold the military at bay as he instituted his political reforms. And early on, Hernández Martínez quelled the split with calls for unity to tackle the communist threat—so clearly expressed in the 1932 uprising. But the dictator lavished the National Guard and National Police to confront insurgent threats, and even called for civilian militias to support a protofascist regime inspired by Mussolini and Hitler. All this sidelined the role and stature of the regular army. Disgruntled graduates of the *Escuela Militar* joined civilian politicians, business groups, and labor leaders seeking opportunity in a more open political system, and attempted a coup in 1944. They failed—and many were executed, but subsequent protests and strikes brought down the government later that year (Elam, 1997b).

The old guard in the military, under General Salvador Castañeda Castro, reestablished control for a period, but was ousted in 1948 by reform-oriented junior officers. Their leader, Lieutenant Colonel Oscar Osario, proclaimed a populist revolution under a new constitution calling for expansive labor and agrarian reforms. Officers dominated the new political party, the *Partido Revolucionario de Unificación Democrática*, which sought to co-opt the middle and lower classes along the lines of the PRI party in Mexico. The populist tenor would remain, but it quickly became little more than rhetoric as military presidents prioritized the communist threat and suspended or reversed reforms as part of the effort to "defend democracy."

The Cold War stiffened the resolve of the armed forces to retain power, and it also brought more intense U.S. involvement. The defeat of the Axis Powers in WWII deadened efforts to emulate the fascist regimes of Europe, and the lure of U.S. military equipment and technology was considerable. As its influence grew, the United States proposed civic action operations under the Alliance for Progress as a reform-oriented approach to revolutionary activity, but it did so with little understanding of how such activities would mesh with existing civil-military relations. From Washington's perspective, things like building schools and roads, digging wells, funding vaccination drives, offering agricultural extension services, and distributing food would dampen the frustration and animosity associated with poverty, and thus deny revolutionary movements their kindling.

But who delivers such services in these civic action programs is just as important as the services themselves. Civic action was nothing new to the armed forces of El Salvador, and while the military appreciated the counterinsurgency aspects of the programs, it embraced civic action just as much for another reason—such operations validated the belief that the armed forces brought civilization to the masses, that they were nation builders. Alliance for Progress funding allowed the military to take a much more methodic approach in the countryside. In 1963, a General Administration of Civic Action was created in the Ministry of Defense to channel civic action programs through the

(continued)

National Guard. If that was the carrot, the stick—the contracting out of repressive services to large landowners—was formalized with the creation of a new paramilitary organization, the National Democratic Organization, or ORDEN (*Organización Democrática Nacionalista*), which reported directly to the president. Reminiscent of the Civic Guards, ORDEN would also co-opt peasants and take on an intelligence function (Walter and Williams, 1993).

Socioeconomic inequities remained at the root of El Salvador's difficulties. The population density of the country has historically been among the highest in Latin America—an unfortunate statistic for the vast majority of the population that is dependent on subsistence farming, but barred from land ownership by expansive estates. Honduras, which is six times the size of El Salvador but with less population, had long acted as a relief valve. But the stream of Salvadoran migrants seeking land raised tensions over time, and led to a brief war in 1969. More than 100,000 Salvadorans in Honduras now had to return and most joined the ranks of the unemployed or landless. In addition, the country as a whole could no longer look to Honduras as an outlet for its population. The country had reached its boiling point. Guerrilla groups sprouted throughout the country, and by 1980 united. To underscore the fact that things had not changed much since 1932, they took on the name Farabundo Martí Front for National Liberation (FMLN).

The new Reagan administration in the United States responded aggressively, having just seen the Sandinistas take power in Nicaragua, and supported a military solution to the long-standing socioeconomic ills of the country with vast amounts of military aid (Needler, 1991). The result was a bloody civil war that killed more than 75,000— including at least 50,000 unarmed civilians. Among the more disturbing elements of the war was the extensive use of "death squads." Clandestine units kidnapped, tortured, and disappeared suspected subversives and guerrilla sympathizers. Such organizations were made possible by and should be understood in the context of the history of paramilitaries that had long worked in the shadows of government repression. Many of those involved in death squad activity had "cut their teeth" as members of ORDEN, which had effectively gone underground and remained as vibrant as ever even after it was abolished in 1979.

Three factors brought the combatants to the negotiating table in 1990, culminating in a comprehensive peace accord in January 1992.

First, the war had reached a stalemate, and all Salvadorans were growing war-weary. Second, the end of the Cold War both undermined the revolutionary rhetoric of the FMLN and dampened U.S. support for aggressive military responses to revolutionary action. And the final factor was the presence of a mediator that both sides viewed as neutral—the United Nations. The impact of the accords on the military were nothing short of noteworthy: A special commission was formed to investigate human rights abuses during the civil war and, as a result, just over 100 high-ranking officers were purged from the service; the military was downsized and units merged with FMLN units; the mission of the military was redefined toward external threats; the National Guard and *patrullas cantonales* were dismantled; the National Police and the intelligence system were placed under civilian command; and a new council with civilian members was created to oversee military education.

In fact, what is most intriguing about the accords is the focus on military reform, and the absence of significant socioeconomic reforms. Ironically, the extensive and violent campaign exerted by the military unraveled its relations with the economic elite. The civil war checked growth in the coffee industry, and the violence sent some one million— about one-quarter of the population—abroad. By the 1990s, the most important component of the economy was remittances from abroad, and much of the economic elite had reinvested their capital in financial services located in urban areas. With their wealth rearranged, they no longer required military forces to protect large landed estates (such interests remain, but they are simply less dominant today) (Stanley, 2006, pp. 109–110).

The armed forces of El Salvador look and behave very differently today than they did just two decades ago. Having once been a force of more than 60,000, there are now only 24,000 regular troops. With the old paramilitary forces disbanded, the new national police force has taken a completely civilian face, and even assumed the name "*Policía Nacional Civil*" (National Civilian Police).[17] A new National Academy of Public Security was created exclusively to oversee the training of new police officers. To help bridge civil-military understandings in security affairs, recommendations from the accords led to the College for Higher Strategic Studies, which draws soldiers and civilians to study defense issues together. And civilian expertise improved. A 2006 study of the legislature showed that 10 of the 84 members were proficient in defense affairs, and found "informed, competent staffs" (Bruneau and Goetze,

(*continued*)

2006b, p. 72). Importantly, the accord also spawned the National Council for Public Security, a civilian advisory body to the presidency designed to institutionalize the separate study and assessment of public security, as opposed to national defense. Similarly, the old Ministry of Defense and Public Security was pared to the Ministry of Defense, and public security administration went to the new Ministry of Justice and Public Security (the National Civilian Police reports directly to this body). Today, the armed forces place a priority on humanitarian assistance, and have increased their participation in peacekeeping missions substantially. The country sent 380 troops to support Operation Iraqi Freedom (the final troops were recalled in 2009).

Still, there remain areas of concern. The country still lacks a civilian defense minister, and civilian staffing in the ministry is meager. Generally, civil-military relations have remained calm. Much of the early anxiety in the armed forces decreased when the government issued a general amnesty in March 1993—the same month that a special Truth Commission published its findings on the extent of military involvement in human rights abuses. But as elsewhere in Latin America, memories of past abuses did not fade. Activists continued to pursue justice through international avenues—most prominently in the Spanish courts in a case that implicates 14 superior officers in the 1989 high-profile killings of seven Jesuit priests. And in the 2010 periodic review conducted by the United Nations Human Rights Council, countries such as Argentina and Mexico urged El Salvador to annul its amnesty. Further pressure came from the Inter-American Court of Human Rights in 2013, which issued a ruling on the 1981 El Mozote massacre. The court found the state "responsible for the violation of the right to life" and deemed the amnesty inapplicable due to the scale of the violence (over 1,000 were killed in the massacre). But even the FMLN, which had transformed itself into a political party and gained the presidency in 2009, did not press to overturn the amnesty. As culpable as the military was during the civil war, members of the FMLN also committed atrocities. Indeed, there may even be evidence implicating current FMLN President Sánchez Cerén (2014–). Government officials on both the left and the right were thus stunned in July 2016 when the country's Supreme Court found the amnesty unconstitutional because it "prevents the state form meeting its (constitutional) obligations to prevent, investigate, judge, punish, and offer reparations for serious rights violations" (*NotiCen*, 2016). In a move that further underscored the rise of the judiciary as an influential actor in

Salvadoran politics, in October of 2016, a lower court responded to the Supreme Court ruling by reopening an investigation into the El Mozote massacre.

The nullification of the amnesty will no doubt be consequential and unearth old controversies and tensions. Nonetheless, as demonstrated in countries such as Argentina and Chile that have repealed amnesties, the pursuit of justice can aid national reconciliation and the reduce the culture of fear left in the wake of repressive military rule. In fact, if anything upends the relative calm of civil-military relations, it could be the growing role of the military in criminal matters. El Salvador now has one of the highest murder rates in the world. Much of the violence is linked to the burgeoning ranks of street gangs that fight for control over neighborhoods so that they can extort businesses, collect ransoms through kidnappings, and traffic drugs. The gangs are ironically traced to the 1992 peace accords. The war was so long and brutal that some one million fled to the United States. Many developed connections with street gangs in the marginalized neighborhoods of Los Angeles, and retained those ties when they returned in the 1990s. The gang life is now being passed on to a new generation in the streets of San Salvador. In another ironic consequence of the peace accords, the bold moves to dismantle the repressive police forces left them weakened and easily overwhelmed as gang activity spread. ARENA President Tony Saca instituted the first *"mano dura"* policies in 2003. But the FMLN presidents later announced a series of *"super mano dura"* policies, making gang membership punishable by 10 years in prison, and even placing a general in charge of the Ministry of Justice and Public Security. Some 7,000 troops were given special assignments with the police, and essentially granted impunity under a new rule that prohibited investigations into police shootings when done in "self defense." Though the government brokered a truce that reduced violence from 2012 to 2013, when it began moving imprisoned gang leaders to high-security prisons, the violence returned (Wade, 2016; *The Guardian*, 2015). During this time, back on the Web page of the armed forces, a change was soon made to the menu of topics involving the armed forces. Added to the heading of "national defense" a new concern was duly noted: "maintaining internal peace." Time will tell whether civilian control in El Salvador can withstand a return to public security by the armed forces.

(continued)

Discussion Questions

1   How does the case of El Salvador illustrate the relationship between economic interests and military thought and behavior? Under what conditions does a military act more autonomously?
2   Should we be optimistic about the reentry of El Salvador's armed forces into matters of internal security?

Conclusion

Military intervention was almost ordinary in the Latin America of the past. The move toward democracy and international pressure are likely to prohibit a return to such overt involvement in the politics of the region, but that does not mean that the military will become inconsequential in the new democratic regimes. New security norms and challenges have emerged, and institutions such as the ministry of defense must be arranged to ensure civilian control as the military finds its new role. But these changes cannot and will not take place in a vacuum. The armed forces have their own interpretations of history and views of the past roles they played as builders of the nation and state. In Honduras, the army justified its removal of President Zelaya by declaring that they were simply fulfilling their duties under the constitution, skirting the fact that they had in fact upended the chain of command, taking action in defiance and against their commander in chief. The event illustrates how the image from the past—of the military as the guardian of the state—still influences military behavior. As new institutional procedures emerge to address new security norms and challenges, care must be taken to ensure that they also bridge rather than further the divide between differing civilian and military perspectives on the proper roles, purposes, and contributions of the armed forces.

Key Terms

Costa Rica Consensus   395
professionalization   405
antipolitics   405
National Security Doctrine   406
civilian supremacy   407
political management   408
democratic security   408

human security   408
cooperative security   409
confidence building
    measures   409
ministry of defense   414
national security council   415
joint military staff   415

Discussion Questions

1   Is the Costa Rica Consensus a good idea? Is it justifiable for powerful countries to influence spending decisions in less-developed countries in this way? Would such a policy unfairly discriminate against those

less-developed countries with security challenges such as drug trafficking or criminal activity that may warrant more military spending?

2 Should civilians in Latin America strive for civilian supremacy, or settle with political management of the armed forces? What could be the costs of holding governments in Latin America to the high expectations of civilian supremacy?

3 Which government institutions have the most significant impact on civil-military relations?

4 What are the dangers of allowing a military to take a greater role in domestic security issues such as crime and drug trafficking? What are the costs of not allowing them to do so?

Notes

1 "Spanish Daily Reports Honduran General's Views on President's Overthrow." BBC Monitoring—Latin America. July 29, 2009.
2 For a good analysis of the legalities surrounding the events in Honduras, see Cassel (2009).
3 The HDI is a composite score that measures literacy, life expectancy, and per capita income. It was developed by the United Nations Development Program.
4 This explanation is a bit simplified. Some military regimes withdrew from power on stronger terms than others. See Arceneaux (2001).
5 "Brazilian Government Opposes Trials for Junta's Torturers." *Latin American Herald Tribune*, June 12, 2009. Available at: www.laht.com.
6 "The Brazilian Military Is Back, as It Fleshes Out Its Weaponry and Strategies." Council on Hemispheric Affairs, September 9, 2008. Available at: www.coha.org.
7 Huntington emphasizes that professionalization occurs only among officers, not enlisted men. This is because enlisted men are in a trade, not a profession. They are experts in the application of violence, not its management.
8 MERCOSUR is the Spanish acronym for Common Market of the South. In 2008 the organization united with the Andean Community to create UNASUR—the Union of South American Nations.
9 Article 10, "Framework Treaty on Democratic Security in Central America." Full text available at: www.sica.int/busqueda/busqueda_archivo.aspx?Archivo= trat_33842_2_19032009.htm.
10 Full text available at: www.oas.org/charter/docs/resolution1_en_p4.htm.
11 See Marcela Donadio and Maria de la Paz Tibiletti, 2008, *Atlas Comparativo de la Defensa en América Latina*. Buenos Aires: Red de Seguridad y Defensa en América Latina.
12 See data available on the website of the Secretary of Defense, Mexico: www .sedena.gob.mx/images/stories/D.H/2014/situacionquejasyrecomendaciones.pdf.
13 "'We Have Seen a Significant Amount of Deaths': Inside Latin America's Brutal War on Crime." Business Insider December 12, 2015. Available at www .businessinsider.com.
14 Pablo Scuticchio. "Growing Role of Armed Forces in Disaster Relief a Dangerous Trend for Latin America." Wilson Center: New Security Beat, October 22, 2015. Available atwww.newsecuritybeat.org.
15 As the former administrative center of the Captaincy General, Guatemala was strongly influenced by elite groups with ties to Spain and greater sympathies to conservative thought. El Salvador had always been an outpost of the Spanish Empire. This, along with the denial of a bishopric (which would have given the

country its own bishop), made the area more suspicious of centralized rule and more open to liberal thought.

16 This history is nicely detailed on the website of the armed forces of El Salvador. See *Fuerza Armada de El Salvador-Historia.* Available at www.fuerzaarmada .gob.sv:90/index.php?option=com_content&view=article&id=49&Itemid=84.

17 A quota system was created under the accords to guide the initial staffing of the force: 20 percent of members were to come from the ranks of the FMLN, 20 percent from former paramilitary members, while 60 percent were to be new, civilian recruits.

Suggested Readings

Miguel Angel Centeno. 2002. *Blood and Debt: War and the Nation-State in Latin America.* **University Park, PA: Penn State Press.** The prominent sociologist Charles Tilly wrote, "War made the state and the state made war." This was the case in Europe, where conflict spurred nationalism and the growth of state capacity to mobilize the population and raise revenues. Centeno notes that the administrative structure of the state must meet a minimal level in order to initiate Tilly's dynamic, and Latin America's states did not pass the threshold. Moreover, geography such as the Andes and jungle areas contained military exertions. As a result, Latin American armies remained too weak to even consolidate control within their own borders. The result has been a history of civil conflict.

Brian Loveman. 1999. *For la Patria: Politics and the Armed Forces in Latin America.* **Wilmington, DE: Scholarly Resources Books.** In this wide-ranging historical survey of the armed forces in Latin America, Loveman traces the dominant role the military played not only through the direct control of government, but also, more significantly, in its impact on the political thinking of the region. He illustrates the military impact by showing how military concerns made their way into the constitutions and legal norms of the region.

Julie Mazzei. 2009. *Death Squads or Self-Defense Forces?: How Paramilitary Groups Emerge and Challenge Democracy in Latin America.* **Chapel Hill, NC: University of North Carolina Press.** Overt military intervention and repression may not be likely in Latin America today, but that does not mean military force does not affect the region through other avenues. Paramilitary forces are often found at the forefront of civil conflicts. Mazzei examines the conditions under which paramilitary groups are able to emerge and thrive in case studies of Colombia, El Salvador, and Mexico.

David Pion-Berlin. 1997. *Through Corridors of Power: Institutions and Civil-Military Relations in Argentina.* **University Park, PA: Penn State University Press.** Few countries have a more ominous history of military intervention in politics than Argentina. And yet, few now doubt the strength of civilian control in the country. Pion-Berlin traces how political leaders used institutions and policies to craft this civilian control. He takes a detailed look at policy changes in human rights, military budgets, and defense reform.

References

Agüero, Felipe. 1995. *Soldiers, Civilians, and Democracy: Post-Franco Spain in Comparative Perspective*. Baltimore, MD: Johns Hopkins University Press.

Arceneaux, Craig. 2001. *Bounded Missions: Military Regimes and Democratization in the Southern Cone and Brazil*. University Park, PA: Penn State University Press.

Arceneaux, Craig, and David Pion-Berlin. 2007. "Explaining OAS Responses to Democratic Dilemmas in Latin America." *Latin American Politics and Society* 49:2, pp. 1–31.

Arias, Oscar. 2009, July 9. "Fuel for a Coup: The Perils of Latin America's Oversized Militaries." *Washington Post*.

Bruneau, Thomas C., and Richard B. Goetze, Jr., eds. 2006a. "Ministries of Defense and Democratic Control," in *Who Guards the Guardians and How: Democratic Civil-Military Relations*, pp. 71–100. Austin, TX: University of Texas Press.

Bruneau, Thomas C., and Richard B. Goetze, Jr. 2006b. "Civilian-Military Relations in Latin America." *Military Review* 86:5, pp. 67–74.

Burns, E. Bradford. 1984. "The Modernization of Underdevelopment: El Salvador, 1858–1931." *Journal of Developing Areas* 18, pp. 293–316.

Cassel, Doug. 2009. "Honduras: Coup d'état in Constitutional Clothing?" American Society of International Law Insight 13:9. Available at www.asil.org/files/insight090729pdf.pdf.

Centeno, Miguel Angel. 2002. *Blood and Debt: War and the Nation-State in Latin America*. University Park, PA: Penn State University Press.

Diamond, Larry, Juan J. Linz, and Seymour Martin Lipset, eds. 1995. "Introduction: What Makes for Democracy?" in *Politics in Developing Countries: Comparing Experiences with Democracy, 2nd ed.*, pp. 1–66. Boulder, CO: Lynne Rienner.

Donadio, Marcela. 2016. *Atlas Comparativo de la Defensa en América Latina*. Buenos Aires: Red de Seguridad y Defensa en América Latina.

Elam, Robert V. 1997a. "The Army and Politics in El Salvador, 1840–1927," in Brian Loveman and Thomas M. Davies, Jr., eds., *The Politics of AntiPolitics: The Military in Latin America*. Wilmington, DE: SR Books.

———. 1997b. "The Army and Politics in El Salvador, 1927–1945," in Brian Loveman and Thomas M. Davies, Jr., eds., *The Politics of AntiPolitics: The Military in Latin America*. Wilmington, DE: SR Books.

Fitch, J. Samuel. 1998. *The Armed Forces and Democracy in Latin America*. Baltimore, MD: Johns Hopkins University Press.

Fleurant, Aude, Sam Perlo-Freeman, Pieter D. Wezeman, and Siemon T. Wezeman. 2016. "Trends in International Arms Transfers, 2015." SIPRI Fact Sheet February 2016. Available at www.sipri.org.

Fournier, Dominique. 1999. "The Alfonsín Administration and the Promotion of Democratic Values in the Southern Cone and the Andes." *Journal of Latin American Studies* 31:1, pp. 39–74.

Giraldo, Jeanne Kinney. 2006. "Legislatures and National Defense: Global Comparisons," in Thomas C. Bruneau and Richard B. Goetze, Jr., eds., *Who Guards the Guardians and How: Democratic Civil-Military Relations*, pp. 34–70. Austin, TX: University of Texas Press.

The Guardian. 2015. "One Murder Every Hour: How El Salvador Became the Homicide Capital of the World," August 22. Available at www.theguardian.com.

Inter Press Service. 2010, June 8. "Distrust Hinders Disarmament in Latin America." Available at www.ipsnews.net.

Los Angeles Times. 1995, April 26. "Argentine General Says Army Killed Leftists in 'Dirty War.'"

Loveman, Brian. 1999. *For la Patria: Politics and the Armed Forces in Latin America*. Wilmington, DE: Scholarly Resources Books.

Loveman, Brian, and Thomas M. Davies, Jr., eds. 1997. *The Politics of AntiPolitics: The Military in Latin America*. Wilmington, DE: SR Books.

Manuela Estrada, Isabel. 2014. "Eleven CFAC Countries Complete UN Peace Operations Training in Guatemala." *Diálogo*, December 16. Available at www.dialogo-americas.com.

Needler, Martin C. 1991. "El Salvador: The Military and Politics." *Armed Forces and Society* 17:4, pp. 569–88.

New York Times. 2010, June 6. "Latin America Still Divided over Coup in Honduras."

NotiCen. 2016. "Supreme Court Voids 23-Year-Old Amnesty Law." July 28. University of New Mexico: Latin American Database.

Pereira, Anthony W., and Jorge Zaverucha. 2005. "The Neglected Stepchild: Military Justice and Democratic Transition in Chile." *Social Justice* 32:2, pp. 115–31.

Perlo-Freeman, Sam, and Catalina Perdomo. 2008. "The Developmental Impact of Military Budgeting and Procurement—Implications for and Arms Trade Treaty." SIPRI Working Paper. Available at www.sipri.org/research/armaments/milex/publications/unpubl_milex/mili_budget.

Pion-Berlin, David. 2005. "Political Management of the Military in Latin America." *Military Review* 85:1, pp. 19–31.

———. 2009. "Defense Organizations and Civil-Military Relations in Latin America." *Armed Forces and Society* 35:3, pp. 562–86.

Pion-Berlin, David, and Harold Trinkunas. 2007. "Attention Deficits: Why Politicians Ignore Defense Policy in Latin America." *Latin American Research Review* 42:3, pp. 76–100.

Robin, Marie-Monique. 2005. "Counterinsurgency and Torture: Exporting Torture Tactics from Indochina and Algeria to Latin America," in Kenneth Roth, Minky Worden, and Amy D. Bernstein, eds., *Torture: A Human Rights Perspective*, pp. 44–54. New York: The New Press.

Stanley, William Deane. 2006. "El Salvador: State Building Before and After Democratisation, 1980–95." *Third World Quarterly* 27:1, pp. 101–14.

Stockholm International Peace Research Institute (SIPRI). 2016. *SIPRI Yearbook 2016*. New York: Oxford University Press.

Wade, Christine. 2016. "El Salvador's 'Iron Fist': Inside Its Unending War on Gangs." *World Politics Review*, June 6. Available at www.worldpoliticsreview.com.

Walter, Knut, and Philip J. Williams. 1993. "The Military and Democratization in El Salvador." *Journal of Interamerican Studies and World Affairs* 35:1, pp. 39–91.

Index

 Taylor & Francis eBooks

Helping you to choose the right eBooks for your Library

Add Routledge titles to your library's digital collection today. Taylor and Francis ebooks contains over 50,000 titles in the Humanities, Social Sciences, Behavioural Sciences, Built Environment and Law.

Choose from a range of subject packages or create your own!

Benefits for you

» Free MARC records
» COUNTER-compliant usage statistics
» Flexible purchase and pricing options
» All titles DRM-free.

Benefits for your user

» Off-site, anytime access via Athens or referring URL
» Print or copy pages or chapters
» Full content search
» Bookmark, highlight and annotate text
» Access to thousands of pages of quality research at the click of a button.

 REQUEST YOUR **FREE** INSTITUTIONAL TRIAL TODAY | **Free Trials Available** We offer free trials to qualifying academic, corporate and government customers.

eCollections – Choose from over 30 subject eCollections, including:

Archaeology	Language Learning
Architecture	Law
Asian Studies	Literature
Business & Management	Media & Communication
Classical Studies	Middle East Studies
Construction	Music
Creative & Media Arts	Philosophy
Criminology & Criminal Justice	Planning
Economics	Politics
Education	Psychology & Mental Health
Energy	Religion
Engineering	Security
English Language & Linguistics	Social Work
Environment & Sustainability	Sociology
Geography	Sport
Health Studies	Theatre & Performance
History	Tourism, Hospitality & Events

For more information, pricing enquiries or to order a free trial, please contact your local sales team:
www.tandfebooks.com/page/sales

 Routledge Taylor & Francis Group | The home of Routledge books | **www.tandfebooks.com**